The International Politics of the Nigerian Civil War
1967–1970

The International Politics
of the Nigerian Civil War
1967–1970

JOHN J. STREMLAU

PRINCETON UNIVERSITY PRESS
Princeton, New Jersey

For Carolyn

CONTENTS

PART III. ISOLATING THE CONFLICT

LIST OF MAPS

PREFACE

Civil wars, with varying degrees of external involvement, have become the principal form of violence in the international system. Most of these conflicts erupt in Third World countries. Thus far, very little has been published about how the local parties in a modern civil war seek to attract or discourage foreign intervention.

My interest in focusing on the policies of those embroiled in armed civil strife was aroused by stark realities; since World War II millions of lives have been lost in the pursuit of essentially domestic political objectives during conflicts that have frequently also imperiled international peace. In Africa alone, there have been no fewer than twelve civil wars between 1960 and 1976. Among the most severe and internationally significant of these was the 1967–1970 war between the federal government of Nigeria and the secessionist eastern region of Biafra.

The possible disintegration of Africa's most populous country, a state that had previously been widely regarded as the continent's outstanding parliamentary democracy and that had enjoyed the bright economic prospect of becoming one of the world's major oil producers, affected a wide range of foreign interests. Many African leaders faced the issue of whether the Biafran example might inspire secessionist forces within their own newly independent and still fragile states. Questions were raised about how events in Nigeria would affect the latent competition between France and Great Britain for influence over their former West African territories. And it was conceivable that the struggle might somehow become another test of strength between the United States and the Soviet Union or precipitate United Nations action similar to the controversial involvement in the Congo. The internationalization of the Nigerian civil war, however, bore little resemblance to situations elsewhere.[1] In this case, foreign intervention resulted primarily from humanitarian rather than from political or ideological concerns.

Barely a year after Biafra's secession, and despite a lack of substantial diplomatic recognition or even covert help from foreign powers,

[1] For general background reading see: James N. Rosenau, ed., *The International Aspects of Civil Strife* (Princeton: Princeton University Press, 1964); Richard A. Falk, ed., *The International Law of Civil War* (Baltimore: Johns Hopkins University Press, 1970); Louis G. M. Jaquet, ed., *Intervention in International Politics* (The Hague: Netherlands Institute of International Affairs, 1971); and John Norton Moore, ed., *Law and Civil War in the Modern World* (Baltimore: Johns Hopkins University Press, 1974).

the war ranked as the most important foreign issue in public opinion surveys throughout Western Europe, and it was regarded as second only to Vietnam among the majority of Americans. In contrast to the lack of popular attention accorded other civil wars of comparable or greater violence, the specter of mass starvation in Biafra brought forth unprecedented amounts of private foreign assistance that substantially altered the nature and duration of the struggle.

Given the intense passions aroused by Biafra, perhaps I should not have been surprised when my decision in 1969 to become a research associate at the Nigerian Institute of International Affairs in Lagos was criticized and strongly discouraged by several academic colleagues. Not only were there warnings about the risks of becoming too partisan and jeopardizing all claim to scholarly credentials; some went so far as to insist that by merely affiliating with a Nigerian institution, one would somehow dignify a regime that many believed to be guilty of genocide. Such sentiments, and the demands for intervention to save Biafra, contrasted sharply with the views that I had encountered in 1968 during a series of visits to African universities in eleven countries.

Concern about the suffering and welfare of the civilians inside Biafra was evident throughout Africa, but so were the apprehensions about the Balkanization of Nigeria, especially if this were to be achieved through foreign intervention. The fundamental difference between the prevailing attitude in Africa and public opinion in Western Europe and the United States centered on the issue of whether the survival of the Biafran state was a necessary condition for the survival of the Ibo people. A desire to understand how Nigerian and Biafran authorities tried to deal with the political implications of differing positions on this issue sparked the research for this book.

During a two-year residency in Lagos my wife completed a doctoral study of the sensitive and complex economic issues associated with indigenization of management in foreign-owned corporations, while I assembled most of the material for this book. Neither of us was ever harassed, censored, or in any other way constrained from conducting hundreds of interviews and gathering our data. Following the cessation of hostilities in January 1970, we traveled freely throughout the former Biafran territory. The degree of candor and willingness to recall wartime experiences differed among individuals although, in general, those who had been responsible for Nigeria's and Biafra's foreign relations were equally forthcoming. Several leading Biafrans who contributed to this study were interviewed while in exile; they were as cooperative as those who chose to remain or return to Nigeria soon after the war.

I have chosen not to dwell on the righteousness of either side, and I remain ambivalent about many aspects of the Nigerian civil war and the various ways that the international community reacted to the conflict. Nevertheless, implicit but important value judgments will be evident in every chapter that follows, and no doubt it will be these, as much as the factual presentation and organization, that will concern many readers.

A list of those interviewed appears after the Note on Sources, but special thanks are due to the following: Yakubu Gowon, C. Odumegwu Ojukwu, Allison Ayida, Godwin Onyegbula, Okoi Arikpo, Uche Chukwumeriji, and Dike Nworah. After imposing on so many for so much assistance—particularly Emeka Ojukwu, who agreed to several all-day conversations—I only hope that all concerned will judge this book to be fair and accurate.

Lawrence Fabunmi, as Director General of the Nigerian Institute of International Affairs, provided innumerable courtesies. I also owe much to his successor, the late Olusupo Ojedokun, who became a close friend and mentor. The help of the Institute's library staff under the direction of the late Irene Kluzek certainly eased the task of secondary research. Among my friends in Lagos none was more valued for thoughtful advice and encouragement than my two colleagues at the Institute, Oluwale Idris and Mohammed Brimah.

Robert L. West of the Fletcher School of Law and Diplomacy deserves credit for helping to inspire this study and for closely following its development. As early drafts began to take shape, W. Scott Thompson offered extensive suggestions and selflessly devoted countless hours to strengthening its presentation.

I was fortunate to have the benefit of comments from three other readers who have written extensively about Nigeria. My thanks to David Williams extends well beyond the many improvements that he has made in this manuscript. The insights and incomparable coverage of the Nigerian civil war that he provided as editor of *West Africa* were essential to the development of a framework for this book. John de St. Jorre's revisions of the final draft were only the most recent contributions that this outstanding journalist and author of *The Nigerian Civil War* has made to this project. Finally, I want to express appreciation to Pauline Baker for her frequent and wise counsel throughout my period of research in Nigeria and for prompting several valuable changes in the final draft of the book. I owe her and her husband, Raymond, a great debt of gratitude.

Field research was financed by a Shell International Fellowship that was awarded and administered by the faculty of the Fletcher School of Law and Diplomacy. I am also pleased to acknowledge Penny Gosdigian's generous help in preparing the manuscript for publication.

Above all, I am indebted to my wife, Carolyn, who has shared this entire adventure with me. Her belief in the study, regardless of my own periods of doubt and frustration, was a constant source of strength. Throughout, she has been my most constructive critic, and I have gratefully accepted her many suggestions to improve the style and content of every draft. Without her love and support this book would not have been completed.

CHRONOLOGY OF IMPORTANT EVENTS IN THE NIGERIAN CIVIL WAR

1966

January 15 First Republic overthrown by military. J.T.U. Aguiyi-Ironsi forms military government; C. Odumegwu Ojukwu appointed governor of the Eastern Region and Yakubu Gowon becomes army chief of staff.

May 24 Ironsi issues decree establishing unitary state; followed by riots in the North.

July 29 Second military coup. Yakubu Gowon emerges to succeed Ironsi, who is assassinated.

Late Sept./ early Oct. Rioting and Ibo massacres in North; many Ibos flee to Eastern Region.

1967

January 4–5 Gowon and Ojukwu meet at Aburi, Ghana.

May 27 Gowon issues decree dividing Nigeria's four regions into twelve states. State of emergency declared.

May 30 Ojukwu declares secession and establishment of "Republic of Biafra."

June 12 Eleven civilians appointed commissioners in Federal Executive Council.

June Federal government sends delegation to Soviet Union following rejection by British and U.S. governments of requests for aircraft and arms.

July 6 Fighting breaks out between Biafran and federal troops.

July 10 Ogoja captured by federal First Division, commanded by Col. Mohammed Shuwa. Biafran aircraft bombs Lagos with little damage.

July 15 Nsukka captured by First Division.

July 25 Federal Third Marine Commando Division, commanded by Col. Benjamin Adekunle, captures Bonny ocean terminal, thus controlling access to the sea from Port Harcourt.

July 27 Shell-BP manager arrested in Biafra; released following month.

August 9 Biafran forces invade Midwest, capture Benin, and advance to Ore in the West, thus threatening both Ibadan and Lagos. Two incendiary bombs dropped by Biafran aircraft on petrol storage tanks in Apapa with little damage.

August 10 Gowon announces that what had previously been "police action" against secession is now "total war." Kaduna bombed by Biafran aircraft.

August 11 Biafran aircraft bombs Lagos, causing some civilian casualties.

August Crated MIG–17s brought into Kano airport by Soviet Antonov–12 transports. L–29 Delfin jet trainers arrive at Apapa by sea.

August 10–21	Federal response to loss of Midwest includes formation of the Second Division under Col. Murtala Mohammed. Elements of this division start to move into northern part of Midwest in mid-August.
August 29	In major turning point of war, federal Second Division troops recapture Ore, thereby halting Biafran advance on Lagos.
September 14	OAU summit in Kinshasa agrees to send mission to Lagos for discussions with federal government. Capture of Ikom by federal First Division.
September 20	Benin, Midwest State capital, falls to advance elements of federal Second Division.
October 4	Enugu, Biafran capital, captured by First Division.
October 9	Asaba, on west bank of the Niger River, captured by Second Division. Two spans of Niger River bridge blown up by retreating Biafrans.
October 18	Naval amphibious task force commanded by Adekunle captures Calabar and Parrot Island. Federal forces start to move north to link up with First Division at Ikom to seal Cameroon border.
October/ December	Second Division makes two abortive attempts to cross the Niger River.
November 22–23	OAU Consultative Mission under Emperor Haile Selassie opens talks with Gowon in Lagos.
December 20	Pope Paul's special mission arrives in Lagos.

1968

Early January	Federal Second Division crosses Niger River at Idah and starts advance toward Awka and Onitsha. Federal government replaces existing currency notes.
January 29	Biafran authorities begin issue of their own currency and postage stamps.
February 9–10	Visit to Lagos by Arnold Smith, secretary general, Commonwealth Secretariat.
March 21	Onitsha captured by Second Division.
April 5	Abakaliki captured by First Division.
April 13	Tanzania recognizes Biafra.
April 21	Afikpo captured by First Division.
Late April	Entire Southeastern State captured by Federal forces, with occupation of Ikom, Uyo, Eket, Abak, Ikot Ekpene, and finally, Opobo.
May 6	Bomu oilfields captured by Third Marine Commando Division.
May 6–15	Enaharo and Mbanefo meet in London under Commonwealth auspices.
May 8	Gabon recognizes Biafra.
May 15	Ivory Coast recognizes Biafra.
May 19	Third Marine Commando Division captures Port Harcourt, having already taken the oil refinery at Okrika; Biafrans cut off from the sea.

May 20	Zambia recognizes Biafra.
May 23–31	Kampala peace talks.
May 26	Murtala Mohammed replaced as commander, federal Second Division, by Ibrahim Haruna.
May 27	Czechoslovakia announces embargo on supply of arms to federal government.
June 5	Gowon states federal troops will not advance into the Ibo heartland unless all appeals for a settlement fail. Holland announces embargo on supply of arms to federal government.
June 12	Debate on arms supplies in British House of Commons. France announces embargo on supply of arms to federal government.
June 20–24	British minister of state, Lord Shepherd, visits Lagos; also travels to Enugu and Calabar.
July 5	Belgium announces embargo on arms supply to federal government.
July 15–26	OAU Consultative Committee meeting at Niamey, attended by federal government and Biafran delegations. Adjourned to Addis Ababa.
July 29	Ahoada, last major town in Rivers State, taken by federal Third Marine Commando Division.
July 31	French cabinet statement supports Biafran claim to self-determination.
August 5–9	Peace talks in Addis Ababa.
August 15	Gowon announces "final offensive" into Ibo heartland to begin August 24.
August 28	Federal government requests Britain, Canada, Sweden, Poland, and OAU and UN each to nominate an observer to report on the behavior and conduct of federal troops in Ibo areas.
September 4	Aba captured by federal Third Marine Commando Division.
September 10–11	Federal Fifteenth Commando Brigade captures Oguta.
September 13	Commando brigade elements moving toward Uli airstrip cut off Biafran troops.
September 13–16	Fifth summit of OAU held in Algiers.
September 15	Biafrans retake Oguta.
September 16	Owerri taken by federal Sixteenth Commando Brigade.
September 25–30	Lord Shepherd's second visit to Lagos; he also flies to Port Harcourt and Uyo.
September 30	Okigwi taken by First Division.
November/ December	Nigerian air force starts air strikes on Biafran airstrips with little success.
December 11–17	Lord Shepherd makes third visit to Lagos.
December 15	Tax riots in Western State.
December 21–24	A Biafran offensive to recapture Owerri and Aba fails.

1969

February 22	President Nixon announces appointment of C. Clyde Ferguson as special coordinator for Biafran relief.
March 6	Russian warships pay first courtesy visit to Lagos.
March 12–13	British House of Commons debates Nigeria.
March 26	Federal First Division advances on two axes: the first from Afikpo, aimed at Bende, and the second from Okigwi, south to Umuahia.
March 27–31	Visit of British Prime Minister Harold Wilson and HMS Fearless to Lagos. Wilson also visits Enugu, Port Harcourt, and Calabar, and on March 31 flies to Addis Ababa to discuss civil war with Emperor Haile Selassie.
April 18–20	OAU Consultative Committee on Nigeria meets in Monrovia.
April 22	Umuahia, the Biafran seat of government, captured by federal First Division.
April 25	Biafran troops reoccupy Owerri.
May	Noticeable increase in Biafran activity between the Niger and Ase Rivers in the Okpai and Aboh areas.
May 4	Lieutenant Colonel Ojukwu assumes rank of general.
May 9	Biafrans attack AGIP oil drilling sites in Okpai area, Midwest State; Italian oilmen held as hostages.
May 12	Federal Supreme Military Council announces redeployment of senior field commanders: Obasanjo assumes Adekunle's command over the Third Division, Jalo replaces Haruna in the Second Division, and Bisalla succeeds Shuwa in the First Division.
May 22	Air attacks by Swedish MFI–9B minitrainer aircraft, led by Count Carl Gustav von Rosen, begin against Port Harcourt, Benin, and oil fields in the Rivers and Midwest states.
May 30	One-day visit by Gowon to Togo.
June 1	First indication that Uga airstrip (north of Orlu) used by Biafrans for relief and arms flights.
June 1	Ojukwu issues Ahiara Declaration.
June 5	Swedish Red Cross plane shot down by Nigerian air force near Eket, in Southeastern State. ICRC flights from Cotonou suspended until federal policy clarified.
June 19	Federal government announces approval of a large-scale land relief route into rebel territory.
June 30	Lagos announces that the federal Rehabilitation Committee will coordinate relief in the future.
August 1	Pope Paul meets both federal and Biafran representatives in Kampala.
August 7	Gowon visits Ghana.
August 12	Gowon meets President Zinsou in Dahomey (Benin).
August 13	Tax riots in Western State.
August 17	Former President of Nigeria, Dr. Nnamdi Azikiwe, pays surprise visit to Lagos and has talks with Gowon. They travel to Liberia for 48 hours of further discussion.

August 28 Azikiwe declares support for a united Nigeria at a London press conference.

September 4 Federal government agrees in principle to ICRC plan for daylight flights of relief.

September 5 Azikiwe's formal homecoming to Lagos; later in September he visits all twelve states.

September 6–10 Sixth OAU summit conference held in Addis Ababa.

September 13 Agreement signed by ICRC and federal government for daylight relief flights into Uli airstrip.

September 14 Ojukwu rejects ICRC-Lagos daylight relief flights agreement.

October 15 Western State government announces tax and associated concessions to rioters.

October 25 Gowon visits Congo (Zaire).

Mid-November Marked signs of federal buildup for new offensive.

December 5–10 Maurice Foley, British parliamentary undersecretary, in Lagos for talks with federal government.

December 14 Federal army prepared for offensive and reported waiting authorization from Lagos.

December 15–18 Effort to launch peace talks in Addis Ababa.

December 17 Ojukwu again rejects daylight relief flights.

December 27 Federal Third Division elements from Aba link up with First Division at Umuahia, cutting off more than 500 square miles of Biafran enclave.

1970

January 7 Owerri falls to federal Third Division.

January 11 Ojukwu leaves Biafra for Ivory Coast.

January 12 Uli airstrip captured. Federal First and Third Divisions meet at Orlu. Major General Philip Effiong, officer administering the Biafran government since Ojukwu's departure, broadcasts surrender over Radio Biafra.

January 13 Gowon accepts Biafran surrender.

January 14 Biafran armistice mission arrives in Lagos.

PART I

AN AFRICAN AFFAIR

· 1 ·

NIGERIA'S PREWAR FOREIGN POLICY

In June 1966, less than twelve months before Biafran secession, Nigeria's head of state, Major General Aguiyi-Ironsi, summoned his ambassadors from their diplomatic posts in Africa for six days of consultations in Lagos. The meeting was to have been the start of a series of ambassadorial gatherings leading to a comprehensive review of foreign policy, the first since Nigeria achieved independence from Britain in 1960. The decision to begin with an assessment of the federal government's interests in Africa was explained by General Ironsi:

> In the whole sphere of Nigeria's external relations, the Government attaches the greatest importance to our African policy. We are aware that because of our population and potentials, the majority of opinion in the civilized world looks up to us to provide responsible leadership in Africa; and we realize that we shall be judged, to a very great extent, by the degree of success or failure with which we face up to the challenge which this expectation throws on us. We are convinced that whether in the political, economic or cultural sphere, our destiny lies in our role in the continent of Africa.[1]

Seven weeks later, Ironsi was dead, a victim of Nigeria's second military coup in less than seven months, and the country slipped to the brink of anarchy. Aspirations for leadership in Africa had to be abandoned, as the formulation and execution of a coherent foreign policy became impossible under conditions of domestic chaos. Not until late 1967, well into the civil war, did the federal military government under General Yakubu Gowon succeed in establishing a policy framework for the conduct of international relations, and Africa emerged as the central focus of Nigeria's civil war diplomacy. The basic strategy, which prevailed until the end of the conflict in January 1970, was defensive, aimed at limiting Biafra's penetration of the international system. Nigeria—the would-be giant of Africa—ironically found itself tied to a foreign policy that depended in large measure on the willingness of other African governments to maintain a solid front of

[1] Remarks by the Head of State to the Regional Conference of Heads of Missions in Africa (cited hereafter as RCHM-A), Lagos, June 9, 1966, Cn 1/21/I, 114.

3

diplomatic support as a means of discouraging intervention that would foster Biafran independence.

Unlike the Congo crisis a few years earlier, the Nigerian civil war did not polarize Africa or seriously intensify tensions between the United States and the Soviet Union; nor did it bring an influx of United Nations peace-keeping forces. To understand official foreign reaction to the conflict in Nigeria, black Africa's richest and most populous country, one should be aware of the federal government's role in international affairs prior to Biafran secession on May 30, 1967. Diplomacy, after all, is a cumulative process, and Nigeria's previous behavior influenced foreign reaction to the civil war. The federal government's experience during this earlier period also helped shape its effort to control the degree of external involvement in its domestic conflict. This chapter will present a brief outline of Nigeria's prewar foreign policy, with special emphasis on intra-African relations, and it will conclude with a description of how the federal government conducted its diplomacy.

NATIONAL INTERESTS AND FOREIGN RELATIONS

In the years following Independence, Nigeria's civilian leaders became increasingly embroiled in conflicts resulting from their attempts to consolidate national authority over some 250 linguistically distinct groups, which are scattered across the country's 356,699 square miles—an area comparable to Italy, France, Belgium, and Holland combined. Nigeria was the epitome of what William Zartman referred to as the new "state-nations" in Africa: a former colonial territory that had acquired the formal institutions and sovereign rights of a modern state, but was so badly fragmented that national allegiance remained in doubt.[2] Under these circumstances, Nigeria's political elite was too preoccupied with domestic affairs to pay much attention to international issues. Once the British had withdrawn, the various political groups within Nigeria sought to consolidate their positions and to seize control at the center by engineering a series of lavishly financed and ethnically rooted coalitions that were progressively disruptive and untenable. Shortly after the first military coup in January 1966, the Ministry of External Affairs undertook an analysis of Nigeria's global interests. The result of this exercise was not a report but a set of tables (see Appendix I). Nigeria's interests were divided into eighteen categories, and each state in the international system was graded, according to its relative interest to Nigeria, on a scale from one to ten in each of the eighteen categories. A foreign power's composite score

[2] Zartman, "Characteristics of Developing Foreign Policies."

thus could range from 18 to 180. Not surprisingly, Britain led the list (163), followed by the United States (145), West Germany (106), Canada (104), and France (101).

The table provides an interesting insight into official perceptions of the scope and intensity of Nigeria's external relations barely a year before the outbreak of civil war. The perspective is much broader and more diverse than the British had projected when the Nigerian foreign office was created on the eve of Independence, and the subsequent institutional changes reflect the growing role Nigeria played in African affairs. In 1960, only two of Nigeria's seven diplomatic posts were in Africa, but by 1966 twenty-four out of a total of forty-two resident missions were located on the continent. If one refers back to the 1966 table of interests, and aggregates Nigeria's foreign concerns by region, Africa scores higher than the total for Europe and North America combined, primarily because of the importance ascribed to racial affinity.

At the global level, Lagos sought unabashedly to maintain close relations with Britain and other Western governments, for this was seen as the way to maximize economic development, a key element in promoting greater domestic integration. "Moderate" and "pragmatic" are the terms that Western scholars most frequently invoke to describe the international conduct of Sir Abubakar Tafawa Balewa's government (1960–1966).[3] From 1960 to 1968, Nigeria received $273 million in technical and capital assistance from the Organization for Economic Cooperation and Development (OECD) countries—Western Europe, the United States, Canada, and Japan.[4] Nigeria was the biggest recipient of OECD funds in Africa. While this figure pales when compared with the enormous oil revenues that accrued to the federal government in the 1970s, Western foreign aid and investment contributed significantly to the 5.7 percent annual rate of economic growth in real terms attained during the early 1960s. This economic input was considered vital by those political leaders who influenced the distribution of aid projects and federal revenue so as to reward important constituencies.

In addition to foreign aid, 85 percent of Nigeria's exports were sold to OECD countries, and close to 75 percent of Nigeria's imports came from that group. Nigeria offered the largest market in Africa,

[3] See Phillips, *The Development of Nigerian Foreign Policy*; Coleman, "The Foreign Policy of Nigeria"; and Cowan, "Nigerian Foreign Policy." Unpublished works that stress the same underlying attitudes in Nigeria's post-Independence foreign policy include: Gray, "The Foreign Policy Process in the Emerging African Nation: Nigeria"; Azikiwe, "Nigerian Foreign Policy 1960–1965"; and Idowu, "Foreign Policy of Nigeria 1960–1965."

[4] Nelson *et al., Area Handbook for Nigeria*, pp. 376–379.

and its capitalist economy was among the most hospitable to Western investments.[5] A further indication of Nigeria's steadily improving economic standing was the July 1966 agreement that provided for associate status with the European Economic Community, the first non-francophone African country to receive such consideration.[6] Nigeria had for many years been the world's second leading exporter of cocoa and groundnuts, the foremost exporter of palm products, and the fifth largest seller of natural rubber. Earnings from these and other primary products financed most of the country's early development, and later helped pay for the civil war. Table 1–1 highlights the aggregate trade flow between Nigeria and her major partners during the war years, a pattern that had been established during the early 1960s.

Petroleum was a relatively insignificant source of foreign exchange until 1969, when it accounted for most of the sharp rise in export earnings that appears in the table.[7] Approximately 400,000 barrels a day were produced in 1966, compared with 2,000,000 barrels a day seven years later. Yet the prospect of great oil wealth—even without any premonition of the sharply rising prices of the 1970s—naturally affected the rosy economic outlook in 1966, and was another reason for strengthening ties with Europe and America. The federal government sought to be recognized as a nonaligned power because, as the prime minister explained in his first foreign policy address, such a status "will ensure that full attention is paid to the opinions expressed by our representatives."[8] Nigeria's overwhelming foreign economic interests were, however, with the major Western powers.

Economic dealings with the Communist bloc, by comparison, remained negligible throughout the 1960s. Little development assistance was sought or forthcoming, and only some 6 percent of Nigeria's imports came from the Soviet Union, China, and Eastern Europe combined. Barely 3 percent of the country's exports were sold to the Eastern bloc. On a more basic level, there was in Nigeria a deep national commitment to a free enterprise system, a widespread admiration for

---

[5] See Kilby, *Industrialization in an Open Economy, Nigeria 1945–1966*, chapters 1 and 2.

[6] The agreement lapsed in 1969 because the French declined to sign. This was assumed to reflect the pro-Biafran policies of Charles de Gaulle. In fact, there was probably more at stake than a "show of humanitarian concern." Nigerian Ministry of External Affairs records show that Lagos believed the reason it took so long to draft the initial agreement was because of French obstructionism within the European Economic Community, which grew out of de Gaulle's desire to perpetuate the special relationship with the former French colonies already enjoying associate status.

[7] See Pearson, *Petroleum and the Nigerian Economy*, for a discussion of this period.

[8] Statement by the Prime Minister, *House of Representatives Debates*, August 20, 1960 (Lagos: Federal Government Printer, 1960).

TABLE 1-1

Principal Trading Partners of Nigeria 1967-1969
(value in millions of Nigerian pounds)*

Country of Origin or Destination	Imports			Exports		
	1967	1968	1969	1967	1968	1969
United Kingdom	64.6	59.9	86.3	70.3	61.9	87.7
Netherlands	9.3	7.8	11.6	30.8	27.0	42.8
United States	27.8	22.3	29.3	18.5	16.0	40.0
West Germany	25.2	21.2	26.4	25.1	17.9	19.3
Italy	10.7	13.8	13.5	14.1	13.1	14.5
France	9.4	7.2	8.0	22.4	11.5	31.9
Soviet Union, Eastern Europe, and the People's Republic of China	13.8	12.1	14.3	7.5	12.2	12.3
African countries	2.6	4.3	5.5	2.8	2.0	3.0
Other countries	60.1	44.0	53.8	46.6	44.9	66.6
Total	223.5	192.6	248.7	238.1	206.5	318.1

Source: adapted from Nigeria, Federal Office of Statistics, Nigerian Trade Summary, December 1967, 1968, 1969 (Lagos, 1968, 1969, 1970). Table appears in Nelson, et al., Area Handbook for Nigeria, p. 370.

*One Nigerian pound equals U.S. $2.80.

Western democracies, where many of the modern elite had been educated, and a suspicion of Soviet intentions in Africa. The latter feeling was particularly strong in the Northern Region, where Communism was considered by a Moslem elite to be synonymous with atheism. This wariness was reflected in the federal government's decision to delay opening an embassy in Moscow until 1963.[9]

When a group of social scientists conducted an extensive survey of the attitudes of Nigerian legislators in late 1962 and early 1963, they uncovered an international outlook that held few surprises.[10] Regarding the cold war, the legislators were asked whether Nigeria

[9] When the Soviet embassy was established in Lagos in 1961, the number of its diplomatic staff was limited to ten, whereas no such restriction was placed on the diplomatic missions of Britain and the United States. While only five diplomatic car plates were allocated to the Soviet embassy, one hunderd each were given to the British and Americans. Aluko, "The Civil War and Nigerian Foreign Policy."

[10] Free, The Attitudes, Hopes and Fears of Nigerians. One hundred members of the Nigerian federal House of Representatives were selected by random sampling from a list of all such legislators.

7

should: (1) side with the United States, Britain, and their allies; (2) side with Russia and its allies; or (3) side with neither. The responses were as follows:[11]

	Legislators
side with United States, Britain, etc.	41%
side with Russia, etc.	2
side with neither	50
qualified answers	6
no opinion	1
	100%

Asked to indicate their opinions of various countries on a ten-to-one, high-to-low scale, the composite results were:[12]

	Composite Score
United States	8.3
Great Britain	6.9
Russia	4.6

The attitudes behind these figures revealed that "usefulness" was a principal criterion. The British had helped Nigeria before Independence, but they were less helpful currently. Six out of ten of the respondents gave as the reason for the high rating accorded the United States that "Americans have helped Nigeria" and "are prepared to continue to help us." The Soviet Union was admired for its science and space achievements, but criticized, first because it was Communist and totalitarian, and second because Russia had done nothing to help Nigeria.[13]

By mid-1966, relations with Moscow seemed to be improving, although few would have predicted that when the civil war erupted, only the Soviet Union would agree to supply the federal government with the aircraft it considered necessary for preserving the integrity of the country.[14] When the Conference of Nigerian Ambassadors met in June 1966, the Nigerian embassy in Moscow prepared a lengthy analysis of Soviet intentions in Africa, especially toward Nigeria.[15] While noting that "Soviet leaders have never at any time repudiated the messianic communist doctrine," the report confidently observed that "Soviet cam-

---

[11] *Ibid.*, p. 5.   [12] *Ibid.*, p. 9.   [13] *Ibid.*, pp. 11–18.

[14] This will be discussed in Chapter 3 below. The Soviet Union seemed pleased by the change of government in Nigeria, which brought a southern Ibo to power in January 1966. See Legvold, *Soviet Policy in West Africa*, pp. 269–274.

[15] "Soviet Political Intentions in Africa," report prepared by the Nigerian embassy in Moscow preparatory to the June 1966 Conference of Nigerian Ambassadors in Africa and forwarded to the Ministry of External Affairs by Ambassador Ifeagwu, May 16, 1966, pp. 2–3.

paigns in Africa so far have not met with any real or apparent success; [and] in the face of this unbroken record of failures, the architects of Soviet policy have been compelled to adjust the special ideological spectacles through which they had looked at Africa in the past . . . current Soviet policy lays increasing emphasis on encouraging the image of the USSR as a benevolent industrial power whose only desire is to live and trade in peace . . . while maintaining the same long-run strategy and goals . . . the eventual victory of communism."[16]

It was recommended that Nigeria take steps to exploit this change in Soviet tactics toward Africa in order to further two specific interests. The first suggestion was that the federal government sign an economic and technical cooperation agreement with Russia. In the absence of such an agreement, Lagos had learned that it could only take advantage of Soviet technical assistance on a commercial basis and that the Soviet contracts had proven exorbitant.[17] Second, it was urged that Lagos sign a cultural agreement with the Soviets. At the time, more than five hundred Nigerian students were studying in Russian universities, most of them sponsored by Nigerian trade unions rather than by the Nigerian government. To get to Russia, the students usually secured travel permits to visit nearby West African countries, whence they could then depart for Moscow. The federal government considered this illegal, and the report concluded that a cultural agreement was essential "to force an undertaking that all offers of scholarships and recruitment of students should be done only through Nigerian government and approved channels."[18] The cultural agreement was initialed in Lagos in March 1967 and signed in August of the same year; the agreement on economic and technical cooperation was not concluded until November 1968.[19]

[16] *Ibid.* Examples of these setbacks were given as follows: "The Soviet attempt to subvert the Government of Guinea was detected in good time and this led to the expulsion of the Soviet Ambassador from Guinea in 1961. They have suffered other setbacks. The Communist Party has been banned in the Sudan. In the U.A.R. several communists have been arrested and charged with plotting to overthrow the Government of President Nasser. In Algeria the underground communist movement is being repressively suppressed by the authorities. It will be remembered that also in Kenya the Government turned back Soviet arms apparently supplied at the request of somebody in Kenya. Similarly, the overthrow of President Nkrumah during the recent military coup in Ghana marks another setback for the Soviet diplomacy in Africa."

[17] *Ibid.*, Part II, "Nigerian-Soviet Trade and Economic Relations," p. 7. The embassy staff was especially irked at a contract signed August 25, 1965, between the former government of Eastern Nigeria and the Soviet trading organization, "Techno-export," for a feasibility study with a view to establishing a specialist hospital in Enugu by Soviet technicians. The undertaking proved to be an "expensive commercial proposition" and, apparently to its surprise, the Eastern Region government found it had to pay for nearly all the work in foreign exchange.

[18] *Ibid.*, Part III, "African Education in the USSR," p. 11.

[19] Nigeria, Ministry of Justice, *Nigeria's Treaties in Force*, Vol. I.

Aside from these interests and the concern about possible Soviet influence among radical African states, Nigeria's relations with Moscow during the prewar years were correct but limited.

As for the close ties to Western powers, the Balewa government came under severe domestic criticism on only one occasion. This concerned a defense agreement with Great Britain that was arranged prior to Independence and was passed by the Nigerian legislature in November 1960. The agreement contained a secret understanding granting Nigeria military assistance as a quid pro quo for British air staging facilities, which would have remained under British control. Leaked information about the secret clause caused such a furor in Lagos that the treaty was abrogated by mutual consent in early 1962.[20] Otherwise, there were few strains between Lagos and London during these early years.

When Ian Smith unilaterally declared the independence of Southern Rhodesia on November 11, 1965, Nigeria discouraged other African governments from breaking diplomatic relations or taking other reprisals against Britain.[21] In return, Prime Minister Wilson agreed to devote the major portion of the January 1966 Commonwealth Prime Ministers' Conference to the Rhodesian question, and the meeting was held in Lagos, the first time that the heads of government had convened outside London.[22] The session helped to quell international criticism of the Wilson government; but if it enhanced the prestige of the Nigerian government, this was obscured by the military coup two days after the conference adjourned.

The most overt conflict between Nigeria and a Western power prior to the civil war occurred shortly after Independence, when France persisted in testing atomic weapons in the Algerian Sahara. After several warnings, the federal government suddenly broke diplomatic relations with Paris on January 5, 1961, imposed a complete embargo on all French goods, and gave the French ambassador forty-eight hours to leave the country.[23] The action was uncharacteristically abrupt, and was taken soon after the embarrassing revelations about the British defense agreement, at a time when the opposition in Parliament was sounding increasingly radical and appeared to be gaining strength. The break with France was popular domestically, and may have helped the Balewa government. As a diplomatic move, however, the gesture appears to have

[20] Ojedokun, "Nigeria's Relations with the Commonwealth, with Special Reference to Her Relations with the United Kingdom, 1960–1966."

[21] This was recalled approvingly by the Conference of Heads of Mission in Africa, which met in Lagos, June 9–14, 1966.

[22] Commonwealth of Nations, Meeting of Commonwealth Prime Ministers, Minutes of Meetings and Memoranda, Lagos, January 11–12, 1966.

[23] For an account of this incident, see Phillips, *The Development of Nigerian Foreign Policy*, pp. 124–126.

been a serious mistake. In the short run, it caused enormous economic hardship for Nigeria's improverished, land-locked francophone neighbors to the north and for tiny Dahomey (Benin) on the west coast. Moreover, Nigeria's rebuke failed to stop the atomic tests and did not encourage other African governments to sever relations with Paris.

The expulsion of the French ambassador also contradicted Nigeria's more basic policy of striving quietly to supplant France as the dominant power in West Africa.[24] As will be noted in later references to Nigeria's relations with its francophone neighbors, Lagos has never entertained any delusions about the extent of French influence over the former colonies or about the federal government's limited financial capability —at least before the era of oil wealth—to offer these countries sufficient incentives to lessen their dependence on France.[25] Nevertheless, a fundamental assumption of Nigeria's foreign policy has been that over the long term, France's interests in West Africa would gradually recede and the former colonial areas would look to Nigeria for leadership in the areas of international security and economic development. In the meantime, Lagos sought to avoid exciting any fears among her weaker neighbors that might have encouraged them to seek closer ties with the former colonial protector.[26]

The moderate to conservative diplomacy which, with the exception of the expulsion of the French in 1961, typified the foreign policy of the Balewa government also reflected the need to maintain a viable coalition in Lagos. Given the severe internal strains and constant readjustments that had to be made to sustain such a coalition, the prime minister usually sought to avoid becoming embroiled in world issues that might have afforded his domestic opposition an opportunity to stir up debate. Unless East-West tensions intruded on Africans affairs, they were generally ignored by the prime minister and his foreign office.

Nigeria's self-avowed political interests related almost exclusively to the changing conditions in Africa. In the broadest sense, Nigerian leaders viewed their country's international prestige as a function of the extent to which Nigeria was considered a leader of black Africa. As one

[24] Whether the affront had any bearing on President de Gaulle's inclination to support Biafran secession can only be surmised. M. Raymond Offroy, the French ambassador who was so unceremoniously deported, seven years later became one of the most prominent figures in the pro-Biafran lobby in France.

[25] This entire matter was reviewed in great detail in preparation for the June 1966 Conference of Nigerian Ambassadors. RCHM-A, "The Economic Dependence of the Afro-Malagasy States on France, A Working Paper," Lagos, June 3, 1966.

[26] A strong endorsement to continue this policy of restraint is set forth in RCHM-A, Working Paper No. 1, "Nigeria's Relations with Other African Countries," Section C, "Nigeria's Bilateral Relationship with Individual African States: French Speaking Africa," Lagos, June 1966.

of the working papers for the 1966 policy review conference for Nigerian ambassadors flatly asserted, "Africa is Nigeria's natural sphere of influence. To shirk this manifest destiny is not to heed the logic of history."[27] Yet beneath these assertions there have been more immediate concerns. To quote from another of the documents prepared for the ambassadors' conference: "Our interest in African affairs has naturally been far from altruistic. Indeed, our African posture and attitude has been respectively shaped and guided by the traditional concept of protecting and promoting our vital national interests, the most important of which is to create conditions at home and around us conducive to political stability.[28]

It was often said during the Nigerian civil war that African leaders felt compelled to support the federal government out of a fear that if Biafra were successful, this might inspire secessionist movements elsewhere in the region; a similar attitude certainly lay at the heart of Nigerian foreign policy before the war. Given the fragility of the country's federal structure, Nigeria's leaders were anxious that the surrounding international environment in West Africa should be conducive to domestic tranquility. Regarding the right of a people to self-determination, a Ministry of External Affairs briefing paper had this to say: "This principle [self-determination] underlies our efforts to secure the decolonization of those parts of Africa still under the colonial yoke. . . . But a word of caution here is necessary: the principle of self-determination in its purely theoretical context may be at variance with the other important principle of territorial integrity. This means that some sections of existing states may claim self-rule on the principle of self-determination. This, however, is not what is meant by the principle in the context of our African policy."[29]

Nigeria's true national interest, in the opinion of the country's ambassadors, were the same in 1966 as they had been in 1960, and these were reiterated in the conference report as follows:

I. to ensure political stability and internal security, the *sine qua non* for orderly and progressive development of Nigeria's resources for the benefit of Nigerians;

[27] RCHM-A, Working Paper No. 2, "Nigeria's Role in the OAU," Lagos, June 1966.

[28] RCHM-A, Working Paper No. 1, Section A, "The Place of Africa in Nigeria's Foreign Policy," Lagos, June 1966.

[29] The context for this commentary was a paper prepared by the embassy staff in Khartoum, Sudan, which refers specifically to the attempted secession by the Negroid southern Sudanese from a state dominated by Arab northerners. Throughout the 1960s the federal government invariably refused to aid or even talk to representatives from the southern part of Sudan. See "Nigeria's African Foreign Policy, Purposes, Principles and Practices," prepared by the embassy of Nigeria, Khartoum, for the Conference of Nigerian Ambassadors, undated.

II. to insulate Nigeria from external subversion;

III. to ensure respect for Nigerian sovereignty and territorial integrity;

IV. to create suitable conditions for cooperation with African countries in economic, technical, cultural and other fields;

V. to protect the interests and dignity of those [tens of thousands of] Nigerians residing in [West] Africa.[30]

The ambassadors further concluded that Nigeria should pursue these interests according to five basic principles. The first of these was "pragmatism . . . to work on the basis of what is clear, practicable and realistic."[31] That the conference should elevate "pragmatism" to the level of high principle reflects an implicit rejection of ideological debate and a belief that if Nigeria were to play an effective role in international affairs, it had to remain sufficiently flexible to adapt to changing conditions.

The second principle committed the federal government to "respect existing boundaries in Africa [which] . . . must, in the interest of peace in Africa, remain the recognized boundaries until such a time as the peoples concerned decide of their own free will to merge into one unit."[32] Nigeria would not support international integration by force or coercion. Complementing this pledge was the principle of "non-interference in the internal affairs of other states," and a fourth principle that demanded "respect of the sovereign equality of all states no matter their size, population, military or economic might."[33]

The fifth and final principle may sound rather hollow in light of subsequent developments within Nigeria: the ambassadors reaffirmed the federal government's firm support for the peaceful settlement of disputes by negotiation, conciliation, and arbitration, adding that "we refuse to take or encourage dogmatic stands from which no compromise is possible."[34] In fact, the government's approach to settling the civil war was not completely inconsistent with this principle of foreign policy, as the chapters on civil-war negotiations will indicate.

The June 1966 ambassadors' conference also recommended that Nigeria pursue four objectives in Africa:

I. maintenance of good neighborly relations with all states in general and with our immediate neighbors in particular;

II. cooperation with other African states to prevent Africa from becoming an area of crisis and world tension;

---

[30] RCHM-A, Summary of Recommendations and Conclusions, CN 1/21/II, Lagos, June 14, 1966.

[31] *Ibid.*   [32] *Ibid.*   [33] *Ibid.*   [34] *Ibid.*

III. dedication to fostering the systematic evolution towards unity in the Continent; and

IV. emancipation of all African territories under foreign domination, and the eradication of racial discrimination.[35]

The above objectives were stamped "Top Secret," along with all the other documents from the 1966 ambassadors' conference. Actually, these objectives and the principles behind them were neither new nor unknown. Nigeria's leaders had been espousing them publicly for five and a half years and, as will be discussed in the succeeding pages, the conduct of Nigeria's intra-African relations—the most dynamic and politically important element in the country's foreign policy—was rarely, if ever, at variance with these objectives.

PROMOTING STABILITY IN AFRICA

Nigeria was born in an age when the internal upheavals in the former Belgian Congo had become the cutting edge of the cold war. In his 1960 foreign policy address, Prime Minister Balewa declared: "It is true that Africa is changing every day . . . but with the good developments are bound to be some bad ones and we are troubled by the signs which we see of the ideological war between the Great Powers of the world creeping into Africa. We shall therefore take steps to persuade the African leaders to take serious note of this distressing trend and we shall make every effort to bring them together, so that we may all find a way to unite our efforts in preventing Africa from becoming an area of crisis and world tension."[36] The statement was indicative of the federal government's pragmatic approach to African unity as a means of achieving greater political independence and security for all nonwhite countries of the region. In pursuit of this objective, the federal government would take the lead in promoting the formation of a pan-African alliance that, in May 1963, became the Organization of African Unity (OAU).

The greatest challenge to Nigeria's views of what would constitute a desirable and feasible level of regional political cooperation was raised by President Kwame Nkrumah of Ghana, who preached the establishment of an African military high command and continental "union government."[37] Nkrumah's charisma and the aggressiveness of his foreign policy produced a mixture of contempt, envy, and occasional apprehension in Lagos. Although Nigeria's leaders never doubted

[35] *Ibid.*

[36] Statement by the prime minister, *House of Representatives Debates*, August 20, 1960.

[37] For a definitive study of Nkrumah's foreign policy, see Thompson, *Ghana's Foreign Policy 1957–1966.*

14

Nkrumah's lack of realism, they considered his actions to be a threat to international peace and stability in Africa as well as to Nigeria's own internal security and prestige.[38] The main concern of Nigeria's diplomacy in Africa during the early 1960s was thus to isolate Nkrumah and make certain that his initiatives did not shatter the emerging regional consensus or directly subvert the fragile federal coalition in Lagos. Well-documented revelations in 1962 about Nkrumah's links with Nigeria's leading opposition party, and the widespread suspicion that he was somehow responsible for the assassination of Togolese President Sylvanus Olympio, nearly caused a break in diplomatic relations with Accra, and spurred Nigerian efforts to win the allegiance of governments throughout Africa.[39]

Because Nigeria's vulnerability to subversion was shared by many other newly independent states in the African region, the federal government's role in organizing diplomatic opposition to Nkrumah earned the respect and confidence of many prospective members of the Organization of African Unity. Eighteen months before the OAU was formed, the federal government invited all independent African states to send their foreign ministers to a meeting in Lagos which, in Ghana's absence, reached a tentative agreement on the formula for the OAU Charter.[40]

When the federal delegation left for the first pan-African summit in May 1963, it carried a brief prepared by the Ministry of External Affairs that outlined the basic objectives as follows:

[38] Looking back on this era shortly after Nkrumah was deposed, an analysis prepared by the Nigerian Ministry of External Affairs notes: "On attainment of independence, Ghana was quick to sever all the common links which existed between British West Africa and so the very foundation on which West African Unity could have been built was shattered. . . . They not only discriminated against Nigerians [living in Ghana] in the matter of employment but even engaged in subversive activities against Nigeria and heaped unbearable insults on our leaders. Jealous of Nigeria's resources and her size which marked her out for leadership in Africa, they did everything possible to discredit us the world over." RCHM-A, Working Paper No. 1, Section C, "Nigeria's Bilateral Relationship with Individual African States: Ghana," Lagos, June 1966.

[39] For an account of Nkrumah's role in Nigeria's internal affairs, see Thompson, *Ghana's Foreign Policy*, pp. 237–244. While evidence exists concerning Nkrumah's earlier attempts to overthrow Olympio, his complicity in the actual event remains unclear. *Ibid.*, pp. 308–313.

[40] Lagos Conference of the Heads of African and Malagasy States Organization, Verbatim Report of the Plenary Sessions, Lagos, January 25–30, 1962. Those attending the December 1962 meeting included: Cameroon, the Central African Republic, Chad, Congo (Brazzaville), Congo (Zaire), Dahomey (Benin), Ethiopia, Gabon, Ivory Coast, Liberia, Madagascar, Mauritania, Nigeria, Niger, Senegal, Sierra Leone, Somalia, Tanganyika (Tanzania), Togo, and Upper Volta. A useful background study in this field is Legum, *Pan Africanism: A Short Political Guide*; also, Wallerstein, *Africa, the Politics of Unity*.

Prior to any discussion of a Common Charter, all the participants at the conference should be asked to affirm the following principles:

(a) sovereign equality of African and Malagasy States, whatever may be the size of their territories and the density of their populations, or the value of their possessions;

(b) non-interference in the internal affairs of Member States;

(c) respect for the sovereignty and territorial integrity of each State and for its inalienable right to independent existence;

(d) peaceful and harmonious settlement of all disputes arising among the African and Malagasy States;

(e) unqualified condemnation of any subversive activity on the part of neighboring or other States;

(f) the constant promotion and fostering of all available means of cooperation in the fields of economics, health, nutrition, education, and culture; and

(g) dedication to the total emancipation of the remaining dependent territories of Africa.[41]

With the exception of principle (f), which was replaced by a plank affirming "a policy of non-alignment with regard to all blocs," the seven points in the Nigerian brief reappear almost verbatim in Article III of the OAU Charter.[42]

Elaborating on Nigeria's position during the summit proceedings, Prime Minister Balewa reminded his fellow heads of state that

Nigeria's stand is that if we want unity in Africa, we must first agree to certain essential things; the first is that African States must respect one another. There must be acceptance of equality by all the States. No matter whether they are big or small, they are all sovereign and sovereignty is sovereignty. The size of a State, its population or its wealth should not be the criteria. It has been pointed out many times that the smaller States in Africa have no right to exist because they are too small. We in Nigeria do not agree. It was unfortunate that the African States have been broken up into different groups by the Colonial powers. In some cases, a single tribe has been broken up into four different States. You might find a section in Guinea, a section in Mali, a second in Sierra Leone and perhaps a section in Liberia. That was not our fault because, for over sixty years, these different units have been existing and any attempt on the part of any

41 Ministry of External Affairs (cited hereafter as MEA), Brief on the Addis Ababa Conference of Africa and Malagasy Heads of State and Government, Lagos, May 15, 1963.

42 For a detailed analysis of the OAU Charter, see Cervenka, *The Organization of African Unity and Its Charter*.

country to disregard this fact might bring trouble to this Continent. This is the thing we want to avoid.[43]

Not only did acceptance of Balewa's view of African unity help to contain Nkrumah—thereby serving Nigeria's immediate interests in 1963—but the subsequent formation of a regional alliance based on the principles set forth in Article III of the OAU Charter was to offer the federal government a line of defense that proved very useful in its civil war diplomacy.

During the three years following the creation of the OAU, the Balewa government lobbied vigorously to ensure its viability. In 1965, when the organization was very nearly destroyed by another intra-West African dispute over allegations of Ghanaian subversion, Nigeria arranged for an extraordinary session of the OAU Council of Ministers in Lagos,[44] which set in motion a series of diplomatic compromises that tended to limit Nkrumah's ability to interfere with the domestic politics of other OAU members, thus strengthening the norms of mutual respect for sovereign equality and territorial integrity. In light of the deep ideological cleavages that had polarized Africa during the previous five years, the establishment of a credible regional organization was a major diplomatic achievement for which Nigerians claim considerable credit.[45]

The Federal Ministry of External Affairs' perceptions of the OAU's importance were reiterated during the 1966 Conference of Nigerian Ambassadors in Lagos. A policy paper prepared for that meeting flatly rejected any suggestion that Nigeria was self-sufficient enough to withdraw from the OAU, or that the regional body was no more than a debating forum. Noting that the dissolution of the OAU was "unthinkable," the policy paper concluded with several a priori assumptions that held that if the organization were ever to disappear, "many more states would fall upon each other's throats and that Africa would become a battleground without an umpire for the big world powers. Reduced to a lone wolf, Nigeria cannot hope to effectively shield herself from international intrigues either by her size or natural resources.

[43] Proceedings of the Summit Conference of Independent African States, Vol. I, Section 2, Addis Ababa, May 1963. Statement by the Rt. Hon. Prime Minister of Nigeria, Sir Abubakar Tafawa Balewa.

[44] Verbatim and Summary Record of the Fifth Extraordinary Session of the Council of Ministers of the Organization of African Unity, Lagos, June 10–13, 1965.

[45] Reviewing the formative years of the OAU, a 1966 working paper prepared by the Nigerian Ministry of External Affairs concluded that: "Nigeria's contribution has been to keep the OAU from drifting from the principles which inspired its creation. We have by our words and deeds emphasized over and over again the vital importance of the need to eschew interference in the internal affairs of other states," RCHM-A, Working Paper No. 2, Lagos, June 1966.

. . . With all its manifest faults, the OAU provides a forum for the collective expression of African opinion on matters affecting the destiny of the continent as well as the international community. Should it disintegrate, Africa's voice will count for little in a world impregnated with enlightened self-interest."[46]

The prospects for international peace and security in Africa seemed especially promising in the spring of 1966. The conflict in the Congo (Zaire) had subsided, and with it much of the divisive bitterness that had undermined regional cooperation during the early 1960s. More importantly for Nigeria, Kwame Nkrumah had been deposed. The Ministry of External Affairs noted hopefully that "with Nkrumah and his inordinate ambitions out of the scene, the way may now be open for a new happy chapter in the history of Nigeria/Ghana relations, and indeed, West African cooperation."[47] A delegation representing the new Ghanaian head of state, General Joseph Ankrah, came to Lagos shortly after the coup and, according to Nigerian records, "expressed Ankrah's strong desire to resume the positive cooperation of the colonial years."[48]

Nigeria's relations with her immediate neighbors also appeared in 1966 to be better than ever before.[49] The irredentist rhetoric that occasionally surfaced in the federal legislature, notably with regard to the possibility of Nigeria annexing the Spanish island of Fernando Po, where thousands of Ibo laborers worked on plantations, disappeared with the advent of military rule in Lagos.[50] The thousands of Yorubas living in Dahomey (Benin) and the mix of Hausa/Fulani along the long frontier with Niger facilitated smuggling, and the escape of fugitives and even of some dissident local politicians, but the international political tensions were minor. Of slightly greater concern to Lagos was the notion that the Cameroon Republic harbored ill will toward Nigeria as a result of the United Nations-administered referendum (1961) in Sardauna Province (formerly Northern Cameroon). By 1966 the ceding of this territory was still being commemorated by a day of national mourning throughout the Cameroon Republic. In addition to this issue, the international frontier between Cameroon and Eastern Nigeria remained undefined, and the arbitration of the boundary had become complicated by the prospects of oil reserves in the Calabar riverine border areas. Aside from these issues, however, relations with Yaoundé had been steadily im-

[46] *Ibid.*

[47] RCHM-A, Working Paper No. 1, Section C, "Nigeria's Bilateral Relationship with Individual African States: Ghana."

[48] *Ibid.*

[49] RCHM-A, Working Paper No. 1, Section C, "Nigeria's Bilateral Relationship with Individual African States: Nigeria's Immediate Neighbors," Lagos, June 1966.

[50] See Akinyemi, "Nigeria and Fernando Po, 1958–1966, The Politics of Irredentism."

proving, a fact of enormous political significance at the time of Biafran secession.

Elsewhere in West Africa firm political links had been established with a generally conservative francophone community, forged in part by the common opposition to Nkrumah. Lagos very much wanted to strengthen these ties so as to encourage these countries "to come voluntarily to the realization that their economic and political destiny lies with Nigeria."[51] There was very little that could be done in the short run to reduce the continued influence of the French in their former colonies, although Radio Nigeria did acquire external broadcasting facilities and commenced extensive French language programming in the mid-1960s.

The basic position of the Ministry of External Affairs acknowledged that it would be many years before Nigeria possessed the economic strength to provide an alternative to dependence on France and that, in the meantime, if Nigeria appeared too ambitious this would prove counterproductive. To quote from a 1966 ministry working paper on relations with francophone West Africa: "Opportunities will present themselves for closer cooperation. Nigeria should take time by the forelock; but in doing this she should be seen to be guided not by the "Big Brother" ambition to dominate but by the desire to promote stability in Africa and interstate friendship. Thus she would be creating a favorable atmosphere which would enable her to develop closer relations with the states when the French influence has declined . . . sooner or later, the Afro-Malagasy states will be laid open to the influence of a wider world . . . if the economic situation of the states so improves as to reduce economic dependence on France."[52] Nigeria's decision to strike a benign but cordial position vis-à-vis the constellation of former French colonies paid off handsomely during the civil war, when the strong support for the federal government that was shown by these states helped to offset General de Gaulle's inclination to assist Biafra.

Beyond West Africa, the federal government had traditionally enjoyed good but rather limited relations with the OAU member governments of north, east, and central Africa. Dealings with Arab states had been complicated by the federal government's opposition to any attempt to draw the OAU into the Arab-Israeli dispute and by Nigeria's willingness to allow the establishment of an Israeli embassy in Lagos. There were rumors following the January 1966 coup that President Nasser of Egypt and other Arab leaders were preparing to break relations with Nigeria because of their anger over the deaths of a Moslem prime minister and

[51] RCHM-A, "The Economic Dependence of the Afro-Malagasy States on France." Lagos, June 1966.
[52] Ibid.

the northern premier, the Sardauna of Sokoto who, unlike the prime minister, had openly denounced the state of Israel. Shortly after Ironsi came to power, however, he sent a large delegation of prominent Northerners on a hastily arranged tour of Middle East capitals and, according to Ministry of External Affairs records, President Nasser subsequently informed Nigeria's ambassador in Cairo that he would like to develop closer ties with Lagos, because in the past Prime Minister Balewa had resisted his overtures.

Regarding the situation in southern Africa, Nigerians have always felt deep and bitter resentment about any continuation of the status quo, but during the 1960s they felt powerless to affect the situation. In the table of national interests presented in Appendix I, the Republic of South Africa does not even appear and, for the most part, the federal government preferred to be identified as a "moderate" on the issue of continued white minority rule rather than to engage in what it knew would be regarded internationally as merely symbolic gestures of protest. This same attitude influenced Nigeria's dealings with the OAU's Committee for the Liberation of Africa office in Dar es Salaam.[53] When the committee was established in 1963, Nigeria contributed $280,000, but by 1965/1966 the committee's total annual receipts from all member governments amounted to only $358,000 out of a total annual budget appropriation of $2.4 million,[54] and the Ministry of External Affairs recommended that further Nigerian contributions be withheld on the grounds that much of the earlier money had been seriously mismanaged, a fact that was confirmed by a specially appointed OAU board of auditors that visited Tanzania in November 1966.[55]

Compared with the international entanglements that confronted Nigerian foreign policy makers during the civil war, the difficulties in managing the country's external relations during the five years following Independence appear to be insignificant. While there had been some notable challenges to Nigeria's interests, especially in Africa, these had been resolved to the federal government's satisfaction.

The federal government was proud, too, of its contribution of troops as part of the United Nations peace-keeping operations in the Congo (Zaire) and later to the Republic of Tanzania, where President Nyerere was confronted by a domestic insurrection.[56] On a less dramatic scale,

[53] RCHM-A, Working Paper No. 3, "Aid to African Countries, Nigeria's Relations with Unliberated African Countries," Lagos, June 1966.

[54] OAU, "Estimates for the Budget of the Special Fund of the Coordinating Committee for the Liberation of Africa for the Fiscal Year 1967/68," Appendix I.

[55] OAU, Report of the Board of Auditors, Coordinating Committee for the Liberation of Africa, Annex I, "Report of the OAU Coordinating Committee for the Liberation of Africa to the Council of Ministers at its 8th Session," Addis Ababa, February 1967.

[56] The Congo operation began in December 1960 under the auspices of the

Lagos also had quietly initiated its own bilateral foreign economic assistance program in Africa[57] (see Appendix II). The sums were not large—Nigeria's per capita income was less than $100 at the time—but the gifts were another demonstration of the federal government's determination to foster friendly and peaceful relations on the continent.[58]

Against this background of expanding linkages, both in Africa and the wider international system, it is useful to know a little of the brief history of Nigeria's overextended and generally inexperienced foreign policy establishment as it developed prior to the civil war. One tends to think of diplomacy as a carefully calculated set of moves and countermoves analogous to chess. But Nigeria's capacity to analyze alternative foreign policy options was hampered by a lack of extensive and reliable information from around the world and an inadequately trained and understaffed diplomatic corps.

The Management of Nigeria's External Relations

The development of the federal government's foreign policy institutions paralleled the country's growing international interests. By necessity, the process was rapid. The first indication of any planning for the conduct of foreign relations under an independent Nigerian government did not appear until 1956, when a sessional paper anticipating a future foreign ministry was prepared under British advice.[59] Nigeria would have only six permanent missions with embassy status: London, Washington, New York, Accra, Khartoum, and one Western European capital. In addition, there would be a consulate to service Moslem pilgrims in Jedda, Saudi

---

United Nations. Nigeria provided two infantry battalions, and these became the backbone of the UN contingent. They continued to serve with great distinction until June 1964, when they were the last troops to leave. The federal government also supplied four hundred policemen to assist with civilian security and to train Congolese police. In April 1964 Lagos dispatched a battalion of soldiers to help President Julius Nyerere restrain mutinous Tanzanian troops. Although the operation took less than six months, the Nigerians played a vital role in training Tanzanian forces loyal to Nyerere, and thereby helped to keep him in power. Needless to say, the Nigerians were particularly incensed by Nyerere's 1968 recognition of Biafra, which they considered an outright betrayal. For an evaluation of the Nigerian army's performance of peace-keeping operations, see Miners, *The Nigerian Army 1956–1966*, Chapter 5.

[57] RCHM-A, Working Paper No. 3, "Aid to African Countries," Lagos, June 1966.

[58] In 1966, Nigeria's ambassadors recommended that the allocation for foreign aid be increased substantially, to 1 percent of the country's annual budget, which in that year would have amounted to a commitment of approximately $3.5 to help other African governments. The decision had to be deferred for the duration of the civil war because of the shortage of foreign exchange. *Ibid.*

[59] Nigeria, *The Training of Nigerians for the Representation of Their Country Overseas: A Statement of Policy* (Lagos: Government Printer, 1956).

Arabia, and one on the Spanish island of Fernando Po for the thousands of plantation workers from Eastern Nigeria. The foreign missions and the tiny home ministry of three divisions—Protocol and Training, Economic, and Consular—would be staffed by forty bureaucrats. Anything larger than this was dismissed by the British as "prohibitively expensive in men and money" and, as the sessional paper paternalistically suggests, "There are many countries in the world where the older Commonwealth countries . . . are content to leave the diplomatic representation of their interests to Her Majesty's government in the United Kingdom."[60]

Between 1960 and 1965 the number of resident Nigerian missions in foreign cities grew from two to forty-two, while the corps of foreign service officers increased from forty to two hundred.[61] The size of these permanent missions and the ranking of ambassadorial posts within the ministry hierarchy reflects, to a degree, the table of interests indicated in Appendix I.[62] It is noteworthy, however, that Lagos chose not to open missions in several European capitals where foreign investment and

[60] *Ibid.*, p. 2.

[61] Nigeria, *Federal Staff Lists*, No. 8 to 1st April 1960; No. 9 revised to 1st January 1961; No. 11 revised to 1st January 1963; No. 13 as at 1st January 1965; No. 15 as at 1st August 1966; No. 16 as at 1st August 1970. No *Federal Staff Lists* were published during the war years, 1967–1969, and there appears to have been no substantial change in the size of the ministry during this period. The figures refer only to external affairs officers grades 1–9, and not to executive officers, secretaries, and typists.

[62] Nigeria's foreign missions are ranked in clusters of declining order of importance from Class A–1 to A–2, B–1 and B–2. Of the forty-two missions established by 1966, only three were in the A–1 category—New York, London, and Washington—and each was staffed by approximately eighteen people. The positions of high commissioner in London, ambassador to Washington, permanent representative to the United Nations, and permanent secretary of the Ministry of External Affairs were the highest in the service. They were interchangeable, and often were retirement posts. The most prestigious post was that of permanent representative to the United Nations and, within the ministry, New York was considered the country's most important foreign mission, a global listening post and forum to project Nigeria's concerns onto the world stage.
At the time of the civil war, the federal government maintained twelve class A–2 missions, six of which were located in Africa. The list included: Addis Ababa, Cairo, Abidjan, Leopoldville (Kinshasa), Nairobi, Accra, Rome, Moscow, Tokyo, Ottawa, Paris, and Bonn. When embassies were later opened in Peking and Rio de Janeiro, they were placed in this second tier. The largest number of embassies were rated B–1, with staffs of between five and ten. There were twenty-one such posts on the eve of secession, namely: Dublin, Geneva, New Delhi, Karachi, Jeddah, Khartoum, Bamako, Bathurst, New York (consulate), Conakry, Freetown, Monrovia, Dakar, Lomé, Cotonou, Niamey, Fort Lamy, Lusaka, Yaoundé, Kampala, and Dar es Salaam. The lowest category, B–2, was reserved for the consulates in Hamburg, Liverpool, Port Sudan, Buea (West Cameroon), Edinburgh, and Fernando Po. Based on a "Working Paper on the Administration Organization of the Ministry," prepared in March 1966 by the head of administration, Ministry of External Affairs.

other economic interests were actively being pursued, but the federal government did open twenty-four missions in Africa, and six of them—Abidjan, Accra, Addis Ababa, Cairo, Kinshasa, and Nairobi—were given the same status by the ministry as the embassies in Paris, Bonn, and Moscow.

Within the headquarters in Lagos there was a proliferation of substantive and administrative divisions reflecting Nigeria's widening international interests.[63] Nearly three-fourths of the foreign service officers were posted to foreign missions, which meant that the staff complement in Lagos amounted to only forty or fifty professional officers. The policy-oriented divisions—Africa, Asia, Euro-Western (including the Americas), and International (United Nations and other non-African international organizations)—each could claim only a handful of staff.[64] The ministry's budget for home and field operations grew from $2.7 million in 1960/1961 to $9.9 million in 1965/1966.[65] It then leveled off during the war years because of the foreign exchange constraints.[66]

The number of foreign service officers remained at approximately two hundred throughout the civil war, despite the flight of Ibo staff during the spring of 1967. As the domestic crisis worsened, the demands on the Ministry of External Affairs increased. The situation was especially frantic in Lagos, where overburdened staff not only had to cope with the cable traffic to Nigeria's foreign missions but also serviced the fifty embassies, nine high commissions, thirteen consulates, and nine international agencies, which were all based in the federal capital. The number of foreign service officers in the federal Ministry of External Affairs was about equal to the professional staff of the American embassy, excluding the two hundred or so USAID and information officials scattered around the country. It is not surprising, therefore, that Western diplomats in Lagos became exasperated when, during the height of international pub-

[63] After 1966 the Ministry of External Affairs was organized into the following divisions: Protocol, Administrative and Establishment, Accounts, Research, Africa, Asia, Euro-Western, Consular and Treaties, Economic, International, Information, and Military.

[64] Among the policy-oriented divisions, Africa had an establishment of eight officers, while Asia had three officers, Euro-Western (including the Americas), four; and International (United Nations and other non-African international organizations), seven. These basic arrangements prevailed with minor changes through the civil war years. One notable development was the diversification and expansion by 1969 of the Africa Division, which grew to ten officers, each of whom had a subregional area of specialty. The Euro-America Division, as it was renamed, shrank from four to three officers, and Asia dropped from three to two over the same period.

[65] Nigeria, *Estimates of the Federation of Nigeria 1960/61* and *1965/66*.

[66] Nigeria, *Estimates of the Federation of Nigeria 1970/71*. By comparison, the budget of the United States Department of State was approximately $450 million in 1970.

lic concern over the civil war, the ministry was slow to respond to the flood of demands for clarification of policy. In addition to the shortage of staff at the ministry headquarters and in Nigeria's missions in foreign capitals, there were also problems related to a history of poor morale within the foreign service and the disruptions caused by the sudden changes in government and the advent of civil war.

During the 1960s the most experienced and talented group of foreign service officers came from the initial class or thirty-seven that had been carefully recruited immediately prior to Independence.[67] When they entered the service in 1960 their average age was thirty-three, and all but five had the equivalent of at least a B.A. degree. Because the appointments were based on merit as reflected in the level of academic training, the vast majority were southerners, where advanced formal education was more readily available than in the north. As the ministry expanded following the departure of the British, there were strong pressures from Northern Region political leaders to achieve a greater ethnic balance in the foreign service. Despite recommendations to the contrary, the Balewa government declined to require written examinations for the new recruits, and whereas the first class of officers had been closely examined and seconded to British embassies for practical training, subsequent entrants had only to pass an interview and survive a series of lectures and a brief familiarization tour of Nigeria's four regions.

The sudden increase in the size of the ministry meant that experienced personnel had to be rotated quickly to assist with the opening of new missions and to supervise new staff. Diplomats and their families who had expected to serve in a post for the normal two years suddenly were sent—often without warning—to a new location within a year or six months. A further detriment to professional esprit during the early 1960s was the practice of appointing politicians to ambassadorial posts. In 1965 approximately 75 percent of Nigeria's foreign representatives were noncareer appointees, compared with only 27 percent by the end of the civil war in 1970. Not surprisingly, a survey of the federal civil service in 1967 found that 71 percent of the senior respondents in the Ministry of External Affairs cited political considerations in appointment and promotion as the greatest contributor to inefficiency in the foreign service. This figure was the highest reported by any federal ministry.[68]

[67] Nigeria, *Federal Staff List*, No. 8, pp. 32—33. Among the outstanding examples from this group were: Permanent Secretaries P. C. Asiodu and I. J. Ebong; and Ambassadors V. A. Adegoroye, L. Harriman, O. Jalaoso, E. O. Ogunsulire, and C. O. Hollist. Interestingly, while many Biafran emissaries formerly served in the Ministry of External Affairs, few came from this core group. A notable exception was Godwin Onyegbula, Biafra's permanent secretary of foreign affairs and Ojukwu's chief foreign policy adviser.

[68] Nigeria, *Training Needs of the Federal Civil Service*, p. 41.

Until the military seized power, the civil servants in the Ministry of External Affairs had little influence over the formulation of foreign policy.[69] Throughout the 1960–1965 period, Prime Minister Balewa dominated the foreign policy-making process. He was assisted, at first, by his Hausa-speaking British secretary, Peter Stallard. From August 1961 until December 1964 the foreign affairs portfolio was assigned to the flamboyant Ibo politician Jaja Wachuku, with help from two junior ministers of state, northerner Nuhu Bamali, and a non-Ibo easterner, Dr. E. A. Esin. When Wachuku was relieved of his duties the foreign affairs portfolio was reclaimed by the prime minister, and remained there until he was deposed in January 1966.

When the military seized power they were warmly greeted, not only by the population at large, but by the civil servants in the Ministry of External Affairs. With the cabinet abolished, the permanent secretary reported directly to the head of state. General Ironsi had had no real experience in foreign affairs, aside from his service as the last United Nations commander in the Congo, and thus he depended on the ministry for the formulation and execution of foreign policy. But the optimism and sense of renewed purpose that characterized the Ministry of External Affairs during the spring of 1966 was short-lived. Ironsi's successor, Lt. Col. Yakubu Gowon, also preferred initially to defer to the Ministry of External Affairs, although during the internal upheavals following the second coup d'état, Nigeria's foreign policy was paralyzed.[70]

As the Eastern Region moved toward secession, at least twenty-five Ibo diplomats transferred to the Eastern Nigeria public service, while scores of other officers resigned or went into exile abroad.[71] To fill these vacancies, the government did not recruit from outside the service but, in most cases, simply shifted executive or administrative officers to "Branch A" foreign service officer status. Many of these were Northerners who had previously failed to qualify for "Branch A."[72] These changes also undermined the efficient conduct of foreign relations, and meant that the government's position was often not adequately explained in response to official inquiries by representatives in Lagos and in capitals around the world.

[69] See Aluko, "The Foreign Service."   [70] Interview: Yakubu Gowon.

[71] A check of *Federal Gazettes* for 1967 indicates that there were at least sixty-eight Ibo transfers and secondments from the Ministry of External Affairs, although many of these were among the secretarial and executive ranks. The list is incomplete, as many officers merely went on indefinite leave or left without formal severance. Biafra's foreign affairs establishment will be discussed in Chapter 4.

[72] This can be surmised by comparing *Federal Staff List* No. 15, as at 1st August 1966 with *Federal Staff List* No. 16, as at 1st August 1970.

Shortly after secession, Gowon appointed a twelve-member cabinet of distinguished civilian advisers, who were each assigned ministerial portfolios but were called commissioners, not ministers, with membership on a Federal Executive Council. They were accountable only to the supreme military commander, and served purely in an advisory capacity. Their participation in the government was meant to signal the military's commitment to restore civilian rule and, within the hierarchy, they were prominently situated directly between the senior technocrats and the Supreme Military Council.[73] Any state business relating to defense procurement, military strategy, or administration of the armed forces remained the exclusive domain of the military junta. On other matters, however, the civilian commissioners could wield considerable personal influence. Several had had extensive international experience: most notably, Commissioner of Finance Chief Obafemi Awolowo; Commissioner of Information and Labour Chief Anthony Enahoro; Attorney General and Commissioner of Justice Dr. T. O. Elias; and Commissioner of External Affairs Dr. Okoi Arikpo.

By the time that the civilian commissioners were appointed, the close alliance between the army and the civil servants had been fairly well established and, with few exceptions, this continued. At the very center of power were a handful of permanent secretaries, sometimes referred to as the Oxford tribe because three of their most prominent members —Allison Ayida, Philip Asiodu, and A. A. Atta—all took degrees at that university. When one of this group was asked for his assessment of the extent to which the commissioners initiated policies within their given ministries, he replied that "initial" rather than "initiate" was the more appropriate term for their work.

During the civil war, this small cadre of permanent secretaries, together with a few high-ranking military officers, commissioners, and other influential civil servants, would meet informally with the head of state for after-dinner coffee on Monday and Wednesday evenings to discuss major policy issues, foreign and domestic. Because the Ministry of External Affairs was so thinly staffed and never developed a policy planning group,[74] the formulation of options and the establishment of

[73] The Supreme Military Council included the head of state and commander-in-chief of the armed forces; the heads of the army, navy, air force, and national police; and the military governors of the four regions (of the twelve states after May 1967).

[74] The ministry's Research Division, which might have performed a policy planning function, consisted of only one officer, whose responsibility was to monitor the security of overseas missions. The ministry library was housed in one small room, and consisted of a few hundred volumes, most of which were outdated American and British political science studies. There was also a rudimentary press file, and the library was responsible for posting Nigerian newspapers to all missions. The Nigerian Institute of International Affairs, which does possess what

priorities usually took place at these semi weekly gatherings. Attendance at any one time was difficult to predict because it might include one or more military governors or field commanders who happened to be visiting Lagos, a federal commissioner recently home from an overseas mission, or anyone else of influence who had a special interest in some particular issue of current concern. Policy formulation and implementation thus reflected the interplay of personalities, frequently without much regard for nominal bureaucratic or military assignments, and members of the Lagos diplomatic corps claim to have been generally unable to discern, much less forecast, whose opinions within the federal government might hold sway on any given issue of foreign policy.

Gowon maintains that dividing responsibilities between his Federal Executive Council of civilian commissioners and his Supreme Military Council of governors and armed forces chiefs of staff posed few difficulties because he was able to uphold the separation of powers outlined in the 1963 federal constitution, and as chairman of both groups he alone controlled the two agendas.[75] In practice he appears to have functioned more as a chairman of a board of directors than as a supreme military commander. His state governors enjoyed broad freedom to manage local affairs, and Gowon always preferred to have any issue settled informally between himself and a given governor or among those governors most directly affected. He handled the Federal Executive Council in a similar manner, meeting often with individual commissioners or urging ministries to settle their various problems directly without having to raise a potentially contentious issue before the full council. The Supreme Military Council of state governors met only infrequently, and Gowon would try to limit consideration of recent actions by the Federal Executive Council to a simple briefing from the chair. Gowon operated as a conciliator and a broker for conflicting interests, which was no doubt exactly what the badly shaken federal system required prior to and during the civil war.

Between 1967 and 1970 General Gowon changed only one of his civilian commissioners and none of the members of his Supreme Military Council. The permanent secretaries of the "kitchen cabinet" were also retained. The conduct of foreign relations was relatively immune to domestic pressures, especially under military rule. On issues of strong and often conflicting local interest, Gowon had to balance many forces carefully, including potentially explosive ethnic jealousies. Because he was not experienced in politics and had only disdain for the extrava-

---

is perhaps the finest international affairs library in Africa, has the potential for providing the ministry with a variety of services to assist policy planning, but these were not developed during the civil war period.

[75] Interview: Gowon.

gances demonstrated by politicians of the civilian regime, he preferred to stand aloof from most of the squabbles of domestic government. Foreign affairs provided an opportunity for what he came to regard as the higher pursuits of statesmanship. Increasingly, Gowon assumed a personal interest in the day-to-day flow of diplomacy, surprising officials at the Ministry of External Affairs by his prompt and thorough reading of all briefs. He also had a Reuters News Service telex installed in Dodan Barracks in order to follow both international events and the reports by Western journalists of developments in Biafra during the civil war.

As his confidence in foreign affairs grew, Gowon continued to depend, nonetheless, on his "kitchen cabinet" of advisers and his commissioner of external affairs, Dr. Okoi Arikpo. Gowon was drawn to Arikpo by the latter's unpretentious and scholarly demeanor, which masked a deep resentment over racial injustice in southern Africa and what he also felt was the oppression of minority ethnic groups in the old Nigerian federation. Arikpo, who prior to his appointment to the Federal Executive Council had been head of the National Universities Commission, had been born near Calabar in eastern Nigeria. For years he had been agitating for a redistribution of power in Nigeria, which Gowon would finally effect. With his long record of opposition to Ibo domination of Eastern minorities, he proved to be an effective international spokesman for the new federal government, and his close personal rapport with Gowon permitted him to play a major role in shaping civil war foreign policy.

Before turning to the international politics of the civil war, it is necessary to look briefly at the breakdown of domestic authority. Nigeria's foreign policy makers had very little opportunity to initiate international action during the civil war. They largely waged defensive diplomacy in reaction to Biafran attempts to penetrate the international system, and in response to the demands emanating from foreign powers who were concerned about the deteriorating conditions within Nigeria. These early international reactions to the escalating conflict were shaped by the history of interethnic struggles inside Nigeria and by estimates of the new federal government's capacity to resolve these extreme differences.

· 2 ·

THE LOSS OF AUTHORITY
AT HOME AND ABROAD

"Foreign policy is authoritative or it is nothing," a scholar once observed.[1] The degree of international confidence that a sovereign elicits varies directly with the extent to which he is perceived to speak for his polity, and the success of his foreign policy varies directly with the degree of confidence elicited. If the polity is in such a degree of turmoil that its essential structures are no longer identifiable, the conduct of international relations will also break down. Foreign powers do not know to whom to listen, and the presumed sovereign cannot be certain of the allegiance of those he purports to represent. To speak of the success or failure of a country's foreign policy under such conditions is almost meaningless.

When a thirty-one-year-old lieutenant colonel named Yakubu Gowon succeeded Major General Ironsi as head of state following the collapse of the first military government on July 29, 1966, his first address to the world was one of low-key desperation. To "all true and sincere lovers of Nigeria and Nigerian unity both at home and abroad," Gowon declared, "putting all considerations to test—political, economic, as well as social—the base for unity is not there or is so badly rocked, not only once but several times. I therefore feel that we should review the issue of our national standing and see if we can help stop the country from drifting away into utter destruction."[2] In reality, Lieutenant Colonel Gowon commanded only a modicum of allegiance from three of Nigeria's four regions, while one military governor, thirty-one-year-old Lt. Col. Chukwuemeka Odumegwu Ojuwku, refused to recognize Gowon as head of state and adopted a position of de facto secession in behalf of the predominantly Ibo Eastern Region.

From August 1966 until August 1967, governments in Europe and

[1] Jones, *Analyzing Foreign Policy*, p. 17.

[2] This excerpt is taken from the broadcast monitored by the British Broadcasting Corporation ME/2229/B/1, and reproduced in entirety in Kirk-Greene, *Crisis and Conflict in Nigeria*, I, 196–197. Later government accounts sometimes deviated from the original by omitting the crucial "not" from the phrase "the base for unity is not there." Cf. Nigeria, *The Struggle for One Nigeria*. Nigerians argue, and with good reason, that Lieutenant Colonel Gowon's reference to the "base for unity" implied only a rejection of Ironsi's May 24, 1966, unification decree, and did not suggest a rejection of the old federal arrangement. The unification decree and Gowon's subsequent policies are discussed below.

North America, which had played such a prominent role in the political and economic development of Nigeria prior to the second coup, adopted a "wait and see" attitude, unable to determine the probable outcome of Nigeria's escalating domestic conflict. A major source of this foreign ambivalence was the realization that the former Eastern Region, which on May 29, 1967, finally proclaimed itself the sovereign Republic of Biafra, appeared at least as viable as the remnants of the federal Nigerian coalition based in Lagos.

Separatist agitations had surfaced intermittently in various parts of Nigeria since the colonial amalgamation in 1914,[3] but this sporadic political turmoil was ignored by the international community. The successive coups in 1966 and the attendant violence in the various regions cast Nigeria's political development in a new light that tended to enhance the credibility and apparent legitimacy of Biafra's claim to self-determination. The following pages review the dynamics of Nigeria's prewar politics and the paralysis of foreign policy making that persisted during the closing months of 1966 and well into 1967.

RISING POLITICAL CHAOS AND THE THREAT OF SECESSION

The structural arrangement of the Nigerian federation was determined long before independence was even contemplated; the River Niger formed a natural boundary for the eastern and western administrative divisions of the coastal area, while the north/south split was derived from a charter grant to the Royal Niger Company to exploit the hinterland (see Map 2–1). Indirect rule was made easier for the British by the dominance in each of the regions of one nation: Hausa in the North (estimated by 1963 to total 11.6 million), Ibo in the East (approximately 9.2 million), and Yoruba in the West (approximately 11.3 million).[4] The half million Ibos residing on the west bank of the Niger were largely ignored until after Independence, when a fourth region, the Midwest, was carved out of the predominantly Yoruba West in 1963. Altogether, the three major groups made up barely 60 percent of the country's total population, a central political fact that was largely overlooked by foreign observers before the creation of the twelve states in May 1967 and the emergence of minority influence in a more pluralistic federation.

Throughout the period of colonial rule, two parallel developments

[3] Tamuno, "Separatist Agitations in Nigeria since 1914."

[4] These figures are based on the 1963 national census, the only one taken between 1953 and 1973. The total was estimated to be 55,558,163. The figures are believed to be exaggerated due to the allocation of parliamentary seats according to population. The 1963 census precipitated a partial but major boycott of national elections and brought the country to the verge of crisis. See MacKintosh, *Nigerian Government and Politics* for a discussion of this period.

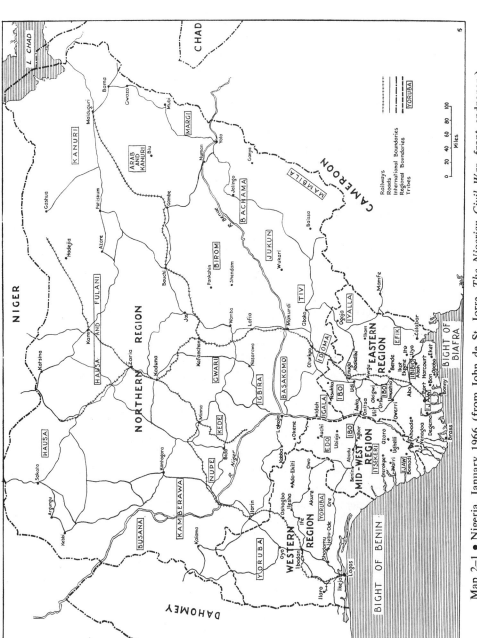

Map 2–1 • Nigeria, January 1966 (from John de St. Jorre, *The Nigerian Civil War*, front endpaper.)

occurred, one functional and one dysfunctional, that influenced the growth of national unification. The relatively unified administration with its legal system, common currency, and expanding systems of communications, trade, and education fostered a new sense of belonging together. At the same time, however, this interaction tended to awaken a new consciousness of cultural differentiation.

Except for occasional wars of conquest, interethnic competition had previously been minimal.[5] The processes of political and administrative modernization radically changed this. As new elites, particularly bureaucratic elites, began to compete for the acquisition of modern skills, jobs, and promotions, they appealed increasingly for the political support of their ethnic groups in the struggle. For a while these growing cleavages were masked by the common cause of ridding Nigeria of colonial rule. But once the withdrawal of the British became an inevitability, the phenomenon of "tribalism" became a central feature of the Nigerian political game.

The form and content of Nigerian national politics took shape during the decade immediately preceding Independence.[6] From the enactment of the Local Government Ordinance in 1950 until October 1, 1960, the British instructed Nigerians in the operation of the Western parliamentary democratic system. The latter readily accepted the form, but held to their own views on the content, preferring to write their own rules according to the political realities inherent in the tripartite administrative arrangement. Reinforcing this, the British allowed each region to retain its own system of local government and law. The intranational bargaining that followed was based on three principal considerations: 1) the Hausa/Fulani leadership possessed the strength to control the people of the Northern Region, and thus a plurality but not a majority of the national population; 2) the majority of the country's trained manpower, those in a position to administer the allocation and development of the national wealth (excluding private capital, which was primarily under foreign control), were of southern origin; and 3) the federal army was too small and too dominated by the British to be a significant factor in determining the outcome of interregional disputes during the first five years of independence.

The federal election of 1959 set the stage for post-Independence politics.[7] Each of the three major parties enjoyed the overwhelming support of the dominant ethnic group in one of the three regions,[8] and

[5] See Crowder, *The Story of Nigeria*. Some tribes, notably the Hausa and Yoruba, trace their civilizations back 2,000 years.
[6] See Coleman, *Nigeria: Background to Nationalism*.
[7] Post, *The Nigerian Federal Election of 1959*.
[8] See Sklar, *Nigerian Political Parties*, for the full historical development of the three parties.

all pursued two main objectives: achieving consolidation within the home region and winning support from minority ethnic elements in each of the other two regions. None of the parties succeeded in establishing a broad national base of constituents, and the newly independent government in 1960 was a prearranged coalition of the predominantly Hausa/Fulani northern party and the predominantly Ibo party from the East. Throughout the five years prior to the January 1966 military takeover, the essence of Nigerian politics was the struggle for control at the center, in which the northern party sought to maximize its power by encouraging competition between the two smaller southern parties, who could only hope for a role as minority partner in running the federal government. The post-Independence stakes were higher than ever before for federal patronage, construction contracts, international loans, university scholarships, development projects, and a host of personal and group amenities. And with the departure of the British overseers, the institutional restraints on competitiveness and the use of power—which had been inherently artificial because they were imposed by a colonial power—dissipated rapidly.

Attempts by the Western and Eastern Region political elites to appeal to minority ethnic groups in each other's region and in various areas of the North led to violent confrontations and allegations of widespread voting fraud, bribery, and corruption. Meanwhile, the North was able to enter into a more advantageous coalition with insurgent elements in the Western Region by exploiting a series of treason trials and the jailing of several of the Western Region's most popular political figures. By late 1965 national politics in and around the federal capital of Lagos were fraught with labor unrest, political assassination, paralysis of the judicial system, forfeiture of revenues, and the breakdown of public administration.[9]

Constitutional legitimacy had all but disappeared when, on the night of January 15, 1966, an army revolt, led by a cadre of young majors, broke out in the Northern command post at Kaduna.[10] The majors succeeded only in taking Kaduna, although rebel elements managed to kill the Northern and Western premiers, the prime minister, the minister of finance, and a number of high-ranking—predominantly Northern—army officers. The head of the army, Major General Aguiyi-Ironsi, an Ibo, remained loyal to the federal government and, following a cabinet crisis over succession, he assumed power. Ironsi appointed military

[9] *West Africa*, No. 2483, January 1965.

[10] For a detailed account of the coup, see the confidential "Special Branch Report of the Events of 15 January 1966," purportedly prepared by the Intelligence Division of the Lagos Police and reprinted in Kirk-Greene, *Crisis and Conflict*, I, 115–124. Noteworthy analyses by outside observers include Schwarz, *Nigeria*, and First, *Power in Africa*.

governors for each of the regions, which were then renamed provinces.

General Ironsi's federal military government was headed by a Supreme Military Council, including the chiefs of staff of the army (Yakubu Gowon), Navy (Akinwale Wey), and air force (George Kurobo), the inspector-general of police (Kam Selem), and the four regional military governors (Hassan Katsina, North; Odumegwu Ojukwu, East; Adekunle Fajuyi, West; and David Ejoor, Midwest). Ironsi served as chairman and, with the legislative provisions of the constitution suspended, ruled by decree. Political parties were banned, freedom of the press restored, political appointees were removed from public boards and statutory corporations—a per annum saving of approximately $8.5 million—and some prices and taxes were cut.

Immediate public reaction to the coup was relief and optimism. This feeling soured, however, during the following months. The first shock came when Ironsi broke an agreed moratorium on promotions within the army and announced the promotion of twenty-one officers, eighteen of whom were Ibo. A second point of contention was the failure to bring to trial those responsible for the deaths of senior Northern officers and the Sardauna of Sokoto, while at the same time keeping the popular Yoruba nationalist, Chief Obafemi Awolowo, in prison. Finally, open hostility to the Ironsi regime erupted with the killing of hundreds of innocent Ibo civilians in the North following Ironsi's May 24, 1966, decree (No. 39), which stipulated that Nigeria "shall cease to be a Federation and shall accordingly as from that day be a Republic . . . all officers . . . in a civil capacity shall be officers of a single service."[11] This was interpreted in the North as an attempt to impose the pre-Independence Ibo preference for a unitary state that Ibos would dominate through their control of the army and the bureaucracy.

The growing tensions culminated in a hastily planned and executed countercoup on July 28–29, 1966. Ironsi and a number of Ibo officers and troops were killed. A Yoruba from Western Nigeria, Brigadier Ogundipe, was chief of staff and second in rank to Ironsi. He tried to restore order and dispatched the head of the army, Lieutenant Colonel Gowon to Ikeja International Airport on the outskirts of Lagos. Gowon was detained by the well-armed mutineers, who continued to negotiate with Ogundipe. The governor of Eastern Nigeria, Lieutenant Colonel Ojukwu, remained at his post and offered Ogundipe his full support, but the latter concluded that he lacked sufficient backing within the army and relinquished his command.[12]

[11] Federal Republic of Nigeria, *Constitution (Suspension and Modification)* (No. 5), Decree 1966, *Official Gazette*, No. 51, Vol. 53, May 24, 1966.
[12] Interview: Ojukwu.

The insurgents were badly divided over whether to dissolve the Nigerian federation; a British commercial aircraft bound for London was ordered to fly the families of Northern Region soldiers to the Moslem city of Kano, as several commissioned officers from the far North argued that a political union with southern Nigeria was no longer possible.[13] Those who favored a new attempt to promote national unity finally asked Gowon to become their spokesman and leader. Reluctantly he agreed, and on August 1, 1966, more than three days after the outbreak of mutiny, Gowon emerged as the new commander-in-chief and head of the federal military government.

There has never been any evidence to suggest that the thirty-one-year-old army chief of staff was directly involved in the army revolt or harbored any plan to become Nigeria's third head of state. Even Ojukwu does not accuse him of complicity in the coup.[14] Gowon's immediate and obvious appeal for the plotters was that he was the most senior Northern officer in the army[15] and the vast majority of infantrymen and noncommissioned officers, whose loyalty was a prerequisite for any military regime, were, like Gowon, from the minority ethnic groups of the northern middle-belt area around Jos.

Gowon's reluctance to assume command came from a concern that he would not have the loyalty of enough of the armed forces to govern. But he was implored by representatives of the federal civil service not to allow the country to disintegrate. It was the cadre of technocrats from Lagos who set out arguments regarding the economic and social costs of northern secession—and who argued that the most disadvantaged would be the many minority groups, such as Gowon's own tiny Angas tribe, that together comprised nearly half of Nigeria's population. The American ambassador, Elbert Mathews, and the British high commissioner, Sir Francis Cumming-Bruce, also visited Gowon at the Ikeja barracks and pleaded with him to try and pull the country together. "They told me," Gowon later recalled, "that not another dime in foreign assistance would come to Nigeria" if the regions were allowed to separate.[16] In the final analysis, his determination rested on the belief

[13] Kirk-Greene, *Crisis and Conflict*, I, 53–54.

[14] Interview: Ojukwu. Writing at the height of the civil war, Ojukwu did refer at least once to Gowon as "leader of the coup," Ojukwu, *Biafra*, I, 31.

[15] Although Gowon was the senior Northern officer in the military, he was outranked by Ogundipe, Commodore Wey of the navy, and Colonel Adebayo. Three lieutenant colonels, Bassey, Imo, and Njoku, had greater seniority. A major reason why Ironsi was declared "missing" and not officially pronounced dead until six months after the coup was the new government's unwillingness to admit that the regular chain of command, legitimized by rights of seniority, had been arbitrarily broken. When Ironsi assumed power he had been the country's highest ranking officer.

[16] Interview: Gowon.

that he had sufficient support from his military colleagues to form a viable junta. Gowon concedes, however, that he did not really feel secure with this judgment until June 1967, nearly a year after he officially assumed power.[17]

The coup was effective in all regions but the East. One of Gowon's first decisions sought to restore the federal regional system while Ironsi appointee, Lieutenant Colonel Ojukwu, adopted a position of de facto secession; the links of common services and revenue allocation were maintained, but federal authority ceased to exist.[18] Reflecting on this after the civil war, Ojukwu maintained that he had wanted to lead the East into immediate formal secession and that had he done so Biafra would have survived. He claimed that his advisers persuaded him of the dangers of trying to evict the six hundred Northern troops stationed in the East, and that a wiser course would be to wait until the Gowon regime collapsed for lack of support in the south.[19]

In his first address to the nation, Gowon rested his claim to legitimacy as sovereign on "the consent of a majority of the members of the Supreme Military Council." How large the majority was, was not explained.[20] Gowon's own commanding officer, Brigadier Ogundipe, pledged his support for the new regime in return for the post of high commissioner in London.[21] Among the four military governors, Gowon could count on Hassan Katsina in the North and David Ejoor in the Midwest, the latter a close personal friend. The presence of a large Ibo population in the Midwest, however, raised questions about Ejoor's own security.

The situation in the Western Region was also problematic because the very popular Lieutenant Colonel Fajuyi, the governor under Ironsi, had been murdered. Gowon moved quickly and adroitly to consolidate his authority in the West by appointing a new governor, Colonel Robert Adebayo, while immediately freeing Chief Awolowo and other popular former political leaders from prison.[22] As a further precaution, loyal

---

[17] *Ibid.*

[18] Within hours of Gowon's first broadcast, Ojukwu answered over Eastern Nigeria Broadcasting Service by stressing the East's need to define for itself any further relationship with Lagos, and noting that the only point of Gowon's speech was to help restore peace while immediate negotiations began to allow the people of each region to determine the form of any future association. The Ojukwu statement is reprinted in Kirk-Greene, *Crisis and Conflict*, I, 198–199.

[19] Interview: Ojukwu.

[20] Among the eleven members of the Supreme Military Council, Ironsi and Fajuyi were dead, and Ojukwu and Kurobo withheld support.

[21] At least this was the account that Ogundipe gave to several members of his staff at the Nigerian High Commission in London.

[22] Gowon personally greeted Chief Awolowo when he was flown into Lagos. The release of Awolowo after three years of detention prompted thousands of Yorubas to line the streets of the federal capital upon his return shouting "Awo!

Northern troops were maintained in sufficient numbers at the Abeokuta and Ibadan garrisons to restrain any popular uprisings. It was not an auspicious beginning and, as far as the outside world was concerned, Gowon was unknown and untested.

Any hopes that Gowon might have had to win the Eastern Region's allegiance to his still fragile regime failed to materialize. First, there were reports of continued killing of Ibo sergeants and enlisted men by Northerners within the army. Although there has been no suggestion that Gowon knew of the purges in advance, or in any sense condoned such actions, he appeared powerless to stop the carnage, and this further undermined his pretense of authority.[23] To reduce immediate tensions Gowon felt compelled to respond to Ojukwu's persistent requests that the six hundred predominantly Northern troops stationed in the East be withdrawn from the Enugu garrison; to leave these understaffed troops under an Ibo commander in a hostile environment would threaten a disaster from which the country might not recover. The withdrawal of the troops suddenly gave new reality to the bifurcation of power in Nigeria. Ojukwu's de facto secession now appeared much less presumptive.

In September 1966, Gowon formally abolished the Unification Decree and reinstated a federal system as it had existed before May 24, 1966.[24] He then convened an ad hoc constitutional conference for delegates from the four regions and urged them to consider four alternative forms of government:

1. a federal system with a strong central authority;
2. a federal system with a weak central authority;
3. confederation; or
4. "an entirely new arrangement which will be peculiar to Nigeria and which has not yet found its way into any political dictionary."[25]

On the eve of the conference, Ojukwu informed the Consultative Assembly of representatives from the Eastern Region that he expected the assembly to conclude that the basis for unity, aside from economic cooperation, no longer existed, and that the East should expect to field its own army, manage its own economic resources, and conduct its own

---

omo 'luwabi, Adupe l'owo 'lorun. Adupe lo 'wo Gowon!": Awolowo! Gentlemen, Thanks be to God. Thanks be to Gowon! *Morning Post*, August 8, 1966.

[23] *New York Times*, August 20, 1966.

[24] Federal Government of Nigeria, Decree No. 59, Supplement to Official Gazette Extraordinary, No. 85, Vol. 53, September 1, 1966.

[25] Nigeria, *Nigeria 1966*, pp. 37–40.

foreign policy.[26] In reply, the assembly mandated Ojukwu to "take all such actions that might be necessary to protect the integrity of Eastern Nigeria."[27]

The constitutional conference in Lagos failed to seize the basic issue, although it did serve as a vehicle to sort out certain differences between the West and the North.[28] Eastern participation, however cool initially,[29] was withdrawn in late September following news of widespread atrocities in the North against Ibo civilians. On what is now referred to in Nigeria as "Black Thursday," September 29, 1966, mob violence broke out against the tens of thousands of Ibos who until then had been shopkeepers, civil servants, and service workers throughout the North. Estimates of the number of deaths range from 5,000 to 50,000, and the number of Ibos who subsequently returned home as refugees from around the federation may have ranged from 700,000 to 2,000,000.[30] There were also reprisals against Northerners living in the East, although there had been relatively few Hausa/Fulani in the region.[31]

"If Nigeria survives the last week's killings," a noted British Africanist wrote at the time, "it can survive anything."[32] While the violence may have been politically inspired, it was more like anarchy than genocide.[33] After the initial killings, Ibos were allowed to leave the North without much further bloodshed. It was obvious that they were no longer wel-

[26] Ojukwu, *Biafra*, address to the Consultative Assembly, August 31, 1966, I, 36–40.

[27] "Ojukwu's Mandate from the People of the East," August 31, 1966, reprinted in Kirk-Greene, *Crisis and Conflict*, I, 216.

[28] For an informed analysis of the complex changes taking place in the Western Region at this time, see Dudley, "Western Nigeria and the Nigerian Crisis." Texts of the proposals submitted by each of the regions, including the crucial "Northern Delegation's Supplementary Constitutional Proposals" of September 20, 1966, are included in Kirk-Greene, *Crisis and Conflict*, I, 216–256.

[29] According to the former head of the Eastern Nigerian Civil Service, N.U. Akpan, the instructions issued to the Eastern delegation had as their sole aim "the abolition of the central government for the country and its replacement with a loose and scarcely effective common services organization." Akpan, *The Struggle for Secession*, p. 44.

[30] During the Supreme Military Council's discussions at Aburi, Ghana, in January 1967, Ojukwu claimed that 10,000 people had been killed in the massacres of 1966. Nigeria, *Meeting of the Military Leaders at Peduase Lodge* (cited hereafter as Aburi Meeting), p. 5. The figure most frequently used is 30,000 deaths, although some estimates have run as high as 200,000. See Baker, "The Emergence of Biafra."

[31] According to former President Azikiwe, who is himself an Ibo from Onitsha, "hundreds of Hausa, Fulani, Nupe and Igalla speaking people of Northern origin residing in Eastern Nigeria were abducted and massacred in Aba, Abakaliki, Enugu, Onitsha, and Port Harcourt." Azikiwe, *Origins of the Civil War*, p. 7.

[32] Colin Legum in the *Observer*, October 16, 1966.

[33] For a thoughtful attempt to isolate the socio-economic variables contributing to the violence, see O'Connell, "The Anatomy of a Pogrom: An Outline Model."

come in vast areas of the federation, as Northerners eagerly vied for the hundreds of job openings that the evictions had created.[34] Regardless of what Nigerian apologists later argued, the massacres could never be erased, and their international impact was constantly aggravated by Ibo propagandists eager to justify the legitimacy of Biafran secession. The massacres in the North and the return of refugees, however atrocious, also benefited Ojukwu's military regime in the East. The immediate effect was to traumatize much of the population and, as Ojukwu later recalled, the shock enabled him to consolidate support that carried him through the secession.[35] The refugees were largely absorbed by the extended family system that predominates in Iboland, and in this process much of the population became personally touched by tales of horror from the North. Many of those who returned also brought much-needed skills that could be used by the expanded regional bureaucracy. Ojukwu welcomed this talent, particularly the senior civil servants, because he believed that their departure from the federal civil service would further undermine the already fragile cohesiveness of Gowon's government.[36]

Nigeria's Military Leaders Meet in Ghana

As conditions deteriorated following the violence in the North, Britain's roving ambassador, Malcolm MacDonald, made several trips to Lagos, Enugu, and Accra. MacDonald urged conciliation, regardless of the procedural arrangements. Similar lobbying had been underway by the British high commissioner in Lagos, Sir Francis Cumming-Bruce, who had previously served in Accra and could speak with personal knowl-

[34] In Kaduna, one foreign correspondent observed more than 1000 northerners waiting in line to apply for about 200 vacancies at the Post and Telegraph Exchange within hours of the Ibo exodus. *New York Times*, October 10, 1966.

[35] When he was appointed military governor by General Ironsi in January 1966, Ojukwu believes he was regarded as a "small boy" by the deposed civilian leaders. The situation changed dramatically with the second coup and the subsequent violence. This provided him with an opportunity to demonstrate his leadership, primarily by taking a tough, defiant stand against the federal government. Interview: Ojukwu.

[36] Ojukwu concedes that he underestimated the resiliency of the federal bureaucracy and is rather bitter about his early dealings with those Ibo civil servants who returned from Lagos. In spite of the atrocities in the North they were, he recalls, reluctant to relinquish their positions in the federal bureaucracy, which paid higher salaries and offered more prestige than the regional civil services. Ojukwu maintains that he had to assure them personally that they would receive comparable perquisites in Enugu. Interview: Ojukwu. This was further confirmed by the deputy to the head of the Eastern Nigerian civil service, who also recollects the many arguments and rivalries that developed over the difficulties in integrating the high-ranking returnees. Interview: F. U. Emeghara.

edge of the Ghanaian government's desire to assist with any reconciliation. Ojukwu claims to have been suspicious of British intentions, but on November 23, 1966, he announced his willingness to go to Accra, the Spanish offshore island of Fernando Po, Monrovia, or Addis Ababa to meet with his military colleagues.[37]

Gowon repeatedly and publicly rejected a Supreme Military Council meeting outside the country, and branded such suggestions "unpatriotic."[38] The young head of state was anxious to avoid doing anything that would give further credibility to Ojukwu's claim that the federal government lacked sufficient authority to guarantee the personal security of an Ibo leader. Meanwhile, the British were urging concessions to allay Ojukwu's fears, and they were supported in this by the Americans, who also maintained a consulate in Enugu with direct access to the Eastern governor.[39] Most of the suggestions for talks outside of the country were immediately dismissed by Gowon.[40] The one option that he could not easily dismiss was the persistent offer of good offices from Nkrumah's successor in Ghana, General Joseph Ankrah.

The Ghanaian head of state was uniquely well placed to serve as intermediary between the young Nigerian lieutenant colonels. A brother officer who had been promoted through the ranks during the days of the British colonial Royal West African Frontier Force, Ankrah enjoyed a personal—almost paternal—rapport with Gowon.[41] For nearly five months, Ankrah made repeated informal overtures to bring the adversaries together.[42] These initiatives, which had the strong back-

[37] Ojukwu, *Biafra*, address to the Eastern Consultative Assembly, November 23, 1966, I, 68–85. Ojukwu preferred Addis Ababa because, as the home of the Organization of African Unity and the United Nations Economic Commission for Africa, it offered a much wider international platform from which to broadcast the East's grievances. Ghana, after Nkrumah, on the other hand, was believed to be too much a British client, and the Eastern Nigerian press was already full of accusations about the formation of an "Anglo/Hausa" alliance that intended to repress the East.

[38] *New Nigerian*, November 23, 1966.

[39] The United States maintained consulates in the North, West, and East, but not in the Midwest. In early 1967 there were only three diplomatic missions in the Eastern capital of Enugu: the British, American, and Cameroonian representatives.

[40] American Ambassador Elbert Mathews, for example, reportedly returned from one trip to Enugu with a query of whether the federal government would welcome the provision of an American aircraft carrier as a neutral site for talks; Gowon is said to have rejected the suggestion as "utter nonsense." Interview: Edwin Ogbu, permanent secretary of external affairs at that time.

[41] For a sketch of the "old boy network" that existed among the members of the Ghanaian and Nigerian military establishments, many of whom had trained together at the British-run West African training school at Teshie, Ghana, see Cameron Duodu, "Old Boy Network Brings News Service of Nigerian Peace Talks," *Observer Foreign News Service*, No. 23417, January 9, 1967.

[42] Interview: General Joseph Ankrah.

ing of the British and the Americans,[43] were direct and personal. Ghana's high commissioner in Lagos at the time recalls that the contacts between Ankrah and his Nigerian comrades were so restricted that he did not learn of the outcome until it appeared in the Lagos *Daily Times*.[44]

As 1966 drew to a close Gowon was finding it increasingly difficult to resist the Ghanaian overtures. The Supreme Military Council had been unable to meet in full session since he had assumed power on July 29. Frustrated in his attempt to reestablish a unified high command over the Nigerian army, and facing a rising tide of militant secessionism in the East, Gowon finally decided that a meeting outside the country offered the only immediate alternative to an untenable situation. Ojukwu maintains that when he telephoned Gowon to wish him well on Christmas Eve, the federal leader suggested they meet in Accra, and the bargain was struck.[45] On January 4–5, 1967, the Supreme Military Council convened at Peduase Lodge, a sumptuous hilltop retreat built by former President Nkrumah in Aburi, Ghana.

Aburi would be the last face-to-face encounter between Gowon and Ojukwu, as representatives of the two factions in the Nigerian conflict. To understand better the nature and outcome of the January 1967 meeting and to place the roles of the two men in a more personal perspective, we should look briefly at the differences in their background and style of leadership. Elsewhere in the book little attention will be given to the possible significance of such factors in actually shaping government policy, because this is not a study of decision-making processes. It should be noted that the following paragraphs are based on impressions received during post-war interviews with the two former military commanders.

At first glance, Gowon and Ojukwu would appear to have been unlikely enemies. They were born within a year of each other, raised as Christians in families that revered most things British, trained as military officers in England, served with the United Nations peace-keeping forces in the Congo, and enjoyed rapid promotions in Nigeria's tightly knit and well-disciplined 9,000-man army. In 1963, not yet thirty years old, the two officers achieved the rank of lieutenant colonel. Ideologically, Gowon and Ojukwu's general views were practically indistinguishable: each believed in capitalism and saw military rule in Nigeria as an unfortunate but necessary step along the road to western-

---

[43] Ankrah boasts that at this stage he was talking to Washington and London, and that Lyndon Johnson and Harold Wilson were listening. Interview: Ankrah.

[44] Interview: Alhaji Yakubu Tali, Ghanaian high commissioner in Lagos.

[45] Interview: Ojukwu. Ojukwu's chief secretary has since published that the arrangement was actually sealed by Britain's roving ambassador, Malcolm MacDonald. Akpan, *The Struggle for Secession*, p. 51.

style democracy. Communism was considered by both to be undesirable for Nigeria. Neither man could be described as "tribalistic."

Beyond these shared characteristics, however, there were well-known differences in their demeanor. Yakubu Gowon, the nonsmoking, non-drinking, soldier's soldier, was slow and deliberate in conversation. He is a man devoid of pretentions who, after nine years of service as head of state of the world's tenth most populous country, enrolled as a freshman student at Britain's University of Warwick.[46] Out of uniform, Gowon seems shy, but without self-doubt, and he is eager to impress the listener with the importance of such ideals as trust, honesty, hard work, service, and love of country in enabling him to persevere in office. The frequent invocation of these symbols has often been privately dismissed by even his warmest admirers as naive and of little use in guiding policy, but few have challenged his sincerity.[47]

Ojukwu, by contrast, is a charismatic figure who possesses a towering ego, a quick mind, and a keen appreciation of political intrigue. He is a natural conversationalist who will allow an interview to run for nine or ten hours without faltering or missing an opportunity to score a point with wit or sarcasm. He is more powerfully built than Gowon, and his full beard and piercing stare became a symbol of Biafran resistance that was recognized around the world. Ojukwu's sense of historical mission and grandeur may have been inspired by childhood experiences and what appeared to be a prophetic but initially difficult choice of careers.

He was born the son of a self-made Ibo millionaire who had been knighted by the Queen of England and who was determined that young Emeka would receive the finest education that money could buy. After attending secondary school at Kings College, Lagos, and Epson College, Surrey, England, he went to Oxford, where he majored in modern history and received a B.A. degree in 1955. He returned home and joined the Eastern Nigeria Public Service as an administrative officer but, to the shock and dismay of his father, he resigned two years later and enlisted in the army. His reason for doing so, he later said, was that he felt Nigeria was "headed for an upheaval and that the army was the place to be when the time came." He thus became the first Oxford graduate in the Nigerian armed forces and, after a two-year officer training course at Eaton Hall, Chester, was assigned to the Fifth Batallion in Kano. Following a series of additional training courses in Britain, including the Joint Services Staff College, and a stint as the Nigerian

---

[46] Reflecting on the difficulties he encountered during his first year at the university, he commented that running the affairs of state was a good deal easier and more comprehensible than analyzing the works of Plato.

[47] As a close aide once remarked, "Every time I see the General he tells me 'speak the truth, always the truth, and everything will turn out all right.' I tell him 'yes sir' and then do what I have to do!"

army's quartermaster general, he returned to command the Fifth Battalion at the end of 1964.

Ojukwu never considered himself to be a professional soldier and saw the army as only a way to achieve political power. He was contemptuous of the civilian politicians, for their corruption and ineffective government, and he was eager to see an end to their extravagances. When the majors instigated the January 1966 coup he was strategically located in Kano, but astutely avoided joining the rebels. Instead, he supported Ironsi and was rewarded by being appointed governor of the Eastern region. Ojukwu had never been enamored with the radical politics of Gamal Nasser, but he perceived a situation in Nigeria analogous to the Egyptian revolution and, just as the young lieutenant colonel succeeded Major General Naguib in Cairo, Ojukwu entertained hopes of replacing the inept Major General Ironsi.

At this stage, Gowon had a much more limited vision of himself and his potential for service to the nation; his objective was to be a good soldier and that, in the best British tradition, meant staying out of politics. Gowon's father was an Anglican catechist who had raised his family at Wusasa in Zaria, although they were from the small group of Angas who live on the Jos Plateau. His first language was Hausa, and he never learned to speak proper Angas. As a result, he was detached from both his home village and the Moslem population in which he grew up, a factor that later allowed him freedom from the ethnic and kinship networks that have often led to corrupt behavior by Nigerian officials. Gowon's family was poor, but his father's affiliation with the Church Missionary Society allowed Yakubu and his ten siblings to attend church schools and, after graduating from Zaria Government Secondary School in May 1954, he went directly into the army. The transition from strict parental authority to military discipline went smoothly.

Training at the Royal Military Academy, Sandhurst, was, for aspiring military officers of Gowon's generation, what an Oxford B.A. was for ambitious civil servants—a ticket to quick promotions and a secure career. Gowon derived enormous pride and a sense of professional identity at Sandhurst. There was, of course, no access to the intellectual excitement or the social life of sports cars and trips to London theaters that marked Ojukwu's period at Oxford. Gowon was sent back to England for several further training courses during the 1960s, and had returned from the Joint Services Staff College only two days before the Balewa government was toppled in January 1966. He respected Ironsi's rank and agreed to try to reestablish military discipline and an orderly chain of command as army chief of staff.

Gowon attributes what he regards as Ojukwu's biggest weakness to a failure to adhere to the ethics of a professional soldier; Ojukwu

43

blithely asserts that he has always regarded himself as an amateur in military matters.[48] The federal leader accuses Ojukwu of trying vainly to foment a coup in 1964 and, more importantly, believes that he was involved with the plotting that resulted in Balewa's murder and the killing of senior Northern military officers two years later. Gowon was one of those marked for assassination and was spared only because he was not in his Lagos hotel room when the contingent of rebels arrived to kill him. He was, instead, taking his girl friend home to her father's residence in the suburb of Apapa. The woman was a member of a prominent Ibo family, and the romance might have resulted in marriage had Gowon's father not objected. That love for an Ibo woman possibly saved Gowon's life is one of the more poignant ironies in Nigerian history.

Ojukwu's perceptions of Gowon are also unflattering, but they do not evoke similar allegations of deceit, arrogance, or insatiable ambition. He views his federal adversary, however condescendingly, as "a decent enough chap" who was the tool of Northern interests and really did not comprehend his situation. When Ojukwu was asked once whether he believed Gowon was bluffing with his threat to invade Biafra, he replied: "No, I don't think he is bluffing. Bluffing presupposes a certain amount of intelligence."[49] Even after the fall of Biafra, Ojukwu maintained that he simply could not take Gowon seriously.

The image of Nigeria's head of state as barely in control of his government was not without foundation. During the war he tolerated a surprising degree of decentralization in military operations. At times divisional commanders not only made tactical decisions but behaved like feudal barons, quarreling over supplies, attacking without prior consultation, and ignoring orders from Lagos. Gowon's style of leadership by consensus was often indecisive and obtuse, and in many cases he seemed to believe that if he ignored difficult problems long enough they would resolve themselves. He constantly tried to stay aloof from the ethnic rivalries and sub rosa political machinations that plagued his administration. Viewed more positively, his low-key approach and emphasis on conciliation in resolving internal conflicts was undoubtedly an important factor in holding together the diverse interests that composed his government.[50]

Ojukwu's rule was quite different. He relished the exercise of political power, and was actively engaged in shaping policies at all levels of his

[48] Lloyd Garrison in the *New York Times Magazine*, July 22, 1969, quotes Ojukwu to this effect at the height of the civil war.

[49] From an earlier interview that Ojukwu granted to Stanley Meisler of the *Los Angeles Times, International Herald Tribune*, January 16, 1970.

[50] O'Connell, *Yakubu Gowon: A Political Profile.*

government. In the process he sometimes became bogged down in the morass of Ibo kinship and clan rivalries that hampered his regime, but there was never any doubt that he was in control of events in Biafra. Because of Biafra's size and relative homogeneity, he had an easier task than he would have had in Nigeria but, unlike Gowon, he was a consummate politician. He could be ruthless in removing opposition and, when necessary, he could inspire his troops by leading the charge into battle. At the Aburi talks in Ghana he showed himself to be a sophisticated, single-minded negotiator; his opponent was no match for him.

When Nigeria's military leaders assembled on January 4, 1967, Ghana's head of state, General Ankrah, sought to remain in the background in deference both to Gowon's sensitivity to the international implications of meeting outside Nigeria on an essentially domestic matter,[51] and because Ghana was in reality powerless to affect the situation. At the outset of the discussion Ankrah carefully rejected any inference that he might try to sit in judgment or even presume to mediate.[52] He also sought to avoid any conflict over protocol by describing his presence at the conference as merely that of a "brother officer," and he set a tone of jocular informality more appropriate to a coffee break in an officers' mess than to high-level diplomacy. This format, however artificial, held for two days of talks.

Unfortunately, the warm hospitality and friendly asides among old friends belied the lack of any agreement on the basic issues dividing the two camps. Ankrah later recalled watching Nigeria's young colonels clink their champagne glasses at the end of the conference and thinking with satisfaction that the matter was "finally settled." In his mind at least, Ojukwu had accepted Gowon as Nigeria's head of state and commander-in-chief, and as long as the "army boys" kept to themselves and out of the clutches of the former politicians, Ankrah was convinced that peace would prevail in Nigeria.[53]

General Ankrah was not the only one to mistake form for substance at Aburi. Malcolm MacDonald was immediately pleased with the apparent success, and informed David Hunt, who was about to arrive in Lagos as Britain's high commissioner that "It's simple and that's its merit: the Constitution is to be further amended to give each region almost complete autonomy, and in return the East acknowledges the unity of Nigeria and recognizes the Federal Military Government with

---

[51] The significance of Gowon's concession to meet Ojukwu at a foreign venue was not overlooked by the international press, whose comments seemed to justify earlier fears among federal officials that the gathering would be interpreted abroad as a convocation of equals rather than as subordinates with their commander-in-chief. See, for example, *The Times* (London), January 5, 1967.

[52] Aburi Meeting, Opening Remarks by General Ankrah.

[53] Interview: Ankrah.

Gowon as its head."[54] Even Gowon was relieved and has said that he returned from Aburi fully willing to issue a public statement endorsing the accord without reservations; he did not do so because he was ill with a fever, which he has since recognized as a most fortunate indisposition.[55]

Anyone who has read the highly controversial Aburi transcripts cannot deny that Gowon was immediately put on the defensive by his adversary from the East who, through careful preparation and quick wit, extracted a series of apparent concessions that could be construed as leaving Nigeria without a central government.[56] It is difficult to fault Frederick Forsyth's assertion that "intellectually, Ojukwu towered over the rest."[57] But the Aburi showdown was no academic exercise; Ojukwu was on the attack politically. He correctly assumed that in the wake of the shameful massacres, the growing concern in London, and the rising disaffection in the Western Region, the other members of the Supreme Military Council might be in a mood to be conciliatory. He arrived at Aburi with a cadre of advisers, briefs to distribute to his colleagues, and a well-tuned sense of the opportunities.

Gowon approached the conference with an entirely different perspective. "We did not get to Aburi," he later declared, "to write a new constitution for Nigeria."[58] Throughout the Aburi discussions he remained preoccupied with what he apparently believed were purely military issues; namely, would Ojukwu agree to respect the new military command structure, and would he assist with the reintegration of the Nigerian armed forces? Gowon does not appear to have fully understood Ojukwu's point that "the Army problem is mixed up very closely with the political problem . . . it depends on what form of Government you have for you to decide what sort of Army should serve that Government."[59]

Gowon's implicit assumption was that if the army could find a basis for internal consensus and respect for central authority, then the "legal boys" and civilian representatives of the four regions should and could work out the constitutional arrangements. Restoration of the army as a national institution was, at least for him, the whole point of Aburi. Complicating his task were the differing views exhibited by the other military governors, aside from Ojukwu. At best, Gowon could only be

---

[54] Hunt, *On the Spot*, p. 178.   [55] Interview: Gowon.

[56] One comes away with this conclusion regardless of which version is read—the one published by the Federal Government Printer or the more complete text released by the Eastern Nigerian Information Service.

[57] Forsyth, *The Biafra Story*, p. 86.

[58] *Morning Post*, January 27, 1967. Report of Lieutenant Colonel Gowon's press conference on the meeting at Aburi.

[59] Aburi Meeting, p. 17.

a broker for the conflicting local interests. Ojukwu's side was united, a pattern that would be repeated throughout the subsequent civil war, while Gowon had to forge a coalition government by steering a middle course. He was even unsure at this stage how to reorganize the federal army so as to minimize further tension and possible bloodshed. This left Ojukwu plenty of room to maneuver—to exploit differences among the other governors—and he played his hand skillfully.

As an international public relations exercise, the Aburi meeting must be considered an important victory for Ojukwu. "On Aburi We Stand" became the diplomatic and propaganda battle cry of Biafran spokesmen throughout the ensuing civil war, and it seemed to strike a responsive chord in the world press. The political argument behind the slogan, briefly stated, held that at Aburi there had been unanimous renunciation of force to settle Nigeria's internal differences, and that there had also been unanimous approval of a decentralization program, which should have given each region full control over its internal affairs and a veto over any policy decisions taken by the central government in Lagos. Gowon, Ojukwu later claimed, had flagrantly reneged on both counts. The federal government, not surprisingly, interpreted the Aburi records differently.

Substantively, Ojukwu's victory proved to be hollow. The final communiqué did pledge a renunciation of force, but it also included the following: "On the powers and functions of the Federal Military Government the [Supreme Military] Council reaffirmed its belief in the workability of the existing institutions subject to necessary safeguards."[60] The "necessary safeguards" were enumerated in a separate document that was never released. The crux of Ojukwu's argument turned on a paragraph of the final communiqué which stated that "any decision affecting the whole country must be determined by the Supreme Military Council. Where a meeting is not possible such a matter must be referred to the Military Governors for comment and concurrence."[61]

Once the civilian officials in Lagos had digested the Aburi communiqué, the cadre of permanent secretaries closest to Gowon, together with Attorney General Dr. T. O. Elias, drafted a lengthy memorandum warning of the full implications of "concurrence." Their case boiled down to the following: "The introduction of the element of Regional Military Governors' consent in the Federal Legislation will leave the Federal Executive Council with virtually no functions, and the powers of the Federal Military Government vis-à-vis the Regional Military Governments no longer exist."[62] Over the next two weeks a series

[60] Aburi Meeting, Final Communiqué, signed at Aburi on January 5, 1967.
[61] *Ibid.*
[62] The highly controversial memorandum was reprinted by Ojukwu's govern-

of meetings were held among the principal legal officers, civil servants, and military secretaries of the regional governments, all with a view to reaching a more realistic compromise regarding the operational meaning of the Aburi accord. The various exchanges were an exercise in futility. Toward the end of January 1967, Gowon issued a clarification of the Aburi discussions, stressing that the bottom line had been a unanimous pledge of allegiance to the Nigerian army under a unified command, with himself as the supreme commander, adding that: "we definitely decided against regional armies."[63] Several weeks later he further clarified his position to a closed-door meeting of the Lagos corps of African ambassadors when he flatly declared: "I emphasize that it was never the intention that any Military Governer should have the power to veto decisions taken by the Supreme Military Council."[64]

Ojukwu's response to the Lagos interpretation came in a personal note to Gowon denouncing the federal commander for not keeping his word, and vaguely threatening secession by the Eastern Region.[65] Once it became apparent to the East that Ojukwu's tactical victory at Aburi would not be upheld, secession was almost inevitable. From January 1967 until the formal declaration of Independence on May 29, 1967, the Ojukwu government was preoccupied with preparations for secession and the possibility that other regions might be persuaded to follow this course, thereby precipitating the complete dissolution of the Nigerian federation.

Ojukwu and his associates claim that when the Northern troops were withdrawn from the East in August 1966, the weapons that remained in the region amounted to only 120 rifles of bolt-action type.[66] Regardless of future constitutional arrangements, the East felt powerless to defend itself against physical intimidation from Lagos and, because of this, a secret arms procurement program began immediately. The first

---

ment as an appendix to the Eastern Region's version of the Aburi talks. The document's authenticity has never been denied. It was dated January 20, 1967, and was circulated under the signature of S.I.A. Akenzua, Acting Secretary to the Federal Military Government. *The Meeting of the Supreme Military Council*, Appendix IV, pp. 56–63.

[63] *Morning Post*, January 27, 1967, Gowon's Press Conference on the Aburi Meeting. Reprinted in full in Kirk-Greene, *Crisis and Conflict*, I, 352–354.

[64] MEA, "Remarks by His Excellency the Head of the Federal Military Government and Supreme Commander of the Armed Forces to Heads of African Diplomatic Missions in Nigeria on the Nigerian Situation," March 1, 1967.

[65] "Unilateral Action"—A personal letter from Ojukwu to Gowon, in Kirk-Greene, *Crisis and Conflict*, I, 359–362.

[66] Interview: Ojukwu. The figure appeared so frequently in conversations with former Biafrans that it has assumed the quality of legend, which may or may not be true. Frederick Forsyth refers to 303 police rifles (*The Biafra Story*, p. 115) and, whatever the true figure, it is a fair assumption that the Eastern Region arsenal in 1966 was negligible.

clear evidence that Ojukwu's agents were buying military equipment appeared in October 1966, when an aging DC-4 commanded by an American gunrunner, Captain Henry Wharton, crashed in northern Cameroon en route to Eastern Nigeria with a load of small arms and ammunition.[67] The purchase of such equipment was not easy. Eastern agents lacked previous contacts with black market dealers in Europe, and Ojukwu was unable to authorize purchases in foreign exchange without alerting the central bankers in Lagos. Asked about this, Ojukwu says that the only way he was able to acquire arms during 1966 and early 1967 was to buy them himself. When his father, Sir Odumegwu Ojukwu, died on September 13, 1966, he left an estate of several million pounds.[68] Some of this was safely banked in Europe, and his son claims to have used all of it, approximately one million pounds sterling, to purchase arms.[69]

Ojukwu had been quartermaster general in the Nigerian army before becoming governor, and he felt that he knew what he was buying and what was required to contain any military threat from Lagos. The materiel actually received fell short of expectations, however, because his civilian buyers were frequently deceived and overcharged by unscrupulous dealers.[70] Nevertheless, the arms that did reach the East provided a crucial boost to morale and lent a feeling of self-reliance. This sense of independence grew throughout the spring of 1967, stimulated to a large degree by the apparent weakness of the federal government.

On February 25, 1967, Ojukwu promised his people that he would not allow them to be slaughtered in their beds, that the East was militarily ready to resist any threat, and that unless the Aburi accord was implemented by the end of the fiscal year, March 31, 1967, the East would unilaterally withdraw from the prevailing federal arrangement.[71] This brought a quick response from General Ankrah, who, less than a week later, invited Gowon to Accra to determine what if any-

[67] The incident is described in Thayer, *The War Business*, p. 162. British High Commissioner David Hunt, who was in Lagos at the time, claims that Francis Nwokedi, the former Nigerian permanent secretary of external affairs, and Christopher Okigbo, the poet, went to France to buy arms in August, shortly after the second coup. Hunt, *On the Spot*, p. 172.

[68] Sir Odumegwu Ojukwu, O.B.E., K.B.E., L.I.D., was the founder, chairman, and managing director of Ojukwu Transport Limited, one of the largest transport companies in Nigeria. He was also chairman of the African Continental Bank, the Eastern Nigerian Marketing Board, the Nkalagu Cement Company, and the Nigerian National Shipping Company.

[69] Interview: Ojukwu.

[70] For a fascinating description of the uncertainties and frustrations of dealing for the first time in the illicit international arms trade, as recounted by one of Biafra's envoys, see Mezu, *Behind the Rising Sun*, chaps. 1–4.

[71] Ojukwu, *Biafra*, "Breach of Aburi Accord," broadcast February 25, 1967, I, 107–113.

thing was being done to meet Ojukwu's demands and to urge him to take whatever steps were necessary to placate Eastern fears.[72] Ankrah received assurances that new concessions would be forthcoming at a planned meeting of the Supreme Military Council in Benin on March 16, and he relayed these assurances to London and Washington.[73] Ankrah also secured Gowon's permission to send a high-level fact-finding delegation directly to Ojukwu's headquarters in Enugu.[74] The diplomatic maneuvers gave added prominence and legitimacy to Ojukwu's grievances, but failed to lure the Ibo leader to attend the Supreme Military Council meeting on March 16, 1967.[75]

The outcome of the rump session of the Supreme Military Council was viewed by the East as further evidence of a weak and indecisive federal government. The next day a decree was published in Lagos that prescribed a major decentralization of the country's administration. Apparently, Ojukwu's demand for the concurrence of all military governors on such matters as trade, commerce, industry, transport, the armed forces, and higher education, was finally acceptable.[76] There was, however, a key reservation. The provision in section 70 of the constitution that gives powers to the Supreme Military Council "to take over the legislative functions of a Regional Government during any period of emergency which might be declared in respect of that Region by the Supreme Military Council" was upheld; so, too, was the provision of Section 71 granting the Supreme Military Council "the power to take appropriate measures against a Region which attempts to secede from the rest of the Federation."[77]

The Northern governor, Hassan Katsina, hailed the March 17, 1967, Decentralization Decree as evidence of a common front that would contain the East;[78] but a week later Ojukwu published an edict giving himself emergency powers to declare the region a disturbed area.[79] With the approach of March 31, 1967, the day on which Ojukwu would declare secession unless his demands regarding the Aburi agreements

---

[72] *Daily Graphic* (Accra), March 5, 1967.

[73] Interview: Ankrah.

[74] The delegation, led by Major General Ocran, spent several hours with Ojukwu on March 8. *Daily Graphic* (Accra), March 10, 1967.

[75] In a lengthy interview with the London *Sunday Times* (March 13, 1967), Ojukwu restated his determination not to deal with the federal government on any basis other than the arrangements outlined in the Aburi communiqué.

[76] Federal Republic of Nigeria, *Constitution (Suspension and Modification)*, Supplement to the Official Gazette of the Federation of Nigeria, Vol. 54, A91–92. Decree No. 8 promulgated on March 17, 1967. Explanatory Note attached to the decree reprinted in Kirk-Greene, *Crisis and Conflict*, I, 401–402. The decree was later rescinded.

[77] *Ibid.*   [78] *New Nigerian*, March 21, 1967.

[79] *Daily Times*, March 25, 1967.

were met, there were strong indications that the rest of the federation lacked the strength to resist. On March 30, the governor of the Midwest Region, David Ejoor, told reporters in Benin that the federal military government did not intend to use force on any region that wanted to secede, a position that was also endorsed by the Western governor, Robert Adebayo.[80]

With the cohesiveness of the rest of Nigeria apparently weakening, Ojukwu decided not to force the issue with an announcement of formal secession on March 31. His immediate objective became the removal of Northern troops from the Ibadan and Abeokuta garrisons in the Western Region. If he could generate sufficient domestic and even international pressures to have all troops reassigned to their region of origin—as recommended in the Aburi communiqué—then the prospect for a new, independent southern alliance, or merely the fragmentation of the federation, would be enhanced. Thus, instead of seceding, Ojukwu signed a revenue collection edict directing that all revenues derived from the Eastern Region be diverted from the federal authorities in Lagos and paid into his regional treasury.[81] This latest demonstration of the East's autonomy was followed by Ojukwu's call for a summit meeting of Nigeria's military leaders in the presence of Emperor Haile Selassie of Ethiopia, General Ankrah, President Nasser of Egypt, and President Tubman of Liberia.[82] Ojukwu's envoys had quietly been touring African capitals for several weeks in an attempt to win foreign support for their interpretation of the Aburi agreement. The envoys had discovered that the reports of the October 1966 massacres in the North had generated much sympathy among African leaders. Ojukwu hoped to convert this sympathy to political pressures that would restrain the federal government from taking any reprisals, while enhancing his own status internationally as an independent actor.

Lagos retaliated against Ojukwu's seizure of federal revenues by suspending all Nigerian Airways flights to the East, halting postal and money-order transactions, and canceling the diplomatic passports of thirty prominent Ibos who were known to be lobbying against the federal government overseas.[83] In response to the call for mediation by African heads of state, Gowon summoned the Lagos diplomatic corps to

[80] *Ibid.*, March 31, 1967.
[81] Eastern Nigeria Government, *Revenue Collection Edict*, March 31, 1967; *Morning Post*, May 1, 1967; also, Kirk-Greene, *Crisis and Conflict*, I, 88–89.
[82] *West Africa*, No. 2603, April 22, 1967, p. 539.
[83] An extraordinary issue of the *Federal Gazette* published in Lagos showed that the passports were canceled on various dates between April 20 and May 3, and included such prominent Ibos as Dr. K. O. Mbadiwe, Dr. Pius Okigbo, Francis Nwokedi, Flora Azikiwe, and a number of diplomats suspected of engaging in arms purchases abroad. *West Africa*, No. 2607, May 20, 1967, p. 673.

a briefing session during which he outlined his reasons for rejecting the suggestion:

a. the current situation in Nigeria is an internal affair;
b. the invitation, emanating from Lt. Col. Ojukwu as it does, has the undertone of seeking de facto recognition by these African Heads of State. It also implies that there is a dispute between two sovereign and equal states;
c. to avoid possible division in the ranks of the OAU, and especially among those who would be genuinely interested in assisting Nigeria;
d. the fact that Lt. Col. Ojukwu refuses to recognize the existence of the Federal Government and myself as the Head; and
e. the invitation to any Head of State must, as a matter of protocol, emanate from me as Head of the Federal Military Government. In reaching such a decision I would, of course, consult my colleagues on the Supreme Military Council.[84]

Gowon sought to assure the ambassadors that the situation in Nigeria, which he compared to the threat of Katanga's secession in the Congo, was "well within the capacity of my government to resolve."[85] The governments represented had shown little enthusiasm for becoming openly involved unless specifically invited by the federal government, and those African leaders named in Ojukwu's proposal either ignored his call or deferred to the federal government.[86] Even the Ghanaians withdrew from further efforts at mediation, although primarily for domestic reasons.[87] Regarding Gowon's assurances of his government's viability the ambassadors undoubtedly were less sanguine, and the events of the ensuing several weeks would be even more dismaying.

The greatest shock was a direct challenge to the Gowon regime issued by the Western Region's most prominent Yoruba politician, Chief Obafemi Awolowo. On May 1, 1967, Awolowo told a major gathering of Yoruba elite that "if the Eastern Region is allowed by acts of omission or commission to secede from or opt out of Nigeria, then the

[84] "Gowon Addresses Heads of Diplomatic Missions in Lagos," reprint of speech made in Lagos on April 24, 1967, Kirk-Greene, *Crisis and Conflict*, I, 410–414.

[85] *Ibid.*

[86] Of the three, only President Tubman acknowledged any contact with the Easterners. The Liberian president said that he was willing to do anything he could to help the federal government resolve the situation. *West Africa*, No. 2603, April 22, 1967, p. 539. For a discussion of interest among East African leaders to play a mediatory role, see Anglin, "Zambia and the Recognition of Biafra."

[87] On April 17, 1967, there was an attempted coup in Ghana in which Lieutenant General Kotoka, general officer commanding, was killed by rebel forces. *West Africa*, No. 2603, April 22, 1967, p. 541.

Western Region and Lagos must also stay out of the Federation."[88] Responding to Awolowo's remarks, the Western "Leaders of Thought," the most representative body of Yoruba opinion then in existence, passed a resolution declaring that if any region seceded, "the Federation as we know it shall cease to exist" and "Western Nigeria shall automatically become independent and sovereign."[89]

When Gowon tried to convene the Supreme Military Council three days later, both Ojukwu and the Western regional governor, Colonel Adebayo, failed to attend. The Western governor made it plain that he would not participate as long as Northern troops remained in the West.[90] It appeared as though an East-West alliance was developing that might force Gowon's abdication and result in the dissolution of the Nigerian federation into two or possibly three sovereign states, one dominated by the Ibos, another by the Yorubas, and a third—landlocked and impoverished—under the control of the Hausa/Fulani.

Respect for Ojukwu's position was apparently on the rise, not only within Nigeria, but in Britain as well. Ojukwu never expected the British government to support the breakup of the federation, but he did hope for British neutrality, which obviously would make secession a less risky venture.[91] Neutrality would not only deprive Gowon's regime of any access to British military assistance, but it would be tantamount to a vote of no confidence in the federal government. When Gowon forced their hand, apparently inadvertently, the British signaled their appreciation of the political realities in Nigeria.

At issue was a possible venue for a last-ditch conference of all military governors to forestall secession. Following the humiliation of May 8, when both the Eastern and Western governors declined to attend the Supreme Military Council meeting, Gowon sent the following cable to the governors: "Tentative arrangements made for British assistance military personnel one or two companies strictly to create neutral zone for us to meet. Suggest Benin/Naifor ideal venue. Alternative offer British aircraft carrier/frigate. . . ." Ojukwu released the cable and condemned the suggestion of a British force as "inimical to the security of the Eastern Region."[92] The Western governor joined in rejecting British involvement, and renewed his appeal for the withdrawal of Northern troops from Ibadan and Abeokuta.[93] An embarrassed federal government later released the text of the cable with the caveat that

[88] *Daily Times*, May 2, 1967. Also reprinted in Kirk-Greene, *Crisis and Conflict*, I, 414–418.
[89] *Daily Sketch*, May 3, 1967.
[90] *Daily Times*, May 13, 1967 and May 21, 1967.
[91] See Hunt, *On the Spot*, pp. 178–179.
[92] *Sunday Times* (Lagos), May 21, 1967.
[93] *Ibid.*

"no official request has been made to the British Government in this context. Only tentative feelers were made."[94]

The British were evidently displeased with the implications that they were prepared to backstop Gowon's efforts to revive the federation, and they took steps to disassociate themselves from his faltering regime. According to a statement issued by the British High Commission in Lagos: "No such request [for a security force] has in fact been made to the British Government. If all four Military Governors and the Federal Government wished for a meeting of this sort and a request was made to the British Government it would receive careful consideration; but it would only be given consideration if it was the unanimous wish of all Nigerians from all parts of the country."[95] The stipulation that there had to be unanimity among the regional governors before Britain would consider becoming involved was tacit recognition that the federal government possessed only nominal authority, and that the country was already functioning, de facto, as a confederation of separate entities. Britain's unwillingness to interfere with this arrangement was viewed in the East as a very encouraging omen.

Faced with an untenable situation, Gowon tried to forestall Eastern secession by granting a series of dramatic concessions during the third week of May. First, the federal government removed the economic sanctions taken against the East, restored normal postal and telecommunications services, and permitted the resumption of normal shipping and air traffic, effective from May 23.[96] Two days later the police inspector-general announced that soldiers of non-Western Nigerian origin would be removed from Ibaban and Abeokuta within a few days' time.[97]

The East's reaction was to treat Gowon's concessions as a sign of weakness and to claim that sanctions had failed and the federation was on the verge of collapse.[98] Secession was at hand. Lagos appeared to lack the power and the will to resist. The allegiance of the Western Region was in serious doubt and the British seemed resigned to a "wait and see" policy. On May 26 Ojukwu addressed a joint meeting of Chiefs and Elders and the Consultative Assembly and offered the members three choices: "(a) accepting the terms of the North and Gowon and thereby submit to domination by the North, or (b) continuing the

[94] Nigeria, Federal Ministry of Information, Press Release No. 1108, May 18, 1967.

[95] *Morning Post*, May 19, 1967, also reprinted as "British High Commission Denies Dispatch of British Troops," Press Release of the U.K. High Commission, Lagos, and included in Kirk-Greene, *Crisis and Conflict*, I, 424–425.

[96] *Morning Post*, May 21, 1967.   [97] *Ibid.*, May 25, 1967.

[98] *Nigerian Outlook*, May 22, 1967, and a major statement by Cyprian Ekwensi, director of Information Services of the Eastern Region, Radio Enugu, May 23, 1967.

present stalemate and drift, or (c) ensuring the survival of our people by asserting our autonomy."[99] The assembly, to no one's surprise, endorsed independence the following day.

TWELVE STATES MINUS THREE

Instead of announcing the birth of Biafra on May 27, 1967, Ojukwu paused once again to see if this latest threat would prompt the federal government to withdraw all Northern troops from the West. For the first time in the ten-month war of nerves, Ojukwu overplayed his hand. Rather than offering new formulae or gestures to mollify the East, Gowon counterattacked: four hours after the news of the Consultative Assembly's mandate for secession reached Lagos, he issued a constitutional decree that transformed the Nigerian political system. The decree superseded the six-week old decentralization decree (No. 8) and replaced the four regional governments with twelve federated states.[100] While the far-reaching decision would take thirty-two months to implement fully, in retrospect the creation of twelve states was a major turning point in the country's history. The decision established the administrative units listed in Table 2–1 and shown in Map 2–2.

Creating twelve states eventually facilitated three major shifts in political power. At the regional level, the redistricting delimited Hausa/Fulani hegemony over the northern half of the country and, by the end of the civil war, prevented any further Ibo domination in the non-Ibo areas of the East. Nationally, the new arrangement marked the ascendancy of representatives from the minority tribes, which composed nearly 40 percent of the country's population. Nigeria had changed domestic alliances with the possibility of building a more politically viable nation. The immediate instigation for such a dramatic move was, of course, the threat of Eastern secession.

By announcing the creation of twelve states prior to Biafran secession, Gowon established first claim to the loyalties of several million non-Ibos in the former Eastern Region. As later events would show, nothing contributed more to the isolation of the Ibo-led rebellion than the disaffection of the Eastern minorities. Had these small ethnic groups in the riverine areas of southern Biafra resisted federal liberation—either directly or through aid and comfort to Biafran guerrillas—the rebellion might have been a success.

Anyone who was familiar with Nigeria's political history would have known that the seemingly arbitrary decision by the federal gov-

[99] Ojukwu, *Biafra*, I, 173.
[100] Federal Republic of Nigeria, *The Constitution (Repeal and Restoration)*, Decree 1967, No. 13, Supplement to Official Gazette Extraordinary, No. 37, Vol. 54, May 27, 1967.

TABLE 2-1

The Twelve States

	Capital	Area in sq. miles	Population
Eastern Region	*Enugu*	*29,479*	*12,395,000*
East Central State	Enugu	11,548	7,469,000
Rivers State	Port Harcourt	6,985	1,545,000
Southeastern State	Calabar	10,951	3,381,000
Western Region	*Ibadan*	*30,481*	*10,931,000*
Western State	Ibadan	29,100	9,488,000
Lagos State	Lagos	1,381	1,443,000
Midwestern Region	*Benin*	*14,922*	*2,536,000*
Midwestern State	Benin	14,922	2,536,000
Northern Region	*Kaduna*	*281,782*	*29,609,000*
North-Central State	Kaduna	27,108	3,878,000
Northwestern State	Sokoto	65,143	5,734,000
Northeastern State	Maiduguri	105,025	7,793,000
Kano State	Kano	16,630	5,775,000
Kwara State	Ilorin	28,672	2,399,000
Benue-Plateau State	Jos	39,204	4,230,000

Source: adapted from the statistics in Federal Government of Nigeria, *Nigeria Handbook 1970* (Lagos, 1970), p. 85. The population figures reflect the controversial 1963 census.

ernment had been foreshadowed and was not without legitimacy. Pressures to free the minority tribes from the domination of the three major ones had surfaced periodically during the previous twenty years. British indirect rule generally respected local interests and institutions, with the result that until the prospect of political independence became a certainty, there were few instances in which one cultural group was coercively made subordinate to another cultural group.[101] The growth of nationalism and party rivalry changed interethnic relations. As noted earlier, each of the three major tribal groups created a political party, which sought simultaneously to consolidate its authority over the local region and to appeal to dissident groups elsewhere.

Nowhere in Nigeria was minority agitation as strenuous as the Ibibio-led anti-Ibo movement to form a COR region encompassing the Calabar, Ogoja, and Rivers provinces. The movement was based in the eastern port city of Calabar, near the Cameroon border, where British missionaries had established one of their earliest footholds in

[101] Coleman, *Nigeria: Background to Nationalism*, p. 385.

Nigeria: The Twelve States

Map 2–2 • Nigeria: the Twelve States (from A.H.M. Kirk-Green, *Crisis and Conflict in Nigeria*, frontispiece)

Africa.[102] The indigenous Efiks and Ibibios were among the best educated and most politically aware groups in Nigeria. Calabar was for many years the East's most important economic center, as the principal outlet for the region's major cash crop, palm oil. The marketing and refining of this lucrative crop was dominated by Ibos, a factor long resented by the indigenous peoples. The Efiks, Ibibios, and Annangs of Calabar and Ogoja provinces made up approximately one-quarter of the East's twelve million people.

A fourth minority group, the one million Ijaws, inhabited the Rivers

[102] For a fascinating account of early mission work in Calabar, see Livingstone, *Mary Slessor of Calabar, Pioneer Missionary*.

Province west of Calabar. For years they had fished in the creeks surrounding the industrial port city of Port Harcourt, enduring Ibo domination. By 1966, however, these same marshy creeks were producing nearly two-thirds of Nigeria's 400,000 barrels per day of high-quality crude petroleum. Moreover, the channel island of Bonny near Port Harcourt was Nigeria's only export terminal for petroleum, and the country's sole refinery was also in the Port Harcourt area. If Biafra was to be viable it was essential that Port Harcourt and the oil-rich environs remain under Ojukwu's control. Conversely, statehood for the Rivers Province seemed to offer the Ijaws a far better opportunity to enjoy the wealth accruing from locally mined petroleum.

The individual most identified with the campaign for more states was Chief Obafemi Awolowo. In 1953 he had called for a redivision of the country into nine states: four in the North (to free the middle-belt Yorubas from Hausa domination), two in the West, and three in the East.[103] The arrangement was strikingly similar to the one imposed in 1967, but throughout the intervening fourteen years Awolowo's efforts were resisted. President Azikiwe objected particularly to the COR-State movement because he felt that the claim was based primarily on anti-Ibo sentiment.[104] When Awolowo was released from prison in 1966, he immediately called public attention to the plight of the minorities should any of the four regions try to secede, and suggested anew the need for a more broadly based federation.[105]

Gowon was not unsympathetic to the need for more states. As a member of a tiny ethnic group and a Christian from the predominantly Moslem North, he was personally aware of the inequities of the old system. In November 1966 he told the nation: "It is quite clear that our common need in Nigeria is that no one region or tribal group should be in a position to dominate the others . . . there is no doubt that without a definite commitment on the states question, normalcy and freedom from fear of domination by one region or the other cannot be achieved. . . . Given the present size and distribution of the Nigerian population and resources, the country could be divided into not less than eight and not more than fourteen states."[106] It is also significant that following Gowon's assumption of power there were threats of

[103] Coleman, *Nigeria: Background to Nationalism*, p. 388.

[104] *Ibid.*, p. 395.

[105] "Awolowo's Speech to the Western Leaders of Thought on Accepting the Title of 'Leader of the Yorubas,'" *Morning Post*, August 12, 1966. Reprinted in Kirk-Greene, *Crisis and Conflict*, I, 202–203.

[106] "Towards a New Nigeria," an address to the nation by the head of the federal military government, November 30, 1966, reprinted in Nigeria, *Faith in Unity*, p. 5.

resistance to any Ibo-led secession, and public demonstrations in favor of the federation erupted in the Calabar/Rivers areas of the East.[107]

By the spring of 1967 Gowon was openly invoking the states issue to counter Ojukwu's talk of secession. Summoning the Lagos diplomatic corps on April 24, he assured them, "I want to make it abundantly clear that in the event of Lt. Col. Ojukwu carrying out his threat to secede, this will be a clear signal in the first place to create a COR-State for the protection of the minorities in Eastern Nigeria whom we know do not want to part from the rest of the country. This action of creating the COR-State will be backed by the use of force if need be."[108] In the event, the decision to create the twelve states preceded the declaration of secession by less than forty-eight hours.

Under the new administrative arrangement, twelve military governors were appointed. The phasing out of the old regional governments was to take one year to allow for the establishment of local administrative institutions. Each state would have the same degree of local control as the old regions had under the 1963 federal constitution. In his charge to the new governors, Gowon declared, "Each State is an autonomous unit within the Federation of Nigeria. Each State is equal in all respects to other States. You, as Military Governors, therefore, have full powers over all constitutional responsibilities allocated to the States. No one Military Governor is subordinate to another in the discharge of his constitutional responsibilities."[109] A week later, Gowon announced the creation of a Federal Executive Council composed of twelve civilians, representing each of the new states. The list of appointees included numerous outstanding leaders from minority and antiestablishment political movements of the 1960s.[110]

[107] On October 1, 1966, the government-owned *Morning Post* reported: "Leaders of minority areas in the Eastern Region have sent an SOS to Lt. Col. Gowon asking for the withdrawal of armed troops sent to occupy certain towns in Old Calabar and Rivers. . . . [It was alleged] that these troops were sent to these areas to intimidate the people and force them to abandon their demand for separate states. During the past week the Eastern Nigeria Broadcasting Service and all official information media in Eastern Nigeria have mounted massive propaganda campaigns against the creation of new states."

[108] "Series of Provocations," an address by the head of the federal military government to the heads of diplomatic missions in Lagos, April 24, 1967, reprinted Nigeria, in *Faith in Unity*, p. 42.

[109] "New Leaders for New States," an address by the head of the federal military government to the military governors, May 31, 1967, reprinted *ibid.*, p. 59.

[110] Gowon retained the chairmanship of the Federal Executive Council. His vice chairman and commissioner of finance was Chief Obafemi Awolowo. The other wartime commissioners—several of whom were not announced immediately —included: Okoi Arikpo (External Affairs); J. S. Tarka (Transport); Anthony Enahoro (Information and Labour); Aminu Kano (Communications); Wenike Briggs (Education); J. E. Adetoro (Health); T. O. Elias (Justice); Yahaya Gusau

With the creation of the twelve states, the formal announcement of secession was an anticlimax. Shortly after midnight on May 30, 1967, Odumegwu Ojukwu and a crowd of his closest advisers, family, and friends, gathered at the sprawling governor's mansion in Enugu to hear the following declaration:

> Fellow countrymen and women, you, the people of Eastern Nigeria . . . aware that you can no longer be protected in your lives and in your property by any government based outside Eastern Nigeria . . . THEREFORE I . . . DO HEREBY SOLEMNLY PROCLAIM THAT THE TERRITORY AND REGION KNOWN AS AND CALLED EASTERN NIGERIA TOGETHER WITH HER CONTINENTAL SHELF AND TERRITORIAL WATERS SHALL HENCEFORTH BE AN INDEPENDENT SOVEREIGN STATE OF THE NAME AND TITLE OF THE REPUBLIC OF BIAFRA.[111]

At 3 A.M. on May 30, Ojukwu summoned the Enugu diplomatic corps, which consisted of the American consul, Mr. Barnard, the British deputy high commissioner, Mr. Parker, and the Cameroonian consul, Mr. Nkuo, to inform them of his decision to declare Biafra an independent nation. Two hours later the message was relayed in a sixty-five–minute radio broadcast to the twelve to fourteen million Ibos, Efiks, Ijaws, and Ibibios whose lives would soon be ravaged by one of the most violent conflicts in African history.

After nearly a year of political maneuvering, the issue was finally engaged. Ojukwu, who had never recognized Gowon's sovereignty over the East, was at last prepared to test his own independence. The prospects were indeed grim. Secession is, after all, a zero-sum proposition, and the likelihood that Ojukwu could be persuaded voluntarily to rejoin the federation diminished sharply with the announcement of the twelve-state structure. For the East to accept such an arrangement would deprive Ojukwu's government of 60 percent of its agricultural revenues and 95 percent of the income from petroleum. Cut off from Calabar, Ogoja, and Port Harcourt provinces, the overpopulated Ibo heartland would thus become land-locked, underfed, and relatively impoverished. While one could reasonably question the fighting capability of Ojukwu's untrained and poorly equipped five thousand-man army, the commitment to resist the reimposition of federal authority was beyond doubt.

Interested foreign actors, confronted with the prospect of having

---

(Economic Development); Olufemi Okunnu (Works and Housing); R.B.O. Dikko (Mines and Power); and Ali Monguno (Trade and Industry).

[111] Ojukwu, *Biafra*, "The Declaration," May 30, 1967, I, 193–196. For an hour-by-hour account of the events surrounding Ojukwu's declaration, see *West Africa*, No. 2610, June 10, 1967, pp. 773–774.

to choose sides, could derive very little confidence from their contacts in Lagos. The power and determination of the federal government to impose the new twelve-state system could only be surmised. The performance of the Gowon regime since July 1966 certainly did not bode well; even strongly profederal civil servants had questioned their government's capacity to survive. Toward the end of 1966, for example, the head of Nigeria's Ministry of External Affairs had told Ojukwu with exasperation, "I have been announced as a delegate to the OAU Meeting at Addis Ababa but I am not going anywhere until I am sure of what I am representing."[112] The twelve-state decree provided only a tentative answer, although it would remain the central point of reference for Nigerian foreign policy makers until the rebellion was finally crushed. In June 1967, however, the new state system was merely a political blueprint, and before the federal government could begin to reassert itself internationally, a clear show of strength at home was absolutely essential.

[112] Edwin Ogbu, permanent secretary, Ministry of External Affairs, from the transcript of a meeting between Lieutenant Colonel Ojukwu and a delegation of federal civil servants held in Enugu on October 27, 1966.

· 3 ·

THE WORLD DECLINES
TO TAKE SIDES

Britain's ambivalence toward the Gowon regime, which surfaced public-ly over the issue of security guarantees for a meeting of the Supreme Military Council in May 1967, had been building for several months. When David Hunt arrived in Lagos during February as the new British high commissioner, he brought a message from the Queen that carefully hedged the possibility of future support from London. According to Hunt, the message "began by expressing our support for the *concept* of Nigerian unity, assuring the Federal Government that Britain would do nothing to encourage secession. The rest of the message was taken up with exhortations to the Government to stick to its policy of negotiation rather than coercion and to go to the utmost limits of conciliation. He [Gowon] naturally asked me what our attitude would be if that policy failed, and I could only reply that I hoped things would not come to such a pass."[1]

The unwillingness of Nigeria's oldest and closest foreign ally to offer assurances was reinforced by a similar attitude adopted by the United States. When Gowon summoned David Hunt and the United States ambassador, Elbert Mathews, to his Dodan Barracks headquarters in late May and asked for a joint pledge of support from the two govern-ments, Mathews is said to have replied that while Washington hoped Nigeria would remain united, he was equally sure that the United States government would decline to take sides in what it regarded as a purely internal dispute.[2] Since the answer was likely to be negative, the ambas-sador suggested that Gowon not ask for an endorsement. The high com-missioner indicated that the British government was likely to adopt a similar position.

For the federal military government, which was universally recognized as the legitimate authority over all of Nigeria, the aloofness by the two Western powers had a chilling effect. Gowon had hoped that the Americans, in light of their own history of civil war, would be sympathetic to the federal cause. Less than a year earlier Mathews and David Hunt's predecessor had pleaded with Gowon in the wake of

[1] Hunt, *On the Spot*, pp. 174–175.
[2] Interviews: Edwin Ogbu, permanent secretary of external affairs, who was present at the meeting; and Gowon.

the second coup not to abandon the quest for a strong and united Nigeria. Gowon later described his dealings with the Americans and the British at the time of Biafran secession as "deeply disappointing," an experience that taught him the validity of John Kennedy's dictum, which he paraphrased as "governments have no friends or enemies—only interests."[3] Many in Lagos believed that a stronger show of confidence in the federal government by Britain and America might have deterred Ojukwu's bid for independence.

Although the Americans and British were not prepared to give Gowon open-ended commitments of support, they did make assurances that they would not intervene in the event that secession was declared. The federal government had also taken the precaution of eliciting formal pledges not to assist Ojukwu from other governments during the spring of 1967. In March Gowon called together the African diplomatic corps in Lagos and during a closed meeting asked that their respective governments agree to "do nothing whatsoever tending to give any form of recognition or support to dissident elements opposed to my Government."[4] The assurances were given, as were similar pledges from the various non-African powers represented in Nigeria, including the French. Later in the year the commissioner of external affairs, Dr. Okoi Arikpo, even paid a secret visit to Lisbon, where he also received a promise—however disingenuous—that Portugal would do nothing to encourage the breakup of Nigeria.[5]

When secession was declared Gowon immediately issued a pro forma public call to all countries and international organizations to "respect the territorial integrity of the Federal Republic of Nigeria."[6] This same message along with a warning that "any attempt to recognize the so-called Republic of Biafra as a sovereign state will amount to interference in the internal affairs of my country and will be regarded as an unfriendly act," were conveyed in identical notes to the secretariats of the United Nations and the Organization of African Unity for distribution among all members of both organizations.[7]

Incredibly, a Radio Biafra newscaster announced on the day of secession that Ghana, Togo, the Gambia, Ethiopia, and Israel had all

[3] Interview: Gowon.

[4] MEA, Remarks by His Excellency the Head of the Federal Military Government and Supreme Commander of the Armed Forces to Heads of African Diplomatic Missions in Nigeria on the Nigerian Situation, March 1, 1967.

[5] Interview: Dr. Okoi Arikpo.

[6] A Statement by the Head of the Federal Military Government on May 30, 1967, reprinted in Nigeria, *Faith in Unity*, p. 57.

[7] Text of a Letter from the Head of the Federal Military Government to the Secretary General of the United Nations, released by the Federal Ministry of External Affairs on May 30, 1967.

extended diplomatic recognition to the new republic and that more countries would follow shortly. The director of information for Biafra, who nearly lost his job because of the mistake, attributes the claim to the irresponsible enthusiasm of a young announcer.[8] His director of programming, in a separate interview, asserts that the announcement went on the air without prior clearance but blames the error on "the pressure to produce good news."[9] Whatever the source, Ojukwu and the head of his newly created Ministry of Foreign Affairs were furious, knowing that this would lead Nigeria to demand that the governments so named publicly repudiate the Biafran claim and pledge their support for the federal government. As soon as the Nigerian request was made, the five quickly complied.[10]

Elsewhere in Africa the initial commentaries regarding Biafran secession were generally muted.[11] Radio Guinea was the most acerbic, denouncing Ojukwu as the "Tshombe of the Eastern State." But this analogy was explicitly rejected by President Julius Nyerere of Tanzania and, more importantly, by Congolese President Joseph Mobutu.[12] Those countries most directly affected, the Republic of Cameroon and the other states contiguous to Nigeria, withheld judgment on the merits of the dispute, although President Hamani Diori of Niger publicly assured Gowon that he would not recognize Biafra.[13]

Most of the world's governments simply ignored Biafra, and those compelled to take a stand issued statements that were carefully hedged. In Washington, a State Department spokesman declared in response to press inquires that American policy was opposed to the balkanization of Africa, but should Biafra become "a going concern accepted by the Organization of African Unity, by its neighbors and by Britain, it is quite conceivable that the United States reluctantly would extend

[8] Interview: Cyprian Ekwensi, director of Biafran Information Services.

[9] Interview: Obi Odo, director of programming, Radio Biafra.

[10] Interviews: Ojukwu and Godwin Onyegbula, permanent secretary, Biafran Ministry of Foreign Affairs. It is possible that the radio announcer had learned from someone at the Ministry of Foreign Affairs that the five countries had not unequivocally ruled out future recognition of Biafra, but had made this contingent on prior recognition by other powers, notably Britain and America, and in light of the much talked-about neutrality already shown by London and Washington, the announcer jumped to conclusions.

[11] *West Africa*, No. 2610, June 10, 1967, pp. 772–773; and No. 2611, June 17, 1967, p. 806.

[12] Statement issued by the Tanzanian High Commission in London, DTX/ 746, June 1, 1967. President Mobutu reportedly declared upon receipt of the diplomatic credentials of Nigeria's ambassador, Alhaji Muhamadu Bayero, that the secession of Eastern Nigeria could not be compared to Katanga because that secession was brought about by foreign financial interests, while the secession of Biafra was the result of internal forces acting against Nigeria. *West Africa*, No. 2611, June 17, 1967, p. 806.

[13] *Ibid.*

recognition."[14] In June 1967 Chief Enahoro was sent to Washington to brief American officials, and he recalls sardonically that he found "diminishing comprehension of the Nigerian crisis the higher up the hierarchy one went."[15] The State Department, Enahoro discovered, "did not think we meant what we said. . . . They did not grasp the realities of the twelve states . . . they doubted if we could win and suggested that the Ibo area was capable of standing on its own. Ibos were thought to have all the talent. They [U.S. officials] tended to dismiss me as a dreamer and not representative of the real power in Nigeria. One had to keep one's patience. They tended to gauge us by a double standard: what was right for the American federation in 1860 did not hold for the Nigerian federation."[16] Nigeria's disappointment and frustration with the American policy turned to anger over a wire service report that quoted Secretary of State Dean Rusk to the effect that the Nigerian crisis was primarily a British responsibility.[17]

If Nigeria was a British concern, London initially did not appear ready to assert any leadership in defense of Nigerian federal unity. George Thomas, minister of state for Commonwealth affairs, carefully avoided condemning either side when he spoke to the Royal Commonwealth Society two days after Biafran Independence. Describing the crisis as purely an internal matter for Nigerians to settle among themselves, he declined to make any further comment.[18] The first statement of policy by the Labour government was offered to the House of Commons by the Commonwealth secretary on June 6, 1967. Measuring his words, Mr. Bowden stated that "in the interest of British nationals there [inside Biafra], there is some association between our representatives in Enugu and the break away regime, but at this stage there can be no recognition of the Eastern Region by ourselves, nor has any other country recognized it."[19] "British policy," one close observer later wrote, "seemed to be out of gear if not totally immobilized."[20]

Reinforcing the "wait and see" attitude among the major Western powers were more immediate concerns that preoccupied them elsewhere. Barely a week after Ojukwu announced secession, Israeli jets launched a preemptive strike against Egypt, thereby triggering the Six Day War in the Middle East. Nigeria, for the moment, was a distant secondary concern. With the closure of the Suez Canal, the strategic importance of Biafra's petroleum reserves became more obvious, and this consideration may have further discouraged the British and other European con-

[14] Melbourne, "The American Response to the Nigerian Conflict," p. 33, quoting the *Baltimore Sun*, June 1, 1967.
[15] Interview: Anthony Enahoro.   [16] *Ibid.*
[17] *Daily Times*, July 13, 1967.   [18] *Ibid.*, June 3, 1967.
[19] Great Britain, *Parliamentary Debates*, Vol. 747, June 6, 1967, cols. 810–812.
[20] De St. Jorre, *The Nigerian Civil War*, p. 296.

sumers from identifying too closely with the federal government until the military situation became clarified.[21]

Above all, Nigeria was not of vital interest to the two superpowers, who were maneuvering toward detente. Neither was anxious to become entangled in local West African politics. Unlike so many other insurgencies in the cold war period after World War II, Biafra was not a liberation or revolutionary movement with foreign ties. When President Lyndon Johnson and Soviet Premier Alexei Kosygin met in late June 1967 for two days of informal talks in Glassboro, New Jersey—against the background of the Six Day War in the Middle East—Nigeria was not a priority issue.

Further evidence of British and American fence-sitting was the decision by both governments not to withdraw their consul generals from Enugu once secession had been declared. They also agreed to allow their technical assistance personnel, information services, and youth corps volunteers to remain in the East, so long as conditions permitted. These actions enhanced the respectability of the Biafran regime and caused much discomfort in Lagos, where officials regarded any official contact with Ojukwu as an affront to Nigeria's sovereignty over the rebellious territory.[22]

BIAFRA'S FIRST APPEAL

Ojukwu's lengthy address justifying secession, as well as the actual declaration of independence, dealt primarily with internal grievances and the determination to resist federal encroachment. There was no foreign policy plank and no direct appeal for international recognition. The only references to foreign concerns were several reassurances that Biafra would honor all international treaties and obligations previously negotiated by the federal government on behalf of the Eastern Region, that the lives and property of all foreigners residing in Biafra would be protected, that the charters of the Organization of African Unity and the United Nations would be faithfully adhered to, and that Biafra intended "to remain a member of the British Commonwealth of Nations in our right as a sovereign independent nation."[23]

When later asked to explain Biafra's foreign policy during this early period, Ojukwu replied that he had no foreign policy because events were moving so quickly and the need to mobilize for a possible military confrontation was so great that he had little time to dwell on foreign

---

[21] *The Times* (London), July 7, 1967. By early 1967, London bought nearly 30 percent of Nigeria's petroleum exports, which met approximately 10 percent of British needs.

[22] Ogunbadejo, *Nigeria and the Great Powers.*

[23] Ojukwu, *Biafra,* I, 196.

affairs.[24] The ministries that he claims most preoccupied his attention were Defense, Internal Affairs (i.e., police and domestic security matters), and Information. The Ministry of Information, which was later overshadowed by the Directorate of Propaganda, engaged primarily in domestic work: the overriding concern at this stage was to convince local province leaders that Biafra was invincible.[25] Ojukwu also asserts that he did not expect immediate diplomatic recognition, given the little that Biafra had to offer any prospective ally, but that this would follow eventually should Biafra prove to be a viable proposition—a situation that would necessarily include retention of control over the oil fields in the Rivers area.[26]

Evidence suggests that Ojukwu's recollections are somewhat over-simplified. While Biafra lacked a proper network to conduct normal diplomatic relations and Ojukwu was no doubt preoccupied with matters of military security, early attempts to penetrate the international system did conform to a basic strategy that could be adapted to the few available opportunities for gaining influence. Soon after war broke out, Biafran spokesmen began appealing for internationally supervised unconditional negotiations under the auspices of the United Nations, the Organization of African Unity, or any other group of countries interested in a peaceful settlement. The underlying political objective in this internationally popular theme was to freeze effectively the status quo of two independent power centers in Nigeria and, to the extent that the talks were sanctioned by the international community, Biafra—as an equal party to the dispute—would acquire a degree of de facto recognition.

Ojukwu and his advisers knew that secession ran counter to the prevailing norms in Africa, and the collapse of the continent's most promising democracy had already dismayed Nigeria's traditional friends, namely, Britain and the United States.[27] The most that Biafra could reasonably hope for was Anglo-American neutrality, including a denial

---

[24] Interview: Ojukwu.

[25] Interview: Uche Chukwumerije, head of Biafran Directorate of Propaganda. The early work in reinforcing the siege mentality within Biafra has been detailed by another of the participants, Onu, in *Domestic Propaganda in the Biafran Adventure*.

[26] Interview: Ojukwu.

[27] Godwin Onyegbula, Ojukwu's chief foreign policy adviser, had previously served for several years in the Nigerian foreign service and, while stationed in Lagos, had participated in the numerous consultations that consistently rejected any overtures for support from the rebels of southern Sudan. On the basis of this experience and his earlier assignment as chargé d'affaires in Washington, Onyegbula maintains that he harbored no illusions about the difficulties Biafra could expect in its struggle for recognition, regardless of the personal sympathies of various officials. Interview: Onyegbula.

of military sales to the federal government. Without foreign help, Ojukwu was convinced that Gowon's regime lacked the necessary domestic support and military competence to restrain Biafran secession. On the other hand, should London be provoked, for example, into mounting an air-rescue operation ostensibly to protect the safety of the five thousand British citizens in Biafra, Ojukwu's regime would have been practically powerless to stop the intervention.

A limited campaign to project the East's grievances into the international arena started months before the advent of secession. In addition to the numerous tours by distinguished Ibos aimed at winning foreign support for Ojukwu's interpretation of the Aburi accord, two public relations firms were retained. The New York agency of Ruder and Finn began to represent Eastern interests in February 1967 and, in London, Economic Development Services undertook similar efforts to advertise alleged federal injustices. The British effort was the most extensive and best disguised, with EDS shepherding journalists to Eastern Nigeria and arranging for seemingly spontaneous newspaper advertisements by Ibo students in Britain.[28]

Once secession was declared, the handful of former Nigerian diplomats who had been attached to the governor's office in Enugu regrouped as the Biafran Ministry of Foreign Affairs and Commonwealth Relations. Within a few weeks the staff grew to nineteen officers, and remained at that level for most of the war. Organizationally, the ministry was a less complex version of the one in Lagos. The principal divisions were Political, International, Information, and Protocol. There were no regional divisions such as Africa, Euro-America, and Asia.[29] By the time war broke out in July 1967, the ministry maintained an international network of six tiny but active offices in Lisbon, London, Paris, Geneva, New York, and Dar es Salaam.[30]

---

[28] In a letter to B. O. Odinamadu, permanent secretary of the Eastern Region's Ministry of Information, dated March 10, 1967, Grenville Jones of Economic Development Services writes: "it is essential that when George Knapp of EDS arrives with the journalists that he is referred to throughout as a commercial adviser and a commodity expert and not in any way connected with the political and propaganda side. The reason for this is that any reference to this firm's political as opposed to our commercial role will jeopardise our efforts on your Government's behalf in the U.K. . . . . We want to keep our opponents 'on the hop' and running around in circles. At the moment they are saying 'how can these East Nigerian students organize and write these advertisements, pay for them, distribute leaflets and mount a fairly massive lobby?' So we would be grateful if the Government referred to us as their commercial advisers in the U.K. as well as our role in purchasing office equipment, books, etc."

[29] Republic of Biafra, Ministry of Foreign Affairs and Commonwealth Relations, Internal Telephone Directory, Enugu, 1967.

[30] Republic of Biafra, Ministry of Foreign Affairs and Commonwealth Relations, List of Offices Abroad, August 1967.

The Biafran Ministry of Foreign Affairs actually paid scant attention to international politics during the opening stages of the crisis. It functioned primarily as the vehicle through which Ojukwu coordinated his frantic efforts to locate, purchase, and arrange for the delivery of military equipment. The Ministry of Foreign Affairs was also responsible for operating Biafra's lone telecommunications link to Europe via Lisbon.

The political impact of Biafra's initial efforts to awaken international concern, beyond that aroused by the reports of independent journalists who regularly covered West Africa, is difficult to gauge. The head of the press section of the Nigerian Ministry of Information asserts that the propaganda battle with Biafra was lost in Europe and America before secession was even announced, but he attributes the success to pro-Ibo sympathies justifiably aroused by the bloody reality of the 1966 pogroms in the North, a view which he shares with General Gowon.[31] American and British officials generally agree that the news of Ibo pogroms, amplified by Ojukwu's special envoys and publicists, stirred a small but vocal lobby that discouraged too close an identification with the federal government. Compared to the efforts of pro-Biafran groups at the height of the war, the political influence of these early supporters was negligible. More importantly, Gowon's inability to curb the violence in the North or to restrain Ojukwu from secession called into serious question the capacity of the federal government to prevail in the event of a military confrontation with the East.

THE ABSENCE OF MILITARY SUPERIORITY

Among Western diplomats who served in Lagos during this period, few are bold enough to claim that they were able to foresee the outcome of the Nigerian crisis in June 1967. Britain's high commissioner, David Hunt, takes great care in his memoirs to refute his critics who claimed he had misled the British government into supporting the Nigerians with his overly optimistic reports of a quick victory. He pleads that this was not the case and that he was at pains to remind London of Foch's remark: "La guerre est une chose aléatoire."[32] The capacity of Biafra's tiny untrained army to resist any federal incursions was untested but Hunt quotes approvingly of a May 1967 report from an *Observer* correspondent in Enugu: "Everyone knows it is not possible for what remains of the Nigerian army to make any successful attempt on the East."[33] Ojukwu's determination to lead the East to full independence

---

[31] Interviews: L. E. Scott-Emuakpor, head of press section, Ministry of Information; and Gowon.

[32] Hunt, *On the Spot*, p. 181.   [33] *Ibid.*

was manifestly credible. In addition to Nigeria's presumed military weakness, Biafra possessed numerous logistical advantages that would increase the effectiveness of its growing army. The secessionists also boasted about the prospect of a viable economy[34] and the presence of hundreds of skilled and adaptable technocrats who seemed fully able to operate the new state system.[35]

Biafra claimed only a twelfth of Nigeria's territory and a quarter of the country's population, but its 30,000 square miles were comparable to the state of South Carolina or the country of Sierra Leone (see Map 3–1). Also, Biafra encompassed one of the most densely populated areas in black Africa, and among the forty sovereign members of the Organization of African Unity, it would have ranked as the fourth largest in population. The East's road and bridge network was the most developed in Africa, with three major airports, several smaller landing strips, and two highly developed seaports. A railroad transversed Biafra, and Ojukwu had seized much of Nigeria's rolling stock. Inland water routes in the southern areas also eased the conveyance of goods through the thick bush. The Niger River formed a natural defensive perimeter along the western border, and the southern frontier was entirely seacoast. The eastern boundary was shared exclusively with the Republic of Cameroon. Only the 200-mile northern border with Nigeria was easily vulnerable to a federal invasion.

On the eve of secession, Ojukwu declared confidently that "there is no power in this country [Nigeria], or in black Africa, to subdue us by force,"[36] A few days later he made the following prediction for the benefit of a British journalist: "Gowon will hum and haw for some time. The North will be impatient and start to hare down here with a ramshackle army. Once they cross [into Biafra] we'll take the war straight to them. I have the wherewithal to ensure that a large part of what is the North is completely destroyed and put under the control of Biafra."[37]

The mass jubilation in Enugu and other major cities immediately upon

[34] The Biafran government estimated its volume of trade to be approximately one-half billion dollars per year, with a GNP of 1.5 billion dollars. Biafra, *The Case for Biafra*. These figures were later challenged by O. Aboyade and A. A. Ayida, who argue that they were based on presecession economic interdependencies with the other regions in Nigeria, and once these ties were broken, even if Lagos had not imposed a blockade, the East's GNP would have dropped precipitously as a result of numerous economic discontinuities. O. Aboyade and A. A. Ayida, "The War Economy in Perspective."

[35] The East claimed to have 600 engineers, 700 lawyers, 500 doctors, and thousands of experienced civil servants, railway operators, and technicians of various skills. Biafra, *The Case for Biafra*, p. 4.

[36] Ojukwu, *Biafra*, I, 173.

[37] De St. Jorre, *The Nigerian Civil War*, p. 132.

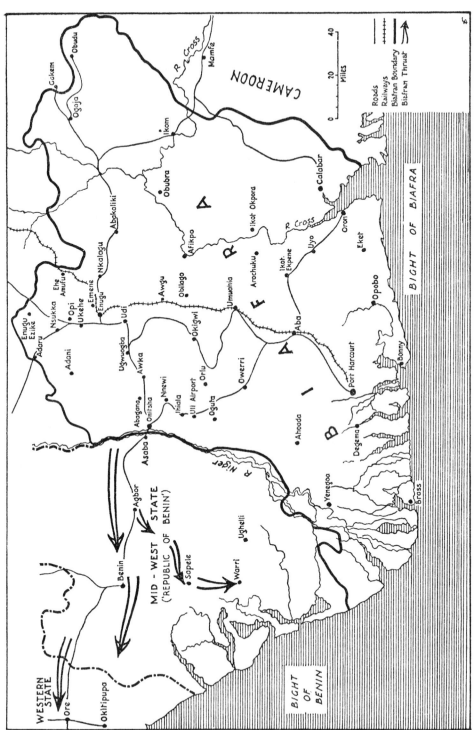

Map 3-1 • Biafra at the Height of Its Power, August 1967 (from John de St. Jorre, *The Nigerian Civil War*, p. 155)

secession indicated that at least many urban Ibos believed and supported him. Although Ojukwu did not appear to have the military
capability to launch a major offensive against the rest of the federation,
there was ample reason to believe that with the planeloads of arms
hastily acquired over the previous nine months, Biafra could take care
of itself.

The Nigerian army of seven thousand men was only slightly bigger
and better equipped than the rebel militia. Moreover, a full battalion
of federal troops had been stationed in the Western State, where the
predominantly Northern soldiers served virtually as an occupation force.
Gowon, who raised himself to the rank of general the day after secession was announced, could not count on the support of a single major
ethnic group comparable to the mass of Ibos who backed his adversary.
The disruption within the Nigerian army since January 1966 also raised
questions about Gowon's capacity to confront Ojukwu. Of the fifty-
seven senior officers who had been commissioned prior to Independence,
only five were available for duty on the federal side.[38] Eighteen of the
original fifty-seven served Ojukwu, and the rest had either left the
service or had been killed in the two coups.

Most of the junior officers on both sides had fewer than seven years
of experience. At Independence in 1960, 70 percent of the officers
serving in Nigeria were British.[39] Gowon and Ojukwu thus faced somewhat similar command problems, although the latter would not have to
contend with long supply lines into hostile areas.

The Nigerian army was equipped with only light armor, no tanks,
and a small number of personnel carriers. Adding to Gowon's difficulties in the short run was the onset of the summer rainy season,
which renders the majority of roads leading to Eastern Nigeria almost
impassable for two or three months.

Predictions regarding the probable success of a federal blockade
also had to be carefully hedged. In 1967 the Nigerian navy consisted
of only one frigate, two small coastal defense vessels, and three coastal
launches to patrol the East's two hundred-mile coastline. During a news
conference in London shortly after secession was declared, Matthew
Mbu, who later became Biafra's foreign minister, asserted that no
Nigerian vessels had penetrated Biafra's twelve-mile limit. Asked about
the threat posed by the Nigerian navy, Mbu quipped: "What navy?

[38] Miners, *The Nigerian Army*, p. 230.
[39] *Ibid.*, ch. VI. British colonial administrator John Smith suggests that
Nigeria's "secret weapon" in the war against Biafra turned out to be hundreds of
reservists and warrant officers who had served in the Burma campaign during
World War II and returned to duty in 1967 to manage the complex logistical and
supply problems that confronted the federal army. Oyinbo (pseud.), *Nigeria:
Crisis and Beyond*, p. 82.

I was Minister for the Federal Navy."[40] Nigeria's air force appeared similarly impotent. It comprised some twenty-six unarmed Piaggio trainers, ten Dornier trainers, twenty-seven communications aircraft, ten Noratlas transports, and four Dakotas—in other words, the federal air force had no bombers or fighters.[41] Biafra, on the other hand, had two World War II vintage B–26 bombers, plus six French-built Alouette helicopters and a few civilian aircraft seized from Nigerian Airways.

"TOTAL WAR"

The federal government's first response to Biafran secession was to re-impose severe economic sanctions, including a blockade of the East's air and sea ports, a ban on foreign currency transactions, and a halt to all incoming post and telecommunications. The only international business excluded from the sanctions was the continued export of crude petroleum from Port Harcourt; the reason for this was that the semi-annual payment of royalties was not due until July 10, and both sides hoped to collect the full revenue. Aside from the economic blockade, there were no direct reprisals, and during the first five weeks of secession the initial confrontation appeared to be, in the words of one experienced journalist, a "phoney war."[42]

Economic sanctions had a particularly bad reputation in Africa because of Britain's failure to bring down the Ian Smith regime in Rhodesia. The prospect that they would ever work against Biafra was even more dubious, given the thousands of Ibos who lived in West Cameroon and across the Niger River in the Midwest State. For the most part, these people had never paid much attention to domestic and international frontiers except in the rare instances that these conformed to tribal law and custom.[43] It also appeared likely that illicit international shipping could be offloaded by small craft in the hundreds of estuaries that sliced through the vast riverine regions of Nigeria's newly-proclaimed Southeastern and Rivers states.

Nigerian authorities defended the credibility of the economic threat by stressing the East's traditional economic dependence on the rest of the federation, and by suggesting that Ojukwu really did not have the

[40] *West Africa*, No. 2612, June 24, 1967, p. 838.

[41] Hanning, "Lessons from the Arms Race."

[42] De St. Jorre, *The Nigerian Civil War*, ch. 5, "The Phoney War, June–July, 1967," pp. 123–144.

[43] Interview: E. O. Kolade, Nigerian consul, Buea, Cameroon, who estimates that there were approximately 200,000 Ibos in west Cameroon at the time of Biafran secession.

strength or tenacity to resist.[44] In fact, the application of economic sanctions was the federal government's only immediately available option. Nigeria's army was so poorly deployed and equipped that the government had to limit its initial response to the economic sphere while the mobilization of forces got underway.

International respect for the federal blockade was generally good. All major foreign shipping lines agreed not to enter the prohibited areas, and several with ships bound for Eastern Nigeria had them rerouted to federal ports.[45] The strength of this paper blockade was much greater than Biafra's leaders had expected and, however undramatic, the effective closure of the Eastern ports was a major defeat for the secessionists.

The handful of stray cargo vessels willing to smuggle goods into Biafra dwindled with the shelling and capturing of two ships by the Nigerian navy in early July.[46] A further important indication of foreign willingness to support the federal quarantine of Biafra was an early agreement between the governments of Nigeria and Cameroon to restrict movement of persons and goods across their respective borders.[47] While it proved difficult to enforce the new regulations until the federal army had occupied the Southeastern State, President Ahidjo deployed Cameroonian troops along the frontier and sent his secret police into border villages to monitor and interdict unusually large purchases of local and imported goods.[48]

The real test of the blockade's viability focused on the behavior of

[44] Summarized, for example, by Dr. O. Aboyade, one of Nigeria's leading economists and an adviser to the federal government, in "Economic Sanctions against the Eastern States," Radio Nigeria, *Newstalk*, June 1, 1967.

[45] *Morning Post*, June 3, 1967, and June 6, 1967.

[46] For details of the actual seizures, see *New Nigerian*, July 8, 1967, and *Daily Times*, July 13, 1967.

[47] *Morning Post*, June 8, 1967.

[48] Interviews: Kolade and Hadj Hammadou Alim, ambassador of the Federal Republic of Cameroon in Lagos. The Ibos control much of the economy of west Cameroon, and, according to Kolade, there were rumors that Ojukwu had sent representatives to west Cameroon offering support for any secession there. President Ahidjo took a strict position of neutrality along the frontier; his security forces would not allow Biafrans or Nigerians to transverse Cameroonian territory, although it was several months before this was fully operational. He even denied a Nigerian request to use the small portion of the Ikom-Calabar road that cuts into Cameroon for a few miles. There is considerable anti-Ibo feeling in west Cameroon, which in 1961 voted to side with Yaoundé so that the majority of west Cameroonians would not have to remain under Ibo domination. To reduce tensions in these border areas during the war, Ahidjo passed restrictions that forbade listening to Radio Nigeria or Radio Biafra at high volume. The wearing of native cloth with pictures of Ojukwu or Gowon was also banned. Internationally, Ahidjo remained one of Nigeria's strongest supporters as will be noted in later discussions of the role of the Organization of African Unity in the Nigerian crisis.

Nigeria's largest oil concessionaire, Shell-British Petroleum.[49] When the July 10 deadline for royalty payments passed without any action from Shell-BP, the federal government announced a "Petroleum Control Decree" that extended the blockade to oil tankers.[50] The amount involved was close to twenty million dollars, and Biafra tried to assert its claim through a combination of legal arguments and unabashed extortion. In Washington, Ojukwu's lawyers drafted a lengthy memorandum for all major oil companies operating in Nigeria to show why the Biafran government, with de facto control over the East, should, according to British and American practice, receive all taxes and other revenue payments from any company interested in operating there.[51] The oil representatives listened politely to the legal briefs but did not respond, preferring instead to continue dealing with the federal government.[52]

Shell-BP was dealt with separately and more aggressively. The most dramatic—if overpublicized—episode in Biafra's brief exposure to oil politics was the arrest of Shell-BP's local managing director, Stanley Gray, and his incarceration in the plush Presidential Hotel in Enugu. Nigerian officials believe the incident was a mere ruse to allow the company a way to make at least a token payment to Ojukwu without burning all its bridges with the federal government. Ojukwu, however, relishes his recollection of the browbeating late-night sessions with Shell-BP officials, during which he claims to have come close to extracting major concessions.[53] In the end, he was promised a "token" payment of approximately two million dollars, which would have been equivalent to the amount of revenue earned during the seven weeks of Biafran secession, with the rest of the obligation to be held in escrow. Apparently, the payment was never actually made.[54]

[49] Gulf Oil, the second largest producer, operated in the Midwest State, and thus paid its obligations promptly to the federal government. Other fields inside Biafra had not begun to produce, so the revenue issue really applied only to Shell-BP.

[50] *Daily Times*, June 15, 1967.

[51] Surrey, Karasik, Gould, and Greene, Memorandum re: International Law of State Succession with Respect to Concession Agreements between Petroleum Companies and Nigerian Government Relating to Petroleum Exploitation within Biafra, as well as Taxes and Other Revenue Payments in Connection with Activities in Biafra, July 21, 1967. The Nigerian position has been carefully explained by Federal Chief Justice T. O. Elias in "The Nigerian Crisis in International Law."

[52] Davis, "Negotiating about Biafran Oil."

[53] Interview: Ojukwu. The most theatrical confrontation is said to have taken place when McFadzean, Gray's superior, flew in from London. The Biafran leadership was split over what would amount to "reasonable" demands, and Ojukwu asserts that his tough talk was undermined by one of his senior advisers, who privately phoned McFadzean to assure him that compromise was possible.

[54] There has been endless speculation about whether or not Shell-BP made the

The imposition of the federal blockade against oil tankers left the question of future payments unresolved, although not for long. On July 5 and 6, 1967, armed conflict erupted for the first time. Who fired the first shot is a matter of dispute, but within a week federal troops had launched their first major offensive as they pushed southward on two flanks, toward the town of Ogoja near the Cameroon border and against the university town of Nsukka, fifty miles due north of Biafra's capital. Both objectives were achieved in a matter of days, and on July 25, 1967, a southern front was dramatically opened when a federal naval amphibious task force captured the ocean oil terminal intact at Bonny. Federal forces could now claim de facto control over the country's major petroleum outlet. Although actual production could not be resumed until Biafran forces were evicted from Port Harcourt and the surrounding drilling fields of the Rivers State, the victory at Bonny convinced the British government and Shell-BP of where their true interests lay.

The British high commissioner, David Hunt, returned home during the first week of August and met with Prime Minister Wilson at Number 10 Downing Street. Hunt recounts that:

> The crunch came only about a month after the war started. . . . The Federal Government had placed orders for arms with manufacturers in the United Kingdom and these had applied for the necessary export licenses. . . . Mr. Wilson listened carefully to our arguments but to him the nub of the matter was that Nigeria was a fellow Commonwealth country in difficulties, that we had equipped her in the first place and; she could therefore expect a continuity of supply and, on the other side, that a refusal would be equivalent to intervention in favour of the rebels. He saw very quickly and attached great importance to the point that such an act would damage our interests not only in Nigeria but also in the rest of Africa.[55]

The decision in London was reached just as the Biafrans were about to launch their most daring military adventure of the war. On

---

payment and, if so, how much and to whom. The most plausible explanation—namely, that Gray made the pledge but the British government refused to release the foreign exchange for transfer to Switzerland—appears in de St. Jorre, *The Nigerian Civil War*, p. 141, and in Cronje, *The World and Nigeria*, pp. 166–171. Interview: Ojukwu, who maintains that Biafra never received payment.

[55] Hunt, *On the Spot*, p. 194. According to a summary report on Anglo-Nigerian relations that was filed with the federal Ministry of External Affairs by the Nigerian high commission in London toward the end of 1967: "Britain's shift to unequivocal support of Nigeria came suddenly when Nsukka fell and then Bonny. During that time Nigeria received the full and official assurances from representatives of the Foreign Office in behalf of Her Majesty's government."

August 9, 1967, Ojukwu ordered a surprise counterattack to the west, across the Niger River, to draw federal troops away from his capital at Enugu and to discredit the impression of Nigerian invincibility. Fewer than a thousand men were involved, and the maneuver was hastily planned in total secrecy. The eighty-mile road from Onitsha to the Midwest capital of Benin was defenseless, due to a well-timed minicoup by Midwest Ibo officers who dominated the federal garrison. Within nine hours, the Biafran troops occupied virtually the entire state, some 15,000 square miles. Before nightfall Biafra had augmented its size by nearly 50 percent, and had once again discredited the federal government's claim of authority over a major section of Nigeria. More-over, the assault was carried out with a paucity of modern equip-ment, as Biafran troops had to be transported by private cars, com-mercial "mammy" wagons, and an assortment of police and army vans.[56]

Ojukwu had given a Yoruba, Lt. Col. Victor Banjo, command of the invading Biafran army in the hope that this would placate non-Ibos in the Midwest and facilitate a linkup with dissidents in Western Nigeria. Once in control of Benin, Banjo announced that the Midwest would be independent of both Nigeria and Biafra, but first he would liberate Lagos and Western Nigeria from Northern domination. Ojukwu was furious with the suggestion of an independent Yoruba state, and recalled Banjo for consultations. A full week passed before the Biafran offensive resumed, and the critical delay may have cost Biafra a prime opportunity to achieve independence.

Ojukwu now contends that his single greatest mistake of the war was not to rush personally to Benin with his best battalion, remove Banjo, and then head straight for Lagos. With hindsight, it seems pos-sible that his forces might have broken through to Lagos and, at a minimum, forced Gowon's abdication to the North. Ojukwu also believes he might have been able to extend his control over the south-ern half of Nigeria and eventually the entire country.[57]

The news of the Midwest invasion caused panic in Lagos, a mood that was exacerbated by several crude explosives dropped on the capital

[56] Ghana's head of state, General Ankrah, asserts that he personally warned General Gowon that the most likely point of counterattack by Biafran forces would come through the Midwest, and that he was surprised by the lack of federal re-sistance. Interview: Ankrah. But David Ejoor, the military governor of the Mid-west, had told Lagos that in light of the large Ibo population west of the Niger River, the greatest service that the state could serve would be to remain neutral. As it turned out, he correctly suspected the treachery of his Ibo subordinates, but was powerless to stop them. A detailed chronology of these events is recorded in *Africa Research Bulletin*, August 1–31, 1967. Also, see de St. Jorre, *The Nigerian Civil War*, pp. 153–165.
[57] Interview: Ojukwu.

city by a single B–26.[58] General Gowon's response was to declare "total war."[59] Hastily, a new army division (the Second) was formed under the command of Lt. Col. Murtala Mohammed, a tough Sandhurst-trained Northerner who would later wage some of the war's bloodiest campaigns. Gowon also imposed a dusk-to-dawn curfew over Lagos and Ibadan, and on the political front dispatched the vice-chairman of the civilian Executive Council, Chief Awolowo, on a personal tour through the West to rally Yorubas in behalf of the Federal government.

The week's hiatus in the fighting thus offered the Nigerians an absolutely vital opportunity to establish defensive positions 135 miles east of Lagos near the village of Ore. When the Biafrans entered the Western State on August 17, they encountered increasing resistance for seventeen miles, until they were stopped at Ore on the following day. Intense fighting between federal and Biafran forces, which together numbered less than two thousand, continued for several days. Once the rebel retreat began, it moved slowly eastward until the last contingents were forced back across the Niger River and into the Ibo heartland on October 6, 1967. Biafra never again mounted a major offensive or seriously threatened the federal government. Military historians are likely to conclude that the outcome of the Nigerian civil war was determined at Ore, nearly two-and-a-half years before Biafra finally surrendered.

Although Biafra had been unable to retain control over the Midwest, rebel forces had shown surprising panache, which gave Ojukwu's military leadership a new credibility in Lagos and abroad. Crushing the rebellion would not be, as Gowon had forecast, a simple "police action."[60] Current indications were for a long, hard struggle, which most likely would have to be carried into the densely populated Ibo heartland. Millions of innocent lives might be jeopardized and, in the event of protracted guerrilla warfare, the fighting could conceivably drag on for months and years. One obvious alternative was a negotiated settlement, which Ojukwu urgently proposed when he was at the height of his military power. With his forces still at Ore, he appealed to the international community to assist in arranging for a cease-fire and peace talks.[61] It was a call that met with the growing sympathy in Africa, Europe, and North America, where authorities were not only appalled by the specter of rising death tolls, but were also worried about the political side effects of "total war" in Nigeria.

[58] *Morning Post*, August 10, 1967.
[59] *Morning Post*, August 12, 1967, text of General Gowon's declaration of "total war."
[60] *Daily Times*, July 14, 1967.
[61] Radio Biafra, August 21, 1967, and restated in greater detail in Biafra, *The Case for Biafra* released on August 29, 1967. Ojukwu's terms for negotiations are discussed in detail below.

While it was becoming evident that Nigeria would probably win, an outcome that was widely approved internationally, two aspects of the way the war was unfolding caused particular alarm to many foreign governments. The latest projections regarding the intensity and duration of violence necessary to crush the rebellion endangered the fragile stability of inter- and intra-state relations in Africa. Memories of the recent disasters in the Congo (Zaire) were still fresh and, as will be discussed later, there were inevitable fears that Biafran resistance might eventually inspire secessionist movements elsewhere. The increased violence in Nigeria also threatened to become a political issue in Europe and America, where there were already signs that Biafra's struggle for self-determination might appeal to many of the highly politicized groups that had been angered by events in South Vietnam.

A second development was of more immediate concern to the Western powers, as well as to several African governments. Soon after war broke out, the Nigerian government imported from the Soviet Union a squadron of twelve reconditioned MIG-17 fighters and another twenty-nine trainers. The decision to purchase Soviet equipment was not taken lightly. There was a deep strain of anti-communism in the British-trained Nigerian military, and Soviet involvement in the Congo (Zaire) and in Nkrumah's Ghana had cast long shadows over official thinking in Lagos. Federal leaders also did not want unduly to alarm Western interests, despite their irritation with Washington and London.

Intense pressure within the Nigerian armed forces to acquire fighter aircraft followed from the knowledge that Ojukwu had purchased two aging B–26 bombers in Europe which, as expected, began bombing Lagos shortly after the fighting erupted.[62] After the bombers had been observed at Eastern airfields, Gowon turned first to the British and Americans and told them that he had to have a credible air force and would "deal with the devil" if necessary.[63]

Britain declined to sell him the requested squadron because the Wilson government decided that public reaction would be highly critical, and that the Nigerians really did not need such sophisticated equipment.[64] The United States similarly rejected Nigeria's request to purchase arms. Washington's decision was a triple affront: first, the United States had been one of Nigeria's traditional suppliers; second, the State

[62] See Hunt, *On the Spot*, pp. 179–180.
[63] Interview: Gowon.
[64] British Conservative MP John Cordle reportedly announced with indignation on August 14, 1967, that Lagos had asked for a squadron of fighter aircraft just prior to the start of the war. He said that this request had been rejected, and that a second request was pending, which also would be declined. Cronje, *The World and Nigeria*, p. 32. When Northern leaders in Kano learned of the British refusal they were so incredulous that they sent their own man straight to Whitehall to see if what Lagos had told them was true. Interview: St. Elmo Nelson.

Department's decision came just after the Johnson administration had agreed to provide the Congo (Zaire) with aircraft; and third, Lagos was offended by the way the decision was announced to the press—as though Nigeria had asked for assistance rather than simply permission to buy arms.[65] After a fruitless check with the smaller West European powers, Gowon decided to approach the Soviets as a last resort.[66]

The Soviet arms deal was negotiated in Lagos by General Gowon and his closest military advisers.[67] There was never any suggestion of outright Soviet assistance, and the Nigerians resisted proposals for long term bartering arrangements. A key element in the negotiations was the adroit diplomacy of Soviet Ambassador Alexander Romanov, a warm and mildly gregarious individual who appeared at ease in his large Mercedes-Benz and at the socially prominent Ikoyi Club, where he frequently played an enthusiastic game of tennis. Romanov was sensitive to Gowon's needs, as well as to the latter's apprehensions, and the two developed a cordial rapport. By July a bargain had been struck in principle, and Chief Enahoro traveled to Moscow to complete the arrangements.[68] The formal signing of a cultural agreement that had been pending for some time pleased the Russians and eased the military transactions.[69]

The planes began arriving at Kano airfield in mid-August, together with approximately two hundred Soviet technicians. In practice, the fast-moving fighters proved to be unsuitable for military conditions in Nigeria and, as instruments of terror, they probably did more to consolidate Biafran resistance than to weaken it. Politically, however, the decision to deal with the Russians proved to be one of Gowon's wisest foreign-policy moves of the war. Nigeria's nonaligned status instantly acquired new credibility, and for the duration of the conflict Gowon could use the threat of greater reliance on Moscow to ensure the flow of British small arms and to restrain the Western powers from pressing

[65] United States Department of State, statement by Robert J. McCloskey, released July 10, 1967, F–347, LRS–12. For Nigerian reactions: *Daily Sketch*, July 13, 1967; *Sunday Post*, July 16, 1967; and *New Nigerian*, July 17, 1967.

[66] For analyses of Soviet policy in this regard, see Legvold, *Soviet Policy in West Africa*, pp. 311–330; "The USSR and the War in Nigeria," *Mizan*, No. 70/71 (Winter/Spring 1969), pp. 31–38; Klinghoffer, "Why the Soviets Chose Sides," pp. 47–50; and Cronje, *The World and Nigeria*, Ch. 12.

[67] Interviews: Gowon; Ogbu; and Peter Onu, political officer, Nigerian embassy in Moscow. In June Ogbu visited Moscow, and many press reports linked the trip to arms procurement. Ogbu maintains that the reason for the journey was to try to reorganize the embassy staff and security arrangements in the wake of an internal crisis precipitated by the abrupt departure of Ambassador C. O. Ifeagwu, an Ibo who—among other acts—threw an Independence Day celebration for Biafra at the Nigerian embassy.

[68] Interview: Enahoro.   [69] Interview: Gowon.

too vigorously for a compromise settlement on terms he considered contrary to the national interest.

Initiatives to promote a peaceful settlement became pronounced during the summer of 1967, and the federal government grudgingly allowed the Organization of African Unity to consider the issue. But with Nigeria's successful military defense of the Midwest and the knowledge that the Soviet Union was prepared to sell additional equipment to assist the federal army, Gowon's regime suddenly enjoyed a degree of confidence and authority at home and abroad that had been lacking since the July 1966 coup d'état.

· 4 ·

THE OAU BECOMES INVOLVED

As the violence in Nigeria increased, so did the level of diplomatic activity surrounding the conflict. Evidence of this appeared throughout Africa, where preparations were underway for the Fourth Annual Summit of the Organization of African Unity, scheduled to convene in Kinshasa on September 10, 1967. Behind the various approaches was a widely shared concern that secession in Nigeria threatened the stability of the region. With the introduction of Soviet aircraft, many governments feared the return of cold war rivalries to Africa.

East African Initiatives

The first public moves on behalf of a peaceful settlement appeared in East Africa soon after secession was announced. Leading these efforts were two Commonwealth members, President Kenneth Kaunda of Zambia, and President Julius Nyerere of Tanzania.[1] Neither government had vital interests to protect in Nigeria, and both were renowned proponents of African unity—although in light of their unhappy experience with the Federation of Rhodesia and Nyasaland, Zambians retained a deep suspicion of any federal arrangement inherited from the British. Nyerere and Kaunda apparently felt that as pan-Africanists with long-standing personal contacts among Nigerian leaders, many of whom were now Biafrans, they were well suited to provide good offices. Believing that General Ankrah's government in Ghana was too closely identified with British interests to deal effectively with the Biafrans, Zambia began in June 1967 to assert publicly that Nigeria's internal difficulties were a legitimate concern to the rest of Africa, and should be immediately reviewed by the heads of state of the East African Community with a view to arranging a just and peaceful solution.

Initial efforts by Ojukwu's envoys to present Biafra's case before senior foreign officials were successful only in East Africa. The reasons for this were partly accidental, and reveal much about the highly per-

[1] For an analysis of Zambian perceptions, see Anglin, "Zambia and the Recognition of Biafra." A similar but less detailed account of the Tanzanian outlook is set forth in Butler, "Tanzania's Decision to Recognize Biafra." For reports on East African fears that Nigeria might become another Congo, see *Financial Times*, June 21, 1967, and *Observer Foreign News Service*, June 23, 1967.

sonalized diplomacy that transpired among Africa's loosely linked political units.

Prior to the secession, Zambia's high commissioner in Lagos, Matiya Nglande, became deeply concerned about the plight of the Ibos, and traveled to the East for fact-finding discussions with Ojukwu.[2] As tensions mounted, he was regarded by the federal government as an Ibo partisan, although no attempt was made to have him recalled. With Nglande's encouragement, Ojukwu sent Professor Chike Obi, a leading Ibo intellectual and well-known leftist, on a tour of East Africa in early 1967. Obi carried bundles of propaganda dramatizing federal acts of injustice and, contrary to the experience of envoys sent to Europe, Obi encountered little difficulty in placing this material in the hands of cabinet members and other high officials in the capitals of East Africa.[3] Obi's visit was followed by a more substantive initiative by Austin Okwu in early June.[4] Okwu was a seasoned diplomat who had opened Nigeria's formal contacts with Tanzania in 1962, and he enjoyed a warm personal friendship with President Nyerere.[5]

While the Biafrans were quietly making inroads in East Africa, the federal government all but ignored that area. Relations with Kenya were excellent, and Nigeria's few interests were well represented by High Commissioner Leslie Harriman. The post in Dar es Salaam was considered less important, and the high commissioner there was considered ineffective and awaiting retirement.[6] The federal government had no high commissioner in Lusaka, and failed to send a special envoy to the area until after secession. Throughout the late spring and early summer, Lagos concentrated on Europe, where the security in many embassies had broken down following the defection of Ibo personnel. This situation, in turn, had complicated the negotiation, purchase, and importation of urgently needed arms and other military equipment. Until September 1967, Gowon retained the Foreign Ministry portfolio, and during the crucial month of June 1967 his permanent secretary of external affairs, Edwin Ogbu, was carrying out special assignments in Europe.[7] Ogbu later admitted that federal inattentiveness to East

---

[2] *Morning Post*, April 26, 1967.

[3] Interview: Leslie Harriman, Nigeria's high commissioner in Nairobi.

[4] *Financial Times*, June 15, 1967.

[5] Okwu remained in Tanzania throughout the civil war and was instrumental in negotiating Tanzanian and Zambian recognition of Biafra.

[6] The kindest word offered by ministry officials in this envoy's behalf was that the large rose garden that he assiduously cultivated while stationed in Dar es Salaam brought Nigeria prestige by winning several prizes in local garden shows.

[7] Many of Nigeria's embassies abroad had become badly politicized, with Ibo envoys sometimes serving as arms agents for Ojukwu and more often acting to ensure that top-secret cables were routed to Lagos via Enugu. Edwin Ogbu, the

African opinion was a serious oversight, particularly in light of the central role that Africa came to play in Nigeria's strategy to contain Biafra's penetration of the international system; in mid-1967, however, priorities lay elsewhere.[8]

Gowon dispatched Dr. Okoi Arkipo and a delegation of civil servants in late June to tour East Africa and explain the federal position. By the time they reached Lusaka, President Kaunda was on a state visit to China, and those ministers with whom the delegation met claimed to be hearing the full background of the Nigerian crisis for the first time.[9] At the same time, the Zambian government announced that at its instigation there would be a meeting of the four East African presidents in early July to discuss the Nigerian conflict. Arikpo told the press, somewhat lamely, that Nigeria did not object to the proposed summit so long as the leaders dealt exclusively with the federal government.[10] Remarks by President Nyerere a week later made plain that he, at least, was intent on "preventing the United Nations or the big powers from intervening in Nigeria" and that this would necessitate some form of consultation with both sides in the dispute.[11]

The federal government had hitherto taken African support for granted.[12] When news of the forthcoming East African summit reached the federal capital, the official response included this barbed reminder: "Africa's interest in the Nigerian crisis is readily understandable. Every single African country, with the possible exception of Somalia, is plagued by tribal problems. . . . This country applauds President Kaunda's heroic efforts to build the Zambian nation. For this reason he had the sympathy of Nigerians when he dealt ruthlessly with the Lumpa sect."[13] On the day before the summit opened, Radio Nigeria further warned that the East African initiative could "wreck the already shaky foundation on which the OAU now rests."[14]

Shadows much darker than any cast by Radio Nigeria obscured the East African peace initiative. Prior to the summit, President Milton Obote of Uganda sent a message to General Gowon asking for assur-

---

permanent secretary of external affairs, spent most of his time in Europe administering oaths of allegiance to representatives of the federal government, ensuring that lines of communication were secure, and moving personnel around to fill the gaps opened by departing Ibos. Interviews: Ogbu and several Nigerian diplomats involved in the process.

[8] Interview: Ogbu.

[9] Interview: Victor Adegoroye, a member of the Arikpo delegation and Nigeria's high commissioner to Ghana during the civil war.

[10] *Standard* (Tanzania), June 27, 1967.

[11] *Ibid.*, July 5, 1967.   [12] Interview: Ogbu.

[13] Radio Nigeria, *Newstalk*, June 28, 1967.

[14] Radio Nigeria, *Newstalk*, July 7, 1967.

ances that war would not erupt while the four East African leaders were meeting.[15] Lagos declined, and on July 6, 1967, less than forty-eight hours prior to the summit, federal troops launched their first major offensive, against Ogoja and Nsukka. When the summit convened, the four East African leaders sent an urgent request to Lagos to allow a peace mission to visit Nigeria immediately. The suggestion was quickly rejected on the grounds that it was premature and unnecessary.[16]

Among the four East African leaders there were considerable differences over what could or should be done. Tanzania and Zambia were the most interventionist and the most sympathetic toward Biafra. President Jomo Kenyetta of Kenya was more cautious, and federal officials credit him with protecting Nigeria's interests in this instance.[17] Kenya's stand was supported by President Obote of Uganda, who at the time faced a serious secessionist challenge from the Baganda. The final communiqué thus reflected these conflicting pressures and realities. No mention was made of the two parties to the dispute, which would have pleased Biafra, but the desire to play the role of mediator was clearly evident: "Mindful of the approaches already made by Nigerian leaders to the four Presidents, they expressed their concern about the Nigerian situation which is highly explosive . . . [and] the Four agreed that it was not too late to offer their good offices to the Government of Nigeria on their own or in conjunction with other African leaders."[18]

The East African summit proved to be only the first in a series of attempts to internationalize the Nigerian conflict within Africa. By merely meeting, Kaunda, Nyerere, Obote, and Kenyatta had shown their concern over Nigeria's internal problems. And before the East African initiative had run its course, President Mobutu of the Congo (Zaire) dispatched special delegations throughout Africa to seek support for a Congo-led peace initiative in conjunction with the September OAU summit.

THE KINSHASA CONFERENCE

While Mobutu's envoys were touring Africa, Dahomey's (Benin's) foreign minister, Emile Zinsou, flew to Lagos in late August to express

[15] Interview: Leslie Harriman who, as high commissioner to Kenya with accreditation to Kampala, conveyed the message to Gowon on President Obote's behalf.

[16] Interview: O. Adeniji, head of the Africa Division, Federal Ministry of External Affairs.

[17] Kenyatta had served as chairman of the ten-member OAU ad hoc commission on the Congo crisis in 1964, and could speak from first-hand experience of the frustrations and humiliations of trying to mediate without the support of the parties to the dispute.

[18] Standard (Tanzania), July 11, 1967.

his willingness to mediate, and Ghana's military leaders hastily sought to arrange a West African minisummit to discuss the Nigerian conflict in advance of the OAU meeting in Kinshasa.[19] Throughout, the federal government took the position that the secession was a purely internal matter, and that if any initiative were to emerge within Africa it should come from the Organization of African Unity and not from one or more self-appointed mediators.[20] Zinsou replied to the rebuff by saying that the suggestion of OAU involvement was "not a bad idea and that if the matter was raised by Nigeria at Kinshasa he was certain there would be a fruitful discussion."[21] Meanwhile, relations with Ghana were becoming strained, and according to a federal official who met with Ankrah, the general was increasingly prone to "tantrums over how Nigeria did not show enough appreciation of his peace efforts."

The federal tactic of referring all suggestions of mediation to the OAU summit was pursued with the knowledge that under normal summit procedures any attempt to discuss a member's internal affairs could be foreclosed on a point of order; should a member call for a vote, the federal government was certain it could command the necessary majority. Nigeria did not wish, however, to alienate African opinion, and carefully refrained from criticizing those who proposed some form of mediation. Ojukwu was portrayed as being in collusion with European imperialists, and as seeking to exploit the good will in Africa by raising false hopes that a compromise was possible on Biafra's terms.[22] Quietly, Nigeria's ambassadors in Africa elicited reassurances from Emperor Haile Selassie and other leaders that the crisis would not be allowed to intrude on the OAU summit without the full consent of the federal government.[23]

Of far greater concern to the federal government was the danger that non-African powers—notably the United States—might try to promote an OAU peace initiative contrary to Nigeria's interests. Washington had already taken the position that the Nigerian crisis was an African affair, and the Johnson administration was becoming nervous about the sale of Soviet aircraft and the increased level of violence.[24]

[19] Delegations were sent to Cameroon, Chad, Niger, Liberia, Togo, and Dahomey (Benin). Interview: Adegoroye.

[20] See Gemuh E. Akuchu, "The Organization of African Unity Peacemaking Machinery and the Nigerian-Biafran Conflict."

[21] *Daily Times*, August 24, 1967.

[22] Radio Nigeria, *Newstalk*, August 8, 1967.

[23] Interview: A. Haastrup, Nigerian ambassador to Ethiopia.

[24] *Washington Post*, June 1, 1967. America's irritation over the Soviet arms sale was evident when State Department spokesman Robert McCloskey criticized Moscow on August 21, 1967, for not showing the same "forebearance" as the United States. Library of Congress, Legislative Reference Service, "The Nigerian Civil War," LRS–15, August 21, 1967.

Lagos did not want to be pressured into any cease-fire or negotiations with Ojukwu until the Midwest had been fully liberated and the predominantly minority areas—the oil-rich Rivers State and the Southeastern State—could be occupied by federal troops. Thus, when the American embassy in Lagos submitted an aide memoire on the eve of the Kinshasa summit that suggested the creation of an ad hoc team of OAU conciliators, the federal government assumed that the United States was signaling that the groundwork had been done for a major diplomatic offensive.[25]

Further complicating the federal government's position was a major appeal from Ojukwu for immediate peace talks under the auspices of the OAU. While declaring that such talks could only take place if Biafra's sovereignty were recognized, Ojukwu held out the prospect of future association with the federal government, and published a short White Paper to this effect on the eve of the Kinshasa summit.[26] The memorandum recalled the "common experience of over fifty years of political, economic, social and cultural ties" between Biafra and the rest of Nigeria. It proposed that the Republic of Biafra would be willing to resume economic cooperation on rail, road, harbor, aviation, post and telecommunications, customs, and currency matters. The institutional arrangements would be comparable to the East African community of four sovereign states, which had gone into effect only recently. It was a clever move, one that was intended to appeal to Presidents Kaunda and Nyerere, while creating a favorable impression in Europe and America.

General Gowon replied to the Biafran White Paper on future association in a major broadcast to the nation two days before the start of the OAU Council of Ministers meeting in Kinshasa. The speech was a hardline defense of Nigeria's military policies, which concluded that "there is no alternative to a Federal Union of Nigeria. The only possible alternative is the emergence of several armed camps in this country and continuous fighting for many years to come. There will then be the chaos of an arms race and the tyranny and the petty dictatorship of war lords already exhibited by Ojukwu and his clique. In such a chaos Nigeria will be converted into a theatre for cold war and other disastrous adventures."[27] To represent these views at the Ninth Ordinary Session

[25] Interview: Philip Asiodu.

[26] Ojukwu's call was broadcast over Radio Biafra on August 21, 1967, and the same message was cabled to the OAU Secretariat on August 27, 1967. The White Paper was published as "Memorandum on Future Association between Biafra and the Rest of the Former Federation of Nigeria" (Enugu: Government Printer, 1967).

[27] "Gowon's Address to the Nation on the Progress of the War," September 2, 1967, reprinted in Kirk-Greene, *Crisis and Conflict*, II, 167.

of the OAU Council of Ministers, Gowon named Commissioner of External Affairs Okoi Arikpo to lead the delegation to Kinshasa.[28]

Dr. Arikpo carried a simple but tough brief from General Gowon: under no circumstances allow the Nigerian crisis to appear on the agenda for the OAU summit.[29] The federal delegation would stand rigidly on Article II (2) of the Charter, would threaten to walk out or even withdraw from the OAU if the crisis were inscribed on the agenda, and would welcome—but not press for—a general resolution condemning secession in any form. In his annual report, OAU Secretary General Diallo Telli reinforced the Nigerian view that the prospects for a discussion of the crisis had been foreclosed: "the only initiative, by the Lesotho Government, to bring the matter before the OAU, for the latter to 'consider ways and means to avoid the Nigerian crisis degenerating into civil war' was very short-lived. The Nigerian Federal Government being categorically opposed to this initiative because of the purely domestic nature of the situation obtaining in Nigeria."[30]

Rumors that a high-level Biafran delegation would be permitted to visit Kinshasa during the summit proved baseless.[31] President Mobutu also ensured that the forty Ibos attending Louvanium University in Kinshasa were restrained from demonstrating. Inside the ministerial conference chamber, however, it became clear that the host government was strongly in favor of raising the issue at the forthcoming summit, and that the Congo (Zaire) would be supported by Ghana, Uganda, and Tanzania.[32]

[28] The federal delegation was ethnically representative of the new Nigeria: Arikpo, an Ekoi from Calabar in the east; Commissioner of Education Weinke Briggs, an Ijaw from Port Harcourt, also in the east; Commissioner of Trade and Industry Alhaji Ali Monguno, a Kanuri from Borno in the north; and Permanent Secretary of Trade and Industry Philip Asiodu, an Ibo from the Midwest. The fifth delegate, Col. Olufemi Olutoye, a western Yoruba, was military undersecretary in the Ministry of External Affairs, and had the unenviable assignment of explaining to skeptical OAU members why earlier assurances from the federal government that the conflict would amount to only a brief police action had failed to come true.

[29] Interview: Gowon.

[30] OAU, "Report of the Administrative Secretary-General Covering the Period from February to August 1967," Addis Ababa, September 1967, C/M 157, p. 25.

[31] It was reported in the Nigerian press that the former premier of the Eastern Region, Michael Okpara, had arrived in Kinshasa with a delegation that included Aaron Obonna, Michael Ibekwe, and Uloma Wachuku, and that they met with Foreign Minister Justin Bomboku. *Daily Times*, September 9, 1967. This was never confirmed, and none of the federal delegates interviewed had uncovered any evidence that the delegation had been allowed entry to the Congo (Zaire). When Chief Awolowo arrived for the actual summit he was told by President Mobutu that Biafran emissaries had flown into Kinshasa but were turned back at the airport.

[32] MEA, Report of the Federal Delegation to the Ninth Ordinary Session of the OAU Council of Ministers, September 4–11, 1967.

Council meetings are usually only a testing ground for arguments that must ultimately be resolved by the Assembly of Heads of State. In this instance the Nigerians encountered little difficulty in resisting efforts to place the crisis on the summit agenda. As one federal delegate candidly observed, "The Council of Ministers is much more open and easier to manipulate than the Assembly of Heads of State where there is much more deference to procedure. Such tactics as shouting 'shame . . . shame' or openly invoking the names of other potential secessions elsewhere in Africa to discredit opponents would not have been acceptable within the Assembly [but prevailed in the Council]." It was understood, of course, that the Assembly would not be bound in any way by the agenda recommended by the Council of Ministers.

The council meeting lasted from September 4 through September 11, 1967, and was immediately followed by the three-day summit. Eighteen of the thirty-nine members were represented by their respective heads of state.[33] Absent from the proceedings were the cluster of Moslem states that could have been counted on to support Nigeria, but who decided to stay away for reasons related to the unlikelihood that the OAU would adopt a strong pro-Arab stand condemning the recent Israeli victory in the Middle East.

Because of the highly personal way that summit diplomacy is carried on within the OAU, those heads of state who choose to attend tend to dominate the proceedings of the annual conference, frequently at the expense of governments represented by lesser officials. The 1967 summit seemed likely to be controlled by the host, President Mobutu, and such elder statesmen as Selassie of Ethiopia, Tubman of Liberia, and perhaps Kaunda of Zambia. The combination seemed fully capable of raising an OAU peace initiative, quite possibly with the United States or other outside backing. Gowon's attendance was never seriously considered, for domestic military and political reasons. The question was whether to allow his commissioner of External Affairs, Dr. Arikpo, to represent Nigeria at the summit, or to send a more senior delegation. At the last minute Gowon delegated the highest-ranking civilian in his government, Chief Obafemi Awolowo, to represent him in Kinshasa. The assignment would prove to be most difficult, even for one of Nigeria's most adroit and internationally well known political leaders.

Gowon's instructions to Awolowo were again to prevent the civil war from being placed on the official agenda or in any other way from becoming an issue of formal consideration at the summit. Awolowo

[33] Those represented by their chief executive included: Cameroon, Central African Republic, Chad, Congo (Brazzaville), Congo (Zaire), Dahomey (Benin), Ethiopia, The Gambia, Ghana, Liberia, Mauritania, Niger, Rwanda, Somalia, Uganda, Upper Volta, and Zambia.

left for Kinshasa fully expecting to hold the line against any open discussion of Nigeria's internal affairs.[34] As soon as he arrived he began lobbying, and immediately found that the African heads of state were less concerned about Nigeria's domestic politics than whether the federal government possessed the will and the power to win. Awolowo was on the defensive from the outset, and describes the diplomatic maneuvers already underway:

> The day I arrived, just before the opening session, the [francophone] OCAM [Organisation Commune Africaine et Malagache] group plus Mobutu were holding a lengthy closed door session during which we strongly suspected Nigeria was a major point of discussion. Fortunately, President Diori's [the current chairman of OCAM] chalet was directly opposite mine so I was able to establish close contact with him. We learned soon after that OCAM and Mobutu and the East Africans wanted the matter brought up. I also discovered that there was much ambivalence among the heads of state. Obote, Kaunda, and Mobutu each wrote letters to me proposing the question be raised. I answered each refuting the suggestions. Kaunda's was the most hostile while Mobutu's was the mildest. I therefore answered each in kind.[35]

A further affront to the federal position came from Ojukwu, who had managed, probably with the help of the Zambians or Tanzanians, to provide each head of state with a formal letter of appeal supported by another Biafran White Paper.

At the time, Biafran troops were still in control of most of the Midwest, and the thrust of the White Paper was that "neither side can achieve complete military victory . . . hence we [Biafra] have always stood for a negotiated settlement . . . [but] Nigeria has demonstrated her utter contempt by spurning fraternal offers of mediation from several of the Continent's most distinguished elder statesmen."[36] In his covering letter Ojukwu detailed the successes of the Biafran army on the western front, and reiterated his determination to continue fighting until Nigeria agreed to a negotiated settlement. The letter ended with the following challenge: "Should they [the Federal Government] stubbornly persist in spurning African appeals for a settlement, it would then be for African Heads of State and Government individually or collectively to determine how best to bring about a just and lasting peace and thus redeem the good name of the Continent."[37]

---

[34] Interviews: Gowon; Chief Obafemi Awolowo.

[35] Interview: Awolowo. [36] Biafra, *The Case for Biafra*.

[37] Text of letter drafted by the Biafran Ministry of Foreign Affairs, September 4, 1967.

According to his account, Chief Awolowo continued to respond firmly to these initial pressures: "I went from head of state to head of state explaining our case; taking the line that if they raised the matter I would be very rough on them and Nigeria would walk out of the conference if necessary. We would not be pilloried. Every one of the members had its own skeleton in the closet and we would not hesitate to raise it. No one had the right to question the internal affairs of another state. If Biafra succeeded all Africa would suffer. I lobbied the night before the opening session, all day and well into the next night with no rest."[38] Awolowo was only partially successful. When the current chairman, Emperor Haile Selassie, opened the summit, he referred to the Nigerian crisis and expressed the hope that "there will soon emerge a lasting solution which will serve the interests of the Nigerian people as a whole, and the entire Continent of Africa."[39]

Aside from the Emperor's reference, there was never any formal discussion of the Nigerian crisis.[40] But outside the conference chamber Awolowo finally agreed to participate in an ad hoc gathering of seven heads of state who were determined to involve the OAU in the search for a peaceful settlement of the conflict. Thus, on the morning of September 12, 1967, Presidents Mobutu, Tubman, Kaunda, Ahidjo, Diori, Emperor Haile Selassie, and General Ankrah met for the first of several marathon discussions, which became popularly known as the "Caucus of Heavyweights." No formal records of these conversations were kept, and Chief Awolowo and Dr. Arikpo sat in on the discussions only when invited by the heads of state.[41]

The federal delegation was surprised and concerned by the involvement of Presidents Diori of Niger and Ahidjo of Cameroon. The continued support from both leaders, whose states adjoined Nigeria, was of vital strategic importance to the federal government. Besides, Diori was chairman of OCAM and both men had close ties with Paris. The Nigerians already had reason to believe that the United States might have influenced Mobutu, Tubman, and Emperor Haile Selassie; now there was the added fear of pressure from France. As the caucus proceedings got underway, the federal delegation learned of a draft

---

[38] Interview: Awolowo.   [39] *Daily Times*, August 9, 1967.

[40] This contrasts with the 1968 and 1969 summits, when the Nigerian crisis was part of the regular agenda. Analyses of these discussions, based on the proceedings of the Assembly of Heads of State and Government, will appear in later chapters.

[41] When the caucus became a consultative committee, greater care was taken to keep records, although only of the formal closed-door sessions. The author has had access to these records and, as we shall see, they reveal where each head of state stood on the matter of greater international involvement in the Nigerian crisis as the war progressed.

resolution proposed by Kaunda of Zambia with the backing of the OCAM states, which would have had the OAU call for an immediate cease-fire, endorse direct negotiations between Nigeria and Biafra, and "find a formula to permit de facto recognition of Biafra without coming out and actually saying so."[42] Awolowo maintains that he thwarted this plan by strictly adhering to "the technical point that the OAU had no jurisdiction to interfere in our affairs and if it did so it would open a flood gate of future interferences which few of the others present could afford themselves. At one point I even implied that if such a precedent were set Nigeria would feel free to support dissidents in other countries."[43]

Inside the caucus, Awolowo found President Kaunda of Zambia to be the most difficult to deal with, and the first few hours of discussion were acrimonious. Kaunda finally left the room, to be replaced by President Obote of Uganda.[44] Before Kaunda's departure, it was made plain to the Nigerians that if they refused OAU involvement they faced the threat of Zambian and Tanzanian recognition of Biafra, a development that also raised fears among many other members of the organization who did not want to see African ranks divided on the Nigerian question. In Kaunda's absence, tensions subsided. Emperor Haile Selassie and President Tubman emerged in control of the proceedings and worked to develop a consensus that would accommodate the federal government while carving out a role for the OAU, to establish the organization as the foremost judge of the international implications of the Nigerian civil war.

By the late afternoon of September 13, agreement within the caucus was reached for the establishment of an ad hoc committee of African heads of state to deal with the Nigerian crisis. Contrary to Kaunda's wishes, the committee would not be constituted as a mediatory body but would be called only a "Consultative Committee," in deference to the federal government. Credit for this compromise approach belongs to President Tubman of Liberia who may have been familiar with a similar arrangement within the Organization of American States.[45] Awolowo accepted the suggestion of a "Consultative Committee," which, in his view, implied only "their participation in an advisory capacity . . . coming to Nigeria to offer their solidarity in support of

[42] MEA, Report of the Federal Delegation to the OAU Summit, September 12–14, 1967.

[43] Interview: Awolowo.

[44] Douglas Anglin also refers to this tension between Awolowo and Kaunda in "Zambia and the Recognition of Biafra," p. 113.

[45] Interviews: Awolowo; Leonard de Shields, head of Africa Section, Liberian Department of State.

Nigeria."[46] Having made the crucial concession of allowing the OAU to become involved with Nigeria's internal difficulties, Awolowo spent the rest of his time in Kinshasa ensuring that the resolution creating the Consultative Committee conformed to his conception of the committee's limited terms of reference.

Agreement on the text of the resolution was finally reached by 3:00 A.M. on the last day of the summit, September 14. Chief Awolowo wanted General Gowon's approval before any vote was taken by the assembly. Efforts to telephone Dodan Barracks failed. With the assistance of the United States embassy in Kinshasa, a call was routed at 5:00 A.M. direct to General Gowon through the American embassy in Lagos.[47] Gowon, somewhat reluctantly, consented to the OAU formula. Later that morning the following resolution was accepted by acclamation and without debate by the Assembly of Heads of State and Government:

> The Assembly of Heads of State and Government meeting at its First Ordinary Session in Kinshasa from 11th to 14th September 1967;
> Solemnly reaffirming their adherence to the principle of respect for the sovereignty and territorial integrity of member states;
> Reiterating their condemnation of secession in any member state;
> Concerned at the tragic and serious situation in Nigeria;
> Recognizing the situation as an internal affair, the solution of which is primarily the responsibility of Nigerians themselves;
> Reposing their trust and confidence in the Federal Government of Nigeria;
> Desirous of exploring the possibilities of placing the services of the Assembly at the disposal of the Federal Government of Nigeria;
> Resolves to send a consultative mission of six Heads of State (Mobutu, Tubman, Ankrah, Ahidjo, Diori, and Haile Selassie) to the Head of the Federal Government of Nigeria to assure him of the Assembly's desire for the territorial integrity, unity and peace of Nigeria.[48]

The Kinshasa Resolution was later viewed as a major diplomatic advantage for the Nigerians, although General Gowon and his advisers in Lagos were privately very nervous about the development. Initial press

[46] Interview: Awolowo. Awolowo used virtually the identical words in a statement to the press on the final day of the summit in Kinshasa. *Daily Sketch*, September 16, 1967.

[47] Interviews: American officials at the embassies in Lagos and Kinshasa.

[48] OAU Communiqué issued at Kinshasa, September 14, 1967, reprinted in Kirk-Greene, *Crisis and Conflict*, II, 172–173.

and radio reports were rather misleading; "OAU to Mediate in Nigerian War" was the headline in one respected British paper.[49] "A number of us here were worried," recalled a close confidant to Gowon, "until we saw the text of the resolution . . . the technical aspects of the resolution were very important."[50] The composition of the committee—the "Caucus of Heavyweights" minus President Kaunda of Zambia—was also reassuring to Lagos because none of the six was considered sympathetic to Biafra despite their members' varying views regarding a cease-fire and negotiations.

Awolowo won several key points while the resolution was being drafted. The most important of these appears in the last paragraph, where the Consultative Committee's purpose is described as merely to "assure" General Gowon "of the Assembly's desire for the territorial integrity, unity and peace of Nigeria." There were several attempts to introduce more neutral language, such as to empower the committee "to look into the matter." Awolowo rejected this formula and also insisted on the omission of any call for a cease-fire or for negotiations between the two sides. Missing, too, was the call for a peaceful settlement of the dispute, because the Nigerians argued that this would imply the de facto existence of Biafra as a party to the conflict. Finally, Awolowo scored an important diplomatic point when the caucus agreed to include a formal condemnation of secession in the OAU resolution.

By allowing the OAU to take up the Nigerian question, the federal government at last conceded that the conflict was not a purely domestic issue. Now it could be treated as a matter that was of legitimate concern to all of Africa. The question that remained, however, was whether the threat of greater international involvement could be controlled at the regional level. An indication that this would indeed be the case appeared even before the delegations had left Kinshasa, when, during the closing ceremonies, United Nations Secretary General U Thant addressed the assembly and warmly endorsed the decision to form a Consultative Committee on Nigeria.

The secretary general reaffirmed his belief that regional organizations should provide the first and foremost forum for assessing the international significance of a local dispute, strongly implying that this would preempt United Nations involvement in the Nigerian crisis.[51] With the conflict under consideration by the OAU, whose forty-one members composed nearly a third of the votes in the UN General Assembly,

[49] *Financial Times*, September 15, 1967.

[50] Interview: Allison Ayida.

[51] For a full discussion of the relationship between the United Nations and the Organization of African Unity, see Cervenka, *The Organization of African Unity*, Ch. 5.

there was little chance that Biafra's foreign supporters would ever succeed in placing the matter on the United Nations agenda. And, as the conflict dragged on through 1968 and 1969, U Thant consistently took the position that, so long as the regional body remained united in its approach to the Nigerian question, the UN Secretariat would decline to become involved.[52]

The second immediate benefit accruing to the federal government as a result of the OAU's action was less apparent; Tanzania's recognition of Biafra was postponed for another seven months, while the East African states were now on record supporting an OAU resolution that condemned secession. The threat of Tanzanian recognition had been a useful lever to push the federal government into accepting the formation of the Consultative Committee. Although President Kaunda was no doubt irked by the treatment he received from Chief Awolowo, and disappointed by what he considered to be a watered-down resolution, he was nevertheless sufficiently satisfied to continue to withhold recognition of Biafra, and advised President Nyerere to do likewise.[53]

Kaunda's ambivalence toward the results of the Kinshasa summit was shared in Biafra. Official reaction by the secessionist radio was muted pending some indication of how the Consultative Committee would proceed. Within the Biafran Ministry of Foreign Affairs a memorandum was prepared that dealt with the OAU's performance, and it reflects Ojukwu's dilemma:

> The acceptance of the OAU resolution on the Nigeria/Biafra crisis for diplomatic intervention is a triumph for Biafra because it was a vindication of the fact that the dispute was no longer internal. The resolution did, however, go out of its way to placate Lagos, probably in order to make mediation possible, hence the relevant portion refers to the Conference's desire for "expressing the possibility of putting the services of the Conference at the disposal of the Federal Government of Nigeria." The pains taken, however, to assuage the feelings of Lagos heighten the fear that our cause could be compromised, and it is for this reason that this Government has maintained an attitude of discreet silence towards the OAU initiative.

[52] U Thant's frankest statement in this regard was made in early 1969, when he told a press conference: "If the Heads of African States have asked all members of the United Nations and all members of the OAU to refrain from any action likely to endanger the peace, unity and territorial integrity of Nigeria, I do not see how UN member states, or for that matter the Secretary-General, can be actively involved." *UN Monthly Chronicle*, VI (February 1969), p. 39. For an earlier comment in the same vein see: *UN Monthly Chronicle*, V (August-September 1968), p. 104.

[53] Anglin, "Zambia and the Recognition of Biafra," p. 114.

Above all, the OAU intervention will now have the effect of delaying individual initiative by those states as in East Africa, which would have given us recognition.[54]

Regrettably for Biafra, these uncertainties would be resolved when the Consultative Committee finally convened in Lagos and chose to identify itself fully with the federal government's campaign to repress the rebellion.

CONSULTING WITH AFRICAN HEADS OF STATE

The announcement of the Consultative Committee gained wide international attention.[55] Speculation focused on how soon the committee would meet and, given the vagueness of its mandate, to what purpose. As the delegations left Kinshasa on September 15, 1967, President Mobutu reportedly declared that the committee should arrange to be in Lagos within a week, for if they delayed, "early October would be too late."[56] A similar note of urgency was struck when President Tubman and U Thant stopped in Lagos en route from the summit, and the federal government announced that it had agreed to receive the full committee by the first of October.[57] Press reports a few days later further indicated that Emperor Haile Selassie would arrive in Nigeria on September 21 to prepare the way for the formal meeting,[58] and the United States Department of State announced that President Diori intended to cut short his state visit to Washington in order to participate in the Lagos proceedings.[59] These hopeful signs to the contrary, the Consultative Committee waited for over two months, until November 23, 1967, to visit Lagos.

Officially, the reasons given for the repeated delays were various conflicts in the schedules of one or more of the members. In actuality, the postponements related more to the military developments within Nigeria than to matters of diplomatic protocol. When the committee was created, the federal government was asked to refrain from further military aggression against Biafra so as not to embarrass the committee during its peace mission. This Gowon declined to do because his

---

[54] BMFA, "Foreign Policy Objectives: A Policy Memorandum," prepared in Enugu, September 1967.

[55] For a brief review of editorial comment by the major British, American, and French newspapers, see *West Africa*, No. 2625, September 23, 1967, pp. 1223–1224.

[56] Radio Brazzaville, September 17, 1967.

[57] Nigeria, Federal Ministry of Information Press Release, September 15, 1967.

[58] *Daily Times*, September 19, 1967.

[59] *West Africa*, No. 2626, September 30, 1967, p. 1285.

forces were currently engaged in three crucial operations: liberating the Midwest, capturing the Biafran capital of Enugu, and sealing the Cameroon border from Ikom to Calabar.

Federal officials were also displeased with much of the foreign publicity given to the establishment of the committee. To quote one official Nigerian commentary entitled "Let's Get This Straight";

> There seems to be some jubilation in Enugu over the impending visit of . . . six African Heads of State to Nigeria . . . the External Service of Radio Ghana referred to the mission as coming to mediate in the Nigerian conflict. Both Radio Yaoundé and the quack experts on the Manchester Guardian have also made similar references. . . . This may be as a result of an honest misunderstanding of the object of the mission or yet another deliberate attempt to falsify issues and undermine the campaign to halt Ojukwu's rebellion. . . . There can be no turning back on the task of crushing Ojukwu and keeping the nation one."[60]

Within the military establishment there were also those who felt, as one officer put it, that the committee was proceeding with "indecent haste," and many suspected this was intended to assist Ojukwu in achieving an immediate cease-fire.

For a while it appeared that the committee would meet on October 5, but as the federal First Division was about to seize Enugu, the date was pushed ahead to October 31.[61] The Nigerians had hoped that the fall of Biafra's capital would convince the Ibo elite to surrender, with or without Ojukwu. During September there had been considerable fighting around the city, but on October 3-4, 1967, the city was quickly evacuated and came under federal control without any resistance. This naturally encouraged many in Lagos to believe that a renunciation of secession might be obtained in advance of any meeting of the OAU Consultative Committee.

Unlike other wars, the invasion and fall of Biafra's capital did not bring about a rapid end to the war. While the loss may have damaged Biafra's prestige, it did not prove to be as strategically important as might have been expected. Enugu, after all, had been largely a British creation to facilitate the colonial administration of the region east of the Niger River, and was never regarded as truly an Ibo city. As discussed in Chapter 5 below, Ojukwu was easily able to relocate his government

---

[60] Editorial in the government-owned *Morning Post*, September 23, 1967.

[61] For announcements of rescheduling and the "official" reasons for postponements, see *West Africa*, No. 2627, October 7, 1967, p. 1317; No. 2630, October 28, 1967, p. 1409; and No. 2632, November 11, 1967, p. 1565.

in Umuahia, deep in the traditional Ibo heartland, and from there wage a remarkably tenacious war of attrition.

Throughout October, the federal offensive continued, marked by the Second Division's capture of Asaba on the west bank of the Niger River, and the Third Marine Commando Division's dramatic assault and occupation of Calabar, which opened the way for a linkup with the First Division at Ikom, thereby sealing off the Cameroon border and completing the initial encirclement of Biafra. With each advance the European and American press raised the specter of wanton massacre if federal troops overran Biafra, and they decried the committee's failure to meet.[62] *The New York Times* editorialized: "With so much at stake it is inexcusable that the heads of government have so long delayed their OAU mission. . . . These men need to remember that the standing and perhaps the future of the OAU are at stake along with Nigeria's fate. . . . The hour is terribly late and there can be no higher priority for Africans."[63]

In an effort to prod the federal government, President Tubman sent a highly publicized message to the UN and OAU secretariats, which called on the members of the two organizations to try and contact the Biafrans in order to persuade them to lay down their arms, and to convince the federal government of the dangers in trying to realize its political objectives through military means.[64] The initiative infuriated the editors of the government-owned *Morning Post* in Lagos, who accused the Liberian president of being a "Horse of Troy" and sabotaging the OAU committees.[65] The quick reaction from the *Morning Post* displeased the Ministry of External Affairs, whose commissioner had recently returned from a visit to Washington and knew that Tubman was under great pressure to demonstrate Africa's concern over developments in Nigeria. A special commentary was prepared for Radio Nigeria that praised the Liberian's good will.[66] Tubman, however, regarded the *Post* editorial as an affront and promptly tendered his resignation from the OAU committee to Emperor Haile Selassie. He was subsequently prevailed upon to withdraw his letter of resignation, and General

[62] A commentator for the West African Service of the British Broadcasting Corporation's *Newsreel* of October 24, 1967, ominously concluded, "the great danger is that there might be a massacre in the last stage of winning, not through any wish of General Gowon or through the wish of the federal government . . . or the federal commanders but the danger is that you get a small army in an overwhelmingly hostile Ibo territory and inevitably there is going to be guerrilla activity against the army and inevitably, these guerrilla activities will have reprisals . . . it could be very difficult to control the troops."

[63] *New York Times*, editorial, November 15, 1967.

[64] Text of the message was reprinted in the *Daily Sketch*, October 23, 1967.

[65] *Morning Post*, editorial, October 24, 1967.

[66] Radio Nigeria, *Commentary*, October 26, 1967.

Gowon sent a special team to Monrovia, headed by Commissioner of Mines and Power Dr. R.B.O. Dikko, to apologize for any insult.[67]

An unexpected military slowdown in mid-November and the Tubman/Lagos altercation helped to break the diplomatic logjam over when the committee would meet. The Liberian president decided to stay home, and President Mobutu, who long ago had become disillusioned with the committee's chances for success, also declined to attend.[68] President Ahidjo, who had previously threatened not to attend,[69] changed his mind and joined Ankrah, Diori, and the Emperor in Lagos on November 23, 1967.

In spite of numerous assurances, the Nigerian government remained apprehensive that the committee might press for negotiations on terms it would deem unacceptable, but presented in such a way that to refuse would tend to discredit the federal cause. Thus, when General Gowon welcomed the African leaders to the committee's opening session, he carefully presented his interpretation of the situation:

> your Mission is not here to mediate . . . your consultations with the Federal Military Government can be fruitful only if we all recognize the nature of our crisis. There was fear of domination by one region over the other and by one ethnic group over the rest. The only way to remove this fear and the structural imbalance in the Federation is by creating more states. . . . It is just not possible to avoid friction through any arrangement based on the four former regions. The former Northern and Eastern regions had to be split up in order to remove the imbalance in the country's political structure. . . . We cannot cease current military operations to end the rebellion . . . until the rebels renounce secession. . . . A new leadership of the East-Central State must accept the new structure of the Federation based on twelve states.[70]

The Emperor replied briefly by declaring that he "unreservedly supports Nigerian national unity," but refrained from any reference to the issues dividing the country. The meeting then proceeded into secret session.[71]

Once inside the conference chamber, it became apparent that neither the committee nor Nigeria was quite sure how to proceed. There was

[67] For the most complete published account of this sequence, see *Agence Cameroun Presse*, December 27, 1967.

[68] Mobutu's stated reason for not attending was that he had to be in Kinshasa on November 24 for the second anniversary of his coup d'état.

[69] *La Presse du Cameroun*, October 27, 1967.

[70] "Welcome Address to the OAU Consultative Mission by the Head of the Federal Military Government," November 23, 1967, reprinted in *Report on the OAU Consultative Mission to Nigeria* (Lagos: Nigerian National Press, 1967).

[71] *Ibid.*

no agenda and really no diplomatic precedent. They had come to consult, but consult on what? The Emperor announced that their purpose was to "consider the Nigerian situation on the basis of the OAU Resolution" adopted at the Fourth Summit, and then promptly called on General Gowon to "explain to us the problem we are facing and his views on the matter under consideration."[72] Gowon replied that he had outlined the problem in his opening public address, and therefore suggested that the committee "ask me what you feel about the situation."

The Emperor then proceeded to set the tone for the discussions that followed for nine hours. First he sought to reassure the federal government: "the situation in Nigeria is of concern to all of us. It concerns us because secessionist tendencies are to be found in almost all African states. This is the legacy we have inherited from the colonialists who tried ruling Africans by dividing them. We know that secession, if it were to be tolerated on our continent would lead to the destruction of what Africans hold in high esteem—their independence and their progress." Then came the Emperor's appeal for greater international involvement in the search for a peaceful settlement, a plea echoed by each of the three other visiting heads of state:

> Our aim is to help the federal government and the people of Nigeria to resolve their problems in a peaceful way. But in order to discharge this heavy responsibility and mandate we carry from the Assembly of Heads of State and Government, we must find a way of communicating with the other side which is conducting the hostilities against the Federal Government of Nigeria. If we could find another way by which this commission could discharge its responsibility faithfully . . . then it would have been a worthwhile task to inquire into the possibilities. But my personal opinion is that in order to discharge effectively the mandate we hold, it is necessary to somehow, I do not know what particular procedure, communicate with Col. Ojukwu. Through that communication we hope to be in a position to persuade the secessionist group that the consequences of their actions are inconsistent, not only with the interest of the Nigerian people but the interest of all of Africa.

Opening statements by the other members of the Consultative Committee all endorsed the Emperor's call for Nigerian approval of OAU/Biafra contacts. Differences were evident, however, regarding the appropriate level and expressed purpose of such contacts.

President Diori believed the committee's task should be to find

[72] Verbatim Records of the meeting of the OAU Consultative Committee on Nigeria, held at the Nigerian Institute of International Affairs, Lagos, Nigeria on November 23, 1967.

out from the Biafrans what minimum conditions they would accept in return for a renunciation of secession. Since Gowon's previous pleas for surrender had been rebuked, despite increasing military pressure, President Diori pondered: "What are the safe-guards; what are the guarantees that the mission would be able to tell the rebels if they do not readily agree to return into Nigeria and respect the territorial integrity of Nigeria?" To which General Ankrah promptly added: "The federal government can also tell us whatever guarantee they may be able to give us, if any individuals are to go there (Biafra) or to make contact, and also finally if all went well where the federal government are prepared to meet the rebels." The purpose of the OAU/Biafra dialogue would have been, in Ankrah's view, to communicate the three demands contained in Gowon's opening address—renunciation of secession, acceptance of the twelve states, and repudiation of Ojukwu's leadership—so that the rebels "may use our good offices to let them lay down their arms and renounce secession."

President Ahidjo completed the first round of proposals by suggesting a more carefully graduated OAU initiative. Initially there should be only radio contact with the rebel leaders, who would be informed of the OAU's unanimous endorsement of the principle respecting the territorial integrity of member states. Ahidjo further urged that the rebels be implored to make a statement that "they are ready to be integrated into the great Nigerian family." Once the OAU received this declaration "in principle" from the rebels, then "perhaps it would be necessary for the OAU to use its good offices to intervene between the two parties . . . to bring them together at a political level." Ahidjo's scenario would have had Nigeria drop its precondition that required Biafra to accept the twelve-state system prior to the commencement of negotiations.

The Emperor then called on General Gowon to "elucidate further about the ways and means of achieving initial contact" with the rebels, adding that such contact "does not mean that we hold any sympathy for them." But before Nigeria's head of state could reply, President Diori intervened to suggest a short recess for "contacts and discussions." Diori apparently sensed that the committee might be pushing the federal government too quickly down the road to further internationalization, and thus asked a stint of informal off-the-record bargaining, a common practice in OAU conference diplomacy. Diori proposed a break of fifteen minutes, but Gowon countered with an offer of lunch, noting that the subjects raised during the course of the morning "require quite a lot of thought." The meeting thus adjourned for three hours.

When the Consultative Committee reconvened for the afternoon session, Gowon spoke first. Nigeria, he said, "accepted the need to transmit a message on behalf of the OAU, consisting of the text of the Kinshasa resolution, to the rebels." But he added the following conditions: "I would expect the message to contain the conditions which my government considers essential . . . the twelve-state structure . . . and a new [Ibo] leadership . . . then military operations can cease, negotiations can begin, and for us on our part we pledge that representatives of the East Central State can then take full part on a basis of equality in discussions regarding the constitutional arrangements of the country."

Gowon was determined that any contacts with the Biafran regime should not be construed as the first round of substantive mediation. Even in the unlikely event that secession was renounced in principle, Gowon's pledge for open and full constitutional discussions on the basis of twelve states was meaningless, at least in the short run. The predominantly Ibo East Central State would amount to less than 40 percent of the territory still under de facto Biafran control. Yet Gowon insisted that any OAU communication with Ojukwu begin with endorsement of Nigerian reunification and the twelve-state system and a call for new Ibo leadership. "We would expect," Gowon said in closing, "that this message will be given publicity in order to avoid misinterpretation outside Africa."

General Ankrah became irked with the rigidity of the federal position and intervened to lecture his junior military colleague: "We know the federal government demands twelve states . . . perhaps the rebels will accept three or two or one [states in the East] but the best thing would be to get around the table and argue out the two sides." In Ankrah's view, the proper role of the Consultative Committee would have been to transmit the OAU's condemnation of secession, as well as Nigeria's conditions for a cessation of hostilities, listen to the rebel rebuttal, and then try to mediate the differences.

The more experienced statesmen—Ahidjo, Diori, and the Emperor—rejected Ankrah's plan as unnecessarily clumsy. Rather than tabling all of the federal government's demands at the outset, they sought to limit the committee's role to the one issue that most concerned the rest of Africa, namely, a renunciation of secession. Who represented the Ibos in any negotiations and the internal administrative arrangements resulting from those negotiations were of no immediate interest to the Consultative Committee. As President Ahidjo observed,

Basically it is the territorial integrity of Nigeria which is of concern to us. The rest is entirely a domestic affair. How can we in our contacts with the rebels discuss the number of states within the territorial boundaries of Nigeria itself? How can we really talk to them about the status of this or that Nigerian citizen or of this or that region? If we take the other [federal] terms, that there should be other leaders instead of the present leaders [of Biafra] how far can they claim authority over the areas they control? The OAU Commission lacks the authority to make such a determination. Responsible authority exists in the Eastern Region. We cannot ask them to renounce secession and then say that there are other conditions such as the need for someone else instead of Colonel Ojukwu.

In a similar vein, President Diori also implored that the committee stick to basics: "We would like to tell the world that our brothers of the federation have all good faith but the hindrance lies with those [Biafrans] who sought to resort to force. I think this would be a considerable moral force. The territorial integrity of Nigeria is the important thing, the rest is purely domestic . . . after the battle you may find that you need other [than twelve] divisions." "The point of our task," the Emperor declared in summing up, "is to end secession," which he denounced—no doubt with a view to his own domestic troubles in Eritrea—as a "dangerous precedent" for Africa. Once the secession had been ended, the Emperor concluded, "then Nigerians can take up other problems such as the division of the country into twelve states."

Following the Emperor's remarks, the committee adjourned for a second round of informal off-the-record discussions aimed at producing a final communiqué that would be acceptable to the federal government. During the informal exchange, Gowon dropped his demand that the committee, in any dealings with Biafra, stipulate that a repudiation of Ojukwu's leadership be a precondition for direct peace talks. When the committee resumed sitting later in the evening, Emperor Haile Selassie opened the session by reading the following draft communiqué:

1. The Mission reaffirmed the decision of the OAU Summit embodied in its resolution condemning all secessionist attempts in Africa. The Mission also reaffirmed that any solution of the Nigerian crisis must be in the context of preserving the unity and territorial integrity of Nigeria.
2. The Mission considered the terms of the Federal Military Government for the cessation of military operations.
3. The OAU Consultative Mission agreed that as a basis for return to peace and normal conditions in Nigeria the secessionists should renounce secession and accept the present administrative structure of the Federation of Nigeria.
4. H. E. Lt. General Ankrah was mandated by the Mission to convey the text of the OAU Kinshasa summit resolution as well as discus-

sions and conclusions of the first meeting of the Mission in Lagos to the secessionists and report back to the Mission urgently the reaction of the secessionists. The Mission will decide on the next course of action on the receipt of His Excellency Lt. General Ankrah's report.

5. It was also agreed that the OAU Consultative Mission will remain in constant touch with the Federal Military Government.

6. The Federal Military Government was in complete agreement with the conclusions reached at the meeting and the action to be taken to ensure the unity, territorial integrity of, and peace in Nigeria.

As soon as the draft communiqué had been presented, Gowon rose with an amendment. In addition to calling upon the secessionists to "accept the present administrative structure of Nigeria" (Par. 3), Gowon wanted to include the phrase "as outlined on the basis of the twelve states." General Ankrah entered a plea for vagueness in the unlikely event that it might "trap" Ojukwu into negotiating on the basis of a united Nigeria. Gowon, still believing he had been the one who had been "trapped" by the Aburi accords, wanted no room for ambiguity. The term "present administrative structure," as it appeared in the draft communiqué, could be interpreted as referring only to the relationship between the center and the federated parts—whether there be four regions or twelve states. Furthermore, Ojukwu could argue that since he never accepted the twelve state system, the "present administrative structure" could only refer to the Constitution Suspension and Modification Decree No. 1 of January 1, 1966, which confirmed him as governor of the Eastern Region. Gowon adamantly refused to deal with his adversary on the basis of the former regions, even if Ojukwu renounced secession in advance of negotiations.

Emperor Haile Selassie reminded Gowon that they had "extensively exchanged points of view on this tactical point" during the informal after-dinner discussions, and he urged the Nigerian leader to let the draft stand. At this juncture, President Diori intervened with a rather clever compromise. Since the federal decree establishing the twelve states allowed for certain adjustments in the future, Diori suggested the inclusion of a reference to the twelve-state decree rather than mentioning the actual administrative arrangement. Given that the decree stipulates a minimum of twelve states, Gowon readily agreed, and paragraph three of the draft communiqué was changed to read:

The OAU Consultative Mission agreed that as a basis for return to peace and normal conditions in Nigeria the secessionists should renounce secession and accept the present administrative structure of the Federation of Nigeria, as laid down by the Federal Military Government in Decree No. 14 of 1967.

General Ankrah was mandated by the committee to communicate the text of the final communiqué to Ojukwu by means of a two-way radio link. Ojukwu's response could then be relayed to the other members.

The Biafran government withheld comment about the Lagos meeting until the outcome was known. When news of the final communiqué reached Enugu, the reaction was immediate and sharp. Quoting a government statement issued within hours of the committee's adjournment, Radio Biafra declared, "it is obvious that the reported conclusions are an attempt by a few African states to use their position in the Committee to blackmail and discredit the Organization of African Unity. By so doing these African states have fallen prey to the British-American imperialist conspiracy to use the Committee's recommendation as a pretext for a massive arms support for their puppet and tottering neo-colonialist regime in Lagos."[73] When General Ankrah tried to reach Ojukwu through the radio channel that they had maintained intermittently since the time of the Aburi meeting, the Biafran leader ignored the signal.[74]

Nigerian foreign policy makers had reason to be satisfied when they reviewed the position adopted by the OAU's Consultative Committee. True to its mandate from the Assembly of African Heads of State and Government, the committee had placed its services at the disposal of the federal military government. By referring to the twelve-state decree in its final communiqué, the committee had further blurred the distinction between the domestic and international aspects of the conflict, but this particular initiative was a major gain for the federal government. The explicit endorsement of the twelve-state decree conferred international legitimacy on Gowon's claim to the allegiance of all Nigerians, and it reaffirmed his sovereign prerogative to impose whatever administrative structures his government deemed vital to the preservation of Nigeria's national interest.

The committee's decisions carried broad political implications for the future of Biafra. The Consultative Committee purported to represent the interests of the African region, and because of this the Nigerians expected that the strong profederal stand taken during the Lagos meeting would stifle any further criticism from individual leaders within Africa. President Diori's participation was additionally important because, as the current chairman of the OCAM group, he was in a position to speak for the francophone community and, in turn, in-

[73] Radio Biafra, November 25, 1967.   [74] Interviews: Ankrah; Ojukwu.

fluence the French government. Similarly, the views of Emperor Haile Selassie were expected to count for something in Washington, while General Ankrah's support meant that members of the Commonwealth —especially Britain—now had one more reason to ignore Biafra.

By the end of 1967 a Nigerian victory appeared increasingly probable. The Biafran thrust through the Midwest had been repulsed, the Cameroon frontier, including the nearby port city of Calabar, had been sealed, and the Biafran capital at Enugu had fallen. Biafra was completely cut off from international discourse, save for a lone telex link to Lisbon and six partly chartered, partly Biafran-owned DC–7s and aging Super Constellations that shuttled between Port Harcourt and Portugal several times weekly. "What concerns us," Ojukwu bemoaned to his people, "is that the reaction of the world to the genocidal war being waged by Nigeria against Biafra has, for the most part, been one of silence, indifference and occasionally of veiled hostility to Biafra."[75]

[75] Ojukwu, *Biafra*, "Genocide," address to joint meeting of the Consultative Assembly and the Council of Chiefs and Elders, January 27, 1968, I, 228.

PART II

THE ISSUES
TRANSCEND SECESSION

· 5 ·

BIAFRA PENETRATES
THE INTERNATIONAL SYSTEM

Withdrawal from the Midwest and the loss of the capital at Enugu forced the Biafran government to undertake a major reassessment and reorganization of the war effort. The confident self-image of Biafra as a military power invulnerable to federal attack had to be abandoned, along with the notion that the war would be a brief affair. Instead, the realization that the Ibos were a people under siege began to take hold.

The new emphasis would be on Biafra's determination to fight on, regardless of the cost. To enhance the credibility of the threat to wage an indefinite "people's war" against Nigeria, Biafran spokesmen redefined their struggle as a defense against genocide, rather than a fight for political self-determination. International and domestic support for the Biafran state would increasingly be portrayed as a sine qua non for the survival of the Ibo people. More immediately, however, the secessionists had to confront the reality of continued international isolation, a lack of foreign exchange with which to purchase military equipment, and a well-armed federal army that appeared ready to invade. Beginning in early 1968, the Ojukwu regime intensified its campaign to awaken international concern to the plight of the civilian population, and to convert this growing interest into political pressure that would force Nigeria to accept an unconditional cease-fire and thereby halt the federal military offensive.

For a brief period, May to August 1968, it appeared that a cease-fire and negotiated settlement might be possible as representatives from the two sides met for formal discussions.[1] The talks in Kampala and Addis Ababa sponsored, respectively, by the Commonwealth Secretariat and the Consultative Committee of the Organization of African Unity, tacitly acknowledged Biafra's de facto independence of federal authority, and were the high point of Biafra's attempt to penetrate the inter-

[1] Formal discussions were actually held only twice during the war: May 23–31, 1968, under the auspices of the Commonwealth Secretariat in Kampala, Uganda, and August 5–September 6, 1968, under the auspices of the OAU Consultative Committee in Addis Ababa, Ethiopia. In each case there were extensive preliminary meetings between representatives of the two sides. A third round of direct negotiations was held April 18–20, 1969, under the auspices of the Consultative Committee in Monrovia, Liberia, but it failed to establish a sufficient justification for the resumption of full-scale talks.

national political system. This chapter will analyze Biafra's efforts to mobilize international support for an unconditional cease-fire and the subsequent diplomatic recognition from four African states, which helped set the stage for the much-publicized "peace talks" in Kampala.

THE DIRECTORATE OF PROPAGANDA

With the growing appreciation of vulnerability to federal attack came indications of domestic disaffection with Ojukwu's regime. On October 11, 1967, the Biafran leader addressed a joint meeting of his Consultative Assembly and the Council of Chiefs and Elders. He admitted for the first time that his troops had been "ill-prepared, inadequate and poorly equipped" for the war.[2] His frankness contrasted sharply with the assurances of military invincibility that he had conveyed to the same group during their last meeting, six months earlier.[3] "We had expected to finish the war . . . by the end of August," he reminded the assembly in October, and he blamed the failure on unnamed "saboteurs and traitors" who foiled the successful Midwest invasion and "opened the door" to Enugu. Ojukwu acknowledged that there were those who wished him to step down, and he offered to do so. Predictably, the Consultative Assembly rejected the suggestion.

Although the Consultative Assembly was not an independent body, its pronouncements served to remind any dissidents that there was no immediate alternative to Ojukwu's leadership. The only individual of comparable stature, the charismatic leader of the January 1966 coup, Major Nzeogwu, was killed under mysterious circumstances on the northern front shortly after the war broke out; and Nzeogwu's principal associate, Major Ifeajuna, was publicly executed as a Biafran traitor following the collapse of the Midwest invasion.[4] The combination of these actions helped to consolidate Ojukwu's authority, but there was still a need to reinforce public awareness and support for what now promised to be a long and immeasurably painful war.

As soon as the government was relocated in Umuahia, major and rapid changes were made in the structure and content of Biafra's propaganda operations in order to overcome past criticism and win greater favor at home and abroad. Until the loss of Enugu, responsibility for Biafran propaganda rested with the Ministry of Information, a direct descendant of the Eastern Region's ministry, and its staff of

[2] Ojukwu, *Biafra*, address to joint session of the Advisory Council of Chiefs and Elders and the Consultative Assembly, October 11, 1967, I, 211–218.

[3] *Ibid.*, I, 146–176, address to the Joint Meeting of Chiefs and Elders and the Consultative Assembly, May 26, 1967, in which he declared, "there is no power in this country, or in Black Africa, to subdue us by force."

[4] *West Africa*, No. 2626, September 30, 1967, p. 1285.

seventy civil servants. Ojukwu had not been satisfied with the ministry's work, which he considered inefficient, pedestrian, and not sufficiently in tune with the hopes and fears of the Biafran people.

In an effort to bypass the rigidities of the civil service, a Directorate of Propaganda was established. For a while the directorate operated within the ministry, but as the director for propaganda later recounted;

> The collapse of the Midwest offensive and the withdrawal from Enugu threw the information operations off balance. The claim that Nigeria could not survive or press a war without Ibos lost meaning. We realized Biafra was collapsing faster than we thought. The population was becoming panicky and was not getting the proper encouragement from the Ministry of Information. The Directorate of Propaganda made a successful bid for more power at Umuahia and got it. We had plenty of money to do what we wanted so we expanded fast at the same time the government was starving the Ministry of Information funds and functions. The directorate expanded to forty-one committees with at least four or five people per committee, but with some as high as eleven or twelve.[5]

Filling the senior positions in the directorate were scores of displaced faculty members from the University of Nigeria, Nsukka, which had been occupied by federal troops shortly before the fall of Enugu.[6] Within a few weeks, the directorate had entered what one participant later described as "the golden age of Biafran propaganda."[7]

The basic challenge confronting Biafran propagandists was the need to strengthen Ojukwu's argument that unless there was a cease-fire followed by a political settlement, the war would continue until every man, woman, and child in Biafra died either of starvation or at the hands of federal troops. To give this threat credibility, the Directorate of Propaganda's first objective was not to convince the outside world that Lagos was bent on mass slaughter, but that the people of Biafra believed this to be so, and therefore would never willingly agree to the restoration of federal authority. The Biafran leadership assumed that if their countrymen demonstrated this determination to resist in the face of widespread suffering and loss of life,

[5] Interview: Chukwumerije.

[6] Among the cadre of young university lecturers who served the Biafran public relations effort were: Dr. Ifeagwu Eke (humanities), commissioner of information; Dr. Michael Echerue (English), head of war information bureau; J. Onuoha (physical education), head of public enlightenment; Dr. O. Anya (zoology), editor, *Biafra Newsletter*; Dr. Ifemesia (history), director of research and documentation. The twelve-man Propaganda Analysis Committee was also entirely staffed by university personnel.

[7] Interview: A. Anafulu, head of the directorate of propaganda's documentation center. See, by him, "An African Experience."

then the United States and other Western democracies would be compelled for moral and political reasons to press Nigeria for a cease-fire that would respect Biafra's autonomy.

The work of the directorate proceeded on two levels: first, the consolidation of the popular will to continue the war regardless of the hardships; and second, the projection of this determination to as wide an international audience as possible. An effective domestic program thus became a precondition for success overseas. Any sign of domestic dissent would adversely affect Biafra's international image. And as increasing numbers of journalists, religious leaders, and international fact-finding teams visited the beleaguered secessionist enclave, it was essential to Biafra's foreign interests that the public demonstrate their indomitable will. Those responsible for Biafran propaganda consider their achievements in maintaining domestic support for the rebellion to have been more important and difficult than the mobilization of international public opinion.

There is no reason to suppose that the secession was unpopular, but it was significant that the initial demonstrations of support in the spring of 1967 occurred mainly in the urban areas. Those who participated recall that the mood approached a victory celebration, with no premonition of the sacrifices that would be required in the months ahead. Aside from the shocking reports of anti-Ibo persecutions in the North and influx of refugees, rural life in Biafra had not been seriously disrupted by the political upheavals during the past year, and the local authorities had done little to mobilize and discipline the masses for war. Biafra had no ideology.

Contrary to the impression created overseas, Ibo villages are highly individualistic, with their own dialects and customs. As the euphoria of Biafran independence yielded to the realities of widespread fear and deprivation, many urban dwellers returned to the relative safety and isolation of their villages. With commercial life dwindling to a standstill as the blockade tightened, the state became the principal employer but, even if one includes Biafra's 40,000-man army, the public work force amounted to no more than one-half of one percent of the population. To counteract the trend toward isolation, alienation, and social fragmentation, the Directorate of Propaganda took steps to solidify opinion.

Biafran propaganda actually went through two phases between January 1968 and the end of the war. The first, which lasted until the spring of 1969, stressed the fear of "genocide," while the second phase, which will be discussed in Chapter 11, sought to redefine the determination to resist in terms of Biafra's "self-reliance." According to those responsible for the public relations campaigns, "genocide" proved to be the most powerful and effective theme of the war. As one participant later wrote, "The genocide propaganda was designed to confirm and instill in the public's mind that nothing short of a sovereign Biafra could guarantee security of life and property. . . . It terrorized the home public and alarmed and alerted the entire world for it conjured up an image of the Nazi regime and its Jewish victims."[8]

The term "genocide" was not a new entry in the civil-war vocabulary. The former governor of the Eastern Region, Francis Ibiam, had referred to the threat of genocide in a radio broadcast shortly after secession was proclaimed.[9] As Biafran propagandists readily admit, however, the systematic killing of a whole people that was carried out during World War II bore no resemblance to the brief bloodlettings and migrations in Nigeria's ethnic conflicts. A major task for the Directorate of Propaganda was to give the threat of genocide greater force in the Ibo homeland.

The centerpiece of the genocide propaganda was the reality of the 1966 pogroms in the North. But although the Ibos had had to flee in terror from their homes in *sabon garis* (stranger's quarters) in cities across the North, once the initial outbursts of violence had subsided, the majority was allowed to leave the region physically unhurt. The question now was whether Ibo and non-Ibo villagers in the East could be convinced that the Nigerians were preparing to slaughter them in their own villages; to give this threat greater plausibility, the directorate portrayed the war as a religious conflict between Christians and Moslems. Nigeria was accused of prosecuting a religious vendetta or *jihad*, and while the image was intended to stir sympathies among foreign missionaries inside Biafra and among Christians around the world, the first objective was to arouse the Biafran masses.

The specter of a holy war derived some plausibility from historical analogy. From 1804 to 1830, the Moslem Fulani under Usman dan Fodio forcibly extended their control over vast pagan areas north of the Benue River.[10] By the middle of the twentieth century, Christianity had become an important element in the social life of southern Nigeria, particularly in the East (see Table 3–1). Christianity provided a new source of common identity for the fragmented village society in the East, and the hundreds of mission schools throughout the region became the principal route for acquiring modern skills and personal advancement under the British colonial system. Biafran propagandists therefore appealed to the Ibo sense of Christian superiority, and described the

---

[8] Paul E. Onu, "Domestic Propaganda in the Biafran Adventure," p. 52.
[9] Radio Biafra, July 21, 1967.
[10] See Crowder, *The Story of Nigeria*, Ch. VI, pp. 90–107.

TABLE 3-1
Religious Distribution by Region

	East	Midwest	North	West
Moslems	29,964	106,857	21,386,450	4,753,225
	(.3%)	(4.2%)	(71.7%)	(43.5%)
Christians	9,573,622	1,393,009	2,881,437	5,359,075
	(77.2%)	(54.9%)	(9.7%)	(49.0%)
Others	2,790,876	1,035,973	5,540,773	818,793
	(22.5%)	(40.9%)	(18.6%)	(7.5%)

Source: data from the controversial 1963 census.

Nigerian war effort as engineered by backward Northerners who were intent on imposing Islam on the East in order to deprive Ibos of any further opportunities for self-advancement.

To confirm the religious ambitions of the northern Moslems, atrocity stories were developed that accused federal troops of systematically desecrating holy places, raping Catholic sisters, and machine-gunning worshippers as they prayed. Whether exaggerated or not, a Biafran information officer later wrote that

> tales such as these conjured up great fear, even among sects traditionally apathetic toward politics and could be used to support underlying themes. . . . Religious victory appeared codeterminant with political ascendancy. . . . The propaganda argued that this stabilization [Moslem domination] could not be effected except by the decimation of the population, especially of the intelligentsia who constituted the main threat to the Hausa-Fulani tradition. . . . Hence the origins of the most powerful and effective propaganda theme, the genocide propaganda.[11]

The key to the success of Biafran domestic propaganda was village-level contact. This work was carried out by the Political Orientation Committee, which organized hundreds of university students and secondary school leaders who would introduce, explain, and justify government policy to small groups of peasants. They would lead criticism of Nigerian atrocities as described by Radio Biafra, and provide exaggerated praise of Biafran military success in order to raise morale. These so-called "agitator corps" would also perform surveillance roles, induc-

[11] Onu, "Domestic Propaganda," pp. 48–49.

ing conformity and exposing recalcitrants and saboteurs. American-trained social scientists reportedly employed various sampling and survey techniques to enable members of the "agitator corps" to conduct weekly opinion polls so that the directorate would know when certain "atrocity arguments were running thin."[12]

The content of Biafra's propaganda was determined by the Psychological Warfare Committee, which normally met every Tuesday to review and plan the major themes to be introduced each month. The committee also decided on four variations of the main theme, one of which was presented each week and ran for seven days. The same themes and subthemes were used for domestic and international audiences. Three elements remained endemic to propaganda during the final two years of the conflict: (1) an emphasis on alleged Nigerian atrocities; (2) the impossibility of any compromise with the implacable enemy; and (3) the indomitable will of the Biafran people.[13]

International considerations frequently influenced the deliberations of the Tuesday meetings of the Psychological Warfare Committee, but it is impossible to generalize about their significance. Reports would be presented by Biafran emissaries, businessmen, or others who had been abroad recently. Sudden military developments would also affect deliberations, and could lead to a shift in the scheduled themes; quite often Ojukwu would intervene to offer a personal assessment of what was or was not working.

Foreign distribution of the directorate's daily and weekly output of propaganda was handled by the Overseas Press Service, which had also been established shortly before the evacuation of Enugu. Cyprian Ekwensi, the internationally renowned author and the former director of Information Services for the Eastern Region, became the head of Biafra's Overseas Press Service in January 1968. Ekwensi's responsibilities included the censoring of all nonofficial news stories transmitted from Biafra[14] and the forwarding of the Directorate of Propaganda's daily news bulletins and other materials to a Geneva public relations firm, Markpress News Feature Services.

When the Biafra story finally began to receive widespread press coverage in Europe and America in mid-1968, those who supported the federal government tended to attribute the public uproar to Markpress. Harold Wilson later described the Markpress effort as "a success

---

[12] *Ibid.*, p. 56.   [13] Interview: Chukwumerije.

[14] There were no resident foreign journalists assigned to Biafra, and most of those who spent time in the enclave did not file their stories until returning home. The international wire services tried to maintain stringers in Biafra, and Ekwensi's office monitored their dispatches. Similar censorship applied to news reports transmitted from Lagos.

unparalleled in the history of communications in modern societies."[15] And on the floor of Parliament, a pro-Nigerian MP summed up the exasperation he shared with many of his colleagues: "In the propaganda field the Ibos have often seemed to be winning the war of words while losing the battle of arms. Behind this success is a highly professional operation conducted by an advertising agency in Geneva."[16]

Markpress is owned and operated by an American, William Bernhardt, whom the London *Daily Mail* once hyperbolized as the "man who sold a war."[17] The role that Markpress played in internationalizing the war was also described in exaggerated ways by politicians in Britain and America who wished to discredit Biafra's appeal for support, but who preferred not to challenge directly the similar case being made by church groups and other Biafran partisans representing large blocs of voters. Actually, the plush Markpress headquarters, which were located in a nineteenth-century mansion on the outskirts of Geneva, served primarily as a transmission point for material that had been written in Biafra by Biafrans. Between February 1968 and January 1970, Markpress relayed a total of 740 news bulletins from Biafra (via the Lisbon telex link) to 3,200 newspapers, parliamentarians, church leaders, and other opinion makers in Great Britain, Western Europe, and North America.[18]

By comparing random selections of Radio Biafra transcripts and subsequent Markpress releases, one discerns very little difference in wording. Because the primary objective of the Psychological Warfare Committee was to maintain a siege mentality within Biafra, the tenor and substance of its propaganda was especially virulent. When this material was relayed abroad it lost credibility, despite efforts by Markpress officials in Geneva to tone down some of the most extreme exaggerations of Nigerian atrocities.[19] Not surprisingly, few who were on the Markpress mailing list would admit that they considered the releases to be a reliable source of information about the war.[20] What the propaganda did accomplish, however, was to remind the outside world that it would be extremely difficult for the Biafran government to compromise its autonomy through negotiations with the federal government.

The Directorate of Propaganda's role in generating international con-

[15] Wilson, *The Labour Government 1964–1970*, p. 557.

[16] Great Britain, *Parliamentary Debates*, August 27, 1968, col. 1523.

[17] *Daily Mail*, January 21, 1967.

[18] Interview: Bernard Preston, Markpress executive in charge of the Biafran account. Great Britain was the most important target audience, and received approximately 22 percent of all mailings.

[19] *Ibid.*

[20] This was confirmed in numerous interviews with British and American scholars, journalists, and legislators. Also see: Wiseberg, "The International Politics of Relief," pp. 572–579.

cern for Biafra's plight can only be surmised. Uche Chukwumerije, who ran the directorate, is highly critical of all the attention accorded Markpress. Chukwumerije refers to the Bernhardt office as merely a "maildrop," and adds that it would be naive to assume that sophisticated opinion leaders would be significantly influenced by a public relations firm, regardless of the number and quality of its releases. In retrospect, he believes that a much more important catalyst for world opinion were the first-hand accounts by foreigners who lived in or visited Biafra and then returned home to describe conditions. As the situation deteriorated in 1968, the number of journalists, religious leaders, and parliamentarians who were flown into the enclave increased dramatically.

It was the task of the directorate, through the Internal Publicity Department, to manage these visits and to ensure that any public demonstrations, meetings with Biafran officials, or press conferences focused attention on the need to preserve the Biafran state as a prerequisite for the survival of the Ibo people. Until the influx of foreigners, Ojukwu's personal involvement in the propaganda effort had been limited to the strategy sessions within the Psychological Warfare Committee. This changed in early 1968, as he began to take a direct interest in the daily operations of the Internal Publicity Department.

FOREIGN PRESENCE IN BIAFRA

The political significance that Biafra's leaders ascribed to visits by religious and other nongovernmental delegations from abroad reflected their desperate sense of isolation. Although a small number of Biafran spokesmen and arms buyers always managed to travel to Europe, international commerce and other foreign contacts virtually ceased. Shortly after the outbreak of hostilities, Eastern Nigeria's small but important diplomatic corps comprising representatives of the British, United States, and Cameroon governments, left Biafra, along with 90 percent of the East's seven thousand non-African residents.[21] Communications with the outside were reduced to a lone telex link with Lisbon and, aside from the occasional journalist who passed through the Cameroon frontier at Mamfe, the only way to reach Biafra was on one of the half-dozen aging DC–6 or DC–7 cargo planes that intermittently flew the grueling seventeen-hour trip between Lisbon and Port Harcourt via Portuguese Guinea.

During the latter half of 1967, Biafra's only prominent visitor was

[21] The estimate of non-African population is based on interviews and on the only available census figures, which are contained in Nigeria, Federal Census Office, *1963 Census*, I, Population by Nationality and Ethnic Group, Eastern Nigeria, Table 3.

the former United Nations representative in Katanga, Irish scholar-diplomat, Conor Cruise O'Brien, who arrived from New York with two American scholars, and spent the latter part of September touring the enclave.[22] The trip was a hastily arranged affair that was funded by small American private foundations, and it coincided with the start of the federal offensive against Enugu. In spite of his military preoccupations, Ojukwu held three long meetings with O'Brien. According to one of the American participants, the topic of greatest concern to the Biafran leadership was how to gain access to foreign governments with a view to securing eventual diplomatic recognition.[23]

At this stage, Biafran officials appeared to have no foreign influence and no ideas about how to acquire any. Ojukwu had hoped that his visitors would be able to mobilize international support for Biafra's political goal of self-determination, and that O'Brien, in particular, would appeal to influential politicians in Britain. Such hopes were unrealistic.[24] When the team returned to New York they did call publicly for an immediate unconditional cease-fire and political negotiations, but this produced very little attention.[25] The foreign press and other opinion leaders still did not take Biafra seriously, in part because the level of human suffering had not reached dramatic proportions, but also because the Biafran government had not yet found a catalytic agent with enough international influence and credibility to sound the alarm.

Despite the upheavals of war, one expatriate group did remain in Biafra, and their transnational links were extensive. When the secession was declared there were approximately 1,050 expatriate Roman Catholic missionaries in Nigeria, and of this total at least 600 were in the East. As Laurie Wiseberg has documented, expatriate Catholics in the East responded to the escalating conflict in three ways that were important to the subsequent internationalization of the conflict.[26]

First, most priests decided to remain with their parishes when secession was declared, and did not evacuate with other foreigners. As federal troops advanced, expatriate missionaries faced a second important decision: whether to stay with their parishioners when evacuation became necessary. Again, most priests chose to be with their parishioners.

[22] Joining O'Brien were Professors Stanley Diamond and Audrey Chapman, both of New York. For a personal account of the visit, see Stanley Diamond, "A Faculty Member's Journey to Biafra."

[23] Interview: Audrey Chapman.

[24] The delegation was invited to Washington for a debriefing at the State Department, but the official view was that Biafra was on the verge of defeat.

[25] Only a handful of journalists attended the group's press conference, and the Biafran mission in New York produced very little follow-up publicity. An October 5, 1967, press release by Aggrey Oji, Biafra's special representative in the United States, actually misrepresented the mission's findings with the headline, "Team Recommends Nigerian Ceasefire, Recognition of Biafra."

[26] Wiseberg, "Christian Churches and the Nigerian Civil War."

In the minority areas of Biafra almost everyone chose not to leave, and thus many expatriate clergy—perhaps two hundred—soon found themselves in federally-held areas, where they remained for the duration of the conflict. Those in predominantly Ibo areas, such as the Nsukka/Enugu sectors, joined the march into the Ibo heartland. Historically, Iboland had been served primarily by one order: the Holy Ghost Fathers from Ireland. Not only were they the largest bloc of missionaries in Nigeria—three hundred men plus another eighty Irish Holy Rosary Sisters—but, unlike other religious orders, the Holy Ghost Fathers were all on one side of the battle line.

A third important response by the expatriate missionaries, especially the Holy Ghost Fathers in Biafra, was the reporting they provided the outside world on conditions and the issues at stake in the conflict. They wrote to fellow churchmen, newspapers, and to political leaders. The foreign editor of the *Catholic News Service*, which supplies 90 percent of American Catholic newspapers, recalls that the majority of their stories on the Nigerian civil war were supplied by missionaries, and that most of these were sympathetic to Biafra.[27] They were also the only expatriate witnesses inside Biafra, and therefore figured prominently in the stories that visiting correspondents filed with home offices in Europe and America. And as conditions deteriorated within Biafra, increasing numbers of Holy Ghost Fathers journeyed abroad to offer first-hand accounts of the suffering.[28]

Commenting on the international impact of these activities, a summary of the discussions during the Fifth Anglo-American Parliamentarians' Conference on Africa noted that "with the introduction of the Holy Ghost missionaries to the United States (in March 1968), touring the country, speaking before church, school and social groups, the constituency for Biafra relief increased a thousand fold. Ignoring political questions as much as possible, Catholic officials attempted to present the question as purely a humanitarian one, and presented the American public with the option of saving lives or being guilty of allowing genocide. Large numbers of people responded."[29]

[27] Rothmyer, "What Really Happened in Biafra?" p. 44, cited in Wiseberg, "Christian Churches and the Nigerian Civil War," p. 13.

[28] Interview: Abigail McCarthy. Mrs. McCarthy, whose husband was then challenging Lyndon Johnson for the Democratic presidential nomination, recalls her unwillingness to come out publicly in support of intervention to save Biafra because this might have detracted from the thrust of the senator's campaign. Only when approached by Irish missionaries who based their appeal on first-hand accounts of the deprivation in Biafra did she agree to devote time to addressing Biafran fund-raising rallies and to participate in teach-ins.

[29] "Nigerian-Biafran Lobbies in the United States," Fifth Anglo-American Parliamentarians' Conference on Africa, St. Croix Island, 20–24 March 1969, unpublished conference proceedings.

Personal appeals from Holy Ghost Fathers serving in Biafra carried special weight at the Vatican and doubtlessly influenced Pope Paul's decision to become the first world leader to send an official delegation to Biafra. But there were at least two other related factors contributing to this important February 1968 diplomatic breakthrough for the Ojukwu regime. The first was the pontiff's personal interest and experience in Nigeria. For thirty years, from 1923 to 1954, he had served in the Vatican State Department, and in the summer of 1962, as Cardinal Montini, he had visited Nigeria while making a tour of Africa. This was the first visit to sub-Sahara Africa by a European cardinal, and he was reportedly deeply moved by his reception from Nigeria's Catholic population.[30]

The second factor was historical. The Catholic Church enjoyed a wider following among the Ibos of Eastern Nigeria than anywhere else in Anglophone Africa, and evangelical interests doubtlessly influenced the extent of the church's involvement in helping Biafra. Catholic missions were not established in Nigeria until long after the Protestant sects had attracted a wide following along the West African coast. By the 1960s, only 2.4 million, or roughly 12 percent of Nigeria's 20 million Christians were Catholics, and approximately 68 percent of the Catholics resided in the eight dioceses of the Eastern Region.[31] Contrary to the popular impression in Europe and America during the height of the Nigerian war, only 1.6 million, or 13 percent, of the East's 12.4 million people had been counted as Catholics during the 1963 census, compared with nearly 8 million Protestants. The East may have been 77 percent Christian, but only 17 percent of those were Catholics, and 80 percent of the East's Catholic population could be found in the four predominantly Ibo dioceses of Owerri, Onitsha, Umuahia, and Enugu. In the long and sometimes ardent history of evangelical competition between Protestants and Catholics across southern Nigeria, Catholicism had made its greatest inroads in Iboland.

Pope Paul's initial public acknowledgment of concern over the plight of the Ibos was a thinly veiled reference in his October 31, 1967, "Message to Africa-Africae Terrarum." Without mentioning Nigeria by name, the pontiff declared, "What are We to say when violence reaches such proportions that it becomes almost equivalent to genocide and pits tribe against tribe within the borders of a single nation? And it has come to that."[32]

---

[30] Hatch, *Pope Paul VI: Apostle on the Move*, p. 114.

[31] Percentages based on figures published by the Catholic secretariat in Lagos in *Catholic Church in Nigeria*, 1968–1969, Special Centenary Issue.

[32] *L'Observatore Romano*, November 1, 1967, cited in Wiseberg, "Christian Churches and the Nigerian Civil War," p. 14.

In December 1967, the Vatican launched its first serious effort to mediate the Nigerian dispute when the pope dispatched two envoys, Monsignors Conway and Rochau, on a tour of Nigeria's three ecclesiastical provinces—Lagos, Kaduna, and Onitsha. Conway was rector of the Irish College in Rome, and had earlier served for five years as a missionary in Eastern Nigeria. Rochau represented the Vatican's relief agency, Caritas Internationalis. In deference to the federal government, the mission went first to Lagos, and upon arrival declared that their purpose was not political, religious, or diplomatic, but merely humanitarian, and that they wished only to arrange for the distribution of food and clothing for displaced persons.[33]

The monsignors were given a cool but proper reception in Lagos, including an audience with General Gowon, but the Nigerians made it plain that they considered the mission to be a private one and not related to civil war diplomacy. When the clerics asked Gowon if he would agree to a temporary cease-fire, thereby enabling them to visit the East with a view to opening indirect negotiations about a possible settlement, the Nigerian leader declined to issue a cease-fire order, and a public appeal from the pope for a Christmas truce did not cause him to change his decision.[34] Any visit to Biafra would have to be at the prelates' own risk.[35] The Commonwealth Secretariat had quietly but unsuccessfully tried to arrange talks between Nigerian and Biafran representatives in October and November, and Gowon had been prepared to cooperate with this initiative,[36] but not with the Vatican, which was already considered in Lagos to be pro-Biafran.

The papal delegation encountered difficulty in arranging transportation into Biafra because the federal government refused to give air clearance to private air-charter companies. To reinforce the Vatican's resolve, Biafra's bishops met and mandated Holy Ghost Father Anthony Byrne to fly to Rome and lobby for the visit. When news of the favorable decision reached Biafra, the bishops sent an immediate note of gratitude, noting that "the arrival of the Papal Mission will be a source of the greatest solace to our people . . . at a time when they felt abandoned by the whole world."[37]

The two monsignors flew into Biafra from Lisbon February 7, 1968, aboard one of the chartered gun-running cargo planes that serviced

[33] *West Africa*, No. 2640, January 6, 1968, p. 25.

[34] Nigeria, *Faith in Unity*, address by the head of the federal military government, December 25, 1967, pp. 86–93.

[35] *Morning Post*, January 6, 1968.   [36] See Ch. 6 below.

[37] Memorandum submitted to the pope on behalf of the archbishop and hierarchy of Onitsha Ecclesiastical Province by Bishops James Moynagh of Calabar and Godfrey Okoye of Port Harcourt, cited in Wiseberg, "The International Politics of Relief," p. 117.

Ojukwu's poorly equipped army. At last an official delegation from a foreign sovereign—the Holy See—had defied the blockade. As the Biafran Ministry of Information's overseas newsletter quickly noted, "By merely coming here they have done what some 'peace-seeking' organizations considered unsafe, risky, impossible and undiplomatic. . . . This visit of the Papal Envoys . . . has thrown the door wide open. Biafra is accessible."[38]

Biafra's reception contrasted sharply with the welcome the prelates had encountered in Kaduna and Lagos. Ojukwu announced a unilateral cease-fire for the duration of the visit, and there were enormous public demonstrations of thanksgiving. As the delegation later reported to the pope, "a tumultuous welcome awaited the envoys: roads lined with joyful people waving palm branches greeted them as they passed, sometimes for an unbroken distance of twenty miles . . . garments were strewn before them . . . churches were filled with over-flowing congregations . . . they crowded town-halls with representatives of the civil authorities . . . all sectors of the community hailed them."[39]

The public demonstrations were not without political overtones, and the mood of the people contrasted sharply with the appearance of "normalcy" that had so impressed members of the Conor Cruise O'Brien team four months earlier. To quote the report of the papal delegation, "On every occasion the deep conviction of the Ibo people that they are fighting for survival against a campaign of genocide manifested itself in forests of placards held aloft and poured forth in every address of welcome. It was the anguished cry of a caged people, denied the forum of world opinion, striving to express its plight to the conscience of the world, which for them the envoys represented."[40]

During their meeting with Ojukwu, the Biafran leader asked the monsignors to "please tell His Holiness that we of Biafra, without further consultations, without further discussions, are prepared at any time to accept a cease-fire and to go round the table to negotiate an honorable peace," a pledge that was simultaneously relayed to the world by Biafra's overseas press service.[41] The monsignors conveyed this message, adding that "the political issues can be solved by negotiation and only by negotiation. . . . If armed hostilities continue against all right reasons, the political issues will still have to be talked out unless violence is criminally allowed to reach the point where the whole of

[38] *Biafra Newsletter*, Vol. 1, No. 8, March 1, 1968.
[39] The Papal Mission of Peace and Relief to the Ecclesiastical Province of Onitsha, 7–12 February 1968, unpublished report, p. 5.
[40] *Ibid.*, pp. 7–8.
[41] Biafra Overseas Press Service, Gv 4, February 9, 1968.

Iboland is but one vast cemetery."[42] And as they completed their mission to Biafra, the papal delegation issued a communiqué that read in part, "We would hope and pray that not only the voice of Christian communities but the voices of those world powers who exercise influence on the African scene be raised on an issue of fundamental human rights to prevent the appalling danger of the general massacre of innocent civilians.[43]

Biafra at last had found a voice of authority on the international stage. The papal envoys were the first official delegation to breach the federal blockade, and they were followed five weeks later by a similar delegation from the World Council of Churches Secretariat in Geneva. Although the coalition of Protestant churches lack the Vatican's sovereign identity and are unable to act decisively or speak with one voice, they represent a huge transnational constitutency from whom Biafra also sought help.

There were only a handful of expatriate Protestant missionaries in Nigeria by 1967, and few of these served in pastoral capacities, especially in the East. The Protestant sects were much less paternalistic than the Catholic hierarchy, and they had not resisted the post-Independence pressures for indigenization. Nearly all the Protestant churches were run by local ministers, and over the years several successful public figures had served simultaneously as political and religious leaders.

The two most outstanding examples were Ibos. Sir Francis Ibiam, who served as governor of the Eastern Region and subsequently a personal adviser to Ojukwu, was the first African vice president of the World Council of Churches. Biafra's Chief Justice, Sir Louis Mbanefo, was another respected church elder who, at the time of the war, was also chairman of the Anglican province of West Africa. While Mbanefo traveled abroad on Ojukwu's behalf, and frequently met with Anglican church leaders, his role was primarily diplomatic. The more important lobbying of Protestant groups was carried out by Francis Ibiam.

The Central Committee of the World Council of Churches first signaled its concern over the Nigerian crisis when, in August 1967, it adopted a resolution expressing "sympathy with member churches throughout all the territories," and specifically sent "greetings and an assurance of prayers" to Ibiam.[44] As the situation in Biafra deteriorated toward the end of the year, Ibiam and Ojukwu discussed the need to make a direct appeal to the members of the World Council, and decided that Ibiam would travel to Geneva, Germany, Sweden, Norway, Britain,

[42] The Papal Mission of Peace, p. 10.　[43] *Ibid.*, p. 12.
[44] Report of the Central Committee of the World Council of Churches, Meeting Held in Crete, August 1967, cited in Wiseberg, "The International Politics of Relief," p. 120.

the United States, and Canada. He left in January 1968 for several weeks, and has described the gist of his messages as encompassing the following mix of religion and politics:

"Look, I am here to tell you Biafra's side of the story. The Nigerian side has already been represented by the BBC, the OAU and the United Nations who backed Nigeria without knowing why. Regardless of other considerations, the killing must be stopped." Then I told them in response to the question "what can we do?": "1. influence governments to stop the war and tell Britain and the BBC to stop lying; 2. seek political recognition for Biafra; 3. tell the United Nations to move; 4. ask the OAU what are they doing; and 5. send medicine, food, and clothing through the blockade. If the church can help, we will survive."[45]

Help did not come as quickly as Ibiam and Ojukwu would have liked, but on March 22, 1968, the World Council of Churches sent a two-man delegation composed of Reverend B. T. Molander and Geoffrey Murray to meet for a week with representatives of the "Christian Council in Biafra." The World Council, which was much more sensitive to Nigerian and OAU opinion than the Vatican, considered the visit to be strictly ecclesiastical, and Molander and Murray later expressed surprise over being received as "official guests of the [Biafran] government."[46] Ojukwu, of course, made every attempt to amplify the political significance of the trip.

Throughout their tour of the enclave, the two churchmen were accompanied by a "conducting officer" from the Ministry of Information, although as they later reported, they had succeeded in persuading the ministry official to alter his preplanned itinerary to enable them to spend more time in renewing pastoral relations with Biafran churches and less with civil authorities. Nevertheless, they later informed the World Council Secretariat in a confidential memorandum that they had been "embarrassed by the amount of press publicity that attended our visit" and reported being "dragooned" into a television interview upon their arrival, which generated a spate of press reports "distorted beyond recognition."[47]

On the eve of their departure they were invited to Ojukwu's new

---

[45] Interview: Sir Francis Ibiam. Sir Francis renounced his royal honors in protest over Britain's support for the federal government.

[46] Report of the Reverend B. T. Molander and Mr. Geoffrey Murray as a Delegation from the World Council of Churches to the Christian Council in Biafra, March 22–29, 1968, unpublished report [cited hereafter as Molander and Murray], p. 2.

[47] Ibid., p. 7.

headquarters, the former premier's lodge in Umuahia.[48] In such encounters with foreign representatives, Ojukwu's personal qualities appear to have been a factor in inspiring confidence in Biafra. Without exaggerating the importance of Ojukwu's charisma and his personal rapport with Europeans, the following excerpt from the Molander/Murray report is suggestive: "We found the Chief of State to be completely relaxed and showing no signs of strain or worry. He seemed to have no doubt about the ultimate outcome of the war. We were convinced of his innate sincerity, his mental capacity, vision, and concern for his people, and believe that he has immense potentiality as an African leader."[49] When the churchmen asked Ojukwu to enumerate Biafra's most urgent needs, they reported that he "replied frankly that absolute top priority was for arms and ammunition and all other shipments including humanitarian relief must give way to those."

The separate reports by the Catholic and Protestant delegations agreed on two points: the Biafrans were prepared to die fighting, and conditions among the civilian refugees were serious and likely to become much worse. How serious was a matter of conjecture. The papal envoys estimated that the number of refugees was approaching four million, while the Protestant delegation put the figure closer to two hundred thousand. Whatever the total, huge numbers of people were indisputably ill-clothed and lacking in adequate medical supplies, and there were growing signs of widespread malnutrition—especially protein deficiency among the children. A need for external humanitarian relief was perceived, but no one suggested that this would have to be of the enormous magnitude that began in earnest five months later with the rapid expansion of the Jointchurchaid Biafran airlift in August-September 1968. The most immediate concern of the church leaders was to promote an end to the fighting.

On March 20, 1968, the Vatican and the World Council of Churches issued a joint appeal to the federal and Biafran governments and to the entire international community. The religious appeal was a milestone in Biafra's quest for international attention and eventual recognition, and it addressed Ojukwu's most urgent military concerns:

The Roman Catholic Church and the WCC unite in one voice in a most urgent appeal to both contesting parties for an immediate ces-

[48] *Ibid.*, p. 4. Further indication of the political significance that the Biafrans ascribed to the visit was the presence of French cameramen who filmed the delegation's formal introduction to Ojukwu for the American public relations firm, Robert S. Goldstein Enterprises, which the Biafrans had contracted to produce a documentary on the war.

[49] *Ibid.*

sation of armed hostilities. . . . We appeal in particular to the African Chiefs of State to offer the contribution of their counsel, their suggestions and, should the case arise, their mediation . . . we . . . urge governments and international agencies in a position to act effectively in this matter to secure a denial of external military assistance to both parties, an immediate cessation of hostilities, the necessary assurances of security to both sides on the laying down of arms, and a negotiated peace.[50]

Biafra's public reaction to the appeal was prompt and positive. When the World Council of Churches delegation formally delivered the message to Ojukwu he immediately pledged his full cooperation, declaring that the churches and Biafra were in near perfect agreement. But when Molander and Murray met privately with the Biafran leader and asked him about a suitable venue for peace talks, he ruled out any country that had taken a stand in the conflict, adding that Biafra was willing to help the Nigerian government in economic matters but no negotiations at all were possible unless his country's independence were recognized.[51]

A week later, on March 31, 1968, General Gowon issued his public reply to the churches and stated, in part, that "the difficulty in a ceasefire without any agreement by the secessionist leaders to retract and to remain part of Nigeria, is that Ojukwu and his foreign backers will certainly use the ceasefire pause to re-arm and prepare for a bloodier conflict in which more innocent lives will be lost. Is that what the Christian world wants for Nigeria?"[52]

The international debate over the possibility of a negotiated settlement of the Nigerian civil war had suddenly come alive and would become more intense as the fighting continued. Articles in the European and American press proliferated in March and April and reflected a growing concern for the fate of the Ibo people. Within the Biafran government, the role of the churches in crystalizing world attention was seen as vital.

Excerpts from two confidential reports prepared by the Propaganda Analysis Committee in March 1968 are indicative; first:

The pronouncements of Monsignor Conway were extremely important, stressing the urgent need for negotiations . . . we should remember that the Pope wields important moral force in the world.

[50] Statement issued simultaneously in Geneva and Rome, March 20, 1968, reprinted in Kirk-Greene, *Crisis and Conflict*, II, 201.

[51] Molander and Murray, p. 4.

[52] Nigeria, *Faith in Unity*, address by the head of the federal military government, March 31, 1968, p. 97.

. . . If through the many contacts that the Papacy has in influential world capitals . . . our case is brought to the notice of those who can help to end the conflict with the recognition of our independence, that would be good.[53]

And from another paper:

The various pronouncements of the Church clearly indicate great psychological satisfaction for Biafrans. . . . It shows that if our cause were put on the altar of public morality we would be vindicated. Our cause has acquired new legitimacy. . . . The Church has no army to enforce a truce but it can achieve much if it sent its emissaries to the world's capitals. . . . It is doubtful for example that Britain can face hostile Christian masses demanding an immediate halt in arms to Lagos.[54]

DIPLOMATIC RECOGNITION

Biafra's campaign to mobilize foreign support for an unconditional cease-fire and a reduction in arms sales to the federal government went beyond the publicized warnings of genocide and the private appeals to church leaders to lobby in their home capitals. It also encompassed a new quest for diplomatic recognition, which, to the dismay of Nigeria and her allies, succeeded in disrupting African solidarity. Between April 15 and May 20, 1968, four members of the OAU—Tanzania, Gabon, Ivory Coast, and Zambia—recognized Biafra as a sovereign state.

Although international law does not provide machinery for ruling on the question of recognition, a new state traditionally comes into existence when "a community acquires, with a reasonable probability of permanence, the essential characteristics of a state, namely an organized government, a defined territory, and such a degree of independence of control by any other state as to be capable of conducting its own international relations."[55] By any reasonable appraisal, the blockaded and shrinking Biafran enclave could not be considered a state in international law.[56] But in this case, diplomatic recognition was

[53] Republic of Biafra, "The Biafra-Nigeria War: Peace Plans and Moves," Propaganda Analysis Committee, Research Bureau of the Biafra Propaganda Directorate, March 15, 1968, unpublished policy background paper, p. 4.

[54] Republic of Biafra, "The Nigeria-Biafra Conflict and the Psychological Force of the Church's Intervention," Propaganda Analysis Committee, Research Bureau of the Biafra Propaganda Directorate, March 15, 1968, unpublished policy background paper, pp. 14–15.

[55] Brierly, *The Law of Nations*, p. 137.

[56] Ijalaye, "Was 'Biafra' at Any Time a State in International Law?" pp. 551–559.

neither sought nor given on the basis of Biafra's presumed viability then, or in the foreseeable future.

The recognition of Biafra did not result in the establishment of normal diplomatic relations, and no embassies were ever opened in the secessionist enclave. Instead, the four recognitions were directed against the federal government's policy of military repression, in the hope that this would weaken Nigeria's resolve to prosecute the war and inspire greater international support for an immediate cease-fire. As an act of intervention, however, recognition is more restrictive than other sanctions because it cannot be regulated according to the level of response by the other side. Since this form of diplomatic protest is so extreme, the timing and defense of the four recognitions appear to have been well coordinated so as to have maximum impact. Recognition was portrayed by those responsible as an act of last resort, in light of the dire human conditions inside Biafra, and as a means of pushing Nigeria into direct negotiations with Ojukwu's government.

The policy reviews underway in those African governments that were inclining toward recognition of Biafra must be seen against the background of military developments in Nigeria that were brought into sharp focus by the federal government's failure to win the war by March 31, 1968. That date had acquired symbolic importance internationally because it had been given as a target date for total victory by the federal army in General Gowon's New Year's address to the Nigerian people three months earlier.[57] Gowon's timetable was keyed to the start of the federal government's fiscal year, which, on April 1, 1968, also entailed the institutionalization of Nigeria's new twelve-state administrative structure. By calling for an end to the war by that date, Gowon was signaling to the nation his determination to see the new federal system put into full operation. The Biafrans, however, interpreted the call as a promise of victory and, when April 1 passed with no abatement in hostilities, Ojukwu again claimed that a stalemate had been achieved, and appealed for intervention to bring about a cease-fire.[58]

Gowon's exhortation to his field commanders to bring down the rebellion by March 31 was not as rash as it appears in retrospect. During February and March, it seemed that the federal army's 1968 spring offensive might prove decisive. The Biafrans were forced to yield important ground on three fronts: Abakaliki Province, one of the major food-producing areas of Biafra immediately north of the Ibo

[57] *Morning Post*, January 2, 1968. In a special broadcast to his field commanders and the chairman of the Northern States Interim Administration, Gowon declared, "I am resolved this crisis won't continue for long. Let's all put our shoulders to the wheel and end it by 31 March 1968."

[58] Ojukwu, *Biafra*, "Gowon's March 31 Deadline," An address by the head of the Republic of Biafra broadcast March 31, 1968, I, 246–251.

heartland; the entire Southeastern State—some 13,000 square miles —including the strategically important riverine coast from Calabar to Opobo; and Biafra's largest commercial center, Onitsha, on the east bank of the Niger. The most dramatic breakthrough was the overland capture of Onitsha after several costly attempts to attack across the Niger River, and had the federal Second Division shown more dash it could have pushed southward into the traditional Ibo heartland, thereby ending the war.

Biafran military leaders concede that the Second Division nearly forced them to surrender in March 1968, but they were able to forestall the military onslaught by cutting the Nigerian supply line from Awka to Onitsha in one brief—almost miraculous—fire fight. On March 25, 1968, a handful of Biafran commandos ambushed a Nigerian supply column of approximately a hundred vehicles that were en route to Onitsha, and with one of their few remaining mortars struck a gasoline truck that was so negligently close to ammunition and other fuel carriers that the chain reaction quickly destroyed the entire convoy.[59] Because of the enormous logistical difficulties in resupplying front-line federal troops, the interdiction removed any immediate threat to the Ibo heartland, and ensured that Gowon's much-publicized goal of victory by March 31, 1968, would not be met.

Although Biafra had been reduced to a land-locked, overcrowded, and frightfully impoverished area of seven to ten thousand square miles, the passing of April 1 added new credibility to Ojukwu's claim that a stalemate had been reached. Biafra still controlled Port Harcourt, the center of Nigeria's petroleum industry, although the town and the surrounding oil-rich Rivers State were coming under increased military pressure from Nigeria's Third Marine Division. If the federal advance could be halted until the onset of the summer rains, Biafra would have several months of relative security and the opportunity to mobilize greater international political and material support.

Ojukwu and his foreign affairs advisers knew that as long as the Organization of African Unity continued without open dissent to support the federal government's reunification policies, intervention by European and American powers to force an unconditional cease-fire was unlikely. Opinion in Biafra differed over whether the 1967 Kinshasa Resolution by the OAU accurately reflected the views of member governments, or were more a result of big-power machinations. It was generally agreed, however, that the unanimous OAU support for the federal government served at least three major political functions that were

[59] Interviews: Generals Philip Effiong, Alex Madiebo, Mike Okwechime. Also reported in *Biafra Newsletter*, Vol. 1, No. 10, March 29, 1968. After the war had ended the remains of this encounter were still visible along the Awka-Onitsha road.

seriously detrimental to Biafran interests: it strengthened the resolve of the non-African powers who otherwise wished to identify with Nigeria; it allowed those who did not want to become more directly involved with arranging a cease-fire to plead that this was a matter for the OAU; and it inhibited those who were tempted to aid the secession.

In Britain, the OAU's pro-Nigerian unanimity helped to legitimatize the Labour government's policy of increased arms sales to Lagos, and insulated Harold Wilson from growing criticism from within his own party. African unity had been a popular symbol among British socialists, and the prime minister hoped that African solidarity against Biafra would restrain the mounting antiwar sentiment among British liberals. Wilson did not expect his profederal policies to be challenged by a Conservative opposition that was committed to the need to offset the Soviet presence in Lagos, and was anxious about the future of British investments in Nigeria.

Similar forces were at work in the United States, where the Johnson administration was deeply embroiled in Vietnam and clearly wanted to avoid any entanglements in Africa. Biafran officials were confident that Washington would continue to refuse to assist the Nigerian war effort, but they now wanted to co-opt enough of the Vietnam peace movement to bring Washington into a more active role in arranging a cease-fire in Nigeria. According to officials in the Biafran Ministry of Foreign Affairs, in all indirect and informal contacts, State Department officials referred them to the OAU. African diplomatic recognition therefore came to be viewed in Biafra as the only way to shatter this case for noninvolvement.

Finally, and perhaps most importantly, the Biafrans sought African recognition as a way of encouraging French intervention. As noted earlier, the initial reaction in Paris to Biafran secession was to adopt a "wait and see" attitude, and to refuse to sell military equipment to either side. By early 1968, the central message reaching Ojukwu and his advisers through numerous informal contacts in Paris was one of sympathetic concern that nevertheless made plain that de Gaulle was unwilling to become more directly involved until there was a greater display of pro-Biafran sentiment among francophone African leaders. So far, the only public expressions by government spokesmen in French-speaking Africa had been in support of Nigerian unity. The most notable of these had come from de Gaulle's close friend, President Hamani Diori of Niger, the current chairman of OCAM and a member of the OAU Consultative Committee on Nigeria. Limited French assistance to Biafra, which finally arrived in the closing months of 1968, will be discussed in Chapter 8. It should be noted, however, that this assistance was carefully managed by de Gaulle and his successor so that other long-standing French interests in Africa would not be unnecessarily affected by the intervention. The crucial link between African opinion and greater French involvement was not overlooked by the Research Department of the Biafran Propaganda Directorate, although the emphasis in this instance was optimistic: "It does not seem too much to expect that France can be persuaded by those French-speaking African states already sympathetic to our cause to come out in open support of our struggle. . . . Patient and friendly negotiations between these countries and Biafra should facilitate France's effort to intervene."[60]

As Biafran leaders surveyed the African region in January 1968 for possible diplomatic support, five governments appeared most receptive: Senegal, Ivory Coast, Tanzania, Zambia, and Uganda. It was a curious mix of political and economic systems, colonial backgrounds, and ideological outlooks. None of these small states possessed the capacity to intervene militarily to assist the Biafran war effort, but they did possess the power to break the diplomatic quarantine of Biafra and to make support for the secession more acceptable to other members of the international community. Each of these governments had previously indicated its acceptance of the Biafran premise that the latter's differences with Nigeria could not be settled by military means. With similar sentiments on the rise in Europe and America, Ojukwu's advisers believed that a diverse cluster of African diplomatic recognitions would serve as the necessary political catalyst for greater non-African intervention.

At the pinnacle of this diplomatic offensive Ojukwu placed former Nigerian president Dr. Nnamdi Azikiwe, who in March 1968 was sent to meet with five African heads of state during visits to Dakar, Abidjan, Dar es Salaam, Lusaka, and Kampala. He concluded his tour with a stop in Paris for discussions with senior French officials.[61] Azikiwe was Biafra's biggest international celebrity, and as one of Africa's best-known and earliest nationalist leaders, he was granted direct access to African heads of state, several of whom had been personal friends for more than twenty years. When secession erupted he had remained in the background, and toward the end of 1967 there was press speculation that he was about to defect to the federal side or might succeed Ojukwu in order to preside over a peaceful surrender.[62] Foreign perceptions of the importance of Azikiwe's allegiance may have been exag-

---

[60] Republic of Biafra, "Biafra's Case and France," Propaganda Analysis Committee, Research Bureau of Biafra Propaganda Directorate, unpublished briefing paper prepared for the head of state (Umuahia, June 1968), p. 2.

[61] *Le Figaro*, April 11, 1975.

[62] *Christian Science Monitor*, October 14, 1967.

gerated, but in the case of Tanzania, President Nyerere informed Ojukwu that a visit from the former Nigerian president was a precondition for a final decision on the recognition issue.[63]

Dr. Azikiwe's approach to lobbying for African support was highly personal and informal. A lengthy document from Ojukwu setting forth the arguments for diplomatic recognition was delivered to all five governments. The essential argument of the appeal appears in the introduction:

> Nigeria has succeeded in prolonging the war and in bringing great suffering and hardship to Africa chiefly because the support which Biafra has received so far has fallen short of *Diplomatic Recognition*. Such concrete action is necessary if Nigeria's war of extermination is to be brought to an immediate end. Biafrans appeal to your country and to those other countries in Africa, which believe that it is morally wrong for one group of people to seek to wipe out another entirely from the face of the earth, to come forward in the interest of humanity and accord recognition to the Republic of Biafra.[64]

Recognition was not being sought in return for any promise of political, strategic, or economic gains, but for the "enthronement of morality in human, in intra-national and inter-African relations." The more immediate objective, however, appears in the final sentence of the aide-mémoire: "The recognition of Biafra will be a salutory influence which may persuade Nigeria to go to the conference table."[65]

The decision to send Azikiwe on this carefully scheduled search for African recognition was based on an assessment of new diplomatic opportunities that several of Ojukwu's less prominent envoys had skillfully nurtured over many months.

As noted in Chapter 4, the first indications of an official willingness to deal openly and sympathetically with Biafra appeared in East Africa. Tanzania's President Julius Nyerere permitted Austin Okwu to open a Biafran information office. For nearly a year the charming and energetic Okwu was Ojukwu's only resident representative in Africa, and he concentrated on building political support for Biafra within the closely linked Tanzanian and Zambian foreign affairs establishments.[66]

Unlike President Kenyatta in Kenya and President Obote in Uganda,

[63] Interview: Ojukwu.

[64] Republic of Biafra, "The Recognition of Biafra," an aide-mémoire prepared by the Office of the Head of State and Commander in Chief of the Armed Forces, March 25, 1968, p. 1.

[65] *Ibid.*, p. 10.

[66] Anglin, "Zambia and the Recognition of Biafra," and Butler, "Tanzania's Decision to Recognize Biafra."

Nyerere and Kaunda did not at that time confront large ethnically based dissident groups who might have been inspired by a Biafran success. Although as members of the OAU each was committed in principle to respect the territorial integrity of member states, Tanzania had split earlier with Nigeria and most other African governments over secession in the Congo.[67] First, Nyerere's stand against Tshombe's insurrection in Katanga had been more outspoken than Nigeria's, and then, to the latter's dismay, he had strongly endorsed the 1964 attempt by Lumumba's followers to set up an independent regime in Stanleyville. Nyerere's view then and in 1968—which was shared by Kaunda—held that each secession had to be judged on its merits and not according to abstract principles.

The drive toward recognition of Biafra was further preconditioned by the news of anti-Ibo pogroms in Nigeria and the sequence of military coups that seemed to confirm Nyerere's and Kaunda's deep suspicions about the viability and justice inherent in any federation that was a creation of imperial Britain. When the two East African leaders made their assessments of conditions in Nigeria, they did not have the benefit of field reports through their own intelligence organizations. Instead, they had to rely on whatever information might be passed along by diplomats from the major powers, contacts with Nigerian and Biafran representatives, and the clippings from Western newspapers that were accumulating in the press files of their foreign ministries. Few tangible relations exist across Africa, and the only East African resident mission in Lagos in 1966/1967 was the Zambian High Commission, with a staff of three. Kaunda in 1962 and Nyerere in 1965 had visited Nigeria in connection with Rhodesian developments, and both reportedly came away disturbed by the high level of internal discord, the complaints of rampant corruption, and the apparent degree of British influence over a Northern-led federal government. That Britain and the Russians now supported the Nigerian war effort could have only helped Biafra's cause in Dar es Salaam and Lusaka.

Nigeria was not unaware of the Biafran inroads in East Africa, as Kaunda and Nyerere had actively sought to play a mediatory role in the crisis before war erupted in July 1967. Relations deteriorated when Zambia held an East African summit only two days after Lagos had turned back Kaunda's call for restraint and commenced military action against Biafra. Kaunda's efforts to mediate were further thwarted by Chief Awolowo's sharp rebuffs during the OAU summit in Kinshasa, although Nigerian, Biafran, and East African diplomats later agreed that Awolowo's acceptance of the OAU Consultative Committee fore-

[67] Singleton, "Conflict Resolution in Africa: the Congo and Rules of the Game."

stalled Zambian and Tanzanian recognition of Biafra in late 1967. But aside from this, the federal Ministry of External Affairs did little to counter the Biafran diplomatic offensive in East Africa.[68]

As Nyerere's impatience intensified over the escalating violence and the ineffectiveness of the OAU Consultative Committee, he began to consult with other African leaders. In February 1968 the Tanzanian president paid his first state visit to Ivory Coast and, although Nyerere and Ivorian president Felix Houphouet-Boigny had been at opposite ends of the African political spectrum for years, they agreed about Biafra, albeit for somewhat different reasons. Their final communiqué did not refer explicitly to the Nigerian conflict,[69] but a few weeks later, Houphouet-Boigny issued his first strong public statement on the war, which he described as a "murderous and genocidal struggle."[70]

Houphouet-Boigny had hitherto been less critical publicly of Nigeria's military policies than either Nyerere or Kaunda, but the Biafrans for months had regarded Ivorian recognition as a primary diplomatic objective because of Houphouet-Boigny's close relationship with de Gaulle, and because they believed that Biafran independence would appeal to Abidjan's political and economic interests in West Africa.

Among African leaders, Houphouet-Boigny remained very unimpressed with the concept and practice of the Organization of African Unity, and he usually did not attend the annual summits. He was also known to be deeply suspicious of "unnatural" federal arrangements—especially those that threatened his interests—and he had played a decisive role in sabotaging the Senegal-based French West African Federation as well as subsequent attempts to establish the post-Independence Mali Federation.[71] The Biafrans assumed that Houphouet-Boigny would want his thesis about the inviability of large federations reconfirmed in Nigeria, if only because of a possible long-term threat to Ivorian markets and political influence in francophone West Africa. Even if Biafra failed to achieve total independence, a confederal or

[68] While the Biafrans sent several senior delegations to Tanzania and Zambia, including two led by the former Eastern Nigerian premier, Dr. Michael Okpara, the Nigerians failed to send anyone following Chief Enahoro's meeting with President Nyerere in Tanzania in October 1967. Following Tanzania's recognition, a delegation was sent to East Africa, but did not reach Lusaka until May 20, 1968, a few hours after Zambia also had recognized Biafra. The delegation, which arrived from Nairobi, was led by Chief H. O. Davies, an old politician who had served briefly as a junior minister in the last civilian government, and who was chosen for the East African visit primarily because of his personal links to Kenya's President Jomo Kenyatta, whom he had once served as legal counsel during the 1953 Mau Mau trials.

[69] The full text of the final communiqué appears in *Fraternité Matin*, February 27, 1968.

[70] Baker, "The Role of the Ivory Coast in the Nigeria-Biafra War."

[71] See Zolberg, *One Party Government in the Ivory Coast*, Ch. VII.

similar compromise that ensured a continuation of two autonomous and mutually suspicious power centers in Nigeria could benefit the Ivory Coast and, for this reason, the Biafrans hoped they could persuade Houphouet-Boigny to exert a maximum diplomatic effort on behalf of a cease-fire. The Biafrans also appealed to Houphouet-Boigny's deep belief in Roman Catholicism, his abhorence of violence,[72] his staunch anti-communism,[73] and the traditional fear among coastal West African leaders of greater Moslem domination from the northern hinterland.

The Biafrans considered Ivorian support to be critical because of Houphouet-Boigny's personal stature, and not because his agricultural country of 4.5 million people, with total armed forces of only 4,500 men, possessed the means to intervene materially. If any African leader could persuade de Gaulle to take Biafra seriously, it would be Houphouet-Boigny, whose prominence in French politics extended back to his first election to the French Constituent Assembly in 1945. He later served as a full cabinet minister in several French governments, until resigning in 1958 to become prime minister and later president of the Ivory Coast. He had remained closely tied to France, where he retained a wide popular following that was reinforced by the reports of his humane rule conveyed by the international press and the more than 40,000 French residents in the Ivory Coast.

Houphouet-Boigny is above all a cautious leader, and he declined to rush to Biafra's aid. Professor Kenneth Dike, one of Ojukwu's most distinguished emissaries, met with the Ivorian president at the latter's summer villa in Switzerland in July 1967 and was very warmly received. But Houphouet-Boigny declined to issue a condemnation of the war until March 27, 1968, when he was en route to a meeting with de Gaulle in Paris.[74] During the ensuing six weeks he shuttled between the French capital and his Swiss villa, listening to French opinions, conferring with other francophone African leaders, entertaining Biafran representatives, and exposing himself to the increasingly grim European press and television reports of the suffering inside Biafra. Because of the difficulty in gathering official intelligence on conditions in the secessionist enclave, the first-hand accounts by European journalists no doubt played an important part in shaping the justification for Ivory Coast's eventual intervention.

Under these conditions, and against the background of military

---

[72] Although Houphouet-Boigny ruled his country as a dictator, he had a reputation for benevolence. No one had been executed for criminal or political offenses, and in 1966 he released 96 of the 106 persons arrested in a 1963 attempted coup and assassination plot.

[73] In 1969, for example, he summarily broke relations with the Russians by expelling the Soviet mission for allegedly fomenting student riots.

[74] Interview: Kenneth Dike.

developments in Nigeria, Houphouet-Boigny finally indicated to the Biafrans that he was prepared to extend diplomatic recognition, but he stipulated that the Ivory Coast should not be the first state to do so. Because of his close association with de Gaulle, he conveyed to the Biafrans that the first act of recognition should come from a nonaligned anglophone state so as to minimize the risk that his decision would be denigrated by Nigeria and her allies as a new form of neocolonial interference. The focus of Biafran diplomacy therefore shifted back to Dar es Salaam, where President Nyerere also had been following reports of the military standoff and mounting human deprivation among the Ibo people, and had concluded that recognition was necessary to call attention to this situation. On April 13, 1968, his government formally recognized "the State of Biafra as an independent sovereign entity and as a member of the community of nations."[75]

Julius Nyerere, whose personal integrity and independent brand of African socialism were widely admired in Europe and America, provided the keynote for the break in African ranks over Nigeria. In a carefully written article for the *Observer* (London), Nyerere explained his action in the following terms:

> Leaders of Tanzania have probably talked more about the need for African Unity than those of any other country. . . . Unity can only be based on the general consent of the people involved. . . . For ten months we have accepted the federal government's legal right to our support in a "police action to defend the integrity of the State." . . . We watched the federal government reject the advice of Africa to talk instead of demanding surrender before talks could begin. . . . It seemed to us that by refusing to recognize the existence of Biafra we were tacitly supporting a war against the people of Eastern Nigeria. . . . We could not continue doing this any longer.[76]

Houphouet-Boigny was still in Paris as the news of Tanzania's decision reached Europe. For the next four weeks he would skillfully amplify Nyerere's case without committing himself. Before the Ivory Coast took the ultimate step of recognition, he wanted to be certain that the world was listening and prepared to accord his action the full significance that he felt it deserved. The day following Nyerere's announcement, the Ivorian was asked by reporters for his reaction, but again declined to state his government's intentions. In response to a question concerning the compatability of recognizing Biafra within the terms of the OAU charter, he did manage to signal his agreement with Nyerere: "What we desire is peace and that is the goal that will guide

[75] Republic of Tanzania, *Statement on the Recognition of Biafra*.
[76] *Observer*, April 28, 1968, "Why We Recognized Biafra," by Julius Nyerere.

my decision. The problem of Biafra is a human rather than a political one."[77] A week later Houphouet-Boigny issued a statement explicitly praising Nyerere's action, but reiterating that there would be no decision until he had had an opportunity to consult fully with his people.[78] Through this procedure he presumably hoped to demonstrate his independence from France, while emphasizing that African support for Nigeria was crumbling.

International interest in Houphouet-Boigny's intentions rose in early May, when his close friend and admirer, President Albert Bongo of Gabon, suddenly recognized Biafra. Gabon's concern over the Nigerian conflict had not been indicated previously, and the Biafrans had not paid much attention to the attitude of this coastal ministate that borders on the eastern side of Cameroon. Prior to the OAU summit in Kinshasa, the Nigerian government had included Gabon in a list of those states that had sent enthusiastic pledges of support and who did not want to see the OAU become involved in Nigeria's domestic affairs.[79] And when Bongo was asked by French reporters in Paris for his reaction to Tanzania's recognition of Biafra, he again declared that the conflict "was purely a Nigerian affair."[80] Intense discussions with Houphouet-Boigny in the days that followed evidently changed his mind.

Houphouet-Boigny's personal prestige among Gabon's political elite was enormous. His speeches were reproduced verbatim in the official party newspaper, *Union Gabonaise*, and were frequently posted on billboards for public enlightenment. Suzanne Cronje's description of the Ivorian leader as a "sort of super-president of Gabon" seems no exaggeration.[81] Furthermore, the thirty-two-year-old Bongo was free to follow the doyen's advice on Biafra because, unlike other conservative leaders of former French colonies, he was not seriously constrained by domestic interethnic pressures or economic dependence on Nigeria. Aside from a brief military coup in 1964, which Bongo's predecessor aborted with the help of French paratroopers, tiny Gabon, with a population of 450,000, had remained politically stable while boasting one of the highest per capita income levels in Africa, due to the country's rich deposits of uranium, iron and manganese ore, oil, and natural gas.[82] The desire to protect these revenues had caused Gabon to pull out of the old federation of French Equatorial Africa, just as Houphouet-Boigny had sabotaged the federation of French West Africa.

[77] *Fraternité Matin*, April 16, 1968.   [78] *Ibid.*, April 22, 1968.
[79] BBC ME/2558/ii, August 31, 1967. Cited in Cronje, *The World and Nigeria*, p. 289.
[80] BBC ME/2748/ii, April 18, 1968. Cited *ibid.*, p. 300.
[81] *Ibid.*
[82] For historical background, see Weinstein, *Gabon, Nation-Building on the Ogooue.*

And when Bongo announced his recognition of Biafra on May 8, 1968, he too explained this action as humanitarian, based on his lack of confidence in the viability and justice of post-colonial African federation.[83]

The day after Gabon's action, Houphouet-Boigny summoned reporters to what one observer described as possibly the most crowded and emotional press conference ever held by an African leader in Paris.[84] He began by noting that this was only his second Paris press conference since his departure from the French cabinet in 1959. The first had been given during an official visit to France and the second, he said, was justified by the "inexplicable and culpable indifference of the whole world about the massacres which have been taking place in Biafra for more than ten months."[85] Speculation about Ivorian recognition had spurred public interest, but his first concern seems to have been to destroy the credibility of the Organization of African Unity's role in the Nigerian conflict, and arouse public opinion in Europe and America against those governments that thus far had protected their profederal policies by referring critics to the resolution unanimously adopted by the OAU summit in Kinshasa.

The political significance in Europe of the Ivorian statement was due partially to the fact that it was delivered by a non-Biafran African and dealt with issues that many liberals may have been reluctant to raise for fear of appearing anti-African or at least patronizing:

> What is it that justifies our culpable, I would even say criminal, indifference in the face of the massacres of our brothers. . . . An internal problem, respect for the territorial integrity of every member of the OAU, the sacrosanct respect of unity. . . . Nothing of the sort excuses our apathy in the face of the kind of crimes perpetrated by black brothers against other black brothers. . . . We have all inherited from our ancient masters not nations but states—states that have within them extremely fragile links between different ethnic groups. . . . Unity should not be imposed by force. Unity is for the living and not for the dead.[86]

At a time when the Vietnam antiwar movement had aroused storms of protest throughout the United States and Europe, Houphouet-Boigny alleged that the war in Nigeria was a far greater horror, and that more people had died in Biafra over the past ten months than in all of Vietnam during the previous three years.

[83] For a full text of the recognition statement, see *Fraternité Matin*, May 9, 1968.

[84] *West Africa*, No. 2659, May 18, 1968, p. 571.

[85] *Fraternité Matin*, May 10, 1968. Full text also reprinted in English in *African Scholar*, I, No. 1 (August-November 1968), 10–13.

[86] *Ibid.*

Houphouet-Boigny's statement was the most dramatic manifestation of Biafra's emergence as a major international issue. It was a catalyst for public opinion and provided a new secular legitimacy for the church-led campaign on behalf of humanitarian intervention. More than any other leader, Houphouet-Boigny symbolized the cultural, political, and economic ties between Europe and Africa and, because of this, his appeal enjoyed unique credibility in Europe, thereby further undermining the Nigerian argument that the war was an African matter to be managed and settled by Africans.

The Ivorian leader returned to Abidjan on May 13, and the following day the National Council of his country's only political party, met for three hours and "by acclamation" issued a mandate for recognition. The formal announcement, a brief four-line declaration published the next morning, was somewhat anticlimactic.[87] In fact, the main thrust of the Ivorian's international protest already had been made in Paris, and the question now was whether the international momentum in Biafra's favor would continue to build until the federal government agreed to a cease-fire and peace talks aimed at reaching a political settlement.

A week later, on May 20, 1968, Zambia became the fourth and last African state to recognize Biafra. Zambia's defense of this intervention echoed the lengthier statement by Tanzania.[88] The decision to recognize actually had been agreed to in principle when Kaunda and Nyerere had met on April 4, but no dates for the announcements had been set.[89] The two leaders had planned that Tanzania would act first, and that Zambia would not follow until at least one West African state recognized Ojukwu's regime. It was also determined that the timing of Zambia's announcement would be keyed to the prospect of peace talks, for it was hoped the additional recognition would strengthen Ojukwu's bargaining hand and encourage Lagos to make concessions. Formal recognition by Kaunda's government was, in fact, granted just three days before the opening of the Commonwealth-sponsored meeting between Biafran and Nigerian representatives in Kampala, Uganda.

The four recognitions during April and May 1968 were a major breakthrough in internationalizing the civil war. After a year of isolation, Biafra finally enjoyed open diplomatic support and credentials. The recognitions split the solidarity of the OAU, thus easing the way for greater non-African involvement. Taken together, the cluster of recognitions carried important credibility among a wider international com-

[87] *Fraternité Matin*, May 15, 1968. Text of statement plus a lengthy account of the May 14, 1968, meeting.

[88] For a full text of the Zambian statement, see Anglin, "Zambia and the Recognition of Biafra," pp. 117–118.

[89] *Ibid.*, p. 116.

munity because they encompassed anglophone and francophone states from East and West Africa, which were known to hold radically different ideological outlooks.

If the recognitions were meant, however, to persuade Nigeria to agree to a cease-fire, to enhance Biafra's leverage and flexibility at the conference table, and to warn Britain and Russia that their military sales to the federal government were alienating them from important segments of Africa, none of these hopes materialized. As a leading Biafran diplomat, Raph Uwechue, later wrote, "It is a lamentable irony that rather than bring the war to an end and so terminate the sufferings of the Biafran masses, recognition provoked an intensification of both. . . . Not only did it encourage the hawks on the Biafran side to unnecessary intransigence as far as peace negotiations are concerned, it also provoked in the federal military government an increased determination to make nonsense by military means of whatever gains Biafra may have scored diplomatically."[90] And as Suzanne Cronje has carefully documented, the supply of military equipment reaching Lagos from Britain and other sources rose sharply in May 1968, in anticipation of the federal army's next offensive.[91]

Diplomatically, the four interventions also failed to produce the trend of recognitions that the Biafrans had anticipated. While the Tanzanian initiative probably helped to nudge the two sides into an agreement to meet formally in Kampala, the scheduling of this meeting gave other governments that might have been considering recognition a reason to adopt a "wait and see" attitude. This was certainly the case with President Obote of Uganda, whom the Biafrans had regarded as a friendly prospect, but who would have destroyed his opportunity to host the Commonwealth-sponsored peace talks had he declared himself to be an ally of Ojukwu's.

The most bitter disappointment for the Biafrans was the failure of Senegal to recognize. Ojukwu's special envoy, Professor Kenneth Dike, had assiduously lobbied President Leopold Senghor and believed that he had received assurances that Senegal would join Tanzania.[92] A communiqué issued in Dakar on March 3, 1968, at the conclusion of President Nyerere's visit with Senghor, encouraged high hopes in Biafra because it called attention to the "deteriorating situation" in certain parts of Africa and asserted that "genocide" and the "oppression of minorities" were holding back progress towards African unity.[93] Yet Senghor, who seems to have been under considerable domestic pressure

[90] Uwechue, *Reflections on the Nigerian Civil War*, p. 89.
[91] Cronje, *The World and Nigeria*, Appendix 2.
[92] Interview: Dike.
[93] *Nationalist* (Tanzania), March 3, 1968.

from his large Moslem constituency, decided to await further military and diplomatic developments. By mid-July General Gowon was publicly praising Senghor for his "maturity" and for not being "carried away by sentiment" regarding the conflict.[94] There is no indication that Dakar ever reconsidered recognizing Biafra.

No other African government ever joined the four in openly supporting Biafra, and the only non-African state to extend diplomatic recognition was the tiny Caribbean country of Haiti. Why President-for-Life Duvalier decided in March 1969 to intervene is unclear. The action was taken after a series of informal contacts between Haitians living in the United States and members of former President Azikiwe's family. According to Ojukwu, when his representatives finally visited Port au Prince, the Haitian leader asked only whether it was true that Biafra was a state under the sole control of black Roman Catholics, and when the delegation acknowledged this, he simply said, "all right, I will recognize you."[95]

In retrospect, the real significance—if any—of the diplomatic recognition accorded Biafra remains difficult to gauge, and is perhaps best regarded as one more indication of the rising international anxiety over the fate of the Ibo people rather than as any endorsement of Biafran secession. As an expression of protest, however, recognition was an unacceptable diplomatic option for European and American governments, that were facing growing domestic criticism of their pro-federal policies, but that wanted to protect long-term political and economic interests in Nigeria and elsewhere in Africa. The obvious alternative to a continuation of the fighting was a political settlement and, even if the prospects for meaningful negotiations remained dim, the Western democracies—especially Britain—eagerly sought to convince their publics that they were working to bring about a peaceful solution to the Nigerian war. How the first phase of this peace-talk diplomacy unfolded is the subject of the next chapter.

[94] Nigeria, Federal Ministry of Information, Press Release No. F 1324, July 16, 1968.
[95] Interview: Ojukwu. Speculation in Lagos diplomatic circles seemed to favor the almost plausible theory that the recognition was Papa Doc's way of getting back at the British for Graham Greene's portrayal of Haiti in *The Comedians*, which had only recently been made into a much-publicized film.

· 6 ·

PEACE CONFERENCE DIPLOMACY,
PHASE I

To understand the course of negotiations during the Nigerian civil war, one must bear in mind that during the final two years of the conflict secession was not the real issue dividing the two sides. Following the collapse of Biafra's August 1967 invasion of the Midwest and the subsequent tightening of the federal blockade, Biafra's chances of achieving complete and lasting sovereignty were negligible. Unless the rebel army miraculously received enough heavy equipment to mount a major counteroffensive or the Gowon regime in Lagos suddenly dissolved as a result of internal political discord, some form of Biafran surrender was inevitable. Accordingly, by 1968 Ojukwu's overriding concern was to ensure maximum opportunities for Ibo political and economic self-determination within a new Nigerian entity.

Biafra's most important bargaining chip in negotiations with the federal government was the power to terminate the secession, and this obviously could only be played once. Ojukwu insists that Biafra was prepared, in principle, to reunite with Nigeria, and that he communicated this to Commonwealth Secretary General Arnold Smith, among others, during the closing months of 1967.[1] The challenge facing any prospective mediator was how to get the two sides in the conflict to agree on a price for the renunciation of secession. The much publicized slogan of the Gowon regime, "To Keep Nigeria One is a Task that Must be Done," was sufficiently ambiguous that the search for a "One Nigeria" solution became a cliché among those who wished to provide good offices without prejudice to future constitutional arrangements.

Nigeria and Biafra took obverse positions on how the negotiating process should unfold. Ojukwu's first objective was to secure an immediate and unconditional cease-fire which, he argued, could provide the proper atmosphere for talks but, in effect, would have frozen the status quo of two independent centers of power and halted Nigeria's military advance. In the event of a cease-fire, the Biafrans looked forward to a full-scale peace conference aimed at working out Nigeria's

---

[1] Interview: Ojukwu. In a separate interview, Arnold Smith confirmed that he had received the signals through contacts with Kenneth Dike and Michael Okpara in London.

future constitutional arrangements. Ojukwu refused, under any circumstance, to renounce secession until negotiations on all other matters of substance pertaining to the economic and political security of the Ibo people had been completed. Biafran representatives invariably insisted they could never agree to a reconstituted Nigeria until they were assured of precisely what they were joining.

The federal government wanted to see the bargaining process begin, rather than end, with a renunciation of secession, and always regarded the conference table primarily as a forum for determining the mechanics of surrender. Gowon asserts that he was fully prepared, from the outset of the conflict, to negotiate the distribution of power within a One Nigeria framework, but never suggested that Ojukwu or his representatives could participate in such discussions except on an equal basis with the eleven other members of Nigeria's Supreme Military Council.[2] He consistently opposed any suggestion for an unconditional cease-fire on the grounds that it would permit the consolidation and rearming of rebel forces, thereby increasing the danger of a longer and more severe conflict should negotiations break down and the fighting resume. In the wake of the adverse publicity generated by the January 1967 prewar talks in Aburi, Ghana, when Lt. Col. Gowon and his military colleagues were embarrassingly outmaneuvered by the East, Lagos remained forever suspicious that any further sessions with Ojukwu or his representatives would somehow become a Biafran public relations success.

Efforts to promote a cease-fire and substantive negotiations were limited to various techniques of diplomatic persuasion. In the absence of more forceful international action or a decisive change in military fortunes, the federal and Biafran regimes failed even to approach agreement on a formula for the renunciation of secession. Biafra's delegations to each of the peace talks were instructed to accept a "One Nigeria" solution only if it entailed full and complete equality for the people of Biafra.[3] Equality in Ojukwu's view meant a return to the status quo ante of four regions. Within this framework, Ojukwu's maximum demands would have been for a separation of power along the lines of his January 1967 interpretation of the controversial Aburi accords, whereby each regional military governor would have retained veto power over all national policies, including defense, security, and foreign affairs.

Since the war Ojukwu has asserted privately that he had been prepared from the middle of 1968 to accept a four-region solution with a

---

[2] Interview: Gowon.

[3] Interviews: Ojukwu; Sir Louis Mbanefo, head of the Biafran delegations to the Kampala and Monrovia talks; and Professor Eni Njoku, head of the Biafran delegation to the Addis Ababa talks.

distribution of authority along the lines contained in the 1963 federal constitution.[4] Because the powers then held by the twelve states did not differ substantially from those formerly retained by the four regions, the essence of Ojukwu's fall-back bargaining position would have been a renunciation of secession in return for federal abandonment of the twelve-state arrangement, plus provisions for at least interim local control over Biafra's security forces. Ojukwu was certain that had Gowon been forced to accept a return to the four regions, this concession would have so undermined the viability of the wartime federal coalition that the ensuing political chaos would have opened the way for a full revival of the "Biafran spirit" and possibly the forging of an Ojukwu-dominated southern alliance.

How far the Biafrans actually would have compromised, had they been offered encouragement, cannot be known. The federal military government had very clear political aims in the war, which were simply nonnegotiable. Throughout nearly two years of intermittent peace talks, Nigerian representatives refused to allow the fundamental question of twelve states to appear on any agenda, arguing that any discussions of the country's constitutional arrangements could only take place among representatives of all the present states. Federal negotiators carried no brief to discuss the future of the twelve states, and consequently never formulated any fall-back positions, as bargaining was not anticipated.[5] On less substantive issues pertaining to the physical safety and welfare of the Biafran people, Federal delegations were always instructed to use their own discretion in determining what seemed necessary and proper to convince the other side and any interested foreign observers that the current military campaign was directed against the Biafran state and not the Ibo people.[6]

Despite the tremendous differences that always separated Nigerian and Biafran delegations, both regimes eventually regarded peace-talk diplomacy as the cutting edge of the internationalization process. While the plight of Biafra's starving masses captured the attention of world public opinion, the parties to the conflict sought to use the conference

[4] Interview: Ojukwu.

[5] Interviews: Anthony Enahoro, head of the Nigerian delegations to the Kampala and Addis Ababa talks; and Femi Okunnu, head of the Nigerian delegation to the Monrovia talks.

[6] Allison Ayida, an important member of every negotiating team fielded by the federal side, describes Gowon's style of instructing his delegations in the following manner: "What Gowon does is give a full mandate to any delegation. He calls the leader aside and says 'I trust you. I cannot be there myself so do what you can for us. Afterwards if I disagree with what you've done, I can always fire you.' In that sense Gowon is very much like Balewa [Nigeria's first prime minister] . . . he likes to give his delegations a relatively free hand, so that they can make concessions in pursuit of overriding objectives, if necessary on the spot." Interview: Ayida.

table as a forum to convince interested foreign governments that the opposition was responsible for the continuing violence. Leaders in both camps held the view that if America, Britain, or other European powers were serious about promoting a peaceful settlement of the conflict they would eventually feel compelled to intervene directly or indirectly to force a compromise. They further assumed that those who chose to become involved would apply the greatest pressures against that side in the dispute which—according to Western values and interests—appeared to be the most inflexible and unreasonable. As a result of these fears, posturing by Nigerian and Biafran representatives during the peace talks acquired a significance for their respective foreign policy establishments that was much greater than the actual proceedings deserved.

CONTACTS WITH THE COMMONWEALTH SECRETARIAT

The serpentine path leading to the Commonwealth Secretariat's May 1968 staging of formal peace talks in Kampala, Uganda, began nine months earlier in London. During the height of Biafra's military success, the August 1967 occupation of the Midwest State, Ojukwu dispatched his chief justice, Sir Louis Mbanefo, to the British capital to lobby for a cease-fire and negotiations. Mbanefo, a renowned international jurist with innumerable contacts in Britain's ruling circles, failed to make any headway. An August 21, 1967, report by Radio Biafra that Ojukwu was willing to enter into peace talks only on the condition that Biafra's sovereignty was recognized[7] apparently caused the Foreign Office in London to await developments before taking a position.

Eight days after Ojukwu's call for recognition and a negotiated settlement, the federal government announced that the Biafran invasion of the Midwest had been decisively halted at the town of Ore, just 135 miles east of Lagos.[8] Shortly thereafter, General Gowon went on nationwide radio to declare that military operations would cease immediately if Ojukwu renounced secession and accepted the twelve-state structure.[9] This change in military fortunes apparently prompted the British Foreign Office to inquire from Sir Louis Mbanefo whether he could say publicly that Biafran sovereignty was not a precondition for the start of negotiations.[10]

After telegraphing Ojukwu for verification, Sir Louis gave an exclusive interview with the London *Financial Times*, which appeared on September 11, 1967. The front-page article, headlined "Recognition of Biafra Not a Ceasefire Condition," attributed the following remarks

---

[7] Radio Biafra, August 21, 1967. Ojukwu reiterated the statement on August 28, 1967, before an international press conference. Ojukwu, *Biafra*, I, 208.
[8] *Morning Post*, August 29, 1967.   [9] Radio Nigeria, September 2, 1967.
[10] Interview: Mbanefo.

to the chief justice: "The recognition of Biafra's sovereignty by Lagos was not as had been reported, a precondition for ceasefire or negotiations. Biafra was not prepared to give up her sovereignty, but did not insist on having this position accepted before the beginning of talks provided Lagos made no conditions either."[11] Mbanefo's interview generated considerable attention in the international press, and was seized by Commonwealth Secretary General Arnold Smith as the opening gambit for a British-backed diplomatic offensive intended to bring the two sides together around the conference table.[12]

Arnold Smith's mandate for intervening in Nigeria's affairs was never explicit. Unlike the Organization of African Unity or the United Nations, the Commonwealth is bound more by tradition than contract; it has neither charter nor treaty, and confers no legal rights or obligations on its members. Hence, the secretary general's position is less circumscribed than his counterparts' at the OAU and the United Nations. Smith assiduously exploited his standing outside the normal chain of diplomatic protocol in an attempt to convince the Nigerians that Commonwealth contacts with Biafran representatives in no way implied greater international recognition of Biafra. He insists, perhaps a bit disingenuously, that throughout the conflict he acted purely in a personal capacity. He even refers to himself as a "Dutch uncle" in dealings with the parties to the dispute.[13] It was a useful political fiction, but one that was not taken very seriously by either the Nigerians or the Biafrans, who considered the Commonwealth secretary general to be little more than a stalking horse for British interests.[14]

Initial efforts by the Commonwealth Secretariat to promote exploratory talks between Nigerian and Biafran representatives were overshadowed by military events and a need to await the outcome of the OAU Consultative Committee's November meeting in Lagos. During the final months of 1967, Arnold Smith quietly stepped up his contacts with Biafran representatives through a series of informal meetings at his London flat, and became convinced that the possibility existed for a political settlement that would permit the reunification of Nigeria.[15]

[11] *Financial Times*, September 11, 1967.

[12] Interview: Smith. The Commonwealth secretary general had established channels of communication directly to Gowon and Ojukwu prior to the outbreak of hostilities, and asserts that his offers of good offices had been warmly welcomed by both leaders. He had last visited Lagos at General Gowon's invitation in July (*Financial Times*, July 7, 1967), but with the outbreak of war the contacts lapsed.

[13] Interview: Smith.

[14] Republic of Biafra, "Commonwealth Peace Moves," a confidential memorandum prepared by the Directorate of Propaganda, March 1968; and *The New Nigerian*, an authoritative analysis by Adamu Ciroma, "Arnold Smith and Prospects for Peace in Nigeria," February 17, 1968.

[15] Interview: Smith.

The Biafrans provided Smith with no details about the kind of arrangement they envisaged, saying they would prefer to discuss such matters directly with the other side.[16] Encouraged by these contacts, the Commonwealth secretary general met at length with Nigeria's commissioner of foreign affairs, Dr. Okoi Arikpo, during the twenty-second session of the United Nations General Assembly in New York. Smith succeeded in convincing the commissioner that the Biafrans were ready to negotiate on the basis of "One Nigeria," but was informed that the federal military government was constrained from participating in any new peace offensives until the Organization of African Unity's five-member Consultative Committee completed the work assigned to it by the Assembly of African Heads of State.[17]

The results of the OAU's November 23, 1967, meeting in Lagos that supported Nigeria, gave impetus to Arnold Smith's behind-the-scenes campaign to promote negotiations. By its actions, the Consultative Committee appeared to foreclose any future role as intermediary between the two sides.[18] Since the United Nations would make no attempt to circumvent the regional authority of the OAU, the Commonwealth Secretariat remained the only intergovernmenal body actively engaged in trying to arrange a peace conference.[19] Encouragement for such a meeting, however, did not come from the federal military government, but primarily from the Biafrans and, less overtly, from the British government.

The Biafrans, at this stage, were frantically trying to gain an international platform from which to mobilize pressure against Nigeria's impending invasion. Repeated delays in convening the OAU Consultative Committee caused Ojukwu to conclude that the committee might be holding back until the current federal offensive had run its course. To break the diplomatic impasse, but without offering any prior concessions, Ojukwu sent to London his commissioner of health, James Udo-Affia, a non-Ibo who belonged to one of the Eastern minority

---

[16] Interview: Ojukwu. Because of the loss of Biafra's capital and related confusion in the enclave, a bargaining strategy had not been carefully developed.

[17] Interview: Arikpo.

[18] As noted earlier, the committee did mandate Ghana's head of state, Gen. Joseph Ankrah, to establish radio contact with Ojukwu to inform him of the committee's decision, but the Biafrans failed to acknowledge Ankrah's radio signals.

[19] There were several private initiatives that ran parallel to the efforts by the Commonwealth Secretariat. The most important of these was a bid by John Volkmar and Adam Curle on behalf of the Quakers, which facilitated an indirect exchange of views between Gowon and Ojukwu during February and March 1968. This communication was couched in such general terms that it did not constitute an exploration of any formulae for a settlement. While Quaker offers to mediate were tendered discreetly, public calls for a negotiated settlement by the World Council of Churches and the Vatican had even less chance of success, for reasons that will be discussed in later chapters.

tribes. The commissioner held a press conference on November 7, 1967, in a committee room of the British House of Commons in order, he asserted, to correct any impression in Britain that the Eastern minorities were not loyal Biafrans.[20] He went on to attack the Organization of African Unity's failure to listen to both sides in the conflict, and urged that the time had come for the Commonwealth Secretariat to "explore ways and means of securing a basis on which both parties in the dispute might be brought together, and a cease-fire agreed upon whilst talks proceed." Lest anyone fail to appreciate what was uppermost in Biafra's mind, the commissioner concluded his remarks in the House of Commons committee room by declaring that Britain "as the mother country, must be completely neutral: military aid to either side should cease whilst the exploratory talks are in progress."[21]

With federal troops apparently en route to victory, the British government was not inclined to change its basic support of the federal military government, and would continue to sell the Nigerian army whatever infantry and other lightweight field equipment was required.[22] At the same time, London's enthusiasm for a cease-fire nearly approached Biafra's. Britain had much to lose from a protracted war, and hoped that the enforcement of the blockade and the loss of Enugu would convince Ojukwu of the folly of continuing the war. Now, in late 1967, with the federal army engaged in liberating the minority areas of the Rivers and Southeastern states, the next major objective would be Port Harcourt, where British companies had more than $250 million invested in oil installations. Not only was there a growing threat to Britain's residual financial interests, but the political risks of a continuation of the war also loomed large.

Public opinion in Britain was not yet aroused over the sufferings of Biafran civilians, but interest was growing and the questions in Parliament were becoming more hostile toward the government's policy.[23] Furthermore, on October 16, 1967, Soviet Premier Alexei Kosygin sent a much publicized personal note to General Gowon assuring the federal government of "Soviet support and cooperation in

[20] Press conference delivered by Mr. James Udo-Affia, November 7, 1967, reproduced in Kirk-Greene, Crisis and Conflict, II, 190–192.

[21] Meanwhile, Radio Biafra continued its strong attacks against "British Imperialists" in Nigeria. Newstalk, "Let London and Lagos Come Out Clean," reprinted in Biafra Newsletter, October 27, 1967.

[22] Great Britain, Parliamentary Debates, Vol. 755, December 5, 1967, cols. 1111–1113; Statement by British high commissioner in Lagos reported in the Daily Times, November 8, 1967; and Wilson, The Labour Government 1964–1970, pp. 555–556.

[23] Great Britain, Parliamentary Debates, Vol. 756, January 19, 1968, cols. 2106–2107.

preserving Nigeria's unity."[24] A prolongation of the conflict could bring greater Nigerian dependence on Soviet military supplies, a development that would not please Her Majesty's government.[25]

Despite the recent successes by the federal army, prospects for a quick end to the conflict were not encouraging to military planners in Britain. Attempts in October by the Second Division to invade the Ibo heartland east of the Niger River proved disastrous.[26] Nigeria's other two divisions, strung out along Biafra's northern and eastern perimeters, suddenly appeared rather vulnerable. A year-end report of Britain's authoritative International Institute of Strategic Studies offered the following bleak assessment of Nigeria's chances for a successful military campaign in 1968:

> Within the last decade, no such country has conducted a successful invasion against a neighbour of remotely comparable strength. At least two problems appear to prove insuperable. First, logistics—supply, communications and maintenance—make enormous demands on a modern army and in a hostile environment they seem to be too much for developing countries. Second, few such armies have developed a sufficient number of leaders in the field to stand up to casualties without a breakdown of the command system. Both considerations applied with special force to the Nigerian army of 8,000 men . . . it was never intended as an instrument of invasion.[27]

Against this background, Arnold Smith dispatched an urgent letter to Nigeria's Commissioner of External Affairs on December 29, 1967, inviting the federal military government to begin secret discussions with the Commonwealth Secretariat so as to discover whether or not a basis existed for more direct negotiations with Biafran representatives. The Nigerians were dubious, but did not want to offend the British.[28] In his New Year's message, Gowon reiterated his preference for a negotiated settlement, providing the twelve-state structure was respected.[29] Exactly one week later, he sent three of his most able and trusted advisers to London in order to brief the Commonwealth secretary general on

[24] *Soviet News*, November 7, 1967.

[25] Biafran publicists tried their best to exploit any latent cold-war apprehensions in Britain. For example, "Anglo-Soviet Collusion: An Enigma," by Gogo Anozia in *Biafra Newsletter*, November 24, 1967; and "Russian Bridgehead in Nigeria," Radio Biafra, *Newstalk*, November 16, 1967.

[26] See de St. Jorre, *The Nigerian Civil War*, pp. 184–189 for a detailed account of the mismanaged assault on Onitsha.

[27] International Institute for Strategic Studies, *Strategic Survey 1967* (London: 1968), p. 37.

[28] Interview: Arikpo.   [29] *Morning Post*, January 2, 1968.

Nigeria's full position, and to determine if the Biafrans were prepared to concede.

The Nigerian delegation comprised three permanent secretaries, Allison Ayida from Economic Development, Philip Asiodu from Industry, and Ahmed Joda from Information. All three were members of Gowon's kitchen cabinet. Ever since their hasty but accurate analysis of the full implications of Gowon's acceptance of the Aburi formula, the Nigerian head of state had come to rely heavily on these three civil servants' interpretation of any Biafran or third-party suggestion for a negotiated settlement. But because they were less well known internationally than several of Nigeria's former politicians who served Gowon as federal commissioners, the delegation was able to slip into London for a six-hour meeting with the Commonwealth secretary general on January 7, 1968, without drawing any attention from the British press. They returned to London for a second and final meeting on January 20, 1968. The two sessions provided Arnold Smith with a definitive explanation of Nigeria's position on matters he had hoped might be negotiable.

Smith greeted the Nigerian delegation with predictable assurances. He stressed that he was not acting as an arbitrator, nor was there any question of treating "the authorities in the East" on parity with the federal military government.[30] Ojukwu's accredited representatives in London, he continued, had been informed by the Secretariat that "any compromise proposals would have the maintenance of the Nigerian political entity as their central point. . . . If there was to be a cease-fire there would have to be a prior understanding on the objectives of subsequent negotiations and it would have to be agreed that secession would not be an issue."[31]

Immediately, the Nigerian delegation wanted to know what changes if any the secretary general discerned in the Biafran position. Smith's reply contained no specifics. The Eastern representatives, he reported, had shown a willingness to talk about a "future Nigerian political entity," but this would depend on other, as yet unknown, conditions. For the moment, Smith added, his contacts only said they would welcome proposals from the secretary general and, in Smith's view, they appeared nervous of any diplomatic undertaking that might displease

[30] *Summary Record of Discussion*, 3:30 P.M., Sunday, January 7, 1968. Present: Allison Ayida, Philip Asiodu, and Ahmed Joda (for Nigeria); Arnold Smith, A. L. Adu, and Gerald Hensley (for the Commonwealth Secretariat).

[31] *Ibid.* Although Smith did not refer to the representatives by name it was understood that they included, in addition to Biafra's resident representative in London, Ignatius Kogbara; the commissioner of internal affairs, C. C. Mojekwu; special envoy Kenneth Dike; and James Udo-Affia.

Ojukwu and lead to personal reprisals once they returned to Biafra.[32] Smith nevertheless claimed to detect a new air of flexibility on the other side, and wanted the federal government's views on both the substance and "face saving arrangements" for a settlement that could be offered to the East.

For the next several hours Arnold Smith and his associates tried to elicit from the Nigerians a variety of concessions. Seven items were covered in detail: the terms of any cease-fire, acceptance of the twelve states, the possibility of holding plebiscites in the disputed areas, economic opportunities for Ibos in Nigeria, the status of Port Harcourt, guarantees for internal security once the fighting stopped, and the format for renunciation of secession. The brief summaries of replies to the Commonwealth Secretariat's inquiries reveal the underpinnings of the federal military government's negotiating position, a position that did not alter substantively for the duration of the civil war.

Terms for a Cease-Fire

All questions relating to a cease-fire elicited the familiar standard reply from the Nigerians: any halt in the fighting could only take place after Biafra had resolutely renounced secession and embraced the twelve-state structure. As Philip Asiodu unequivocally told the Commonwealth secretary general, there "could be no question of a temporary cease-fire with the possible resumption of hostilities if peace talks failed.[33] In fact, Nigeria would have preferred that all preliminary negotiations be kept secret to avoid raising false hopes domestically and internationally. It quickly dropped this latter condition, but never altered the basic requirement for a cease-fire as conveyed to the Commonwealth Secretariat on January 7, 1968.

Acceptance of the Twelve States

While the Commonwealth secretary general seemed to accept as reasonable the Nigerian position that a political agreement on reunification should precede any cease-fire, he appeared more skeptical about the federal government's justification for not compromising on the issue of

[32] Ojukwu's emissaries were under very strict instructions at all times. Whether they genuinely feared physical retribution if they in any way exceeded, or created the impression of having exceeded, their instructions, is moot. After the war it was convenient to claim service to Biafra was under duress, and during the war conveying such fears made refusals to compromise somewhat easier at the personal level. Whatever the actual situation, it was not uncommon for Biafran envoys to inform their foreign diplomatic contacts that they were doves at heart, but feared for the safety of their families if their true feelings were expressed.

[33] *Summary Record of Discussion*, January 7, 1968. The following information on the negotiations is all from this source.

the twelve states. He strongly implied a major breakthrough might be possible if the federal government would signal to the other side a willingness to discuss the matter, adding that since the Ojukwu regime had not been represented in the original decision to subdivide the four regions, to reopen the question now would make an agreed settlement easier to achieve, and would be easier for the international community to understand. Could Lagos, he asked, accept fewer than three states in the East?

The Nigerians firmly ruled out the twelve states as a bargaining point at any conference table. To do so, they argued, would threaten the stability of the entire federation. Allison Ayida gave the following explanation:

> The Federal Government insists on the acceptance of the twelve states not for any mythical attachment to the number twelve but because it was necessary to avoid neither Eastern domination or blackmail from the West. If the North was not to remain one, and this decision was now irreversible, the East for its part could not expect to remain as a single large entity. . . . The federal government rejected special arrangements between the Eastern states because in that event other states in the West and North would demand the same thereby returning to the *status quo ante* of January 15, 1966 with all concommitant dangers.

One small concession that the federal military government was prepared to make would have allowed the three states of the former Eastern Region to operate under an interim Administrative Council, such as already functioned among the six northern states for the purpose of establishing an equitable rationalization of hitherto common facilities. The federal military government would not, under any circumstances, allow one state to join another of its own volition. What Ayida described as "marginal boundary adjustments" might be possible, but they would have to await the eventual establishment of a national boundaries commission.

Plebiscite

Tied to Arnold Smith's inquiry about federal willingness to allow the twelve states to become a subject for negotiations with the Biafrans was the suggestion that questions about the loyalties of the minorities in the eastern areas be determined by plebiscite. The Nigerian response, once again, reflected the fear that to accord special political status to the disputed areas might disturb the careful balance of political forces

152

that now formed the Nigerian federation. The domestic political risks were considered too high, regardless of whether the gesture might please democratically minded foreign powers.

If the creation and abolition of states in the East were to be left to plebiscite, it would be, in Mallam Joda's view, "very difficult to stop other minority groups from asking legitimately for the same rights." "Testing opinion on the existence of any of the three states in the East," Allison Ayida noted apprehensively, "would open a Pandora's box of separatist demands through Nigeria"; and, there was the matter of administrating a plebiscite. The current military thinking in Lagos, according to Philip Asiodu, was that "if a cease-fire were adopted, then rebel forces would have to entirely evacuate the Rivers and Southeastern states." To do otherwise would leave the Biafran administrative and military apparatus in a position to dominate political expression in those areas. This the army and the country would not tolerate.

Economic Opportunities for Ibos in Nigeria

The Nigerians conceded Arnold Smith's point that the Biafrans would need reassurances about their future economic security before agreeing to rejoin the federation voluntarily. But it was equally apparent that Lagos was not prepared to guarantee any rights beyond those that already applied to all other Nigerians. When Smith asked if there could be guarantees for equal access to jobs, Ayida replied that federal jobs were open to anyone qualified, but that civil service posts at the state level were filled predominantly by candidates from that particular area. Commercial firms would continue to hire whom they wished.

Assurances regarding Ibo property rights could be made more easily. There would be no reparations, and major Ibo holdings abandoned elsewhere in the federation were being held by the state governments in anticipation of being returned to their owners once the war had ceased. Asiodu told of $11.2 million that the government had put aside to compensate Ibos for private property that had been destroyed or lost during the 1966 disturbances in the North.[34] Ibos who had decided to remain on the federal side, and Asiodu was one, had been allowed to continue their professional pursuits without interruption or discrimination.

More basic an issue than either personal property or jobs was the future control over the East's mineral and agricultural resources, much of which lay in the minority areas of the Rivers and Southeastern states. Asiodu asserted that the question of export revenues was so

[34] *Ibid.* For details of the earlier dispute over compensation, see Kirk-Greene, *Crisis and Conflict*, I, 86–94.

central that he was certain the Ojukwu regime would renounce secession if they could somehow be assured that the non-Ibo oil-bearing and agricultural areas could be retained. In lieu of this, the Nigerians would only promise that once the secession ended, a revenue allocation commission would decide the exact breakdown of national wealth among the twelve states. The commission's terms of reference would be established by a constitutional assembly, in which representatives from the East Central State (Ibos) would participate on an equal basis with other national groups.

The economic prospects for the Ibos were undeniably bleak, given the crowded conditions and an almost total lack of mineral and agricultural resources in the Ibo heartland. Allison Ayida, as permanent secretary for economic development and reconstruction, acknowledged this and told the Commonwealth Secretariat that Lagos expected to provide substantial compensatory financing for the poorer states. He also conceded that the predominantly Ibo East Central State would be among the one or two states requiring the greatest federal assistance. Ayida's frank appraisal of future Ibo dependence prompted the secretary general to state the obvious conclusion that the current federal position would only underline the Biafrans' own view of a diminished role if they agreed to return to the federation, and this "would not make it any easier for Eastern authorities to accept One Nigeria."

Status of Port Harcourt

On another issue related to Ibo economic security, Arnold Smith said he was certain the Biafrans would insist on guaranteed access to Port Harcourt. At that moment, Biafra still held the port and its oil refinery, although the federal blockade had been in effect since the war broke out. Nigeria's position, as summarized by Allison Ayida, was that future access would pose no problem for the Ibos or anyone else, but if Smith implied that the East Central State would control operation of the port, which in normal times was a federal responsibility, this raised other issues. In order to protect interests of landlocked states in the North, all port facilities in Nigeria would have to remain under the jurisdiction of the federal military government.

Internal Security

The Nigerians acknowledged that the Ibos in Biafra had genuine fears that would have to be allayed prior to any renunciation of secession. Smith wanted to know what the Nigerians were prepared to offer, both on the question of individual security, which would allow the Ibos to travel freely within the federation, and on the more immediate question of physical safety in the event of a cease-fire. Ayida, Asiodu, and

Joda once again had very little to propose. Senior military officers in Lagos, Ayida bluntly remarked, planned only for a federal occupation once rebel forces had been disarmed and disbanded. Special security guarantees, he added, were only conceivable for the predominantly Ibo areas of the East Central State, since Lagos firmly believed that the minority areas in the Rivers and Southeastern states were more fearful of continued Ibo domination than of federal invasion. The delegation specifically did not rule out the possibility of introducing foreign troops to reassure the Ibos in the event of a negotiated surrender, but Ayida stressed that such a foreign presence could only be token. The federal government, he concluded, might accept an observer team but definitely not a peace-keeping force.

Renunciation of Secession

Arnold Smith remained preoccupied with devising a face-saving formula to permit the Biafrans to renounce secession without really appearing to do so. The Nigerians, however, considered the issue to be ephemeral. When asked if the new Nigeria could be called something other than a federal republic, Asiodu replied that as long as the result was in fact a federal union, the term used to describe it could be worked out later. As for the appearance of surrender, Ayida suggested that rather than renouncing secession all the rebels need do was to announce their "unequivocal acceptance of One Nigeria," and that would be the end of it. He added that the citizens of the East Central State would be perfectly free to call their state by whatever name suited them, provided they did not use the name Biafra.

The federal government's intransigence left the Commonwealth secretary general with very little to offer the Biafrans in his bid to promote direct negotiations. Smith concluded the January 7, 1968, discussion by reiterating his conviction that the "essential problem was to find enough practical inducements within the basic framework of a federal government to enable the East to accept One Nigeria." But as he reviewed the day's proceedings, the only inducements he discerned were of a "psychological nature": future Ibo access to Port Harcourt and the freedom to rename the East Central State. The basis for serious negotiations of more substantive issues obviously had not coalesced. Yet Smith appeared determined to press on with mediation efforts, and secured Nigerian approval for maintaining informal contacts with Biafran representatives in order to "discuss possible formulae" for overcoming the current impasse. As the meeting broke up, Allison Ayida warned that the federal government "could not afford to give much in advance in an attempt at political bribery."

The Impasse Confirmed

Two weeks later, on January 20, 1968, Ayida, Asiodu, and Joda stopped briefly in London en route home from the United States and held three hours of further discussions with officials of the Commonwealth Secretariat. Arnold Smith did not participate, designating his deputy, A. L. Adu, to chair the meeting. Adu reported that after extensive contacts with Biafrans in London, the Secretariat had concluded that the only way for the two sides to begin to bridge the major outstanding issues was through direct negotiations.[35] The East insisted on a prior cease-fire, if only temporary, and the Secretariat now wanted to know from the Nigerians their minimum set of essential prerequisites for a cease-fire or whether it would be possible to contemplate a "simple" cease-fire followed by direct talks. Before replying, the Nigerians asked whether any change had been perceived in the basic Biafran position regarding self-determination.

During the secretary general's recent contacts with Ojukwu's representatives, according to Adu, he had "pushed them hard on the question of acceptance of One Nigeria and they had indicated again that they were prepared to go some way towards accepting a Nigerian entity." When asked about the Biafran views regarding the substance of such an arrangement, Adu said they had stipulated such an entity "should consist of a supra-national authority responsible for certain areas of common concerns but without sovereign international personality"; in short, little more than a customs union, presumably with Biafra retaining full authority over the three eastern states.[36]

In the Secretariat's view, the Biafran position was not rigid, and they might yet be enticed back into the federation after a period of disengagement. Adu again acknowledged that the federal government's commitment to the twelve-state structure would make reintegration difficult, but he suggested once more that if Lagos could provide a clearer picture of the powers and degree of autonomy that the individual states would enjoy, particularly in the areas of internal security and economic opportunities, the process of persuading the Biafrans to lay down their arms might proceed to the next stage.

The Nigerians would not budge. Allison Ayida repeated the presentation made two weeks earlier, ruling out a cease-fire—however temporary—without a prior renunciation of secession and acceptance of the

[35] *Summary Record of Discussion*, 5:30 P.M., Saturday, January 20, 1968. Present: Allison Ayida, Philip Asiodu, and Ahmed Joda (for Nigeria); A. L. Adu and Gerald Hensley (for the Commonwealth Secretariat).

[36] *Ibid.* For an earlier version of Biafra's view of the customs union, see Republic of Biafra, Memorandum on Proposed Future Association. A White Paper released in Enugu on August 29, 1967.

twelve states. Direct talks, he added, could begin immediately while the fighting continued. The federal delegation would offer no suggestions regarding possible topics for negotiation other than to express an openness to proposals that might reassure the Ibo people of their security. Retaining police under local Ibo control was cited as an example.[37]

On Monday, January 21, 1968, Ayida, Asiodu, and Joda returned to Lagos convinced that prospects for meaningful negotiations with the Biafrans were nil, although they were uncertain whether or not the Commonwealth Secretariat fully appreciated the depth of the impasse.[38] Their report to General Gowon had a rather sobering effect on the more dovish members of his government, who had hoped that Arnold Smith's optimism signaled an imminent Biafran surrender. A prominent member of that group, External Affairs Commissioner Okoi Arikpo, insists he never again believed there was a chance for a negotiated settlement, despite all of the maneuverings that took place around the conference table later that year.[39]

When Arnold Smith visited Lagos in mid-February to make final arrangements for the fourth session of the Commonwealth Education Conference, due to open in that city on February 26, 1968, the British press was replete with speculation about a possible role for the Commonwealth as a peace maker and peace keeper. The boldest and least correct interpretation of the visit appeared in *The Guardian*, where it was asserted that the secretary general's visit set the stage for a plan to bring about a cease-fire by sending a Commonwealth force of 3,000 men from a half dozen countries to occupy and police the battle zone.[40] Smith's office immediately issued a denial of the report.[41] Nigerian commentators meanwhile complained bitterly about the growing tendency of the British press to treat the question of a cease-fire as somehow divorced from the issue of secession, and questioned the presumption that a European authority could simply step in to restrain an independent African government from suppressing an illegal domestic rebellion.[42] Nevertheless, the incident dramatized the growing impatience in Great Britain over the prolongation of the conflict, a matter of concern for the Labour government and, secondarily, for Nigerian foreign policy makers.

The publicity surrounding Nigeria's failure to win the war by April 1, 1968, included reports of increasing diplomatic pressures in Lagos

[37] *Ibid.*
[38] Interviews: Ayida, Asiodu, Joda.
[39] Interview: Arikpo.
[40] *The Guardian*, February 12, 1968.
[41] Statement issued by the Commonwealth Secretariat, February 13, 1968.
[42] Radio Nigeria, *Newstalk*, February 14, 1968. On the same day Gowon took the highly unusual step of publicly complaining about "unsubstantiated speculation and false claims" by the British press. *Daily Sketch*, February 15, 1968.

for immediate negotiations. This speculation intensified with the news of Tanzania's recognition of Biafra on April 13, 1968.[43] In its official statement justifying recognition, the Tanzanian government held that "the people of Biafra have announced their willingness to talk to the Nigerian authorities without any conditions. They cannot renounce their secession before talks, but they do not demand that the Nigerians should recognize it. . . . But the federal authorities have refused to talk except on the basis of Biafran surrender. And as the Biafrans believe they will be massacred if they surrender, the federal authorities are really refusing to talk at all."[44]

Nigerian officials were skeptical of the assertion that Ojukwu was prepared to talk without conditions, particularly since Dr. Azikiwe's March 30, 1968, statement in Paris had specifically stipulated that Biafra was "ready to agree to an immediate ceasefire to be *followed* by negotiations for a peaceful settlement without preconditions."[45] At no time had Biafra previously indicated its acceptance of the Tanzanian assumption that talks could proceed without a prior cease-fire. The federal government already had informed the Commonwealth Secretariat during the secret January 1968 meetings in London of its willingness to talk with Biafran representatives unconditionally.[46] Commissioner of External Affairs Okoi Arikpo has said he did not believe Ojukwu was prepared to drop his long-standing insistence on a prior cease-fire and, on the basis of the indirect contacts with the secessionists in January, he did not expect any softening in the Biafran negotiating position until the fall of Port Harcourt.[47] But in view of the new wave of international interest in promoting negotiations, the federal government decided to call Ojukwu's bluff. Five days after Tanzania's recognition of Biafra, Dr. Arikpo announced that Nigeria was prepared to meet with Biafran representatives "at any time and at any venue acceptable to both sides."[48] The statement created a minor sensation in the British press, where it was described as a major breakthrough on the road to peace.[49]

Inside the Biafran regime, reaction to Arikpo's statement was ambivalent. On the one hand, there was a wariness that the offer was only a subterfuge instigated by third parties, primarily the British, who

[43] *Christian Science Monitor*, correspondent's report from Lagos, April 10, 1968.
[44] Tanzania, *Statement on the Recognition of Biafra*, p. 2.
[45] Statement reprinted in Kirk-Greene, *Crisis and Conflict*, II, 205–206. Emphasis added.
[46] *Summary Record of Discussion*, January 20, 1968.
[47] Interview: Arikpo.   [48] *Morning Post*, April 18, 1968.
[49] For example, *Financial Times*, April 20, 1968, front page story entitled: "Pressure Mounts on Lagos to Ease Talks Conditions."

sought to take the steam out of the Biafran diplomatic offensive, thereby forestalling further recognitions. At the same time, however, Biafra was also under mounting foreign pressure to accept unconditional talks, that is, to drop the demand for a prior cease-fire. As the head of the Biafran Ministry of Foreign Affairs later described the situation, "Ultimately there was no possibility of not attending peace talks, which is why we could not hold out for tougher conditions. It was always expected that the weaker member to the dispute would, rationally speaking, concede. We could not show ourselves to be overly keen on talking with the Nigerians or third parties would think we were ready to give up. Yet we also had to worry about the impact our uncooperation would have on Western public opinion which was at last rallying to our cause. . . . Both sides [Nigeria and Biafra] were walking a tight-rope. The trick was always to shake the other man's tight-rope."[50]

When Ojukwu responded to Nigeria's challenge to meet without preconditions, he did so with an air of alacrity, hoping to push the federal government off balance. Speaking at a press conference in Aba on April 22, 1968, he dropped his insistence on a prior cease-fire, but declared that the question of an immediate cease-fire be the first item on the agenda of any negotiations.[51] He further proposed that the talks begin within forty-eight hours, that they be conducted at the ministerial level at a venue in Africa mutually agreed upon, and that they be held under the joint chairmanship of two African heads of state selected separately by each side. It was an audacious attempt to advance the internationalization process and, at a minimum, the Biafran leader hoped to force the federal government into the role of obstructionist, while demonstrating to the world that he was quite capable of taking the lead in any dealings with Lagos.

The federal government replied to Ojukwu's plan within hours, predictably rejecting it as "unrealistic," and noting that in the event of negotiations, consideration of cease-fire proposals would be the final and not the first item on the agenda.[52] Dr. Arikpo, who was already in London, was immediately summoned to Downing Street for talks with the prime minister. Harold Wilson apparently had decided to take a more visible role in trying to promote negotiations, given the rising criticism of Nigerian intransigence and British complicity in the war.[53] When Arikpo emerged from the meeting he informed the press that "the federal military government are prepared to embark on talks without

50 Interview: Onyegbula.
51 Markpress Release, Gen. 68, April 25, 1968.
52 Daily Sketch, April 24, 1968.
53 BBC, Review of the British Press, West Africa Service, April 24, 1968.

preconditions . . . as soon as the other side are ready. This should be possible by May 1 at the latest [i.e., within five days]. . . . Once the talks start we can agree on an agenda and other related matters."[54]

Dr. Arikpo's posture of moderation and conciliation was plainly meant for foreign consumption. Back in Nigeria, the federal Ministry of Information immediately issued a statement clarifying the government's position regarding peace talks for the benefit of the army and to reassure the population of the prevailing determination to crush the rebellion. The statement included the following seven major points, which were to remain at the heart of the federal government's negotiating position:

1. acceptance by the rebels that Nigeria should remain one sovereign united country;
2. acceptance by the rebels of the new twelve-state administrative structure of the federation;
3. arrangements for restoring and maintaining law and order in the East Central State such as would remove any genuine Ibo fears about personal safety;
4. guarantees of equal economic opportunities for all Nigerian citizens regardless of ethnic origin;
5. arrangements for rehabilitation of persons displaced during the crisis;
6. arrangements for a Constituent Assembly of representatives of the federal government and of the twelve states to work out a new federal constitution;
7. arrangements for the review of revenue allocation and such matters.

The press release concluded that "agreement on the above matters will lead to a cessation of hostilities and a lasting settlement."[55]

Ojukwu issued a blanket rejection of Nigeria's proposed agenda, and declared that if Lagos were serious about peace it should send representatives to Dakar, Senegal, within forty-eight hours to discuss a cease-fire.[56] As for the Wilson-Arikpo talks in London, Radio Biafra branded them an exercise for transmitting "fresh directives on Nigeria's war of genocide against our people."[57] This outpouring of vilification prompted Gowon to condemn his adversary for not being genuinely interested in

[54] *Daily Times*, April 25, 1968, Dr. Arikpo's Statement to the Press issued in London.

[55] Nigeria, Federal Ministry of Information, Press Release, April 26, 1968.

[56] Radio Biafra, Statement by the Head of State and Commander-in-Chief of the Armed Forces, April 27, 1968.

[57] Radio Biafra, *Newstalk*, April 29, 1968.

peace talks, but merely trying to exploit the world's desire for peace for propaganda purposes.[58]

On the basis of the above exchanges, one might have concluded that the conditions for meaningful talks were at best inauspicious, even allowing for the hard-line public posturing that inevitably precedes serious bargaining. The Commonwealth secretary general, however, was undeterred and, with strong backing from the British government, continued with arrangements for what were now described as merely preliminary talks to discuss purely "technical" questions such as a mutually acceptable venue, operating procedures, and a possible agenda for more meaningful talks. On May 6, 1968, Arnold Smith succeeded in initiating direct talks between Nigeria's commissioner of labour and information, Chief Anthony Enahoro, and the Biafran chief justice, Sir Louis Mbanefo.[59] The meetings, which were held in Mr. Smith's London flat, lasted for nine days, May 6–14, 1968.

PRELIMINARY DISCUSSIONS IN LONDON

The first item settled during the preliminary talks in London was an agreement to hold any further substantive negotiations in Kampala, Uganda.[60] The Biafrans would have preferred Dakar,[61] but the

[58] *Morning Post*, May 3, 1968.

[59] Chief Enahoro was selected to be Nigeria's principal negotiator for three reasons: 1) to have chosen a more senior commissioner, particularly Arikpo of External Affairs, would have unnecessarily elevated the status of the talks; 2) as a Midwesterner and a former deputy leader of Chief Awolowo's Action Group party, Enahoro had sought political allies among Eastern minority groups and was unequivocally committed to the new twelve-state structure; and 3) perhaps most importantly, Enahoro's name was a household word in England as a result of the highly unpopular decision of the British government to deport him in 1963 to face politically motivated charges of treason levied by the Northern-dominated government of Tafawa Balewa. Sir Louis Mbanefo, as noted earlier, was one of Biafra's leaders most respected internationally, and a former member of the World Court.

[60] *Summary Record of Discussion*, May 6, 1968. Present: Chief Anthony Enahoro, Allison Ayida (for Nigeria); Sir Louis Mbanefo, Ignatius Kogbara (for Biafra); and Arnold Smith and Gerald Hensley (for the Commonwealth Secretariat).

[61] According to an official Biafran memorandum, Dakar was chosen because: "1. Senegal is a francophone African state in which the influence of friendly France and not that of the hostile Anglo-American world would be felt; 2. Senegal's head of state, President Senghor, is not hostile to Biafra; 3. Senegal is a member of the OCAM which Biafra favors as a possible international organization under whose auspices the Peace Talks can be held; 4. Senegal in her official statements on the conflict has shown she is non-partisan in the dispute and in light of this Dakar may appeal to Lagos." "Comments about the Choice of a Suitable Venue for the Nigeria-Biafra Peace Talks," a memorandum prepared by the Propaganda Analysis Committee for the Head of State, undated.

Nigerians argued that, for obvious reasons, the meeting should be in a Commonwealth capital. To break the deadlock, Smith suggested that each side submit by private letter a list of all acceptable locations, and Kampala was the only city that appeared on both lists.[62]

After agreeing on Kampala, the Biafran delegation made a brief and obviously futile gesture in support of replacing the services of the Commonwealth Secretariat with those of the East African Common Services Organization. Once the delegates decided to continue using the Secretariat's services, for secretarial and administrative matters only, they turned to the more intractable problem of choosing a chairman for the Kampala talks. The matter was discussed intermittently—often acrimoniously—during six of the nine days of preliminary meetings. When compromise proved impossible, Arnold Smith managed to keep the talks alive by urging the two sides to "agree to disagree" and postpone further consideration of the question until they convened in Kampala. The struggle over procedural matters such as "chairman" vs. "chairmanship" or "observers" vs. "observers (foreign)" came down to whether Biafra could achieve an image of equality with the Federal Republic of Nigeria. The pattern continued as the two sides struggled over an agenda that the Commonwealth Secretariat hoped would provide "a framework for substantive negotiations."[63]

Justice Mbanefo initially insisted that the agenda reflect formal acceptance of the Biafran assumption that a military solution was impossible. Chief Enahoro immediately demurred, noting that a military

[62] Chief Enahoro's letter to Arnold Smith, May 7, 1968. The capitals designated were, in alphabetical order: Accra, Ghana; Bathurst, Gambia; Bridgetown, Barbados; Canberra, Australia; Colombo, Ceylon; Freetown, Sierra Leone; Kampala, Uganda; Kingston, Jamaica; Kuala Lumpur, Malaysia; Nairobi, Kenya; New Delhi, India; Ottawa, Canada; Port of Spain, Trinidad and Tobago; Rawalpindi, Pakistan; Singapore, Singapore; Valetta, Malta; and Wellington, New Zealand.

Also Sir Louis Mbanefo's letter to Arnold Smith, May 7, 1968. The Biafrans proposed only three alternatives: Dakar, Kampala, and the Tanzanian town of Arusha, the site of the secretariat for the East African Economic Common Services Organization. An official Biafran memorandum gives the following pros and cons for Kampala: "negative, 1. British and American influence is present in Uganda and neighboring Kenya; 2. the Buganda question constitutes a serious threat to the unity of Uganda; and 3. anti-Biafra sentiments have been expressed by the Uganda press; positive, 1. as Uganda is a member of the Commonwealth, the OAU, and the East African Common Services Organization, Kampala may be a compromise choice that appears to reconcile the claims of Lagos that peace talks should be held under the auspices of the Commonwealth or the OAU and our claim that it should be held under the auspices of OCAM or EACSO; 2. the Ugandan head of state, Dr. Obote, has not shown any hostility towards Biafra since the struggle began; and 3. the influence of our vocal East African friends will be around the corner to strengthen Biafra's position." "Comments about the Choice of a Suitable Venue," Propaganda Analysis Committee for the Head of State, undated.

[63] *Summary Record of Discussion*, May 10, 1968.

solution—however undesirable—was now viewed by his side as inevitable unless Biafra were ready to negotiate a settlement within the framework of a united Nigeria. He could see no reason, however, for not opening the discussions in Kampala with a consideration of the "military questions attendant on ending the hostilities."[64] This could lead to a second stage dealing with "broader and more fundamental political and constitutional issues." If the general progression was acceptable to the other side, Enahoro urged that agreement on an eight-point agenda beginning with "One Nigeria" be adopted as a framework for negotiating the cessation of hostilities.[65]

The Enahoro eight-point agenda was almost identical to the seven points already published by the federal government and branded "terms of surrender" by the Biafrans; and they were, once more, immediately rejected. Mbanefo refused to discuss the details of any agenda, claiming that this would touch matters of substance that should be delayed until Kampala. He would only propose a two-item agenda: "(i) how to stop the fighting; and (ii) how to live together in peace."[66] An overriding concern of the Biafran side, as the weaker party to the dispute, was to arrive in Kampala with a minimum of constraints on the number of subjects that might be raised. The secessionists were, after all, seeking an international platform from which to present their case. With little to bargain with, they understandably feared becoming entrapped on matters of substance. Hence, in rejecting Chief Enahoro's proposals, Sir Louis argued that the first concern of the peace conference should be an agenda "such as to allow either side to state fully its position."[67]

The secretary general, sensing an impending deadlock, intervened in favor of the broad two-item agenda "so as not to preclude either side's position or prejudge the conclusions which might emerge from the talks."[68] Borrowing from Mbanefo's proposals and Enahoro's summation of a settlement in "two stages," the Commonwealth administrator suggested an agenda formula encompassing "conditions for ending hostilities" followed by "political and economic settlement."[69] The first

[64] *Ibid.*, May 8, 1968.

[65] Contained in a letter from Enahoro to Smith, May 9, 1968. The wording of the eight points was altered so as "not [to] prejudice the conclusions to be reached on each item" and were listed as follows: "1. One Nigeria; 2. Twelve States structure; 3. Law and Order and administration in the East Central State; 4. Security of life and property; 5. Freedom of movement and equal economic opportunities; 6. Rehabilitation of displaced persons and damaged areas; 7. Future constitutional conference; and 8. Cessation of hostilities."

[66] Letter to Commonwealth Secretary General Arnold Smith from Sir Louis Mbanefo, May 10, 1968.

[67] *Summary Record of Discussion*, May 8, 1968.

[68] *Ibid.*   [69] *Ibid.*, May 10, 1968.

was later accepted without alteration, and the second became the final item on the agenda, "arrangements for a permanent settlement."[70]

The crucial ambiguity in the agenda, which allowed the talks to proceed, was the term "conditions" in "conditions for ending the hostilities." For Enahoro the term continued to imply the resolution of the basic issues dividing the two sides prior to a cease-fire. The Biafrans, on the other hand, interpreted "conditions" to be no more than the mechanics of arranging a cease-fire.[71] Mbanefo covered his position carefully by insisting successfully that the first sentence in the paragraph after the agenda headings state: "It is agreed that either side may, under each item, propose for discussion such subjects as it wishes." This gave the agenda an "Alice-in-Wonderland" quality, allowing the two sides to define the terms of references to suit their interests. For the Biafrans, whose only real leverage at the Kampala talks would be the power to refuse to cooperate, the insurance of a totally nonbinding agenda was a sine qua non.

While accepting the unrestricted nature of the Kampala agenda, Enahoro argued strenuously for a formal recording in the London communiqué of the federal government's intention to raise its eight points under "conditions for ending the hostilities." Mbanefo refused even to comment, because "they were not in an area of agreement,"[72] although he did allow that the federal government was as free as any other government to write to his government to inform Ojukwu of its intentions. Not wishing to imply that Lagos was prepared to deal directly with an independent Biafra, Enahoro won reluctant approval of the following addition to the communiqué: "Either side may at any stage before the peace talks convene, serve notice, through the Commonwealth Secretariat, of the subjects it proposes for discussion under each item. It is agreed that the Secretary General will transmit such notice to the other side and that he will not publish it."[73]

The one remaining question, when to convene in Kampala, nearly aborted what had been accomplished to date. Enahoro said he needed

---

[70] *Ibid.*, May 11, 1968.

[71] *Ibid.* The following verbatim exchange is highly relevant in this regard: *Sir Louis*: Would it be better to keep to the word "arrangements" on item 1, "arrangements for cessation of hostilities?" *Chief Enahoro*: Well, the difficulty about that is that whereas arrangements in item 2 flow from an agreement on conditions in paragraph 1, we still have agreement on certain conditions. *Sir Louis*: But everything is subject to agreement. *Chief Enahoro*: No, no, you see the conditions [for a cease-fire] must first be agreed before arrangements [for a permanent settlement] can be made. It is only arrangements that are then needed . . . because you have established the basis for item 2 by agreement on item 1. *Sir Louis*: All I want to make sure is that the proposal does not in any way restrict the discussion.

[72] *Ibid.*, May 12, 1968.   [73] *Ibid.*, May 14, 1968.

two weeks to prepare for the conference; Mbanefo insisted that the two sides should meet again in no more than three days. Timing was no minor concern. The federal army's Third Marine Division was currently mounting a seaborne invasion against Port Harcourt, Biafra wanted the talks to begin before Port Harcourt fell, in the hope of mobilizing international pressure against Nigeria's war policies. Lagos, on the other hand, anticipated new bargaining advantages—even the possibility of outright surrender—if Biafra were forced to enter negotiations following a severe military setback.

After two days of haggling, the Biafrans appeared determined to hold out for a six-day recess. Enahoro insisted he needed a full week for consultations in Lagos and, since he would be traveling by commercial airlines, anything less than eleven days off would be impossible. At this point Sir Louis stated that unless Nigeria compromised further Biafra "might wish to reserve its position on the whole conference."[74] Mbanefo's threat prompted Arnold Smith to intervene and, armed with airline timetables, he eventually persuaded the two sides to split the five days separating their preferred dates, three to two in favor of Biafra. Preliminary talks finally adjourned on the evening of May 14, 1968, with full-scale peace talks scheduled for May 23, 1968.

Port Harcourt fell to Nigerian forces during the eight-day break between negotiating sessions.[75] With its airport, docks, oil refinery, and commercial facilities, the city was Biafra's only real vestige of earlier claims to economic viability. Nigerian military men regard its capture as a major turning point in the war, and General Gowon has claimed that, had Biafra held the city for another two weeks, no fewer than twelve countries were prepared to grant recognition in order to force the federal government to negotiate on Biafra's terms.[76] No one doubts the strategic importance of the battle, but its immediate political impact is difficult to assess. Biafra did not surrender at Kampala, as the federal government had hoped, nor did her representatives appear any more conciliatory. Sir Louis Mbanefo's attitude at Kampala was that Port Harcourt really had not fallen, and therefore was not a consideration.[77] One can only speculate what would have happened had the city remained in Biafran hands for several more weeks or even months; given Nigeria's inherent military superior-

[74] *Ibid.*

[75] *West Africa*, No. 2660, May 25, 1968, p. 621, for a full report of the battle.

[76] *Daily Times*, July 17, 1968, text of General Gowon's Address to the OAU Consultative Committee at Niamey, Niger, on July 16, 1968. On the basis of numerous interviews with Biafran officials, the claim appears to have been exaggerated. In the weeks that followed, only Zambia actually granted recognition.

[77] Interview: Mbanefo.

ity, however, it is doubtful that the federal government would have abandoned its basic objectives.

THE KAMPALA CONFRONTATION

The closer Nigerian and Biafran representatives came to addressing directly the substantive issues that divided them in war, the more difficult it was for the Commonwealth Secretariat to promote even the appearance of progress toward a negotiated settlement. International pressures brought them together for what amounted to nine formal meetings during the period May 23–31, 1968, but the pressures were never enough to force significant concessions or even to sustain the discussions.

Public Positions

The opening ceremonies in Uganda's gleaming new Parliament Building offered Biafrans their first opportunity to present the case for independence in the manner of a sovereign power, apparently enjoying the same rights and privileges as the Federal Republic of Nigeria, and in the presence of the Ugandan head of state.[78] Also present were approximately fifty members of the world press. The Biafran and Nigerian delegations were again led by Sir Louis Mbanefo and Chief Anthony Enahoro. Each delegation was carefully balanced ethnically, so as to promote at home and abroad the legitimacy of their respective claims to the disputed territories.[79]

Sir Louis offered Nigeria and the world a tough opening address, which recalled a long series of atrocities allegedly perpetrated by the federal government.[80] The justification for including these references

---

[78] The Ugandan government made certain that the Nigerian delegation was lodged in the premier hotel, was assigned the most prestigious automobiles, and was invariably the first to be addressed.

[79] The official delegations were, for Nigeria: Chief Anthony Enahoro; Alhaji Aminu Kano, federal commissioner and former head of the old leftist Northern Elements Progressive Union, which had been in alliance with the Ibo-dominated National Council of Nigerian Citizens; Col. George Kurobo, ambassador to Moscow, a Rivers State man who had served briefly as the head of Ojukwu's air force; Ukpabi Asika, administrator of the East Central State and an Ibo from Onitsha; and Dr. B. J. Ikpeme, public service commissioner in the Southeastern State and an official in the Nigerian Red Cross; for Biafra: Sir Louis Mbanefo; C. C. Mojekwu, commissioner for internal affairs and Ojukwu's most trusted adviser; Chief James Udo-Affia, commissioner of health from the Southeastern State; Professor Eni Njoku, vice chancellor of the University of Nsukka; and I. S. Kogbara, Biafran representative in London, former Shell-BP executive, and a resident of the Rivers State.

[80] The Biafran delegation also used the occasion to distribute hundreds of atrocity pictures, with captions recalling the persecution of German Jews, to the members of the press. *The Times* (London), May 24, 1968.

was to substantiate why Biafrans would never again live under Nigerian authority and, somewhat less convincingly, to show that no amount of force could ever resolve current differences. His one concession to the "spirit of conciliation" was: "[although] only sovereignty can guarantee to Biafra the minimum security required, the Biafran delegation will be prepared to examine any other formula put forward by Nigeria which equally and effectively guarantees to Biafrans, by clear and inviolable institutional arrangements, the control of their own security."[81] The chief justice then unveiled, for the first time, his government's basic proposals intended to foster conditions conducive to a negotiated settlement:

1. Before discussion takes place on proposals put forward by us or by Nigeria, we propose that there must be: (a) immediate cessation of fighting on land, sea and air; (b) immediate removal of the economic blockade; and (c) the withdrawal of troops behind the prewar boundaries.
2. Biafra believes that the most essential ingredient in a lasting peace is a political arrangement which gives Biafra full control of the security of the lives and the property of her citizens in and out of Biafra.
3. We believe that sovereignty is the only political arrangement which can give us the required security.
4. Given agreement on a satisfactory political arrangement, we would be prepared to go on to discuss: (a) maximum economic cooperation and common services; (b) the sharing of the assets and liabilities of the former Federation of Nigeria; (c) the payment of compensation for the lives and the property of Biafrans; . . . (d) the holding of a plebiscite in disputed areas both in Nigeria and Biafra.[82]

Chief Enahoro's opening address dwelt less on the past than on the "new realities" of an inalterable twelve-state federation and avoided reiterating Nigeria's well-known proposals for a peaceful settlement. "In military terms," Enahoro confidently declared, "the concept of Biafra is now dead . . . the rebel regime is now confined to two or three towns and their environs in the interior of what journalists like to describe as the Ibo heartland. In these circumstances I suggest we address ourselves here at this meeting to the need to lay a sound foundation for a political solution at a later stage."[83]

[81] Sir Louis Mbanefo, Opening Address, May 23, 1968.
[82] *Ibid.*
[83] Chief Anthony Enahoro, Opening Address, May 23, 1968.

The Chairman and Foreign Observers

Behind closed doors, the discussion returned to the questions of procedure and protocol that had consumed the delegates' attention in London. Enahoro continued to resist the Biafran proposal to instate President Obote as the conference chairman, although he dropped his previous opposition to foreign observers, conceding that they could "help by influencing both sides behind the scenes." He then proposed that there be two observers, one nominated by the OAU and one nominated by President Obote, with heads of state excepted. The Biafrans, who were still seeking every opportunity to maximize their international standing, demanded that the observers be three heads of state nominated by an authority other than the OAU. On the third day of the conference the two sides agreed:

1. that President Obote would be invited to nominate an observer;
2. that Arnold Smith should inform him of the views of Chief Enahoro that the nominee should not be a head of state, and the view of Sir Louis Mbanefo that his discretion in this respect should be unfettered; and,
3. to record disagreement on the question of additional observers.[84]

President Obote appointed his foreign minister, S. N. Odaka, to serve as the only observer, and point three remained unresolved.

Conditions for Ending Hostilities

When the conference finally considered the "conditions for ending hostilities," on May 25, 1968, the Biafran approach to the negotiations revealed a new urgency. Mbanefo was under strict instructions not to discuss anything directly bearing on the substantive relations between Nigeria and Biafra until a cease-fire had been secured.[85] In the wake of losing Port Harcourt, the news reaching Kampala via the world media described a Biafra on the verge of surrender. Communications with Ojukwu were always difficult in periods of heightened military activity, and the delegation in Kampala faced the added problem of having to depend on the limited facilities and circuitous routing provided by the Tanzanian high commission. Under these circumstances, Biafra's representatives said it was impossible to deviate from their original instructions, and limited all remarks to reiterating denunciations of Nigerian brutality while pressing strenuously for a

[84] Kampala Peace Talks, *Summary Record of Discussion*, May 24, 1968, Meeting No. 4.
[85] The author is grateful to Sir Louis Mbanefo, Professor Eni Njoku, and I. S. Kogbara for giving their personal recollections of this period.

reply on the procedures to put into effect an immediate cease-fire.[86]

The mood in the federal delegation, by contrast, was much more relaxed and confident.[87] The longer the talks dragged on against a background of reports about Biafra's imminent collapse, the greater would be the chances—or so the Nigerians hoped—of a graceful surrender at the conference table.[88] Federal delegates also say that they wanted to delay confrontation over the cease-fire issue in order to soften the resolve within the Biafran delegation through personal off-the-record contacts with "old friends."[89] Thus, when Chief Enahoro received Biafra's demands, he immediately asked for time to prepare his reply and to consult with Lagos on grounds that the rebels had chosen not to give the federal government advance notice of their cease-fire proposals.[90] Unfortunately, very little was gained by the delaying tactic.

Relations between the two delegations, already strained, nearly reached the breaking point following the third day of talks and Chief Enahoro's announcement of the apparent abduction of an aide to his delegation, Johnson Banjo. Banjo had been mimeographing Chief Enahoro's opening address in the delegation's suite of offices in the Apollo Hotel when he vanished. The bizarre development provoked charges of Biafran subversion and countercharges of Nigerian delaying tactics.[91] Over the weekend of May 25–26, Chief Enahoro announced that he had received instructions from Lagos to suspend the talks until the Banjo case was solved, while Mbanefo wrote a sharp note to Arnold Smith informing him of an intention to leave Kampala within twenty-four hours.[92]

Of the two threats, Mbanefo's was the more serious. Ojukwu was

[86] Especially Njoku and Mbanefo presentations on May 25, 1968 during Meeting No. 6, Kampala Peace Talks, *Summary Record of Discussion.*

[87] See *West Africa*, No. 2662, June 8, 1968, pp. 655–656.

[88] Njoku recalled: "If the Nigerians had known we had an alternative airstrip, they might not have been so patronizing. They misjudged the immediate strategic importance of Port Harcourt and could not stop asking us 'but how will you get home?' "

[89] The author is grateful to Chief Enahoro, Allison Ayida, and Ukpabi Asika for giving their personal recollections of this period.

[90] Kampala Peace Talks, *Summary Record of Discussion*, May 25, 1968.

[91] Banjo had served as Allison Ayida's confidential secretary for five years. According to Ayida, the Ugandan police eventually discovered Banjo's body in a swamp outside Kampala, long after the conference, and from the autopsy concluded he had been murdered, although the death was immediately due to drowning. The federal government had no idea who the abductors were, but suspected the crime was somehow linked to Ugandan domestic politics and the then incipient secessionist movement among the Buganda.

[92] Enahoro's statement reported in *West Africa*, No. 2661, June 1, 1968, p. 627. Mbanefo's threat was conveyed in a letter to Arnold Smith, Sunday, May 26, 1968, and reported in Markpress Release, Gen. 141, May 27, 1968.

wary of any delays in the Kampala proceedings that might convey internationally the impression that Biafra was close to surren&er. The break could also mean that secret negotiations were underway, contrary to Ojukwu's instructions. By Sunday, May 26, the Biafran leader had managed to telex Mbanefo via the Tanzanian high commission in Kampala and called for his return unless formal talks resumed immediately. Throughout the following day, President Obote, Arnold Smith, and Ugandan Foreign Minister Odaka struggled to keep the talks alive. On Tuesday, May 28, the delegates reconvened for their seventh meeting behind closed doors to hear Chief Enahoro's formal reply to the cease-fire proposals.

In a detailed four thousand-word statement, Enahoro accepted a current theme of Biafran propaganda that claimed that the *security* rather than the *sovereignty* of the Ibo people was the real issue. He then went on passionately to challenge the Biafran position that adequate security presupposed sovereignty.[93] Enahoro acknowledged he "could see difficulties for the other side in simply being asked to lay down their arms" but the way out of the impasse was "to devise a formula which would allow a number of things to happen at one and the same time." He then offered Nigeria's plan for a settlement, the points of which he stipulated had to be implemented simultaneously:

1. A date shall be agreed as Cease-Fire Day.
2. A time on Cease-Fire Day shall be agreed as Cease-Fire Hour.
3. Twelve hours before Cease-Fire Hour:
   (a) the Rebels will renounce secession, order their troops to lay down their arms as from the Cease-Fire Hour and announce the renunciation and the order publicly and simultaneously.
   (b) The Federal Government will order the Army, Navy and Air Force to cease military operations as from the Cease-Fire Hour and announce the order publicly.
   (c) The Commonwealth Secretariat will make the same announcements as at (a) and (b).
4. At Cease-Fire Hour all troops will be frozen in their positions. An Observer Force drawn from a source agreed at this meeting shall take position at the Cease-Fire Lines.
5. Twenty-four hours after Cease-Fire Hour, a Mixed Force shall enter Rebel-held areas for the purpose of supervising the disarming of Rebel forces. The Mixed Force shall consist of: elements of the Observer Force, elements of the Federal Army and Police,

[93] Kampala Peace Talks, *Summary Record of Discussion*, May 28, 1968, Meeting No. 7.

Ibo policemen from the Police units established in the Liberated Areas. The Mixed Force shall cooperate with elements of the Rebel Forces.

6. Not later than Seven Days after Cease-Fire Day, the Administration of Rebel-held areas will be handed over to the Federal Government.

7. Pending arrangements to bring the administration of the East Central State into line with the rest of the country, the Federal Government will appoint a Commission to administer Rebel-held areas. The Commission shall consist of a Chairman who is Ibo appointed by the Federal Government and a number of other members appointed by the Federal Government, half of whom shall be appointed in consultation with Rebel leaders.

8. Law and order in the Rebel Areas will be the normal responsibility of the Police.

9. The Federal Government will recruit persons of Ibo origin and integrate them with the Nigerian Army.

10. As soon as possible, a person of East Central State origin will be appointed to the Federal Executive Council.

11. The Federal Government will, in respect of the organizers of the rebellion, grant amnesty in appropriate cases and will, in respect of other persons connected with the rebellion grant general amnesty.

12. Prisoners of war held by both sides and hostages taken by the Rebels will be released.

Enahoro had offered his adversaries a solution that still obviously amounted to surrender. They were invited to discuss the proposals in any order, but a cease-fire would necessitate agreement on all twelve points. Mbanefo tried to isolate points 1, 2, 3(b), 3(c), 4, and 12 as germane to the "conditions for ending the hostilities," under agenda item 3, and ruled the rest "out of order," that is, only for consideration under "arrangements for a permanent settlement," agenda item 4. Arnold Smtih intervened at this point to suggest that private off-the-record exchanges of view might lead to "greater flexibility." This was accepted, and the delegates reconvened informally later that evening, May 28.

When the Kampala talks suddenly aborted two days later, the special Tuesday night session became the focus in the debate over which side was responsible for the collapse. Exactly what transpired during the informal session is unclear. Arnold Smith believes that the two sides showed enough "conciliation and flexibility" in private sessions to bring about "a loose federal solution with safeguards for Ibo rights" and blames Ojukwu for the breakdown.[94] If a settlement was indeed possible in May 1968, then whose obstructionism caused the unnecessary deaths of hundreds of thousands of people over the next nineteen months? The following brief assessment of the May 28 encounter and the immediate aftermath is a synthesis of the recollections offered by the Nigerians and Biafrans directly involved.[95]

As had happened so many times previously, the Commonwealth secretary general took the lead both in setting up the meeting and in suggesting how the discussion might proceed. Seizing on Enahoro's twelve points, he tried to develop the same kind of formula that had succeeded in bringing the two teams to Kampala, i.e., one that was sufficiently vague to obscure, temporarily, mutually exclusive positions. Chief Enahoro and Professor Eni Njoku—the latter having gained ascendency as the most skillful negotiator in the Biafran delegation—agreed to play along, so long as vital interests were not directly challenged. By the end of the evening, Chief Enahoro had accepted a proposal to "begin serious negotiations regarding the possibility of creating One Nigeria." Both sides agreed that the implementation of a cease-fire should be the first order of business. Enahoro maintains Njoku informally "conceded the eventuality of One Nigeria" even though "we never got to the stage of discussing what it would look like." Njoku corroborates this, but cites "eventuality" as the key to understanding his position. Both spokesmen frankly dismiss Arnold Smith's hope for a "loose Federal solution" as totally unrealistic at that stage.

The Talks Collapse

As the talks bogged down, Gowon sent instructions to Chief Enahoro in Kampala to ensure that the federal delegation conceded nothing of substance. The instructions were the result of Enahoro's request for verification of the twelve-point cease-fire proposals that the federal delegation had tabled on May 28, 1968. Whereas Enahoro had left acceptance of the twelve-state structure implicit in his proposals (point 7), Gowon insisted that before any agreement was reached the rebels must *explicitly* embrace the twelve states. In addition, Gowon stipulated that there would be no question of an interim commission for the rebel-held areas, there would be no recruitment and formation of Ibo units into the federal armed forces, and no elements of the rebel troops or police would be allowed to retain their arms.[96] Gowon's

[94] Interview: Smith.
[95] Interviews: Enahoro; Ayida; Asika; Mbanefo; Njoku; and Kogbara.
[96] Cable: Gowon to Enahoro, May 28, 1968. The text of the instructions, sent

instructions, which did not reach Kampala until shortly after Enahoro had made his presentation, clearly reflected the views of the more hawkish elements in the federal government. By this time, however, the Biafran hard-liners also had grown impatient with the lack of visible progress in Kampala.

On May 29, 1968, Ojukwu issued the coup de grâce to the Kampala talks. In a dramatic midnight radio broadcast celebrating Biafra's first anniversary, he attacked the federal government's "bad faith," declaring, "They believe in nothing but a military solution and would prefer that to peaceful negotiations. Their insincerity about the current talks has been borne out by Nigeria's delaying maneuvers, first during the preliminary talks and now during the full-scale negotiations. Nigeria and Britain will bear full responsibility for the failure of the talks."[97]

A few hours later, Sir Louis Mbanefo called publicly for a plenary meeting, thereby signaling the imminent collapse of the Kampala talks. Overtures from Arnold Smith and the Ugandan government succeeded only in postponing the meeting until the following morning, Friday, May 31. After an hour of pleading by Smith, including a proposal to adjourn for one week to permit each side to consult with their principals, Sir Louis read a final statement. The Biafran delegation, he said, could see little purpose in continuing talks while people were dying and, since the Biafran army was not yet defeated, they would not surrender.[98] Sir Louis left for London that evening.

Chief Enahoro stayed behind for several days "in the hope that something might happen."[99] Before leaving Kampala he held a final meeting with President Obote. The Ugandan leader said he wanted to assure General Gowon that Uganda would not recognize Biafra, and

---

to the delegation via Nigeria's high commission in Kampala read: "The federal government must insist on the following: 1. There must be explicit reference to acceptance by the rebels of the twelve state structures; 2. No elements of the rebel forces can be included in a mixed force for disarming rebel troops. Rebel police must also be disarmed; 3. Ibos will, like other Nigerians, only be recruited as individuals into the armed forces. There is no question of recruitment and formation of Ibo units for integration into the armed forces; 4. There will be no question of an interim commission for rebel-held areas. As soon as possible after renunciation of secession and establishment of a cease-fire, the federal government will appoint a military governor for the East Central State; 5. Cease-fire lines should be demarcated on the map and accepted as part of a cease-fire arrangement; 6. With regard to an observer force, this may come only at the invitation of the federal government."

[97] Ojukwu, *Biafra*, "State of the Nation," broadcast May 30, 1968, I, 269. See also: Markpress Release, Gen. 149, May 30, 1968.

[98] Kampala Peace Talks, *Summary Record of Discussion*, May 31, 1968, Meeting No. 9. Also: Markpress Release, Gen. 155, Mbanefo Statement to the Press, May 31, 1968.

[99] *West Africa*, No. 2662, June 8, 1968, p. 655.

understood Nigeria's difficulties; at the same time, he strongly urged the federal government to consider a unilateral cease-fire for about a week. He remarked that the Nigerian government was in a strong enough position militarily and politically to be magnanimous, and should accept the Biafran challenge, thereby giving them a week to talk meaningfully, adding that this would also "strengthen the hands of Nigeria's friends." Enahoro thanked Obote but told him this was not possible. With nothing further to be accomplished in Kampala, Chief Enahoro flew to London, where representatives from both sides were engaged in publicizing their respective post-mortem analyses of why the talks had failed.[100]

British Efforts to Revive Kampala

The collapse of the Kampala peace talks created widespread dismay in Britain. The political issues at stake in the Nigerian crisis remained, in the popular mind, irrelevant. "The world is only concerned," in the view of one outspoken Member of Parliament, "with bringing this senseless war to the quickest possible end."[101] In the race to assign blame for the demise of negotiations and the continuation of hostilities, Biafra held the public relations advantage. According to Radio Biafra's review of the talks, "Nigeria's refusal to agree to a cease-fire has clearly shown that country's long-standing preference for a military solution to a problem which is essentially a human one."[102] Nigeria's reply, broadcast four days later, could scarcely have captured the hearts and minds of concerned Europeans: "The Kampala talks broke down because the rebel leaders wanted a cease-fire—the mere shadow of peace."[103]

The political backwash confronting the British government in the wake of the Commonwealth Secretariat's inability to arrange a settlement in Kampala consisted of new and more intense demands for an

---

[100] Biafra was, characteristically, ahead of the federal government in distributing its case overseas. Markpress was mailing 3,200 copies of Mbanefo's opening address to editors and opinion makers in Europe and America within hours of its delivery (Markpress Release, Gen. 136). By contrast, the Federal Ministry of Information's booklet, "Framework for Settlement," featuring Enahoro's opening address, was not available in Nigerian embassies for weeks. There were, of course, immediate statements and press interviews given by the delegates, for example, Mbanefo on the BBC June 2, 1968, and Enahoro's interview with Howard Johnson of the London *Daily Mirror* the same day. And Radios Nigeria and Biafra were especially vituperative; for example, Radio Nigeria, "Ojukwu's Sabotage of the Kampala Peace Talks," June 3–4, 1968, and Radio Biafra, "The Anglo-Nigerian War of Total Extermination of Our People," June 1, 1968.

[101] Great Britain, *Parliamentary Debates*, Vol. 766, June 12, 1968, col. 245.

[102] Radio Biafra, *Newstalk*, June 2, 1968.

[103] Radio Nigeria, *Newstalk*, June 6, 1968.

immediate halt of all further arms sales to Nigeria.[104] In response to this public pressure, Prime Minister Wilson sought to show his government's concern over the continued violence in Nigeria while not doing anything that would hurt the federal government's chances for an early victory.

Soon after Sir Louis Mbanefo arrived in London from Kampala, he was invited for discussions with Lord Shepherd, the minister of state at the Commonwealth Office. This was the first official contact between the British government and the Biafran regime. The British government spokesmen were at pains to inform the public that Chief Enahoro had been "consulted in advance," and emphasized that the contact "did not imply any formal recognition of Biafra," but this could hardly detract from what was a significant acknowledgment of Biafra's growing international importance.[105] Mbanefo was perfectly aware of the Labour government's wish to create the impression that "delicate negotiations" were still underway.[106] And it was no coincidence that the day after the Shepherd-Mbanefo contact was announced, the prime minister called for the first parliamentary debate on British arms sales policy to Nigeria.[107] Sensing his temporary advantage, Sir Louis insisted that there must be a cease-fire before the resumption of talks, and demanded written assurances from Lord Shepherd of his government's full support for this condition.

Chief Enahoro, temporarily Nigeria's principal spokesman in London, sent a detailed letter to each member of Parliament on the eve of the debate over whether arms sales to Nigeria should be continued.[108] Regarding the international arms traffic, he recalled that "when the British Government refused to sell aircraft to the Nigerian Air Force, the Federal Government had no difficulty in obtaining them from other sources," and to cut off sales at the current stage of hostilities would again "compel the Federal Government to turn to other sources of supply at a cost which could conceivably involve British interests." An embargo, he concluded, would not affect rebel sources of supply and would only incite them to more intransigence.

The three-hour parliamentary debate was spirited, and nearly all who spoke asked for a ban on arms. Wilson's foreign minister, Michael

[104] *The Times* (London), Editorial, June 1, 1968. The same week the Catholic Archbishop of Westminster, John Heenan, gave a much publicized sermon, the first by a Catholic cardinal in Westminster Abbey since the Reformation, which was devoted to the plight of the Biafrans, and severely attacked the supply of British "instruments of death." *West Africa*, No. 2662, June 8, 1968, p. 678.

[105] BBC, June 11, 1968.   [106] Interview: Mbanefo.

[107] Great Britain, *Parliamentary Debates*, Vol. 766, June 12, 1968, cols. 243–300.

[108] Chief Enahoro, Letter to all Members of British Parliament in Westminster, June 12, 1968.

Stewart, stressed that a general ban would be impossible to administer internationally, and that unilateral action would only alienate the federal government.[109] He assured the members that the British government was doing everything it could to promote a peaceful settlement. While reviewing the support given Arnold Smith, he strongly implied that the Kampala talks would not have been held had Her Majesty's government not intervened.[110] The talks, he maintained, had not broken down but were in "a state of suspense," and he promised the members that Lord Shepherd would be resuming his efforts shortly to pull the two sides back to Kampala. The debate ended without a vote.

When Lord Shepherd met with the Biafran chief justice after the House of Commons debate, Mbanefo continued to insist on assurances of British support for a cease-fire prior to the resumption of talks. Biafra, Mbanefo told the minister, was becoming impatient, and unless the British government were willing to take decisive action, they would terminate further discussion.[111] Shepherd then pledged, in writing, his government's endorsement of a cease-fire, but insisted this be conveyed privately to the federal military government.[112] On June 19–20, 1968, he flew to Lagos to present his proposals directly to Gowon.

The suggestion of the Shepherd mission caused concern and irritation in Lagos, where the leadership assumed the move was intended to confirm or at least threaten an imminent discontinuation of British arms sales. When the minister arrived for what he expected to be no more than a one-day visit he discovered his first scheduled appointment with the head of state had been unceremoniously postponed for twenty-four hours. The principal meeting, on June 21, 1968, was attended by Gowon and eleven of the most influential members of his government.[113] Several of those present have described the first of a series

[109] Great Britain, *Parliamentary Debates*, Vol. 766, June 12, 1968, cols. 289–299.

[110] After reviewing the government's role in the Kampala talks, Stewart continued: "it is not an exaggeration to say that in every field in which there has been any approach to, or hope of settlement, it has been our action which has pushed things forward, and any hopes there are of settlement spring in the main from action we have taken." *Ibid.*, col. 293.

[111] Interview: Mbanefo. Meanwhile, Radio Biafra declared in a June 20, 1968, *Newstalk* entitled "No More Negotiations with Britain" that "there is little doubt now that the Lord Shepherd/Justice Mbanefo negotiations are being used by Britain to delay further recognition of our country by other peace loving states. . . . The government and people of Biafra demand an immediate end to the Lord Shepherd hypocritical negotiations in London. We call on Britain to either stop the arms supply to Nigeria and be thinking seriously on her peace moves or continue the supply of arms to Lagos and drop all pretences at playing the role of peace-maker."

[112] Interview: Lord Shepherd.

[113] The list, in the order it was recorded, reveals the dimensions of the foreign policy establishment as well as the implicit ranking of its leading members: Gen-

of wartime visits by Lord Shepherd as a landmark in civil war foreign relations because it confirmed that Lagos was in a much stronger bargaining position vis-à-vis the Labour government than hitherto realized.

Shepherd began by announcing that Her Majesty's government "was impressed by the military campaign of the federal government, early difficulties have been surmounted and considerable military success achieved." He assured Gowon there had been no change in British policy toward Nigeria, but urged the federal government to recognize that public pressures had been building in Britain against the Labour government's policy, adding that the Biafran press in London had been effective, whereas the federal press effort had not.

Because the federal government had "already won militarily," the British government believed that "any further advances by federal troops [into the Ibo Heartland] would provoke costly guerrilla resistance and hostile public opinion . . . it was now as important for Nigeria to win the psychological victory or the military victory would be hollow." Shepherd, therefore, proposed the following:

1. Informal talks should begin in London outside the glare of the press.
2. Since Mbanefo had no negotiating powers but only could serve to carry messages back and forth from Ojukwu it was therefore important that Arnold Smith be allowed to go to Biafra to talk sense to Ojukwu.
3. The chairman of the British Red Cross should also be allowed to go to Biafra to assess the medical and food needs.
4. The federal government should be ready for offer a cease-fire provided no arms would be imported into Biafra.
5. In the event of a cease-fire, Britain would be prepared to provide a contingent to a Commonwealth Observer Force.[114]

The minister said he felt Ojukwu was already "in a tight corner," his ability to reinforce his troops was extremely limited, and the alternative to continuing the fighting would only lead to chaos. When asked

---

eral Gowon; Vice-Chairman of the Federal Executive Council and Commissioner of Finance Chief Awolowo; Chief of Staff Brigadier Ekpo; Army Chief of Staff Brigadier Katsina; Lagos State Military Governor Colonel Johnson; Commissioner of External Affairs Dr. Arikpo; Attorney General Dr. Elias; Secretary to the Federal Military Government H. A. Ejueyitchie; Permanent Secretary Economic Development A. Ayida; Permanent Secretary External Affairs Baba-Gana; Permanent Secretary Ministry of Industry P. Asiodu; and Deputy Permanent Secretary of External Affairs Edward Enahoro (Edward's senior brother, Chief Anthony Enahoro, later joined the meetings upon arrival from London). *Summary Record of Discussion between Minister of State Lord Shepherd and the Federal Military Government*, June 21–23, 1968.

[114] *Ibid.*

for Mbanefo's terms for the resumption of talks, Lord Shepherd could offer nothing new, to wit, an immediate unconditional cease-fire and the withdrawal of federal troops from liberated areas. This, he suggested, was only a "talking position," and he assured his listeners that the British government was "in a position to apply pressure for concessions." In any case, it was "necessary" for him to return to London with "some positive result, that is, at least the promise of talks beginning soon."

Following their initial meeting, Lord Shepherd was sent on a tour of the country, most notably to see the liberated areas around Calabar in the Southeastern State. Meanwhile, the federal government prepared a detailed reply which, in summary form, read as follows:

1. Not to accept a cease-fire until the rebels accept a United Nigeria on the grounds that to do so would be unacceptable to the nation.
2. Not to approve a visit by Arnold Smith to the rebel-held area because it would be used by Ojukwu to portray a measure of recognition and might offend the OAU Consultative Committee which the federal government already had disuaded from sending representatives to Ojukwu.
3. That the chairman of the British Red Cross be allowed to visit the rebel-held area at his own risk.
4. That informal talks be commenced in London as soon as possible without preconditions and, if they succeeded, fuller talks would be resumed in Kampala.[115]

The above points, as well as a reference to the Nigerian people's impatience for a military victory, were incorporated in a formal reply for Lord Shepherd to convey to Prime Minister Harold Wilson.

On June 26, 1968, two days after his return from Nigeria, Lord Shepherd stood on the floor of the Upper Chamber and boldly announced that: "As a result of my discussion [in Lagos] I am satisfied that meaningful talks are possible and Her Majesty's Government hopes that Sir Louis Mbanefo will shortly return to London to take up this offer."[116] Before the week was out, a speech by Ojukwu made Lord Shepherd's optimistic report appear ridiculous.

During a June 30, 1968 speech at a joint meeting of the Consultative Assembly and the Council of Chiefs and Elders on the failure of the Kampala talks, Ojukwu analogized Lord Shepherd's efforts in Lagos to Chamberlain's 1938 visit to Munich, and accused him of maneuvers

---

[115] *Ibid.*
[116] Great Britain, *Debates in the House of Lords*, June 26, 1968, cols. 1409–1411.

intended to "assuage and stultify the mounting tide of British and world public opinion . . . to allow Nigeria time to achieve the Anglo-Nigerian aim of a military solution."[117] The discussions between Lord Shepherd and Sir Louis Mbanefo were never resumed. According to Ojukwu's chief secretary, N. U. Akpan, the Biafran leader had concluded that "as long as the impression was given that talks were going on, no country would take action [favorable to Biafra] for fear of being accused of trying to undermine the success of the peace talks."[118]

The Biafrans were not the only ones who looked askance at Lord Shepherd's attempt to revive Kampala. Commenting on the significance of the minister's recent trip to Lagos, one of the Nigerian principals in the June 21–23, 1968 discussions wrote to a colleague: "The Shepherd visit was not an independent British initiative. It is meant to supplement Arnold Smith's outfit and the publicity stunt has been dramatized over the BBC for projecting Britain's image. We were quite firm with him."[119] The only significant aspect of the visit, according to the same official, was the question of British arms sales; a matter that, he notes, was never formally raised beyond Lord Shepherd's unsolicited and unambiguous expressions of continued support. For those in the Federal Executive Council who had feared that the Labour minister had come to Lagos—in one commissioner's words—to "blackmail us into accepting a dialogue with the rebels" under threat of an arms embargo, the meeting revealed that "the British Government was more intelligent than the mass of the British people."[120]

Although the British government failed to bring the two sides back to the conference table in Kampala, this did not deter London from urging others to undertake new initiatives in behalf of negotiations. On July 12, 1968, the British embassy in Addis Ababa sent the chairman of the OAU Consultative Committee, Emperor Haile Selassie, an aide-mémoire giving London's assessment of the situation. Blame for the lack of any progress was assigned entirely to Ojukwu, who was condemned for refusing to agree to the resumption of unconditional negotiations and for not making a "gesture" on "the key issue of unity to match concessions by the federal government."[121] The British implicitly acknowledged that they and the Commonwealth Secretariat had lost contact with the Biafrans. The OAU Consultative Committee, of course, had encountered similar difficulties following its November 1967 endorsement of Nigerian reunification in strict accordance with the federal

[117] Ojukwu, *Biafra*, "Failure of the Kampala Talks," June 30, 1968, I, 281.
[118] Akpan, *The Struggle for Secession*, p. 137.
[119] Private correspondence, June 27, 1968.
[120] Interview: Dr. T. O. Elias.
[121] Embassy of Great Britain, Addis Ababa, Ethiopia aide-mémoire, July 12, 1968.

government's demands regarding the twelve states. Nevertheless, the aide-mémoire concluded that Her Majesty's government considered that it would be "extremely valuable" if the Consultative Committee mounted a new diplomatic offensive to break the deadlock, and suggested the committee enlist the good offices of the four OAU member states that had recently recognized Biafra.

The real point of this initiative could not have been to secure a political settlement. Neither the Nigerians nor the Biafrans gave any serious indication that they were prepared to resolve at the conference table what they had so far failed to resolve on the battlefield. What appears to have concerned London, above all, was Biafra's growing threat to convert international humanitarian concern into political pressure. To quote the July 12, 1968, aide-mémoire: "Her Majesty's government are being forced to conclude that the Ibo leadership, as their military position becomes worse, appears all the more determined not to make any concessions evidently in hopes that world opinion will force the federal government to give them what they want. Indeed, it seems that the Ibo leadership are virtually in a position of using the plight of their refugees as a political lever to obtain independence when other means have failed."[122]

World opinion, or more precisely Euro-American opinion, could not alone force Nigeria to accept Biafra's terms. The initial impact of hostile public pressures would be felt not in Lagos, but in Western capitals where the party in power could be held accountable at the polls. The British government was especially eager for renewed peace talks, regardless of who sponsored them, because they might at least provide a diversion for the press and public.

One would have thought that the prospects of a significant OAU initiative were slight, in light of the positions taken by the two sides during and after Kampala and considering the Consultative Committee's unambiguous endorsement of the federal military government in November 1967. Yet within six weeks of the collapse of the Kampala talks, Nigerian and Biafran representatives returned to the conference table at the invitation of Emperor Haile Selassie.

[122] *Ibid.*

PEACE CONFERENCE DIPLOMACY,
PHASE II

African interest in promoting Nigeria/Biafra peace talks peaked sharply during the spring of 1968. The intrusion of the Commonwealth Secretariat into what had been widely acknowledged as an African matter was quietly resented. Although the Commonwealth of Nations and the Organization of African Unity have a partially overlapping membership, they are grounded in opposing political traditions. The OAU seeks to forge international linkages where none previously existed in order to create a new, self-determined, and eventually self-reliant, regional political order. The Commonwealth, by comparison, stands as the remnant of a former imperial system. By successfully bringing the two sides together in Kampala, the Commonwealth Secretariat created the impression that Africans were unable or unwilling to promote peace on their own. Ironically, however, the Commonwealth initiative may have actually served the interests of the OAU by providing those African governments that might have been leaning toward recognizing Biafra with a rationale for doing nothing.[1]

Once the solid front of pro-Nigerian support in Africa had been cracked by Tanzania, Gabon, Ivory Coast, and Zambia, disagreement over Biafra threatened to destroy the fragile OAU alliance that had existed since 1963.[2] Reports of extreme suffering among Biafran civilians and the apparent weakening of the OAU consensus to defend Nigeria's territorial integrity raised the probability of greater non-African involvement in the civil war. Emperor Haile Selassie and others, therefore, began to push for OAU-sponsored negotiations to underline their own desire for peace, and to discourage further recognition or other unilateral actions that might weaken the OAU's international standing and Nigeria's case for reunification. Most African leaders also accepted Nigeria's claim that defiance of the federal blockade by non-governmental humanitarian relief agencies was an affront to the country's sovereignty,[3] and agreed that the OAU should seek to establish

---

[1] *Daily Telegraph*, May 23, 1968, named Congo-Brazzaville and Burundi as "probable" recognizers of Biafra, with Ghana and Senegal as "uncertain."

[2] See Zartman, "Africa as a Subordinate State System in International Relations."

[3] Nigeria, Records of the OAU Fifth Summit—Algiers, *Debate on the Nigerian Crisis*, 5 P.M. to 10:30 P.M., Sunday, September 15, 1968.

guidelines for international relief activities that would satisfy the federal government.

This chapter will analyze the resumption of African efforts to revive negotiations and the subsequent exchange of views between the two sides. It will conclude with a brief discussion of Haile Selassie's futile bid to mediate the terms for providing large amounts of humanitarian aid to Biafra.

New Pressures in West Africa

Those countries with interests most directly affected by developments in the Nigerian crisis were in West Africa.[4] The recognition of Biafra by Ivory Coast and Gabon shook the foundations of the francophone community, not only because they gave comfort to Biafra, but because they also opened the possibility that one day the small and impoverished West African states might have to choose between alienating the federal government of Nigeria and yielding to pressures from within the francophone community.

President Gnassingbe Eyadema of Togo was in Paris on the day Gabon recognized Ojukwu's regime, and he immediately held a press conference to warn that the "Biafran question was threatening African unity," and called for a special session of the fourteen-nation Organisation Commune Africaine et Malagache (OCAM) to discuss the Gabonese action.[5] Before the week had ended, however, the diplomatic crisis deepened when the doyen of the French West African community, President Houphouet-Boigny, also recognized the secessionists. Togo's proposal for a special session of OCAM went unheeded, but Eyadema succeeded in arranging a meeting of the smaller Conseil de l'Entente for the last weekend in May. Thus the Presidents of Ivory Coast, Niger, Dahomey (Benin), Upper Volta, and Togo gathered in the Togolese capital of Lomé to discuss the Nigerian crisis on the same weekend that peace talks were breaking down in Kampala.

The Nigerian government was apprehensive about the specter of French/Ivorian influence over the weaker members of the Entente.[6] In

[4] Chad and Cameroon were resisting local secessionist movements, and had declared national emergencies. Togo and Dahomey (Benin) were profiting from a booming smuggling trade into Nigeria, but authorities in those two ministates worried vaguely about the threat of pan-Yoruba irredentism should Nigeria dissolve into major tribal groups. Niger, of course, suffered the greatest hardship because the war disrupted vital produce export routes to the sea.

[5] Broadcast over BBC News of the African World, May 11, 1968.

[6] The Entente was formed in 1959 by Houphouet-Boigny as a counterpoint to the Dakar-led Mali Federation. A loose association providing for economic harmonization, political consultation, and a development fund, the Entente has been dominated by the greater wealth of the Ivory Coast and the leadership of Houph-

an extraordinary move, General Gowon flew to Lomé on May 27, 1968, for several hours of private discussions with Eyadema. It was the Nigerian head of state's first trip outside the country since his January 1966 meetings with Ojukwu in Aburi, Ghana. Gowon briefed the Togolese president on the lack of progress that was being made in Kampala, but stressed that his government would not participate in any new initiatives from within Africa unless they were undertaken by the Organization of African Unity under the terms of the 1967 Kinshasa Resolution. Then, as an encouragement to greater Togolese/Nigerian solidarity, General Gowon gave his host a promise of a two million dollar "reward" for having returned a plane load of outdated federal currency seized in Lomé six months earlier.[7] The two governments also announced the dropping of all visa requirements for visits under ninety days, a gesture that amounted to foreign assistance for Togo's thriving smuggling industry.

Details of the Entente discussions on May 29, 1968, are sketchy. The final communiqué said only that the meeting was devoted to "solving common economic problems."[8] Nigeria was, however, the principal topic. According to the Nigerian foreign affairs official charged with monitoring entente affairs, President Houphouet-Boigny held the brief for Biafra, but did not press very hard for a major policy change by his colleagues, realizing early the futility of such efforts. When asked for his government's views, Chairman Hamani Diori of Niger reportedly answered that while he sympathized with the plight of "les pauvres Biafrans," if Niger made any overt move toward greater recognition, his people would not allow him back into the country.[9] Colonel Alley

---

ouet. The Entente's Solidarity Fund achieved its present form in 1966 with an initial capital contribution of 1.3 million CFA (approximately $5.5 million at current exchange rates), of which the Ivory Coast's contribution was 77 percent. Abidjan so far has declined to use its drawing rights, thereby establishing an important source of capital for its four poorer partners. Among the Entente states, only the Ivory Coast survives without major budget supplementations from the French government, which are necessary on an annual basis in order to cover basic recurrent costs such as salaries to civil servants.

[7] The plane, a DC–7 captained by Rhodesian John Malloch, was en route to Europe from Biafra on January 18, 1968, with suitcases and cloth sacks of old Nigerian notes nominally valued at 7.4 million Nigerian pounds, or about $21 million, when it landed in Lomé for refueling. Eyadema had returned the notes, and Nigeria sent him a $200,000 gratuity in appreciation. During the May 27 meeting this was quietly raised tenfold and was later used for the construction of a new presidential palace in Lomé.

[8] The communiqué was reported in *West Africa*, No. 2662, June 8, 1968, p. 676. General Gowon was more to the point when he told reporters his trip to Lomé had dealt with the forthcoming "meeting of francophone nations on the Nigerian situation." *New Nigerian*, May 28, 1968.

[9] Interview: Olufemi Olutoye. The majority of Niger's southern population are Hausas with close ties to Northern Nigeria.

faced similar pressures in Dahomey (Benin), only from Yorubas rather than Hausas. For President Lamizana of Upper Volta, a Moslem from a Moslem state, support for Biafra was equally unthinkable.

One issue the five leaders could agree on was the need and desirability for a new attempt to promote a cease-fire and a peaceful settlement through direct negotiations—this time to be arranged among "brother Africans." A major diplomatic stumbling block was the question of sponsorship. President Houphouet-Boigny reported that Ojukwu could not consider an OAU Consultative Committee initiative so long as the committee remained bound by the terms of the September 1967 Kinshasa resolution and the communiqué of November 23, 1967. Biafra preferred that any further suggestions for renewed initiatives be referred to the East African Common Services Organisation, OCAM, or the Entente itself. Since these alternatives were certain to be ruled out of order by Lagos, President Diori was mandated by the Entente to try and work out a new formula with the other members of the Consultative Committee, whereby Biafrans would join any further discussions with the federal military government. It was felt that the Kampala precedent of internationally supervised negotiations might provide the OAU with an opening previously denied by Nigeria's strict interpretation of the terms of the charter.

President Diori played the opening gambit in his bid to reactivate the Consultative Committee immediately upon returning to Niamey. In a gesture clearly aimed at impressing the Biafrans, Diori told a waiting press conference that Niger might support a move to change the Consultative Committee's terms of reference to "make it a conciliation committee if events required."[10] Nigeria had agreed to the formation of an OAU committee only on the condition that its mandate explicitly preclude any pretense of its eventually assuming the role of mediator or conciliator. Diori was now hinting that the committee should free itself of that constraint and become something more than a "consultative" body to the federal military government.

Diori contacted the Consultative Committee chairman, Emperor Haile Selassie, during the first week of June 1968, and found him eager to play a leading role. Suggestions for an OAU initiative had already begun pouring into Addis Ababa from outside the region, but the Emperor did not want to step out front until he had quiet assurances that his efforts would be welcomed by the principals in the dispute.[11] He therefore urged Diori to seek Ojukwu's views through Houphouet-Boigny's good offices, while striving to maintain General Gowon's cooperation.

[10] Radio Nigeria, May 31, 1968.
[11] Interview: Ato Araya Ogbagzy, Ethiopian ambassador to Nigeria.

Within a week of the Entente meeting, President Diori flew to the northern Nigerian city of Sokoto for several hours of discussion with General Gowon. The latter recalled the course of events in Kampala, which indicated that Ojukwu would not negotiate within a "One Nigeria" framework. Nigeria, however, was willing to return to the conference table without preconditions. Gowon acknowledged that the prevailing terms of reference for the Consultative Committee did, in fact, constitute preconditions, but he noted the impossibility of changing those terms without the full approval of the Assembly of Heads of State and Government. If Ojukwu were truly serious about a peaceful solution, then, in Nigeria's view, he should agree to meet with the committee as constituted.

Through contacts with Houphouet-Boigny, President Diori learned that Biafra was unlikely to participate in any future OAU gathering unless the committee's terms of reference were broadened. A further polling of the other members of the committee revealed that only General Ankrah of Ghana was prepared to consider ways to circumvent the committee's original mandate.[12] Mobutu of Zaire and Ahidjo of Cameroon were unequivocally opposed to making OAU offices available to both sides in the war. Ahidjo now maintained that the time was ripe to reassert the committee's support for the federal government, and proposed that the members come to Yaoundé on July 5, 1968, for that purpose.[13] The Emperor, Diori, and President Tubman of Liberia held that there were diplomatic advantages to meeting in Niger, given Diori's established means of communication with Ojukwu through Abidjan.[14] Ahidjo, therefore, deferred, and after a week of further consultations the Emperor informed the federal government of the committee's intention to meet on July 15, 1968, and invited General Gowon to attend. No further effort was made to communicate with the Biafrans at this stage.

Preliminary Discussions in Niamey

The Nigerian government was not enthusiastic about another international initiative so soon after the futile exercise in Kampala, although it did not wish to alienate those who had given Nigeria important diplo-

[12] Interview: Ankrah.

[13] Interview: Hadj Hammandou Alim, Cameroonian ambassador to Nigeria. The recognition of Biafra by Gabon, without prior consultations, reportedly miffed President Ahidjo, who was one of Nigeria's strongest supporters in Africa. Shortly thereafter he issued a major policy statement endorsing the federal government's policy to end the rebellion by whatever means proved necessary. *Cameroon News*, Special Edition, May 1968.

[14] Interview: Boulama Issa, ambassador of Niger to Nigeria.

matic support in the past. Unless Ojukwu indicated his readiness to surrender, many officials—particularly in the army—could see little point in joining another round of talks. The Third Marine Division was now in control of Port Harcourt and pushing rapidly northward through the River State. Biafra's massive airlift was still several months away. From a Lagos perspective, the final offensive appeared imminent, and the proposal for more talks raised inevitable fears of possible Great Power machinations seeking to compromise a total Nigerian victory. The conference host, President Diori, was considered to be personally disposed to the federal cause, but Niger remained heavily dependent on France[15] and there was some concern in Lagos that de Gaulle might be looking for an excuse to recognize Biafra. Thus the federal government decided to approach the Niamey meeting in a typically cautious manner so as not to offend Diori, or any of the major powers who might have been monitoring his progress, while carefully avoiding any new commitments to a peaceful settlement.

Instead of agreeing to go himself, General Gowon delegated the highest ranking member of his civilian cabinet, Chief Obafemi Awolowo, to represent him and, in the chief's words, to "listen and consider suggestions put forward by the members of the Consultative Committee."[16] The Nigerian head of state would take no chance of being trapped in any diplomatically embarrassing encounter with representatives from the other side. As an added precaution, Gowon flew to Cameroon to meet with President Ahidjo on July 8, 1968, to report on the war and win assurances of neighborly help in making certain Nigeria's interests were not compromised in Niamey. "The difficulty in approaching Niamey," a member of the Nigerian delegation later recalled, "was not that the Committee members would reopen the basic issue of 'One Nigeria.' Everyone was in favor of that [reunification] and besides the military had made it no longer an issue. The real question was not 'to be or not to be' but 'on what terms,' and we felt some might have weakened since their November meeting in Lagos."[17]

Chief Awolowo arrived in Niamey, a city of 80,000 on the banks of the upper Niger River, on July 15, 1968.[18] He was formally welcomed by the Emperor, who told him that the Kinshasa mandate of September

[15] In 1971 the French government underwrote approximately $5 million of the $40 million Niger budget. France also bought most of the country's major export crop (peanuts), staffed 250 key positions in the government bureaucracy, and had several thousand teachers and technicians in the country.

[16] *Morning Post*, July 16, 1968.   [17] Interview: Joda.

[18] Other members of the Awolowo delegation included: Alhaji Audu Bako, military governor of Kano State; Dr. T. O. Elias, federal attorney general; A. A. Baba-Gana, permanent secretary, External Affairs; Ahmed Joda, permanent secretary, Information; Allison Ayida, permanent secretary, Economic Development; and E. O. Sanu, ambassador to Ethiopia.

1967 obliged the committee to pursue two objectives: "1. assist the Federal Government to maintain the unity and territorial integrity of Nigeria; and 2. bring peace to Nigeria in the shortest possible time."[19] Each head of state, in turn, implored Awolowo to advise General Gowon that it would be in Nigeria's and Africa's best interests if he personally came to Niamey and joined the discussions.[20] The committee had identified two major points for consideration: 1. the short-term solution, that is the question of relief supplies to the needy; and 2. the long-term objective of a permanent settlement of the crisis.[21] They also wished to have Gowon's approval before any direct contacts were made with the other side, noting that Biafran cooperation with the committee appeared unlikely in any event, because there would be no tampering with the terms of reference. On this basis, the Nigerian head of state flew to Niamey on July 16, 1968, and returned again the following day to consult on the committee's final resolution.

Gowon informed the committee of his government's determination to "prevent any diplomatic maneuver or political initiative which will enable the rebel leaders to sustain the rebellion and secession which they have lost in the battle field."[22] The twelve-state structure that had so preoccupied the Consultative Committee during its November 1967 meeting was de facto no longer at issue; the territory of the East Central State and the territory still under Ojukwu's control were practically identical. Nigeria, Gowon declared, would concede nothing that might jeopardize the security and self-determination of the five million minority peoples recently freed from Ibo domination.

Predictably, no one on the Consultative Committee tried to challenge the Nigerian position, but the chairman inquired whether the federal government was prepared to participate in direct negotiations with the other side under the committee's auspices. Gowon replied that he was prepared to send a team with full negotiating powers, provided the Consultative Committee did nothing that might be construed—either internationally or by the other side—to be at variance with their

[19] Nigeria, *Report on the Niamey Session of the OAU Consultative Committee*, July 15–26, 1968, submitted to the government by the delegation on July 28, 1968 (cited hereafter as *Report on Niamey Session*).

[20] *Ibid.* The heads of state in attendance were: Emperor Haile Selassie, General Ankrah, President Tubman, President Ahidjo, and the host, President Diori. President Mobutu snubbed the meeting by delegating his deputy foreign minister.

[21] *Report of the OAU Consultative Committee on Nigeria*, prepared by His Imperial Majesty Haile Selassie I for the Fifth Ordinary Session of the Assembly of Heads of State and Government, Algiers, September 1968 (cited hereafter as *Report on Nigeria*).

[22] Nigeria, Federal Ministry of Information, Press Release No. F.1317, "Statement by His Excellency Major-General Gowon to the Resumed Conference of the OAU Consultative Committee in Niamey," July 16, 1968.

mandate "to assist the Federal Government to maintain the unity and territorial integrity of Nigeria." If the reports of suffering in Biafra were true, and the regime was near enough to surrender to accept the OAU framework, then Gowon agreed that there could be progress.

President Diori and the Emperor then asked if Gowon could approve an invitation for Ojukwu to come to Niamey so the committee might appeal directly for a renunciation of secession. Echoing the recent Commonwealth experience, the Emperor argued that no one less than Ojukwu would do, since he held all the power and his underlings had consistently shown themselves to be powerless when asked to address the basic issues. The suggestion caused considerable discomfiture on the federal side. According to diplomats in attendance from Ethiopia and Niger, the key arguments employed to win Gowon's permission were that Biafran propaganda had effectively exploited the image of African leaders unwilling or unable to listen to both sides before passing judgment. If the Consultative Committee were to become an effective advocate for Nigerian and pan-African interests, it seemed necessary to preempt further criticism by formally entertaining Biafra's case.[23]

"The Consultative Committee made it clear that they would not see Ojukwu if Gowon said no," Allison Ayida recalled afterward, adding quickly, "when five heads of state who are patently your friends ask you, how can you refuse? In that sense we were presented with a fait accompli."[24] Later that evening, July 16, President Diori publicly invited Ojukwu to come for talks two days hence.

General Gowon returned to Niamey on July 17, one day ahead of Ojukwu, to review the committee's final resolution. The Nigerian leader found little that was objectionable, and the few alterations that he proposed were adopted. The resolution, as amended, states in part that the OAU Consultative Committee:

> Requests both parties, as a matter of urgency, to resume peace talks in order to achieve a final solution of the crisis prevailing in their country, with the objective of preserving Nigeria's territorial integrity and to guarantee the security of all its inhabitants;

> Decides that the OAU Consultative Committee shall remain at the disposal of both parties to help them in this direction. The Consultative Committee will remain in contact with the Federal Government of Nigeria. Colonel Ojukwu or his accredited representatives may at any time contact any of the Member Governments of the OAU Consultative Committee.[25]

[23] Interviews: Ogbagzy and Issa.   [24] Interview: Ayida.
[25] Nigeria, Federal Ministry of Information, Text of the Resolution passed by the

With Gowon's full consent, the committee unanimously passed the resolution, although publication was to be held in abeyance until after Ojukwu had made his appearance. Ojukwu would not be consulted about the scope or contents of the final resolution. Thus reassured, Gowon returned to Lagos on the evening of July 17, leaving Allison Ayida, his permanent secretary of economic development, in charge of a conspicuously low-ranking delegation that had instructions not to be seen anywhere outside the hotel during Ojukwu's stay in Niamey.

Confirmation of the Committee's invitation reached Ojukwu's headquarters in Umuahia via the BBC's seven o'clock evening news on July 16, 1968. It was reconfirmed in cables from Biafran representatives in Dar es Salaam and Abidjan within the hour. Radio Biafra broadcast Ojukwu's acceptance during the regular ten o'clock news on the same evening.[26] Ojukwu credits the invitation to the belief among the committee's members that he would never accept under the prevailing terms of reference, and that the invitation was merely a ploy to make Biafra appear inflexible.[27] He rushed to accept, however, because it promised to enhance his image as a sovereign leader and would allow him to seek support just when conditions at home were becoming desperate; the committee's terms of reference were simply ignored.[28]

In addition to the opportunity for Ojukwu to inject himself into the Consultative Committee's proceedings, the Biafrans believed there was cause to hope for a shift of policy among some of the members. A memorandum, prepared for Ojukwu by the Directorate of Propaganda on the eve of Niamey Conference, cited a variety of recent developments elsewhere—such as the Czech and Dutch arms' embargoes, the defiance of the federal blockade by growing numbers of relief flights, and the popular demonstrations in Europe and America—that would contribute to changing attitudes within the OAU. Above all, the memorandum noted hopefully that "recognition of Biafra by four members of the OAU might have been seen by the Consultative Committee as a threat to the unity and continued existence of the OAU. To save the organization, a compromise solution that incorporates the wishes of these friends of Biafra might be imperative."[29]

The Biafrans had one other reason for hoping conditions in Niamey

---

Organization of African Unity Consultative Committee on Nigeria on July 17, 1968, and released on July 18.

[26] Radio Biafra, July 16, 1968.   [27] Interview: Ojukwu.

[28] Radio Biafra, for example, referred to the Consultative Committee as simply the "OAU Committee" so as to make it appear less partisan.

[29] Republic of Biafra, "Biafra and the OAU Consultative Committee," July 1968, a memorandum prepared for the head of state by the Research Bureau of the Biafran Propaganda Directorate.

might be more favorable than previously. General Ankrah of Ghana was expected to table a resolution that ostensibly would deal with matters related to relief but, if approved, would carry crucial political and strategic benefits for Biafra.[30] The resolution contained three recommendations, the most important of which was for a "limited truce" in order to establish a demilitarized zone for importing massive quantities of relief.[31] The other points referred to the introduction of "an international police force" acceptable to both sides and the establishment of air and sea corridors for relief. Unbeknown to Ojukwu, Ankrah already had tabled the motion, and it had been killed by the rest of the committee on the grounds that it was out of order.[32]

On July 18, 1968, Lieutenant Colonel Ojukwu and a high-powered Biafran delegation left the enclave for Libreville, Gabon, in an old DC–3 gunrunner.[33] In Libreville they transferred to President Houphouet-Boigny's private Mystère 20 jet and took off for a short stopover in Abidjan en route to Niamey. Ojukwu met briefly with the Ivorian president, who informed him that the prospects for any major shift in the committee's attitude were slim. At this point Ojukwu learned of the contents of the committee's "final" resolution, which already had been approved and cleared with the Nigerians.[34]

On the day prior to Ojukwu's arrival, Algerian Foreign Minister Bouteflika unexpectedly visited Niamey to convey President Boumedienne's displeasure over the open contact with Biafra. More importantly, one of the committee members, President Ahidjo of Cameroon, departed in advance of the Biafrans, thus leaving only Selassie, Diori, Tubman, and Ankrah to entertain Ojukwu. When the Biafran delegation finally reached Niamey, it was carefully cordoned off from all contact with the press and was hustled under armed escort

[30] Exactly how Biafra learned about the draft resolution is unclear, but it was probably relayed by Arthur Nzeribe, allegedly a financial crony of General Ankrah, who was for a time the head of the Biafran lobby in Accra. There was considerable pro-Biafran sympathy on the ruling National Liberation Council, and much agitation in Accra from the thousands of Ibos in residence.

[31] The draft resolution was never made public, but a copy was given to the Nigerians and later shown to the author by a member of the federal delegation to Niamey.

[32] Interview: Ankrah.

[33] Those included in the delegation were the former president of Nigeria, Dr. Nnamdi Azikiwe; the former premier of Eastern Nigeria, Dr. Michael Okpara; Chief Justice Louis Mbanefo; a former federal minister, Matthew Mbu; Chief Secretary to the Government N. U. Akpan; Vice Chancellor of the University of Nsukka, Professor Eni Njoku; Commissioner of Home Affairs C. C. Mojekwu; Commissioner of Information Dr. Ifeagwu Eke; Commissioner of Agriculture Eyo Ndem; and the London representative, Ignatius Kogbara. Mbu, Akpan, Ndem, and Kogbara were all from minority areas in the East.

[34] Interview: Ojukwu.

to the airport hotel, where it was kept quarantined until summoned for discussions. Inside the conference chamber the Biafran leader ignored the previous ignominies and became, according to federal records, almost contrite.[35]

During his forty-five minute extemporaneous address, Ojukwu apologized to the committee for any shame the secession had brought to those committed to the cause of African unity.[36] He conceded his military situation was hopeless against Nigeria's bigger battalions and heavy equipment, but he warned that the Biafran people would not and could not agree to return to a united Nigeria until their many grievances had been redressed. As an interim solution, he proposed a limited truce, air and sea corridors, and an international peace-keeping force—a plan very similar to the one tabled by General Ankrah and already rejected. At the heart of his plea was the suggestion that the only way to save Nigeria and the good name of Africa was for himself and Gowon to sit down face to face and work out their differences as they had once tried to do in Aburi, Ghana, back in January 1967.

The call for a meeting of the principals—Gowon and Ojukwu—as the quickest means to ending the suffering and restoring mutual trust apparently appealed to the Emperor and his colleagues. They suggested that preliminary talks begin immediately in Niamey. Ojukwu accepted the invitation, but sought to extract two concessions.

First, he proposed that any talks be held under the auspices of an individual head of state rather than in the name of the OAU Consultative Committee. Ojukwu naturally wished to avoid creating the public impression that by agreeing to meet at the prompting of the Consultative Committee that he thereby endorsed the committee's terms of reference, which included respect for the territorial integrity of Nigeria. The Emperor allowed, with Nigerian approval, that President Diori would chair the preliminary sessions in Niamey, but insisted that he do so in the name of the committee. Thus, in contrast to the Kampala talks, Biafra's status would be enhanced by the presence of a sovereign in what would appear to be the role of a mediator but, at the same time, the chairman's point of reference would remain the goal of Nigerian reunification.

Secondly, Ojukwu tried to persuade the committee to issue a separate communiqué announcing the forthcoming talks, since Biafra obviously did not wish to be associated with the committee's blatantly profederal final resolution. The committee acquiesced in principle to Ojukwu's

[35] Report on Niamey session.

[36] Members of the Biafran delegation insist that the speech was never written down because the time was so short between receipt of the invitation and the departure. According to the delegates, no recording was kept by the OAU Secretariat.

request for a separate communiqué and, on the evening of July 18, 1968, issued a brief announcement of the agreement between "the Federal Military Government and Colonel Ojukwu to initiate preliminary talks" under the chairmanship of President Hamani Diori and "to resume peace negotiations . . . under the auspices of the OAU Consultative Committee on Nigeria."[37] Simultaneously, the committee released its final resolution, which had been slightly amended to "include an expression of gratitude to the two sides for agreeing to resume talks." The impression created by the final resolution was that Biafra had agreed to negotiate "with the objective of preserving Nigeria's territorial integrity." Ojukwu immediately summoned Secretary General Diallo Telli and denounced the release of the final resolution as "premature and provocative," and threatened to abort the talks.[38] When he left Niamey the following morning, July 19, 1968, the resumption of peace talks was still in doubt.

The squabble over how to announce the start of talks caused a delay of twenty-four hours. Ojukwu flew to Abidjan en route home and appealed for Houphouet-Boigny's intercession. By the end of the day the presidents of Ivory Coast and Niger had worked out a compromise. President Diori subsequently released a "final communiqué," superseding what was now called the "special communiqué of July 18, 1968." Since the rest of the Consultative Committee had left Niamey, no attempt was made to alter the substantive paragraphs announcing the beginning of renewed talks. Diori, however, appended a 350-word clarification—with the Emperor's approval—in which he described his task as "to bring together the representatives of the two sides, each one elaborating his own case before me and I shall try on behalf of the Committee to reconcile the two viewpoints. . . . We are convinced . . . a solution of unity can ensure the rebirth of this great country."[39] The formal acknowledgement of "two viewpoints," as yet unreconciled, was sufficient to stay Ojukwu's hand and allow the preliminary talks to proceed on the evening of July 20, 1968.[40]

Preliminary discussions in Niamey lasted for six days. President

[37] "Special Communiqué," released by the Consultative Committee on July 18, 1968. Reprinted as Annex IV in *Report on Nigeria*.

[38] The point was not that Ojukwu was unprepared to negotiate "with the objective of preserving Nigeria's territorial integrity." He, in fact, conceded as much during his discussions with the committee, for reasons that will be elaborated shortly. Naturally, however, he did not want this publicized for fear it would be misunderstood at home and abroad.

[39] "Final Communiqué," released July 20, 1968. Reprinted as Annex V in *Report on Nigeria*.

[40] The clarification did not deter Radio Nigeria from reminding its listeners that, by agreeing to meet under the auspices of the OAU, the rebels had accepted the goal of preserving Nigerian unity. Radio Nigeria, *Newstalk*, July 23, 1968.

Diori opened the first session, but did not attend again until the ceremonial closing on July 26, 1968. In the interim, his chef de cabinet, Gadijo Maitourare, presided.[41] The Nigerian and Biafran delegations were led by Allison Ayida and Professor Eni Njoku, respectively.

Agreement was reached very quickly on the following agenda:

1. Concrete proposals for the transportation of relief supplies to areas of civilian victims;
2. conditions for the cessation of hostilities;
3. conditions for a lasting solution of the Nigerian crisis;
4. procedures to be adopted for the Addis Ababa talks; and
5. a date for the Addis Ababa talks.[42]

Given this modicum of progress, the federal government upgraded its delegation on July 22 with high-ranking officials familiar with the logistical and military aspects of relief, namely, Federal Commissioner of Rehabilitation Timothy Omo-Bare; Federal Commissioner of Works Femi Okunnu; and Colonel Bissala, military secretary to the federal government. Any hopes for success in Niamey were, however, short-lived.

The two sides made no progress whatever on the first three points of the agenda. Most of the discussion concentrated on alternative routes for the introduction of humanitarian relief but, in an exercise that fore-shadowed the drawn-out talks in Addis Ababa, the competing proposals were more concerned with outflanking major troop emplacements than with the shortest distance to the greatest concentrations of civilian suffering.[43] When the negotiators turned to planning for the Addis Ababa talks, however, the Biafran delegation was surprisingly cooperative, and gave in to each of Nigeria's demands. This was in sharp contrast to the experience in London prior to the Kampala talks.

Formal peace talks were scheduled to begin on August 5, 1968, "under the auspices of the OAU Consultative Committee"; the Biafrans made no effort to have the Emperor designated as the sole sponsor. A three-point agenda was adopted that reversed the priorities followed in Kampala:

1. Arrangements for a permanent settlement;
2. terms for cessation of hostilities; and

[41] President Diori continued to work actively behind the scenes, but as the Nigerian delegation's report notes gratefully, he "did not in any way interfere in the proceedings as much as Mr. Smith at Kampala!"

[42] By prior agreement, the preliminary agenda was never released, a major factor expediting early agreement. *Report on Niamey Session.*

[43] The specific alternatives and their political/military implications are discussed below in the context of the Addis Ababa talks, where they were resubmitted in the same form.

3. concrete proposals for the transportation of relief supplies to the civilian victims of the war.[44]

Procedures for the talks were also adopted without difficulty, although these were never published.[45] The progress made during the closing hours in Niamey led to the following assessment by the federal delegation, included in its final report to General Gowon: "The rebels appear to have reordered their priorities and are now prepared to deal with the main political question of secession . . . before proceeding to consider the mechanism for a cease-fire. There is faint possibility that the rebels may be prepared to give up secession under Item I, but they may expect to see the framework of 'Arrangements for a Permanent Settlement' and agree to the outlines with the federal government so that they can be sure of the step by step reintegration of Ibos into the New Nigeria framework."[46]

OJUKWU GOES TO ADDIS ABABA

"If Gowon had gone to Addis," Ojukwu recalled after the war, I would have been able to force him to sign a cease-fire in Africa Hall in front of the Emperor."[47] This bold assertion may sound like a postwar fantasy, but for a brief period following the Niamey meeting Ojukwu believed he might be on the verge of trapping Gowon into accepting a political settlement favorable to Biafra. He left Niamey convinced that the Consultative Committee had agreed with his premise that only a meeting of the principals could produce meaningful negotiations, and that Emperor Haile Selassie would urge Gowon to attend the Addis Ababa formal sessions. Upon arriving home from Niamey, Ojukwu told a press conference, "Gowon will come with his [delegation]," and then added with characteristic bravado, "I think I cut the ground from under his feet!"[48] During the next two weeks (July 20 to August 4, 1968), Biafra's foreign affairs establishment worked feverishly to lay the

[44] Reprinted in Annex VI in *Report on Nigeria.*

[45] The federal delegation's report lists the following points of agreement: 1. the Emperor would be invited to address the opening session with appropriate courtesy replies by each head of delegation; 2. the administrative secretary general of the OAU would service the talks and keep the records; 3. the size of the delegations would be limited to five each, with unlimited advisers; 4. each head of delegation would include concrete proposals for reaching a permanent settlement in his opening remarks; and 5. the meeting would be held under the auspices of the Consultative Committee, with matters of detailed procedures left in the hands of the committee and the host government.

[46] *Report on Niamey Session.*   [47] Interview: Ojukwu.

[48] Radio Biafra, July 23, 1968, replay of press conference given by Lieutenant Colonel Ojukwu on July 20, 1968. Also summarized in *West Africa*, No. 2669, July 27, 1968, p. 882.

groundwork for what it hoped would be a major turning point in the internationalization of the conflict.

Preparations for the encounter, which Radio Biafra invariably referred to as the "Addis Ababa summit," proceeded on two levels. In the Biafran capital of Umuahia a special committee of senior officials from all sectors of the government was formed.[49] It met on a daily basis to prepare elaborate proposals and counterproposals for the delegation. And externally, Biafran representatives mounted a diplomatic offensive aimed at generating official foreign support for Biafra while also pressing Nigeria to cooperate fully with the Emperor.

The planning exercise for the negotiations in Addis Ababa was reminiscent of the approach to the Aburi Conference twenty months earlier; Ojukwu would seize the initiative and overwhelm his opposition with rhetoric backed by detailed proposals that the Biafrans presumed the Nigerians would not only not have anticipated, but would not adequately comprehend. A key element in the strategy was to develop proposals that, in principle, would also appeal to foreign powers in a position to influence the federal government and/or lend greater support to Biafra's cause.

If Ojukwu could have written the scenario, he would have "thrown Gowon off balance" by suggesting to the Emperor that an internationally supervised plebiscite be held in the minority areas of the Rivers and Southeastern states. To carry out the plebiscite would require a cease-fire, of course, and Ojukwu was certain that both suggestions would appeal to the Emperor and, more importantly, to the British and Americans. The fact that Biafra no longer controlled the minority areas failed to diminish the hopes of those charged with drafting the bargaining proposals for the Addis Ababa negotiations. During the brief period between the Niamey and Addis Ababa meetings, the Ministries of Defense, Internal Affairs, and Foreign Affairs turned out briefs detailing Biafra's forward and reserve positions on matters ranging from the local voting procedures in the event of a plebiscite to the feeding and housing of an international peace-keeping force.[50]

The idea of a plebiscite tantalized Ojukwu's imagination because it

[49] The committee was chaired by the commissioner of foreign affairs, M. T. Mbu, and included Commissioners S. J. Cookey (special duties in charge of relief) and Eyo Ndem (Agriculture); Attorney General J. I. Emembolu; Inspector General of Police P. I. Okeke; Professor Eni Njoku; Chief Secretary to the Biafran Government N. U. Akpan; Permanent Secretaries Onyejepu (Defense) and Onyegbula (Foreign Affairs).

[50] Republic of Biafra, "International Peace-Keeping/Observer Force," prepared by the Ministry of Defense, July 1968; "Biafran Proposal for a Plebiscite," prepared by the Ministry of Foreign Affairs; "Interim Administration of Disputed Areas," prepared by the Ministry of Internal Affairs.

could have legitimized his authority, at least in those areas still under Biafran control. If the federal government insisted that the entire former Eastern Region was disputed territory, then Ojukwu planned to counter with an attack on the legitimacy of Gowon's assumption of power in 1966 and the creation by fiat of the twelve states. In short, if the Nigerians challenged his authority over the Ibo heartland, Ojukwu would demand a plebiscite over the entire federation in the expectation that Gowon would back down. "The offer of a plebiscite," a briefing paper for the Biafran delegation confidently notes, "distracts attention from the fact of Biafran sovereignty. . . . It places emphasis rather on the issues of suzerainty, and this presumes the question of sovereignty to be settled. . . . Biafra . . . will thus gain a clear-cut and much more effective criterion for soliciting open world support."[51]

Questions relating to the political relations between the Ojukwu and Gowon regimes, according to Ojukwu's scheme, could be worked out through subsequent negotiations. If, to secure Nigerian acceptance of the cease-fire and an internationally supervised plebiscite in the minority areas, it appeared necessary for Biafra to renounce secession, then Ojukwu was prepared to do so in principle before the Emperor. Given the widespread international acceptance of the legitimacy of Biafran fears, Ojukwu expected that his insistence that he retain an absolute veto over any federal policy affecting the internal or external security of the Ibos would enjoy the backing of the major foreign powers. Unity, Ojukwu would argue, could only be achieved through stages over a period of years. This, of course, was the theme he had effectively promoted during and after the January 1967 Aburi meeting. Now, more than eighteen months later, he hoped that the international furor created by the continuing conflict and specter of human deprivation would ensure that any Nigerian agreement to a confederal solution would be under close scrutiny by Western powers.

Underlying the expectations for a breakthrough in Addis Ababa were several exaggerated assumptions about the impact that the Biafran drama was having on the international community. According to a Biafran Ministry of Foreign Affairs briefing document, "the world wants the wanton destruction of life and property going on now in Biafra to stop forthwith . . . [and] is aware of a dangerous arms race between Russia and Britain." Above all, the analysis concluded that "with Biafra now getting recognition from strong African states which are backed by certain world-powers, notably China [Tanzania] and France [Ivory

[51] Republic of Biafra, "A Propaganda and General Policy Outline on the Biafran Proposal of a Plebiscite and Insistence on an Immediate Ceasefire," a briefing paper prepared by the Ministry of Foreign Affairs for the Biafran delegation to the Addis Ababa Peace Talks, July 1968, p. 2.

Coast], and with the increasing possibility of recognition by some European countries as a result of British intransigence, the war will enter a lengthy, internationalized phase if the present disposition of both sides to effect negotiation is lost."[52] During the two weeks prior to the start of the Addis Ababa talks, Biafran lobbyists and envoys made a concerted effort to generate demonstrations of official international support. The evidence, if not the effect, of the diplomatic offensive is rather impressive.

Ojukwu's strongest hopes rested with the French and the Americans. From the former he sought a major demonstration of outright support in advance of the talks. His resident representative in Paris, Raph Uwechue, together with the Ivorians, failed to convince the French government to recognize Biafra, but they did achieve an important symbolic victory. On July 31, 1968, five days before the start of the Addis Ababa talks, French Information Minister Joel le Theule declared that "the French government believes that the present conflict should be settled on the basis of the right of peoples to self-determination and should entail putting into action the appropriate international procedures."[53] This was the most direct endorsement of the legitimacy of Biafra's claims to date by a major power, and was viewed by the American press as a move certain to strengthen Biafra's position psychologically at the forthcoming talks.[54] The British Broadcasting Corporation referred to the statement as "implied recognition," while a London newspaper interpreted it as a veiled threat to dispatch French paratroopers currently on maneuvers in Gabon.[55]

Gestures by the United States prior to the Addis Ababa talks were more circumspect, but still encouraging to the Biafrans. During his July 20, 1968, press conference, Ojukwu had called on America to help stop the "crime of genocide." He called on President Johnson "not to intervene physically but to bring [his] influence to bear in getting peace."[56] Ten days later the American secretary of state, Dean Rusk, publicly urged both sides to restrain their military operations in order to facilitate negotiations.[57] This, however, was insufficient for presidential candidate Eugene McCarthy, who called on the Johnson administration to "press for an immediate ceasefire and most forcefully urge our British allies to stop the shipment of arms to Nigeria." Echo-

---

[52] Republic of Biafra, "A Propaganda and General Policy Outline on the Biafran Proposal of a Plebiscite and Insistence on an Immediate Ceasefire," p. 7.

[53] *Daily Times*, August 1, 1968.   [54] *Washington Post*, August 1, 1968.

[55] BBC, West African Service, *Commentary*, August 1, 1968; and *Daily Express*, August 2, 1968.

[56] Radio Biafra, July 23, 1968, rebroadcast of Ojukwu's July 20, 1968, press conference.

[57] *New York Times*, July 31, 1968.

ing Ojukwu, McCarthy declared that the United States government "should also be prepared diplomatically to back a division of Nigeria according to the principles of self-determination, at least temporarily, and until such time as the Biafrans and Nigerians may agree on an alternative political settlement."[58] On the eve of the Addis Ababa talks, President Johnson sent a special message to Emperor Haile Selassie that was interpreted, at least by the press, as further evidence of America's interest in promoting a political compromise.[59]

Among Biafran efforts to maximize foreign pressures during the two weeks preceding the Addis Ababa meeting was a fresh series of reports of the horrendous death rate in the enclave. After his meeting with Ojukwu, President Houphouet-Boigny again claimed that more people had died in the Nigerian civil war than in Vietnam.[60] Meanwhile, Biafran estimates put the current death rate at 3 percent of the population per week, or between five and six thousand per day.[61] Radio Biafra further reported that more than 100,000 civilians had been killed by Nigeria's Soviet-built MIGs; this claim also was wildly exaggerated, but no less poignant, given Biafra's incapacity to retaliate or adequately defend itself.[62]

Juxtaposed to the campaign to incite the moral indignation of world opinion over the escalating violence, Ojukwu announced on the eve of the Addis Ababa talks that as "a gesture of sincerity" Biafran forces would observe a unilateral cease-fire. He concluded his statement with the observation that the Nigeria/Biafra war was "fruitless and futile" but "happily, though belatedly, the world has finally come to accept this fact."[63] On the same day the Nigerian government announced that federal forces would not consider a truce until the Biafrans renounced secession.[64]

A thirty-five member delegation, featuring many of Biafra's most prominent officials, left for Addis Ababa on August 4, 1968.[65] To enhance Biafra's international status, President Bongo of Gabon con-

[58] "McCarthy for President," Press Release, August 2, 1968.

[59] *The Times* (London), August 6, 1968.

[60] *Washington Post*, July 21, 1968.

[61] *Washington Post*, July 22, 1968. The same article reported that this rate "wildly exceeded" the estimates of private relief agencies, and that neutral observers saw the new estimates by Biafran authorities as "close to preposterous."

[62] Radio Biafra, July 30, 1968.

[63] Radio Biafra, Lieutenant Colonel Ojukwu's Broadcast to the Nation, August 3, 1968.

[64] *Morning Post*, August 3, 1968.

[65] The delegation included former President Azikiwe; Commissioners Matthew Mbu (External Affairs), S. J. Cookey (special duties in charge of relief), C. C. Mojekwu (Home Affairs), Chief J. Udo-Affia (Health), and Eyo Ndem (Agriculture); Mr. N. U. Akpan, chief secretary; Dr. Pius Okigbo, economic adviser; and Professor Eni Njoku, vice chancellor of the University of Nsukka.

tributed to Ojukwu's entourage his minister delegate in charge of information and an air force captain in full dress uniform.[66] Concerned that the delegation create the right impression as it stepped on to the world stage, Ojukwu's office had issued a special "Code of Conduct" for each official to follow. The Biafran leader had been angered by press reports of conviviality displayed during the Kampala and Niamey talks. All delegates were put on notice that "This is no jamboree; no time for wine, women and songs. Incalculable damage to our image abroad can be done by the appearance of debauchery, irresponsibility and squandermania by people whose kith and kin are dying in hundreds every day. . . . There must therefore be absolutely no fraternisation with any member of the Nigerian delegation. You should discourage, scorn or repulse any attempts at friendliness by any Nigerian."[67] The "code" also exhorted the team to make optimal use of the international exposure offered by the conference and predicted that it would be the center of world attention: "The universal interest which has been aroused by our conflict with Nigeria and the promise which the Addis Ababa conference holds forth of a confrontation between Nigeria and Biafra would certainly make, for the duration of the conference, a veritable press jamboree. . . . Every member of the Biafran delegation is also engaged in public relations duties for his country. He should seek to utilize every opportunity to explain our case to the outside world."[68]

By the time Chief Anthony Enahoro arrived later the same day in Addis Ababa at the head of the federal delegation,[69] Biafran public relations efforts were already underway. In a preliminary report to General Gowon later that day, Enahoro observed sardonically that the "rebels are showing horror films to all comers in their hotel rooms." As for the "press jamboree," Enahoro discerned much less international attention surrounding the talks than expected. In the same report, Enahoro estimated that there were only about ten overseas pressmen, plus four who normally were stationed in Africa, which was fewer than half the number that had flown in from Europe for the Kampala talks. Enahoro concluded that "the overseas press was not inclined to pay

[66] *West Africa*, No. 2672, August 17, 1968, p. 943.
[67] Republic of Biafra, "Code of Conduct for the Biafran Delegation to the Addis Ababa Conference on the Nigeria/Biafra Conflict."
[68] *Ibid.*
[69] Other senior members of the Nigerian delegation were: Federal Commissioners Alhaji Aminu Kano (Communications) and Olufemi Okunnu (Works and Housing); the administrator of the East Central State, Ukpabi Asika; Attorney General T. O. Elias; Colonel T. D. Bissala; Permanent Secretary of Economic Development Allison Ayida; and several lower-ranking officials from the Ministry of External Affairs.

maximum attention to the events in Addis Ababa because they feel the talks will fail."[70]

Consistent with Ojukwu's expectations, Emperor Haile Selassie summoned Enahoro to the Jubilee Palace almost immediately, and repeatedly urged him to convey to General Gowon his fervent wish to see the Nigerian head of state in Addis Ababa. The Ethiopian monarch stressed that the only way to achieve significant progress toward peacefully reuniting the country was for Gowon and Ojukwu to meet directly. Enahoro replied firmly that a visit by Gowon was out of the question, but offered only the vague excuse that conditions at home would not permit the head of state to leave. He assured the Emperor that the Nigerian delegation had a wide and flexible mandate to reach a settlement within a framework of "One Nigeria."[71] This was the closest Ojukwu came to achieving his much-desired "summit."

Despite Gowon's absence, the Emperor convened the talks without delay on the morning of August 5, 1968. As planned, Selassie opened the session with a word of welcome and briefly appealed to both sides to seize this "last chance" to find a peaceful solution.[72] Chief Enahoro's reply was equally brief. He identified the "central issue" as "whether or not the parts of the East Central State of Nigeria, still under the control of the other side, can be reintegrated into Nigeria through these talks," adding that the present circumstances "may well be our last chance to resolve our conflict through a negotiated settlement."[73] Ojukwu then rose and surprised his audience by deviating from the agreed procedures and supplanting the expected exchange of courtesies with a two-hour impassioned indictment of the federal military government.

Ojukwu decided to upstage his adversary. He describes his performance thus:

> We carefully managed our appearance, arriving second to the conference hall after the Nigerians had entered. When I arrived at the head of the delegation I entered the hall and froze at attention until everyone felt compelled to stand up. I glared around at the lot and then entered. Nigeria had lost any psychological advantage. Enahoro knew

[70] Cable: Enahoro to Gowon, August 4, 1968.

[71] Summary of the meeting with Emperor Haile Selassie contained in a cable from Chief Enahoro to General Gowon, August 5, 1968.

[72] "Opening Statement of Welcome, by H.I.M. Haile Selassie I at the Inaugural Meeting of the Peace Negotiations on Nigeria, August 5, 1968," summarized in *West Africa*, No. 2671, August 10, 1968, p. 937. In deference to Nigerian sensitivities, the Emperor wore only a dark European suit rather than his formal uniform, and chose not to use the presidential chair in Africa Hall.

[73] "Statement by Chief Anthony Enahoro at the Inaugural Meeting of the Peace Negotiations on Nigeria, August 5, 1968." Text from Nigerian Federal Ministry of Information, approximately 650 words.

he was on a weak wicket. . . . At the start of the conference, while the Emperor was speaking, Enahoro thought I might make an effort to speak first. I fidgeted, moved papers and made it look like I was about to jump up. Then, when the Emperor finished, Enahoro started immediately to talk. And when he finished, I began to pile on the pressure.[74]

The dramatic presentation notwithstanding, his address contained no hint of compromise on the basic issue of secession.[75] It began by astutely invoking the Emperor's own words before the League of Nations when Ethiopia had stood alone against Italian aggression in 1936. Ojukwu ended with a heavy-handed indictment of Gowon for "aspiring to be the Hitler of Africa." Otherwise, his remarks consisted of detailing Biafra's version of Nigerian history to substantiate his basic contention that the physical survival of the Biafran people could not be separated from the sovereign independence of the Biafran state.

Assessments of the Biafran leader's immediate impact, particularly on the Emperor's disposition, vary according to the allegiance of the observer. The political reality, however, was that without Gowon, Ojukwu's presence in Addis Ababa was quickly becoming untenable. The longer he remained, the more he appeared as an equal to Gowon's subordinate, Chief Enahoro. So he submitted an ultimatum: unless Gowon responded positively to the Emperor's invitation within twenty-four hours, he would return to Biafra. On August 6, 1968, Ojukwu flew home, leaving Professor Eni Njoku behind as the head of Biafra's downgraded delegation.

Ojukwu's performance and sudden exit foreclosed any possibility for substantive negotiations, although the issues on the agenda were yet to be addressed, and the appearance of negotiations would be sustained for another month. A "preliminary assessment" of the talks, cabled back to Lagos on August 8 by a member of the federal delegation, described the conference as "virtually over." Ojukwu's speech was taken as evidence that the Biafran leader continued to believe that foreign intervention would save his regime, and the report stressed that "only a quick military solution can keep Nigeria one." Because of the Emperor's presence, the struggle for propaganda advantage, and "Professor Njoku's better conferenceship compared with Mbanefo's," Gowon was accurately advised that the Addis Ababa meetings might limp along for a few weeks before collapsing. But "One Nigeria," it

[74] Interview: Ojukwu.
[75] "Statement by Lt. Col. C. O. Ojukwu at the Inaugural Meeting of the Peace Negotiations on Nigeria, August 5, 1968." Text from Biafran Ministry of Information, approximately 15,000 words.

was bluntly noted, "remains unattainable through the Conference Table."[76]

The same August 8 cable also warned the Nigerian leader that the failure in Addis Ababa would probably lead to renewed attempts by Biafra's supporters to arrange a direct meeting between Gowon and Ojukwu, and that Gowon should publicly foreclose such a possibility, as a matter of principle, without delay. Following this recommendation, less than two weeks later Gowon granted an exclusive interview with the editor of *West Africa*, in which he laid firmly to rest any possibility of meeting Ojukwu. Commenting upon the Emperor's invitation, he declared: "I cannot enter discussions on equal terms with a man who, even before he became a rebel, was only one of my military governors."[77]

The absence of Gowon and Ojukwu did not deter Emperor Haile Selassie from continuing to press for an exchange of views regarding the two substantive items on the negotiating agenda, that is, "arrangements for a permanent settlement" and "terms for the cessation of hostilities." On Wednesday, August 7, 1968, the two sides met for their first closed-door meeting, and Chief Enahoro outlined a nine-point set of proposals that were practically identical to those tabled in Kampala two and a half months before. Aware of the futility of this undertaking, Enahoro wired Gowon on August 9 the following advice while awaiting the Biafran reply: "There is a strong feeling among the federal delegation that if, as expected, Njoku turns down our proposals at today's [August 9] session, we should not waste more time here. Enahoro has to be mindful of your charge that we must not in any circumstance break up the talks. In fact, this is one of the reasons why we did not walk out and return home when Ojukwu was insulting you. If the talks break down our delegates will hold press conferences at various capitals on way home.[78]

The seventy-six-year-old monarch lobbied strenuously to head off a further downgrading of the talks. He met separately with each side on four occasions during the next two days. The results of these discussions were summarized on August 13, 1968 in a cable that the Emperor sent to the other members of the Consultative Committee. The Nigerian proposals show a somewhat greater sensitivity for Ibo fears of physical abuse at the hands of an occupying force, and the federal government indicated a new flexibility regarding the possible introduc-

[76] "A Preliminary Assessment of the Addis Ababa Peace Talks," Cable sent by Allison Ayida to Secretary to the Federal Military Government H. A. Ejueyitchie, August 8, 1968.

[77] "General Gowon Talks to the Editor," *West Africa*, No. 2673, August 24, 1968, p. 971.

[78] Cable: Enahoro to Gowon, August 9, 1968.

tion of an "external force" after the fighting had ceased. The other guarantees for the future safety and well being of the Ibo people are worth noting, because they were all honored in good faith when the conflict finally ended with a federal military victory in January 1970.

The Emperor's cable to the OAU Committee members reads, in part:

The peace proposals of the Federal Government of Nigeria as submitted in camera are as follows:

1. the renunciation of secession by a joint declaration which would proclaim the unity of Nigeria, but would not require the other side to make a unilateral pronouncement of renunciation;
2. in the view of the federal government such a joint declaration, given agreement in other areas, could be immediately followed by the cessation of hostilities and should be followed by disarming the rebel forces;
3. after disarming the rebel forces, the normal policing of rebel held areas should be the responsibility solely of the police, and that the police units in these areas should consist mostly of persons of Ibo origin;
4. until mutual confidence is restored and external force should be stationed in Iboland composed of units from Ethiopia, India, and Canada and the functions, its composition, numbers, command, financing, and the duration of the force could be negotiated;
5. the military governor and members of his executive council should be Ibos. The Executive Council should be drawn in part from among persons who supported the rebel cause in proportion to be agreed by negotiations;
6. a general amnesty will be granted in most cases; other claims for amnesty could be examined at the talks;
7. public servants will be reabsorbed into public employment and that the Ibos as a people will be assured a fair share of employment in federal public services, including Federal Statutory Corporations;
8. arrangement will be made for a constitutional conference. The composition of such a conference, selection, procedures, etc. could be negotiated;
9. once there is agreement on the reunification of Nigeria, all routes will be open for rushing relief to the needy areas.[79]

In response to the Nigerian proposals, Professor Njoku submitted Biafra's minimum requirements for a settlement. They were briefer and, in light of Gowon's refusal to meet Ojukwu, they were merely pro

[79] Full text of the cable appears as Annex VII in the *Report on Nigeria.*

forma. Biafra's position amounted to three basic and well-known demands, namely:

1. *Internal Security*: the maintenance of law and order in Biafra must be the sole responsibility of the Biafran government.
2. *External Security*:
   (A) Armed Forces: in order to defend ourselves against invaders from outside Biafra, whether Nigerians or other people, we must have our own armed forces.
   (B) International Personality: Biafra must be a member of international organizations to enable her to present her case anytime she has cause to do so.
3. *Economic Security*: Biafra must have the right to enter into international contracts on her own right to ensure that her economic development is not impeded by any authority as Nigeria did before and during the crisis.[80]

After the Biafran demands were shown to the Nigerian delegation, the Emperor pleaded for "new maximum guarantees on security" from the federal government on the grounds that Njoku had not turned down flatly the federal suggestion for some form of joint declaration renouncing secession.[81] Enahoro informed him that the federal delegation "had stretched its mandate as far as it could and it would not be possible to give more concessions as long as the central question of secession remains unresolved." He had not, Enahoro added curtly, "come to liquidate Nigeria." His delegation's task was "not to determine how strong or weak the future structures of the government of Nigeria would be; this would be left to a constitutional conference."[82] On August 13, 1968, Chief Enahoro left Addis Ababa for Lagos. In his stead, Olufemi Okunnu was elevated to head the federal delegation. Okunnu, then only thirty-five years old, was commissioner of works and housing, and the youngest member of Gowon's Federal Executive Council.

---

[80] *Ibid.*   [81] Cable: Enahoro to Gowon, August 12, 1968.
[82] Before leaving Addis Ababa, Eni Njoku met informally with a small Quaker delegation and told them that Biafra was prepared to become part of a Nigerian union and that the concept of Biafran sovereignty was more a symbol of defiance than a political necessity. Njoku added that Biafra was also ready to compromise on such issues as cease-fire lines, territorial boundaries, the composition of a peace-keeping force, etc. On two points Njoku said Biafra could not compromise. They would continue to insist on maintaining an independent armed force behind any cease-fire line, and Biafra would require some degree of international standing independent of federal authority. Quaker representatives carried this message to Lagos and delivered it directly to Gowon. The Nigerian leader questioned Njoku's authority to speak for Ojukwu, and after consulting with his military colleagues, declined to pursue the matter further on the grounds that there could not be two independent armies within the country. Interview: John Volkmar.

Faced with a stalemate over substantive issues and an obvious erosion of authority at the conference table, Haile Selassie invited the other members of the Consultative Committee to meet in Addis Ababa on August 19, 1968, to "exert our influence and that of Africa on both sides . . . and to consult further to what steps should be taken to discharge the mandate entrusted to us by the OAU."[83] It is not clear whether the Emperor actually expected a favorable response, or was merely demonstrating his concern and willingness to pursue all diplomatic alternatives in his efforts as a peace-maker. In any event, he received no encouragement from the committee members, as each one quietly turned down the invitation, noting that it would be more convenient to meet during the OAU summit in Algiers only a month away.

Unilateral Authority over the Biafran Airlift

Having failed to promote any meaningful discussion regarding the two substantive points on the negotiating agenda, the Emperor doggedly turned his attention to the third and final item: "concrete proposals for the transportation of relief supplies to the civilian victims of the civil war." Talk on this subject began on August 14, 1968, and dragged on for three weeks, until the Emperor at last signaled for an adjournment in order to prepare for the OAU summit, which was due to open in Algiers on September 13, 1968.

For the federal government, relief per se was not the issue. Shortly after the war broke out the International Committee of the Red Cross asked for permission to penetrate the federal blockade and fly a plane load of medical supplies into Port Harcourt. Gowon immediately approved the request[84] and throughout the war he remained committed to the principle of allowing food and medical supplies to reach the civilians in Biafra. He supported these endeavors in order to alleviate the human suffering, to promote international good will, and to facilitate what he always believed would be the inevitable transfer of popular allegiance from Biafra to Nigeria once peace was restored.

By mid-1968 the need for massive humanitarian aid was indisputable. The former Eastern Region had historically been a substantial food importer, particularly of protein (primarily beef from northern Nigeria and stock fish from Iceland).[85] In Onitsha, Owerri, and Umuahia provinces, the few thousand square miles making up the Ibo heartland, protein scarcity and general malnutrition had threatened the wel-

---

[83] Text of the cable appears as Annex VII in the *Report on Nigeria*.

[84] *Morning Post*, July 22, 1967.

[85] See Helleiner, *Peasant Agriculture, Government, and Economic Growth in Nigeria*.

fare of the poor and overcrowded population for generations.[86] The traditionally low land-to-man ratio was reminiscent of the Nile Valley and parts of Asia long before the civil war, and by July 1968, after a year's blockade and the crushing inflow of millions of Ibo refugees, mass starvation appeared to be imminent.[87]

Biafra's immediate food crisis was not, of course, the result of some natural disaster such as drought or pestilence, although the spectacle of human misery among the Ibos was often compared to other tragedies, including the Irish famines of the nineteenth century,[88] that were not the direct result of a political conflict. Aid for suffering Biafrans raised political and strategic as well as humanitarian issues. The foreign relief agencies that wished to provide assistance faced difficult choices of policy that are normally not raised when they rush to help the victims of an earthquake or similar "act of God." The obvious risk in the Nigerian situation was that anyone who intervened—regardless of motive—was likely to be seen as a party to the political dispute. Realistic churchmen and other relief personnel acknowledged this fact and many found the risks acceptable. As one religious leader concluded: "When you fed the first Biafran child you made a political decision . . . but the more pressing comment is the citation from the New Testament, 'Feed my sheep'!"[89]

The issue that first concerned Nigerian authorities related to the way relief to Biafra was delivered, and it was over this matter that the initial conflicts with the international humanitarian agencies arose. Ojukwu wanted an arrangement with the agencies that he could control, one that would neither imply any dependence on the federal government nor jeopardize the delivery of military supplies. The relief agencies would have preferred, and repeatedly called for, a combination of land and sea corridors plus unrestricted daylight relief flights. Such arrangements would have allowed the maximum amount of food and medicine to reach the enclave at a minimum cost and danger to relief personnel. These proposals were endorsed in general by the federal government.

[86] A relief worker, long familiar with conditions in the East, remarked to the author during the latter's visit to Owerri in July 1970 that one benefit from the horrors of war had been the recent awareness of the importance of protein-rich foods, and that through wartime programs Ibos had been taught to grow and consume foods high in protein, thereby bringing nutritional standards in Owerri to the highest point in memory.

[87] See Wiseberg, *The International Politics of Relief*, "The Development of Famine Conditions in Eastern Nigeria," pp. 76–82.

[88] The comparison was frequently and effectively evoked by Irish Holy Ghost Fathers in their fund raising efforts for Biafran relief in the United States.

[89] James MacCracken, Executive Director, Church World Service, in a confidential report, "Disaster Report and Response," No. 88–X, to the Church World Service Department Committee, April 2, 1969.

But much more was at stake for Biafra than matters of cost and convenience.

As Nigeria and Biafra maneuvered to establish acceptable ground rules for foreign relief operations, it became apparent that the degree of responsiveness to federal pressures correlated positively with a given humanitarian organization's institutional development and the extent of its formal linkages to recognized governments in the international system, including the Gowon regime in Lagos. Among the potential humanitarian interventionists, the United Nations was most easily deterred from any action regarded in Lagos as contrary to Nigeria's interests. At the other end of the spectrum were the churches, particularly the Nordic group, which provided the foundation for the Jointchurchaid airlift that will be discussed in the next chapter; their intervention was ad hoc and extralegal. They responded only to the dictates of their own moral imperative, without regard to any formal charter of procedures and without any fear of establishing a precedent in the Nigerian conflict that might limit their effectiveness elsewhere. More ambivalent than either the United Nations or Jointchurchaid in defining its rightful obligations in the Nigerian crisis was the International Committee of the Red Cross (ICRC). Of those agencies actively involved in the Biafran air bridge, the ICRC was the most vulnerable to Nigerian pressure. It was also the first to become involved in the Nigerian crisis, and was prepared to work through the OAU in seeking arrangements that would satisfy the federal government.

The ICRC is not an intergovernmental body such as the United Nations, the OAU, or even the loosely-knit Commonwealth organization. It does, however, act as the wartime conscience of the signatory powers to the four Geneva Conventions.[90] In so doing, the committee is obligated to uphold certain standards of procedure. The "Geneva Convention Relative to the Protection of Civilian Persons in Time of War," to which Nigeria is a party, states inter alia, "the International Committee of the Red Cross or any other impartial humanitarian organization may, subject to the consent of the Parties to the conflict concerned, undertake for the protection of civilian persons and for their relief." Historically, the ICRC's work had been devoted primarily to verifying that the conventions were not violated. The massive intervention that the ICRC eventually accomplished in Nigeria was unprecedented.

[90] The Four Conventions are: I. Geneva Convention for the Amelioration of the Condition of the Wounded and Sick in Armed Forces in the Field; II. Geneva Convention for the Amelioration of the Condition of Wounded, Sick and Shipwrecked Members of the Armed Forces at Sea; III. Geneva Convention relative to the Treatment of Prisoners of War; and IV. Geneva Convention relative to the Protection of Civilian Persons in Time of War. Since August 12, 1949, they have been signed by 125 governments.

In December 1967, Nigeria had agreed to a plan for the establishment of an ICRC operational base on the nearby Spanish island of Fernando Po, where there was a Nigerian consul general who could check all cargoes leaving for Biafra. While the secessionists mulled over this proposal, the number of gunrunning aircraft from Portugal increased. Lagos reacted on January 15, 1968, by banning all air traffic to Biafra not specifically cleared by federal authorities.[91] The ICRC was informed that in the future its flights would have to be routed through Lagos to avoid becoming intertwined with Biafra's illegal military supply planes. Two days later, the Biafrans announced their acceptance of the original Fernando Po arrangements. An impasse ensued for three months, and all ICRC planes remained grounded.

Between April 9 and July 15, 1968, ICRC planes made only thirteen flights to Biafra, all of them after dark.[92] The ICRC urgently wanted to increase substantially the flow of supplies to Biafra. On May 23, 1968, it launched a campaign—tactlessly named "SOS Biafra"—that entailed a request from the Geneva headquarters to some thirty national Red Cross societies imploring them to intervene with their respective governments and mobilize public support, in order to obtain massive material and financial support.[93] Simultaneously, the ICRC delegate general for Africa, Georg Hoffman, was sent to Kampala to lobby Nigerian and Biafran representatives who were then meeting under Commonwealth auspices. The initiative, which included a public call for lifting the federal blockade barely a week after the fall of Port Harcourt, was made without any prior consultations with the federal government, and Nigerian authorities were sharply critical of the unexpected intrusion into the political talks.[94]

Toward the end of June 1968, Hoffman went to Lagos and met with General Gowon in an effort to smooth relations and pave the way for greater humanitarian intervention. The federal government was prepared to give the ICRC facilities to deliver huge quantities of relief, but insisted that supplies destined for Biafra be conveyed through the blockade along land corridors. As a stop-gap measure, Lagos agreed to tolerate daylight relief flights to Biafra's only known air strip, a two-mile

---

[91] *West Africa*, No. 2642, January 20, 1968, p. 82.

[92] ICRC, *Annual Report 1968*, p. 13.

[93] ICRC, *Information Notes*, No. 107b, May 31, 1968. The text also notes that the ICRC planned an immediate campaign to enlist the help of the world press. An earlier, less publicized, appeal in April 1968 had been sent to all Red Cross societies, and asked specifically for medical supplies. By June 1968 only nineteen of the national societies had responded. ICRC, Press Release, No. 889, Geneva, June 3, 1968.

[94] *Morning Post*, May 29, 1968; Radio Nigeria, *Newstalk*, May 31, 1968; and, a particularly bitter commentary, *The New Nigerian*, "Dubious Role of the ICRC in our Crisis," June 4, 1968.

stretch of reinforced highway running north and south between the villages of Uli and Ihiala on the Onitsha-Owerri axis. This was the soon-to-be-famous Uli airstrip, Biafra's principal link with the outside world, and the entry port for its clandestine arms shipments. Hoffman was enthusiastic about alternatives to the current arrangements for relief delivery. Night flights were exorbitant in cost and dangerous; an ICRC plane was to crash on approaching Uli during the early hours of June 30.

The talks sponsored by the OAU's Consultative Committee in Niamey and Addis Ababa offered the ICRC an opportunity to arrange a compromise solution for the delivery of relief that would satisfy both federal and Biafran authorities. In principal, the ICRC endorsed the federal proposals for a combination of land corridors and daylight flights as reasonable and desirable.[95] All proposals, for stepped up relief, however, touched complex political and strategic issues that were invariably given top priority by the parties to the dispute. In Niamey, each team had submitted alternative routes for land, sea, and air relief corridors, which raised sensitive questions related to the implied rights of sovereignty, the current deployment of armed forces, and the length, width, and international supervision of demilitarized zones. Nothing was settled, but the federal delegation had left Niamey with the impression that agreement on a land corridor was still possible.[96]

The atmosphere in Niamey had been definitely influenced by Ojukwu's eagerness to meet Gowon in Addis Ababa and, therefore, his delegation was reluctant to raise any serious obstacles at that stage. The situation had changed by mid-August, and the Biafrans quickly made it clear that they would in no way compromise the safety of their nightly airlift of vital military and other supplies. This resolve was first tested on August 14, 1968, when Emperor Haile Selassie initiated the discussion of the relief issue by tabling his own plan for simultaneously opening land and air relief corridors into Biafra, with the federal capital of Lagos as the principal staging area, so as to ensure that Nigeria's sovereignty would not be violated.[97] The plan also included elaborate provisions for international inspections during all phases of the operations.

Apparently moved by the enormity of human suffering in Biafra, even after allowing for any politically motivated statistical inflation, the Emperor seemed to think the time was right to press for alternatives to the limited and, at this stage, erratic night airlift.[98] His objective, as re-

---

[95] *Report on Nigeria.*   [96] *Report on Niamey Session.*

[97] *Report on Nigeria*, pp. 13–14, gives a verbatim account of the first compromise proposals on the transport of relief to Biafra.

[98] By mid-July, the Red Cross estimated that there were up to 4.5 million civil-

ported to Gowon in an August 14 cable from the Nigerian delegation to the Addis Ababa talks was to "assist the federal government by removing the humanitarian issue [from the issue of secession] and to prevent Ojukwu from playing politics and winning world opinion in our internal affairs. . . . The Emperor believes that a solution of the relief question will give the federal government a breathing space to carry on operations outside the glare of world publicity."[99] The Emperor presumably shared with the Nigerians a keen desire not to allow uncontrolled foreign intervention, for whatever reasons, in the internal affairs of an independent African state.

In developing his comprehensive proposals, Selassie had the advice of Mr. August Lindt, the commissioner general on Nigerian relief for the International Committee of the Red Cross, who had been sent to Addis Ababa as "an adviser on logistical questions."[100] It appeared that the federal government, the ICRC, and the Emperor were in sufficient agreement to dictate to the Biafrans the terms for bringing needed humanitarian relief into the enclave. On August 10, 1968, the ICRC halted its night relief flights to Biafra, citing Nigerian antiaircraft fire, and the Biafrans interpreted the move as a power play to force acceptance of a federally approved plan for overland relief.

Had the ICRC been the only humanitarian agency prepared to intervene, Ojukwu would have been left with a choice between accepting relief on Nigeria's terms or bearing the responsibility for any further civilian starvation. On matters related to relief, however, Ojukwu was able to play from a very strong position. The same day Lindt announced the interruption of the ICRC airlift, August 13, 1968, Dr. Edward Johnson of the Canadian Presbyterian Church informed a press conference in Geneva that a "decisive" break in the blockade had been carried out by Carl Gustav von Rosen in a Transair Sweden DC–7B on behalf of the German churches.[101] The Canadian church leader said he had personally flown from Biafra with von Rosen, in the company of *New York Times* correspondent Lloyd Garrison.

Defying all warnings from the Nigerian government, von Rosen had flown into Biafra at tree-top level, and was immediately embraced by Ojukwu who now had an alternative to the ICRC for nightly relief supplies conveyed strictly on Biafra's terms. This was the real beginning of the largest privately-run airlift in history. The impact of this venture on the Biafran economy will be recounted in Chapter 8. In Addis

---

lians displaced and suffering from varying degrees of undernourishment in the Biafran enclave. ICRC, Press Release, Geneva, July 19, 1968, No. 109b.

[99] Cable: Okunnu to Gowon, August 14, 1968.

[100] ICRC, *Annual Report 1968*, p. 14.

[101] Lloyd *et al., The Nordchurchaid Airlift to Biafra 1968–1970*, p. 10.

Ababa, the news reduced the need for a compromise, and ultimately precluded any African influence over this aspect of the internationalization process.

Church defiance of federal authority placed the ICRC in an awkward position. Two days later, on August 16, 1968, the committee threatened to take "every possible step" to deliver food and medical supplies to the civilians in Biafra, and called for federal approval of a new proposal already endorsed by Ojukwu, which would have neutralized a second stretch of highway for exclusive use by the ICRC. Under the plan, Uli airstrip would be free of ICRC planes, although the churches and Biafra's military transports would presumably continue their nightly operations. The major obstacle preventing the federal government from accepting the ICRC's request was that the airstrip that the ICRC was helping to construct was located on the Okigwi/Afikpo road, directly in front of Nigeria's advancing First Division.[102]

Bargaining over alternative arrangements for the delivery of relief supplies had become deadlocked, with Biafra calling for a second airstrip to be placed under international control, and the federal government proposing daylight flights to Uli. Meanwhile, the churches' nightly air shuttle was expanding, in defiance of the federal blockade and without regard for Emperor Haile Selassie's mediating efforts in Addis Ababa. To salvage some semblance of traditional international respect for sovereign authority by enabling the ICRC to operate in Biafra without violating the letter of its convention, Selassie prevailed upon the federal military government in a diplomatic note to Gowon on September 1 to permit the ICRC to resume nightly flights from Fernando Po directly to the secessionist enclave.[103]

Publicly, Nigeria's commissioner of external affairs accused Catholic Relief Services (CARITAS), the World Council of Churches, and "certain national Red Cross societies," of exerting "unhealthy political pressure on the ICRC."[104] The Ministry of External Affairs privately instructed the Nigerian consul on Fernando Po to inspect ICRC planes before taking off for the rebel enclave; as far as the ICRC was concerned, the resumption of night flights was with the private consent of the federal military government, which, under an exchange of notes

[102] Nigeria's detailed rejection of the alternative airstrip was explained to Dr. Lindt in Lagos, and relayed to the federal delegation in Addis Ababa on August 29, 1968. The controversial strip of highway between Okigwi and Afikpo was not overrun by federal troops until September 20.

[103] The Emperor argued that if the federal government had allowed direct mercy flights in the past from Fernando Po after inspections, it should be able to authorize such flights as "a special concession," and that this should be done in advance of the September OAU summit in Algiers so as to defuse the humanitarian argument.

[104] *Daily Sketch*, August 21, 1968.

with the ICRC, declined any responsibility for the safety of the flights, but then also agreed to refrain from doing anything to jeopardize those flights.[105] In a note to Emperor Haile Selassie on September 2, 1968, Gowon indicated his impatience with this arrangement:

> Your Imperial Majesty will appreciate the difficulties and embarrassment we have overcome in submitting to your request considering the activities of the ICRC in other world capitals. They have, in effect, presented us with an ultimatum and a *fait accompli* to over fly positions held by my troops in taking supplies to rebel held areas without agreement. . . . *This is a flagrant attempt against all the conventions and history of the ICRC; to do in an African country what they have never dared to do in many other more disastrous theatres of current world conflict.* Irrespective of international illegality involved and possible incidents for which my government cannot accept responsibility, their action can only increase the intransigence of the rebels, postpone peace and the solution of the Nigerian crisis indefinitely, entail more suffering, and in effect defeat the humanitarian purposes which they claim to serve.[106]

For the public record, on September 3, 1968, the ICRC and the Nigerian government announced an agreement permitting ten days of unrestricted daylight flights to Uli airstrip as an interim emergency measure to alleviate the worst civilian suffering.[107] The federal government thus formally lifted its air blockade, but only during the day, and only for a specified period. Haile Selassie sent a message of congratulations and personal appreciation.[108] When Ojukwu refused to accept this arrangement, the ICRC within forty-eight hours launched a much expanded all-night air shuttle from Fernando Po to Biafra called "Operation INALWA" (International Airlift West Africa) in the hope that the federal government would continue to be tolerant.[109] The full scope and political significance of the ICRC operation will be reviewed in the chapter that follows.

When the talks in Addis Ababa adjourned sine die on September 9, 1968, few abroad took much notice, although Nigerian and Biafran publicists were quick to distribute long treatises purporting to detail

---

[105] Cable, Ayida to Ejueyitchie, August 29, 1968.

[106] MEA, Text of Note from H. E. Major-General Yakubu Gowon to His Imperial Majesty, conveyed by Olufemi Okunnu on September 2, 1968.

[107] ICRC, Press Release No. 906, Geneva, September 3, 1968; and Nigeria, Federal Ministry of Information, Press Release No. F1565, September 3, 1968.

[108] Nigeria, Federal Ministry of Information, Press Release No. F1569, September 4, 1968.

[109] ICRC, Press Release No. 910b, Geneva, September 10, 1968.

who was to blame for the lack of any substantive agreement.[110] At the time the talks collapsed, Western Europe was reeling from the August 20–21 Soviet invasion of Czechoslovakia, and America was consumed with the violence of the Democratic National Convention in Chicago.

The Addis Ababa meetings were, nevertheless, the most protracted and complicated of the war; the Emperor ultimately met separately with each delegation on at least thirty-five occasions.[111] Yet the OAU Consultative Committee's efforts, which for the most part consisted of personal initiatives by the Emperor, brought the two sides no closer to a negotiated settlement than the earlier moves by Arnold Smith and the Commonwealth Secretariat.

Defiance of the federal blockade and the lack of progress in Addis Ababa encouraged the hawks on both sides to press for tougher policies. In Lagos, Gowon summoned his senior field commanders for consultation on August 14, the day after von Rosen's much-publicized flight into Biafra. After a full review of the military situation, the decision was taken to pursue the war into the Ibo heartland. For the moderates, including Gowon, who had hoped that with the fall of Port Harcourt and federal occupation of the minority areas Ojukwu would agree to surrender, this was a final and difficult turning point. Ten days later, on August 24, 1968, Gowon formally announced that a "final push" into the Biafran enclave was unavoidable and underway.

If ever Ojukwu stood a chance of converting international humanitarian concern into political action, it was during the summer of 1968; the intensity of pressures from the many pro-Biafra groups in Europe and North America would not be duplicated.[12] Whether and under what conditions the popular outcry to save Biafra might have moved Western governments to forsake their more abiding interests in Nigeria and risk a major rift with the federal military government, can only be guessed. One element in the equation, which allowed these same governments freedom from having to act decisively on the Nigerian question, was the convening of direct talks between federal and Biafran

[110] Nigeria, Federal Ministry of Information, *Federal Peace Efforts* (Lagos, 1968), and Republic of Biafra, *Biafran Government Statement on Peace Talks with Nigeria* (Enugu, 1968).

[111] *West Africa*, No. 2676, September 14, 1968, p. 1085.

[112] The most obvious, if not always the most reliable, indicator of public interest in Biafra was the burst of coverage by the Western media. Most notable in Britain were special supplements in the *Sunday Times* (June 9, 1968) and the *Daily Telegraph* (August 22, 1968). In the United States a special pictorial feature of the suffering in Biafra appeared in *Life* (July 12, 1968) and reportedly caught the attention of President Lyndon Johnson. And in late August, Lieutenant Colonel Ojukwu received the ultimate media recognition when he became the fourth African since 1960 to appear on the cover of *Time* (August 23, 1968).

representatives. As grass-roots pro-interventionist lobbies mushroomed in Western countries, harassed officials could always excuse their inaction by pleading an unwillingness to disrupt "delicate negotiations."

Reflecting on the political significance of the 1968 peace talks, Nigeria's commissioner of external affairs has concluded: "The peace talks accomplished what we wanted. While they did not influence those who supported the rebels they did a great deal to reassure our friends, particularly the British Labour government which was under great pressure from their Left Wing and public opinion. Our willingness to talk had an important impact because by not insisting on a military solution we spiked much of the criticisms."[113] Not surprisingly, Arikpo's perceptions closely match those offered by General Gowon: "We were ready to talk [with the Biafrans] as long as the war continued. It was the only way to parry the threat of greater foreign intervention. As long as you talk people will wait."[114]

With the benefit of hindsight and in the bitterness of defeat, Ojukwu and his principal advisers later regarded the 1968 peace talks as an Anglo-American subterfuge that successfully took the steam out of Biafra's most powerful diplomatic offensive. At the time, however, Biafra's leaders were preoccupied with staving off the threat of widespread starvation and what appeared to be an imminent federal invasion of the Ibo heartland. The following chapter discusses the collapse of Nigeria's fall 1968 offensive, and how the secessionists were able to acquire internationally the means to sustain a war of attrition in the hope of ultimately bringing about a political settlement that would preserve Biafra's political and military self-determination.

[113] Interview: Arikpo.   [114] Interview: Gowon.

· 8 ·

A WAR OF ATTRITION

September 1968 passed without peace and national reconciliation, as
General Gowon's latest "final offensive" again proved inconclusive.
Elements of Colonel Adekunle's 35,000-man Third Marine Division
succeeded in pushing north from Port Harcourt, and captured two of
Biafra's three remaining towns, Aba and Owerri, but the victories produced few strategic advantages. More importantly, a third prong in
Adekunle's northward push came within seven miles of capturing Uli
airstrip before being stopped by a Biafran counterattack. Had the airstrip fallen, Biafra might have surrendered. Instead, the war dragged
on for another fifteen months. Before returning to a discussion of
foreign involvement one should know the military developments that
lay behind the conduct of international relations (see Map 8–1).

When Aba fell on September 4, 1968, Biafra lost its last major commercial center and the former Eastern Region's fourth most populous
town.[1] Aba offered virtually no resistance to advancing federal troops,
whose forty-one-mile march from Port Harcourt had been almost entirely through friendly areas of the Rivers State.[2] For several months,
Aba had been in virtual insurrection against Ojukwu's authority; Biafran
forces had been sent to maintain order, and the town's leading political
figure, former Minister of External Affairs Jaja Wachuku, had been
placed in detention. When Nigerian troops arrived, the Biafrans had
already withdrawn to take new positions north of the town, and most
of Aba's 131,000 inhabitants had gone into hiding in the surrounding
bush.

A second column of Adekunle's forces advanced twenty miles west
of Aba, and captured the smaller town of Owerri on September 15,
1968. Once again, Biafran troops and all but a handful of the 50,000
prewar population withdrew to the outskirts of town in advance of
the Nigerian army. Owerri was the first major town to fall inside the
traditionally overcrowded Ibo heartland, and its capture caused considerable self-congratulatory publicity by the federal government. In
fact, Nigerian troops controlled only the inner township, and constant
harassment from the intensely hostile surrounding areas forced a with-

---

[1] Only Port Harcourt (180,000), Onitsha (163,000), and Enugu (140,000)
were larger than Aba (131,000) in population, according to the 1963 census.
[2] *West Africa*, No. 2676, September 14, 1968, p. 1065.

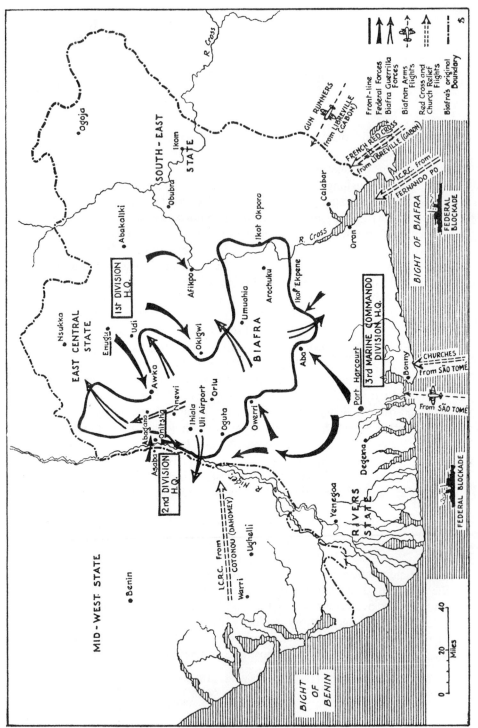

Map 8–1 • Biafra, October 1968 (from John de St. Jorre, *The Nigerian Civil War*, p. 221)

drawal in April 1969 from Owerri, the only Biafran town to change hands during the war.

While the fall of Aba and Owerri attracted press headlines, a third contingent of Adekunle's forces was engaged in a far more strategic battle twenty-five miles west of Owerri—a daring and ultimately disastrous attempt to capture the Biafran landing strip at Uli. On September 10–11 the Fifteenth Commando Brigade occupied Oguta, a village located only ten miles southwest of the airstrip. Had the commandos succeeded in securing their position 3 miles beyond Oguta, medium-range artillery would have been able to close down the airstrip ahead of advancing troops.

When Ojukwu received word that Oguta had fallen, he rushed twenty-three miles from his headquarters near Owerri to lead a counterattack. Overnight he moved in six pieces of field artillery, one of the largest batteries ever assembled by Biafra's poorly equipped forces.[3] He positioned his forces on the east bank of Orashi River, the only natural defensive position on the road between Oguta and Uli airstrip. With a battalion of nine hundred soldiers under the command of Col. Joe "Hannibal" Achuzie, Ojukwu waited for Adekunle's troops to cross the water at daybreak, September 12. As the Nigerians embarked in canoes and other small craft the Biafrans opened fire, sinking most of the vessels. In the confusion that followed, the remnants of the Fifteenth Brigade retreated quickly to positions twenty miles south, just outside the Ibo heartland near the village of Ebocha.

Ebocha is the northernmost outpost in the Rivers State, and its attractiveness as a point of retreat for the federal troops confirmed, however ironically, the political significance of dividing Eastern Nigeria into three states. The episode also shed important light on why Nigeria took so long to win the war. According to a Nigerian army Lt. Colonel who was familiar with the event: the loss of Oguta was "a tragic blunder" due primarily to the lack of experience and the particular ethnic composition of the Fifteenth Commando Brigade. The brigade had been formed shortly after the capture of Port Harcourt in May 1968, and comprised Rivers State troops whose principal commitment seems to have been to rid their homeland of the traditional Ibo domination. When the brigade reached Oguta, the first sizable village inside Iboland, discipline fell apart, with uncontrolled looting and drunken celebrations. When the word came from the forward elements that the Biafrans had counterattacked, brigade members fled in disarray back to the safety of their homeland in the recently liberated Rivers State. Summarizing the debacle, the Nigerian officer concluded: "So the Rivers

[3] The battery consisted only of two 105mm howitzers, a 12mm mortar, and three 81mm mortars.

troops argued, 'o.k., we have our state which we wanted and helped get . . . the Ibos now have their state and that's fine with us. Just don't get us shot!' Then they faded. What did they think they were doing? We Yorubas had our own state long before anyone even thought of a Rivers State and we were willing to go on fighting. But that is Nigeria."[4]

The loss of Oguta was a major factor in the prolongation of the war. By mid-September 1968, the Third Marine Division held a ragged perimeter along Biafra's southern front, running from the Niger River 150 miles eastward through Owerri and Aba to the Cross River, which separates much of Iboland from the Southeastern State. With the exception of the withdrawal from Owerri in April 1969, these positions changed very little during the remaining fifteen months of war.

The progress of the two other federal divisions also bogged down. The First Division, composed of 40,000 troops, including many from the old prewar Nigerian army, was based in Enugu. Between October 5, 1967, and September 30, 1968, the forward positions had moved fifty-five miles south to Okigwi. In the process, vast areas of predominantly Ibo but relatively underpopulated northeastern Biafra were occupied. These included Abakaliki Province, a vital agricultural area for the overcrowded Ibo heartland, where rampant Biafran infiltration and rearguard ambushes posed security problems. The immediate reason for a halt in the offensive at Okigwi, however, appears to have been an acute shortage of ammunition.[5] The reserves in Enugu were nearly exhausted, and the supply route, a 170-mile laterite road south from Makurdi, had become impassable during the 1968 rainy season.[6] The First Division failed to mount another major advance until it finally pushed thirty-five miles southward and captured Umuahia, Biafra's interim capital, on April 22, 1969.

During the August 1968 offensive, the least successful of Nigeria's three divisions was the Second, known in Lagos as the "tortoise division." Created in the aftermath of Biafra's July 1967 invasion of the Midwest, the Second Division was nearly destroyed during the spring of 1968 as a result of several abortive attempts to cross the Niger River and mount a frontal assault against the city of Onitsha. Having finally encircled the city in March and established a divisional headquarters on

[4] Interview: a Nigerian officer.

[5] To compensate for the vulnerability of their forward position and for the lack of competent junior officers at the company and platoon level, Nigerian commanders chose to amass huge quantities of military supplies before continuing with any offensive. In August 1968, federal operational planners determined that, as a minimum, each division would need a reserve of five million rounds of small arms ammunition. Such quantities were beyond the reach of the First Division by the time it reached Okigwi.

[6] *New York Times*, article by Lawrence Fellows in Onitsha, October 4, 1968.

the east bank of the Niger, the Second Division tried unsuccessfully to push seventeen miles south in order to capture Ojukwu's home village of Nnewi. While Ojukwu's village was of little strategic value, it was symbolically important and was not far from Biafra's vital Uli airstrip. To protect Nnewi, all roads to the area were trenched, and a rather elaborate network of bunkers was installed to impede the federal advance.

Failing to move southward, the Second Division tried to build an effective offensive perimeter by linking up with the First Division along the 150-mile axis between the Niger and the Cross Rivers. Here too, Biafran defiance had a decisive short-run effect. By disrupting Nigerian efforts to establish a solid northern front, the Biafrans were able to maintain crucial supply lines of local foodstuffs from the northern areas of the former Eastern Region through Agula and Adazi in the Awka Division.

Inside the 5,000 square miles of territory still under effective Biafran control, Ojukwu's forces enjoyed several immediate tactical advantages. The excellent network of asphalt roads in populous Ibo areas greatly facilitated military logistics. Although petrol had to be carefully rationed and vehicles were scarce, Ojukwu's headquarters were never farther than fifty miles from the front lines. This compared with the 300 to 400 miles separating General Gowon from his field commands. Ojukwu's ease of military communications and field logistics, plus the advantages of a tightly linked command structure and an ethnically homogeneous army, permitted the rapid and flexible deployment of Biafra's limited fire power against the weakest links in the poorly coordinated and overextended federal offensive.[7]

BIAFRA APPROACHES BANKRUPTCY

The measure of Biafra's precarious military posture in terms of the scarcity of equipment has been given by those who visited the front.[8] Behind such assessments, however, was the equally critical question of

[7] Nigerian attack forces were equipped with armored vehicles—including Saladin AML–60 and AML–90 armored cars, Ferret Scout cars, and Saracen APCs—but their effectiveness was challenged by the Biafrans, who had excavated and mined the main roads essential to any Nigerian advance. Also, Biafran defensive positions, particularly along the northwestern perimeter, proved to be greater obstacles than Lagos had expected. The positions depended on a number of well-sited concrete bunkers, which were connected by a series of trenches with fire steps cut wherever visibility permitted. They were well drained during the 1968 heavy rains, and held firm against the perils of weather and federal shelling.

[8] See, for examples, Nwankwo, *Nigeria: The Challenge of Biafra*, ch. III; and Forsyth, *The Biafra Story*, ch. IX.

Biafra's continuing ability to finance vital overseas procurement of arms and ammunition. Throughout the thirty-month conflict, Biafra had to import virtually all of its meager military and medical supplies, and did so without any visible means of paying for them. Furthermore, during the second half of the war, much of the army's food rations also had to be imported.

The following pages describe the sources and magnitude of the international assistance that facilitated a continuation of Biafra's armed resistance. The presentation emphasizes the particular nature of this assistance that allowed the secessionists to retain a surprising amount of political independence in spite of their growing deprivation. The credibility of Ojukwu's threat to continue fighting indefinitely depended both on the image of unmitigated resolve so evident in the well-publicized sufferings of the Biafran people, and also on the apparent commitment of his foreign backers to continue to aid the rebellion. To understand Biafra's intransigence at the international conference table and the basis of Ojukwu's optimistic belief that he possessed the means eventually to force a more favorable negotiated settlement, it is important to note the various kinds of external resources that became available.

Although imposition of the federal blockade in June 1967 denied the Biafrans any further income from their principal exports of palm oil products and petroleum, Ojukwu was able to procure sufficient military equipment to arm his fresh recruits from the more than twenty million dollars in foreign exchange accounts belonging to the former Eastern Region government.[9] Had the war ended in a matter of weeks, as the Biafrans expected, the funds initially available for military procurement might have sufficed. The greatest constraint facing Biafran military planners during the summer of 1967 was not, after all, a shortage of arms, but the lack of trained manpower.[10] When it became apparent that Gowon would not back away from the challenge of secession, and that a major military confrontation was imminent, Biafra's arms buyers flocked to Europe, where they reportedly were duped into squandering huge sums on faulty and inappropriate equipment.[11] As a result, Biafra's

[9] Six million pounds were transferred abroad by the African Continental Bank just prior to a federal edict prohibiting such overseas conversions in April 1967. A further one million pounds were transferred on May 23, 1967, when the ban was temporarily lifted in response to the recommendations of the National Conciliation Commission. West Africa, No. 2640, January 6, 1968, p. 25.

[10] Interview: Ojukwu.

[11] For a discussion of the deceptions perpetrated against Biafran buyers, see Thayer, The War Business, pp. 161–169. For a personal but fictionalized account, see Mezu, Behind the Rising Sun. Evidence of Biafran confidence during this early period were the various substantial and nonstrategic outlays of foreign exchange

sterling and dollar reserves were rapidly depleted. Soon the only major new source of foreign exchange available to the Biafran government was through the sale of Nigerian currency on the European black market.

When secession was declared, more than thirty million Nigerian pounds were in circulation in the Eastern Region. At the official exchange rate of $2.80, this amounted to approximately eight-five million dollars. In addition, another thirty-five million Nigerian pounds that had never been in circulation were seized by Biafran authorities from the Benin, Enugu, and Port Harcourt branches of the Nigerian Central Bank.[12] How much of this was actually unloaded on the black market, and at what prices, can only be surmised. According to Bank of Biafra officials, the Nigerian pounds were sold at between one-half and one-third of the official exchange rate. Piecing together various accounts of currency transactions, and allowing for the seven million Nigerian pounds seized at Lomé airport, it is doubtful that the Biafrans realized more than fifteen million dollars from the various exchanges made during the latter months of 1967.

In January 1968, the federal military government introduced a new paper currency that immediately rendered valueless some forty-eight million old Nigerian pound notes that were still in Biafran hands. The Biafran government had been slow to sell large quantites of Nigerian notes earlier for fear of depressing the black market price in Europe. Ojukwu later referred to his failure to issue Biafra's own currency months earlier and to dump the supply of Nigerian paper in Geneva for whatever the market would bear, as one of the greatest mistakes of his regime.[13] The Biafran leader blames this error on his economic advisers who, he says, insisted that there was no urgency because the Nigerians lacked the financial competency to change a currency. Whatever the reasons, the loss was staggering for the Biafran treasury—upwards of forty million dollars—and it came at a time when Biafra's other reserves were nearly depleted. Ojukwu insists that from January 1968 until the end of the civil war, he never had more than one million dollars on hand at any one time for military procurement. This figure may be too low but, because Ojukwu was his own minister of finance and minister of defense, it is impossible to corroborate such an assertion.[14]

---

that accelerated the secession's impoverishment. The most prominent of these was the purchase of a Hawker Siddeley DH–125 executive jet for Ojukwu.

[12] *West Africa*, No. 2640, January 6, 1968, p. 25.

[13] Interview: Ojukwu.

[14] Perhaps because he had once served as quartermaster general for the Nigerian army (1963–1964), Ojukwu repeatedly made plain to his subordinates that he needed no help in determining what equipment should be purchased and by

There is, however, ample evidence in the international press and from various accounts by Biafran commanders that the supply of arms reaching the enclave dwindled to a trickle during the first nine months of 1968.

In January 1968, six Super Constellations and DC–7s, some Biafran-owned and others chartered, provided whatever arms reached the secessionists from abroad. Each of the aging aircraft would make about one flight a week, a grueling seventeen-hour trip from Lisbon to Port Harcourt, with a brief stopover at Bissau in Portuguese Guinea.[15] The planes carried an average of ten tons per load, but much of the cargo included medicine, canned goods, and even luxury items that were unobtainable in Biafra. If forty or fifty tons of arms and ammunition reached Biafra in a week, this was considered extremely good. With the decline in Biafra's foreign exchange, the rate of arms deliveries dwindled to only one or two a week in July 1968. At this point the funds available for military procurement were at their lowest point of the entire war. Even if Biafran buyers located small lots of reasonably priced automatic rifles and ammunition, they were increasingly unable to meet the exorbitant transportation costs of $22,000 per flight from Lisbon.[16]

Between July and October 1968, the average flow of military equipment reaching Biafra grew approximately twenty-fold, from around ten tons to two hundred tons per week.[17] Aside from several antiaircraft pieces and ammunition for Biafra's few howitzers and mortars, nearly all of the equipment consisted of small arms and ammunition. The war materiel was a hodgepodge of vintage makes and models of French, Czech, Soviet, Chinese, and British origin.[18] While the supply was never large enough to shift the balance of forces between Biafra and Nigeria, it was sufficient, given Biafra's logistical advantages, to wage a war of

---

whom. Only his most trusted civilian advisers were sent abroad on arms-buying missions. The Biafran Army Chief of Staff, Major General Alex Madiebo, asserts that the military establishment was allowed to participate only in the distribution process once the arms reached Biafra. This made military planning difficult, but had the additional advantage, from Ojukwu's position, of allowing the commander-in-chief to pit one subordinate against another in the competition for scarce military supplies. Interviews: Madiebo, Effiong, Okwechime, and other Biafran officials.

[15] *West Africa*, No. 2645, February 10, 1968, pp. 146–147.

[16] Thayer, *The War Business*, p. 165. See also de St. Jorre, *The Nigerian Civil War*, pp. 321–323.

[17] The figure is a rough approximation based on interviews with Biafran diplomatic and military personnel, including the officer in charge of off-loading operations at Uli Airstrip.

[18] According to several former Biafran soldiers, the British-made Madison automatic rifle remained the most popular infantry weapon. With the exception of the French arms shipments discussed below, most of the equipment was purchased on the international arms market from private dealers.

attrition.[19] From October 1968 until the end of the war, arms and ammunition were never again in dangerously short supply.[20]

Credit for keeping the Biafran resistance alive so long is popularly ascribed to French intervention, with secondary speculation focusing on possible covert assistance from South Africa, Portugal, Israel, China, and the four African states recognizing Biafra. The compilation of such a list merely reflects those members of the international system who, regardless of their ideological or other political differences, stood to gain by the weakening or dissolution of the Nigerian federation. Theoretically, anyone could have quietly deposited foreign exchange in Biafra's overseas accounts, and Ojukwu flatly states that he would have been a fool not to accept aid from South Africa or any other source had it been offered.[21] But very little aid was forthcoming, at least from foreign governments.

The basic reasons for the lack of enthusiasm in official circles are not difficult to discern; Biafra was undeniably an underdog fighting a losing cause for a political objective that all members of the international system reject, if only in principle. Given the probable outcome, and the strong support that the federal government enjoyed throughout the African region, any foreign power contemplating intervention in Biafra's favor would have had to consider a variety of possible political and economic costs. Also, one should not overlook the fact that among Biafra's most likely allies—especially South Africa, Portugal, Israel, and France—there was an abiding fear of Soviet penetration in Africa. The longer the Nigerian civil war dragged on, the greater they saw the chance that Lagos would become dependent on assistance from Moscow.

The most decisive and reliable source of funds that could be used to purchase military equipment abroad was the foreign exchange component in the vast, privately administered, humanitarian relief effort to mitigate the suffering of Biafra's hungry masses. This money not only

[19] David Williams, editor of *West Africa*, recalled in an interview: "Whether it was the French or not, the new rate of arms supply was crucial. From the front line observations, in August 1968, I had concluded that the rebels were finished, saved only by the rain. A French journalist with me reported similarly. The federals were temporarily short of ammunition, but otherwise there seemed little to stop them." When Michael Leapman, diplomatic reporter for the London *Sun*, later visited the Biafran front lines in early 1969, he observed that the troops were able to fire away with an abandon comparable to the style of the Nigerians; see his "Biafra: At the Front."

[20] In fact, Biafra's military supplies were in better shape at the beginning of 1970 than at any time in the previous year. Interviews: Ojukwu, Effiong, Madiebo.

[21] Interview: Ojukwu. In November 1968, the Biafran leader was quoted as saying, "Our major problem is to survive. Anybody who offers assistance for my people is a true friend. Biafra is prepared to accept aid from the devil because the first thing is survival." *West Africa*, No. 2686, November 23, 1968, p. 1393.

enabled the secessionists to procure the minimal arms necessary to maintain their defenses during the darkest days of mid-1968, but the unquestioning support from humanitarians assured Ojukwu of a measure of political independence when dealing with the French government and other prospective benefactors. Before turning to the strategic importance of international humanitarian relief in sustaining the resistance, the role of France and other lesser powers which supported Biafra will be considered.

LIMITED AID FROM FRANCE AND OTHER GOVERNMENTS

Few issues arouse greater bitterness among Biafra's erstwhile military leaders and diplomats than the question of French assistance. At best, it was belated and half-hearted, but to many Biafrans it seemed cynically capricious. Part of the resentment among Biafrans may have been the result of inflated expectations. President de Gaulle's record of support for self-determination, his Roman Catholicism, his sentimental attachment to West Africa dating back to World War II, and most importantly, his reputed Anglophobia, encouraged Biafrans to hope for major French support.[22] Paris traditionally had taken the general position that local nationalism would not permit a federal structure to survive in Africa, and French policy ensured that the former colonies in West and Equatorial Africa would not merge into a federation during the 1960s.[23] Smaller units are presumably easier to control than big ones, and the Biafrans further assumed that de Gaulle would be so apprehensive about the future role of a Soviet/British-backed Nigeria as the dominant power in the midst of tiny francophone West African states, that he would intervene to aid the secession.[24] The Biafrans hoped to reinforce de Gaulle's predilections by offering the French easy access to the East's petroleum reserves.[25]

Ojukwu's interests were well represented in Paris by Raph Uwechue, who functioned as a would-be Biafran ambassador from a suite of offices

[22] For reflective speculation about de Gaulle's motivations, see Cronje, *The World and Nigeria*, pp. 194–209.

[23] France preempted the establishment of a large independent francophone Africa by promoting a new system of direct representation of the individual territories in Paris, which severely inhibited the Dakar-based West African Federation. The French also supported Houphouet-Boigny's successful effort to destroy the Mali Federation and Gabon's opposition to the Equatorial African Federation.

[24] Republic of Biafra, Research Bureau of the Propaganda Directorate, "Biafra's Case and France," briefing paper prepared for the head of state (Umuahia, June 1968).

[25] Republic of Biafra, Research Bureau of the Propaganda Directorate, "Economic Factors Inducing the Present French Attitude to Nigeria/Biafra War," briefing paper prepared for the head of state (Umuahia, June 1968).

known as the "Biafra Historical Research Association," close by the Arc de Triomphe.[26] Uwechue had resigned as Nigerian chargé d'affaires prior to secession; he had originally been sent to Paris in May 1966 to reopen the Nigerian embassy, which had been closed for six years in protest by the Nigerians against continued French atomic tests in the Sahara.[27] De Gaulle's reputed bitterness over this humiliating rebuff by a federal government dominated by Northerners encouraged early hopes among the Biafrans.

"To anyone who was close to the scene," Raph Uwechue later wrote, "it was clear that France was meticulously careful not only to avoid being drawn into the conflict but to discourage the buildup of arms and armaments in any part of Nigeria.[28] Whatever de Gaulle's personal feelings about the breakup of Nigeria, France had other interests to protect. Until May 1968, none of the leaders of French-speaking Africa had embraced the secession, and several were openly hostile to the cause. The principle of self-determination can cut two ways, and de Gaulle was no doubt aware that Biafra's success might well inspire dissident Hausas in southern Niger, thousands of Ibo residents in western Cameroon, and Yorubas in eastern Dahomey (Benin) to seek greater autonomy. More to the point, French troops had to be flown in to Chad at President François Tombalbaye's request in August 1968 in order to help quell rebellious Moslems in the northern provinces who had been agitating for independence for years.[29]

In addition to the political constraints, the French also risked considerable financial loss if they sided openly with Biafra. In 1966, French investments in Nigeria totaled approximately one hundred million dollars.[30] The most publicized commercial interest was their stake in Nigeria's oil industry, although there was considerable public confusion

[26] When peace talks collapsed with little hope for a negotiated settlement, Uwechue left the Biafran foreign service in December 1968, and wrote a book entitled *Reflections on the Nigerian Civil War: A Call for Realism.*

[27] See discussion in Chapter 1.

[28] Uwechue, *Reflections on the Nigerian Civil War*, p. 96. The author notes that requests by the federal government for the purchase of two dozen French Fouga Magisters and bombs were refused soon after secession, and other orders already in the pipeline for armored cars were cut down. The two American-built B–26 bombers deployed by Biafra at the beginning of the war were bought in France, but through third parties to whom they had been sold for aerial survey purposes, and export licenses were obtained months before the conflict developed.

[29] *West Africa*, No. 2674, August 31, 1968, p. 1030. The Moslems of the Tibesti region had never accepted the authority of Tombalbaye, a southern Protestant, and for this reason the Chadian government had retained French military administration in the province until 1965, five years after Independence, thereby forestalling a possible secession.

[30] *West Africa*, No. 2671, August 10, 1968, pp. 929, 938.

regarding the extent of those concessions and their location.[31] The only French company with oil concessions was SAFRAP,[32] whose fields were located both in the Midwest State and in the former Eastern Region. Production had begun on a commercial scale in August 1966, and by June 1967 SAFRAP was producing only 37,000 barrels a day, compared with 486,000 barrels by Shell-BP and 56,000 by Gulf, the other two companies then in operation.[33] The SAFRAP fields were outside the Ibo heartland, and the company's most promising concessions were in the Midwest State. Unless the Biafrans could maintain effective control over the minority areas of the oil-rich Rivers State, the center of Shell-BP operations, they would have little to offer the French.[34] Meanwhile, the Rivers State government, even though still based in Lagos as a symbol of the resistance to Biafran rule, wasted no time in issuing a major White Paper for foreign distribution that called attention to the extent of the oil fields in non-Ibo areas.[35]

During the first year of secession, Raph Uwechue was able to reach numerous important and sympathetic members of the French foreign affairs establishment, including the head of de Gaulle's Secretariat for African Affairs, Jacques Foccart. But the Quai d'Orsay, France's foreign ministry, remained openly hostile to Biafra. When Ojukwu tried to send a high-level delegation to Paris in December 1967, led by the former Eastern Region premier, Dr. Michael Okpara, it was not allowed through customs at Orly airport, and was compelled to depart immediately.[36]

Ojukwu recalls seeking three kinds of assistance from de Gaulle during this period: "arms, recognition to neutralize international support for Nigeria and [mercenary] training to help build our forces." The Biafran leader insists, however, that prior to September 1968 the

[31] For a full discussion of the oil-producing areas, see Pearson, *Petroleum and the Nigerian Economy*, especially ch. 9.

[32] SAFRAP is a wholly owned subsidiary of ERAP, the state-owned Entreprises de Recherches et d'Activités Petrolières formed in 1966 by a merger of two companies. ERAP's chairman was Pierre Guillaumat, a well-known mining engineer and former Gaullist minister.

[33] *West Africa*, No. 2671, August 10, 1968, p. 929.

[34] In July 1967, the Biafrans did try to sell future rights to oil and mineral resources in the Eastern Region to the Rothschild Bank in Paris for $16.8 million. The deal was never consummated, however, allegedly because a Biafran official leaked word of the impending transaction to the Nigerians.

[35] *The Oil-Rich Rivers State*, published by the Information Unit, Office of the Governor, Rivers State (Lagos: National Press, 1967).

[36] *West Africa*, No. 2638, December 23, 1967, p. 1657. The same report noted that Nigeria's commissioner for external affairs, Dr. Arikpo, had recently visited Paris en route home from New York, and that the French foreign minister, Couve de Murville, had used the opportunity to reiterate France's policy of non-recognition of Biafra.

only significant help from France was in connection with the recruitment of approximately fifty white mercenaries, who played a critical role in restoring Biafran morale following the evacuation of Enugu.[37] Through informal diplomatic channels the Biafran Ministry of Foreign Affairs received the following message from French authorities: "We would like to help you but your position looks hopeless."[38]

When de Gaulle finally made a public show of support for Biafra, he did so, in Raph Uwechue's view, primarily in response to French domestic pressures.[39] On July 31, 1968, de Gaulle directed his secretary of state for information to announce that the Biafrans had "demonstrated their will to assert themselves as a people" and that the conflict "must be resolved on the basis of the right of peoples to self-determination."[40] The precise timing of the statement, as noted earlier, was meant to coincide with the commencement of peace talks under the auspices of the OAU Consultative Committee. Perhaps a more important determinant was the general tenor of French politics in the wake of the May 1968 national strike, which had precipitated a number of hastily arranged reforms that narrowly saved the de Gaulle regime. A public opinion poll taken in the summer of 1968 had revealed that Biafra ranked number one, ahead of Vietnam, as the international issue of greatest concern to the French people.[41] Sentiment was overwhelmingly pro-Biafran, and was led by the French left that, not incidentally, had been at the vanguard of the student and workers' protest in May.[42]

A second factor prodding the French government were the appeals by the Ivory Coast and Gabon immediately following their recognition of Biafra. Dr. Kenneth Dike, Ojukwu's representative in Abidjan, and Raph Uwechue, among others, insist that Houphouet-Boigny's

[37] Interview: Ojukwu. Also Oyewole, "Scientists and Mercenaries." Of the fifty-three mercenaries who arrived in late 1967, all but three departed by June 1968. Foreign analysts generally support Ojukwu's contention that the mercenaries provided only a brief psychological advantage to the Biafrans, and that they quickly outlived their usefulness. See also Mockler, *Mercenaries*; Cronje, *The World and Nigeria*, ch. 9; and de St. Jorre, *The Nigerian Civil War*, ch. 12.

[38] Interview: Onyegbula.

[39] Uwechue, *Reflections on the Nigerian Civil War*, p. 96.

[40] *Le Monde*, August 1, 1968.

[41] *West Africa*, No. 2672, August 17, 1968, p. 965. Biafran propagandists had been active in France from the outset of the struggle and, unlike the Nigerians, they saw to it that their materials were printed in French. The Paris press corps also was briefed regularly, and journalists were encouraged to go to Biafra.

[42] Typical of this support was a statement signed by Sartre, de Beauvoir, Kastler et al., which condemned the British, Soviets, Egyptians, the United Nations, and the OAU for patronizing genocide, and concluded that "the struggle in Biafra is today the struggle of the whole Left. If the Left ignores it, if it connives at this genocide . . . the Left will inevitably pervert its other actions, and it will cease to exist as a movement." *Le Monde*, November 20, 1968.

strenuous lobbying in Paris was a crucial element in changing the French position.[43] When asked about the pro-Biafran pressures confronting de Gaulle, a French diplomat in Lagos said he personally believed the lobbying from within Africa was at least as important as the agitation from French public opinion, and unquestionably carried more weight than the French president's anti-British attitude or the private appeals he received from Pope Paul, although the latter considerations figured in the equation. One of the difficulties facing de Gaulle, the same source continued, was that a number of francophone African heads of state were playing a double game: supporting Nigeria within the OAU, but then urging de Gaulle to take a more outspoken position in support of Biafra in order to force a negotiated settlement.[44] If true, this would suggest that the fear of a united and powerful Nigeria in West Africa may run deeper than the record of OAU support for the federal government indicates.

Whether or not the above analysis is correct, the question of Biafra's survival probably was never more than of marginal interest to de Gaulle, and his equivocation reflected this. Although he shared the predisposition of those West African leaders who wished to see the Nigerian federation at least weakened, if not destroyed, he nevertheless could not be insensitive to the preferences of the majority of African states, including, of course, the oil-rich countries of North Africa, which were among the strongest supporters of the federal government. Thus, de Gaulle tried to satisfy both sides while remaining committed to neither.

On June 12, 1968, France announced a total arms embargo. In reality, the French had been refusing to supply military equipment to both sides in the dispute since the outbreak of hostilities twelve months earlier.[45] The public affirmation was presumably intended to placate Biafran supporters at home and abroad, while simultaneously countering pressures for French military assistance to Biafra. The new political support for Biafra, symbolized by the July 31, 1968, endorsement of Biafra's right of self-determination, was also carefully hedged by de Gaulle during a September 9, 1968, press conference. France, he declared, has "helped Biafra within her possibilities. She has not accomplished the act which for her, would be decisive: the recognition of the Biafran Republic. For she thinks that the gestation of Africa is first of all an African business. Already, there are East and West African states which have recognized Biafra. Others seem to be heading toward recognition. It means that for France, the decision which

---

[43] Interviews: Dike and members of his staff in Abidjan. See also Uwechue, *Reflections on the Nigerian Civil War*, p. 97.

[44] Interview: French embassy official, Lagos.

[45] *Le Monde*, June 13, 1968.

has not yet been taken, cannot be considered as excluded in the future."[46] De Gaulle's press conference was held on the eve of Africa's resounding vote of support for the federal military government during the fifth OAU summit in Algiers. The predictable outcome at Algiers left the French president appearing to favor Biafra, while implicitly ruling out such action by publicly deferring to prevailing African opinion.[47]

As de Gaulle sought refuge in a political position that would give France optimum flexibility in dealing with the several contending pressures, he also faced new temptations to assist Biafra militarily. There is no indication that he ever seriously considered intervention on a scale that might have redressed the balance of forces in the conflict. He appears to have been more inclined to the argument that France's long-term interests and those of her former West African colonies would be best served if Biafra were allowed to sustain a war of attrition long enough to force a political settlement. Such a compromise solution would, conceivably, reduce the likelihood that the new Nigeria would enjoy the internal strength necessary if she ever wished to dominate West Africa. Most leaders interviewed on both sides of the civil war embrace this highly cynical view of French policy.

With the growing popular support for Biafra throughout France and the recognitions by Ivory Coast and Gabon, Ojukwu sent former President Azikwe and other well-known Ibos to Paris in the hope of securing more substantial aid. Alluding to the bitter frustrations of this period, the head of the Biafran foreign office recalls: "Instead of assistance we received more expressions of sympathy. We were told that if we held onto Port Harcourt for a while longer then there might be cause to reconsider. But how, we asked, could we continue fighting without arms? Well, we lost Port Harcourt [in late May 1968] but we didn't give up and when we proved that we were a headache which would not disappear quickly, only then did we manage some small headway in Europe. With the French, the intercession of our friends in Africa [Gabon and the Ivory Coast] helped considerably."[48]

When assistance finally came, it was arranged not by the officials in the Quai d'Orsay but through the personal efforts of Jacques Foccart.[49] As head of the Secretariat for African Affairs, Foccart was in close touch with Houphouet-Boigny and, unlike the diplomats in the Quai d'Orsay, he had been for some time in favor of greater French

---

[46] *Le Monde*, September 11, 1968.

[47] De Gaulle's position was partially foreshadowed nearly two months earlier, when the secretary of state for foreign affairs, M. de Lipkowski, in response to a question in the French Senate, stated that the Biafran problem was an African one that was relevant to the OAU's competence much more than to the United Nations. *Le Monde*, July 21, 1968.

[48] Interview: Onyegbula.   [49] Interview: Ojukwu.

intervention to aid the rebellion.[50] Biafra's military high command was informed by Foccart's office in August 1968, just prior to the Addis Ababa peace talks, that efforts would be made to ensure that necessary military equipment would continue to reach the enclave.[51]

At a meeting between French and Biafran officials on September 7, 1968, the latter were reportedly told that France would not abandon its promise of facilitating the importation of arms, but that overt political support would not be forthcoming until more African states had recognized Ojukwu's regime.[52] From their previous travels, the Biafrans knew that the prospects for more recognitions remained dim, and that the most which they could expect from African leaders would be diplomatic support in the event that Ojukwu renounced secession and called for the formation of a Nigerian confederation.[53] This, of course, was unacceptable to Ojukwu.

Substantial deliveries of French arms did not actually commence until late September 1968,[54] almost two weeks after the Biafrans had successfully turned back Nigeria's most serious military threat so far: a bid by elements of the Third Marine Division to push into the Ibo heartland from the Rivers State and capture Biafra's airstrip at Uli. Only after the military situation had stablized to the point where Paris felt the Biafrans were in a position to wage a war of attrition did they provide substantial indirect military assistance.

The French claim they did not supply Biafra with arms or equipment.[55] Ojukwu was informed that the Ivory Coast and Gabon henceforth would be in a position to grant Biafra immediate loans for the purchase of military equipment, and that the French would back these

[50] Informed speculation about the nature of the debate over Nigeria taking place within the French government appears in: Cronje, *The World and Nigeria*, pp. 203–205; de St. Jorre, *The Nigerian Civil War*, pp. 210–218; and *West Africa*, No. 2680, October 12, 1968, pp. 1200–1201.

[51] Interview: Effiong.

[52] De St. Jorre, *The Nigerian Civil War*, pp. 229–231. His account of the meeting is based on interviews with Uwechue and access to some of the latter's relevant files. With Dr. Azikiwe in Paris were the former premier of the Eastern Region, Dr. Michael Okpara; the head of the Biafran mission in Abidjan, Dr. Kenneth Dike; Biafra's representative, Raph Uwechue; and the former Nigerian permanent secretary of external affairs and a close Ojukwu confidant, Francis Nwokedi.

[53] Uwechue, *Reflections on the Nigerian Civil War*, p. 143. Uwechue cites Senegal, Tunisia, Sierra Leone, Uganda, Liberia, Burundi, Rwanda, and Ghana as willing to publicly endorse a confederal solution.

[54] *Washington Post*, October 2, 1968. The report cites reliable diplomatic sources in London, Washington, and West Africa. Ojukwu, in a postwar interview, dated the arrival of stepped-up military supplies at some time during the first week of October 1968.

[55] For a detailed official refutation of the allegations that the French government was supplying arms to either party in the dispute, see *Le Monde* (weekly edition), November 14–20, 1968.

loans. It was, however, made perfectly clear to the Biafran leader that Foccart would determine the amount of loan funds available.[56] According to one foreigner who was familiar with the arrangement, "In the last year of the war French arms rose [from only 10 percent of the arms received from abroad] to about half of the foreign total. With francs from the Ivory Coast Biafra purchased from the government of Gabon arms originally bought from the French government and resold at cost. They were supplied to Libreville and flown to Biafra by French commercial pilots and chartered planes."[57] This procedure allowed the French government to preserve the formality of their June 1968 embargo, and periodically to reassure the Nigerians in "good faith" that they were not aiding Ojukwu.[58]

In addition to the loans, Foccart allegedly told the Ivorians and Gabonese that Paris would not object if they turned over their surplus military stocks to Biafra and that France would replenish them.[59] Since the Ivorian army numbered fewer than 4,000 men, and Gabon maintained only a 900-man force, the two governments were not in a position to make substantial direct contributions.[60] The chief of military planning for Biafra, Mike Okwechimi, later described the arrangement thus: "French weapons came but not French support. The Ivory Coast and Gabon gave us what they could, knowing that France would resupply them. France sent observers to Biafra to see if we were wasting their ammunitions. They must have thought we were one of their colonies."[61] Estimates of the value of this French military equipment run to around five million dollars.[62]

[56] Interview: Ojukwu.

[57] Stanley Diamond in *New York Review of Books*, February 26, 1970.

[58] Nigeria formally accepted this legal fiction. Dr. Okoi Arikpo recalled, in a postwar interview, four separate visits to Paris during the conflict, in which he had to endure elaborate explanations of France's unqualified support for a united Nigeria and denials of complicity in supplying Biafra with arms. Arikpo states that he let these pass without public challenge so as not to play into the hands of Nigeria's enemies within the French government. Interview: Arikpo. For a thoughtful analysis of Nigeria's restraint toward the French, see Roy Lewis' article in *The Times* (London), October 22, 1968.

[59] Interview: Biafran military officers.

[60] Booth, *The Armed Forces of African States*.   [61] Interview: Okwechimi.

[62] Initial reports in the British press placed the inflow of arms from French sources at thirty tons a night (e.g., *The Guardian*, October 2, 1968). By late October, speculation ran to one hundred tons a night (e.g., *The Times* [London], October 22, 1968). Suzanne Cronje has done a comparison of the various figures, and concludes that there is ample reason to suspect exaggeration. She cites high-ranking Biafran sources who placed the total value at "no more than $5 million" (*The World and Nigeria*, p. 197). Kennedy Lindsay also cites "informed sources" and estimates French support in 1968 to have been only about $4.8 million ("How Biafra Pays for the War," p. 27). Ojukwu maintains the loans never were in excess of one million dollars at a time, and "several" were made in 1968–1969. Interview: Ojukwu.

Proud Biafrans bitterly resented French interference and felt entitled to military support without conditions. Upon reflection, Ojukwu asserted: "I was never happy with French arms supplies or any system I could not control. The French were always trying to exert controls with their arms. There were a couple of slow-downs once they began supplying us that were intended to force us to change our policies. . . . The French would have liked to control my entire regime. . . . There could be no question of our becoming totally dependent on the French."[63] The French wanted the Biafrans to route all of their military imports via Gabon and offered to increase their loan scheme in return. Ojukwu refused, however, preferring to ship the equipment that he was able to finance from private sources through Lisbon and the Portuguese island of Sao Tomé. This second staging area was the same one that was being used by the Jointchurchaid humanitarian relief operation.

Suspicions about French intentions did not inhibit the Biafrans from seeking greater military and political assistance from de Gaulle. When the French president appointed a two-man delegation of parliamentarians to visit the enclave in early 1969, Biafran officials were ready with a lengthy and unrealistic list of requests. In addition to asking for a major and immediate increase in arms and ammunition to offset Nigeria's arsenals, they called on the French to provide air support to protect Biafra's landing fields and halt the Nigerian advance. On the diplomatic level, the Biafrans suggested that Paris "initiate a four great-power action to bring about the arms embargo and cease-fire" and urged the granting of diplomatic recognition so that "France will be in a better position to persuade other governments to support Biafra's cause."[64] Nothing came of the visit and there were even press reports that indicated the rate of arms reaching Biafra declined somewhat in the weeks that followed.[65] Reflecting on the French contribution, Biafra's

[63] Interview: Ojukwu. When asked about reductions in the supply of arms reaching Biafra from French sources, Ojukwu mentioned two instances of what he regarded as reprisals for "unfriendly" actions by his government. The first occurred when he deported the German mercenary Rolf Steiner in November 1968. Ojukwu theorizes that Paris was displeased because they felt that without Steiner and a handful of his associates French ammunition would be squandered. A second brief but abrupt interruption in military supplies from Libreville came in May 1969, when Biafran forces attacked AGIP oil-drilling sites in the Midwest, killing eleven Europeans and capturing another eighteen. The public outcry in Europe was immediate, and the French cut off the flow of arms to press Ojukwu into releasing the hostages, which he did. This incident will be more fully described in Chapter 11.

[64] Republic of Biafra, Ministry of Foreign Affairs, "Brief for the Guidance of Biafran Officials on the Occasion of the Visit of Messrs. Raymond Offroy and Jacques Marette, French Deputies, 2nd–9th March 1969," dated February 28, 1969.

[65] *Sunday Telegraph*, April 20, 1969. By June the *Christian Science Monitor* estimated that the weekly quantity of arms reaching Biafra had again reached

chief of staff, Major General Philip Effiong, snapped: "the bastards did more harm than good by raising false hopes and by providing the British with an excuse to reinforce Nigeria."[66]

French military assistance, whether valued at five million dollars or twice that figure, was tiny when compared to the financial contribution that France made to the federal government by continuing to import Nigerian goods. The economic realities are startling and often overlooked. The federal government financed its external military procurement from foreign exchange reserves and from the sale of primary products overseas. With the wartime disruption of the petroleum and palm oil industries, Lagos increasingly depended on revenues from cocoa and, most importantly, groundnuts.[67] France was by far the largest consumer of Nigerian groundnuts, and purchased nearly $100 million worth in 1967–1969.[68] Throughout the crisis the French remained Nigeria's fourth most important trading partner behind the British, Americans, and Dutch. During 1969 alone, Nigeria enjoyed a trade surplus with the French that amounted to slightly more than $66 million dollars, much of which was no doubt used to finance purchases of military equipment from the British and Soviets.[69]

Portugal, South Africa, and Rhodesia

Aside from the French, the number of foreign governments that might have been persuaded to aid Biafra for reasons of political and strategic self-interest could be counted on one hand. The most obvious were the racist regimes in South Africa and Rhodesia, which would doubtlessly have been pleased with the breakup of black Africa's richest and most populous country. Sustained violence and chaos in Nigeria would have given comfort to those who believed that black Africans were incapable of peaceful self-government, and at the same time would have distracted world opinion from conditions in areas under white domination. Similar benefits probably attracted the Salazar government in

---

approximately 150 tons per week, that is, about fifteen deliveries by a DC–7. *Christian Science Monitor*, June 3, 1969.

[66] Interview: Effiong.

[67] Nigeria, Federal Office of Statistics, *Annual Abstract of Statistics, 1970* (Lagos: Federal Office of Statistics, 1971), pp. 88–89. Between 1966 and 1968 revenues from petroleum dropped from $257 million in $104 million, and in 1968 accounted for only 7 percent of Nigeria's export earnings. Earnings from palm oil products fell even more sharply, from $93 million to $29 million. Income from cocoa, on the other hand, jumped from $79 million to $145 million, while the sale of ground nut products remained relatively steady, fetching $155 million in 1966 and $146 million in 1968.

[68] *Ibid.*, p. 77. Groundnut sales to France totaled $29 million in 1967, $23.8 million in 1968, and $45.4 million in 1969. Italy, Nigeria's second largest customer during the same period, purchased roughly one-third as much.

[69] Ogunbadejo, "Nigeria and the Great Powers," p. 23.

Portugal, the last major colonial power on the African continent, which was then heavily engaged in repressing African liberation movements in Guinea-Bissau, Angola, and Mozambique.

Counterbalancing these temptations to intervene in aid of Biafra were broader political considerations of both form and substance. First, there would have been the obvious contradiction of promoting the self-determination of another country while seeking to isolate and defeat similar aspirations within white-ruled Africa. Second, to have openly aided Biafra would have further outraged the majority of black African governments, would have angered the British, and might have led to greater Soviet support for the federal government, developments that would not have been in the interests of either Portugal or South Africa.

The first and most consistent cooperation extended to Biafra by a foreign government came from Portugal, although the relationship was strictly limited. Lisbon's most valuable concession was to grant the Biafrans air landing and communication privileges soon after secession was announced. Ojukwu tried, and would have preferred, to have had his European base of operations elsewhere, but no other government would sanction such activities.

Throughout the conflict, the office in Portugal controlled nearly all of the traffic in and out of Biafra. International arms dealers flocked to Lisbon, and the airport there became the staging area for European materiel. The Portuguese further aided Biafra by allowing the military transports to refuel and to make final entry arrangements at airstrips in their colonies of Guinea-Bissau, approximately fifteen hundred miles northwest of Biafra on the African coast, and Sao Tomé, an island three hundred miles to the southeast of the enclave.

The Portuguese do not appear to have supplied Ojukwu's army with military equipment, and they were never outspoken in support of Biafra.[70] When Nigeria's commissioner for external affairs secretly visited Lisbon in late 1967, he was informed that the Salazar government had no intention of aiding Biafra. Portugal, the commissioner was told, was satisfied that Nigeria had the military capability to terminate the rebellion, and so it was "clearly not in Portugal's best interests to antagonize the federal government."[71] While Lagos had little confidence in these assurances, there is no evidence that the Portuguese ever threatened to intervene more directly. Biafra's representative in Lisbon confirms this, and with noticeable bitterness relates how his government's relations with Portugal were always "strictly business," with the Biafrans having to pay dearly for the use of all air-

[70] Interviews: Egbert Nworgu, Biafra's representative in Lisbon during 1967 and 1968, and later in Sao Tomé; and John de St. Jorre who reported on the Lisbon gunrunning operations for the London *Observer*.

[71] Interview: Arikpo.

234

port and communication facilities.[72] British journalist John de St. Jorre, who covered both the Nigerian and Congolese civil wars, reports that the help Portugal gave to Tshombe in Katanga, and later to the rebellious Congo mercenaries, had been similarly cautious.[73]

Evidence of South African and Rhodesian military assistance to Biafra is also very sparse. There is, for instance, no way to determine whether South Africa ever made covert cash deposits to Biafra's overseas accounts. During the war there were only two published reports of South African involvement; both were written in London by Gordon Brook-Shepherd for the conservative *Sunday Telegraph*, and appeared toward the end of the conflict.[74] According to Brook-Shepherd, South Africa began shipping between twenty-five and fifty tons of arms per week to Biafra in mid-1969. This would have amounted to between fifteen and twenty-five percent of Biafran imports at that time. Biafra's chief of staff maintains, to the contrary, their military imports actually dropped in the summer of 1969, and that when the supplies picked up later in the year this was due to a new round of loans arranged in Europe and to Biafra's improved financial position.[75] Similar suspicions surround Biafra's relations with Rhodesia, but one wonders whether the hard-pressed Salisbury regime was in a position to spare either guns or foreign exchange.[76] More likely, Ian Smith deferred to Pretoria.

Israel

Israel was another country to which Biafra looked for military support, and with much greater enthusiasm than it approached the three governments just discussed. There was enormous popular sympathy in Israel for the self-proclaimed "Jews of Africa," who spoke of a fear of

[72] Interview: Nworgu. The airport facilities on Sao Tomé underwent major improvements during the war, but these were either paid for directly by the relief agencies or underwritten by them at a rate of $16,000 per month in guaranteed landing fees. Otherwise, the churches and the Biafrans dealt with the Portuguese on a strictly commercial basis. Lloyd et al., *The Nordchurchaid Airlift to Biafra 1968–1970*, ch. 12.

[73] De St. Jorre, *The Nigerian Civil War*, p. 219.

[74] *Sunday Telegraph*, August 10, 1969, and November 30, 1969. The two articles were substantively the same. The Brook-Shepherd account later provided the basis for a somewhat embellished attack published by the Nigerian Federal Ministry of Information in Lagos entitled *South Africa's Visible and Invisible Aid to Nigerian Rebels* (Lagos: National Press, 1969).

[75] Interview: Effiong. The impact of the increase in available funds on the Biafran war effort in 1969, particularly with regard to the procurement of aircraft, will be discussed in later chapters.

[76] The author has seen cables from the Biafran Ministry of Foreign Affairs, when it was still in Enugu, which indicate that Ojukwu's representatives did establish contact with the Smith regime early in the conflict and made arrangements with a Rhodesian charter company run by John Malloch to carry arms to Biafra on the Sao Tomé and later on the Libreville runs.

genocide because their record of intelligence and diligence had aroused the wrath of the Moslem North in Nigeria. Because of these public pressures, Foreign Minister Abba Eban sought to assure his critics in the Knesset just after the war by saying that Israel had done all that she could to aid Biafra. The remark, which Israeli officials claim was misquoted and taken out of context, reinforced the belief in Lagos that Israel had, in fact, been a major contributor to the Biafran war effort.[77]

If Israel did help Biafra, her actions were heavily camouflaged.[78] A former American diplomat who followed the Nigerian crisis from Washington believes that the greatest service Israel performed for Biafra was to put Ojukwu's arms buyers in contact with European dealers prepared to unload quantities of outmoded Soviet equipment captured during the June 1967 war with Egypt, and that these purchases were among Biafra's best bargains.[79]

There are more fundamental reasons for surmising that Israel did relatively little to support Biafra. Ojukwu announced secession less than a week before the outbreak of the Six-Day War, and during the months of intense diplomatic activity that followed the Israeli victory, Jerusalem worked strenuously to win the support of the forty-member African bloc at the United Nations. Given the OAU's stand on Nigeria and the growing demands from the organization's Arab members that all African leaders should break relations with Israel over the latter's refusal to withdraw from occupied territories, the Israeli government did not wish to antagonize any country south of the Sahara.

Since the federal government was likely to emerge victorious in the civil war, Jerusalem appears to have been more interested in maintaining good relations with Lagos than in helping Biafra secede. By late 1969 Israeli diplomats in Lagos believed that they were on sufficiently good terms with the Gowon regime that the federal government would soon upgrade its diplomatic representation in Jerusalem by seeking ambassadorial accreditation. Steps in this direction were suddenly aborted, however, by news of the Eban statement in January 1970.

China

Biafran overtures to the Chinese also produced very little, despite a growing Soviet presence on the federal side. Until the spring of 1968,

[77] The statement was given wide coverage in the Nigerian press, and on January 20, 1970 the Israeli ambassador was summoned to the Ministry of External Affairs for five hours of questioning.

[78] The Paris Bureau of the Associated Press on July 19, 1969, cited unnamed "diplomatic sources" who claimed that small arms of Israeli origin were being brought to Biafra by third parties.

[79] Biafran officers say these were distributed as captured federal arms.

no attention had been given to enlisting Chinese support. The Ministry of Foreign Affairs had no Sinologists, and those Ibos who were otherwise well-connected overseas had no experience in dealing with the Chinese. In April 1968, the Research Bureau of the Propaganda Directorate prepared a position paper entitled "Biafra's Quest for Survival and Recognition: The Alternative of Seeking Chinese Aid." The report concluded that "China is perhaps the only major communist country that can intervene effectively on our side" and recommended that Peking "should be approached for aid as soon as possible."[80] The obvious problem was how to proceed.

Dr. Ikenna Nzimiro, an outspoken Marxist sociologist from the University of Nigeria, Nsukka, submitted a confidential blueprint for "Diplomatic Activities with the Socialist Zones," which recommended that the government seek to contact the Chinese in Dar es Salaam, Tanzania.[81] Ojukwu first sent P. K. Nwokedi to Paris, where he met with Chinese representatives, but Nwokedi returned with no more than private expressions of sympathy.[82] Further efforts to reach Peking through Dar es Salaam were somewhat more productive. In response to urgings from the Tanzanians and Zambians, the New China Press Agency issued its first major statement on the conflict in September 1968, which denounced "Anglo/American imperialism and Soviet revisionism" for supporting the Nigerian federation in its "massacres of the Biafran people."[83]

When Ojukwu was later asked about Chinese military aid, he said that Tanzania's consumption of Chinese arms and ammunition more than tripled during the later stages of the war, implying that this equipment was passed along to Biafra.[84] The Tanzanians normally import very little military equipment since their army numbers only 7,500 men, with a total annual defense budget in 1968 of less than $11 million.[85] Even if only one or two million dollars worth of Chinese small arms had reached Biafra via Tanzania, this would not have been an insignificant contribution to Ojukwu's hard-pressed forces. Nigerian army officers report, however, that they captured few Chinese weapons.

[80] Republic of Biafra, Research Bureau of the Propaganda Directorate, "Biafra's Quest for Survival and Recognition: The Alternative of Seeking Chinese Aid," submitted to the Ministry of Foreign Affairs, April 8, 1968.

[81] Ikenna Nzimiro, "Diplomatic Activities with the Socialist Zones," a confidential paper, undated, submitted to the Ministry of Foreign Affairs in the spring of 1968.

[82] Interviews: Onyegbula, Nzimiro.

[83] New China Press Agency, September 22, 1968.

[84] Interview: Ojukwu.

[85] Booth, The Armed Forces of African States, 1970, p. 22. Tanzania's army possessed only twelve light tanks, fifteen armored personnel carriers, some Chinese-made mortars, and Soviet artillery.

Food, Foreign Exchange, and a Relief Economy

Fortunately for Biafra, there were alternatives to foreign government donors. Between April and September 1968, Biafra became a ward of the international community and remained so until the rebellion collapsed in January 1970. This state of dependency was unique in international relations because the necessary intervention was initiated and administered by privately run agencies who could not, and would not attempt to, tie their aid to political conditions. Biafra, and not her benefactors, set most of the terms for this vital assistance.

The avowed objective of the many religious and humanitarian organizations responsible for maintaining Biafra was to alleviate the suffering of millions of innocent civilians trapped inside the Ibo heartland. They succeeded brilliantly under extremely difficult circumstances. In the process they also effected rapid and dramatic improvements in what remained of the Biafran economy, and thereby helped to insulate the Biafran state from the growing threat of national disintegration and military defeat. Possibly the greatest contribution to the Biafran war effort by the humanitarian organizations was actually made prior to September and October 1968, the period when their massive airlift of food supplies finally got underway.

As noted earlier, Ojukwu's financial and military fortunes reached a nadir during the summer of 1968, a situation that would not be duplicated until Biafra's demise nearly eighteen months later. This was the period, prior to the arrival of the arms from Gabon and Ivory Coast, when Nigeria's army successfully occupied Port Harcourt and nearly all of the 20,000 to 25,000 square miles surrounding the 5,000 square miles of Ibo heartland. Military stocks in Biafra were precariously low, and the rebels had no visible means to pay for even the occasional plane load of arms that continued to reach the enclave from Lisbon.[86] The permanent secretary of defense recalls that requisitions were so low that only those among Biafra's 20,000 troops with front-line duty were given ammunition, and at the paltry rate of four rounds per rifle.[87] By dispensing with almost everything except small arms, ammunition, and some mortar, however, Biafran troops success-

[86] Small but important sums of foreign exchange were realized from the philatelic sale of Biafra's recently issued postage stamps and from the collection and sale abroad of gold jewelry from destitute Biafrans. Sums of hard currency were also sent home by the several thousand Ibos living in Europe and North America, plus whatever could be raised from the million or more Ibos who resided elsewhere in West Africa. In Accra, Ghana, for example, leaders of the Ibo community eventually decided to issue identity cards to members at a price of ten dollars per person, and thereby raised $50,000. This did not take place, however, until late in the war, and there is considerable dispute over what portion of these funds actually reached home.

[87] Interview: Onyejepu.

fully held the line against Nigeria's August 1968 offensive. The major battles at Aba and Owerri on the southern front may have cost Ojukwu no more than $500,000 in precious foreign exchange, but at this stage all such expenditures had to be met from Biafra's own accounts.[88]

When asked how Biafra managed to survive through the dark days of battle in July and August 1968, Ojukwu named three factors: the logistical advantages that permitted him to concentrate his limited fire power; the difficulties that the Nigerian high command experienced in resupplying its own forces for a final advance;[89] and the financial aid he received from the churches and other relief agencies. Regarding the latter he added, "the only source of income available to Biafra was the hard currency spent by the churchs for yams and gari. That's all. At this stage we had no loans or anything else. It wasn't much, but enough to sustain us."[90] With the subsequent operation of the relief air lift, the foreign exchange component and the overall contribution to Biafra's economy would increase dramatically, although the timing of the relatively smaller initial investments were strategically at least as important.

Any person or organization wishing to transfer money to Biafra in order to pay for local goods and services would make a deposit into the London or other branch of the Ibo-owned African Continental Bank, and an equivalent sum would be released in local currency that was valueless outside Biafra. The sum paid to the bank immediately became available to the Biafran government as external revenue, and could be invested in military equipment, used to pay Markpress for its propaganda services, or allocated for other foreign purchases.[91]

The exchange rate for the Biafran pound was fixed by the Biafran Central Bank at $2.80. There were never any price controls or rationing in Biafra, and the government collected no revenues internally. To meet the salaries of an estimated 20,000 civil servants and related personnel, plus numerous other expenditures, the total money supply was increased from sixty-three million Biafran pounds in January 1968 to nearly two hundred million Biafran pounds a year later.[92] Inflation was

[88] The estimate was made by Kennedy Lindsay in "How Biafra Pays for the War."

[89] The 1968 rainy season was one of the longest and heaviest in memory, and this further hampered the conveyance of supplies to Nigeria's widely dispersed forces.

[90] Interview: Ojukwu.

[91] As a rule, Biafra's overseas missions were totally self-sufficient. Any salaries of Biafran foreign service officers residing abroad, as well as office maintenance costs were financed by local fund-raising efforts and were never a drain on Biafran foreign exchange. Acknowledging Biafra's foreign exchange difficulties, the secessionists' Washington law firm voluntarily halved its monthly retainer of $4,000 in April 1968.

[92] Interview: Sylvester Ugoh, head of the Biafran Central Bank.

rampant from the outset, and this caused sharp rises in the cost of local purchases made by the international relief organizations.[93]

The biggest foreign exchange allotment by the relief agencies went for the purchase of local foodstuffs. Because of the many different groups participating in the feeding program and the unavailability of budgetary breakdowns for supplies purchased in Biafra and abroad, it is impossible to set an exact aggregate figure for the period between April and September 1968.

By the summer of 1968, the International Committee of the Red Cross was providing assistance to approximately 400,000 Biafran refugees housed in camps, while the consortia of church groups were serving another 250,000 daily meals at more than three hundred feeding stations.[94] The recipients, approximately five percent of Biafra's estimated twelve million people, were served a mixture of imported protein and carbohydrates. Much of the carbohydrates, primarily yams, were purchased locally. The agencies figured that a minimum of 25 yams for 100 refugees were required every two days.[95] If the agencies were feeding 600,000 people during the critical summer of 1968, their yam requirements alone would have totaled more than a million yams every two weeks. When the World Council of Churches representative in Orlu Province was visited by a WCC delegation in mid-November, he informed them that local food purchases had been averaging over $140,000 per month.[96] The WCC had ten other provincial representatives, and although their purchases would have been considerably less because of Orlu's proximity to the food-producing areas, the figure is suggestive. A further clue appears in the October 1968 progress report of Germany's Diakonisches Werk noting expenditures to date on the feeding program had totaled $1.25 million.[97]

In addition to the local food costs, there were the personal living expenses incurred by several hundred expatriates who helped administer

[93] O. Aboyade and A. A. Ayida, "The War Economy in Perspective." For a breakdown of the price increases of specific commodities, see "Food and Agricultural Situation in Biafra," Comité International de la Croix-Rouge, Geneva, May 1969, mimeographed, table, p. 13.

[94] ICRC, Information Note, No. 109b, July 19, 1968; DICARWS-WCC Progress Report on Nigeria/Biafra Conflict, August 8, 1968; and WCC Press Release on Nordchurchaid, Nb/34–68, September 13, 1968. The number of feeding stations would quadruple to 1200 in the coming year.

[95] World Council of Churches, Newsletter, January 1969, Red Cross Distribution Formula, p. 4.

[96] Visit to Biafra, November 9–14, 1968, by a World Council of Churches Delegation led by Canon Burgess Carr. An unpublished report.

[97] Diakonisches Werk, Progress Report No. 16, Appendix III, October 17, 1968. This was in addition to $2.4 million spent during the same period for food, medicine, and other materials purchased abroad.

the programs in Biafra.[98] Ojukwu notes that he could have been, and probably should have been, more strict with foreign relief personnel, but instead allowed them liberal import privileges, thus freeing them from the necessity of living entirely on the Biafran economy.[99] Even so, if each relief worker spent only the equivalent of five dollars per day between April and September 1968, Biafra would have gained $250,000. The actual figure was probably higher, and certainly became so as the agencies expanded their staffs. Furthermore, there were approximately five salaried indigenous staff members for every expatriate, plus innumerable paid helpers.[100] The aggregate wage bill must have reached several hundred thousand dollars.[101]

To deliver relief goods from the airport to the central storage depots and then to distribute them in the provinces, the international agencies had to hire more than two hundred heavy trucks and a host of smaller vehicles from private firms and individual Biafrans.[102] The heavy trucks rented for between four and six Biafran pounds per day. In the months preceding the expansion of the airlift, the foreign exchange generated by truck rentals may not have exceeded $2,500 per day, but the cumulative expenditures were substantial.

A number of organizations also made direct cash grants for specific projects during this crucial period. A few examples are: $24,000 from the Presbyterian Church in Canada to the Presbyterian Church in Biafra; $20,000 from the interdenominational Port Harcourt Project for work in Biafra; approximately $25,000 from American Baptists and related church groups to co-religionists in Biafra for local spending; and $10,000 to hospitals and relief centers from a Quaker relief team during a four-day visit in late August. One Catholic official in Britain estimated that British and Irish churches alone donated approximately $400,000 for local projects prior to September 1968.[103] Special funds were also established by Nordchurchaid in each province to help provide refugee housing at the many camps and, where conditions permitted and the refugees were able to return home, money was made available to

[98] The ICRC claimed 100 Europeans by September 1968. ICRC, Press Release, No. 910b, September 10, 1968. The Protestant Churches fielded another 100 Europeans, mostly medical personnel. "Nigeria/Biafra Emergency," World Council of Churches Progress Report, October 29, 1968. There were also a few hundred expatriate Catholic clergy in Biafra, but their daily expenditures per person were probably less than those incurred by the professional relief teams.

[99] Interview: Ojukwu.

[100] "Nigeria/Biafra Emergency," World Council of Churches Progress Report, October 29, 1968.

[101] The lowest paid professional staff should have received the civil service minimum of £B700 per annum, nominally the equivalent of $1,960.

[102] *The Nordchurchaid Airlift to Biafra 1968–1970*, p. 85 and Appendix 38.

[103] *West Africa*, No. 2681, October 19, 1968, pp. 1228–1229.

buy roofing mats, bamboo, and other building materials. On one hastily arranged twenty-seven hour visit to the enclave during this critical period, for example, delegates from small Protestant sects in the United States arrived with $55,000 in their money belts. They presented the foreign cash to an astonished bishop of Owerri, who presumably turned it over to the Biafran Central Bank in exchange for local currency. By Western military standards such sums would not carry an army very far, but in Biafra's hit-and-run defense of the Ibo heartland, even these small amounts of foreign exchange were crucial.

The foreign exchange contributions cited above composed only the initial fallout from what quickly became the largest privately run international relief operation in history. An estimated $250,000,000[104] was expended to keep Biafra alive during the last fifteen months of the Nigerian civil war, and one may reasonably assume that at least 10 percent of this assistance came in the form of foreign exchange that had to be converted into Biafran currency for local purchases of foodstuff and various services. Biafra certainly was never flush, but beginning in August and September 1968, there was little danger of being unable to purchase enough small arms and ammunition to sustain a war of attrition. The secession became, in the bittersweet words of Ojukwu's army chief of staff, "a commercial venture."[105] Elaborating on this theme the head of Biafran military planning remarked after the war:

> Financing the war was largely accomplished through private and humanitarian contributions. Much was diverted from funds raised abroad. Those who wished to make strictly humanitarian contributions could give to specific agencies but those giving to "Biafra" often didn't ask any questions and that money could be used to purchase arms on the black market. Often funds would be raised for a specific project and then someone comes along and donates the project outright—the Canadians gave a big hospital for example—freeing the funds already raised.[106]

The relief agencies' contribution of hard currency represented only one aspect of their vast campaign to aid Biafra's civilians. The larger but less controversial contributions, up to 100,000 metric tons of essential food and medical supplies, were purchased abroad and airlifted in approximately 7,800 flights to Biafra.[107] Once the August 1968 federal

[104] The estimate was made by Beverly Carl, the deputy chief of the Nigeria-Biafra Relief and Rehabilitation Program, US-AID, in "American Assistance to Victims of the Nigeria-Biafra War."

[105] Interview: Madiebo.   [106] Interview: Okwechimi.

[107] The Biafra airlift was comparable only to the Berlin airlift, although it holds a distant second place. As of May 31, 1949, the total Berlin cargo came to

advance had been halted, food became as important a factor in sustaining a war of attrition as the continuing resupply of military equipment.

Following the loss of Port Harcourt in May 1968, Biafra's only air terminal and point of entry for all arms and ammunition was moved seventy-five miles north to the improvised air strip near Uli. When Uli went into operation, the tarmac was 25 meters wide, about the size of a two-lane highway, and 2,600 meters long. There were only eight parking areas, plus a narrow taxiway running parallel to the runway. The infrastructure had been designed by Biafran authorities, principally for use by military transport aircraft. Ojukwu allowed the relief agencies to land with food and medical supplies as long as their activities did not impinge on the flow of military equipment. In mid-September 1968, Biafra restricted the number of relief flights landing at Uli because of increased arms traffic.[108] The International Committee of the Red Cross was allowed four flights per night, and the churches another six. The cutback in access was not the only constraint, however, as a relief agency report points out, "Uli being a military base the government planes received top priority in the allocation of parking areas and in manpower for offloading . . . forcing the aircraft of the two humanitarian airlifts to waste a great deal of time and fuel, first in holding over the airport waiting for parking areas to be cleared and then on the ground while workers were rounded up.[109]

To improve operating conditions at Uli air strip, the relief agencies quickly undertook several major initiatives. On September 28, 1968, they imported 30,000 square feet of aluminum planking worth $220,000 to surface a new parking area and widen the taxiway to accommodate the larger DC–7C and 1049–H Super Constellations.[110] The World Council of Churches contracted for the building of dirt feeder roads and several other improvements in the parking and off-loading areas.[111] In addition, the four Nordic church organizations provided for a greater sophistication in air traffic technology available to Biafran air force controllers at Uli, including landing lights to replace the kerosene flares, $30,000 worth of radio equipment, a stand-by generator, high-intensity

---

1,738,184 tons, carried in 212,623 flights. Fortunately, Biafra did not require the huge quantities of coal and other heavy goods necessary to sustain Berliners during the winter of 1948–1949.

[108] *The Nordchurchaid Airlift to Biafra 1968–1970*, p. 14.

[109] *Ibid.*, p. 25.

[110] "Report of the First Three Months of Nordchurchaid," Copenhagen, November 25, 1968.

[111] The arrangement between the World Council of Churches and the Biafran Ministry of Works had the former providing diesel fuel, flown in from Sao Tomé, and the latter supplying the heavy equipment and personnel. *The Nordchurchaid Airlift to Biafra 1968–1970*, p. 27.

fog lamps, a $20,000 direction finder, and other navigational equipment.[112] By mid-October 1968, the Uli complex was able to handle up to fifty flights per night, more than three times the previous number. An excerpt from a report filed by an American church official captures the evangelical spirit behind the airlift: "To stand in Uli in the middle of a dark night . . . or to stand in the Sao Tomé airport and watch the planes take off in relays for Biafra, is a wondrous experience indeed! One wonders at the might of the Christian Church and the determination that we are our brother's keeper, and to see so visibly and hear so audibly what has been wrought."[113]

Four airlifts from three staging areas touched down at Uli, flying in from the coast on the same approach. The heaviest traffic originated on Sao Tomé. This was the staging point for Jointchurchaid, an "ad hoc air transport organization" comprising a host of Catholic and Protestant groups from Europe and North America.[114] Between August 26, 1968, and December 2, 1968, Jointchurchaid completed 774 flights, delivering seven thousand tons of relief commodities at a cost of $25 million.[115] The total Jointchurchaid contribution reached 66,000 tons in 5,310 flights, at a cost of $116 million, by January 1970.[116]

Sao Tomé was also a staging point for Biafran arms. In the spring of 1968, when the various church groups were beginning to seek ways of sending medical and food supplies into Biafra, they rented cargo space and planes from Captain Hank Wharton's air charter service.[117] Wharton was the rather notorious operator of Ojukwu's military supply system, and the identification of the churches with the importation of Biafran arms left a bitter legacy in Lagos.[118] Sao Tomé quickly be-

[112] *Ibid.*, Appendix 9. The churches also purchased tracking radar of U.S. military origin, but found it unsuitable for conditions at Uli.

[113] James MacCracken, "Disaster Report and Response No. 88–X," a report to the Church World Service Department Committee from the Executive Director, CWS, April 2, 1969.

[114] Member organizations of Jointchurchaid as constituted in Rome, November 9, 1968, were Das Diakonische Werk, Stuttgart, Deutscher Caritasverband, Freiburg; Caritas Internationalis; Swiss Protestant and Catholic relief groups; Dutch Protestant and Catholic relief groups; Catholic Relief Services; Church World Service; and Nordchurchaid, made up of Folkekirkens Nodhjaelp (Denmark), Kirkens Nødjelp (Norway), Lutherhjalpen (Sweden), and Kyrkans U-landshjalp (Finland). Additional participants included: Canairelief (Canada); Christian Aid, CAFOD, Catholic Women's League, Church of Scotland (all British); and Joint Church Aid-U.S.A. (Composed of the American Jewish Committee, Church World Service, and Catholic Relief Services-USCC).

[115] Nigeria/Biafra Emergency-Material Aid, World Council of Churches, report by H. Reuschle, Geneva, December 3, 1968.

[116] Statistics provided in a personal letter from Ludwig Geissel of Das Diakonische Werk to J. Kennedy Lindsay, January 30, 1970.

[117] *The Nordchurchaid Airlift to Biafra 1968–1970*, pp. 3, 5.

[118] For information concerning the exploits of Henry Wharton as Ojukwu's

came known internationally as a center of relief activities, but it also remained a collection point for arms destined for the enclave throughout the war. The churches accepted this rather embarrassing arrangement because, as one relief worker candidly noted, the Portuguese-controlled island was "free from obstacles imposed by Nigeria or the Organization of African Unity."[119]

A second relief transport organization, ICRC's International Airlift West Africa (INALWA) was based on the island of Fernando Po.[120] The island was less than one hundred miles off the eastern Nigerian coast, on the same axis as Sao Tomé. When Red Cross operations began the island was still administered by Spain, but it achieved independence as part of Equatorial Guinea on October 12, 1968. The Red Cross and the several Protestant church groups that shipped their donations via INALWA preferred Fernando Po, not because it was closer to the mainland than Sao Tomé, but because it was not a Portuguese colony.[121] During the last three months of 1968, INALWA carried approximately 5,000 tons of food supplies into Biafra, and between January and June 1969 another 14,000 tons reached the Ibo heartland by this means.[122]

Two smaller relief airlifts originated in Libreville, Gabon, on the mainland southeast of Biafra. For the last half of the civil war, this was also the primary conduit for arms and ammunition to Biafra.[123] Between the summer of 1968 and April 1969, the French Red Cross supported 163 flights, which carried 1,070 tons of relief supplies from Libreville to Biafra.[124] A parallel operation launched by an interdominational, but heavily Catholic, private Irish appeal called Africa Concern ferried in 3,203 tons of relief in 306 flights from Libreville.[125]

---

principal gunrunner during the first half of the conflict, see Thayer, *The War Business*, pp. 162–168 and de St. Jorre, *The Nigerian Civil War*, pp. 321–323.

[119] Aitken, "On the Airstrip at Uli," p. 14.

[120] In addition to national Red Cross societies, particularly those in Germany, Austria, Canada, Denmark, Finland, U.S.A., U.K., Ireland, Italy, Norway, Netherlands, Sweden, and Switzerland, other agencies using the ICRC airlift included: World Council of Churches; CARE; Lutheran Church Missouri Synod; Methodists; Oxford Committee for Famine Relief (OXFAM); Quakers; Raedda Barnen; Salvation Army; Save the Children Fund; Seventh Day Adventists; International Union for Child Welfare; and UNICEF.

[121] To use the Portuguese facilities at Sao Tomé, a World Council of Churches spokesman noted, would "show a lack of feeling for the spirit of freedom and independence of the new African nations." World Council of Churches/DICARWS Statement, August 23, 1968.

[122] ICRC, *Annual Report 1969*, p. 15.

[123] For an early report on the expanded Libreville shuttle, see *West Africa*, No. 2679, October 5, 1968, p. 1185.

[124] Figures are available only for this period, although the airlift continued until the end of the war. Estimate is based on data assembled by Laurie S. Wiseberg in "Humanitarian Intervention: Lessons from the Nigerian Civil War," p. 11.

[125] *Ibid.*

Africa Concern tried to adopt a "neutral" position, but the French Red Cross operations were openly supported by the French government and, in light of the French military support that was also routed through Gabon, the Libreville airlifts gave credibility to the federal government's assertion that relief flights were providing a cover for Biafran arms shipments. In fact, once the much larger airlifts from Sao Tomé and Fernando Po became fully operative in late 1968, the proportion of gunrunning aircraft reaching Uli on any given night amounted to only about ten percent of the air traffic.

In assessing the strategic importance of the relief agencies' acceptance of Ojukwu's demand that they fly at night, the central fact is that the Nigerian air force lacked the capability to discriminate among incoming aircraft after dark. Not only were Biafra's military transports far fewer in number and interspersed with the relief planes as much as possible, but they were practically identical to the relief aircraft that flew the same flight patterns into the enclave.[126] The typical aircraft on both the arms[127] and relief[128] shuttles were old DC–6s and DC–7s. If Gowon had decided to close down Ojukwu's military airlift, he would have had simultaneously to stop all incoming relief. For reasons that will be discussed in chapter 10, the federal government did not interdict the relief planes until a lone Swedish Red Cross plane was shot down in June 1969.[129] Instead, the Nigerians began in late October 1968 to harass the Uli airstrip with small bombs dropped through the hatch of an aging DC–3 whose pilot called himself "Intruder."[130]

A basic assumption of Biafran foreign policy from the summer of 1968 until the collapse of secession in January 1970 held that international public opinion would not tolerate significant Nigerian interference with the relief efforts to aid starving Biafran civilians. Even after the Nigerian air force interdicted the Red Cross plane in June 1969, the Biafrans remained confident that the major powers would prevent Gowon from stopping the flow of food into the enclave and, as long as the food arrived at night, the clandestine arms shuttle would be protected.

[126] Interview: Onyemelukwe, and *Nordchurchaid Airlift to Biafra 1968–1970*, ch. 6.

[127] Wharton's operation from Sao Tomé used both types of transports, and the Rhodesian-owned charter service from Libreville comprised three DC–7s, a DC–6, and three smaller DC–3s. Interview: Okwechimi.

[128] ICRC, *Annual Report 1968*, p. 15; *Nordchurchaid Airlift to Biafra 1968–1970*, ch. 9.

[129] Propeller-driven aircraft equipped with cannon, light bombs, and machine guns were available to federal buyers and could have been deployed from Benin and Calabar at night against Uli. British intelligence reported that the Soviets were prepared to sell Lagos such aircraft, but the offer was declined.

[130] Aitken, "On the Airstrip at Uli," pp. 13–16.

Harassment by the federal air force was a real threat to Ojukwu only if the relief agencies used this show of hostility to withdraw support for the airlift on condition that Biafra agree to alternative modes of delivery. This ploy was, in fact, adopted by the Red Cross which, under the terms of the 1948 Geneva Convention, eventually felt obliged to respect the wishes of the Nigerian government. Jointchurchaid, however, was under no similar constraint. "I was certain," Ojukwu remarked afterwards, "that the most Nigeria would do to the airlift was shoot down one or two planes. I was assured the Churches would continue to the end—all of them—no matter what. I was also sure the Red Cross would stop, but as long as I had the other two directions it was all right. Hence I opened the Libreville line and I always kept arms coming through from Sao Tomé."[131] Under these circumstances Ojukwu was able to refuse any proposal to neutralize Uli for daylight relief flights. Had he accepted day flights, the Biafran leader points out, "Nigeria would have been free to bomb our alternative airstrip [another stretch of reinforced roadway near Uga sometimes used for gunrunning] with impunity. We were fighting a war and I needed arms."[132]

The debate over whether, or to what extent, the airlift of humanitarian relief provided a cover for arms traffic has obscured another politically significant aspect of the massive influx of food supplies. What has been largely overlooked by those interested in the dynamics of the Biafran resistance was the crucial role this relief played in supporting the Biafran army and bureaucracy, the two main components of the Biafran state system. The salaries of clerks and infantrymen started at under $700 per annum when the war broke out. All wages, up to the civil service ceiling of $7,500, remained constant during the war, while the price of gari (cassava flour) and other staples increased thirty-six-fold or more by early 1969.[133] The only way for Ojukwu to placate the military and civil service as conditions worsened was to allow them direct and ample access to relief materials.[134]

All food entering Biafra or procured from domestic sources (including materials bought behind enemy lines) was monitored and, to some extent managed, by the Directorate of Food Supply. Basically, the directorate was concerned with the distribution of food according to military and security priorities: the army was supplied first, the ten

---

[131] Interview: Ojukwu.   [132] *Ibid.*

[133] ICRC, "Food and Agricultural Situation in Biafra," May 23, 1969, p. 13. Some other examples of inflation: four bananas from three pence to ten shillings; one chicken from seven or nine shillings to four pounds; one hoe from four shillings to four pounds.

[134] Interview: F. U. Emeghara, deputy to the chief secretary of the Biafran government.

directorates second, and the civil service third. The total personnel in these sectors probably amounted to no more than 60,000, or approximately 5 percent of those receiving relief in January 1969.[135] Yet they composed the Biafran state, and their welfare was absolutely essential to the war effort and the administration of authority within the enclave. Unrestricted access to imported relief supplies for members of the government became a fact of life from mid-1968 onward. How much they consumed is impossible to determine. Given the nature of the extended family in Ibo society, any member fortunate enough to hold a government position—the higher the better—was expected to provide for all who could claim even a tenuous familial bond.[136]

The international humanitarian organizations repeatedly denied feeding anyone but the most desperate—pregnant women, nursing mothers, the very young, and the aged. While one cannot doubt their noble intentions, their own records reveal that conditions were often beyond their control. Humanitarian intervention in the Nigerian conflict was an ad hoc affair for which the agencies were unprepared: "It was never envisioned that the requirement for massive relief in the form of foodstuffs would have to be continued for a prolonged period of time. Therefore, the organization for handling this problem sort of 'grew up,' rather than being formally planned for long term, large scale operations. As a result, a rather minimal amount of objectivity in selection of recipients for food relief has been incorporated into the program."[137] There were, of course, variations in the degree of control each agency maintained over the distribution of its contributions.

Protestants, Catholics, and the Red Cross each ran their own feeding stations and relief distribution networks throughout Biafra. Operations overlapped and occasionally evangelical competition for the loyalty of refugees was reported.[138] In general, the agencies cooperated, but they

[135] The number of troops totaled approximately 40,000, but most of these were foot soldiers with relatively small claim per man on relief supplies. There are innumerable stories of troops appropriating crops as the need arose. The bureaucracy, including the directorates, numbered between 15,000 and 20,000 persons, and they were dependent on the allocations from the Directorate of Food Supply.

[136] It was not uncommon for an overworked but highly placed civil servant to face the additional responsibility of feeding his entire village of several families, a task that would entail several trips a week into the bush with the car trunk full of relief materials recently off-loaded at the airport.

[137] From a report prepared by the medical secretary of the World Council of Churches Program in Biafra, August-December 1969, reprinted in *Nordchurchaid Airlift to Biafra 1968-1970*, p. 96.

[138] A World of Churches representative in Okigwi Province reported to a visiting delegation from Geneva in November 1968 that while WCC and CARITAS enjoyed the "finest cooperation" at the top level, "some local Roman Catholic priests are making 'stockfish Catholics.' Some are reported to distribute the stockfish only to Catholics after mass on Sunday. Others first ask the recipient: 'are you a Catholic?' 'No, I am Presbyterian.' 'Do you want to become a Catholic?'

were nevertheless hard-pressed to cope with the widespread confusion and mishandling of relief supplies once they were off-loaded and trucked from Uli air strip.[139] The Catholics, who often seemed the least concerned about the political implications of their intervention, nevertheless held the tightest reins over the distribution of their relief. This was possible because of the church's well-developed administrative hierarchy and the presence of Irish Holy Ghost Fathers and other expatriate clergy who ensured that priority was given to feeding the most desperate.

The Protestants ran a much less well integrated organization. The most widely used name for the local Protestant effort in Biafra was the World Council of Churches. This was somewhat misleading, and caused the World Council's headquarters in Geneva considerable discomfort.[140] When secession was declared, Biafran Protestant clergy immediately announced the formation of the Christian Council of Biafra, with Reverend G. E. Igwe designated as secretary of the "World Council of Churches Refugee Relief, Biafra." This unilateral bid for international affiliation angered the Christian Council of Nigeria and embarrassed the World Council.[141] The Christian Council of Biafra had succeeded in making its authority stick, and attracted substantial cash contributions from national church groups in Europe and America. Some control over the distribution of the various Protestant relief efforts was provided by Dr. Herman Middelkoop, but generally the entire process was run by Biafrans who, understandably had fewer qualms about feeding hungry soldiers or meeting urgent government requests.[142]

If the answer is yes, the person receives the stockfish, if it is no, he does not." Diary of a visit to Biafra compiled by a WCC official.

[139] The Catholics (CARITAS) and those Protestant groups that chose to operate from Sao Tomé rather than to join the World Council of Church's operation on Fernando Po flew in supplies on alternate nights to avoid confusion at Uli. The ICRC/World Council of Churches airlift was run separately.

[140] On December 19, 1968, Dr. E. C. Blake, general secretary of the World Council of Churches, wrote to the secretary of the Refugee Relief Committee in Biafra: "I understand also that the relief programme is being carried out in the name of the WCC . . . we in the World Council are somewhat embarrassed by this for two reasons: 1. We are receiving credit which we do not fully deserve . . . 2. We are concerned that our constituency in Nigeria should suppose that we have taken a political rather than a humanitarian orientation in our World Council policy."

[141] During the World Council of Churches' Fourth Assembly in Uppsala, Sweden, July 4–19, 1968, the Nigerian delegation accused the council of seeming to grant international recognition to Biafra and threatened unspecified reprisals unless the word "Biafra" were dropped from all further correspondence. Subsequently the WCC headquarters tended to refer to the disturbed area of "the former Eastern Region," although the Christian Council of Biafra went right on printing its stationery in the form of a national member of the WCC.

[142] In August 1968, Dr. Middelkoop "emphasized [to Geneva] that the Relief Committee is now giving priority to the employment of indigenous relief per-

The most important food supplier for Biafra's military and civilian elites may have been the nonsectarian International Red Cross. In early August 1968, the ICRC had only three expatriate officials to monitor the distribution of relief materials in Biafra. With the expanded airlift, the number of foreign relief workers jumped to 140 by the end of September. More than half of these were withdrawn by the end of 1968, however, owing to military pressure and Biafran irritation over the ICRC's dealings with the federal government.[143] Meanwhile, the running of ICRC local operations devolved to a newly recruited staff of six hundred Biafrans. The Biafran Red Cross and the Food Directorate worked in tandem to guarantee that the politically relevant elements of Biafran society were well fed, including sufficient largesse to care for the various hungry relatives of the extended families of officials.

The nightly delivery of relief supplies would have been insufficient to sustain Biafra indefinitely. Uli's incapacity to handle the increasing volume of carbohydrates, in addition to less bulky protein-rich commodities, eventually would have led to an untenable situation. The only alternatives would have been to accept Nigeria's offer for a land corridor plus daylight flights or to develop the means to supply the population with locally grown carbohydrates. Ojukwu opted for the second course and was again assisted by the foreign relief agencies.

During the final year of the conflict, there would be the widespread cultivation of cassava, the starchy root crop known elsewhere as manioc, which Ojukwu wryly refers to as Biafra's secret weapon. The plant will grow throughout the year in practically any soil. By late 1968 cassava was being cultivated all over Biafra in small road-side plots and village fields. Although it is relatively low in protein and other nutrients, cassava served as a meager but sufficient supplement to the growing in-

---

sonnel and requested funds to facilitate this." "Nigeria/Biafra Emergency Appeal," World Council of Churches Progress Report August 16, 1968. At that time the WCC had only 48 expatriate staff members in Biafra to administer 600–700 refugee camps. Three months later the head of the Methodist Church in Biafra conveyed his concern to Geneva about "the increasing number of complaints that certain Biafran pastors were using the relief supplies for their own benefit." Diary of a visit to Biafra compiled by a WCC official.

143 ICRC, *Annual Report 1968*, p. 18, cites "the advance of Federal troops" as the reason for the withdrawal. For a strong condemnation of the tactlessness and ineptitude of expatriate Red Cross workers in the Nigerian conflict, see "Relief Effort: Errors and Lessons," *Venture*, XXI (July/August 1969), pp. 17–22. When asked about the pretext used to expel the Swiss Red Cross workers from Biafra, Ojukwu recounts how he dispatched his police to raid a particularly raucous party of expatriate ICRC personnel and their Biafran girlfriends. Having marched them through the streets of Umuahia after midnight to police headquarters, Ojukwu suggested it would be in everyone's interest if those involved quietly left Biafra and the overall number of expatriate staff be drastically reduced. Interview: Ojukwu.

flow of foreign relief. It is the principal reason why Biafra's carbohydrate reserves held out much longer than Jointchurchaid and others had predicted.[144]

As part of this program to increase self-sufficiency in agriculture, Jointchurchaid set up "Food Production Committees" in every province. The aims of the committees were threefold: to create demonstration plots; to ascertain the need for seeds and machinery and to obtain these when possible; and to oversee the distribution of seeds and machinery when obtained.[145] During the first three months of the program, foreign relief agencies imported and distributed 250 tons of planting material and agricultural equipment.[146] CARITAS Internationalis took the lead in these efforts, which included airlifting 100 tons of vital maize seeds from Colombia.[147] The relief agencies also established twelve major farms of 100–150 acres each, and eighteen smaller farms of 10–15 acres each in which Ibos retained ownership of the land but were assisted by expatriates in developing and managing the crops.[148] CARITAS further converted the football fields and adjacent grounds at 1,200 Catholic schools into gardens. Thirty-two thousand hoes and machetes were also flown in to assist Ojukwu's agriculture program.

Capturing the world's attention and attracting sufficient material support to wage a war of attrition were the crowning achievements of the Ojukwu regime, but they satisfied only a first objective. The real issue was whether or not international concern for the survival of the Ibo people could be transformed into political intervention aimed at preserving the integrity of the Biafran state. "Relief, no matter how massive, is at best a palliative," to quote a December 1968 statement by Ojukwu. The Biafran leader continued, "Biafra is rich in food, both protein and carbohydrates, and all that is required is for conditions to become more or less normal for the millions of refugees to return to their areas at present disturbed by enemy presence."[149]

Ojukwu's earlier quest for a cease-fire and a negotiated political settlement that would respect Biafra's claim to self-determination had become bogged down in peace-talk diplomacy during the summer of 1968. Now that Biafra had acquired the means to sustain a war of attrition,

[144] Jointchurchaid, Press Release, No. 40, Geneva, February 25, 1969, corrects earlier dire predictions.
[145] *Minutes*, Fourth Plenary Conference of Jointchurchaid, Lucerne, June 11–13, 1969. Report of Rev. O'Conner of Holy Ghost Fathers.
[146] *Ibid.*
[147] *Ibid.* Also, ICRC, "Food and Agriculture Situation in Biafra," May 23, 1969, pp. 5, 9–11.
[148] *Minutes*, Fourth Plenary Conference of Jointchurchaid, Lucerne, June 11–13, 1969.
[149] Statement by H. E. Lt. Col. Ojukwu, Umuahia, December 29, 1968, reprinted in Kirk-Greene, *Crisis and Conflict*, II, 342–345.

Ojukwu was not inclined to compromise. On September 25, 1968, he issued one of his most defiant speeches of the war and called on the Biafran people to "rededicate yourselves again to the struggle. The future belongs to us, and we can regain lost grounds by renewed effort."[150]

[150] Ojukwu, *Biafra*, Address to a joint meeting of the Consultative Assembly and the Council of Chiefs and Elders, September 25, 1968, I, 356.

PART III

ISOLATING THE CONFLICT

· 9 ·

MAINTAINING INTERNATIONAL
POLITICAL SUPPORT FOR NIGERIA

Nigerian foreign policy adapted to the growing international public concern over conditions in the Ibo enclave by seeking to maintain good relations with those governments facing the strongest pro-Biafran lobbies. At the same time, Lagos pressed the members of the Organization of African Unity for a maximum show of diplomatic support, so as to discourage European and American political interference in what the federal government hoped the major powers would continue to regard as primarily an "African affair." The inherent difficulty in pursuing these two objectives simultaneously was that it necessitated the granting of diplomatic assurances that were sometimes contradictory.

The interests of profederal Western governments and the majority of African states diverged over how Nigeria should conduct the war. Pressure from Europe and America encouraged the federal government to cooperate fully with all peace initiatives, to show restraint in the conduct of military operations, and to allow unrestricted access to Biafra for the various humanitarian organizations. The majority of African governments, on the other hand, sought clear evidence of Nigeria's determination to crush the secession quickly, preferably with a minimum of non-African involvement.

Nigerian spokesmen tried to accommodate official concerns both in Africa and in Europe and North America. The task was much easier in Africa because of the shared belief that the overriding objective for the federal government should be the rapid termination of the rebellion. Fortunately, the annual OAU summits coincided with the end of Nigeria's rainy season, and the federal army's fall campaigns in 1967, 1968, and 1969. Nigeria's delegates to the OAU thus could always point to renewed military activity as indicating their government's determination to prosecute the conflict.

European and American audiences required a different posture, although here, too, a coincidence of circumstances occasionally assisted Nigeria's diplomatic efforts. Public pressures, aroused over the plight of Biafra's civilian population, peaked in Western democracies during the summer of 1968, at the height of Nigeria's worst rainy season in years. With the federal army unable to push forward through the mud, it was somewhat easier for the Ministry of External Affairs to project an image of deliberation and restraint in the government's military policies. There is, however, no evidence to suggest that Lagos ever delayed a major military offensive in deference to foreign policy concerns.

Profederal Western officials frequently complained that Nigeria failed to counteract Biafran propaganda when opportunities were available. To an extent this is true, although there is much more to propaganda than a mere exchange of words. When called upon to show good faith by agreeing to meet Biafran representatives in an international arena or by allowing relief planes to penetrate Nigerian air space, Lagos could be quite flexible. So long as basic military strategy was not compromised, Gowon was fully prepared to demonstrate to Europe and America that his regime was neither bloodthirsty nor inordinately intransigent and, at one stage, he even ordered the grounding of his lone squadron of jet fighters to assuage international public opinion.[1]

This chapter will review the federal government's very limited and ineffective efforts to engage in direct media propaganda, and will then give an account of Nigeria's somewhat strained relations with Britain prior to the Fifth (1968) OAU summit in September. The chapter concludes with an assessment of the breadth of pro-Nigeria support during the deliberations among African heads of state in Algiers and in the twenty-third session of the United Nations General Assembly a few weeks later.

Federal Propaganda

Lagos never established a public relations operation to match Biafra's Geneva-based Markpress, and few citizen "Action Committees" in Europe or America came to the defense of the Nigerian cause. Federal diplomats generally remained aloof from the internal political debates that raged in Europe and North America over how a given government should react to the Nigerian crisis. There were three basic reasons why the federal military government never tried to inspire countervailing public pressures abroad to neutralize the various Biafran lobbyists: the lack of popular receptivity to the federal case; bureaucratic wrangling between the Ministry of Information and the Ministry of External Affairs over who should speak for the federal government overseas; and General Gowon's personal dislike for propaganda.

Many influential Nigerians, including senior officials in the Ministry of Information, believed that the propaganda war was simply a lost cause, and that nothing they said would have erased the reality of the

---

[1] Gowon's willingness to curtail air operations will be discussed in Chapter 11 in conjunction with British Prime Minister Wilson's visit to Nigeria and related developments during the spring of 1969.

1966 pogroms or the human deprivation inside Biafra. They were bitter about what they considered to be Ojukwu's exploitation of Western gullibility by skillfully exaggerating the magnitude of the suffering while completely obscuring the causes of the dispute and the federal government's true intentions. "How can you talk to people who refuse to listen?" was a typical rationalization for the inadequacies of the federal propaganda effort.

When Nigerian spokesmen did try to explain their position to foreign audiences, the exercise was often futile. It was simply impossible to match the imagery of genocide with a discourse on the twelve-state federation. Even the usually popular symbol of "African unity" failed to evoke much enthusiasm, except within the American black community. And when federal officials tried to explain the political and strategic implications of unrestricted humanitarian intervention, they were usually brushed aside. In a December 1968 televised panel discussion in New York, for example, Nigeria's ambassador to the United Nations attempted to show that Jointchurchaid, "with the best intentions," was nevertheless "indirectly" aiding the rebellion and prolonging the war. Before he had an opportunity to elaborate, an irate Irish priest intervened: "If you call innocent children and babies a few days old and babies a week old or a month old who are dying of starvation— they have no milk, no food—if they are rebels, I don't know what."[2]

Faced with such ad hominem arguments, Gowon's representatives were defensive. As one prominent Nigerian diplomat remarked in exasperation after a particularly emotional Washington "teach-in": "If that's democracy in action, who needs it!"

A further reflection of Nigerian impatience with what they considered to be the gross misrepresentation of the Euro-American press and numerous elected officials, were the notes of protest from the Ministry of External Affairs. In the Nigerian view, those best placed to curb pro-Biafran excesses were the respective home governments. Answering the allegations by pro-Biafran Congressmen and Senators was considered by Lagos to be the responsibility of the United States Department of State, and not the Nigerian government. Similar arguments were made with regard to political pressures facing other Western governments. According to one German diplomat:

The Nigerians did little to counter the Biafran propaganda in Germany; in fact, none of their publications were even translated into German until 1969. Yet the Nigerian government showed absolutely no sympathy for the difficulties the German government was encountering in dealing with its public opinion and could not understand

[2] *New York Times*, December 19, 1968.

why we were not doing more . . . when an editorial came out against Nigeria they held us responsible. By contrast, they showed great patience in their diplomacy—beyond what could have been expected.[3]

The heart of the problem, of course, was a lack of credibility. This was compounded in Britain and the United States, where the Wilson and Johnson regimes had already alienated those on the political left who now tended to support Biafra. When asked why the British government failed to speak out more openly in Nigeria's defense, a senior Whitehall official replied, "it would have only brought the do-gooders down on our neck."

Although the undeniable horrors that had afflicted the Ibo people since 1966 ensured that any promises of future reconciliation by the federal government would be greeted with skepticism, there were several symbols that Lagos could have invoked more effectively in appealing to Western audiences; the history of Ibo domination of the Eastern minorities and the support that Nigeria enjoyed throughout black Africa were two examples. There were other reasons, however, for the poor federal showing in the competition for public support. One factor, which has been largely overlooked, was the long-standing bureaucratic rivalry between the Ministry of Information and the Ministry of External Affairs.

According to the Nigeria (Constitution) Order of Council 1960 on the Assignment of Responsibilities to Ministers, the Ministry of Information is responsible for the production of propaganda, domestic and overseas, while the Ministry of External Affairs distributes the latter.[4] This division of labor has never worked very satisfactorily. During the formative years following Independence the relationship is widely believed to have been undermined by a personal animosity between Minister of Information T.O.S. Benson, and his counterpart in external affairs, Jaja Wachuku. Then too, there was the relative prestige of the two ministries: the Ministry of External Affairs traditionally has been the most selective in its recruitment, while the Ministry of Information has had a reputation among university graduates as a bureau of last resort. In 1961, the minister of information invited an undersecretary of state from the British Foreign Office to examine the ministry's capacity to meet the federal government's requirements for overseas publicity and, much to the eternal delight of the Ministry of External Affairs, the undersecretary concluded, inter alia:

[3] Interview: Federal Republic of Germany, embassy, Lagos.
[4] Republic of Nigeria (Constitution) Order of Council 1960 (Government Notice N.2420 dated December 15, 1960, in *Official Gazette* No. 79, Vol. 47, pp. 1594–1600).

There can be no doubt that the Ministry of Foreign Affairs and Commonwealth Relations [as it was then called] must have the ultimate power to control the policy of information services overseas, and [that] it must, above all, have the power to decide in detail what line the information service should take on any issue involving Nigeria's foreign policy or her relations with other countries. It would obviously be an absurd and dangerous situation if Nigeria were to talk to the world with two different and perhaps conflicting voices.[5]

The Ministry of External Affairs successfully retained absolute control over the dissemination of Nigerian propaganda. Yet the ministry, with a war-time hiring freeze and only two hundred foreign service officers, lacked the manpower to cope with the Biafran challenge in the public relations field. The Information Division at the ministry headquarters in Lagos was staffed by only two officers and their secretaries. It functioned as a liaison with the Ministry of Information, and advised on issue priorities, primarily with regard to the propaganda broadcasts of Radio Nigeria. Budgetary limits aimed at conserving foreign exchange during the war further constrained the public relations activities of Nigeria's diplomats overseas, as allowances for individual officers were cut 25 percent across the board and essential services at many missions had to be frozen in order to meet strict budget ceilings.[6]

The Ministry of Information also was forced to operate within tight financial restrictions that precluded additional work abroad. The ministry was allowed to post a press officer in the Nigerian embassies in Paris, London, Washington, and Moscow, but these posts had been established prior to the civil war and were not expanded during the conflict. All initiatives through these outlets had to be cleared in advance by the respective ambassador.

The content of Nigeria's wartime propaganda was shaped at weekly meetings of a special committee comprising several permanent secretaries, notably Asiodu from Industries and Ayida from Economic Development, and chaired by the director of Federal Information Services. The major themes for the week were then communicated to the national and international audiences during three-minute "Newstalk" radio editorials that followed the morning and evening news. This was the heart of the federal government's propaganda effort. Written publications, frequently transcripts of the "Newstalks," were prepared by the

[5] MEA, Report on the Information Division of the Federal Ministry of Information, prepared by R.H.K. Marett, May 26, 1961, para. 35.

[6] Between fiscal years 1967/68 and 1969/70 (with the fiscal year ending on March 31) total expenditures by the Ministry of External Affairs declined approximately 6 percent, from $10.3 million to $9.66 million.

Overseas and Publication Section of the Ministry of Information. This effort to project the substance of the positions contained in "Newstalks" never amounted to very much because the ministry was allowed only six staff positions for this project and had only the manpower to fill five of the posts.

Responsibility for hiring overseas public relations firms also lay with the Ministry of Information, but again the lack of funds and a full mandate precluded any major publicity offensives.[7] The most significant work was done by the London firm of Galitzine, Chant and Russell, which functioned primarily behind the scenes, lobbying parliamentarians on the advice of the Nigerian high commission.[8] A more adventuresome, if less successful, undertaking occurred in France, where a small group of highly vocal Marxists was recruited to stage demonstrations and teach-ins in response to the pro-Biafran Left. Unfortunately, the communist ideology of the profederal agitators soon created apprehensions among the staff of the Nigerian embassy in Paris and, rather than risk offending other important interests within the French business community, the campaign on the Left was quickly dropped.[9]

In 1969, the Ministry of Information drew up an elaborate three-million-dollar budget for overseas work, which would have included the stationing of ministry personnel throughout the world and the establishment of several information centers, somewhat along the lines of the British Council or the United States Information Service. The plan was severely criticized during a meeting of Nigeria's ambassadors in Lagos on June 24, 1969. Among other issues, the ambassadors refused to accept information officers who would operate independently of the chancery staff, and they attacked the proposed allocation of funds on a number of counts that amounted to a plea that the money could be more effectively spent by the Ministry of External Affairs.[10]

The proposal for an expanded international public relations campaign by the Ministry of Information was not put into effect during the war years. Not only was the Ministry of External Affairs resistant to the Ministry of Information's proposed propaganda, but General Gowon also was decidedly unenthusiastic. Those who counseled Gowon regarding new ventures in propaganda maintain that his reactions invariably

[7] A line item for "Public Relations Consultants Fees" does not appear in the Ministry of Information budget until 1970/71, when $462,000 was finally earmarked for this purpose.

[8] Interview: David Russell of Galitzine, Chant and Russell.

[9] Julia and Andre Hervé, the daughter and son-in-law of author Richard Wright, organized the pro-Nigerian movement and were subsequently brought to Lagos as consultants to the Ministry of Information.

[10] MEA, Conference of Nigerian Ambassadors, Report of Discussion held Tuesday, June 24, 1969, CNA/1, External Publicity and Information.

were laced with such homilies as "actions speak louder than words," and "truth shall prevail."[11]

In response to the widening coverage of the Nigerian crisis in the world press during the summer of 1968, a few concrete steps were taken to "educate" the international media. As a gesture to the foreign press corps stationed in Lagos,[12] for example, a director of Federal Information Services was appointed to coordinate the flow of official information from the ministry's various divisions and to expedite interviews between journalists and senior officials. A non-Ibo Easterner was designated to run the office, presumably to draw attention to the lack of multiethnic support for Biafran secession. Unfortunately, the individual selected for this public relations task was so irascible that he quickly became the bane of the Lagos press corps. Somewhat more successful were the two package tours in May and July 1968 arranged by Nigeria's public relations firm in London that brought approximately twenty British journalists to Lagos for a round of interviews and a tour of the battlefronts.[13] Also in July 1968, the Nigerian high commissioner in London began hosting small weekly working luncheons at Nigeria House for journalists and other opinion makers.[14]

The above efforts notwithstanding, Nigeria's relations with the foreign press were never very cordial, and in some instances broke down completely. In 1967 a decree was issued prohibiting all foreign news agencies from publishing or relaying information deemed detrimental to Nigeria, and this general restriction remained in effect until 1971.[15] The federal government tolerated the resident foreign press corps in Lagos, but

---

[11] On October 15, 1968 Gowon told the Inter-Government Conference on Public Information Services: "The Policy of the Federal Government on publicity has always been based on truth and the world is now seeing the truth, which always lasts longer than falsehood. If we keep ourselves together and cooperate at home we shall be able to stand against any external adverse publicity about us." Federal Ministry of Information Press Release, No. F.1875.

[12] Several foreign news agencies maintained bureaus in Lagos, including the Associated Press, Agence France-Presse, Reuters, the Ghana News Agency, TASS, Deutsche Presse Agentur, and the Voice of America. The British Broadcasting Corporation also staffed an office in Lagos until its principal correspondent was deported in June 1969.

[13] The tours included representatives from *The Times, Sunday Times, Observer, Financial Times, Guardian, Telegraph, West Africa,* the *Daily Express* and the BBC. Interview: Russell.

[14] The meetings were organized by Galitzine, Chant and Russell in consultation with the High Commission; that is, officials from the Ministry of External Affairs, and not the Ministry of Information, determined who would be lobbied. Among those attending were members of Parliament, businessmen, and representatives of various labor and other interest groups.

[15] Ojukwu imposed similar restrictions, but the only representatives of foreign news agencies in the enclave were Biafran stringers. Interview: Godwin Ironkwe, Reuters correspondent in Biafra.

rarely took steps to make reporting easier. As the war continued into 1969, however, the government's impatience with reporting it considered biased caused a rise in press harassment.[16]

Nigerian ambassadors in several Western capitals tried to counteract hostile local press reporting by inviting prominent citizens to visit Nigeria in a personal capacity, at the federal government's expense. Beginning in the summer of 1968, delegations of Germans, French, Swiss, British, and Americans came to Lagos on fact-finding missions. Hopes and plans for the program far exceeded its actual scope. On August 16, 1968, for example, Ambassador Joseph Iyalla cabled from Washington strongly endorsing the idea of a "crash effort to secure a better understanding of our case," and he outlined the three categories of American visitors whom he wished to invite:

(i) V.I.P. group of top editors, commentators, influential personalities, members of Congress, Council on Foreign Relations, etc.

(ii) "Middle grade" group of American academicians, Trade Unions, and women editors, etc.

(iii) "General" group of civil rights activists, Negro community representatives, activist student leaders, etc.[17]

By the end of 1968, six Americans had visited Nigeria as guests of the government.[18] None was a movie star or literary celebrity of the type whose trips to Biafra gained wide press coverage in the United States. If the visits to Nigeria had any subsequent impact back home, this was behind the scenes.

The most dramatic success of the visitors' program occurred in Britain, when Dame Margery Perham returned from a meeting with General Gowon and a August 30–September 7, 1968, tour of the fronts. Dame Margery, the renowed Africanist, until that time had identified herself with the plight of the Ibos. Upon leaving Nigeria, and on the basis of her exposure to the minority areas in the East, she dramatically reversed her stand and broadcast a personal appeal to Ojukwu calling for an end to the rebellion.[19] In addition to Dame

[16] Two resident correspondents, Lloyd Garrison of the *New York Times* and Peter Stewart of the BBC, were actually deported for their coverage of the federal government's handling of the war. A third, Ian Laval of Reuters, was briefly detained for the premature release of a government policy statement on relief.

[17] Cable: Ambassador J.T.F. Iyalla to Ministry of External Affairs, August 16, 1968.

[18] The six were: Osborne Elliot, editor-in-chief of Newsweek Magazine; Eugene Foley, former assistant secretary of state for commerce; Arthur Houghton, Jr., president of Steuben Glass Co.; Waldemar Nielson, president of the African-American Institute; John M. Letiche, professor of international economics, University of California; and James Meredith, Black civil rights activist.

[19] Radio Nigeria, "Broadcast Message to Emeka Ojukwu from Dame Margery

Margery, the Nigerian High Commission in London concentrated on helping those members of Parliament who were already profederal to journey to Lagos and rejuvenate their predilections. Two favorites were John Tilney and Nigel Fisher, former Commonwealth Relations Office ministers in the Macmillan cabinet.

STRAINED RELATIONS WITH BRITAIN

Harold Wilson's government needed more substantial indications of federal goodwill in order to quell growing criticism in Parliament. The policy of allowing British arms manufacturers to sell weapons to Nigeria was at issue, and appeals for an embargo against further sales intensified as a full-scale federal invasion of the Ibo heartland began to appear inevitable. Responding in part to diplomatic pressure from London, General Gowon announced on June 5, 1968, that federal troops would not advance into the Ibo heartland "unless all appeals for a settlement failed."[20]

The statement was issued barely a week before the British Parliament was due to debate the government's policy toward Nigeria. Predictably, British Foreign Minister Michael Stewart quoted Gowon's words as indicative of the federal government's goodwill, and also the latter's willingness to listen to the good advice offered by Her Majesty's government.[21] If Britain stopped selling arms to Nigeria, the foreign minister implied, London could no longer serve as a countervailing influence against any hawks in Lagos who might press Gowon for a full-scale invasion. Inside Biafra, one of Ojukwu's aides drafted a memorandum that interpreted Gowon's apparent hesitation to invade as indicating that Lagos had returned to a policy of "encirclement," and that the decision had been precipitated by pressure from Britain and other unnamed powers.[22]

When Gowon made his June 5 statement, he could afford to wait. Port Harcourt had recently been captured following heavy fighting, and his troops needed to consolidate their southern positions while the rainy season peaked. During the ensuing two and a half months, the peace talks in Addis Ababa collapsed and the aerial blockade of Biafra was decisively and openly defied by the relief agencies. Foreign policy

---

Perham," September 7, 1968. See also *The Times* (London), October 30, 1968, "Chance for Nigeria," a letter to the editor from Dame Margery Perham.

[20] *Morning Post*, June 6, 1968.

[21] Great Britain, *Parliamentary Debates*, Vol. 766, June 12, 1968, cols. 297–299.

[22] Republic of Biafra, Ministry of Foreign Affairs, "Some Notes and Suggestions about the Nigeria-Biafra War," June 10, 1968.

priorities had also shifted—back to Africa—with the OAU's fifth summit scheduled for September 13, 1968, in Algiers. As noted earlier, African governments were generally much more hawkish than Nigeria's supporters in Britain. Lagos remained convinced, moreover, that one way to minimize the threat of foreign interference was to encourage a maximum degree of profederal sentiment within the OAU. Thus, with the coincidence of the offensive at the end of the rainy season and the OAU summit, Nigerian spokesmen talked again about a military solution.

During the weeks preceding the Algiers summit, members of Gowon's Federal Executive Council traveled widely throughout Africa to give assurances of a quick end to the rebellion.[23] Meanwhile, Nigeria's military commanders made plain their intention to press on with the fight. The most outspoken, Col. Benjamin Adekunle of the Third Marine Division, bluntly informed visiting journalists that he would soon present Gowon with a special "OAU victory": the successful occupation of Biafra's three remaining towns, Owerri, Aba, and Umuahia.[24] Then, on August 24, 1968, Gowon was asked during an interview with the British Broadcasting Corporation whether reports of a "final" military push were true; he replied, "That's correct . . . all fronts from the north southwards, southwards northward, northwestern pushing southeastern." When pressed for a prediction of the victory date, he said "within the next four weeks."[25]

The timing of Gowon's remark, which appears to have been a spontaneous reply to an unsolicited question,[26] proved to be of considerable embarrassment to Harold Wilson's government in Britain. The BBC aired its interview with General Gowon proclaiming the invasion of the heartland on August 26, 1968, the night before Parliament convened for a special one-day debate on Nigeria. The federal government's readiness to compensate London for this latest and rather unnecessary strain in Anglo/Nigerian relations provides an interesting counter-

[23] Among those who traveled on this assignment were: Alhaji Ali Monguno to Ghana, Sierra Leone, and Liberia; Dr. T. O. Elias to Tunisia; Alhaji Aminu Kano to several North African capitals; Ukpabi Asika to Mali, Upper Volta, Guinea, and Senegal; and Ibrahim Tahir to East Africa. Gowon met directly with the leaders of all neighboring countries during June and July.

[24] *Daily Times*, August 8, 1968; *West Africa*, No. 2676, September 14, 1968, p. 1065.

[25] "Gowon Announces the 'Final Push' "; partial transcript of BBC interview, August 24, 1968, reprinted in Kirk-Greene, *Crisis and Conflict*, II, 316–317.

[26] This, at least, is the view of several of his advisers as well as foreign correspondents who had an opportunity to interview the Nigerian leader during the war. To paraphrase David Williams, editor of *West Africa*, Gowon will either tell you the truth as he perceives it or he will decline comment altogether for reasons of military security; it is as simple as that. Interview: Williams.

point to the more militant tenor of their intra-African diplomacy prior to the OAU summit.

The August 27, 1968, debate in the British House of Commons was often heated and centered on the government's determination to continue authorizing the export of arms and ammunition to Nigeria.[27] Gowon's announcement of an imminent invasion of the Ibo heartland rendered absurd, in the eyes of Wilson's critics, the argument that continued British arms sales were necessary to preserve Britain's residual influence in Lagos, to ensure, among other things, that Nigeria would seek an end to the rebellion through negotiations. Incredibly, Commonwealth Secretary George Thomson tried several times during the August 27 debate to explain that in the government's view, General Gowon's televised remarks were inaccurate and that a "full scale" invasion of Iboland had not really begun. His comments were greeted by jeers from the back benches. Undaunted, the undersecretary of state for Commonwealth Affairs rose in the final minutes of debate to say that the concern over the BBC interview was baseless, because "While this debate has been proceeding we have been in touch with Lagos, and General Gowon has told us personally that when he said that the final push is now in progress he was referring to the continuing preparatory operations for a final push."[28] The distinction, if one existed, was lost on those calling for a change in British policy.

Parliament adjourned without a vote, much to the consternation of the fifty MPs from both parties who had tabled a motion calling on the government to halt the sale of all further arms. Afterward, Biafra's supporters convened a massive demonstration in Trafalgar Square, and later that evening marched to the prime minister's residence at No. 10 Downing Street, where several of the demonstrators very nearly succeeded in battering their way through the front door. The next morning Wilson's minister of state in the Commonwealth Office, Lord Shepherd, was scheduled to see Chief Enahoro to counteract Biafra's successful penetration of British politics. Shepherd recalls preparing for the meeting, in light of recent "nasty incidents," and was determined to "get the heat off." The result was a suggestion that the federal government invite a team of international observers to serve as "umpires," overseeing the conduct of battle for the purpose of discrediting the Biafran lobby in Britain.[29]

The proposal for international observers was not new, but in the past it had been associated with policing a cease-fire. When Shepherd met Enahoro later in the morning, August 28, he claims to have told him

[27] Great Britain, *Parliamentary Debates*, Vol. 769, August 27, 1968, cols. 1433–1533.
[28] *Ibid.*, col. 1522.   [29] Interview: Lord Shepherd.

bluntly: "Look, your propaganda machine is bloody awful. You know what we're up against. What do you think of inviting observers, military men who would report publicly on the situation?"[30] Enahoro agreed to pass along the proposal, and within forty-eight hours Gowon sent his approval. On August 30, 1968, the federal government publicly invited representatives of the United Nations, the OAU, Britain, Poland, Canada, and Sweden to accompany Nigerian troops fighting in Biafra and thereby verify their behavior and conduct in Ibo areas.[31]

Allowing a predominantly European group of military officers to pass judgment over whether Africans could wage a "civilized war" may have smacked of paternalism to some Nigerians. But the gesture illustrates Gowon's confidence and his readiness to make concessions of form, if not substance. Inviting the foreigners to bear witness promised to reduce the threat of interference as the level of military activity increased, but it did not imply any slowdown of the offensive. The day after the federal government alerted the British of their readiness to welcome observers, Gowon informed the nation in a major broadcast that the Supreme Military Council had decided to press on urgently with the invasion to "end the rebellion with the least delay."[32] In a more militant vein, Radio Nigeria proclaimed, "Let the Federal Army march into rebel held areas. . . . Let them crush what remains of the rebellion and liberate the suffering masses. This is what the nation demands. . . . Certain misguided foreign governments and humanitarian and religious organizations of dubious integrity will try to bring pressure to bear on the federal government. But it is up to our leaders to stand firm in the face of these pressures. Only the government of Nigeria can decide what is good for the country."[33]

[30] *Ibid.*

[31] On September 6, 1968, the federal government formally invited the observers from the four countries and two international organizations to visit Nigeria, initially for a period of two months. The representatives of the UN and the OAU issued separate reports, while the delegations from the four countries became known as the "Observer Team" and issued their reports jointly. For the first period, from September 24 to November 23, 1968, see: *No Genocide*, Report of Observer Team to Nigeria (Nigerian National Press, Lagos, December, 1968); also, *No Indiscriminate Bombing*, Report on Activities of the Representatives of Canada, Poland, Sweden, and the U.K. during the period 14th January–6th March, 1969 (Nigerian National Press, Lagos, March 1969); Observer Team Report for March 7–April 30, 1969, Federal Ministry of Information Press Release No. F.496, May 9, 1969; Report on Activities of the Representatives of Canada, Poland, Sweden, and the U.K. during the period 1 May to 27 June 1969, Federal Ministry of Information Press Release No. 692, July 1, 1969; and Report on Activities of the Representatives of Canada, Poland, Sweden, and the U.K. during the period 28 June to 30 September 1969, Federal Ministry of Information Press Release No. 1079, October 8, 1969.

[32] *Daily Times*, September 1, 1968.

[33] Radio Nigeria, *Newstalk*, August 29, 1968.

"British interference" at this stage in the crisis would have meant a discontinuation of arms sales. This would have been a severe political blow to Nigeria's international image, but it would not have been critical to the military campaign or the eventual outcome of the war. Although the small arms that equipped the federal infantry were largely British and vital to the war effort, Nigeria's foreign exchange position was improving with a return to full oil production,[34] and a plethora of private arms dealers were ready to take up the slack. More importantly, Dr. Arikpo had paid a visit to Moscow in July, and reportedly found the Russians prepared to supply Nigeria with whatever was necessary.[35] There was a strong disinclination in Lagos to lean too heavily on Soviet support but, as the British knew perfectly well, the federal government was prepared to purchase this essential infantry equipment. Continued arms sales, one could argue, were more vital to Britain's long-term interests than to Nigeria's. Under no circumstances did the Wilson government wish to see Russia's presence in Nigeria grow any larger, particularly when the federal army seemed close to a final victory.[36]

Regardless of public sentiment in Britain, the Labour government by this time had indicated its unwavering commitment to Lagos by allowing British arms exporters to commit themselves to delivering equipment months in advance so as to aid Lagos with military planning.[37] Gowon was therefore not under any serious pressure to agree to the British suggestion that he invite observers, and went along mainly to show his good faith. A similar flexibility would be demonstrated in later months with regard to the relief issue.

In the short run the announcement of the invitation to the observer team risked undercutting Emperor Haile Selassie's efforts to reassert the authority of the OAU Consultative Committee over the international aspects of the civil war. The federal delegation, which was still meeting in Addis Ababa, was instructed to reassure the Emperor on this and other points, as the following excerpt from a September 1, 1968, cable from Lagos indicates:

Hope the invitation to send observers has not raised scares at your end of dangerous internationalization or slight of the Emperor's committee. The scheme was brought home by Enahoro from London. Useful

[34] Gaston Rimlinger and Carolyn Stremlau, *Economic Survey 1960–1970*, A Report prepared for the Lagos Office of the Ford Foundation, September 1, 1970, pp. 12–20.

[35] The significance of the visit was not lost on the British press, and on August 11, 1968, the *Sunday Telegraph* reported the acquisition of more Ilyushin bombers as an outgrowth of the visit.

[36] Interview: Michael Stewart, British foreign minister.

[37] MEA, internal memorandum, September 1, 1968.

to explain it is not the intention to invite the United Nations to send observers but the idea is for Nigeria to borrow an experienced man from U Thant's staff of military personnel. There should be some delay in assembling the team, British haste notwithstanding.

The support subsequently accorded the federal military government's policies by the member states of the OAU during the September 13–16, 1968, summit in Algiers demonstrated that nothing Nigeria had done so far in the war had significantly alienated the vast majority of African leaders.

RENEWING AFRICAN SUPPORT

The question that most concerned Nigerian diplomats as they prepared for the OAU meeting was whether French President Charles de Gaulle was secretly pressing his weaker colleagues in francophone Africa to endorse Ojukwu's regime, thereby setting up a rationale for French intervention. The same thought had been troubling Emperor Haile Selassie, and in mid-August he summoned the French ambassador in Addis Ababa for a clarification of his government's position. The gist of the reply, which was relayed to Lagos, was that "The French Government had no intention of according recognition to Ojukwu and the French Government also promised to do all in its power to discourage other African countries from doing so."[38] When the Nigerian chargé in Paris sought similar clarification, he too received unequivocal assurances that France was committed to respect the "will of Africa" as expressed by the OAU, and that no attempt would be made by Paris to influence that decision."[39]

While Nigerian foreign policy makers were warming up for what they hoped would be a decisive diplomatic victory in Algiers, Ojukwu was being advised that the summit would not amount to very much. A lengthy memorandum prepared by S. O. Mezu, the chief political officer in Biafra's office in the Ivory Coast concluded that: 1. the Algiers Conference might not even take place; 2. if it did take place, not many African heads of state would attend; 3. in any event, very little would be accomplished, less still about the Nigeria/Biafra question; and, 4. the chances of a postponement should not be ruled out.[40] These conclusions rested on several assumptions. The most important were that many

[38] MEA, Cable: Chief Enahoro to General Gowon, August 12, 1968.
[39] Interview: E. O. Ogunsulire.
[40] Republic of Biafra, Ministry of Foreign Affairs, Memo to G. A. Onyegbula from Dr. S. O. Mezu: Organization of African Unity Meeting in Algiers: An Analysis and Projection Based on the West African Political Scene, Abidjan, August 20, 1968.

members would be discouraged from attending for "security reasons" such as the Tshombe kidnapping, the recent hijacking of an Israeli civilian aircraft to Algiers, and the existence of dissident undercurrents in the Algerian army. If convened, Mezu was certain "it would be paralyzed by dissension over the Nigerian question." He even conjectured that "countries like the UAR, the USSR and Great Britain would not be unhappy if the Algiers conference does not take place since the conference may be critical of their policy in the Nigeria/Biafra conflict."

Contrary to Mezu's projections, the summit convened on September 13 with twenty-two of the thirty-nine delegations present represented by their heads of state or government.[41] It was the most impressive turnout since the first regular summit in 1964. Biafran hopes for greater recognition or diplomatic chaos evaporated overnight. Instead of skirting the Nigerian question, the OAU passed a tough profederal resolution, which called on "all member states of the United Nations and the OAU to refrain from any action detrimental to the peace, unity and territory integrity of Nigeria."[42]

Preliminary diplomatic skirmishes over Nigeria's place on the agenda occurred during the Council of Foreign Ministers meeting, September 9–12, 1968. The position taken by the federal delegation was that the war was nearly over, and Africans should rally behind the cause of Nigerian unity as victory approached. Col. Olufemi Olutoye, military undersecretary at the Ministry of External Affairs, came with maps and charts of all military operations. He set up a "situation room" in the Nigerian suite at the *Club des Pins* conference center, and kept in constant contact with Lagos and the progress of Adekunle's Third Marine Division in order to relay each day's developments to an eager parade of delegates. "The only real questions that mattered for the OAU," Olutoye later recalled, "was who would win and how soon."[43] Adekunle's dramatic capture of Aba on September 4 and Owerri ten days later tended to confirm the credibility of federal assurances in Algiers.

When President Houari Boumedienne of Algeria opened the Council of Ministers meeting, he struck a decidedly anti-Biafran tone. Africa,

[41] The twenty-two countries represented by their sovereigns were: Algeria, Cameroon, Central African Republic, Congo (Brazzaville), Congo (Zaire), Dahomey (Benin), Ethiopia, Gambia, Liberia, Libya, Malagasy, Mali, Mauritania, Mauritius, Morocco, Niger, Rwanda, Somalia, Swaziland, Sudan, Upper Volta, and Zambia. Malawi was the only member not represented at all.

[42] Resolution adopted by the Fifth Assembly of Heads of State and Government, 10:30 P.M., September 16, 1968. Tanzania, Ivory Coast, Gabon, and Zambia voted against the resolution. Rwanda and Botswana abstained. Reprinted in Kirk-Greene, *Crisis and Conflict*, II, 328–329.

[43] Interview: Olufemi Olutoye.

he declared, had repeatedly suffered "colonialist and imperialist offensives characterized by the vilest ignomy and most insolent aggression," including "the plot against Nigeria which is the biggest state in the OAU and in our Continent, a country whose unity and stability was a source of pride for all of us."[44] After a brief discussion, the Council of Ministers decided Nigeria would appear on the summit agenda (Item 5), but only as "The Report of the Consultative Committee on Nigeria." Tunisia's foreign minister challenged the scope of Item 5 as being too limited, and tabled an amendment to replace it with: "Nigeria-Biafra: (a) General Discussion; (b) OAU Consultative Mission; (c) Hearing of the two parties to the dispute."[45] Nigeria's commissioner for external affairs predictably rejected any suggestion of Biafran participation, but allowed that his government would not object to a discussion of the Consultative Committee's report. The Tunisian delegate then withdrew his amendment, reaffirmed his government's support for the federal military government as "the only government in Nigeria," and thanked the federal delegation for its "conciliatory attitude."[46]

Chief Obafemi Awolowo arrived in Algiers on September 12 at the head of Nigeria's delegation to the summit.[47] In contrast to their performance at the Kinshasa summit the year before, the federal delegates were no longer clinging to the fiction that the crisis was purely an internal affair, and went out of their way to explain the situation in Nigeria.[48] Chief Awolowo met separately with all heads of state, including President Kaunda of Zambia, prior to the formal discussion of Item 5 on the final night of the assembly. He sought a strong resolution to tie the organization closely to the goals and policies of the federal military government, so as to discourage any future unilateral support for Biafra, either as a result of non-African pressures or out of frustra-

[44] *West Africa*, No. 2676, September 14, 1968, p. 1063.

[45] MEA, Summary Record, OAU Fifth Summit–Algiers, Debate on the Nigerian Crisis, September 15, 1968.

[46] *Ibid.* Reaction to the Tunisian amendment was particularly hostile from the other North African states, so much so that the Tunisian foreign minister rose during the Assembly of Heads of State and Government to deny Cairo press reports alleging his amendment had been introduced "as a way of supporting the secessionists under imperialists' pressure."

[47] Other members of the Nigerian delegation included: Chief Anthony Enahoro, Commissioner, Labour and Information; Dr. T. O. Elias, attorney general; Alhaji Baba-Gana, permanent secretary, External Affairs; Allison Ayida, permanent secretary, Economic Development; Hamsad Ahmadu, principal secretary to the head of state; Alhaji Ali Akilu, former chief secretary to the Northern Regional government; Professor O. Aboyade, University of Ibadan; and Col. O. Olutoye, military undersecretary, Ministry of External Affairs.

[48] Interview: Kaye Whiteman, deputy editor of *West Africa*, who attended both summits and gives much credit for the federal success in Algiers to more effective lobbying.

tion over any prolongation of the war. Reflecting on his experiences at the two summits, Chief Awolowo describes the 1967 session as being preoccupied with trying to assess the political viability of the federal military government. By 1968, he maintains, attention was focused on the much more limited issue of Nigeria's military timetable: "At Algiers the members were prepared to go all out for Nigeria, but they wanted assurances that results would come quickly."[49]

Biafra's interests were barely represented at Algiers. Among the four states recognizing the secession, Zambia's Kenneth Kaunda was the only sovereign present, and he found himself in such an awkward position that he left for Paris two days before the Nigerian question was discussed formally. Ivory Coast and Gabon were represented by their foreign ministers, and Tanzania by Vice President Rashidi Kawawa.[50] In the series of ad hoc consensus-building diplomatic exercises that typify the drafting resolutions at OAU gatherings, the views of those delegations represented by their head of state or government again dominated the proceedings. The four governments that had recognized Biafra distributed copies of a 3,500-word "personal" message from Ojukwu to the heads of each delegation, but they lacked sufficient influence to lobby in behalf of the position Ojukwu outlined. The heart of the Biafran message was, by now, a well-known disposition:

It is the considered view of the government and people of Biafra that the only scheme which can secure the lives and property of Biafrans while preserving the advantages of the old Nigerian Federation, is an Economic Union of the two independent and sovereign states of Biafra and Nigeria—something like the East African Common Market. . . . From this foundation, as mutual respect and confidence returns through the years, cooperation could extend over a much wider area and develop into some kind of political commonwealth such as that which unites the states of former French West Africa.[51]

[49] Interview: Awolowo.
[50] President Bongo of Gabon told a French television audience in Paris: "I cannot go to the Algiers Conference for I disapprove the default of the OAU in the Biafran affair . . . genocide is underway in Biafra . . . silence is no longer possible. I refuse to make myself an accomplice of this international crime." *West Africa*, No. 2675, September 7, 1968, p. 1055. Presidents Nyerere and Houphouet-Boigny gave no specific explanations, although the former's relations with Algeria had been strained since the 1965 overthrow of Ben Bella, and Houphouet-Boigny risked a further rebuff in Algiers for his close relations with Israel, having welcomed a conference of Israeli ambassadors to Abidjan the month before.
[51] Republic of Biafra, text of personal message from H. E. Lt. Col. O. Ojukwu to the Heads of Delegation to the Fifth Assembly of Heads of State and Government, Algiers, September 1968.

The Consultative Committee met on the morning of September 15 to prepare a draft resolution for the summit's approval and to review the Emperor's report. The members present included: the chairman, Emperor Haile Selassie and Presidents Tubman of Liberia, Mobutu of Congo (Zaire), Diori of Niger, and Ahidjo of Cameroon. General Ankrah did not attend, and was represented by his commissioner for external affairs. Whatever earlier hopes the Biafrans may have had about the Consultative Committee's willingness to entertain their arguments, these were finally set to rest. The proposed resolution, which the Emperor later submitted to the assembly, recalls the OAU's earlier support for the defense of a united Nigeria, expresses concern over the sufferings of the civilian population, and:

1. Appeals to the secessionist leaders to cooperate with the federal authorities in order to restore peace and unity in Nigeria;
2. Appeals for cessation of hostilities;
3. Recommends that the above being accomplished the federal military government of Nigeria declare a general amnesty to cooperate with the Organization of African Unity in ensuring the physical security of all the people of Nigeria alike until mutual confidence is restored;
4. Appeals further to all concerned to cooperate in the speedy delivery of humanitarian relief supplies to the needy;
5. Calls upon all member states of the United Nations and the OAU to refrain from any action detrimental to the peace, unity and territorial integrity of Nigeria.[52]

The Emperor summarized the Consultative Committee's efforts to assist Nigeria find a peaceful solution, and tabled the draft resolution midway through the summit's final evening session, which began at 4:00 P.M. September 15 and ended at 6:00 A.M. the next morning.[53] He was followed by each member of the committee, who explained why he endorsed the resolution and the goal of Nigerian unity. The remarks by Ghana's foreign minister were typical, but particularly reassuring to the federal delegation in light of General Ankrah's "troublesome" behavior in Niamey. The Ghanaian minister sought to draw attention to Article III of the OAU Charter, calling for strict adherence to the principle of noninterference in the internal affairs of member states, appealing to the assembly to discuss the Nigerian crisis within the constraints of Article III, and concluding that only in this way could the

[52] Draft Resolution on Nigeria, Prepared by the OAU Consultative Committee on Nigeria, September 15, 1968.

[53] Organization of African Unity Secretariat, Confidential Report of the OAU Consultative Committee on Nigeria submitted by H.I.M. Haile Selassie, September 15, 1968.

OAU "demonstrate to the outside world that it is a mature organiza-tion."[54]

Tanzania and Zambia, both represented by their vice presidents, intervened to announce they could not vote for the draft resolution be-cause it was only "an endorsement of the firm position of the Federal Government." The original villains responsible for the Nigerian crisis, according to Tanzania, were British imperialists who, by deliberately fostering tribalism, had ensured that the former regions of Nigeria could not live together! The Tanzanian delegate strongly condemned Russian and British neocolonialism, appealed to the assembly to take a firm decision against starvation and killing, and called for an uncondi-tional cease-fire to be followed by a negotiated final settlement. Zambia's vice president seconded his colleague's remarks, but then he closed on a note that stressed that his government's recognition of Biafra was for humanitarian reasons, and should be accepted as nonpolitical. With-out elaborating, he appealed to the summit to understand that "we [Zambians] have nothing against our brothers from Nigeria."

President Boumedienne of Algeria followed with an amendment to the proposed resolution that expressed gratitude to the members of the Consultative Committee, and invited them to continue their efforts within the context of the Kinshasa and Algiers resolutions. The latter point was very much in Nigeria's interest, since the continued existence of the committee would provide a relatively safe forum to which any further non-African peace initiatives could be referred.

The Algerian president moved to close off the debate on the draft resolution as soon as he had tabled his amendment. This was seconded by President Ahidjo of Cameroon, but it prompted sharp protests from Biafra's four allies. The Ivorian delegation threatened to leave Algiers if precluded from presenting its position. After the Emperor intervened, with what the Nigerian records describe as "a passionate plea for free-dom of speech in the interest of parliamentary democracy," Boume-dienne withdrew his motion for closure with the comment that he had no intention of sending the Ivory Coast delegation home, as such a step would be contrary to the tradition of African hospitality.

The Ivorian foreign minister, Arsene Usher Assouan, rose to explain that his government's recognition of Biafra had been a "matter of conscience." It had been "forced" to act on humanitarian grounds and only for that reason. He then submitted a substantive amendment to the committee's draft resolution, the only one of the evening. The Ivory Coast proposed that the OAU drop any further references to the "peace and unity of Nigeria" as the predetermined goal of negotiations, and

[54] MEA, Summary Record, OAU Fifth Summit–Algiers, Debate on the Ni-gerian Crisis, September 15, 1968. The following account is from the same source.

that the assembly recognize that there were two parties to the dispute. The Ivorian amendment received no support, except from the three other members who had recognized Biafra. The suggestion that the OAU acknowledge Biafra's existence by appealing "to both sides to take effective measures to bring about an immediate ceasefire" encountered especially strong criticism from the north and central African delegations, who felt that the Consultative Committee already had gone too far in allowing Ojukwu to present his case on the international stage as an independent political actor.

Criticism of Biafra and her supporters was far more hawkish behind the closed doors of the OAU summit chamber than most of the comments that the members aired publicly. The prime minister of Somalia, for example, asserted that the federal government had "no alternative but to keep Nigeria together by force of arms," and he complained that the committee's draft resolution was "too conciliatory" and "did not go far enough in repeating the condemnation of secession and censuring the four countries who recognized the rebel regime." The predominantly Moslem states of Sudan, Algeria, Morocco, Guinea, and Mali took similar positions. Strong support for Lagos also typified the remarks of sub-Sahara moderates such as Gambia, Sierra Leone, Kenya, and Senegal. The prime minister of Swaziland, then the newest member of the OAU, decried the four recognitions of Biafra as a "stab in the back and a vote of no confidence in the efforts of the Consultative Committee and in the Assembly of Heads of State and Government."

"Too much has been made of the humanitarian aspect of the Nigerian crisis," argued President Keita of Mali. "If Ojukwu loved his people he alone could have saved them from starvation and suffering. Ojukwu has the power to call off the secession and stop the war anytime." "If people are starving," President Ahidjo of Cameroon injected, "why should they lay down conditions under which they are to receive food for their starving population—what does it matter to the hungry if the food is brought into his house through the back door, the window or even the roof?" As for human rights—in this case Ibos within Nigeria—the President of Mali asked rhetorically, but with candor not usually heard in such forums: "which African country here has not placed some limitations on human rights and the rights of its own minorities and opposition groups?"

Chief Awolowo was invited by the chairman to wind up the five and one-half hour debate. Speaking for the first time, the head of the Nigerian delegation sounded contemptuous of the positions taken by the four who had recognized Biafra. If, as Tanzania had argued, the civil war in Nigeria had damaged the image of Africa, that image was similarly damaged by the 1964 military revolt in Tanzania which, Awolowo noted sarcastically, "had to be brought down by President Nyerere sending an S.O.S. for Nigerian troops who saved his regime. There was no call for humanitarian considerations then!" Turning to Zambia, he referred to the subversive elements that had been held in preventive detention in that country, and declared that if those elements had been "armed to the teeth like Ojukwu, President Kaunda would have been fighting a civil war in his country whatever the humanitarian consideration."

By contrast, Awolowo was much less vitriolic in his references to Gabon and Ivory Coast, the two governments that were actually providing major material assistance to Biafra. Unlike the East African countries, Gabon and Ivory Coast were physically close enough to Nigeria to pose a serious strategic threat, at least as staging areas for Biafran supplies. The Nigerians therefore were as cautious in their dealings with the two former French colonies as they were in their dealings with France. Awolowo concluded his remarks, however, with a not-too-subtle allusion to francophone Africa, congratulating the summit, as a body, for its "independence in being able to withstand the pernicious influence of the imperialists and neo-colonialist forces bent on destroying Nigeria by using some OAU members." The federal government, he promised, would implement the resolution submitted by the committee and amended by Algeria. The resolution was then adopted 33 to 4, with 2 abstentions.[55]

Critics of the OAU's performance may claim, with some justification, that Biafra never received a fair hearing. But it is wrong to argue, as novelist Frederick Forsyth has, that "the organization that prides itself on being the repository of the conscience of Africa washed its hands of the biggest conscientious issue in the Continent."[56] The remarks of Tanzanian Vice-President Kawana in Paris immediately following the summit were similarly misleading when he described the Algiers proceedings as the "one clear example in history where eminent leaders decided to evade the real issue by playing the ostrich game."[57] What pro-Biafran critics of the OAU usually ignored was that the vast majority of African leaders cared most about the elimination of the secession, which they regarded as a destablizing influence in the region. Moreover, they rejected Biafra's claim that Nigeria was guilty of genocide against the Ibos. Rather than "playing the ostrich game," African leaders

[55] Gabon, Ivory Coast, Tanzania, and Zambia cast negative votes, and Rwanda and Botswana abstained on the grounds that neither delegation was able to receive adequate instructions from their respective capitals in time for the vote.

[56] Forsyth, *The Biafra Story*, p. 207.

[57] *West Africa*, No. 2677, September 21, 1968, p. 1090.

were ready to throw whatever diplomatic weight they possessed behind the federal government; for those members whose survival depended on French economic and technical assistance, such open support of Nigeria could have entailed considerable political courage.

Within the Nigerian foreign policy establishment, reaction to the summit's decision was one of jubilation. The following extracts from a memorandum on the "Publicity Implications of the Algiers Summit Conclusions on Nigeria" are indicative:

In diplomatic terms our missions and posts in Africa will have to be upgraded and rated as highly as those in Europe and elsewhere as the reward for the massive support Africa has given Nigeria at a time when Western countries and neo-colonialist forces were determined not to appreciate the federal case for keeping Nigeria one.

The OAU recognized that secession is an African problem and that the Nigerian example . . . would have serious repercussions on the Continent if it were allowed to succeed.

Africa has pronounced on the Civil War in Nigeria and the prescribed solution should be respected by all other members of the United Nations, including President de Gaulle. . . .

The successful military operations on the ground influenced to some extent the assessment at the Algiers debate, the military commanders and their men on the ground should receive generous and frequent mention—all Africa has reposed confidence in their ability to crush the armed rebellion with the minimum loss of lives.

Humanitarian aspects did receive mention and due attention at Algiers but members realized that if the rebels were not so bent on using starvation as a political weapon, relief supplies would have reached the civilian victims long ago. . . .

African countries have made it clear to imperialists and neo-colonial forces that they should henceforth desist using the humanitarian issue to divert the attention of the world from the Vietnam war, racism in Rhodesia and Southern Africa and other burning issues of the day, including the ending of secession and armed rebellion in parts of the East Central State of Nigeria.

The four rebel countries have not shown any signs of penitence inspite of the polite tones of the Ivory Coast and Gabonese delegations during the Algiers debate on Nigeria; frequent appeals should be made to them to fall in line with Africa by using their influence to get the secessionists to give up and thereby save lives . . . Tanzania and Zambia should be singled out for presistent attacks for their partnership with Portugal . . . Ivory Coast and Gabon may be treated more leniently although Libreville as the arms supply base should be condemned all the time.[58]

The Algiers resolution was not substantively different from the one passed twelve months earlier by the Kinshasa summit. But in light of the intervening international uproar over Biafra, this latest reaffirmation of support from the African region was enormously gratifying to Lagos. The pan-African alliance had weathered the challenge posed by the four recognitions, and there now appeared to be little prospect of further defections. The wall of diplomatic support raised by the OAU would remain the centerpiece in Nigeria's strategy to contain the process of internationalization. When the 23rd session of the United Nations General Assemby convened the following month, the reality of Biafra's political isolation was again apparent.

NIGERIA AND THE 23RD SESSION OF THE UNITED NATIONS

The federal Ministry of External Affairs anticipated that attempts might be made in the Security Council, the General Assembly, or within any of the specialized committees, to raise embarrassing questions concerning its conduct of the civil war. Ojukwu had sent a personal message to every member of the United Nations in early October that appealed for concerted action by the world body to enforce an immediate cease-fire and stop the genocide.[59] At a minimum, federal officials expected Nigeria to be attacked by the four members that recognized Biafra. The predicted line of attack was summarized in a brief prepared by the Ministry of External Affairs: Nigeria would be indicted for violating the United Nations Charter by using force to "deprive the Ibos of their right of self-determination . . . [and for] committing genocide against the Ibos, whether planned or otherwise."[60]

The Nigerian delegation was instructed to brush aside any suggestion of Ibo self-determination by referring to the internationally recognized territorial definition of the sovereign state of Nigeria and the historical voluntary participation of Ibos and other ethnic groups in the constitutional evolution of Nigeria. To refute charges of genocide, it was recommended that the delegates stress: 1) the peaceful presence of 50,000 Ibos in Lagos, plus over 600,000 indigenous Ibo inhabitants

[58] MEA, Publicity Implications of the Algiers Summit Conclusions on Nigeria, undated.

[59] Ojukwu, *Biafra*, I, 361.

[60] MEA, Brief for the 23rd Session of the United Nations General Assembly: The Nigerian Situation and the United Nations, September 7, 1968.

of the Midwest State; 2) the repeated assurances and substantive proposals made by the federal government allowing an "international presence" into the East Central State to assure the Ibos of their safety; 3) the promise of equality for the East Central State within a twelve-state federation; and 4) the offers made at Niamey and Addis Ababa for land corridors to relieve the suffering inside the Ibo redoubt.

Within the Security Council, Nigeria did not expect to be challenged. Should France or one of the nonpermanent members table a resolution requesting the world body to use its good offices "to bring the two sides together," the federal government planned to ask the Soviet Union to veto the resolution.[61] The Ministry of External Affairs believed, however, that such measures would not be necessary:

> In any case, our assessment is that the Nigerian crisis, if raised, is unlikely to be the subject of a resolution . . . the most likely event is that one of the members will make a general statement on the crisis and seek the Secretary General's good offices in arranging peace talks. The object will be to internationalize the conflict, thus bringing pressure to bear on us to grant concessions to the rebels either in the form of full independence within a confederation or limited independence which will confer a special status on the rebels. Our strategy should be merely to insist that any such discussion would violate the Charter of the United Nations since it will be tantamount to intervention in our internal affairs.[62]

Similar unilateral attempts to raise the issue were foreseen with regard to the addresses at the opening session of the General Assembly. Lagos accepted the fact that little could be done should this happen and advised the delegation, "We cannot stop any country from making oblique or direct references to Nigeria at the General Assembly or in any of the committees of the United Nations. *Our only course of action is always to exercise our right of reply.*"[63] With OAU states accounting for nearly a third of the United Nations membership, and with no hints that major changes in policy were being contemplated elsewhere in the nonaligned world or among Soviet bloc countries, the federal government was confident that all attempts to engage the

[61] *Ibid.* Britain, Nigeria's other ally among the permanent members of the Security Council, was considered to be under such heavy domestic pressure that a veto was improbable, but Lagos expected her at least to abstain.

[62] *Ibid.*

[63] *Ibid.* Dr. Okoi Arikpo, commissioner for external affairs and chairman of Nigeria's delegation, addressed the 23rd session of the General Assembly on October 11, 1968. His address was reprinted in the *New Nigerian*, October 9–11, 1968.

United Nations in a debate of the Biafra question would be easily deflected.

As it turned out, very little mention was made of the Nigerian crisis. Aside from the four African members that recognized Biafra, only France, the Netherlands, Jamaica, Haiti, Honduras, Sierra Leone, and Kenya raised the issue of possible United Nations consideration of the conflict.[64] The submissions were only perfunctory, and no member, including the four maintaining diplomatic relations with Biafra, tried to have the issue inscribed on the agenda.

Outside the General Assembly the only other "pro-Biafran" initiative was a September 1968 open letter from the Canadian government to Secretary General U Thant seeking the latter's views as to how the United Nations might help to relieve the suffering in Nigeria. Canadian diplomats defensively explained that the gesture was merely to placate Canadian public opinion, and that the letter certainly posed no serious threat to Nigeria's interests. U Thant's views were well known and, lest there be any doubt, the secretary general told the press: "If the heads of African States have asked all members of the United Nations and all members of the OAU to refrain from any action likely to endanger the peace, unity and territorial integrity of Nigeria, I do not see how member states, or for that matter the secretary general, can be actively involved."[65]

The official support that the federal government enjoyed within the world community severely limited Biafra's attempts to internationalize the civil war. Yet this working consensus among governments, which was sufficient to deter further recognition or overt political backing of the rebellion, was of little use to the federal government in its attempts to assert authority over the intervention by the non-governmental transnational humanitarian relief agencies. No one at this stage, including General Gowon, openly questioned the need for humanitarian assistance to alleviate civilian deprivation inside the Biafran enclave. But as the war dragged on, the role of the relief agencies in contributing to Biafran resistance became a paramount concern among Nigeria's leaders. How to proceed against the various humanitarian organizations not only raised profound moral and domestic political issues but also entailed the risk of antagonizing friendly governments in Europe and America.

[64] United Nations General Assembly, 23rd Session, Plenary A/PV 1683, p. 8 (France); PV 1681, p. 7 (Netherlands); PV 1679, p. 14 (Jamaica) and p. 2 (Haiti); PV 1692, p. 20 (Honduras); PV 1686, p. 17 (Sierra Leone); PV 1699, p. 20 (Kenya).

[65] *UN Monthly Chronicle*, VI (February 1969), p. 39, Press Conference given by the Secretary General, January 28, 1969.

· 10 ·

INTERNATIONAL REFLECTIONS
OF A MILITARY STALEMATE

Biafra's chances for wider diplomatic recognition were discounted by Nigerian diplomats following the September 1968 military advances by the federal army and the strong vote of confidence from the OAU summit in Algiers. In strictly political terms, Ojukwu's attempt to penetrate the international system had been contained. But on another level, mobilizing foreign humanitarian support, the Biafrans were receiving adequate assistance to withstand the hardships created by the federal blockade, and their capacity to sustain a war of attrition continued to improve during the closing months of 1968.

With the Nigerian army bogged down in what European commentators derisively referred to as a "sitzkrieg," federal spokesmen more openly criticized the international relief agencies for prolonging the conflict, while talk about the inevitability of a political settlement surfaced again in Europe and North America. International public pressure for a cease-fire and resumption of negotiations also increased, amid new reports that Biafra's several million people would face widespread starvation by early 1969 if conditions did not improve dramatically.[1]

The prospect of unprecedented suffering in Biafra meant that the profederal policies of Britain, the United States, and other Western powers would again come under sharp domestic criticism. American policy seemed especially vulnerable during the closing days of the Johnson administration, when President-elect Nixon promised a full review of America's position on the Nigerian crisis. The Biafrans naturally hoped that the apparently deepening humanitarian concern in Washington would finally produce direct political action to arrange an immediate cease-fire, and that if this occurred other Western governments would feel compelled to follow America's lead.

Meanwhile, the diplomatic maneuvering taking place in Britain was reminiscent of the situation one year earlier, when the Labour government tried to insulate its policies by promoting direct negotiations between Nigerian and Biafran representatives. In January 1969, Whitehall strongly hinted that delicate behind-the-scenes initiatives were underway in connection with the Commonwealth Prime Ministers Con-

---

[1] For example, "Human Tragedy of Hitherto Unimagined Proportions Predicted in Biafra," Jointchurchaid, Press Release, Geneva, December 17, 1968.

280

ference and, when nothing materialized, Harold Wilson suddenly paid a surprise visit to Nigeria "in search of peace." Eventually, it fell to the OAU Consultative Committee to bring the two sides together in April 1969 for what turned out to be the final round of direct contacts. These developments, beginning with the federal government's failure to assert its authority, even indirectly, over the Red Cross airlift to Biafra, are discussed here to illustrate how Nigerian foreign policy and the policies of concerned governments elsewhere responded to Biafra's war of attrition.

NIGERIAN FOREIGN POLICY AND THE REALITIES OF HUMANITARIAN INTERVENTION

Throughout the civil war, a major goal of the federal military government's domestic and foreign policy was to convince both the Ibo people and world opinion that the Nigerian army was not bent on genocide but only sought an end to secession and the restoration of national unity. Allowing relief supplies to reach Biafra's civilians was deemed essential, not only to promote international good will, but to facilitate the inevitable transfer of popular allegiance from Biafra to Nigeria once peace returned to the country.

But as the resistance stiffened, federal military leaders became increasingly impatient with the prevailing relief arrangements. Nigerian indictments of the humanitarian agencies have been summarized by one student of the controversy as covering the following points:[2]

1. By dealing directly with Ojukwu's regime and not agreeing to having relief cargoes verified in Lagos the relief actors were according Biafra greater legitimacy.
2. By their highly emotional appeals on behalf of the starving Biafrans the relief agencies were building sympathy and political support for the secessionists.
3. By supporting Ojukwu's persistent calls for a cease-fire partisanship was evinced.
4. By repeating Biafran allegations of genocide Nigeria was unjustly vilified.
5. By portraying the war as a religious struggle between Christianity and Islam (which some of the church personnel were inclined to do) they were distorting the truth.
6. The airlift, in violation of Nigerian airspace and without authorization, was undermining Nigeria's negotiating position on relief.

[2] Wiseberg, "Christian Churches and the Nigerian Civil War."

7. The relief shipments were providing material support to the rebellion.

8. The relief flights were providing a cover for the arms flights.

9. The relief agencies were spending large amounts of foreign currency in the enclave and this provided Biafra with the means to purchase arms.

10. The airlift and related communication facilities undermined Nigeria's attempt to isolate the secession by making it easier for journalists to visit Biafra and for Ojukwu's spokesmen to travel to Europe.

Spokesmen for the federal government aired their complaints over Radio Nigeria and in the local press, but the strategic implications of the humanitarian intervention attracted little attention outside Nigeria. Reports of the suffering in Biafra were so horrendous that the resultant outcry of public opinion in Europe and America constrained Western governments from taking notice of, much less siding with, the Nigerian authorities. Instead, Gowon was urged repeatedly by these governments to tolerate whatever delivery and distribution arrangements the relief agencies were able to negotiate with Biafra.

The private appeals could be blunt; to wit, a September 1968 note from the Danish prime minister warned that "any incident that might occur in connection with the relief flights would be considered a blow against humanity."[3] America's undersecretary of state issued a public statement in a similar vein when he pledged in December that the United States would "help to intensify in every way feasible the existing relief flights."[4] And Britain's Labour government, while less hawkish on relief, also implored Gowon at least to go through the motions of showing the world he could be magnanimous, even though it was quite clear in advance that Ojukwu would not accept the various offers for land corridors and daylight flights. British Foreign Secretary Michael Stewart later acknowledged that Lagos had legitimate cause to object to the partisanship displayed by many of the relief agencies but, recalling the agitation from the left wing of his own party, Stewart remarked: "Nigerian flexibility on relief was really what was at stake for us. We kept telling them you must, if only for presentational reasons, be as generous as you can on the relief matter."[5]

The federal government learned that it could expect little support

---

[3] From the text of a message from the Danish prime minister to Major General Gowon, September 2, 1968. Royal Danish Embassy, Lagos.

[4] United States, *Department of State Bulletin*, December 23, 1968, "The Tragedy of Nigeria," by Undersecretary Katzenbach. Address made at Brown University, December 3, 1968.

[5] Interview: Stewart.

from the Western powers on matters related to the logistics of humanitarian relief. The same statesmen in London or Washington who could be counted on to denounce French intervention for prolonging the conflict generally declined to associate themselves with Nigerian protests over the way humanitarian relief was being handled.[6] Cynics in Lagos took the view that this merely reflected political realities: the Christian churches have powerful constituents where the French do not.

Nigeria's policy toward the Biafran airlift was often quite ambiguous, particularly as pressures for military reprisals intensified within the federal government in late 1968. Gowon's own view throughout the conflict was that for moral and political reasons, civilians in the secessionist enclave deserved to be fed.[7] He met frequently with private individuals who had visited Biafra and, without publicity, elicited and accepted their eyewitness accounts of the starvation, even though he became increasingly convinced that exaggerated claims were made simply to intimidate him into accepting Ojukwu's political demands.[8]

In setting policy on the relief issue, Gowon stood almost alone in urging toleration of the humanitarian intervention. Aside from Commissioner of External Affairs Okoi Arkipo, Attorney General T.O. Elias, and a handful of less prominent officials who argued for a flexible approach toward the foreign relief agencies, Gowon's attitude was opposed by most of his advisers and military colleagues. One of his most trusted aides recalls the feelings shared by the cadre of influential civil servants who helped shape policy: "Gowon was clear in his mind of the symbolic importance of permitting relief in but his advisers thought the whole thing to be rather silly. . . . Ojukwu was playing politics with relief and he would have been a fool to act otherwise. . . . We knew his troops were being sustained by relief supplies; it was only logical."[9]

Had Gowon really wanted to close down Uli airstrip through aerial attack he would have had to acquire different military equipment. The Soviets probably were prepared to sell Nigeria vintage propeller-driven

[6] There were exceptions to this pattern of not calling attention to Biafra's intransigence on the issue of daylight relief flights, but such protests were given scant attention by the western media. (See, for example, the *New York Times*, December 6, 1968, coverage of Robert McClosky's statement on behalf of the U.S. government and the front-page article on Biafra two days earlier.) Western governments did occasionally, without publicity, resist requests from the relief agencies that were likely to irritate Lagos: for example, the Swiss government's refusal in late 1968 to allow Jointchurchaid to establish a direct radio link between Geneva and Biafra, and the Canadian government's November 12, 1968, refusal to provide Jointchurchaid with two air force transports, after checking with Lagos.

[7] Interview: Gowon.

[8] According to Gowon, one of his most reliable contacts was with the Quakers, who managed quietly to visit both sides periodically throughout the war.

[9] Interview: Ayida.

fighter bombers that could easily have halted off-loading operations at Uli with the steady application of force not available to the faster MIG jets or the lone DC–3 transport that occasionally harassed night-time operations. The airstrip was poorly defended by a few Balfor anti-aircraft guns but, unless significantly upgraded, these batteries would not have posed a serious threat to attack aircraft.[10] Locating Uli was not a problem, as it had become the second busiest airport in Africa, after Johannesburg. Gowon discounts, but does not rule out, John de St. Jorre's suggestion that collusion between mercenary pilots, who were working for different sides but were in tacit agreement not to destroy each other, was the reason Uli stayed in business.[11] Nigeria's aircraft, in Gowon's view, were simply inadequate to the task.

The costs of deploying an effective bomber force, however, promised to be considerable. First, there would have been an international uproar, and within Biafra civilian suffering would have increased sharply. Also, it was known in Lagos that the ruling Biafran elite had stockpiles of food and, together with the army, they would have been the last to succumb. Gowon further assumed that Ojukwu had contingency plans for alternative landing strips, and that these could accommodate his gun-runners almost immediately. As a result of these considerations, Gowon concluded that the only effective way to close Uli, with a minimum loss of life, was to capture it on the ground.

Following the Third Marine Division's push northward from Port Harcourt during the fall 1968 campaign, it seemed that a federal control of Uli was imminent. When the offensive collapsed near Oguta on September 12, Gowon encountered fresh demands from the more hawkish elements in his government to take alternative action against the relief operation. He decided on two aproaches. First, the Nigerian air force would continue to harass the nightly off-loading operations so as, in Gowon's words, "to make Uli feel uncomfortable but not to the point of encouraging Ojukwu to build more landing centers."[12] The second tactic was to apply indirect political pressure against the relief agencies by seeking to limit the availability of staging areas close to Biafra.

Materials reaching the enclave from Gabon and the Portuguese colony of Sao Tomé were beyond Nigeria's reach; but on October 12, 1968, the International Committee of the Red Cross and the World Council of Churches operations on the Spanish island of Fernando Po came

---

[10] According to relief agency records, the Jointchurchaid and ICRC airlifts had to be halted briefly in December 1968, not because of Nigerian air attacks, but because of the "undisciplined antiaircraft fire" from Biafra's inexperienced Balfor gunners. *The Nordchurchaid Airlift to Biafra 1968–1970*, p. 76.

[11] Interview: Gowon. See: de St. Jorre, *The Nigerian Civil War*, pp. 317–320.

[12] Interview: Gowon.

under the authority of the independent Republic of Equatorial Guinea. The new sovereign, President Francisco Marcias Nguema, was not happy with the ICRC agreement he inherited from the Spanish, and he eagerly sought close relations with Nigeria both for domestic reasons and to demonstrate his independence from Spain.[13] According to his representative in Lagos, "We suspected their [ICRC's] commitment to humanitarian action was not genuine. We wanted to respect the sovereignty of our friendly next door neighbor. . . . What Equatorial Guinea was after from the ICRC, in the interests of Nigeria, was a rejection in practice of the illegal night flights."[14] On November 29, 1968, the government of Equatorial Guinea forbade the ICRC to carry fuel by air to Uli, claiming it was a strategic commodity essential to the war effort.[15] The ICRC subsequently was ordered to halt its airlift from December 21–22, although through the intercession of Auguste Lindt, Switzerland's ambassador to Moscow, who was also serving as ICRC general commissioner for West Africa, the Equatorial Guineans allowed the flights to be resumed from December 23 for two weeks. President Nguema announced on January 14, 1969, that ICRC night flights were no longer to be authorized, although daylight flights would be permitted.[16] The deteriorating relations between the ICRC and Equatorial Guinea elicited these comments by the government press in Lagos: "Now that the ICRC has been shown the way out of Santa Isabel, it will do well to reconsider the whole issue of its activities in rebel-held areas. One can only hope that the ICRC will now see the sense in the federal government's offer, and henceforth use Nigerian airports for legitimate daytime relief flights into rebel held territory."[17]

The ICRC and its Western backers moved quickly and decisively to circumvent President Nguema's decision to force the issue of daylight flights. On Christmas eve, seventy-two hours after the initial interruption

[13] Approximately 60,000 of Fernando Po's 80,000 people are Ibo contract laborers who come from Eastern Nigeria to work on the plantations. When separatist agitation erupted on the island shortly after independence, the government suspected Biafran complicity. Ibos thought to be active in the separatist movement were arrested and under a later agreement with the federal government were sent for internment in Lagos.

[14] Interview: Jose W. Okori Dougan, ambassador of Equatorial Guinea to Nigeria.

[15] It was common practice for the relief planes to "bleed" their fuel tanks while unloading at Uli, thereby providing the relief trucks with enough petrol to return to their distribution centers in the bush. The ICRC, however, claimed it needed to carry additional in-cabin containers of petrol to supply generators in the hospitals and their fleets of relief vehicles in Biafra. ICRC, *Annual Report 1969* (Geneva, 1970), p. 13.

[16] *Morning Post*, January 21, 1969.

[17] Radio Nigeria, *Newstalk*, January 1, 1969; also: "Bravo Equatorial Guinea," editorial, *Morning Post*, January 21, 1969.

of the ICRC airlift, the American chargé in Lagos informed Gowon that the Johnson administration had agreed to sell eight huge C–97G "Stratofreighter" transports to the relief agencies at the nominal cost of about $4,000 each.[18] Although the request from the churches had been pending for several weeks, the timing of the decision was meant to convey to the federal government America's determination to see that the air bridge—particularly the ICRC component—was not impeded. Gowon most certainly regarded the American decision to provide the C–97Gs as a direct intervention in response to the closing of the Equatorial Guinea relief staging facilities.[19]

Nigeria's ambassador in Washington, J.T.F. Iyalla, immediately protested the sale. He informed the State Department that, in the federal government's view, the C–97G transports would: first, strengthen the rebels' determination to reject land corridors, and second, encourage them to prolong the war in the belief that the U.S. government was preparing the way for a more direct intervention with which to force a political setttlement; and, third, directly or indirectly increase Biafra's capacity to import arms.[20] State Department officials dismissed the charges, and in one stroke provided the relief agencies with the means to double the tonnage of supplies carried into Biafra each night.[21] The larger long-range planes would also allow the ICRC to relocate staging areas farther from the troubled areas if Nguema's decision to eject the ICRC from Fernando Po remained in effect.

It took the ICRC less than a month to negotiate an alternative staging base at Cotonou, the commercial capital of Dahomey (Benin), the tiny former French colony located along Nigeria's western frontier. The new arrangement, which commenced operations on February 1, 1969, reportedly included a $3 million package deal whereby the financially strapped regime of Dr. Emile Zinsou received an outright gift of more than $1 million from the ICRC, with the remaining $2 million to be spent on modernizing Cotonou airport, financing new hotel construction, and providing various medical supplies destined for the Dahomean Ministry of Health and Social Welfare.[22] Dahomey, a poor

---

[18] The public announcement was delayed until December 28, 1968. Four planes were earmarked for the ICRC and four for Jointchurchaid. Jointchurchaid, Press Release No. 23, January 3, 1969.

[19] Interview: Gowon.

[20] Nigeria, Federal Ministry of Information, Press Release No. F.2212, December 30, 1968. *The Morning Post* bitterly denounced the sale in an editorial with the leader "Hostile Act," December 30, 1968.

[21] USIS, Special News Release, No. 545, Lagos, December 31, 1968. The statement contained a promise that the planes would be used solely for the transport of relief supplies and that they in no way connoted a change in basic U.S. policy. The federal government-owned *Morning Post* remained skeptical: "A Reply That Is Not an Answer," editorial, January 4, 1969.

[22] Details of the arrangement are scarce. These figures were used in a wire

country, had a per-capita income below $100 for its 2.7 million people. Sixty-five percent of the government's $38 million budget was allocated to bureaucratic salaries, and an annual subsidy from France was required to balance the budget.[23] The financial incentive to accept the ICRC was strong: in addition to the initial $3 million, projections were for the ICRC to spend approximately $150,000 in Cotonou to cover local housing and other costs, plus whatever money was allocated for the purchase of indigenous foodstuffs used in the airlift to Biafra. Asked about the agreement, Dr. Zinsou remarked that he had been led to believe the ICRC had prior clearance from Lagos, and assumed Nigeria would welcome Dahomey's action *de bonne foi*.[24]

Reactions to the Contonou/Biafra airlift in Lagos were mixed. Representatives of the 10,000 Dahomeans resident in Nigeria immediately sent a much-publicized note of protest to Zinsou, expressing opposition to what they decried as an "unfriendly act."[25] The federal government, however, was restrained in voicing any criticism.[26] The one official commentary on the matter sounded more miffed than angry: Dahomey had not consulted Nigeria in advance, nor had the federal government been given the right to inspect cargoes loaded in Contonou.[27] Before the week was out, Zinsou sent a special envoy to Lagos to invite the federal government to send a permanent mission to Cotonou to check all loadings, but on second thought the Nigerians declined. According to the *Morning Post* the federal government was only prepared to inspect daylight flights because night flights were considered "unauthorized."[28]

Privately, Nigerian diplomats were irked at Zinsou. Although they tended to dismiss their tiny neighbor as being impotent, they admitted having inhibitions about forcing a showdown over the relief issue. Only a week before the agreement with the ICRC was announced, Zinsou had stopped briefly in Lagos en route from discussions with General de Gaulle. Zinsou told waiting reporters that he had once again informed the French president of his government's and Africa's firm support for

---

service story appearing in the *Daily Times* on March 20, 1968, and were verified by American and European diplomats.

[23] "Dahomey Living beyond its Means," Report of the President's Speech to the Nation, *Agence France Presse*, August 1, 1968.

[24] Interview: Dr. Emile Zinsou, president, Republic of Dahomey.

[25] *Daily Times*, February 5, 1969. Similar token demonstrations were also made by pro-Nigerian Yorubas in eastern Dahomey. *Daily Times*, February 10, 1969.

[26] The Nigerians appear to have been caught unawares. Their embassy in Dahomey professed ignorance of the new arrangement, adding that "the Dahomean Government is most friendly and all we can do is wait and see." *Sunday Sketch*, February 2, 1969. An official Radio Nigeria *Newstalk*, a week earlier had listed Dahomey among "Nigeria's True Friends," along with Equatorial Guinea, Niger, Cameroon, and Senegal. January 23, 1969.

[27] Radio Nigeria, *Newstalk*, February 3, 1969.

[28] *Morning Post*, February 11, 1969.

the federal government's campaign to reunify Nigeria.[29] No one doubted that Nigeria was capable of taking reprisals against Dahomey—the latter, after all, had barely a thousand-man army to defend four hundred miles of frontier with Nigeria—but federal authorities were apprehensive about possible wider political repercussions. Lagos briefly imposed severe but undeclared restrictions on travel between the two countries; following foreign press accounts of the sanctions, however, the federal government quickly issued a formal denial and eased the border controls.[30]

Once Dahomey consented to the establishmnet of an ICRC base, Equatorial Guinea began to reappraise its position. The Red Cross presence on Fernando Po had, after all, been a boon to that tiny country's fledgling economy.[31] The ICRC planes, which had been placed at the disposal of President Nguema for flights between his country's two largest cities, were sorely missed.[32] As one official remarked, "we kept asking ourselves why doesn't the Nigerian Government act against night flights?"[33] Following a round of renegotiations with Dr. Lindt, and several personal overtures from United Nations Secretary General U Thant, President Nguema allowed the ICRC to reopen its base on Fernando Po from February 12, 1969.

What had begun as an attempt to force the ICRC to issue an ultimatum to the Biafrans for daylight flights rebounded to Ojukwu's advantage. The ICRC nightly airlift had not only survived the challenge, but, through intervention by the United States, had wound up with four additional C–97G transports and two staging areas outside Nigeria, and was apparently free of federal influence. More importantly from a political standpoint, Biafra's only lifeline for foreign assistance and military supplies seemed secure. From January to June 1969, the air bridge operated without serious interference.

Publicly, Ojukwu continued to invoke the familiar imagery of Biafra appealing to the world's conscience for assistance in the name of humanitarianism. On February 10, 1969, the Biafran leader proclaimed to his followers: "All over the world, ordinary people—men, women, children, both professionals and laborers, farmers, businessmen—have cried out for justice and the rights of our persecuted people. . . . It is our founded belief that this support by the masses all over the world will, in the year

---

[29] *Daily Times*, January 22, 1969.

[30] Nigeria, Federal Ministry of Information, Press Release No. F.234, February 28, 1969. The border closure was confirmed in an interview with Dr. Zinsou.

[31] Equatorial Guinea's population of 280,000 did not receive direct benefits from Red Cross commitments comparable to those received by Dahomey, but the impact of ICRC expenditures in that small economy was substantial.

[32] Santa Isabel, with 37,000 people, is located on Fernando Po, and is the country's largest city. The capital, Bata, is located in the mainland province of Rio Muni, and has 27,000 people.

[33] Interview: Dougan.

1969, be translated into support and positive action by their various governments."[34] At the heart of this dream was the possibility of a major change in United States policy toward the Nigerian conflict following the inauguration of Richard Nixon, which, in turn, might precipitate a series of changes in Europe, Scandinavia, and even in Britain.

THE RESTATEMENT OF POLICY
IN THE UNITED STATES AND EUROPE

Presidential candidate Richard Nixon had issued a statement on September 9, 1968, which called on the Johnson administration to cease a "wringing of hands" about the situation in Biafra where, he asserted, "genocide is what is taking place right now—and starvation is the grim reaper. . . . This is not the time to stand on ceremony or to 'go through channels' or to observe the diplomatic niceties. . . . America is not without enormous material wealth and power and ability. There is no better cause in which we might invest that power than in staying the lives of innocent men and women and children who otherwise are doomed."[35] Radio Biafra devoted much attention to the declaration[36] and subsequently praised Nixon's election in an editorial entitled "The Right Man on the Right Side."[37] As the inauguration approached, Radio Biafra's commentaries continued to attack America's complicity with the British-Soviet alliance that supported Nigeria, but a sharp distinction was drawn between the purported guilt of the Johnson administration and the confidence that the people of Biafra had in the new president.[38] Mrs. Nixon's public appearance at a Biafran fund-raising ceremony held at New York's St. Patrick's Cathedral was warmly praised by Biafra's commissioner for information as a further indication of America's growing commitment to help save Biafra.[39]

[34] Ojukwu, *Biafra*, Address to joint meeting of the Council of Chiefs and Elders and the Consultative Assembly, February 10, 1969, I, 370–371.

[35] "Nixon's Call for American Action on Biafra," September 9, 1969, reprinted in Kirk-Greene, *Crisis and Conflict*, II, 334–335.

[36] Radio Biafra, *Newstalk*, September 14, 1968, September 15, 1968.

[37] Radio Biafra, *Newstalk*, November 11, 1968. The editorial commented in part: "The victory of Richard Nixon symbolizes the rejection by the American people of the unpopular Johnson administration. It shows the maturity of the United States electorate because the antics of President Johnson did not impress anybody as genuine. The election of Mr. Nixon . . . is a glowing tribute to such great aspirations as justice, liberty, peaceful settlement of disputes and the right of all peoples to self-determination . . . the government and people of Biafra earnestly hope that the President-elect will use his position to get the world to observe and abide by these principles. In particular, we hope he will bring pressure to bear on the world to stop the senseless war. . . ."

[38] For example, Radio Biafra, *Newstalk*, November 25, 1968.

[39] Radio Biafra, January 17, 1969, report of a January 16, 1969, press statement by Dr. Ifeagwu Eke, Biafra's commissioner for information. Also, *Newstalk*,

Congressional pressure for a new peace initiative by the Nixon administration also appeared to be on the rise.[40] Senators Kennedy, McCarthy, Proxmire, McGovern, Dodd, and others had made previous statements calling for a greater American role in solving the crisis, but during the first week of January fifty-two Senators and over one hundred Congressmen issued a joint appeal.[41] On January 24, 1969, President Nixon ordered a full-scale review of American policy toward the Nigerian conflict[42] and Radio Biafra quickly reminded Nixon that "only a cease-fire can give meaning to the efforts of humanitarians to alleviate human suffering in Biafra."[43] Meanwhile, Biafra's chief legal counsel in Washington forwarded to presidential adviser Bryce Harlow a copy of a 1,500-word memorandum prepared by the Ministry of Foreign Affairs entitled "The Biafran Viewpoint."[44] The memorandum raised the specter of growing Communist influence in Nigeria and promised continued Biafran resistance, which, in the event of federal occupation, purportedly would drag on as guerrilla warfare "certainly for a decade." In the Biafran view, the United States was the only major power acceptable to both sides, "due to its proclaimed neutrality and policy of providing neither side with arms," and would be able to bring about "meaningful negotiations" and a prior cease-fire. No details of a possible settlement were provided, as Biafra would demand that there be no preconditions, but there was a vague reference to the possibility of a Nigerian Commonwealth.[45] This same appeal for American assistance in arranging a cease-fire was the theme for discussions with two congressional delegations that visited Biafra in mid-February; the first was led by the newly appointed Republican senator from New York, Charles Goodell, and the other was headed by the chairman of the House Foreign Affairs Subcommittee on Africa, Congressman Charles Diggs, a Democrat from Michigan.[46]

The briefing papers prepared by the Biafran Ministry of Foreign Affairs in anticipation of the Diggs mission instructed that every effort be made to divert the delegation's attention from its ostensible purpose,

---

"Biafra Appreciates This Gesture," January 19, 1969, which portrayed a sharp contrast between Mrs. Nixon's action and the "callous indifference" of Mrs. Johnson.

[40] For a review of Congressional concern, see Cronje, *The World and Nigeria*, ch. 11, pp. 225–251.

[41] *New York Times*, January 6, 1969.

[42] *Washington Post*, January 25, 1969.

[43] Radio Biafra, *Newstalk*, January 27, 1969.

[44] Letter and enclosure from Walter S. Surrey of Surrey, Karasik, Gould and Greene to Bryce Harlow, January 28, 1969.

[45] Republic of Biafra, Ministry of Foreign Affairs, "The Biafran Viewpoint," undated.

[46] *West Africa*, No. 2699, February 22, 1969, p. 226; and No. 2700, March 1, 1969, p. 257. Also, Markpress Release, Gen. 502, Umuahia, February 11, 1969.

which was to inquire about the logistics of humanitarian relief, and, instead to emphasize the role Biafra expected America to play in arranging a cease-fire.[47] The permanent secretary, who assembled the briefing papers, had read a recent issue of the Ripon Society's journal that portrayed Mr. Nixon at a crossroads in the course of America's relations with Nigeria.[48] The article, because it was written by a Republican organization, was given much weight, and summarized in detail as background information for those who would meet Diggs. The greatest cause for encouragement in the article was the suggestion that the Nigeria/Biafra conflict should be a "subject for great power diplomacy" because settlement of this issue would facilitate four-power agreements on Vietnam, the Middle East, and nuclear arms limitations.[49]

The Diggs visit was a disappointment to Biafrans. The team spent only two days in the enclave and the majority of its two-week mission traveling around Nigeria.[50] Biafran officials had been briefed to appeal to Diggs' African heritage and to argue that Biafra represented "the true awakening of the African man," but according to General Effiong, the black Congressman had made up his mind before coming: "Biafra is 'the Black man fighting for his dignity', we told him. But Diggs and his Negroes talked only about pride in big units and the modernization of Africa. . . . Diggs was the worst of them all [Americans visiting Biafra]; he only wanted to confirm his predisposition."[51] Before the end of February, a far more serious blow was dealt to Biafra's hopes for American intervention, one that confirmed Ojukwu's decision to alter the course of civil war diplomacy with new tactics of defiance.

Throughout the early weeks of 1969, Ojukwu harbored positive expectations regarding the outcome of the Nixon administration's policy review. Recalling Nixon's campaign statement on genocide, the Biafran leader told a group of visitors in late January: "I am optimistic in that I see in him [Nixon] a man with sympathy."[52] Ojukwu also took com-

[47] Republic of Biafra, Ministry of Foreign Affairs, "General Brief on Visit of American Congressional Delegation," prepared by G. A. Onyegbula, Permanent Secretary, February 13, 1969. Also "Biafran Government Aide-Mémoire on Peace and Relief," undated.

[48] "Biafra and the Bureaucrats: Nixon at the Crossroads," *Ripon Forum* (February, 1969); reprinted in full in Markpress Release, Gen. 505.

[49] Republic of Biafra, Ministry of Foreign Affairs, "General Brief on Visit of American Congressional Delegation," p. 3.

[50] United States Congress, House of Representatives, Committee on Foreign Affairs, *Report of Special Fact-finding Mission to Nigeria*, February 7–20, 1969, by Hon. Charles C. Diggs, Jr., Michigan, and Hon. J. Herbert Burke, Florida, March 12, 1969 (Washington, D.C.: Government Printing Office, 1969).

[51] Interview: Effiong.

[52] Ojukwu, *Biafra*, interview with the American Committee to Keep Biafra Alive, Umuahia, January 21, 1969, II, 216.

fort in Nixon's anticommunism, predicting that with the prolongation of the war Nigeria would become more dependent on Russia and, "once the Soviet involvement launches the struggle along the cold war line, I believe from past records that it is likely that President Nixon would look more intimately into the problem."[53] More immediately, the American president was scheduled to meet with President de Gaulle of France in late February, and the Biafrans hoped for a breakthrough in light of de Gaulle's recent expressions of encouragement.[54] In a conversation with journalist Lloyd Garrison, Ojukwu stated that "President de Gaulle has said he believes in a cease-fire and self-determination. A joint statement when President Nixon goes to Paris might resolve the situation."[55]

Ojukwu suggested that if the United States and France called for a cease-fire, Britain would be forced to join, and most of Africa would follow. According to the full-blown scenario, Nigeria's growing isolation and the prospect of becoming dependent on the Soviet Union would frighten the Moslem northerners and cause a "soul-searching reappraisal in Lagos." Nixon's role, Ojukwu reportedly said, was crucial: "America is the only country that can halt or neutralize the other two powers [Great Britain and Russia] on the side of Lagos. The key to Africa falls upon the United States, whichever way she jumps—and until she jumps, we won't really know where Africa will jump."[56]

Within hours of the above interview, President Nixon announced the results of his foreign policy review of the Nigerian crisis.[57] The president implicitly ruled out any action that might be construed as legitimizing Biafra's claim to self-determination. Instead, he declared that "United States policy will draw a sharp distinction between carrying out our moral obligations to respond effectively to humanitarian needs and involving ourselves in the political affairs of others."[58] To give institutional expression to this crucial—if somewhat overdrawn—dichotomy of interests, Nixon divided the State Department's special task force on Nigeria into two groups.[59] One would remain under a

[53] *Ibid.* This was further elaborated by Ojukwu in an interview with Marvin Kupfer in *Newsweek*, February 13, 1969.

[54] In his New Year's Eve address, de Gaulle again voiced France's support for the Biafran cause, stating that "valiant Biafra's right of self-determination must be recognized." *Washington Post*, January 1, 1969.

[55] *New York Times*, February 23, 1969.

[56] *Ibid.*

[57] *Washington Post*, February 23, 1969. A text of the statement was delivered to General Gowon by America's ambassador in Nigeria, Elbert Mathews, and reprinted verbatim by the Federal Ministry of Information, Press Release No. F.216, February 23, 1969.

[58] *Ibid.*

[59] The State Department had set up the task force on November 26, 1968, to "coordinate and expedite the U.S. response to developments in the Nigerian Civil

career diplomat and retain responsibility for overseeing the conduct of "normal" relations with the federal government.[60] To handle humanitarian matters, the president named Clarence Clyde Ferguson, Jr., a law professor at Rutgers University, as his Special Coordinator on Relief to Civilian Victims of the Nigerian Civil War.[61] Lest there be any misunderstanding in Lagos or Umuahia, the president carefully circumscribed Ferguson's terms of reference: "The special coordinator will not seek and will not accept a charge to negotiate issues other than those directly relevant to relief."[62]

Nixon's decision, in fact, merely reconfirmed the policy adopted during the Johnson administration, but the added flourish of the Ferguson appointment was intended to appease pro-Biafran sentiment in Congress while reassuring London and Lagos that earlier statements during the campaign did not indicate any major new United States involvement. The Nigerian government, which only recently had voiced concern over the political implications of United States actions of self-avowed humanitarian nature,[63] greeted the Nixon announcement with undisguised relief. Radio Nigeria predicted that the decision to separate humanitarian and political matters would "go down in history as one of the wisest decisions taken by the Nixon administration [and] . . . shows cool-headed realism and unmistakable statesmanship," and added that "It is particularly commendable when one views it against the background of recent actions and statements of some misguided American leaders who have been trying to make the new administration get fully involved in Nigeria's internal affairs."[64] The same commentator ended with the not unrealistic hope that other Western countries and organizations would follow Nixon's lead "by staying out of the politics of the Nigerian crisis."

After the war, Ojukwu recalled Nixon's appointment of Ferguson as a watershed in the reformulation of Biafra's approach to the international system. "Nixon," he quipped with bitter irony, "smothered Biafra in relief"—a reference to the president's success in extricating himself from pro-Biafra domestic pressures while sidestepping the

---

War." C. Robert Moore, deputy assistant secretary for African affairs, was named to head the task force. *Washington Post*, November 27, 1968.

[60] Dr. Roy Melborne, country director, West Africa, retained supervision over the diplomatic side of U.S.-Nigerian relations. Interview: Melborne.

[61] Ferguson was actually appointed by Secretary of State William Rogers on February 23, 1969, the same day as the president's announcement. He was given the rank of ambassador.

[62] Text of President Nixon's February 22, 1969 statement. Nigeria, Federal Ministry of Information, Press Release No. F.216, February 23, 1969.

[63] *New York Times*, quoting a statement by federal Commissioner of Information Anthony Enahoro.

[64] Radio Nigeria, *Newstalk*, February 24, 1969.

issue of greater American involvement in behalf of a cease-fire. Then, acknowledging dashed hopes, he snapped, "We all knew the joke that you wouldn't buy a used car from him, but somehow we kept believing that he would come through."[65] Biafran officials declined public comment on the Ferguson appointment and continued to focus their attention on the forthcoming summit in Paris.[66] On the eve of the February 29, 1969, talks, "massive demonstrations" were reported by Radio Biafra in Umuahia and Orlu calling on the American president to reverse the former administration's policy of "rubber stamping British policy."[67]

Nothing favorable to Biafra's interests resulted from Nixon's discussions in Paris and London. Rather, the secession appeared to be even more isolated during the following weeks. Harold Wilson's well-publicized visit to Nigeria in March and the OAU Consultative Committee's willingness to blame Biafra for the continuation of armed conflict, were viewed in Biafra as two more planks in the international conspiracy to abstain from saving Ojukwu's regime. Then, on April 28, 1969, Biafra's most important European supporter—President Charles de Gaulle of France—suddenly resigned. Soon after Georges Pompidou came to power he sent word to Ojukwu via Houphouet-Boigny that the level of support accorded by de Gaulle would be sustained; Biafrans, however, had hoped for more, and these assurances did not arrive until after the French runoff election on June 15, 1969.[68]

Efforts to convert humanitarian concern into official action to help the Biafran government had been even more decisively quashed elsewhere in Europe. Authorities in Italy, Switzerland, and Germany also faced highly agitated religious and civic lobbies, but they were less tempted than de Gaulle to identify with the secession. All three had declined to sell arms to either side at the outset of hostilities, and thus were spared the embarrassment of having to affront the federal government by appearing to shift their political positions when the pro-Biafra popular movement took hold in Europe.

Tensions did arise over the delivery of relief to the enclave and, as the war intensified, these European powers responded in a pattern similar to the policies of the United States. In Switzerland, the government fully supported the intervention by the International Committee of the Red Cross, while quietly assuring Lagos that this connoted neither endorsement of the secession nor declining interest in expanded economic relations with Nigeria. The Italian government behaved in a similar fashion as it maneuvered to identify with the humanitarian

---

[65] Interview: Ojukwu.
[66] Radio Biafra, *Newstalk*, February 28, 1969.
[67] Radio Biafra, February 28, 1969.   [68] Interview: Effiong.

aspirations espoused by the Vatican, while quietly seeking to protect its growing trade and investment in Nigeria, which was becoming an important source for oil.

Germany was given special attention by the Biafrans, and they assigned a "Special Representative" in 1968 to complement their three other would-be European embassies in Lisbon, London, and Paris.[69] The German Protestant churches were among the most militant in Europe; on one occasion they sent a private memo to the Bonn government that reportedly called for the deployment of German tanks, planes, and armed forces to open relief corridors into Biafra.[70] "All the German government wanted," one of its diplomats recalled, "was our political liberty from public opinion and, on the relief question, we were willing to do anything to get it." As for the political merits of the dispute, the head of the Africa Service in the German Foreign Ministry was a former ambassador to Lagos and, he worked strenuously to ensure that his government did not compromise Nigeria's basic interests.

When public concern over Biafra reached a high pitch in Germany during May 1968, Minister for Foreign Affairs Willy Brandt summoned all African ambassadors accredited in Bonn and reminded them, "the Federal Government [of Germany] welcomes the efforts of African States to achieve growing economies and political unity. . . . Furthermore, the OAU, with its principles of respect for the sovereignty and territorial integrity of member States will, in the opinion of the Federal Government [of Germany] be a big help in stabilizing the continent of Africa."[71] Bonn boasted the second largest number of residing African ambassadors in the world, after Washington, and as the world's second largest trading nation Germany had extensive economic interests throughout the African region. Brandt made it plain that until the OAU changed its attitude toward Nigeria, Bonn would not alter its present position. Fortunately for the German government, much of the steam was released from the pro-Biafran movement when the German people suddenly became transfixed by the Soviet invasion of Czechoslovakia on August 20–21, 1968.

The specter of genocide against the Ibos also gained credibility among millions of Scandinavians. Public pressures for political action were especially intense in the Nordic countries. Finland, Norway, Iceland, Sweden, and Denmark maintained a common position on the Nigerian crisis despite slight differences of nuance. Norway was

---

[69] The representative, Dr. F. Obonna, established a Biafran office in Wiesbaden, but he was not accorded diplomatic status by the Bonn government and continued to travel on a Nigerian passport.

[70] Interview: Wilhelm Wagner.

[71] Speech by the Federal Minister for Foreign Affairs, Willy Brandt, to the African Ambassadors accredited in Bonn, May 6, 1968. *Afrika*, IX (1968).

perhaps the most pro-Biafran, with Norwegian parliamentarians repeatedly introducing resolutions calling for the diplomatic recognition of the secessionists. At the other extreme were the Swedes, who strongly supported the federal government and contributed one of their generals to the International Observer Team that helped to undermine the credibility of Biafra's genocide propaganda.[72] When popular pressures reached a crescendo in Scandinavia during August 1968, the prime ministers of the five governments issued a joint statement declaring their full support for the Organization of African Unity as the proper forum for dealing with the political issues at stake in the Nigerian crisis.[73]

While the five Nordic countries refused to intervene politically, they did give their wholehearted support for the humanitarian activities of their citizens in aiding Biafra and between August 1968 and September 1969 they issued six joint public appeals emphatically supporting the intervention by the humanitarian agencies to aid Biafra.[74] At the same time, they apparently never gave serious consideration to the question of diplomatic recognition. To quote Denmark's foreign minister:

> It has been the traditional practice of Danish foreign policy to let recognition depend upon, first of all, the stand taken by the majority of countries in the region [the OAU] and secondly, whether or not the government is recognized by the Big Powers. As you can see Biafra has a long way to go. Danish recognition policy has always been based and still is based on factual circumstances not moral or political values. We will never use recognition as an instrument in order to support or counteract any party in a given conflict.[75]

The Low Countries—Belgium, Luxembourg, and the Netherlands— also coordinated their positions on the Nigerian crisis. There were frequent cries in the Dutch and Belgian parliaments for recognition of Biafra, but as one seasoned diplomat from The Hague described the political realities, "The Nigerian crisis was one issue where the Dutch government did not agree with either Parliament or public opinion . . . our relations with Nigeria always had been very good. We are their second largest buyer, fifth largest seller, and fifth in development aid.

[72] The federal government's decision to invite the governments of Britain, Canada, Sweden, and Poland to send an observer to report on the behavior and conduct of federal troops in Ibo-populated areas was announced on August 28, 1968, and is explained in Chapter 9.

[73] Joint statement issued by the five Nordic governments, August 14, 1968.

[74] Joint statements issued by the five Nordic governments: August 14, 1968; September 2, 1968; January 19, 1969; March 3, 1969; April 24, 1969; September 2, 1969.

[75] Statement by the Danish foreign minister before the House of Parliament, June 12, 1969.

Until June 1968 we were a major arms supplier; we built their principal ship the SS *Nigeria* and supplied the ammunition for their guns."[76]

On June 7, 1968, the Dutch government announced an immediate and total ban on all arms shipments to Nigeria, amid a storm of protest following a detailed report by Biafra's Overseas Press Division that a Dutch company was about to ship twenty-five million rounds of ammunition to Lagos.[77] The Biafrans applauded the decisions as signaling a major shift in Dutch policy toward the crisis, but four months later, after much of the public pressure in The Hague had subsided, Prime Minister Piet de Jong issued a strong statement condemning the secession and pledging Dutch support for the position adopted by the Organization of African Unity.[78]

The government of Belgium followed The Hague and issued a total arms embargo on July 13, 1968. Prior to that time, a Belgian diplomat recalled, a Sabena 707 would carry a full load of arms to Lagos at least once a week, and his government was extremely reluctant to abandon this highly profitable arrangement.[79] The decision to announce an embargo marks the high-water mark of Biafran influence in Brussels —as it was in The Hague—and stands as one of the few instances where the Biafrans were able to convert widespread humanitarian concern into political action. The campaign by Biafra's supporters in Belgium was also spurred by the timely release of a detailed account of an impending arms sale by local merchants.[80] Sources in the Belgian embassy in Lagos later intimated, however, that the Biafran victory was more symbolic than real because the government simply allowed the exporting companies to change the end-use certificates and ship their arms and ammunition to countries, such as Britain, who were not at war themselves but in a position to forward the materiel to Lagos.[81]

BRITISH DIPLOMATIC MANEUVERS

The intensity of public hostility to official policies toward Nigeria on the European continent never approached the levels that confronted the Wilson government in Britain, where the former colonial power

---

[76] Interview: Royal Netherlands embassy, Lagos.

[77] Markpress Release, Gen. 86, May 7, 1968.

[78] Markpress Release, Gen. 166, June 10, 1968. Statement by the Netherlands prime minister before the Netherlands parliament, October 10, 1968, in which Mr. de Jong declared, inter alia, "A granting of independence to all these various ethnic groups would lead to splitting and cutting up of the African Continent, with all its detrimental consequences for the development of that continent and of its inhabitants."

[79] Interview: Belgian embassy, Lagos.

[80] Markpress Release, Gen. 175, June 15, 1968.

[81] Interview: Belgian embassy, Lagos.

eschewed any pretense of neutrality and permitted the open sale of vast quantities of arms and ammunition to the Gowon regime. For a brief period during the fall of 1968 it seemed that the loose coalition of antiwar activists, religious and nonsectarian humanitarian bodies, and the millions of contributors to the Biafran relief effort were fading politically. Following the fresh reports of imminent mass starvation toward the end of the year, however, opposition to the government's position began to coalesce again.

In early December, 130 members of the House of Commons called on the government to halt all further arms sales to Lagos and devote itself to fostering a cease-fire.[82] During the next three months, the prime minister was the object of demonstrations, petitions, and vociferous lectures from the pulpit.[83] For a brief period in January, trade with Nigeria was even threatened by bands of irate British dockers who refused to handle any cargo bound for Lagos.[84] Exacerbating Mr. Wilson's difficulties were a series of shocking reports from Biafra that appeared in *The Times*, among other newspapers, detailing the civilian suffering caused by federal jet aircraft.[85] And, if the reports themselves were not a sufficient embarrassment to the government, federal authorities in Lagos abruptly suspended privileges in January 1969 for the British Broadcasting Corporation, on the grounds that its reporting had been biased.[86]

The pressures facing Mr. Wilson were not all domestic. Britain's international prestige, to a greater extent than for any other external power, had become tied to the outcome of the the civil war. By early 1969 Wilson was again being urged by Washington and several European powers to take a more decisive lead in promoting a negotiated settlement. During February he held separate meetings with President Nixon

[82] Great Britain, *Parliamentary Debates*, Vol. 774, December 4, 1968.

[83] On February 25, 1969, the prime minister was asked on the floor of the House of Commons approximately how many petitions, letters, resolutions, etc., he had received "on Biafra," and he replied that more than 2,000 of all types had recently been delivered to No. 10 Downing Street. Great Britain, *Parliamentary Debates*, Vol. 777, cols. 1275–1277, February 25, 1969.

[84] *The Times* (London), January 11, 1969. The dockers were persuaded to abandon their protest once they had been assured that they would not be required to load any military equipment.

[85] The British press frequently carried detailed accounts of atrocities allegedly carried out by federal aircraft, but none created the public outrage that followed the series of four articles about bombing and civilian casualties written by Winston Churchill, grandson of the former prime minister, which appeared on the front pages of *The Times*, March 1, 3, 4, 5, 1969. The *Guardian* (March 7, 1969) credits the series with provoking the government to yield to a two-day debate of the Nigerian crisis, March 11–12, 1969, an event that is referred to below.

[86] *New York Times*, January 26, 1969. The actual closing of the BBC's West African office, in Lagos, and the arrest and deportation of correspondent Peter Stewart was not ordered until June 15, 1969.

and Chancellor Brandt. Both leaders supported the British commitment to sell Lagos military equipment as an alternative to a Soviet monopoly, but they too faced constituents who were deeply agitated by events in Nigeria. When Mr. Wilson visited Bonn he was met by crowds of pro-Biafran, anti-British demonstrators, and in one dramatic moment two protestors burst through police cordons to throw buckets of blood at him.[87] Meanwhile, in Switzerland the Biafran lobby was busy organizing a national boycott of all British imports as an expression of opposition to London's alleged complicity in the Nigerian war effort.

Wilson's options for engineering a peaceful settlement were rather limited. With Nigeria in control of nearly 90 percent of the territory of the former Eastern Region and preparing for another military offensive, halting the sale of arms was out of the question. The Nigerian economy was in surprisingly good shape,[88] with sufficient funds to buy arms elsewhere if the government wished; the Soviets, particularly, were presumed ready to make up any shortage created by Britain's withdrawal.[89] A further cause for not endangering relations with Lagos was the announcement on December 4, 1968, that Shell-BP had resumed operations and Nigerian oil production was expected quickly to surpass the prewar levels.[90] The Wilson government was resigned to continue its policy of selling military equipment to Nigeria and, as before, tried to persuade its critics that in doing so London retained sufficient leverage to press Lagos on matters related to humanitarian intervention and on the need for a negotiated settlement.

From late 1968 until March 1969, Prime Minister Wilson campaigned publicly for a resumption of peace talks. The Labour government knew that the prospects for a resumption of formal talks and a negotiated settlement were extremely bleak.[91] But press speculation in Britain about an imminent meeting between Nigerian and Biafran representatives was surprisingly optimistic, apparently sparked by a New Year's Eve broadcast in which Ojukwu stressed his readiness to

[87] *The Times* (London), February 13, 1969; more generally, *West Africa*, No. 2698, February 15, 1969, pp. 169–170.

[88] *West Africa*, No. 2691, December 28, 1968, p. 1544; more generally, O. Aboyade and A. A. Ayida, "The War Economy in Perspective."

[89] Wilson, *The Labour Government*, p. 590.

[90] *West Africa*, No. 2688, December 7, 1968, p. 1447; also, Webb, "Then the War Came." Webb was formerly Head of Public Relations, Shell-BP, Port Harcourt.

[91] This view was conveyed to Lord Shepherd by General Gowon, December 11–17, 1968, when the Nigerian head of state rejected any suggestion of an unconditional cease-fire and insisted that any substantive discussions with Ojukwu's representatives would have to be "based on the terms of the Algiers Resolution." Radio Nigeria, December 11, 1968; also, Adamu Ciroma's authoritative commentary, "Lord Shepherd and the Truth," *New Nigerian*, December 18, 1968.

begin unconditional negotiations.[92] A major story, extrapolated from this and based on a rather unrealistic understanding of the dynamics of the conflict, was compiled by *The Times* in early January with the headline "Biafra Peace Talks Nearer." The article asserted that Biafra was prepared to consider a confederal status in return for control of its own police and defense forces. The Nigerians, for their part, were believed to be flexible on the subject of boundaries for the new states, and *The Times* anticipated a "One Nigeria" solution that would incorporate "virtually all Ibo territory in a single state, including large areas of the former Midwest Region." The new arrangement was expected to provide for shared communications, a customs union, and a limited pooling of revenue expenditure, including oil royalties. Both sides, the article concluded, had realized finally that neither could "go it alone," and that a cease-fire and reconciliation was now possible.[93]

The focus for such optimism was a forthcoming meeting of the Commonwealth prime ministers, the first since 1966,[94] which would convene in London during the second week of January. It was assumed, at least by Fleet Street editors and journalists, that the Commonwealth organization would be acceptable to both sides and, unlike the OAU, Commonwealth countries possessed the means to enforce a cease-fire and adequately police any settlement.[95] The May 1968 peace talks in Kampala had been promoted only by the Commonwealth Secretariat and not by the prime ministers, who were expected to be much more effective. Among those who would be present in London were Presidents Nyerere of Tanzania and Kaunda of Zambia, who presumably could represent Biafra's interests at the highest levels of discussion.

The Nigerian government, however, brushed aside all suggestions of a formal peace initiative by the Commonwealth prime ministers, and flatly refused to allow the subject on the conference agenda on the grounds

[92] Markpress Release, Gen. 472, "Text of Lt. Col. C. O. Ojukwu's End of Year Message 1968," January 31, 1968. Actually, the substance of the address, if compared to Biafra's public positions as enunciated during weeks prior to the August 1968 Addis Ababa peace talks, offered nothing new. Ojukwu remained firm in the position that before anything else could be settled, a cease-fire would have to be arranged but, as before, he was prepared to meet to discuss the mechanics of a cease-fire. The most conciliatory remark in his January 31, 1968, address was a reference to the large area of "great mutual advantage" between Nigeria and Biafra and the suggestion that any peace talks might eventually consider economic ties and a possible Commonwealth arrangement.

[93] *The Times* (London), January 7, 1969.

[94] The previous conference had been held in Lagos, January 1966, less than two days before the military seized power.

[95] Nigeria, Federal Ministry of Information, *Commonwealth Prime Ministers Conference 1969: British Newspaper Review*, No. F.17, January 7, 1969; No. F.21, January 8, 1969; No. F.50, January 12, 1969; and No. F.64, January 16, 1969.

that to do so would undermine the authority of the OAU.[96] The head of Nigeria's delegation, Chief Obafemi Awolowo, informed a BBC television audience that he would oppose any attempt to place matters related to the crisis on the conference agenda, but if such matters were raised in general discussion, Nigeria would be prepared to answer them.[97] The federal government, he added, had a good case to make, if the need arose, and there was little danger of a Nigerian walkout. He also assured his audience of planned meetings with the presidents of Zambia and Tanzania, the two Commonwealth members recognizing Biafra, and expressed his willingness to hold private talks with any representative from Biafra who might be in London. As for the chances for a cease-fire, Chief Anthony Enahoro bluntly told a group of Commonwealth correspondents, "There is no way of dealing with armed rebellion in any country than with force of arms. The only way this thing can be brought to an end is if one side or the other gives up. . . . A cease-fire enabling them to regroup and recover from recent revenge would be completely stupid. We have them on the run."[98]

The highlight of the Commonwealth meeting, at least in terms of press coverage, was a skillfully staged reception by Prime Minister Harold Wilson to dramatize his concern—and the Commonwealth's —with developments in Nigeria. Toward the close of the conference he invited the heads of all delegations to an informal out-of-session meeting at Lancaster House, which was officially described as "a discussion over gin and tonic" but exuded pretensions of a British-led initiative to promote Nigeria-Biafra talks.[99] The gathering lasted only an hour, and Chief Awolowo spent most of the time bringing the Commonwealth members up to date on the military situation and prospects for a speedy victory.[100] Aside from general expressions of concern, Awolowo encountered no hostility; even Nigeria's arch-antagonists, Presidents Kaunda and Nyerere, sought to reestablish a degree of amity with the federal delegation.[101]

[96] *Morning Post*, January 6, 1969.

[97] Remarks by Chief Awolowo over British television, January 7, 1969, reported in Nigeria, Federal Ministry of Information, Press Release No. F.23, January 8, 1969.

[98] *Daily Telegraph*, January 14, 1969.

[99] *West Africa*, No. 2694, January 18, 1969, p. 21.

[100] Interview: Awolowo.

[101] According to a Canadian delegate who was present, Nyerere gave the impression that he had reached a point of personal regret over his decision to recognize the secession, and was quietly working to rebuild broken bridges. Interview: John Schioler, Commonwealth Division, Canadian Foreign Office. Chief Awolowo made a similar statement upon arriving home in Lagos, but this was immediately denied by the Tanzanian high commission in London. *West Africa*, No. 2695, January 25, 1969, p. 109.

During the Lancaster House cocktail party, Awolowo reiterated his willingness to meet informally with Ojukwu's representatives if the latter desired. The Biafrans, however, chose to remain aloof. This decision had been made well in advance of the conference, and was subject to change only if Nigeria signaled a fundamental change in its approach to a cease-fire and negotiated settlement.[102] As rumors of impending talks continued to circulate in the British press, Biafra's office in London called a news conference to state that Ojukwu, contrary to reports, had sent no special envoys to Britain. According to the Head of the London office, Ignatius Kogbara:

> I had direct authority to talk to [Chief Awolowo] but my instructions were not to talk but to be around and appear ready to talk. Again and again I emphasized that my point of view was official and that there was no other point of view. We didn't want to talk. Our intelligence was that the British wanted to trick us into a statement with Awolowo. Foley [parliamentary undersecretary, Foreign and Commonwealth Office] tried to arrange a meeting but we said our friends would talk in our behalf.[103]

Biafra's "friends," Tanzania and Zambia, proved to be less helpful than expected, preferring to conserve what little influence they could muster for the protracted debate over Rhodesia. Declining to take the lead as Biafra's surrogate, President Kaunda said before leaving London that the most likely people to succeed in facilitating negotiations were those without a strong commitment.[104] Ojukwu's singular attempt to penetrate the councils of the Commonwealth was routed instead through the new prime minister of Sierra Leone, Siaka Stevens. The initiative quickly dissolved.

Prime Minister Stevens held several discussions with two senior Biafran envoys: Dr. Kenneth Dike, Ojukwu's representative based in the Ivory Coast with responsibilities for West Africa; and Francis Nwokedi, the former federal permanent secretary of external affairs, who eventually became Biafra's representative in Freetown and a confidant of the prime minister.[105] Stevens agreed to circulate a letter to all prime ministers attending the Commonwealth Conference, in which he called for the establishment of a special committee comprising two representatives from the federal and Biafran governments under the

---

[102] Republic of Biafra, Ministry of Foreign Affairs, "Strategy for the Commonwealth Prime Ministers Conference," policy memorandum, December 14, 1968; and "The Demerits of Sending a Delegation to London for the Commonwealth Prime Ministers Conference," policy memorandum, December 18, 1968.

[103] Interview: Kogbara.

[104] West Africa, No. 2695, January 25, 1969, p. 109.

[105] Interview: Dike.

chairmanship of Emperor Haile Selassie of Ethiopia or President Tubman of Liberia.[106] The committee would be given a mandate to act in behalf of the Commonwealth prime ministers in order to "call for an immediate ceasefire, make arrangements for relief supplies and after that to get the two sides around the conference table in order to find ways and means of resolving the difficulties which exist between them."[107]

Awolowo did not see a copy of the letter until the prime minister handed him one at the end of their otherwise cordial meeting on the morning of January 14. In his formal reply circulated a few hours later, the Nigerian expressed surprise at the "unusual way" the matter had been handled and then unequivocally rejected the notion of another special committee.[108] The reasons were obvious. Nigeria resented the implication of de facto parity with the rebel government, and even if "suitable terms of reference could be worked out," the committee would only duplicate the work of the OAU Consultative Committee.[109] Nothing more was heard of the Stevens proposal.

When the conference adjourned on January 15, 1969, after eight days of formal sessions, a 7,000-word communiqué was issued, but Nigeria was not mentioned.[110] Shortly after the conference had ended, the British prime minister made a statement that sought to place blame for the absence of any dramatic breakthroughs toward a peaceful settlement: "The Head of the Nigerian delegation made plain to me and to others privately and to the gathering of twenty-seven of us at Lancaster House, his willingness unconditionally to attend a meeting with Ojukwu's representatives. . . . I regret that there was no move in response from Colonel Ojukwu's representative."[111] In Lagos, General Gowon described the London Conference as "another vote of confidence in Nigeria."[112]

The outcome of the Commonwealth deliberations may have reassured the federal government, but it did little to mitigate Harold Wil-

[106] Text of Circular Letter to All the Prime Ministers Attending the Meeting of Prime Ministers, January 1969, from the Hon. Siaka Stevens, Prime Minister of Sierra Leone, January 13, 1969.

[107] *Ibid.*

[108] Text of Letter to the Hon. Siaka Stevens, Prime Minister of Sierra Leone, from Chief Obafemi Awolowo, January 14, 1969.

[109] The arguments in Awolowo's reply were echoed by Radio Nigeria, *Newstalk*, January 17, 1969.

[110] Meeting of the Commonwealth Prime Ministers: London, 1969, *Final Communiqué*, January 15, 1969.

[111] *British News Bulletin*, VIII (February 26, 1969). A similar statement was made by the prime minister in the House of Commons. *Parliamentary Debates*, Vol. 776, January 21, 1969, cols. 549–554.

[112] Nigeria, Federal Ministry of Information, News Spotlight, "General Gowon Praises Commonwealth Delegation," F.85, January 19, 1969.

son's domestic troubles. During a day-long Parliamentary debate on Nigeria in early March, the fifth since the crisis began, Wilson encountered the severest criticism to date.[113] The vote on the question of continued arms sales was lopsided in favor of maintaining the existing policy (232–62), but more than half (330) of the members abstained and over a quarter of Mr. Wilson's Labour party failed to support him.[114] The outcome might have been less secure but for an apparent sudden increase of Soviet influence in Nigeria and the dramatic announcement that the prime minister planned to visit Nigeria.

Less than a week before the debate, a Russian naval squadron consisting of two missile destroyers, one submarine and one fleet oiler steamed into Lagos harbor on an unprecedented good-will visit. Nigeria's official press heralded the arrival as proof of the country's new-found status as a nonaligned power.[115] While the ships were in port a Russian sailor "fell" into Lagos lagoon and swam to the British merchant vessel *Tweedbank*, where he requested political asylum. Within an hour Nigerian police converged on the *Tweedbank* with the Soviet ambassador and the captain of the Soviet ship, and retrieved the sailor.[116] Many Conservatives interpreted the incident as one more illustration of Nigeria's growing subservience to the Russians. At the same time, rumors were abound in London alleging Soviet intentions to open consulates throughout Nigeria.[117] The latter reports were groundless.[118]

Whether the specter of a greater Soviet presence in Nigeria would have been sufficient, or even necessary, to sustain a vote of confidence in Wilson's arms policy cannot be determined, because the prime minister injected a second, more dramatic, element into the debate when his foreign secretary announced that Wilson planned to fly to Lagos and personally explore the possibilities for a peaceful settlement.[119] It was a bold move that had been cleared with the federal government only two days before. Gowon sought, and received in advance of the visit,

[113] Great Britain, *Parliamentary Debates*, Vol. 779, March 13, 1969, cols. 1571–1696. For a summary of the debate, see *West Africa*, No. 2703, March 22, 1969, p. 330.

[114] Analyzed by *Financial Times*, March 14, 1969.

[115] *Morning Post*, March 5, 1969.

[116] For a discussion of the international legal basis supporting the federal decision to board the *Tweedbank* in the company of Soviet officials, see Elias, "The Nigerian Crisis in International Law."

[117] The rumors, including the assertion that the Soviets were eager to establish a monopoly over the supply of sophisticated hardware to the Nigerian air force and army, were reported by the conservative *Sunday Telegraph*, March 16, 1969.

[118] For a thoughtful analysis that discounted any significant increase in Soviet influence in Nigeria, see *West Africa*, No. 2699, February 22, 1969, pp. 201–203. More generally, see Legvold, *Soviet Policy in West Africa*, pp. 311–330.

[119] Great Britain, *Parliamentary Debates*, Vol. 779, March 13, 1969, cols. 1681–1695.

assurances that the prime minister would not assume the pretensions of a mediator or undertake any other activity that suggested Britain was prepared to deal with the two sides on an equal basis. Wilson arrived in Lagos on March 27, 1969, for four days of fact finding.[120]

The British prime minister sought Gowon's help on four issues that concerned the British people: 1. the resumption of direct talks with Biafran representatives, or at least new assurances of the federal government's willingness to talk so as to render more credible Wilson's allegations that Ojukwu was the real obstacle to a negotiated settlement; 2. guarantees for the safety of Ibos within a reunited Nigeria; 3. increased relief supplies to Biafra; and 4. claims of indiscriminate bombing by the federal air force.[121]

Gowon's most significant concession was a pledge to curtail the infamous strafing by the pair of MIG–17s that made daily sweeps across the Biafran enclave. On other matters, the Nigerian leader reiterated that the basic issues were nonnegotiable, but he remained ready to send a team to meet with representatives from the other side, provided Ojukwu raised no preconditions.[122] Regarding relief, Gowon merely recalled the federal government's standing offer of land corridors and/or daylight flights to Uli. He urged the British prime minister to verify for himself the security of those Ibos under federal rule in the occupied areas of the former Eastern Region.

Fully half of Wilson's time in Nigeria was spent touring the three eastern states. This exercise, which included several enthusiastic impromptu speeches by the visitor, was immensely popular with federal leaders because it implied unqualified British support for the twelve states, including the legitimacy of Ukpabi Asika's rule in the liberated areas of the East Central State.[123] While in Port Harcourt and Calabar, Wilson received much-publicized testimony from eastern minority leaders concerning the history of Ibo exploitation and the new realities

[120] Sir Denis Greenhill, the new head of the Diplomatic Service, paid a hastily arranged visit to Lagos, March 11–12, 1969, to make arrangements for the prime minister's visit. *The Times*, March 11, 1969. Wilson had authorized Lord Shepherd to raise the proposal of a visit during the minister of state's December 11–17, 1968, talks with General Gowon. Wilson wanted to make the trip before or just after Christmas, but Gowon declined to invite him. Wilson, *The Labour Government*, p. 590.

[121] *British News Bulletin*, X (April 16, 1969); also, Wilson, *The Labour Government*, p. 629.

[122] Wilson conveyed to Gowon prior to the visit his assurances that Britain fully adhered to the federal position on the nonnegotiability of "One Nigeria." Wilson, *The Labour Government*, p. 629.

[123] The prime minister later reported to Parliament that the administration of the East Central State was being carried out by a "distinguished Ibo who is in complete authoritative control of the State," Great Britain, *Parliamentary Debates*, Vol. 781, April 2, 1969, cols. 485–500.

of minority self-determination within the Nigerian federation.[124] Radio Nigeria voiced official pleasure over the excursion, and expressed the hope that the prime minister would henceforth be in a better position to "clear the minds of the doubting Thomases in Britain . . . and tell those pro-rebel Parliamentarians in Commons what exactly the situation is in Nigeria."[125]

Wilson's enthusiasm, reminiscent of an election-eve campaign in the hustings, must be weighed in light of a decision pending among Gowon's closest advisers back in Lagos. The prime minister had inquired shortly after arriving whether the federal government would object to a possible meeting between himself and Ojukwu. Such a meeting would doubtlessly have enhanced the Labour party's standing in the polls, but obviously touched sensitive nerves in Lagos. Gowon had asked for time to consult. The prime minister's subsequent efforts to demonstrate his good faith and uncompromising support for a united Nigeria composed of twelve federated states did not go unrewarded. When he returned to Lagos on March 30, Gowon informed him, however reluctantly, that the federal government would not object to a meeting, providing it was not held in Biafra or in any country recognizing Ojukwu's regime.[126] Wilson agreed, and restated his intention to serve only as an intermediary, passing to the OAU any thoughts Ojukwu might express pertaining to the resumption of talks, and otherwise limiting the discussion to matters related to relief supplies.

By accepting Gowon's conditions pertaining to possible venues, Wilson destroyed the groundwork for his meeting with Ojukwu that had been quietly laid the previous week. On March 24, Britain's foreign secretary, Michael Stewart, had initiated a series of exchanges when, in response to a member's question on the floor of Commons, he remarked that the prime minister would not be opposed to visiting Biafra.[127] Within forty-eight hours Ojukwu had sent word through his representative in London, Ignatius Kogbara, that Wilson would be received if he wished to come to Biafra.[128] According to Ojukwu, Wilson dispatched Leonard Cheshire to Biafra to make detailed arrange-

---

[124] Rivers State Government, *Our Case: The Rivers State of Nigeria Welcomes the Rt. Hon. Harold Wilson* (Lagos, 1969); and South-Eastern State Ministry of Home Affairs and Information, "An Address Presented to the Rt. Hon. Harold Wilson by the Members of the Executive Council," Calabar, 1967.

[125] Radio Nigeria, *Newstalk*, March 31, 1969.

[126] Wilson, *The Labour Government*, p. 635.

[127] Great Britain, *Parliamentary Debates*, Vol. 780, March 24, 1969, cols. 1019–1023.

[128] Radio Biafra, March 26, 1969. According to the report a senior official had conveyed the confirmation on March 25, 1969.

ments.[129] Under the plan that Cheshire carried to Lagos and handed to Wilson shortly after his arrival, the prime minister was expected to fly into Uli from Lagos, meet Ojukwu, and together they would drive to Umuahia to survey the situation.[130] This schedule was preempted by Wilson's March 30 cable to the Biafran representative in London, proposing a meeting with Ojukwu on March 31 in any one of seven West African locations.[131] Alternatively, he suggested a meeting in East Africa two or three days hence.

Ojukwu immediately rejected the revised proposition, citing pressing military concerns that made it impossible for him to leave his command post.[132] More to the point, the Biafran leader surmised that nothing could be gained from a meeting outside the enclave. Wilson was expected to try to persuade Ojukwu to surrender peacefully and accept a "One Nigeria" solution, regardless of the venue. But had Wilson gone to Biafra, this would have enhanced the secession's international prestige and opened the possibility for visits by other government officials, including representatives of the United States Department of State.[133]

Failing to reach an agreement with Ojukwu on a suitable venue, Wilson left Lagos March 31, 1969, and flew to Addis Ababa to report to Emperor Haile Selassie as chairman of the OAU's Consultative Committee on the meetings with General Gowon. After two days of talks, which included a ninety-minute session with OAU Secretary General Diallo Telli, the prime minister issued a communiqué stating he had "found the federal Nigerian government in full agreement with Britain's policy supporting the need for a negotiated settlement and the preservation of Nigeria's unity."[134] He then rushed back to London on April 2, 1969, to brief the House of Commons.[135]

Wilson had been stymied, although he made a valiant effort to portray the fact-finding aspect of his foray as a major success, since he had been "reassured" of the wisdom of his government's Nigeria

---

[129] Interview: Ojukwu. Cheshire's access to Biafra was excellent. The British hero of World War II, renowned humanitarian, and founder of the Cheshire Homes for Orphans, had been an activist in Biafran relief.

[130] *Ibid.* British authorities are extremely reticent about the extent of their contacts with Ojukwu, but a later report by Cheshire, published in the *Guardian*, November 17, 1969, tends to support Ojukwu's version of the incident.

[131] Wilson suggested Monrovia, Yaoundé, Accra, Lomé, Dakar, Ascension Island, or aboard the HMS Fearless stationed off Cotonou. To expedite Ojukwu's obvious logistical difficulties, he offered to send an Andover, Hercules, or helicopter to pick up the Biafran leader. Wilson, *The Labour Government*, p. 635.

[132] Markpress Release, Gen. 555, March 31, 1969.

[133] Interview: Ojukwu. [134] *Financial Times*, April 2, 1969.

[135] Great Britain, *Parliamentary Debates*, Vol. 781, April 2, 1969, cols. 485–500.

policy.[136] From the outset, he had accepted the reality that neither side would accept him as a mediator, but even his scaled-down bid to serve as an intermediary between the protagonists and the OAU had fallen short of opening a dialogue with Ojukwu. The parameters for any future initiative from London, he now admitted, were quite narrow: "Anyone who knows anything about Nigeria or Africa [he lectured Parliament] will know that any attempt to get a peace settlement is for the Nigerians and, if help is needed, it should come from the OAU and not from any country outside Africa."[137]

RETURNING TO THE CONFERENCE TABLE
FOR THE LAST TIME

The opportunities for the OAU to play an active role in facilitating a negotiated settlement appeared to be negligible. The organization's well-known and decidedly profederal stand obviously precluded any attempt at bona fide mediation.[138] And Ojukwu's publicly expressed views of the OAU revealed a deep bitterness: "The Organization of African Unity [he told a Biafran audience on December 31], is merely a title—a marionette show—plenty of pomp but no circumstance . . . it might be an Organisation of African Eunuchs . . . The OAU has African skin, but this is only . . . a mask for established imperialism—Arab—British—Russian."[139]

Regardless of such hard-line posturing, Britain, the United States, and a host of smaller European powers continued to press for an OAU peace initiative, if only to deflect domestic criticism from pro-Biafran lobbyists. After months of quiet diplomacy, Ojukwu suddenly agreed to field a team of negotiators for a direct meeting with Nigerian representatives and the OAU Consultative Committee in Monrovia, Liberia, April 17–20, 1969. But once again, events leading up to "peace talks" appear to have been the result of a preoccupation with diplomatic form which, however important to all parties concerned, bore very little relation to the probability of reconciling basic differences between Nigeria and Biafra.

The six heads of state who composed the OAU Consultative Committee were not under the same intense domestic pressures as their

[136] For an elaboration of this point, see *Observer Foreign News Service*, April 3, 1969.

[137] Great Britain, *Parliamentary Debates*, Vol. 781, April 2, 1969, col. 490.

[138] OAU Secretary General Diallo Telli visited Lagos in October 1968, but when asked about the prospects of peace talks he stated that he was only interested in "getting the Algiers resolution implemented." *Daily Times*, October 16, 1968.

[139] Ojukwu, *Biafra*, Interview with Biafra Information Complex, December 31, 1968, II, 183.

counterparts in Europe and America and, in light of past failures to promote meaningful negotiations, they were understandably hesitant about trying to arrange another round of talks. A repetition of the protracted and ultimately futile discussions in Niamey and Addis Ababa could only result in greater embarrassment, and be a source of comfort for Africa's detractors. Subsequent deliberations during the OAU summit, moreover, confirmed that the vast majority of African leaders were primarily concerned with defending Nigeria's sovereignty and territorial integrity, and less with the pursuit of an elusive political settlement. Once burned, the Emperor and his Consultative Committee shied away from assuming the role of peace-maker in the absence of firm indications that the belligerents were prepared to talk meaningfully.

Despite a paucity of good omens, speculation about a renewed peace effort led by Emperor Haile Selassie first surfaced in the Western press during early November 1968,[140] although at this stage there had been no more than preliminary soundings. On November 19, 1968, the Emperor sent a formal inquiry to General Gowon concerning the committee's desire to send delegations to Lagos and to Ojukwu's headquarters in Umuahia to explain "the urgent necessity of ending the conflict in Nigeria."[141] Gowon replied that such a move would be "extremely dangerous," and suggested instead that the Consultative Committee "make use first of the good offices of those countries which have recognized the rebel regime to obtain an undertaking from the rebel leader that he is willing to enter into meaningful talks in the context of the Algiers Resolution."[142] Selassie then sent a message to Ojukwu on December 14, 1968, renewing the committee's previous proposal of attempting "to secure from the federal military government guarantees which would assure the safety and well-being of the Ibos as well as of other minority groups in the East within the context of a United Nigeria."[143] In the same message, the Emperor invited the Biafran leader to meet with him in Addis Ababa to discuss the details of the above proposal.[144] Ojukwu declined the invitation, but suggested a four-week truce, and urged the Emperor to use the truce period to promote a more permanent cease-fire.

Taking a slightly different tack, the Emperor called attention to

---

[140] *New York Times*, November 11, 1968.

[141] OAU, Confidential Report to the OAU Consultative Committee from the Chairman, H.I.M. Haile Selassie I on his activities in pursuit of a peaceful settlement. Monrovia, April 18, 1969.

[142] *Ibid.*   [143] *Ibid.*

[144] At the same time, the Emperor sought to enlist the support of Presidents Kaunda, Nyerere, Houphouet-Boigny, and Bongo by simultaneously urging them "to prevail upon Col. Ojukwu to accept my initiative in finding a negotiated settlement to the crisis." *Ibid.*

the advent of Christmas and the Moslem holiday Id al-Fitir, and proposed a one-week truce to mark the religious days and pave the way for reopening negotiations. Gowon declined, stating that "the rebel leadership are not genuinely interested in any cease-fire arrangements," but he did allow for a two-day truce.[145] Ojukwu immediately upstaged his adversary with a unilaterally declared eight-day Christmas truce, the reality of which was open to question.[146]

Biafra's much-publicized efforts to promote a truce, and related European press coverage of severe economic dislocation and other human suffering, had by early 1969 apparently convinced the Consultative Committee that if they could lure the secessionists back to the conference table, the latter might at last agree to rejoin the federation. Among the six committee members, General Ankrah of Ghana was most inclined to believe in the possibility of winning acceptance of a face-saving formula.[147]

Ankrah visited Monrovia during the first week of January to attend the celebrations honoring the twenty-fifth anniversary of the Tubman regime and used the opportunity to suggest a new attempt to promote peace talks. Tubman, while dubious about the chances for a settlement, thought there might be cause for hope if Ojukwu would agree to participate in person.[148] Even if the invitation were refused, Tubman appreciated the utility of putting Biafra in an awkward position. On the latter point, he was warmly supported by the United States embassy in Monrovia. On January 24, 1969, he sent a message to the Emperor proposing that the OAU Consultative Committee invite both the federal government and the "secessionist leaders to meet the members of the committee for negotiations without any agreed agenda."[149]

Before Selassie had time to sound out other members of the committee, a contingent of francophone African leaders embarked on a duplicate, but curiously separate, undertaking. Meeting in Kinshasa, January 27–29, 1969 the fourteen members of OCAM announced the appointment of a special peace mission consisting of Presidents

---

[145] Ibid.

[146] Nigerian and British spokesmen insisted that the Biafrans broke their own truce on December 21, 1968, when they launched an unsuccessful offensive to recapture Owerri and Aba.

[147] For the fifty-four-year-old veteran of World War II and former ranking African officer in Her Majesty's Gold Coast Regiment, continued Biafran resistance—regardless of the political considerations—was simply suicidal and, since he assumed Ojukwu to be rational, the only reasonable thing for Biafra to do "from a military point of view" was to surrender. Interview: Ankrah.

[148] Interview: de Shields.

[149] OAU, Confidential Report to the OAU Consultative Committee from the Chairman, H.I.M. Haile Selassie I, Monrovia, April 18, 1969.

Hamani Diori and Joseph Mobutu.[150] Both leaders had shown themselves to be among the federal government's strongest proponents, publicly and as members of the OAU Consultative Committee. Their identification with OCAM apparently was meant to reassure Biafra that, at least in a formal sense, any peace moves would not be prejudiced from the outset by the terms of reference prescribed by the OAU. Also, any OCAM proposals would presumably enjoy the backing of Ivory Coast, Gabon, and, implicitly, President de Gaulle of France.[151]

Nothing came of the OCAM Special Mission because Gowon quietly informed the two presidents that his government would only consider negotiating under the auspices of the Consultative Committee, and that Lagos was already cooperating with President Tubman's initiative.[152] When Tubman finally announced that the members of the committee planned to reconvene in Monrovia on or about April 18, 1969, Biafra had not yet agreed to participate.[153] As an encouragement, he proposed that the African states recognizing Biafra be allowed to attend the meeting in order to advise Ojukwu's representatives and assure them of a "fair deal." Two weeks after Tubman's February 6 announcement, the Biafran government publicly dismissed any prospects for meaningful talks, alleging that the committee was powerless to restrain the British from aiding Nigeria, that the members had not yet brushed aside their "incredibly inept" decision to support the federal government in Algiers, and concluded by impugning President Tubman's good faith.[154]

---

[150] *Daily Times*, January 29, 1969.

[151] Radio Biafra hailed the announcement of the OCAM special mission as "a definite change of attitude," adding, "In recognition of the strong case for Biafra, these African leaders are no longer dismissing Biafra with a wave of the hand. Instead they now see the necessity for sending a high-level delegation to Biafra and Nigeria respectively." *Commentary*, February 7, 1969. The federal government "welcomed" the move as a show of "genuine concern which the Organization has for a fellow African country," but stressed that the mission members also belonged to the OAU and therefore were expected not to deviate from the "Algiers Resolution." *Morning Post*, editorial, "OCAM Peace Move," February 10, 1969.

[152] Confirmation of Tubman's efforts to reactivate the Consultative Committee became public on February 6, 1969. *Daily Times*, February 7, 1969. On the same day, the federal government reaffirmed its confidence in the OAU as the "competent authority to resolve the crisis."

[153] *Morning Post*, March 14, 1969.

[154] Radio Biafra, *Outlook*, March 19, 1969; *Commentary*, March 22, 1969. When Harold Wilson visited Addis Ababa in early April, Biafran spokesmen attacked the Consultative Committee as a front for British imperialism. *Outlook*, April 2, 1969. In a related editorial, Biafran authorities condemned Consultative Committee member Hamani Diori of Niger for allegedly serving as a conduit for federal arms purchases in European markets closed to Nigerian buyers by various

Ojukwu came under strong pressure from his friends to accept the Monrovia proposition without preconditions. On March 18, 1969, a delegation from Zambia—the first official visit from an African country —began a five-day tour of the enclave. The mission was led by the Zambian ambassador to the Ivory Coast, Ali Simbula, and took as its theme the need for an OAU solution to the conflict.[155] Less conspicuously, Tanzania, Ivory Coast, and Gabon also urged Biafra's leaders to cooperate with the Consultative Committee.

The basic argument raised by those supporting Ojukwu's regime was that the April 18 meeting in Monrovia would be only preliminary in nature, and therefore did not require acceptance, implicit or otherwise, of Nigeria's demand that all substantive negotiations be conducted on the basis of "One Nigeria." The meeting, they further contended, would provide Biafra with an important opportunity to force a public showdown with Nigeria on the cease-fire issue. The latter point struck a responsive chord among senior officials in the Biafran Ministry of Foreign Affairs. A principal hope underlying their eventual acceptance of the Monrovia invitation was that if Nigeria were too intractable on the cease-fire issue and the talks subsequently broke down, one or more of the committee members would withdraw or renounce the chairman's mandate as too partisan toward the federal government. The dissolution of the Consultative Committee was seen as a crucial objective in Biafra's struggle to break the political logjam that prevented further internationalization of the civil war.[156]

More coercive pressures also weighed in favor of Biafran acquiescence. During late March and early April, President Houphouet-Boigny of the Ivory Coast and Consultative Committee members Hamani Diori and Joseph Mobutu paid separate visits to Paris for discussions with General de Gaulle. They reportedly succeeded in enlisting French support for curtailing arms sales to Biafra during April as a way of encouraging the secessionists to take a more flexible attitude toward negotiations. According to the April 16 issue of the satirical but informed *Le Canard Enchaîné*, Biafran arms deliveries fell from twenty-five tons per day to less than a ton per day by mid-April.[157] Whatever

---

embargoes. Markpress Release, Gen. 566, Statement by the Commissioner for Information, April 4, 1969.

[155] Markpress Release, Gen. 545, "Zambia Says Nigeria-Biafra is an African Problem," undated.

[156] Interview: Onyegbula.

[157] Cited in the BBC's *Morning Show*, West African Service, April 17, 1969; also *West Africa*, No. 2708, April 26, 1969, pp. 461–462. The *Washington Post*, May 10, 1969, reported that according to "informed officials," the United States had asked the French to halt its arms supply to Biafra to further the chances for peace. Ojukwu maintains that the French did curtail arms shipments in late

problems Ojukwu might have had with his foreign friends, however, they paled when compared to the more immediate threat posed by the federal army. On March 26, Nigeria's First Division began to advance on two axes: the first from Afikpo aimed at Bende, and the second from Okigwi south to the current Biafran capital at Umuahia.[158] By agreeing to go to Monrovia, the Biafrans hoped to force a slow-down in the federal offensive, or at least to dramatize to the world that while delegates were talking peace the Nigerian war machine was on the march.[159]

On April 13, 1969, Emperor Haile Selassie met with Ojukwu's East African representative, Austin Okwu, in Lusaka on the eve of the fifth East and Central African summit. The Emperor extended a formal invitation for Biafran attendance at the Monrovia Consultative Committee, and, together with the presidents of Tanzania and Zambia, pleaded for full cooperation. The next day one of Biafra's leading hawks, Commissioner for Internal Affairs C. C. Mojekwu, announced Biafra's readiness to attend "in order to show her genuine willing-ness for a negotiated settlement."[160] The purpose of the forthcoming meeting, in Biafran eyes, was mainly "to explore the possibility of further talks," which could only take place if the discussions in Monrovia culminated with an "immediate cessation of hostilities."[161]

The Consultative Committee reconvened at the Temple of Justice in Monrovia on April 18, 1969.[162] H.I.M. Haile Selassie was in the chair, with Presidents Tubman, Diori, Ahidjo, and Mobutu attending; the only delegation not represented by a founding member of the Com-mittee was Ghana's, owing to General Ankrah's sudden resignation less than two weeks before.[163] The vice chairman of the National Liberation

---

May, but in response to Biafra's capture of eighteen European oilmen and not in conjunction with peace talks. Interview: Ojukwu.

[158] Umuahia fell to elements of the First Division on April 22, 1969.

[159] A similar situation had occurred in May 1968, when Port Harcourt came under strong military pressure on the eve of the Kampala talks. Biafrans joke bitterly that they could always tell when another peace offensive was coming by the escalation of federal military pressure. Nigerians, on the other hand, complain that pressure for talks always increased when they were on the verge of a great victory, and this was symptomatic of the collusion between Biafrans and those abroad who opposed a federal victory.

[160] Radio Biafra, April 14, 1969.

[161] Full statement broadcast over Radio Biafra on April 16, 1969.

[162] The delegations actually began to arrive on April 16, and spent most of the following day in informal consultations to determine the procedure to be followed at the formal opening on April 18.

[163] General Ankrah's resignation was prompted by a scandal that revealed his illegal activities of soliciting, through an intermediary, funds from expatriate businessmen to be used in a planned campaign for the presidency upon return to civilian rule. The intermediary was an Ibo, Arthur Nzeribe, whose close connec-

Council, J.W.K. Harlley, attended in his stead. General Gowon and Colonel Ojukwu declined to attend this "preliminary session"; the former cited personal reasons—on April 19 Gowon was to wed Miss Victoria Zakari—while Col. Ojukwu faced a more compelling need to remain at home to defend his capital from imminent federal attack.

Biafra's delegation was relatively high powered. It was led by the chief justice, Sir Louis Mbanefo, who had been in the background since his role as head of Biafra's negotiating team in Kampala the previous May.[164] Behind the chief justice stood Ojukwu's most trusted adviser, Commissioner for Internal Affairs Mojekwu. Nigeria's team was led by its Commissioner for Works and Housing, Femi Okunnu, who was assisted by the permanent secretary for economic development, Allison Ayida. Okunnu and Ayida had served before on federal negotiating teams, although Okunnu was the youngest man in Gowon's civilian cabinet and his presence in Monrovia was interpreted as a reflection of the federal government's pessimism about the prospects for meaningful talks.

Following brief formal opening addresses by the host, President Tubman, and Chairman Haile Selassie, the committee met in private session and the delegations from Nigeria and Biafra were invited to the conference room, one after the other, to state their positions.[165] The leader of the federal delegation led off with a familiar but very short call for the renunciation of secession in the interests of peace and unity in Nigeria and throughout Africa.[166] The remainder of Commissioner Okunnu's remarks dealt with proposals for guaranteeing the security of Ibos in Nigeria. These were the same assurances that had been conveyed to the Biafrans in Addis Ababa nine months earlier, which allowed for the establishment of an external observer force to provide added confidence and security for Ibos in areas currently under Biafran control.

---

tions with the Biafran lobby in the Accra area raised fears in Lagos that Ankrah and the remnants of his government had fallen prey to Biafran influence.

[164] As on previous occasions, the host government ensured that Biafra's international status as a nonrecognized sovereignty was recognized by protocol and the allocation of housing and other facilities. The Biafran delegation to Monrovia was, for example, housed at the Liberian government's Hospitality Centre, while all other delegations stayed at the Ducor International Hotel.

[165] OAU, *Confidential Report of the OAU Consultative Committee on Nigeria.* Addis Ababa, September 1969, Sixth Ordinary Session of the Assembly of African Heads of State and Government, AHG/41, Address of H.I.M. Haile Selassie I, Monrovia, April 18, 1969, Annex III; and Address of Welcome from H. E. William V. S. Tubman, President of Liberia, Annex II. (cited hereafter as OAU, *Confidential Report of the OAU Consultative Committee*).

[166] *Ibid.*, Statement by the Nigerian Delegation at the conference of the OAU Consultative Committee, Monrovia, AHG/41, Annex IV.

The leader of the Biafran delegation also restated his government's well-known demands, specifically the call for an immediate cease-fire, but unlike his federal counterpart, he offered no proposals.[167] Instead, he made a lengthy review of the historical factors bearing on the secession and devoted the remainder of his address to condemning the federal government, Britain, Russia, Algeria, and Egypt for the continuation of the war. The OAU was also blamed for not taking a stronger stand in favor of a cease-fire. Buried in the final paragraph of his speech was the following sentence, which subsequently became the focus of the committee's interest: "Twenty-one months of war, of indiscriminate bombing, of mass murder by Nigerian troops, have only served to increase not only our anxiety but a feeling of bitterness which makes immediate political unity an impossibility."[168]

When the committee resumed in private session after hearing from both sides, President Tubman was the first to speak and seized Mbanefo's reference to "immediate political unity" as suggesting that the Biafrans were opening the door for eventual political unity.[169] To verify this, the Liberian president proposed that a small subcommittee of two or three members be appointed to meet the Biafran delegation in camera to find out from them whether a face-saving formula could be drawn up for the cessation of hostilities and the opening of substantive negotiations based on an agreement to uphold the territorial integrity of Nigeria. The Consultative Committee agreed to the suggestion, and Tubman and President Diori were designated to meet with Sir Louis Mbanefo.

Before the full session adjourned to enable the subcommittee to carry out its assignment, other members of the Consultative Committee expressed their views on the role of the committee at this stage in the crisis. Presidents Ahidjo and Mobutu reminded the others that, in accordance with the Kinshasa and Algiers resolutions, the committee's only function was to help the federal government maintain the unity and territorial integrity of Nigeria. They urged the committee to be frank with the Biafrans, and tell them they had erred by seceding and should renounce their past mistake immediately. President Tubman intervened again to discourage the apportioning of blame, recommending instead

---

[167] *Ibid.*, Opening Statement by Sir Louis Mbanefo at the conference of the OAU Consultative Committee, Monrovia, AHG/41, Annex V.

[168] *Ibid.*

[169] The following discussion of the closed-door proceedings is based on the Executive Council Information Paper, "Meeting of the OAU Consultative Committee on Nigeria Held in Monrovia—17–20 April 1969," submitted by the vice chairman of the National Liberation Council, J.W.K. Harlley, to Ghana's ruling National Liberation Council (cited hereafter as Harlley Report); and OAU, *Confidential Report of the OAU Consultative Committee.*

a more positive approach in their efforts to persuade Biafra to abandon its secession.

The Ghanaian delegate, J.W.K. Harlley, was the most pro-Biafran member of the committee, and he advocated an immediate cease-fire and the imposition of an embargo on the shipment of arms to both sides in the conflict. Presidents Mobutu and Ahidjo promptly expressed reservations about any embargo placed on the supply of arms to Nigeria, which, they contended, had the sovereign right to buy arms to protect itself. Ahidjo further referred to the massive flow of arms into Biafra in spite of the federal government's efforts, and concluded this was proof that the proposed embargo would achieve nothing. Following this exchange, the meeting recessed for the day to allow the subcommittee to meet with the Biafran delegation.

The Tubman-Diori-Mbanefo talks lasted well into the night, and continued the following morning, Saturday, April 19. The plenary session of the full committee was to have resumed at 10:00 A.M., but had to be postponed until 1:30 P.M. When the delegates finally met, attention was directed to the following formula, which had been prepared by the subcommittee and had the tentative approval of the Biafran delegation:

> Upon the request of the Consultative Committee of the OAU on Nigeria, the *two parties* to the Civil War accept in the superior interest of Africa to initiate negotiations on the basis of *the return to a normal situation in the country* and ensuring all forms of security and guarantee of rights and privileges to the citizens as a whole.
>
> Within the context of this Agreement, the two parties accept an immediate cessation of the fighting and the opening without delay of peace negotiations.
>
> The Consultative Committee of the OAU on Nigeria offers its good offices in order to facilitate these negotiations.[170]

For the Biafrans, the above text represented a major diplomatic advance from the prevailing OAU resolution on Nigeria, which had been approved during the September 1968 summit in Algiers. The resolution, which the Assembly of African Heads of State and Government had approved 34 to 4, had not mentioned the Consultative Committee's good offices and, instead of referring to the "two parties to the Civil War," appealed "to the secessionist leaders to cooperate with the federal authorities in order to restore peace and unity in Nigeria." Although Presidents Tubman and Diori lacked the authority to suggest

---

[170] Text of the Subcommittee's formula is included in the Harlley Report, Appendix V. Emphasis added.

316

that the committee ignore its original mandate and offer to mediate the dispute, thereby exceeding its function as a consultative body to the federal government, they were obviously seeking a formula that would facilitate full-scale peace talks under OAU auspices.

When the Tubman/Diori draft was shown to the Nigerians, Femi Okunnu said that he was prepared to accept it, providing negotiations would not be initiated "on the basis of the return to a normal situation in the country." The phrase was deemed too ambiguous, because it left open the possibility of a return to the four semiautonomous regions that Ojukwu claimed had been ratified by the Supreme Military Council during their January 1966 meeting in Aburi, Ghana. As a "compromise," Okunnu proposed that any future negotiations be undertaken on the basis of a "federally united Nigeria."[171] With the Nigerian army firmly in control of the Eastern minority areas, he conceded that there no longer was a need to refer explicitly to the twelve-state federal structure.

The committee discussed the amendment briefly and agreed to accept it, subject to the dropping of the word "federally" from the phrase "federally united Nigeria." Okunnu accepted the change, and the committee commended the federal delegation for accepting the formula. They promised to try to persuade the Biafrans to accept the revised formula, but before doing so they decided that, if Mbanefo rejected it, the formula should remain as is and be published in the form of a declaration with a brief comment to the effect that the federal side had approved the plan, but it had been rejected by Biafra.

Sir Louis reentered the conference room, read the altered statement, and announced that as a jurist he could not accept anything he did not fully understand. In the present context, he claimed he did not understand what the term "united Nigeria" stood for; with the abrogation of the Nigerian constitution and the assumption of supreme power by General Gowon in 1967, Nigeria had no constitution. If he accepted the formula as it stood, the chief justice continued, he would only be surrendering his people to the final authority of General Gowon.

By previous agreement, the heads of all six delegations, one after another, appealed to Sir Louis to reconsider his position. At one stage, President Tubman, paraphrasing the Bible, reminded the chief justice that "the letter killeth but the spirit giveth life," and said that he should consider the spirit and not the letter of the revised formula and accept it. In reply to all these appeals, Mbanefo firmly reiterated his objections, but offered to submit another draft formula that would make

[171] Text of the federal version of the Subcommittee's formula is included in the Harlley Report, Appendix VI.

the subject of a united Nigeria one of the topics for negotiation at the conference table after a cease-fire had been achieved. This the committee declined to consider.

It was apparent to the committee that, in spite of Biafra's weakening position on the battlefield, Ojukwu would not change the stand he had taken throughout the crisis. The members therefore proceeded to discuss their final communiqué. Presidents Tubman and Diori suggested that the communiqué should indicate precisely what in the proposed formula had been rejected by the Biafrans, but at the insistence of Presidents Ahidjo and Mobutu, it was decided to place the blame for the failure of the meeting squarely on the Biafrans. Two documents were released to the press on the morning of April 20: a "Declaration" setting forth the negotiating formula approved by Lagos, followed by the committee's regrets that the Biafrans did not accept the proposals, and a "final communiqué" giving a brief account of the work done by the committee, blaming the Biafrans for the failure to produce a settlement, and appealing to Biafra's supporters to commit themselves to the goal of Nigerian unity.[172]

Chief Justice Mbanefo later referred to the committee's work when he complained bitterly to the Liberian press that "they [the Consultative Committee] have not advanced beyond their original stand taken at Kinshasa in September 1967, before we were even heard. . . . They are more concerned with the legitimacy of Gowon's regime than stopping the war."[173]

"The Committee of Six," Mbanefo reportedly stated on another occasion, "was ready only to accept a precondition for a cease-fire, instead of a cease-fire before anything else."[174] The precondition in dispute was nothing less than an unequivocal renunciation of secession. Mbanefo's personal commitment, as well as the brief he carried for Ojukwu, was by his own admission no different in April 1969 from what it had been in May 1968, when he had led Biafra's negotiating team to Kampala.[175]

The federal delegation to Monrovia, by comparison, perceived a certain degree of progress in the committee's decisions. Okunnu asserted that the Monrovia communiqué was "historic" because for the first time the committee had specifically endorsed the federal demand

[172] The "Declaration" and the "Final Communiqué" were published on April 20, 1969. The former has been reprinted as the "Communiqué" in Kirk-Greene, *Crisis and Conflict*, II, 375–376.

[173] Markpress Release, Gen. 576, Statement by Sir Louis Mbanefo, April 20, 1969.

[174] Radio Biafra, quoting Sir Louis Mbanefo's remarks, April 21, 1969.

[175] Interview: Mbanefo.

for a renunciation of secession prior to any cease-fire.[176] The outcome of the Monrovia preliminary talks demonstrated that foreign pressure for a truce or cease-fire was unlikely to approach the level so far encountered with regard to the continuation of relief night flights into Biafra. The latter issue was the one remaining aspect of Biafra's bid for self-determination that had not yet been politicized.

During the three months following the collapse of the Monrovia talks, Ojukwu embarked on his boldest attempt yet to internationalize the civil war. In so doing, he forced Gowon into a showdown over the question of continuing relief flights. The sequence of events leading up to the interdiction of a Swedish Red Cross plane on June 5, 1969, and the resulting domestic and international repercussions set the stage for Nigeria's decisive invasion of the Ibo heartland and Biafra's demise.

[176] Press Statement by federal commissioner for works and housing, Olufemi Okunnu, upon his return to Lagos from Monrovia, April 22, 1969.

· 11 ·

THE FUTILITY OF SECESSION

Biafra's strategy for internationalizing the civil war underwent a major shift during the second quarter of 1969. For nearly a year, secessionist forces had sought, in Ojukwu's words, "to delay the enemy until the world conscience can effectively be aroused against genocide."[1] By "effectively," Ojukwu meant governmental intervention to bring about a cease-fire and a political settlement that would guarantee the integrity and self-determination of his regime. Following the collapse of the September 1968 federal offensive, Biafran troops steadfastly defended their positions, while the world's conscience produced an outpouring of material assistance. This, however, was not enough. International political support, so necessary for the long-term survival of the Biafran state, continued to be withheld, causing Ojukwu to alter the basic thrust of his foreign policy.

Ojukwu's exasperation over the limited involvement of the Western powers became increasingly evident as 1968 drew to a close. "Let us not deceive ourselves about this humanitarian aid," he lectured a group of visiting parliamentarians from Western countries, "thousands of people are being killed by the people [of the Gowon regime] who, but for the support of those relief-offering leaders, would not be in a position to do the killing."[2] Somewhat less passionately, the senior staff at the Ministry of Foreign Affairs advised Ojukwu that Biafra's diplomatic efforts had reached a low ebb:

> In Europe and America our case gained considerable sympathy on humanitarian grounds. This was spearheaded by charitable, church and relief organisations. The humanitarian approach has backfired. Ours now is the picture of a pietous starving sickly people unviable and incapable of defending themselves from hunger and war. The image of the Biafran state has been be-clouded by this. There is an urgent need to change this image. The best way to do this would, of course, be to gain a significant military victory, but action in the diplomatic front can contribute to this also.[3]

[1] Ojukwu, *Biafra*, Address to a joint meeting of the Consultative Assembly and the Council of Chiefs and Elders, September 25, 1968, I, 353.

[2] *Ibid.*, Interview with Canadian, Dutch, and Danish parliamentarians and accompanying journalists, Umuahia, November 13, 1968, II, 89–90.

[3] Republic of Biafra, Ministry of Foreign Affairs, "Reviewing our Diplomatic Approach, Summary Conclusions of Heads of Division Staff Meeting," Umuahia, December, 1968, p. 7.

Officials in the Ministry of Foreign Affairs believed that their efforts to convert international humanitarian concern into diplomatic support had been subverted by "Anglo/American propaganda" that prevailed,

1. by showing our case for independence as based on fear of genocide and then trying to prove that Nigeria has no genocidal intentions and therefore our case for independence is baseless; and,
2. by portraying Biafra as an ephemeral state that has lost almost all its territory and is likely to collapse any moment and therefore is unworthy of serious negotiations. . . .[4]

To counter this, it was suggested that the government "play down the starvation issue and the humanitarian aspects of the crisis" and "portray Biafra as a viable state occupied in parts by an enemy but still enjoying the support from a larger part of the territory."[5] No detailed prescriptions were offered for accomplishing this, although the ministry urged government officials to become more visible by issuing statements to the international press that would remind the world that Biafra was, above all, a political entity. "Henceforth," they continued, "we should only emphasize self-determination, British intervention and the imperialist aspects of the conflict."[6]

Ojukwu concurred with the ministry's analysis, but he realized that his ability to manage the international "Biafran lobby" was extremely limited. With no official diplomatic missions beyond the three in Africa,[7] and only seven information offices overseas,[8] Biafra's envoys obviously lacked the trappings of statehood. Before Biafra could engender the respect of foreign powers, however, Ojukwu believed that he had to alter dramatically his military and political policies at home.

BIAFRA GOES ON THE OFFENSIVE

The theme for this fresh attempt to penetrate the international system was Biafran self-reliance, incredible as this may appear in retrospect. Notwithstanding the realities of economic deprivation and a nearly total dependence on humanitarian relief. Ojukwu sought by mid-1969 to

---

[4] *Ibid.*, p. 5.   [5] *Ibid.*, p. 6.   [6] *Ibid.*, p. 7.

[7] Abidjan, Libreville, and Dar es Salaam. The Tanzanian mission serviced Zambia.

[8] By early 1969, Biafra had overseas missions in Lisbon, London, Wiesbaden (Federal Republic of Germany), Amsterdam, Paris, Washington, and Stockholm. In addition, there was a very small office in New York. Matters related to relief and the public relations operations in Geneva were handled from the German mission. Interview: Luke Obi, chief political officer, Biafran Ministry of Foreign Affairs.

infuse his flagging rebellion with an aura of permanency by undertaking a series of aggressive military maneuvers, together with the launching of a Land Army food production program. Rather than continuing to appeal for intervention on humanitarian grounds, Biafra would now seek to demonstrate that it possessed the military capability to attack and destroy targets beyond the Ibo enclave, notably foreign-owned oil installations in the Midwest and Rivers States (see Map 11–1). In addition, the Biafrans would try to convince the world that even if they failed in conventional military terms, they were sufficiently armed and politically mobilized to wage interminable guerrilla warfare in and around the Ibo heartland. All subsequent demonstrations of defiance to the reimposition of Nigerian rule were portrayed internationally as part of a new "Biafran Revolution," the key symbol of the most audacious propaganda effort of the war.

The Biafrans delayed the military phase of their campaign until the start of the rainy season, when Ojukwu's small attack groups would have the advantage and the federal army was likely to be stalled with resupply problems. Also, the enclave's defenses were steadily improving and the Biafrans had developed contingency plans for importing arms, either by air drop or to alternative stretches of reinforced roads, should the federal planes attempt to destroy Uli. Ojukwu continued to count on international public opinion to restrain Britain or any other Western power from stepping in with a major increment to military support for Lagos and, in the event that the Soviets made any dramatic move to upgrade Nigeria's military capability, he anticipated that this might at last force Nixon's hand in his favor.[9]

Another factor in the equation that Ojukwu and his advisers were formulating in early 1969 is worth mentioning briefly. For several months previously, there had been sporadic violence in the Western State of Nigeria over a 5 percent tax increase to cover war costs. Highly speculative reports about the significance of these disturbances appeared in the world press, prompting the governor of the Western State to issue a public denial of claims that the Yorubas were planning to overthrow the federal government.[10] The stories abroad of mounting public

[9] Interview: Ojukwu.

[10] *The Times* (London), September 11, 1968. Reports of mounting dissatisfaction and war-weariness that appeared in the European press bore little relationship to life in Lagos, the predominantly Yoruba federal capital. Perhaps more indicative was a decree issued by the military governor of Lagos State on September 5, 1968, curbing "drumming and other forms of outdoor merriment in Lagos," and deploring "the atmosphere of complacency and frivolity which had become a feature of Lagos and other places far away from the fighting areas." Henceforth, anyone wishing to hold an outdoor wedding, naming ceremony, or other traditional celebration was required to contribute $30.00 to the Armed Forces Comfort Fund. Nigeria, Federal Ministry of Information, Press Release No. F.1575, September 5, 1968.

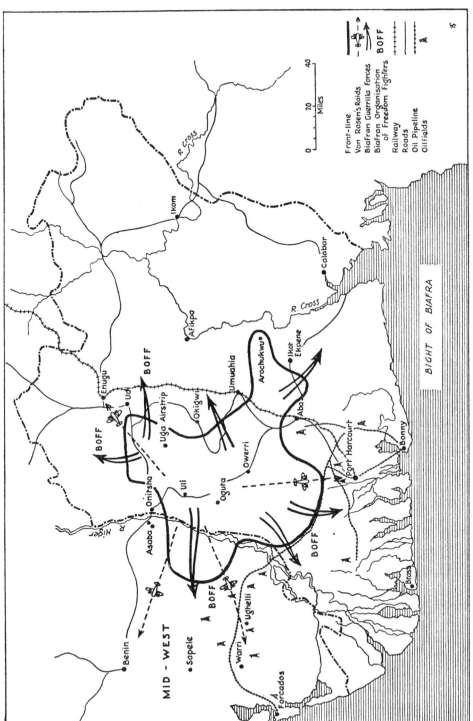

Map 11–1 • Biafra, June 1969 (from John de St. Jorre, *The Nigerian Civil War*, p. 362)

dissatisfaction over Gowon's war policies continued to grow as the year ended,[11] and these, naturally, were read with great interest inside Biafra.[12] Throughout the conflict, the Biafrans fed on rumors of a resurgence of ethnic rivalries on the other side, and they sought to promote dissension in all ways possible. They believed that one way of doing this was to secure a cease-fire, which would open the way for a resumption of political bargaining with all the tension that might entail. By late 1968, Ojukwu sensed that a more immediate way of stirring up chaos, in light of the reports of violence in the Western State, would be to mount new military initiatives in order to undermine further the credibility of Gowon's past promises for a quick end to the war, and thereby exacerbate frustrations elsewhere in Nigeria.

Plans for the revitalization of Biafran resistance evolved quickly during Christmas 1968. A catalyst in these discussions was the Swedish flying ace, sixty-year-old Count Gustav von Rosen, who spent the holidays with Ojukwu.[13] Von Rosen, one may recall, had helped the churches defy the federal blockade by flying a Transair Sweden DC–7B into Biafra on August 13, 1968, thus opening the way for the nightly air bridge.[14] The Count briefly served as chief of operations for Nord-churchaid, but resigned in late September after causing the churches considerable embarrassment by candidly telling a press conference how important it was to bring arms and ammunition to Biafra in addition to food and medicine.[15] Now back in Biafra, he suggested to Ojukwu that by acquiring small propeller-driven aircraft, much damage could be done to federal military and economic targets in the coastal and Mid-west areas. This suggestion matched neatly with the Biafran leader's own plans to infiltrate saboteurs into federally held areas to demonstrate to Lagos and the world that Nigerian claims of control over the oc-cupied areas of the former Eastern Region were invalid.

Five months would pass before Ojukwu would acquire his tiny air

[11] For a detailed analysis of the situation in the Western State, see *Observer Foreign News Service*, October 21, 1968. *The Christian Science Monitor* reported on December 27, 1968, that thirty-five people had been killed as a result of "po-litical infighting among the Yorubas, discontent with the civil war and local grievances."

[12] For a discussion of how the Biafran Ministry of Information monitored the international press coverage of events in Nigeria and forwarded detailed press summaries to Ojukwu, see Anafulu, "An African Experience," pp. 32–40.

[13] For a description of von Rosen's background and activities in the Nigerian crisis, see "Von Rosen" by John de St. Jorre, *Observer Foreign News Service*, No. 26695, July 4, 1969. More generally, de St. Jorre, *The Nigerian Civil War*, p. 334.

[14] See: Lloyd *et al., Nordchurchaid Airlift to Biafra 1968–1970*, pp. 9–10.

[15] Diakonisches Werk, *Progress Report No. 16 on the Nigeria/Biafra Emer-gency*. Reported in a memorandum prepared by the Material Aid Desk, Division in Inter-Church Aid, World Council of Churches, Geneva, October 29, 1968.

force, deploy his guerrilla bands into the Midwest, and formally announce his ideological blueprint for the "Biafran Revolution" on June 1, 1969. In the meantime, preparations were being made. The first step in developing the justification for a claim of self-reliance was taken on January 8, 1969, when Ojukwu convened the Biafra People's Seminar, which met weekly thereafter to discuss the goals of the rebellion. Almost simultaneously, the government announced the beginning of a Land Army, which promised future self-sufficiency in food production.[16] While the Land Army obviously was born of necessity, Ojukwu also emphasized its political significance: the Land Army would prove to Nigeria and the world that the Biafrans were willing and able to care for themselves apart from the humanitarian organizations.[17] The Land Army subsequently became an important part of the propaganda campaign to convince the international community of the vitality of the "Biafran Revolution."

The central element in Biafra's renewed effort to demonstrate its resilience and self-determination, regardless of the odds, was direct military action against the overextended and poorly coordinated federal troops. Ironically, the first clear indication of this new aggressiveness occurred immediately after the fall of Umuahia, which had been Biafra's capital for the previous eighteen months and, more recently, was the only urban center still under Ojukwu's administration.[18] Control of Umuahia did not, however, carry any strategic advantages, and the damage to Biafra's international image as a result of the loss of Umuahia was offset three days later, when Biafran troops suddenly counterattacked and retook the town of Owerri on April 25, 1969.[19] Owerri was the first and only important Ibo township to revert to Biafran control, and it quickly became the new seat of Ojukwu's highly mobile government—the symbol of Biafra's commitment to continue the struggle.[20]

Less than a week after the recapture of Owerri, Radio Biafra announced that Biafran forces had crossed into the Midwest and seized

[16] Ojukwu, *Biafra*, address at the Biafran Agricultural Seminar, Afor-Ugiri, January 17, 1969, II, 66–73; also, *New York Times*, February 12, 1969.

[17] *Biafra Newsletter*, Vol. 2, No. 7, February 28, 1969.

[18] *Morning Post*, April 24, 1969. For accounts of the battle, see *Sunday Telegraph*, April 20 and 27, 1969. Umuahia, which had served as Biafra's capital since the loss of Enugu in October 1967, had a prewar population of 17,000, and when it fell to federal troops it was the only major town of the former Eastern Region under Ojukwu's control.

[19] Markpress Release, Gen. 581, April 25, 1969. For an account of the battle, see *The Times* (London), April 28, 1969.

[20] Actually, while the remnants of Biafra's civil service moved their offices to Owerri, Ojukwu's headquarters—code-named "Madonna One"—were in the compound of a church school in the nearby village of Etiti.

control of the town of Aboh.[21] A few days later, Lieutenant Colonel Ojukwu "accepted" the rank of general from the Biafran Consultative Assembly[22] amid proliferating reports of stepped-up military activity in the Midwest and Rivers States.[23] By late May, the *New York Times* reported that as many as 3,000 Biafran guerrillas were operating west of the Niger River.[24] Much to Nigeria's chagrin, Ojukwu's tattered army had suddenly transformed the normally dreary rainy season into one of the more violent and unpredictable phases of the conflict.

Complementing the infiltration of Biafran troops into the Midwest were the surprise attacks from the air by a squadron of tiny propeller-driven trainer planes equipped with rockets. Biafra had been without an operational air force since the ineffective attempts to bomb Lagos with a World War II B–26 just after the secession started. Following the Christmas 1968 meeting with Count von Rosen. Ojukwu decided that revitalization of the Biafran air force was feasible, and he sent his approval for the purchase in Sweden of five minicon aircraft from a subsidiary of SAAB, for a total cost of only $51,600.[25] Because it is illegal in Sweden to export arms to countries engaged in civil or international conflict, an elaborate smokescreen was contrived whereby the Tanzanian government bought the unarmed MFI–9b version, ostensibly for training purposes.[26] French-made Matra rockets and carriages, twelve per plane, were purchased in France, with the actual fitting and test flights conducted in Gabon. Von Rosen held command over Biafra's operational air staff, which included two other Swedish pilots, two Biafran pilots, a Swedish mechanic, and a Swedish instructor.[27]

Von Rosen's first sortie was on May 22, 1969. The squadron attacked the federal air field and oil installations at Port Harcourt, where the Biafrans claimed to have destroyed two MIGs and one Illyushin 28 bomber on the tarmac, and to have set the oil refinery ablaze.[28] Two days later they rocketed air fields and divisional headquarters at Benin and Enugu. Within a week, the Biafrans claimed to have

[21] Markpress Release, Gen. 586, April 30, 1969.

[22] Markpress Release, Gen. 597, May 11, 1969. The rank was conferred on May 4, 1969.

[23] Markpress Release, Gen. 594, May 9, 1969.

[24] *New York Times,* May 26, 1969.

[25] De St. Jorre, *The Nigerian Civil War,* account of an interview the author held with von Rosen, p. 334. Also, see: Cronje, *The World and Nigeria,* pp. 148–153.

[26] On May 27, 1969, the Swedish government issued a statement disassociating itself from the actions of Count von Rosen. Stockholm *Expressen,* May 27, 1969.

[27] Suzanne Cronje reports that of the two original Biafran pilots, one was killed and the other joined Nigeria Airways as a commercial pilot soon after the war. *Nigeria and the World,* p. 154.

[28] Markpress Release, Gen. 613, May 26, 1969.

destroyed eleven Nigerian planes without taking any ground fire in return.[29] A week later, the minicons extended their field of targets with an attack against the Nigerian power station at Ughelli.[30] This meant that the tiny aircraft had an effective range of at least 200 miles, and would be able to hit Shell-BP's rapidly growing Midwest operations and the principal installations of Gulf Oil, the largest American producer in Nigeria—and the company least affected by the war to date.[31] According to British press reports, Gulf's storage tanks off the Escravos estuary were severely damaged by the minicons in early August.[32]

Emboldened by the initial success of the minicons, Ojukwu announced to the world that he would not be satisfied until the "sinews of war on land and off-shore" were eliminated.[33] This meant not only the Nigerian air fields, communication facilities, and other military targets, but the oil installations as well. "Oil," he declared in early June, "is the mainstay of the Nigerian economy and it is from oil that they obtain all the necessary credits for the prosecution of this futile war."[34] Unstated, but equally important, was the assumption that governments with important oil interests in Nigeria would begin pressuring Lagos to accept an unconditional cease-fire.[35] Underscoring his commitment to the air war, Ojukwu imported another four minicons in July, bringing the total to nine.[36]

The minicon and guerrilla attacks against federal positions must be seen as having only tactical significance; Biafra never acquired the military capability to mount a major counteroffensive sufficient to reoccupy the lost territory of the former Eastern Region. Rebel propagandists

[29] Markpress Release, Gen. 616, May 27, 1969. The minicons flew so irregularly and at such low altitudes that they were out of range of federal antiaircraft fire. Most of the flak, ironically, came from Swedish Bofors.

[30] Markpress Release, Gen. 624, June 2, 1969.

[31] Gulf had invested nearly $200 million in its Midwest concessions by early 1969, and was producing 200,000 barrels per day, or nearly 40 percent of Nigeria's total output at that time. Nigeria, Federal Ministry of Information, Press Release No. F.136, February 5, 1969. The implications of these latest air attacks for British and other foreign investments in petroleum were spelled out in detail by the *Financial Times*, May 31, 1969.

[32] *Daily Telegraph*, August 15, 1969.

[33] Ojukwu, Address on the Occasion of the Second Anniversary of Biafra, June 1, 1969, reprinted in Markpress Release, Gen. 632.

[34] Markpress Release, Gen. 653, June 6, 1969.

[35] Interview: Ojukwu. The Biafran leader discounted the possibility that the affront to foreign interests might prompt them to intervene to help Nigeria win the war because: a. he felt the increment of field equipment necessary to tip the scales was too great, particularly during the rainy season; and b. public opinion would not tolerate any attempt to interdict his vital nightly airlift of humanitarian and military supplies.

[36] By the end of the war only one or two of the minicons remained; most of the others were destroyed on the ground by federal jets.

nonetheless sought to convince everyone that the escalation in military activity posed a credible long-term threat to foreign and Nigerian interests.[37] Simultaneously, Ojukwu tried to transform the image of Biafra as a helpless ward of international philanthropy by issuing a 20,000-word statement entitled, "The Ahiara Declaration: the Principles of the Biafran Revolution."[38] Augmenting the Ahiara Declaration was the publication in New York of a large volume entitled *Biafra: Selected Speeches and Random Thoughts of C. Odumegwu Ojukwu.*[39]

The Ahiara Declaration was intended for two audiences: the international community and the Biafran elite. Regarding the former, Biafra's director of propaganda recalls:

> We had reached the end of our present propaganda line. Within Africa we found it impossible to refute the balkanization argument while Western Europe remained convinced of the benefits accruing from a larger [Nigeria] economic unit. Mere sentiment in our propaganda was getting nowhere . . . the threat of genocide was no longer credible and simply not true. By 1969 we knew that the only question that mattered to foreign governments and investors, however friendly, was: can Biafra survive? Ahiara was meant to answer those questions and to demonstrate that Biafra stood for something . . . [although] its vagueness was its basic fault.[40]

At the same time, he continued,

> Biafra was collapsing under its own weight of corruption. Relief goods were not getting to the people, army officers were commandeering property. . . . If we could have introduced a more just and

[37] Radio Biafra declared, for example: "The times are now more auspicious than they ever were before. To our defence is now being added a new dimension, an operational air force. Our enemy has been shocked by the striking power of the Biafran air force. We assure them that this is but the beginning. The BBC with its lying propaganda has referred to our air power as a mere gesture. We will tell them it will be permanent and enduring." *Newstalk*, May 30, 1969.

[38] Ahiara is the name of the village in which the address was delivered on June 1, 1969. The name sounds suspiciously similar to President Julius Nyerere's famous "Arusha Declaration," which set forth Tanzania's version of African socialism.

[39] C. Odumegwu Ojukwu, *Biafra: Selected Speeches and Random Thoughts of C. Odumegwu Ojukwu* (New York: Harper & Row, 1969), 643 pp. Ojukwu had suggested a compilation of his major speeches in January 1969 and instructed they be organized around themes that would imply an anticipation of the Ahiara Declaration. Interview: Uche Chukwumerije, director of propaganda and the principal editor of the book. Although the preface is dated May 30, 1969, to coincide with Biafra's second anniversary and the launching of Ahiara, the volume did not reach the world market until November 1969, barely two months before Biafra's collapse.

[40] Interview: Chukwumerije.

humane and equitable society then it would have been possible, we believed, to extend the conflict while giving currency abroad to the notion that Biafra had viable prospects.[41]

Thousands of copies of the Ahiara Declaration were published by Markpress and distributed in the form of a little green book, complete with a picture of Ojukwu dressed in Castro-type fatigues, bearing the rank of "General of the People's Army." The statement was a synthesis of the weekly meetings among groups of Biafran intellectuals and "average citizens," which had begun on January 8, 1969.[42] It purported to redefine the structure of Ibo society, but it was merely a *mélange* of vaguely socialist pronouncements anticipating some sort of Christian utopia in a peace-loving Biafra of the future.[43]

Ojukwu's admonishments to the Biafran elite were quite specific: "We have among us some members of the police and judiciary who are corrupt and 'eat bribes.' . . . Even while we are engaged in a war of national survival we see some public officials who throw huge parties to entertain their friends; who kill cows to christen their babies."[44] His socialist prescriptions were, however, very ambiguous. The reference to private property offers a good illustration:

In the New Biafra, all property belongs to the Community. Every individual must consider all he has . . . as belonging to the community for which he holds it in trust. This principle does not mean the abolition of personal property but it implies that the State, acting on behalf of the community, can intervene in the disposition of property. . . . While the Biafran Revolution will foster private economic enterprise and initiative, it should remain constantly alive to the dangers of some citizens accumulating large private fortunes.[45]

The reason for such double talk was the desire not to offend Western capitalists, Eastern socialists, or members of the Ibo elite whose acquisitiveness was justifiably famous, and whose continued allegiance to the

[41] *Ibid.*

[42] Preparation of the Ahiara Declaration was assigned to two socialists from the faculty of the University of Nsukka, Dr. Ikem Enzimiro and Dr. E. Obiechina. They were joined by more moderate intellectuals, such as the commissioner for information, Dr. Ifeagwu Eke, and author Chinua Achebe.

[43] More than one-half of the address was devoted to a familiar account of the history of conflicts with the federal military government. At the heart of the more theoretical closing sections were the Seven Principles of the Biafran Revolution: 1. a belief in the sanctity of human life; 2. rejection of genocide; 3. a belief in patriotism; 4. renunciation of tribalism; 5. respect for civic rights; 6. "power belongs to the people"; and 7. public accountability. Republic of Biafra, *Ahiara Declaration* (Geneva: Markpress, 1969), pp. 27–30.

[44] Biafra, *Ahiara Declaration*, pp. 24–25.

[45] *Ibid.*, pp. 32–33.

regime was absolutely essential.[46] As it turned out, the statement on private property caused such consternation among the Ibo elite that Ojukwu eventually had to clarify his intentions, assuring any wavering supporters that to be against private ownership "would be contrary to the tenets of social justice."[47]

A frequently heard complaint from Biafran intellectuals after the war was that Ahiara failed to have an impact internationally because Western powers saw the document as a veiled move toward communism, or at least a forecast of a hostile investment climate, and this made them less inclined to support Biafra, while the Socialist powers presumably regarded Ahiara as only a primitive version of African socialism, and were contemptuous.[48] In fact, the promulgation of Ahiara was all but ignored abroad.

NIGERIA RETALIATES

Biafra's military exploits were a costly gamble, politically and militarily. The short-run impact on Nigeria's oil production, while serious, was exaggerated by Biafran propagandists. Following the attacks from the minicons and guerrillas, production fell approximately 18 percent to 470,000 barrels per day in July-August 1969, but recovered to 506,000 barrels per day in September and went on to a new high of 663,000 during October.[49] The brief decline in petroleum earnings did not disrupt an otherwise prosperous Nigerian economy.[50] Instead, the attacks provoked a stiffened resolve among Nigeria's leaders to crush the rebellion, and they caused General Gowon to make several difficult but important decisions that he had hitherto resisted.

The loss of Owerri on April 22, 1969, and the Biafran occupation of the Midwestern town of Aboh a few days later prompted Gowon to

[46] Interview: Chukwumerije.

[47] Markpress Release, Gen. 746, "Address to a joint meeting of Chiefs and Elders and Members of the Consultative Assembly," October 31, 1969.

[48] Interviews: Dr. I. Nzimero and Dr. E. Obiechina, who took a leading role in drafting the more theoretical sections of Ahiara, and subsequently headed Biafra's ill-starred "National Orientation College"; also, Dr. Michael Echerue, head of the War Information Bureau; J. Onuoha, head of the Public Enlightenment Committee.

[49] The federal government ceased publishing national oil production statistics in August 1969 for "reasons of security," but the figures eventually appeared in the 1970 monthly figures compiled by the Lagos Chamber of Commerce and Industry.

[50] Ojukwu always overestimated the importance of petroleum in Nigeria's foreign exchange picture and underestimated the strength of the Nigerian economy. While the federal government had to impose severe import restrictions and endure considerable deficit financing internally, the country's foreign exchange position never became desperate because of earnings from agriculture. See Nafziger, "The Economic Impact of the Nigerian Civil War," pp. 233–236.

convene a meeting of the Supreme Military Council in Lagos on May 7, 1969, and to order the most sweeping army reorganization of the war. All three divisional commanders were replaced, and the Second Division was withdrawn from the Onitsha sector and redeployed as a security force in the Midwest.[51] Although the changes of command received very little attention abroad, Nigerian and Biafran policy makers now tend to regard them as a major development with important domestic and international political implications.

The key element in the shakeup was the removal of the fiery "Black Scorpion," Col. Benjamin Adekunle, from the Third Division and his replacement by Col. Olusegun Obasanjo, a military engineer whose fairness and authority was greatly respected among the rank and file. Adekunle had become a war hero following the invasion of Port Harcourt, but he also had acquired a reputation for boundless and reckless ambition, and many of his press statements were politically embarrassing to the federal government.[52] His outspoken antipathy for Ibos played into the hands of Biafran propagandists, who treated such comments as evidence of genocidal intent.[53] Gowon had wanted to remove Adekunle for some months, but was apprehensive about hostile reaction from the Yorubas. The loss of Owerri made the decision easier although to demonstrate that tribal factors were not a consideration, he was compelled to shift his other field commanders simultaneously.

News of Adekunle's reassignment to the directorship of training and planning in Lagos no doubt pleased officials in London and Washington, while inside Biafra the change further reduced the fear of postwar persecutions. The political importance of this change of commanders was summed up by the chief political officer in the Biafran Ministry of Foreign Affairs:

> Obasanjo [Adekunle's replacement] won the war for Nigeria. The change of commanders was crucial. Prior to their replacement

[51] Col. I. D. Bisalla replaced Col. Mohammed Shuwa as the second GOC of the First Division; Lieutenant Colonel Jalo replaced Colonel Haruna as the third GOC of the Second Division; and Colonel Obasanjo replaced Col. Adekunle as the second GOC of the Third Marine Commandos.

[52] One of the most publicized incidents was his mistreatment of the International Observer Team, whose presence he often condemned as another illustration of white paternalism. He publicly denounced Sweden for its pornography, criticized Canada's treatment of Indians, and even threatened to flog one of the team's members for not following his instructions. *Daily Telegraph*, October 31, 1968.

[53] The August 24, 1968, *The Economist* quoted Adekunle as saying: "I want to prevent even one Ibo having even one piece to eat before their capitulation. We shoot at everything that moves, and when our forces march into the center of Ibo territory, we shoot at everything, even at things that do not move." Such statements led the director of Biafran propaganda, Uche Chukwumerije, later to refer to Adekunle as "our secret weapon." Interview: Chukwumerije.

Adekunle behaved in a bloodthirsty vengeful manner which helped us to project the danger to Biafran security internationally and internally. Some of the BOFF [Biafran Organization of Freedom Fighters] infiltrators would come back from the Midwest with terrible tales of atrocities that gave new force to long-standing fears. In 1969 the situation changed dramatically. BOFF infiltrators either stayed or returned with reports of fair treatment, shelter, food, etc. This took much of the fear out of the hearts of the Biafran people.[54]

Another unanticipated side-effect of the Biafran attacks west of the Niger followed the May 9, 1969, raid against the AGIP oil drilling sites in the Okpai area. Eleven Europeans were killed in the process and eighteen captured—fourteen Italians, three Germans, and one Lebanese[55]—thereby touching off the sharpest international criticisms of Biafra to date. Despite demands for the release of the eighteen from the Vatican and German and Italian governments, a Biafran tribunal summarily tried them as spies and sentenced them to death.[56] A flurry of diplomatic activity followed as U Thant, ICRC President Naville, Pope Paul, and the presidents of Ivory Coast, Gabon, Tanzania, and Zambia personally appealed to General Ojukwu for mercy.[57] There were also reports of Portuguese pressure to evict Biafrans from Sao Tomé and from Lisbon should they fail to return the oil men.[58] According to Ojukwu, however, the most serious threat came from the French, who sharply curtailed military shipments to West Africa immediately following the incident.[59]

The Biafran leader bitterly denounced the international furor, telling his people: "For eighteen white men, Europe is aroused! What have they said about our millions?"[60] Privately, he quickly concluded that his enemies were using the plight of the oil men to hide the fact that Biafran troops were able to operate with impunity across federal lines and into the Midwest. While not insensitive to the irony of his predicament,

[54] Interview: Luke Obi, chief political officer, Biafran Ministry of Foreign Affairs, subsequently a representative in Germany, and Ojukwu's principal liaison with the European relief agencies.

[55] *Daily Telegraph*, May 15, 1969, and Markpress Release, Gen. 623, June 2, 1969.

[56] Markpress Release, Gen. 638, June 3, 1969.

[57] U Thant and Marcel Naville issued public appeals while the Vatican dispatched Monsignor Karl Bayer, secretary general of Caritas, to Biafra on May 23. A week later a delegation comprising the Ivorian defense minister, a Gabonese representative, and, most importantly in terms of international prestige, Italy's Foreign Undersecretary Mario Pedini, flew to Biafra for discussions with Ojukwu.

[58] *Daily Telegraph*, June 5, 1969.   [59] Interview: Ojukwu.

[60] Statement over Radio Biafra, June 2, 1969. Also *Newstalk*, June 3, 1969, commented: "One million men are fit for the grave merely because they are black while the twenty-nine are not because they are white."

Ojukwu was furious that his military successes were being obscured by another "human drama." He also believed that the oil-men incident served Nigeria's purposes by distracting international attention from the Ahiara Declaration and the bid to project a new image of Biafran self-reliance.[61]

On June 5, 1969, Ojukwu yielded to foreign pressure and granted the men a reprieve, allowing them to leave Biafra.[62] There were reports of a sizable ranson from the Italian government and ENI, AGIP's parent company.[63] Regardless of the amount, the damage that the incident did to Biafra's moral authority appears to have been considerable. Nigeria's ambassador to Rome asserts that the oil-men dispute "broke Ojukwu's back in Italy," an assessment confirmed by Italian diplomats and reviews of the Italian press. *Il Messagero* compared the death sentence with the verdicts of Nazi courts, and another paper described Biafra as "outside the pale of civilized society."[64]

The killing of eleven European oil men and the related damage by the minicons to the foreign-owned petroleum installations in the Midwest provoked Gowon to order a resumption of attacks by the Nigerian air force. Federal MIGs, which had been grounded since Prime Minister Wilson's visit in March, began hitting targets throughout Biafra during late May.[65] Hostile international reaction was minimal because the attacks were accepted as justified retaliation and, more importantly, they had acquired new accuracy. In the past, federal MIGs had been piloted by Egyptian mercenaries whose notorious disregard for where they dropped their bombs provided Biafran propagandists with many of their most shocking portrayals of Nigerian barbarity.[66] During the spring of 1969, Lagos had quietly replaced the Egyptians

[61] Interview: Ojukwu.

[62] Markpress Release, Gen. 642, June 5, 1969.

[63] The London *Financial Times* quoted Biafran sources as stating that ENI spent $3 million to win release of their men. *Financial Times*, June 21, 1969. During a conference of Nigeria's ambassadors in Lagos, June 24–25, 1969, a figure of $20 million was mentioned. Ministry of External Affairs, Conference of Nigerian Ambassadors, June 1969, Lagos, Nigeria (cited hereafter as MEA/CNA/June 1969), Policy of Nigeria toward Western Europe.

[64] *Observer Foreign News Service*, No. 25268, June 13, 1969.

[65] To quote the confidential minutes of a participant in the Fourth Plenary Conference of Jointchurchaid, held in Lucerne, Switzerland, 11–13 June, 1969: "From April to the first half of May there was no bombing whatsoever but Federal planes have now appeared again." Biafra's first acknowledgment of the resumption was an announcement on June 3, 1969, that federal planes had killed twenty-five people. Markpress Release, Gen. 636.

[66] For a complete listing of every alleged atrocity committed by the Nigerian air force between August 12, 1967, and December 24, 1968, see *Biafra Newsletter*, "Details of Raids on Biafra," Vol. 2, No. 6, January 17, 1969. For a succinct summary of the charges and countercharges, see Cronje, *Nigeria and the World*, pp. 120–122.

with East Germans and other Europeans who were sent to Kaduna for a quick conversion course appropriate for MIG–17s.

International outrage over the oil-men incident further convinced federal officials that the political risks of a direct confrontation with the relief agencies over the continuation of night flights into Biafra were now acceptable. Gowon was under very strong pressure from his field commanders to tighten the blockade, in light of Biafran penetration into the Midwest. The issue was not relief, which Gowon was determined to allow into the enclave, but the need to control the kinds of materiel entering Biafra. The attacks of the minicons became the last straw.

Once Gowon decided to assert greater control over Nigeria's air space, he moved with typical caution, favoring an option that would allow further escalation if conditions warranted. In early June he ordered one of his pilots, an Englishman, to interdict a transport plane destined for Biafra.[67] The pilot was directed to force the plane to land at Port Harcourt for inspection and, in order to permit visual identification and guidance to Port Harcourt, contact was to be made before nightfall. The first flight into Uli air strip on June 5, 1969, entered Nigerian airspace just before dark and was plainly marked "Joint-churchaid-USA." Five mniutes later, a DC–7 with Swedish Red Cross markings followed. A federal MIG–17 picked up the first plane, tailed it for a while, and peeled off. Moments later, the attacker sighted the Swedish plane.[68] According to an American defense attaché in Lagos who claims to have had two days' prior notice of the interdiction and first-hand knowledge of the monitored radio exchanges, the MIG first buzzed the relief plane as the Englishman ordered the Swede to land at Port Harcourt for inspection. The latter refused and headed for cloud cover. The MIG made another pass and fired warning shots across the wing tips of the relief plane. When this also failed to move the Swede toward Port Harcourt, the English flier made a third pass and shot off the whole wing.[69]

The tactical choice of interdicting a Red Cross plane in preference to the Jointchurchaid carrier is explained by the federal director of relief and rehabilitation:

> If we had shot down a JCA plane they were under no legal obligation to announce it and would just go on flying. The Red Cross was obliged to announce the shooting of any of its planes and that was

[67] Interview: defense attaché, U.S. embassy, Lagos.

[68] Details of this sequence were recounted to John de St. Jorre by the pilot of the Jointchurchaid plane, Peter Know. De St. Jorre, *The Nigerian Civil War*, p. 332.

[69] *Ibid*. Also confirmed by American and British diplomats in Lagos.

important. The ICRC presides over government protocol which it feels compelled to respect; after all it has no funds of its own or materials to disperse other than what member governments choose to give it—and Nigeria was continually dealing with those governments.[70]

The fact that the Red Cross plane was of Swedish origin was fortuitous for Lagos, because it reinforced the implicit message that the act was in reprisal for the bombings by Count von Rosen's squadron of Swedish minicons.

The next day, June 6, 1969, a carefully worded, low-key press release was issued to justify the action, while the federal government awaited reaction from abroad. Referring to the downing, disingenuously, as a "case of mistaken identity," the federal government argued that the "disaster" never would have happened had the ICRC agreed to daylight flights. In the Lagos view,

> Ojukwu regarded his clandestine gun-running as more valuable than the lives of those who are feeding his ostensibly starving populace. . . . Since Ojukwu has recently reasserted [in reference to the Land Army] that there is abundant food in the secessionist area, it is difficult to understand why the multiplicity of relief organizations insist on filling the Nigerian sky with their mercy flights.[71]

The statement concluded with an assurance that the federal government was anxious to avoid such incidents in the future and a reiteration of support for the principle of humanitarian relief.

The ICRC protested the interdiction, which it branded "as unexpected as it is inexplicable," but went on to specifically blame Count von Rosen's "sudden intervention against Nigeria" for "the climate of tension and crisis," and demanded authorization from Biafra for daylight flights.[72] Red Cross planes flew two more missions into Biafra on the night of June 10–11, 1969, but then discontinued all further operations from both Fernando Po and Cotonou. Under the terms of the 1949 Geneva Convention, the ICRC could only operate subject to the consent of the parties to the conflict. Although the federal government had not withdrawn its consent in principle, Red Cross officials interpreted

[70] Interview: S. Z. Mohammed, director of Relief and Rehabilitation.

[71] Nigeria, Federal Ministry of Information, Press Release No. F.603, June 7, 1969. For a glowing account of the "massive agricultural efforts by Biafra's Land Army" quoting Donatus Anyanwu, head of the Biafran Relief Services Foundation, see *Washington Post*, July 7, 1969.

[72] Press Release No. 981b, June 7, 1969, and No. 982b, June 11, 1969.

the interdiction as a distinct change of policy, which now precluded night flights.[73] Hitherto, these had been flown at the ICRC's "own risk."

The decision to interdict the Red Cross plane marked a major shift in the political balance within the federal military government. For nearly two years, Gowon had resisted the advice of those who argued that Nigeria's tolerance was without historical precedent and could not be justified. But in the wake of Biafra's recent aggressiveness, hawkish elements were in the ascendancy. Army Chief of Staff Hassan Katsina informed the Lagos press corps in late June that in the future he "would not support feeding anybody we are fighting."[74] And, in a much more widely quoted statement, the government's highest-ranking civilian, Chief Obafemi Awolowo, declared that "all is fair in war and starvation is one of the weapons of war. We should not feed our enemies fat in order to fight us harder."[75]

On June 30, 1969, the Nigerian government convened a special meeting in Lagos with the representatives of sixteen relief agencies in order to establish new guidelines for humanitarian intervention on both sides of the battle lines.[76] The aim of the meeting was "to examine ways and means of ensuring that genuine relief supplies and operations are separated, and seen to be separated, from those so-called humanitarian activities which strengthen the will of the rebels to fight on and reinforce their means of sustaining their rebellion as well as the illusion of world diplomatic approval and *de facto* recognition."[77] The agencies were informed that the Nigerian government planned to assign complete responsibility for the coordination of relief distribution in federally controlled areas to its own National Commission for Rehabilitation, thus relieving the ICRC of that duty. Gowon no longer wished to have the ICRC, a foreign body, appealing to other governments for aid on behalf of deprived Nigerians. The transfer would be gradual so as not to disrupt ongoing programs, but the federal government wanted

[73] ICRC, *Annual Report, 1969* (Geneva, 1970), p. 14.

[74] *Daily Times*, June 27, 1969.

[75] *Daily Times*, June 26, 1969. The Awolowo statement was immediately distributed by Biafra's public relations firm in Geneva: Markpress Release, Gen. 673, June 26, 1969. Typical of the hostile reaction abroad was *The Times* (London), editorial, "A Policy of Famine," June 28, 1969.

[76] Organizations attending the meeting were: Africa Concern, Catholic Relief Services, CARE, Christian Council of Nigeria, ICRC, Muslim International Relief Organization, National Council of Women, Nigerian Red Cross Society, Oxfam, Quaker Friends Service, Catholic Secretariat (Social Welfare Department), St. John's Council of Nigeria, Save the Children Fund, UNICEF, the United Nations Mission of the Secretary General to Nigeria on Humanitarian Activities, and YWCA of Nigeria. Observers from the British High Commission and the United States Agency for International Development were also present.

[77] Opening statement by Chief Anthony Enahoro, federal commissioner for information and Labour, leader of the federal government delegation to the meeting with relief organizations operating in Nigeria, June 30, 1969.

to demonstrate to the world that it alone was ultimately responsible for and able to care for the welfare of the Nigerian people.[78]

Most of the meeting with the relief agencies was devoted to an elaboration of the federal policy toward continued relief operations within Biafra. The familiar ambivalence remained. First, there were domestic political and social imperatives:

> The federal government realizes that it is necessary to demonstrate to the Ibos that federal forces are not fighting them as a people . . . and that it is necessary to demonstrate that after the current war, Nigerians intend to live in peaceful and equal compatriotism with their Ibo brothers. . . . [Therefore] the federal government will continue to allow relief to civilian victims of the civil war in such [rebel-held] areas.[79]

At the same time, however, Lagos wanted an end to night flights and other aspects of the humanitarian programs that enhanced Biafra's international status and bolstered the war effort. Specifically, the relief agencies were ordered to: (a) stop carrying Biafran officials and foreign journalists in and out of Biafra; (b) avoid identification with Biafran political objectives in their fund-raising efforts overseas; (c) cease supplying Biafra with such items as fuel and spare parts for radios, vehicles, and aircraft; (d) tighten relief distribution procedures so as not to continue feeding the Biafran army;[80] and (e) curtail the provision of foreign exchange for local purchases in Biafra.[81]

The final communiqué of the June 30 meeting emphasized Nigeria's ban on night flights, while specifically allowing federally inspected daylight flights to Biafra between 9:00 A.M. and 6:00 P.M. The threat against night flights, however, remained tempered by the following stipulation: "The federal government stated that any aircraft which did not comply with these arrangements would be flying into rebel-held areas at its own risk and its operators would bear the consequences of whatever might happen to it."[82] The representative of the ICRC declined to subscribe to the communiqué.

[78] *Ibid.* The ICRC formally relinquished control over the coordination of relief to Nigeria on October 2, 1969. *Daily Sketch*, October 3, 1969.

[79] *Ibid.*, Opening statement by Chief Anthony Enshoro, June 30, 1969.

[80] A report filed by the International Observer Team asserted, on the basis of interviews with recently captured Biafran soldiers and officers, that military rations in the enclave consisted of food supplied by relief agencies, and this intensified criticism of the humanitarians. Observer Team to Nigeria, Report on Activities of the Representatives of Canada, Poland, Sweden, and the United Kingdom during the Period from May 1, 1969 to June 27, 1969. Lagos, July 1, 1969.

[81] *Daily Times*, June 27, 1969.

[82] Joint Communiqué on the Meeting Between the Federal Government of Nigeria and Relief Organizations, text reprinted in Nigeria, Federal Ministry of Information, Press Release No. 695, July 1, 1969.

For the churches operating in Biafra, little had changed. The Catholic Relief Organizations (CARITAS) had informed General Gowon four months earlier that they were against night flights to Biafra because; "(a) it is illegal; (b) it costs us more; (c) it is dangerous; and (d) night flights are imperfect."[83] But they continued to fly "at their own risk," according to Ojukwu's dictates. Although the federal government was now taking a harder line and had demonstrated a capacity to interdict incoming planes—a threat that was reinforced by reliable reports of Soviet radar ships operating near Calabar and Port Harcourt[84]—the churches were determined to test Nigeria's will.

The military significance, as well as the moral implications, of the ICRC's disengagement from Biafra are ambiguous. In the short run —June to August 1969—the ICRC estimates that the quantities of relief supplies reaching Biafra dropped sharply from an all-time high of 270 tons per night in late May to 100 tons per night in June and July.[85] There was, however, no repetition of the suffering comparable to the summer of 1968. Mitigating circumstances were an abundant cassava crop south and southwest of Owerri, in territory recently regained by the Biafrans, and the good corn crop planted by Biafra's Land Army.[86] By the end of 1969, as the situation again worsened, the Jointchurchaid air lift alone was carrying approximately 250 tons per night to Biafra, slightly less than the combined ICRC/JCA nightly record that had been reached prior to the June 5, 1969, interdiction.[87]

The real issue, of course, turned on the relationship of incoming supplies to the changing needs. Here, one can only rely on the estimates published by the relief agencies and the views of the combatants, none of whom was a disinterested party. Everyone agrees, however, that there was a rising disparity between Biafra's essential needs and available Jointchurchaid relief supplies during the final months of 1969. In May 1969, just before the downing of the ICRC plane, a Red Cross official estimated Biafra's minimum requirements to be

[83] Nigeria, Ministry of Information, Press Release No. F. 228, February 25, 1969 (quote from a statement by Monsignor Rodhnin). For a reaffirmation, see Jointchurchaid, Press Release No. 74, June 23, 1969, and No. 78, July 8, 1969.

[84] *New York Times*, June 28, 1969.

[85] Report by K. H. Jaggi, head of the delegation of the ICRC in Biafra, Topical Red Cross News, *Information Notes*, No. 122b, August 22, 1969. According to the Jointchurchaid records, the ICRC/JCA deliveries in May 1969 were averaging between 300 and 350 tons per night. *Summary Minutes*, Fourth Plenary Conference of Jointchurchaid, Lucerne, Switzerland, June 11–13, 1969.

[86] *Ibid*. Biafra's estimated minimum needs in June 1969 were revised downward by the relief agencies to approximately 60 percent of the projections they had made the previous January.

[87] Jointchurchaid, Press Release No. 125, January 8, 1970.

300 tons per night, a figure roughly equal to incoming supplies.[88] By December 1969, Biafra's minimum needs were judged by the Joint-churchaid to have reached 600 tons per night, an amount more than double what was actually reaching the enclave.[89]

Nigerian officials came to regard the shooting down of the Red Cross plane as a major victory in the final campaign to crush the rebellion.[90] Federal authorities generally assumed that ICRC relief supplies played a major role in feeding the Biafran army, given the massive amounts of commodities they shipped to the enclave and the inadequate supervision by ICRC foreign staff on the ground. The interdiction was expected to make the provision of food for the Biafran army more difficult, and to increase the pressure on Biafra's bureaucrats who did not farm themselves and could not afford the uncontrolled prices for local commodities.

Interviews with Ojukwu and many of his advisers confirm the significance of the ICRC interdiction, although, to the author's knowledge, few members of the Biafran elite encountered personal difficulties procuring food during the final months of the war. The rising deprivation among the masses did undermine morale, however, and caused growing numbers of Biafrans at all levels of society to defect to the federal side.[91] The greatest shock to Biafran authorities was that the federal government had openly challenged the ICRC without incurring the wrath of the international community. For months Ojukwu had rallied the support of those around him with confident assurances that the nightly life line to Biafra was invulnerable to federal attack; the internationalization process, at least in this respect, was held to be irreversible.

---

[88] Jaggi, *Information Notes*, No. 122b, August 22, 1969.

[89] Jointchurchaid, Press Release No. 125, January 8, 1970.

[90] One of the most outspoken is S. Z. Mohammed, federal director of relief and rehabilitation, who has charted the tonnage of relief reaching Biafra against the level of rebel military activity and shown—albeit rather crudely—a distinct positive correlation. Mohammed further believes that had the federal government resisted the establishment of the ICRC airlift in mid-1968, the war would have ended eighteen months earlier and with far fewer casualties. Interview: Mohammed.

[91] Figures on the rate of defections do not exist because of movement between extended families across the battle lines. The trend in rising numbers of people leaving the bush inside Biafra for refugee camps on the federal side was noted, however, by the International Observer Team in late September 1969. Observer Team to Nigeria, Report on Activities of the Representatives of Canada, Poland, Sweden, and the United Kingdom during the Period June 28, 1969 to September 30, 1969. Nigeria, Federal Ministry of Information, Press Release No. 1079, October 8, 1969.

New Elements in
the Emerging International Consensus

Radio Biafra branded the lack of international protest "a conspiracy of silence" and lamented bitterly, "Just a couple of weeks ago, we had in our custody eighteen foreign oil men who were caught collaborating with the enemy. During the brief period they were held the world screamed . . . but Nigeria has brazenly violated the Geneva Convention and almost everyone has kept sealed lips."[92] But there were extenuating circumstances that outsiders found difficult to ignore. The federal government, after all, was prepared to offer Biafra an alternative to night relief flights that was more acceptable to the humanitarian agencies and to the governments that backed their intervention. By agreeing to virtually unrestricted daylight flights, Lagos placed the Biafrans in an increasingly awkward position.[93]

Ojukwu's policy regarding daytime deliveries of relief remained firm but muted. Shortly after the downing of the Red Cross plane, Jointchurchaid dispatched Major General I. Berg, a retired officer of the Royal Swedish Air Force, to meet with Ojukwu and try to win Biafran acceptance of daylight flights. The Biafran leader repeated his objection to daylight deliveries for reasons of "national security"; to wit, if relief planes flew only during the day, the federal air force would be free to interdict all night traffic with impunity.[94] Biafra remained determined to protect the delivery of military supplies, although Ojukwu had invited the churches to build their own airstrip that could be used for relief. Jointchurchaid declined, however, because the Biafrans insisted on a reserve clause permitting them to use the airstrip for military aircraft in the event of an "emergency."[95] Ojukwu's policy, however understandable in strategic terms, was poor public relations. Radio Biafra's assertion that the daylight relief controversy was "invented by the Lagos junta to conceal the conspiracy between Gowon's puppet regime and

[92] Radio Biafra, *Newstalk*, June 17, 1969.

[93] Between late June and early September 1969, the federal government made a series of tactical concessions during protracted negotiations with the ICRC over the degree of cargo inspection. On September 9, 1969, the federal government and the ICRC signed a formal agreement under which relief flights would be resumed from Cotonou, Dahomey, between 9 A.M. and 5 P.M. daily. In Cotonou a Nigerian inspector would have joined two inspectors appointed respectively by the Government of Dahomey and the ICRC to ensure that only bona fide relief goods were transported. Text of the agreement was published in the *Sunday Post*, September 14, 1969. Biafra rejected the offer for reasons of military security. Markpress Release, Gen. 717, September 14, 1969. For an assessment of Ojukwu's rejection in terms of the strategic benefits and political costs, see *West Africa*, No. 2729, September 20, 1969, pp. 1005–1009.

[94] *Summary Minutes*, Fourth Plenary Conference of Jointchurchaid, Lucerne, Switzerland, June 11–13, 1969.

[95] *Ibid.*

the ICRC" did not help, particularly when it was further claimed that "we in Biafra have always known that the assignment of the ICRC in Biafra is that of spying and espionage."[96]

Biafran intransigence on the daylight relief issue played into the hands of several foreign governments, particularly the British. In the House of Commons the foreign minister was asked, "Is it not very generous of the Nigerian government to allow these [daylight relief] flights in view of the fact that international observers reported on 27th June that Biafran troops are being fed on rations supplied by charitable organizations?"[97] To which Mr. Stewart replied, "We must accept that, in the whole history of warfare, any nation which has been in a position to starve its enemy out has done so. As far as I know this is the first occasion on which a government who were in a position to do so have said, 'We are willing not to do so provided our generosity is not exploited for military ends.' That is one of the massive and solid facts in the whole situation."[98] Three days later, Parliament debated the government's arms policy toward Nigeria and barely a third of the 630 members of the House attended. Biafra's sympathizers, could muster only 44 votes in opposition to the prevailing policy.[99]

The vote in Britain was symptomatic of Biafra's slipping credibility throughout Europe and North America. When Nigeria's ambassadors returned to Lagos to review foreign policy in late June 1969, the tenor of their discussions reflected the improved international climate. A rapporteur's summary of the exchange of views among the ambassadors shows a consensus that public opinion in Europe had become increasingly critical of Biafra, and specified that "this was partly because the complexities of the Nigerian situation have begun to dawn on many Europeans who originally saw it in over-simplified terms, and partly because of the Kwale incident [Biafra's seizure of the Italian oil men] which disillusioned many who never believed that the rebels could murder Italian nationals, whose country was so vociferous in her support of the rebels' cause."[100] More importantly, the diplomats discerned a visible trend among Western European governments "to promote their bilateral relations with Nigeria in every field short of supply arms."[101] The decision by the West German government to renew its aid and

[96] Radio Biafra, *Newstalk*, June 17, 1969. *Newstalk*, June 19, 1969, is similarly abrasive.

[97] Great Britain, *Parliamentary Debates*, Vol. 786, July 7, 1969, question from Mr. Wyatt, col. 953.

[98] *Ibid.*, Mr. Stewart, col. 953.

[99] Great Britain, *Parliamentary Debates*, Vol. 786, July 10, 1969, cols. 1588–1712.

[100] MEA/CNA/June 1969, Conference of Nigerian Ambassadors, Policy of Nigeria toward Western Europe, June 24–25, 1969, p. 5.

[101] *Ibid.*, p. 5.

assistance program was cited as a prime example. The Germans, more than other Europeans, were considered by Lagos to be particularly vulnerable to Biafran propaganda because of "the memories of Jewish genocide," which had led them to identify with Biafra "to salve their national conscience."[102]

Nigeria's ambassador in Washington was able to report on similar improvements in the American attitude toward Nigeria, noting that there were "hopeful signs" that growing numbers of influential Americans now questioned the justice of the Biafran cause.[103] Recent testimony by President Nixon's relief coordinator, C. Clyde Ferguson, and Congressman Charles Diggs concerning their experiences in Nigeria were cited as highly beneficial to Nigeria's public image. It was noted that the American government was "agitated" over the humanitarian aspects of the war, but at this stage of the conflict the danger of hostile interference seemed remote.[104] The ambassador concluded confidently that the Nixon administration "strongly supports the sovereignty and territorial integrity of Nigeria."[105]

Although the mood among Nigeria's ambassadors was optimistic, they warned the government that the risk of foreign intervention was likely to increase if the war was allowed to drag on for the remainder of the year. At the conclusion of their review of relations with the United States and Western Europe, they issued a strong recommendation to the military that "every effort be made to suppress the rebellion as expeditiously as possible, [because] Americans in particular . . . were contemptuous of weakness and prove [sic] to meddle in matters where there were elements of Big Power involvement. . . . The government should be able and be seen to be able to demonstrate its capability and, above all, its will to crush the rebellion."[106] For two years Nigeria's representatives had been waging defensive diplomacy against the many foreign actors—governmental and nongovernmental—who wished to influence the outcome of the civil war in ways that the Gowon regime regarded as contrary to the national interest. The ambassadors were impatient, and despite the dim prospects for direct negotiations, the

---

[102] *Ibid.*, p. 3.

[103] MEA/CNA/June 1969, Conference of Nigerian Ambassadors, Policy of Nigeria toward Western Countries, including the Americas (Part II), pp. 3–4.

[104] Elsewhere in the United States Congress, it was noted that: "politicians like Senators Kennedy and Goodell, saw in the furor over the war a fine opportunity to capture the public imagination and affection for their personal political careers. Some segregation politicians used it to further their anti-Negro feelings, while others unable to understand the Black Power movement, used it to salve their consciences on the ground that they were supporting Black self-determination." *Ibid.* (Part II), p. 3.

[105] *Ibid.* (Part II), p. 4.

[106] *Ibid.* (Part II), p. 6 and (Part I), p. 8.

government would be pressed repeatedly by hopeful peace-makers before the war finally ended in January 1970.

A most surprising personal initiative came during Pope Paul's unprecedented visit to Africa in August 1969. Paul's wish to become the first reigning pope to visit Africa had been indicated in March, when it was suggested that the pontiff would be willing to play a mediating role in the Nigerian crisis by flying into the troubled area.[107] The federal government regarded the church as closely identified with the Biafran cause, particularly in Europe,[108] and moved quickly to discourage such an intervention. Lagos also feared that the pope would want to visit Biafra and attempt to undercut the OAU by promoting a meeting between Ojukwu and Gowon.[109] When arrangements for a papal visit to Kampala, Uganda, were confirmed in late July the two leaders were invited to join the pontiff for discussions about ending the conflict, but Gowon immediately declined, citing "prior commitments."[110] Instead, he delegated his commissioner of information, Chief Anthony Enahoro, to lead a team composed of Ukpabi Asika, administrator of the predominantly-Ibo East Central State, and the federal commissioner of transport, J. S. Tarka. All three had a Roman Catholic background, and Enahoro and Tarka had been prominent political champions of the tribal minorities during the era of civilian rule. General Ojukwu sent Professor Eni Njoku, Justice Onyiuke, and his representative in East Africa, Austin Okwu, to represent Biafra.

Before departing from the Vatican, the pope annoyed the federal government by granting a general audience in which he stressed the church's determination to deal with the belligerents as equal parties to the dispute, and he endorsed Ojukwu's call for an unconditional truce.[111] Upon arriving in Kampala he reportedly alleged that two

[107] *Observer*, March 16, 1969.

[108] During the 1969 foreign policy review, the consensus of Nigeria's ambassadors was that "In all countries (Italy, France, Western Germany) where there were predominant Catholic populations, the major motivation was religious. The initial position of the Pope, dictated by Bishops Okoye and Arinze, was instrumental in alienating the feeling of Western Europe for Nigeria. . . . The propaganda of the rebels carried out by Markpress has been so effective and adroit that all important lobbies, intellectuals, Jewish, Christian and political have been persuaded to consider the Rebel cause sympathetically." MEA/CNA/June 1969, Policy of Nigeria Toward Western Europe Including the Americas (Part I), pp. 2–3.

[109] *The Times* (London), March 17, 1969.

[110] Nigeria, Ministry of Information Press Release No. 823, July 27, 1969.

[111] General audience given by His Holiness in the Vatican, July 30, 1969, on the eve of his departure for Uganda, *L'Observatore Romano*, August 7, 1969, and reprinted in Kirk-Greene, *Crisis & Conflict*, II, 412–414. Also *Sunday Times*, July 31, 1969. Ojukwu's truce proposal was released by Markpress: Markpress Release, Gen. 695, July 29, 1969.

Nigerian MIGs had strafed lorries loading food near Onitsha and killed seventy-nine people.[112] The pontiff's apparent readiness to address military questions caused Radio Nigeria to warn of the danger of the visit becoming a "propaganda stunt."[113]

Chief Enahoro and his delegation reached Uganda on July 30, 1969, and immediately began private consultations with Ugandan President Milton Obote to establish the ground rules for the meeting with Pope Paul. Enahoro told Obote that his delegation was in Kampala principally to participate in ecclesiastical ceremonies and had no mandate to hold any peace talks.[114] He reminded the Ugandan leader that the OAU Consultative Committee could not be brushed aside by peace talks under a different aegis. Nigeria would only cooperate in discussions with the pope that sought to establish a common ground for the resumption of negotiations under the terms of the OAU mandate.

Obote remarked that the Ugandan government had no new ideas about the Nigerian crisis, adding that Nigeria's and Biafra's positions had been made perfectly clear, and the most Uganda hoped for was a speedy federal victory. He reported that a Ugandan envoy already had been sent to determine if the pope would offer any new suggestions regarding peace talks, but the envoy had returned empty handed. Obote further reported that Tanzanian President Nyerere, who was in Kampala together with President Kaunda of Zambia, would meet with the pope prior to Enahoro's audience. The Tanzanian president, Obote noted, had been rethinking the Biafra question and was considering a solution that would make Biafra an integral part of Nigeria but with a status similar to the Ukraine in the Soviet Union.[115]

The Nigerian delegation held two private sessions with His Holiness on August 1, 1969. The first, at 3:00 P.M., lasted only twenty minutes, long enough for the pope to inquire how he might serve to bring the two sides together for direct negotiations, and whether the federal delegation would object to submitting its peace terms for papal consideration.[116] Pope Paul then invited the federal delegation for further discussions later that evening, and inquired whether Enahoro could agree to Professor Njoku's attendance. Chief Enahoro agreed to the 9:00 P.M. meeting, promised to supply a copy of the federal peace terms in advance, but rejected the suggestion that Njoku attend.

[112] *Guardian*, August 5, 1969.

[113] Radio Nigeria, *Newstalk*: August 1, 1969.

[114] MEA, Notes of Discussion between Chief Enahoro and President Obote, State House, Entebbe, July 30, 1969.

[115] Enahoro gave no response to the suggestion, as presented by Obote, and the matter never came up in discussions with the pope.

[116] MEA, Summary Minutes of Meeting Between His Holiness Pope Paul and Chief Enahoro, Kampala, August 1, 1969 at 3:00 P.M.

President Obote intervened several hours later, at Pope Paul's behest, to press the federal delegation into agreeing to direct talks with the Biafrans. Enahoro reminded the Ugandan leader of his limited mandate, and noted rather sardonically that the pope really could not expect to arrange an end to two years of war on a three-day visit to Africa, particularly with all the other humanitarian business he had pending.[117] Obote agreed, and promised to go with the federal delegation to the evening session to ensure there would be no embarrassment should the pope proceed to include Njoku anyway.[118]

The federal delegation forwarded a detailed set of peace proposals to Pope Paul prior to the final session on the evening of August 1, 1969. The proposals were substantively identical to those Enahoro had tabled during the OAU-sponsored Addis Ababa talks nearly a year earlier.[119] The pope expressed the belief that a federally imposed military solution was impossible because "protracted war would either lead to foreign intervention or a permanent split of Nigeria."[120] A compromise, he suggested, was the best alternative, and he urged Nigerian acceptance of a truce as a desirable and necessary first step. He declined to comment on what possible arrangements might follow a cease-fire because that was in the area of politics, and he claimed to be concerned solely with restoring the peace.

Enahoro reiterated that a halt in the fighting was only possible if Biafra renounced secession, and urged the pontiff to determine from the other side their minimum terms for rejoining the federation. He went on to criticize the pope's interpretation of military developments in Nigeria, and warned that a federal military victory was the most likely outcome.[121] Pope Paul left Uganda the next day without holding any further discussions.

The pope's August 2 departure placed the Nigerian delegation in an uncomfortable position because the next schedule commercial airliner to Lagos was on August 5. Rather than wait awkwardly in

[117] MEA, Notes of Meeting between President Milton Obote and Chief Enahoro, Kampala, August 1, 1969, at 8:00 P.M.

[118] Ibid.

[119] MEA, Peace Proposals Presented to His Holiness Pope Paul, Kampala, August 1, 1969. The first operative paragraph read, in part, that the federal government would accept: "a formula which provided for the renunciation of secession by the rebels without imposing on them an obligation to declare publicly and in so many words that they had renounced secession." The federal government offered to negotiate: a. such a formula for renouncing secession; b. the joint declaration announcing the formula; c. the authority and mandate of the signatories; and d. the date and time for a cessation of hostilities. The rest of the proposals related to guarantees of Ibo security.

[120] MEA, Summary Minutes of Meeting between His Holiness Pope Paul and Chief Enahoro, Kampala, August 1, 1969 at 9:15 P.M.

[121] Ibid.

Kampala under the glare of the world press, Enahoro decided to go to Nairobi to brief President Kenyatta on the papal meeting. Kenyatta reiterated his opposition to Biafran secession, which he compared to the Shifta rebellion in northeast Kenya, and urged the federal government to press on with the task of reunification.[122]

Enahoro and his party were due to fly to Lagos from Nairobi on August 5, but when they learned that the flight would be diverted through Dar es Salaam, they decided to change carriers and fly home by way of Addis Ababa. The additional stopover permitted Enahoro to assure the Emperor that the talks with Pope Paul in no way undercut the OAU or the special Consultative Committee that the Emperor chaired. Selassie repeated his pledge to continue to back Nigeria and, in an apparent allusion to his own difficulties with rebels in Eritrea, warned that secession would become contagious in Africa if Lagos did not act quickly.[123]

The reason for briefly describing this rather circuitous route back to Lagos is that it illustrates how Nigeria's envoys, who, unlike ministers from major powers, lacked the luxury and freedom of flying by government jet, were able to turn such inconvenience into diplomatic advantage.

While the federal delegation was in Addis Ababa, OAU Secretary General Diallo Telli requested an appointment. Telli informed Enahoro that the OAU's representative in New York had reported that Ivory Coast planned to raise the Nigerian question during the 1969 Fall session of the General Assembly, with possible support from some of the smaller European countries.[124] U Thant had communicated again to Telli that he considered himself bound by the resolution and attitude of the OAU; it was essential, therefore, that the OAU reaffirm its support for the federal government in the strongest possible terms. Telli urged Gowon's personal presence in Addis Ababa for the upcoming OAU Summit to give impetus to this process.

The Nigerian government did not have to be told about the diplomatic importance of OAU summitry. In June 1969, the conference of Nigerian ambassadors had concluded that "the OAU has been the strongest line of our national defense and endeavors . . . the organisation has helped beyond any doubt to contain the tempta-

[122] MEA, Notes of Meeting between President Jomo Kenyatta and Chief Enahoro, Nairobi, August 5, 1969.

[123] MEA, Notes of Meeting between H.I.M. Haile Selassie I and Chief Enahoro at Dire-Dawa, August 6, 1969.

[124] MEA, Notes of a Meeting Between OAU Secretary General Diallo Telli and Chief Enahoro, Addis Ababa, August 7, 1969. The failure of the Ivorian effort to raise interest at the United Nations in the Nigeria-Biafra war is reviewed in *West Africa*, No. 2735, November 1, 1969, p. 1321.

tion of a number of African and non-African states to intefere in the current crisis."[125] Federal hopes for continued support from the OAU had coalesced around two objectives that would further isolate Biafra. First, and most importantly, Lagos would seek a summit resolution that would continue to endorse federal policies of reunification, but that could be endorsed by the four member governments that recognized Biafra and had voted against the Nigerian resolution at the 1968 summit in Algiers. Secondly, the Nigerians hoped they would be able to convince the OAU somehow to admonish the humanitarian bodies that were so actively involved in helping to sustain Biafra.

In seeking the unanimous endorsement of the OAU, the federal government was prepared to be flexible in negotiating the form of a new summit resolution, and had already abandoned any thoughts of trying to duplicate the resolution passed by the Algiers summit. The 1968 resolution, which had been approved 33 to 4, came at a time when Biafra's collapse seemed imminent. Twelve months later the conflict had settled into a war of attrition, with no quick end in sight. Many African leaders continued to favor a military solution. The assurances the Nigerians offered in this regard during the 1968 Algiers summit had played an important role in securing the votes for a strongly worded profederal resolution. Similar promises of decisive military action could not be made in 1969 because they would have lacked credibility. Nigeria could blame foreign assistance to Biafra for the prolongation of the conflict, but found it necessary to yield to those members of the OAU who held that the organization should more actively seek a surrender formula that Biafra would accept.

The framework for the federal government's presummit lobbying effort was determined to a large extent by its previous position taken during the April 1969 meeting of the Consultative Committee in Monrovia. The resulting communiqué had blamed Biafra for the failure to achieve an agreement to begin substantive negotiations, and congratulated the federal government for accepting proposed terms of reference that appeared to be more responsive to Biafra's concerns than had been the case during the 1968 talks in Kampala and Addis Ababa. The key paragraph in the April 1969 communiqué called on "the two parties of the civil war to *accept*, in the supreme interest of Africa, a *united Nigeria*, which ensures all forms of security and guarantee of equality of rights and privileges to all its citizens. Within the context of this agreement the two parties accept an immediate cessation of the fighting and the opening without delay of peace negotia-

---

[125] MEA/CNA/June 1969, Conference of Nigerian Ambassadors, Nigeria's Policy in Africa, pp. 4, 6.

tions."[126] Although this was not acceptable to the Biafrans, the federal government and the members of the Consultative Committee maintained that it was much more conciliatory than the appeal from the 1968 summit "to the secessionist leaders to cooperate with the Federal authorities in order to restore peace and unity in Nigeria."[127]

The federal government's presummit diplomatic offensive opened with the much publicized return to Nigeria on August 17, 1969, of former Nigerian President Nnamdi Azikiwe, Ojukwu's most prominent envoy. Although Azikiwe had been, at best, a lukewarm supporter of secession, he had emerged during the spring of 1968 to lead a delegation of other well-known Ibos on a tour of African capitals in search of diplomatic recognition. He accepted that role, according to friends, because he believed Ojukwu was ready to compromise, and recognition by one or more African states would strengthen Biafra's hand at the conference table. When the 1968 talks failed he became convinced that Ojukwu was as much to blame as Gowon and, in any event, Biafra was doomed. Azikiwe chose to remain quietly in Britain, and he commenced a quiet dialogue with federal representatives. Following the collapse of the Consultative Committee's April 1969 initiatives, President William Tubman met at length with Azikiwe in London and urged him to return to West Africa, specifically to meet Gowon in Monrovia. Azikiwe agreed.

En route to Liberia, Azikiwe's flight stopped briefly in Lagos for a breakfast meeting with General Gowon. He then continued on to Monrovia, where he met formally with Gowon and President Tubman for two days, August 18–19, 1969. The short visit to Lagos and all the attendant publicity obscured the fact that Gowon was actually paying a state visit to Liberia—the first time he had slept outside Dodan Barracks since coming to power in 1966. Thus, in addition to Azikiwe's show of confidence in the Gowon regime, the meeting in Monrovia signaled Gowon's own confidence in the security of his government and his willingness to engage in direct summit diplomacy. Totally unrealistic speculation in the European press about the possible outcome of the Monrovia meeting caused the federal Ministry of External Affairs to cable all Nigerian embassies:

Azikiwe's brief stop-over Lagos was result of informal confidential contacts to persuade him to use his influence to counter Ojukwu's propaganda. There is no change in basic federal conditions for peace

[126] Consultative Committee of the Organization of African Unity on Nigeria, Communiqué, Monrovia, Liberia, April 20, 1969. Emphasis added.
[127] Resolution on the Nigerian civil war adopted by the Assembly of Heads of State and Government at the Fifth Ordinary Session of the OAU, Algiers, September 1968. AHG/Res 54 (v).

and Zik appears convinced of an honorable and equal place for Ibos in United Nigeria. Please destroy any impressions Zik acting as intermediary for rebel regime.[128]

The bilateral communiqué released by President Tubman and General Gowon at the conclusion of their two days of talks expressed Liberia's determination to "work for the restoration of peace and unity in Nigeria" and otherwise contained nothing of substance.[129] As a public relations exercise to enhance the prestige and credibility of Azikiwe's return to the Nigerian fold, the trip to Monrovia was regarded in Lagos as an immense success.

Within three days of the Monrovia gathering, Dr. Azikiwe issued a lengthy public statement from London, which the federal government reprinted as the pamphlet "*I Believe in One Nigeria*"—*Zik* for distribution to Nigerian embassies. Although there was speculation abroad that Azikiwe's defection might lead to other prominent Ibos renouncing General Ojukwu's authority, the federal government's main hopes focused on the impression Azikiwe's actions might create elsewhere in Africa. Thus, with much fanfare, the former president told a crowded London press conference on August 28 of his intention to return to Nigeria for an extended visit, and on September 5, less than twenty-four hours before Gowon departed for Addis Ababa to attend his first OAU summit, Azikiwe flew into Lagos.

Azikiwe's return was the most dramatic element in Nigeria's pre-summit diplomatic offensive, but there were a series of bilateral moves as well. During the latter part of August, at least five federal commissioners went on tour throughout Africa, carrying personal messages from General Gowon to other heads of state.[130] It was Nigeria's most thorough lobbying effort of the war, and one that Gowon carried on personally by meeting privately with each of fourteen heads of delegations while the OAU summit was in session, September 6–10, 1969.[131]

---

[128] MEA, Cable: Permanent Secretary Baba-Gana to All Missions, August 18, 1969.

[129] Text released as Ministry of Information, Press Release No. 907, August 20, 1969.

[130] Some examples of trips made during late August: Federal Commissioner for Trade and Industries Ali Monguno, to Congo (Zaire), Congo (Brazzaville), Malagasy Republic, and Mauritius; Commissioner for Education Wenike Briggs, to Gambia, Sierra Leone, and Mali; Commissioner for Transport J. S. Tarka, to Kenya, Uganda, Ethiopia, Rwanda, and Burundi; Commissioner for Communications Aminu Kano, to Cameroon, Chad, and Central African Republic; and Olufemi Okunnu, commissioner for works and housing, to Sudan, Tunisia, and Algeria.

[131] Gowon held bilateral discussions with the following: Emperor Haile Selassie; President Nyerere (Tanzania); President El Nimeiry (Sudan); President Obote (Uganda); President Ngouabi (Congo-Brazzaville); President Diori (Niger);

Nigeria was one of forty-one African governments represented at the sixth OAU summit, and although the civil war was not formally raised in plenary session until the closing hours of the conference, it was the most important item on the agenda. Aside from Gowon's lobbying effort, the Consultative Committee on Nigeria caucused four times before submitting a draft resolution on the crisis. The committee heard from Biafra's supporters—Tanzania, Zambia, Gabon, and Ivory Coast—and each urged the OAU to call for an immediate unconditional cease-fire. President Nyerere, the only head of state present among the four governments recognizing Biafra,[132] surprised his listeners by personally endorsing the committee's April 20, 1969, Monrovia declaration, which called on Biafrans to accept a "unified Nigeria."[133] The following day the committee interviewed Zambia's vice president, Simon Kapwepwe, who sounded even more conciliatory, and implied a growing desire by the Zambian government to reidentify with the OAU majority. After thanking Nigeria for "patience and broadmindedness, even towards countries which recognized Biafra," Kapwepwe asked the Consultative Committee to "put on record that the Zambian government and people always believed in one and a strong Nigeria. A weak Nigeria will not be a help to Africa. But we have to admit that the Biafrans entertain some fears that have to be allayed. The problem before us is how to bring back the unity of Nigeria. . . . What should be done is to ask the Nigerian authorities to make a heroic decision of declaring a cease-fire."[134]

Gowon responded to this appeal by once again rejecting any suggestion of an unconditional cease-fire, and declared that his government could not agree to engage in any peace negotiations until they had received a "clear indication from Ojukwu that the ultimate aim is Nigerian Unity."[135] He went on to declare that "The Nigerians' fear is that if Ojukwu is allowed to succeed in his secession other states in Nigeria will follow. We shall then end up with a dozen or so independent countries in Nigeria. This will of course serve the interests of foreigners. I am prepared to say that the secessionists enter-

---

President Ahidjo (Cameroon); Vice President Kapwepwe (Zambia); Minister for Presidential Affairs Mongi Slim (Tunisia); a representative of the king of Morocco; Vice President D. Arap Moi (Kenya); minister of national guidance of UAR; foreign minister of Upper Volta; and foreign minister of Gabon.

[132] Gabon and Ivory Coast were represented by their foreign ministers, and Zambia by its vice president.

[133] MEA, Organization of African Unity, Sixth Summit, Addis Ababa, September 6–10, 1969, Summary Record of the deliberations by the OAU Consultative Committee on Nigeria, September 7, 1969, at 7:00 P.M.

[134] *Ibid.* September 8, 1969, at 9:45 A.M.

[135] *Ibid.*

tain fears about their personal security. But I wish to assure the committee that Ibos will not be treated as second class citizens in Nigeria."[136] Gowon defended these assertions by reviewing the administrative changes that had taken place in Nigeria since the creation of the twelve states, and the greater security and equity for all ethnic groups inherent in this diversification. He invited President Nyerere and Vice President Kapwepwe, or their trusted representatives, to visit Nigeria for an extended fact-finding mission, and he also referred his critics to the recent statements by former President Azikiwe and the reports of the International Observer Team.

As the Consultative Committee proceeded to take private testimony, Ethiopia, Liberia, and Niger strongly urged the states that recognized Biafra to assume responsibility for persuading Ojukwu that the security of the Ibo people would be protected in the event that secession was renounced. Of the two francophone governments allied with Ojukwu, only Gabon agreed to meet with the committee, and it adopted a position—later endorsed by Ivory Coast—that was much less conciliatory toward Nigeria than either of Biafra's East African supporters. The Gabonese foreign minister informed the committee that his government was prepared to vote for a resolution that would admit the OAU's failure to solve the Nigeria problem, and that would recommend the task of arranging a cease-fire and negotiated settlement be transferred to "some other authority."[137] Gabon's position was thus much more in tune with Ojukwu's current thinking than the views expressed by Tanzania or Zambia.

Although the Consultative Committee's capacity to arrange a cease-fire and negotiated settlement was severely limited because of its continued support for the federal government, African leaders were not willing to relinquish whatever authority an OAU judgment on the conflict might have in the wider international arena, nor were they enthusiastic about the Commonwealth Secretariat or any other extra-African body providing "good offices." Gabon's reservations notwithstanding, the committee continued to search for a draft resolution that could be unanimously adopted by the OAU summit. Even if such a resolution failed to weaken Biafra's determination to continue fighting, it might at least, in the view of Ghana's foreign minister, discourage foreign powers who were meddling in the internal affairs of Nigeria. With this in mind, a subcommittee was established on the evening of August 8 comprising the Emperor and Presidents Ahidjo and Diori. For the next twenty-four hours the members met intermittently with Biafra's four allies in an attempt to reach a compromise.

[136] *Ibid.*
[137] *Ibid.* September 7, 1969, at 4:30 P.M.

The draft formula that the committee produced before the summit's final plenary meeting on the night of September 10 closely followed the substance of the April 1969 Monrovia Communiqué. Under the terms of the draft resolution, the OAU heads of state would appeal

> to the two parties involved in the Civil War to agree to *preserve* in the over-riding interests of Africa, the *unity of Nigeria* and accept immediately the suspension of hostilities and the opening without delay of negotiations intended to *preserve the unity* of Nigeria and restore reconciliation and peace that will ensure for the population every form of security and every guarantee of equal rights, prerogatives and obligations.[138]

By substituting for "accept . . . a united Nigeria," which appeared in the Monrovia communiqué, "preserve . . . the unity of Nigeria," the Consultative Committee sought to move a step closer to the spirit of the phrase, "return to a normal situation in the country," which the Biafrans had proposed during the April meeting in Monrovia.[139] Gowon continued to maintain that the Biafran terminology was too "ambiguous," but agreed to substitute the verb "preserve" for "accept," and to replace "united" with "unity" because the committee felt these terms might be interpreted by Biafra's supporters as less restrictive. Since Nigeria always had a degree of "unity," the term could be interpreted that the degree of local autonomy within a Nigerian entity was not a foregone conclusion; the two sides would meet to discuss the substance of reunification.

As for the role of foreign involvement in the conflict, the committee accepted Nigeria's contention that the war was being prolonged by the inflow of private humanitarian assistance to Biafra, beyond whatever arms sales and transfers were being arranged by the French. Instead of recommending that the OAU reiterate its 1968 appeal to "all concerned to cooperate in the speedy delivery of humanitarian relief to the needy," the Committee deleted that reference and modified their earlier call for nonintervention by governments to read, "a solemn and urgent appeal to all governments, international organizations, humanitarian institutions as well as to all political, moral and religious bodies in the world to facilitate the implementation of the

---

[138] Resolution, on the Nigerian civil war adopted by the Assembly of Heads of State and Government at the Sixth Ordinary Session of the OAU, Addis Ababa, September 1969, AHG/Res. 58 (vi), reprinted in *Daily Times*, September 11, 1969. Emphasis added.

[139] Republic of Ghana, Executive Council Information Paper Submitted by the Vice Chairman of the National Liberation Council, "Meeting of the OAU Consultative Committee on Nigeria Held in Monrovia, April 17–20, 1969," Appendix V: Secret Draft Resolution accepted by the Biafran delegation.

present resolution and to desist from any action, gesture and attitude likely to jeopardize the efforts of the OAU in finding an African solution to the Nigerian crisis."[140]

The draft resolution was submitted to the plenary session of the summit during the early morning hours of September 10, 1969. It was introduced by President Diori, who reported that

The Nigerian government has so far given full cooperation to the committee and has given all guarantees to the rebels as soon as they agree to rejoin Nigeria. The Nigerian government has even gone to the extent of accepting the stationing of foreign troops in rebel held areas in order to allay fears of the Ibos once the fighting stops. . . . The Nigerian government is prepared to accept a renunciation of secession in any form of words and Gowon has assured us that once this is done he can order a cease-fire within twenty-four hours.[141]

During the subsequent discussion, the four states that recognized Biafra were repeatedly pressed to vote for the resolution. Nyerere began one of the evening's longest presentations with the declaration "I am not General Ojukwu [and] . . . I am not against Nigerian unity if it is the wish of the OAU."[142] Tanzania would abstain, however, because of the president's continued belief in the urgent need for an immediate cease-fire, if only to allow Ojukwu to fly out of Biafra. Nyerere also argued that, while he supported Nigerian unity, inclusion of the term in the draft resolution would only prejudice negotiations. He was joined in this view by Zambia, Gabon, Ivory Coast, Rwanda, and Sierra Leone, while the rest of the OAU members repeated long-standing policies of support for the federal government, with Guinea, Mali, Algeria, Botswana, Cameroon, and Zaire taking the strongest line.

General Gowon spoke last. He did not appeal for support, but offered a personal account of his past association with Ojukwu since their days in military college. It was a rather shrewd attempt to personalize the enemy of Nigerian and African unity in order to convince the assembly that his regime harbored no vindictiveness toward the Ibo people. Ojukwu, he claimed, had invited him to join a budding coup against the Balewa government in January 1965 and, until the

[140] Text of Resolution on the Nigerian civil war, *Daily Times*, September 11, 1969.

[141] MEA, Summary Record of the Plenary Debate of the Nigeria Question during the Sixth Ordinary Session of the OAU Assembly of Heads of State and Government, September 10, 1969.

[142] *Ibid.*

federal army repulsed the rebel blitz through the Midwest in August 1967, Ojukwu's overriding ambition was to rule all Nigeria. Deprived of this option, Gowon suggested that his adversary would exploit any opportunity to remain in power in the East. A cease-fire, he warned, would merely reward Ojukwu's intransigence and thereby prolong the suffering of the Ibo people. If Ojukwu were truly serious about negotiating, Gowon remarked with uncharacteristic sarcasm, "he can come out on any of the aircraft which fly the so-called relief into the airstrip at Uli illegally."[143]

The Emperor pleaded once more for a unanimous vote in favor of the Consultative Committee's resolution, but Biafra's four supporters, plus Sierra Leone, abstained.[144] Thus the resolution passed, 36 to 0. The federal government's reaction to the outcome of the sixth OAU summit was contained in a cable that the Ministry of External Affairs sent to all Nigerian embassies the next day: "Abstention of the four countries which recognize the rebels is considered an improvement over last year's position when they voted against the Resolution thus not accepting the unity of Nigeria in any form. On this occasion their abstention can be construed as their acceptance of one united Nigeria, save that they do not agree with the formula for achieving it."[145]

The satisfaction that Nigerian policy makers derived from the OAU resolution related more to its presumed diplomatic importance than to the likelihood that it would precipitate a major concession by Biafra. Similarly, the Biafrans were under no illusion that the more moderate language of the 1969 resolution implied a willingness by the federal military government to grant special autonomy to Ojukwu's regime within another "new" Nigeria. On September 10, immediately before the Addis Ababa meeting began debating the Nigeria resolu-

---

[143] *Ibid.*

[144] Interviews with diplomats and government officials in Freetown produced the following plausible explanations for Sierra Leone's abstention: 1. parliamentary pressure reflecting popular interest in Biafra's plight, which was stirred up in part by a well-organized resident Ibo community in the capital (Sierra Leone, *Parliamentary Debates*, Vol. I, Session 1969–1970, No. 26, August 6, 1969, Private Member's Motion on Nigeria-Biafra Issue); 2. the June 1969 visit by President Kenneth Kaunda of Zambia to Sierra Leone; 3. President Siaka Stevens' personal admiration for the Ibo people and his close friendship and business association with Francis Nwokedi, Biafra's resident representative in Freetown; 4. the opportunity for Stevens' year-old regime to assert its independence from its neighbors and play a role on the world stage; and 5. President Stevens was to meet Prime Minister Wilson in London in September, and the abstention was seen by some as a threat to embarrass Britain in the hope of securing several economic concessions.

[145] MEA, Cable: Permanent Secretary Baba-Gana to All Missions, September 1969.

tion, Radio Biafra broadcast a statement calling on Nigeria to agree to negotiations about "the type of unity that might be desirable between our two countries."[146] The statement implied that the type of "unity" Biafra would consider promised no more than the customs union Ojukwu had suggested shortly after the outbreak of civil war. The broadcast made plain that Biafra would continue to refuse to enter into any negotiations that required a prior renunciation of secession; thus, it would not accept the Nigerian/OAU condition that the purpose of negotiations be the "preservation of Nigerian unity." After more than two years, the combatants had refined their diplomatic language to the point where, at the most abstract level, the uninformed listener might never have suspected civil war was still raging. The day after the summit adjourned, however, a brief statement was issued in Owerri, Biafra's temporary capital, which dismissed the OAU resolution as "unrealistic, unjust and partisan."[147]

The OAU's vote in support of Nigerian reunification, coupled with the call for noninterference by humanitarian institutions and religious groups, marked another decline in Biafra's already weak international standing. During the previous twelve months, international anxiety over the plight of the Ibos had subsided to the point where African and European diplomats could more openly encourage Biafra to surrender to Nigerian authority. Ironically, Biafra's capacity to sustain a war of attrition against the better-armed Federal Army seemed to blunt the urgency of Ojukwu's assertion that Nigeria was pursuing a policy of unrestrained genocide. The sluggishness of the federal army in prosecuting the war—whether intentional or because of inadequate logistics—and the widespread fraternization across the battle lines that was being reported by foreign journalists[148] and the international military observer team, appeared at variance with Biafra's description of federal troops as "bloodthirsty vandals."

On the issue of daylight relief flights to Biafra, Gowon also scored important diplomatic points while representatives from seventy-seven countries were attending the Twenty-First International Conference of the Red Cross in Istanbul, September 6–13, 1969. The Nigerian leader agreed to a new formula for daylight relief to Biafra that would not have required Red Cross planes to start or land in federal territory.[149] All flights would have originated in Cotonou, where a team of inspectors, including one Nigerian, could verify the cargo, while

---

[146] Radio Biafra *Newstalk*, September 10, 1969.

[147] *West Africa*, No. 2728, September 13, 1969, p. 1075.

[148] *West Africa*, No. 2737, November 15, 1969, p. 1389 summarizes Brian Silk's reports from the war front that appeared in the *Daily Telegraph*.

[149] Full text of the agreement appeared in the *Sunday Post*, September 14, 1969.

Lagos retained the right to call down any aircraft it suspected of violating the terms of the agreement. News of the pact between the federal goverment and the ICRC reached Istanbul on the last day of the conference, and was roundly applauded. Biafra's rejection of the Lagos-ICRC pact within twenty-four hours on the basis that all flights would have to be guaranteed by "a third government or international organization of a political nature"[150] was strongly criticized.

Several weeks later, the World Council of Churches questioned openly for the first time whether the massive Jointchurchaid air lift should continue to operate in defiance of the federal government. During Jointchurchaid's Fifth Plenary Session in Geneva, the World Council's spokesman expressed his "deep distress at the ambiguous position in which the tremendous [relief] effort has put Christian people," and conveyed a sense of frustration over being manipulated by the Biafran government to suit its political purposes.[151]

Biafra's unwillingness to accept daylight relief flights and the increased fighting in the Midwest, including frequent air attacks by von Rosen's minicons, were defended by Radio Biafra as the logical extension of the revolutionary ideology contained in Ojukwu's Ahiara Declaration. But instead of winning wider international respect, this rather ineffective show of militancy lent fresh credibility to the Nigerian claim that secessionist leaders were more concerned about the survival of the Biafran state than the welfare of the Ibo people. Ojukwu, rather than Gowon, was increasingly portrayed in the European and American press as blocking the road to peace.[152]

[150] Markpress Release, No. Gen. 717 September 14, 1969.

[151] World Council of Churches, Communication Nb/30–69, Divisional Committee of WCC Issues Statement on Nigeria/Biafra, December 5, 1969; also, Jointchurchaid, Press Release No. 120, statements made at the Fifth Plenary Session, Sandefjord, Norway, December 12, 1969, which includes the WCC statement and a Jointchurchaid rejoinder pledging continuation of the air lift.

[152] For example, *The Times* (London), editorial, "It is the Children Who Die," September 24, 1969.

· 12 ·

A NIGERIAN AFFAIR

When the Biafran rebellion collapsed in January 1970, the terms of surrender and the subsequent program of reconstruction were managed exclusively by the federal military government. Despite the high degree of international interest and involvement during the conflict, Nigerian reunification was finally achieved without external assistance, foreign mediation, international peace-keeping or security guarantees, and with little regard for the "friendly advice" from those powers that had supported the federal government. The absence of guerrilla resistance and the readiness of the Ibo elite to cooperate in reestablishing federal authority in the secessionist territory reinforced the belief in Lagos that many prominent Americans and Europeans had been duped by Biafran propaganda and had been unfairly critical of federal motives and actions during the conflict. The deference that had often characterized Nigeria's relations with European and American powers in the early 1960s and during the first two years of the Gowon regime disappeared as the federal government acquired self-confidence and sought greater independence from foreign influence.

Nigeria's determination to control the process of national reconciliation was evident in the June 30, 1969, decision no longer to allow the European representatives of the International Committee of the Red Cross to coordinate relief work in federally held territory and to turn this responsibility over to the Nigerian Red Cross.[1] In this same spirit, the federal government became increasingly reluctant to oblige those foreigners who sought further gestures of compromise for the sake of trying to arrange a negotiated settlement. The war already had entered its third year, and domestic pressures for a quick military victory had produced speculation in Lagos that Gowon would be deposed and replaced by a more aggressive leader.

This final chapter traces the diplomatic movements on the eve of military victory and the rapid national reconciliation that followed. These developments provide an appropriate setting for assessing the initial effects of the civil war experience on the conduct of Nigeria's postwar foreign policy, and the extent to which the Biafran example is likely to influence the degree of international involvement in other domestic conflicts.

---

[1] For a progress report four months after the takeover, see *West Africa*, No. 2735, November 1, 1969, p. 1295.

FINAL EFFORTS TO SEEK
A PEACEFUL SURRENDER

As the summer rains subsided and the laterite roads leading to the federal army's forward positions began to harden, the logistical problems of resupplying the troops were gradually overcome. The rate of military imports from Britain suddenly jumped from $2.4 million during the third quarter to $14.7 for the final three months of 1969.[2] In addition to the British equipment, which accounted for approximately 90 percent of the small arms and ammunition used by the Nigerian infantry, Lagos purchased four batteries of Russian 122mm artillery.[3] The large guns were reported to have a range of thirteen miles, and were said to be destined for emplacements that would permit blanket shelling of Uli airstrip. On November 17, 1969, Army Chief of Staff Hassan Katsina announced that a major offensive was underway to liberate the remaining 2,000 square miles of the East Central State before the start of the next rainy season.[4] With hindsight knowledge of Nigeria's total military victory, Katsina's prediction would seem reasonable, but at the time of the military buildup, the prospects were far less certain.

Throughout the latter half of 1969, the battlelines remained stable (see Map 12–1). Nigeria's Third Division under Colonel Obasanjo, which was based at Port Harcourt, concentrated on holding and straightening the 150-mile southern flank. Colonel Jalo's Second Division, which by this time operated only in the Midwest, was preoccupied with Biafran infiltrators across the Niger River who sought assistance from Midwest Ibos in their efforts to attack Nigeria's oil installations. Colonel Shuwa, who still commanded Nigeria's First Division from headquarters in Enugu, had his troops stretched along Biafra's northern frontier from Afikpo to the Niger River. All during the long rainy season small bands of Biafran forces and a growing number of enterprising businessmen who came to be known as "attack traders" had been able to penetrate all fronts in pursuit of food and quick profits. As many as four million people were believed to be struggling for their survival inside the Biafran enclave, and as federal forces tried to advance they only succeeded in pushing greater numbers of Biafran soldiers and civilians through weaker points in the amorphous perim-

---

[2] Cronje, *The World and Nigeria*, Appendix 2, "Nigerian Arms Imports 1967–1969." By carefully analyzing every issue of the *Nigerian Trade Summary*, Table B, Group 951, "Firearms of War and Ammunition Thereof" prepared by the chief statistician, Lagos, Ms. Cronje has charted the inflow of military equipment. She is not able, however, to account for the purchases of aircraft or ships that do not appear in the published statistics.

[3] *West Africa*, No. 2737, November 15, 1969, p. 1389.

[4] *Nigerian Observer*, November 17, 1969.

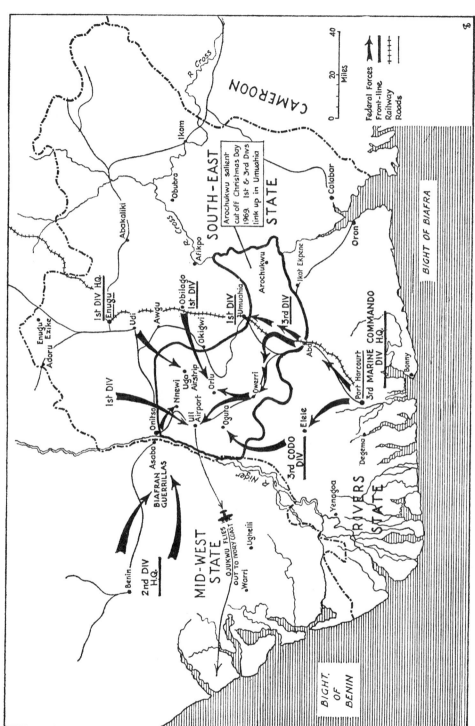

Map 12–1 • Biafra's Final Collapse, December 1969–January 1970 (from John de St. Jorre, *The Nigerian Civil War*, p. 394)

eter. One observer likened this phase of intermittent fighting to squeezing a beanbag.

In subtle ways these battle conditions worked to Nigeria's advantage. The fraternization between opposing forces and the ease with which civilians were able to penetrate the blockade no doubt reduced the fear about federal barbarity, and further undermined Biafra's domestic propaganda. The officer in charge of Biafra's irregular guerrilla forces, which were being hastily trained to operate in the Midwest and behind the First Division's forward positions, recalled that by late 1969 growing numbers of infiltrators "quietly retired" or became refugees as soon as they reached federally held areas; those who came back often wore new boots and other items from the bulging federal stocks.[5]

Reports of the federal military buildup in October and November also may have encouraged defections. The acquisition of the Soviet 122mm guns was especially ominous, even though Ojukwu argued that they lacked the range to carry over the large swamps that had thus far protected Uli airstrip from a ground attack.[6] In fact, the guns were never effectively deployed, but Ojukwu's chief of staff, General Effiong, later maintained that knowledge of their existence affected the debate over the futility of further resistance that raged among Biafra's military elite in the final days of 1969.[7]

Eric Pace of *The New York Times* was one of the few foreign journalists to tour Biafra in the fall of 1969, and he observed the first signs of serious demoralization among the people and within the army.[8] The shortage of food was exacerbated by a harvest of local carbohydrates that was smaller than expected and a cutback in imported protein following the suspension of the ICRC air lift in June. Hunger not only seemed to be undermining the pride of the citizens, but it was also causing class tensions between the tiny but relatively prosperous Ibo elite and the millions of malnourished peasants. Stories of conspicuous consumption by Biafran officials, especially among those in a position to travel abroad, are too numerous and easily corroborated to be dismissed as postwar bitterness.[9] Ojukwu maintains that corruption so threatened the effectiveness of his government that midway through the war he brought in a former British officer to assess the extent of corruption, but when he received the report he concluded that malpractices were so pervasive that to pursue the wrongdoers would cause the collapse of his administration.[10]

[5] Interview: Ukwu I. Ukwu.   [6] Interview: Ojukwu.

[7] Interview: Effiong.

[8] *New York Times*, September 13, 1969, and September 21, 1969.

[9] For published accounts, see Nwankwo, *Nigeria: The Challenge of Biafra*, "The Fruits Rot," pp. 40–45; and Oyewole, *Reluctant Rebel*, Chapter 8.

[10] Interview: Ojukwu. Perhaps the most poignant indictment of Biafran cor-

Meanwhile, from Lagos the federal government engaged in a series of public relations exercises aimed at eroding the solidarity of Biafra's urban workers. In his October 1, 1969 Independence Day speech, Gowon announced a general amnesty for those detained as "security risks" during the civil war. A week later the Statutory Corporations Service Commission, the country's largest employer, announced the regular promotions of railway, ports, authority, communications, and electrical power employees who were still in Biafra but who were "expected to assume their new posts" as soon as the war ended.[11] And although former President Azikiwe was regarded as a traitor by many Biafrans, Radio Nigeria persistently beamed his appeal for surrender into the Ibo heartland. Nigerian aircraft also scattered thousands of leaflets showing General Gowon and the expresident praying together for peace.[12]

The gestures of conciliation did not detract from the preparation to mount a major military offensive, nor did it permit much room for foreign initiatives. A renewed toughness was clearly evident in Nigeria's rebuff to the British when Undersecretary of State Maurice Foley paid a hastily arranged visit to Lagos on December 5, 1969. Characteristically, the trip took place only three days before the British Parliament was due to debate the Labour government's Nigeria policy.

When Foley met with Nigeria's Commissioner of External Affairs Dr. Okoi Arikpo, he opened the meeting with the by-now familiar assurances that the British government remained firmly committed to supporting the federal government. He then proceeded once again to call on the Gowon regime to grant concessions so as to dampen criticism within Britain. Among other things, Foley asked that Nigeria consider a scheme to air-drop relief supplies into Biafra and to allow Prime Minister Wilson to send an official envoy to "plead" with Ojukwu to surrender. Foley then inquired if the federal government had any suggestions that might "help Her Majesty's Government deal with the periodic moral upsurges in Britain." By this stage even Arikpo's exasperation was plainly evident: "Personally, I am getting more and more distressed about the fickleness of British public opinion and the attitudes of highly placed public figures and MP's. . . . Simply because Britain has fought no civil war for so long, the British seem to have forgotten that there is never a civil war without a cause. . . .

---

ruption as a central factor in undermining resistance was offered by Count Carl Gustav von Rosen in a lengthy retrospective interview. *The Times* (London) news article by Suzanne Cronje, "Why Biafra Lost the War: Count von Rosen's Theory," January 27, 1970.

[11] *Daily Times*, October 8, 1969.

[12] *West Africa*, No. 2729, September 20, 1968, p. 1133.

A complete military defeat of the rebels is the only answer to the relief situation."[13]

Regarding the proposal to send a British envoy to meet with Ojukwu, Arikpo conceded that this might have some effect on British public opinion, but he rejected the suggestion on the grounds that it would have no influence on Ojukwu's war policies. Foley noted that the Nixon administration had been able to "hold the line" against the Biafran lobby in America for nearly six months as a result of Ambassador Ferguson's trips to Biafra as a special relief coordinator. Arikpo acknowledged that Ferguson's intervention had turned out to be a "blessing," but then added sarcastically that the position of Britain was not to be compared to the United States which had always acknowledged Britain to be the expert on the Nigerian crisis. The suggestion for air-dropping supplies to Biafra was also promptly rejected, and Foley returned to London with nothing of substance.[14]

Privately and in public Gowon continued to insist that Nigeria would agree to meet formally with Biafran representatives only if the peace talks were explicitly convened on the basis of the OAU resolution, namely, for the purpose of restoring the unity of Nigeria.[15] Ojukwu was also adamant. To the Biafran people he declared that a meeting could be arranged only if there were no preconditions regarding the outcome, and that there be a concurrent cease-fire.[16] He dropped the cease-fire requirement in private conversation with foreigners, but still insisted that the principle of Biafran sovereignty not be compromised in advance of the negotiations.[17]

Optimistic rumors about the likelihood of peace talks in late 1969 nevertheless proliferated in the Western press.[18] This speculation was rooted in the belief that Biafra's situation was indeed becoming

[13] MEA, Minutes of the meeting between the British secretary of state for foreign and commonwealth affairs, Mr. Foley, and the federal commissioner of external affairs, Dr. Arikpo, Lagos, December 5, 1969.

[14] Despite Nigeria's firmness, the threatened revolt among Labour backbenchers in Parliament failed and a heavy bipartisan majority of 170 votes ultimately backed the government's Nigeria policy. Great Britain, *Parliamentary Debates*, Vol. 793, No. 31, December 9, 1969.

[15] On October 10, 1969, Gowon conveyed this position to three Quaker representatives who were quietly exploring with both sides the possibility of a resumption of talks. The Nigerian leader reiterated his demand in an address at the University of Ibadan on November 17, 1969.

[16] Markpress Release, Gen. 746, October 31, 1969.

[17] When the three Quaker representatives who had met with Gowon on October 10, 1969, arrived in Biafra on November 11, they were told that the November 1 speech had been in primarily for domestic consumption and that the only point that Biafra would never concede was that the talks had to be without any "preconditions," which might imply acceptance of a "united Nigeria."

[18] *West Africa*, No. 2735, November 1, 1969, p. 1321; *Economist*, November 9, 1969; and *The Times* (London), November 29, 1969.

desperate, and that Nigeria would concede significant autonomy to Biafra in order to avoid the domestic and international political costs of a violent and possibly protracted confrontation in the Ibo heartland. The signals that inspired the newspaper stories came from Emperor Haile Selassie.

The Emperor apparently believed that by playing a dual role as sovereign of Ethiopia and chairman of the OAU Consultative Committee, he could break the impasse to direct negotiations. In October 1969, he communicated to Ojukwu through the latter's confidant, Francis Nwokedi, who was residing in Sierra Leone and was a friend of Prime Minister Stevens.[19] Selassie sought a private understanding with Ojukwu whereby a Biafran delegation would be sent to Addis Ababa under the presumption that the invitation had come from an African head of state and not from the chairman of the OAU Committee. Under this arrangement, Biafra would be free to regard the outcome of any negotiations as not being prejudiced by the terms of the OAU resolution. Ojukwu agreed.

The Nigerians, on the other hand, assumed that the talks were being arranged by the chairman of the OAU Committee, and accepted the invitation on this basis. On December 8 an Ethiopian spokesman announced that the Emperor was ready to bring the two sides together. But in the absence of any further assurance that the meeting was to be held under OAU auspices, Lagos asked that the tentative starting date of December 10 be postponed. Ethiopia's ambassador in Lagos interpreted the request for delay as indicating that the federal government was increasingly optimistic about the military situation and did not want to be in the awkward position of attending peace talks at the very moment that Nigerian troops were overrunning the Ibo heartland.[20]

To force the issue, Ojukwu sent two of his most trusted advisers, Dr. Pius Okigbo and Godwin Onyegbula, to Addis Ababa. While the delegation was en route, Ojukwu issued a public statement welcoming the Emperor's "personal initiative" to arrange the peace talks.[21] This bald attempt to embarrass the Nigerians infuriated the Emperor. In Lagos Ethiopia's ambassador was summoned to the Ministry of

[19] President Stevens met with the Emperor in Freetown during mid-December in an attempt to work out a formula that would bring the Nigerians and Biafrans together at the conference table. *West Africa*, No. 2741, December 13, 1969, p. 1527.

[20] Interview: Ogbagzy.

[21] Markpress Release, Gen. 766, December 16, 1969. Ojukwu's statement read in part: "His Imperial Majesty has replied that he is taking a personal initiative as an African leader. The proposed talks are to be held under his own auspices and he is acting, not as chairman of the OAU Consultative Committee or even as an agent of the organization itself. The meeting will not be held in the context of the OAU resolution."

External Affairs, where he reiterated that the Emperor would host any peace talks in his capacity as chairman of the OAU Consultative Committee.[22] The federal government announced that it was satisfied there had been no misunderstanding, and that it was prepared to begin talks immediately.[23] By then, however, the Biafran delegation had left Addis Ababa, and Ojukwu refused to reconsider.

"The Biafran delegation had not gone to Addis Ababa to surrender," Onyegbula later recalled. "When it became apparent that Nigeria would insist on negotiations within the OAU framework we had to take the initiative to show we were not yet through."[24] However astonishing it may seem in retrospect, Ojukwu firmly believed in December 1969 that Biafra possessed the means to fight on long enough to force a political settlement with Nigeria, and this would allow him sufficient independence to survive in power and gradually undermine Gowon's authority in Lagos.[25] Going through the motions of peace talks might also have helped to restrain the Nigerian army until the approach of the next rainy season. The key to his gamble was Biafran air power and a presumption of Nigerian war weariness.

During the autumn of 1969, Biafra was able to raise sufficient funds to purchase an additional twenty-four "fighter" aircraft, 18 minisports planes equipped with six rocket tubes on each wing and six Harvard T–6 trainer aircraft adapted with machine guns for strafing raids.[26] More ominously, a squadron of six Mirage fighter-bombers was ordered with sufficient range to attack Lagos. How this equipment was bought is not clear. Biafran officials suggest that the new aircraft were paid for by several unsecured loans that Biafra's African Continental Bank was able to arrange through friendly French banks. Another new source of funds may have been cash gifts from several Latin American governments. Prior to mid-1969, there had been little contact with that region but following Haiti's surprise recognition in March, the possibilities for a round of visits by a senior Biafran official were quietly explored in New York. In the fall of 1969, Dr. Pius Okigbo, Ojukwu's chief economic adviser, led a small delegation around Latin America.[27] Although the governments in that region had no major political or economic interest in the civil war, those familiar with the

[22] Interview: Ogbagzy.

[23] Federal Ministry of Information Press Release, No. 1341, December 19, 1969. Markpress Release, Gen. 777, December 25, 1969, and renumbered Release December 31, 1969.

[24] Interview: Onyegbula.   [25] Interview: Ojukwu.

[26] *Financial Times*, December 31, 1969.

[27] Dr. Okigbo's trip was reported in *West Africa*, No. 2734, October 25, 1969, p. 1290. Among those countries he is believed to have visited are Peru, Chile, Bolivia, Ecuador, Colombia, and Argentina.

fund-raising campaign say that the Biafrans were discreetly but warmly received, and discovered a strong religious sympathy that had been aroused by the Catholic church.

With the new planes, Ojukwu hoped to shut down all oil production in the federal areas, close all ports—including Lagos—to international shipping, and cause panic in the federal capital. At the same time, he planned an increase in Biafran ground resistance, because the Biafran army was as well equipped with small arms and artillery as at any time during the war, with stockpiles in Libreville.[28]

The full complement of air power failed to reach Biafra in time to stop the federal advance, and Ojukwu believes the delays in delivery were the result of sabotage. Planes that were to have been shipped in by air transport for assembly in Biafra arrived from Sao Tomé with critical parts missing or damaged. More importantly, the Mirage fighter squadron was sitting quietly on the tarmac of an isolated air field in southern Sudan when the war ended. The Biafrans suspect that the American CIA bribed the pilots not to make delivery; American diplomats familiar with the incident suggest several reasons, including difficulties in hiring the pilots, fuel shortage, over-flight problems, and Biafra's lack of adequate funds, but they predictably deny U.S. involvement.

On December 31, 1969, Ojukwu issued his third New Year's message of the war.[29] It was a very defiant speech, condemning the OAU's "peace talks charade" and ridiculing Nigeria's frequent "final offensives." "How long," he asked in a rhetorical conclusion, "is the rest of the world going to allow this monstrous inhumanity to go on?"

Within a week the Seventeenth Brigade of Colonel Obasanjo's Third Division suddenly broke through Biafran ranks and linked up with the First Division in Umuahia, thereby isolating the secessionists from their only remaining food-producing areas and effectively cutting the enclave in two.[30] The Nigerian commandos seem to have caught the Biafrans by surprise and once they had entered the heartland they encountered no serious resistance; the opposing Twelfth Division of the Biafran army fled to the bush in disarray.

The collapse of the Twelfth Division opened the way to Biafra's only remaining town, Owerri, which fell to Nigerian forces on January 10, 1970. Around 2:00 A.M. the following morning Ojukwu and his im-

[28] Interviews: Ojukwu, Madiebo, Effiong.

[29] Markpress unnumbered release, December 31, 1969, "Biafra 1969—A Year of Anomalies," General Ojukwu's address to the nation.

[30] The Seventeenth Brigade was led by a 26-year-old major, Samson Tumoye, who later described the offensive in an interview with John de St. Jorre. De St. Jorre, *The Nigerian Civil War,* pp. 395–396.

mediate family flew out of Biafra to exile in the Ivory Coast. Late in the afternoon of January 12, Biafran Chief of Staff Philip Effiong ordered his troops to lay down their arms and offered unconditional surrender.[31] The surrender was formally accepted during an emotion-filled reunion among Nigerian and former Biafran officers at General Gowon's Dodan Barracks headquarters on January 15, 1970. On the same day Ojukwu issued his final statement, an appeal to all governments to "save my people from extermination."[32]

THE ATTRIBUTES OF A FEDERAL MILITARY VICTORY

Contrary to the predictions of Biafran propaganda and innumerable Western journalists, there was no guerrilla resistance. Effiong maintains that the capability for further resistance was there, but he decided it would be futile and cause the unnecessary deaths of thousands of innocent people.[33] Without detracting from the wisdom and decency in Effiong's unequivocal rejection of any inflammatory language or covert efforts to keep Biafran resistance alive, he may have overestimated the possibility. According to the head of the Biafran Organization of Freedom Fighters (BOFF) there was very little "revolutionary" spirit left by January 1970.[34] When another former Biafran official who had served in the ministries of Defense and Foreign Affairs was asked why there had been no guerrilla activity after the war, he replied, "What do you think we [Ibos] are? Barbarians?"

Dire forecasts of rampaging federal troops also proved to be inaccurate. The immediate postwar reporting by John de St. Jorre provides a first-hand objective account of the situation in the East Central State:

> Together with eighty other foreign pressmen I toured the Biafran enclave a week after the collapse. During the tour I also walked for ten miles through a series of "bush" villages north of Owerri in the worst affected area. This and a further two months spent in different parts of Nigeria after the end of the war produced certain firm conclusions. Firstly, there was no "genocide," massacres or gratuitous killings; in the history of warfare there can rarely have been such a bloodless end and such a merciful aftermath.[35]

---

[31] *Radio Biafra,* January 12, 1970.

[32] The statement was issued by Markpress, Geneva, while Ojukwu's whereabouts was still unknown. It warned that unless Nigeria were restrained by international intervention there would be "genocide that would make 1939–1945 in Europe a mere 'child's play.'" Ojukwu said he left the enclave "knowing that while I live Biafra lives." *Financial Times,* January 16, 1970.

[33] Interview: Effiong.

[34] Interview: Ukwu. Soon after the conflict ended Ukwu became commissioner of trade and industry of the East Central State.

[35] De St. Jorre, *The Nigerian Civil War,* p. 404. St. Jorre's assessment con-

De St. Jorre's appraisal of the immediate aftermath contrasts sharply with Pope Paul's widely publicized benediction of January 11, 1970, with its reference to "a kind of genocide" and "possible reprisals and massacres aginst defenseless people in Biafra," and his appeal on the following day for international intervention to prevent "a yet more cruel epilogue of horror."[36] Meanwhile in Paris, French Foreign Minister Maurice Schumann showed a similar concern during an extraordinary Sunday meeting with the United States ambassador, in which he reportedly called for concerted international action to protect Ibo civilians against the danger of a federal massacre.[37] Elsewhere in Europe there were demonstrations demanding that Biafra be opened immediately to international peace-keeping forces.[38]

The threat of genocide carried very little credibility by 1970, especially in light of the ongoing activities of the International Observer Team in Nigeria and General Gowon's public pledge of a general amnesty. Instances of rape, looting, and other examples of misconduct, particularly by the Third Marine Commando Division, were reported by several foreign correspondents who visited the area in January.[39] But thus far nothing has been uncovered by even the most pro-Biafran commentators to contradict the conclusion that the federal army was generally well disciplined.[40] One point of contention that does shadow any evaluation of Nigeria's postwar policies, however, concerns the extent of starvation during the first days of federal occupation and whether authorities responded adequately to human need.

The possibility that mass starvation would follow forced termination of the Biafra air lift caused scores of representatives from international relief agencies and Western governments to rush to Lagos in January 1970 with offers of unlimited aid to alleviate the suffering in eastern Nigeria. Perhaps the most extreme justification for mobilizing a fresh humanitarian relief effort was made by a pro-Biafran group in Sweden which held that if the international community allowed Nigeria to run its own relief program, it would be "wittingly letting three million Biafrans die."[41] Most prospective donors were less adamant, if only to gain Nigeria's cooperation in the wake of Biafra's collapse,

---

forms with the author's impressions received during a similar and completely unrestricted trip through the East Central State in July.

[36] *Herald Tribune*, January 12, 1970, and *West Africa*, No. 2746, January 17, 1970, p. 90.

[37] *Herald Tribune*, January 12, 1970.

[38] For a summary of international reactions, see Wiseberg, "The International Politics of Relief," pp. 426–427.

[39] *Ibid.*, p. 440.

[40] The author's own travels throughout the Ibo enclave in 1970 and 1971 further confirmed this reality.

[41] *Herald Tribune*, January 15, 1970.

but a general lack of confidence in the federal government's capacity to meet the relief needs in Nigeria was reflected on editorial pages throughout Europe and North America.

Nigerian reactions to international humanitarianism in January 1970 proved to be a harbinger of the country's postwar foreign policy, and reflect several of the bitter lessons of civil-war diplomacy. Pope Paul's reference to the possibility of genocide caused unprecedented antipapal student demonstrations, which stunned the archdiocese in Lagos.[42] The mood of defiance toward any further foreign involvement in Nigeria's affairs was reflected in a spate of local press commentaries calling on the government to reject foreign assistance in the name of Nigerian self-reliance.[43]

Lagos was determined to retain full control over all relief operations in the country. An arrangement with an outside agency, such as existed in 1968 when the ICRC was allowed to serve as relief coordintor, would no longer be possible. On January 15, General Gowon declared that Nigeria would seek the assistance of "friendly foreign governments and bodies" but went on to state, "There are, however, a number of foreign governments and organizations whose so-called assistance will not be welcome. These are the governments and organizations which sustained the rebellion. They are thus guilty of the blood of thousands who perished because of the prolongation of the futile rebel resistance. They did not act out of love for humanity. Their purpose was to disintegrate Nigeria and Africa and impose their will on us. . . . We shall therefore not allow them to divide and estrange us again from one another with their dubious and insulting gifts and their false humanitarianism."[44]

In a separate statement, the government identified those actors who would not be allowed to assist with the relief effort. They included France, Portugal, South Africa, and Rhodesia, as well as the relief organizations, Jointchurchaid, Caritas, the French Red Cross,

---

[42] According to the local archbishop, the shock and dismay over press photographs of University of Lagos students with placards proclaiming the "hottest place in hell for the Pope," reached to the highest levels in Rome and were a major factor in convincing the Vatican that the church's standing with the Nigerian Catholic laity might actually be in serious jeopardy. Interview: Archbishop Aggey.

[43] An editorial in the government-owned *New Nigerian* was indicative: "We in Nigeria more than anyone else in the world have been compelled to grasp the meaning and repulsive nature of Western humanitarianism in all its guises. We know that Western humanitarianism is no more than an instrument for subverting the self-respect of its object. . . . Th biggest single lesson from the crisis is learning the art of self-reliance." *New Nigerian*, January 14, 1970.

[44] " 'The Dawn of National Reconciliation'—Gowon's Victory Message to the Nation," broadcast on Radio Nigeria, January 15, 1970, and reprinted in Kirk-Greene, *Crisis and Conflict*, II, 459.

the Nordic Red Cross, and "all other organizations which have operated from Abidjan, Libreville, Sao Tomé, Portugal, South Africa, and Rhodesia."[45] During the weeks that followed, all foreign relief personnel who had sought to remain in the Ibo heartland following Biafra's collapse were deported for illegal entry and working without permits. The majority of these were the fifty-seven foreign Catholic priests, brothers, and sisters.[46] Gowon summoned the archbishop of Lagos, John Kwao Amuzu Aggey, to Dodan Barracks to inform him that the deportations should not be construed as an attempt to restrict the religious freedom of Nigerian Catholic clergy and laity, but that in the future "Nigerians would talk directly to God, without any need for European intermediaries."[47]

Vast quantities of food, medical supplies, and other relief materials did arrive in Lagos during January 1970 from the United States, Britain, and Western Europe. But the federal government rejected numerous other requests for permission to fly relief materials directly to Uli airstrip, and within hours of Biafra's defeat, federal bulldozers returned that much-hated symbol of Ojukwu's independence to the dimensions of a simple roadway.[48] Nigerian authorities also stipulated that any aid reaching the country had to be conveyed by civilian transport piloted by nonmilitary personnel.[49]

Nigeria's restrictions on the flow of relief produced much public criticism in Europe and the United States. Nigerians considered such criticism to be one more example of Western hypocrisy and condescension toward an African government that was presumed ignorant of its own people's needs, or at least was incapable of meeting them. In fact, many outsiders felt justified in pressing Nigeria to accept massive unfettered assistance on the basis of testimony provided by foreign nutritional experts who had been active in Biafra prior to the collapse. The most comprehensive survey had been conducted in late October 1969 by Dr. Karl Western of the United States Department of Public Health, who had concluded that severe malnutrition was certainly not a figment of Biafran propaganda. The trends suggested in Western's report seemed to be confirmed in later testimony by relief workers who had been in the most desperate areas near Owerri before and after Biafra's defeat.[50]

[45] *Financial Times*, January 15, 1970.

[46] *West Africa*, No. 2749, February 7, 1970, p. 177, and No. 2750, February 21, 1970, p. 214.

[47] Interview: Aggey.

[48] Gowon was quoted by a British interviewer as saying "Let me get Uli out of our minds, it has been used too much in international politics already." *Scotsman*, January 23, 1970; cited in Kirk-Greene, *Crisis and Conflict*, II, 463.

[49] *Herald Tribune*, January 15, 1970.

[50] For a full discussion of the Western report and reporting prior to and im-

No one, in fact, has been able accurately to confirm the full extent of starvation that occurred after January 15, 1970, or whether this was significantly exacerbated by Nigeria's refusal to open Uli airstrip or in other ways accommodate the urgent requests from foreign relief organizations. In defense of their policies, Nigerian spokesmen could cite the January 15 report of an official of the League of Red Cross Societies who, after touring the Ibo heartland, concluded that there were sufficient food stocks in Nigeria or en route to meet refugee needs without the necessity of an air lift, and that the Nigerian Red Cross was capable of doing a satisfactory job in carrying out relief operations.[51] A British delegation led by Lord Hunt, which included representatives of Save the Children Fund and the British Red Cross, also toured eastern Nigeria and returned to London with a highly optimistic report.[52] Further praise of Nigeria's relief effort was offered by United Nations Secretary General U Thant[53] and the International Observer Team that continued to monitor developments after the war.[54] Meanwhile, a five-man delegation of Quakers, led by Kale Williams, spent the week of January 13–20, 1970, deep in the Ibo heartland and, without any publicity, prepared a confidential report for the office files that contained the following conclusions:

> There is some severe malnutrition and many people are showing the effects of long periods with inadequate diets. But there was no evidence of large numbers of people faced with imminent starvation. The general amnesty cleared by the Federal Government has been given effect. Former Biafran civilians, soldiers, and policemen are moving freely and many of them had resumed their jobs under federal auspices in the first week. There have been no reports of reprisals or of misuse of weapons by federal troops occupying the liberated areas and lives of civilians and surrendered soldiers had been protected. How can these observations be squared with reports in the World Press of 1000 or 2000 people dying each day from starvation? I would judge that those figures are, and have been

---

mediately after the war see Wiseberg, "The International Politics of Relief," pp. 449–459.

[51] *Financial Times*, January 16, 1970, quoting Henrick Beer, secretary general of the League of Red Cross Societies.

[52] Hunt *et al.*, "Nigeria, The Problems of Relief in the Aftermath of the Nigerian Civil War," Report of Lord Hunt's message, presented to Parliament on January 24, 1970 (London: January 22, 1970), and summarized in Wiseberg, "The International Politics of Relief," pp. 452–454.

[53] *Daily Times*, January 20, 1970.

[54] International Observer Team, Report and Findings of the Representatives of Canada, Poland, Sweden, and the United Kingdom, for the period October 1, 1969 to January 31, 1970 (Lagos, February 14, 1970).

exaggerated, in part honestly by people generalizing from insufficient data, and in part, coldly to serve the political purposes of the war.[55]

So deep was the belief in Lagos that the war had been unnecessarily prolonged through humanitarian intervention, and so discredited were the early forecasts of genocide by starvation, that the Gowon government was absolutely committed to demonstrating its self-reliance domestically and internationally. The Nigerian Red Cross was authorized to handle all private foreign donations and continued to direct field operations, although with considerable technical advice from expatriate Red Cross officials. The National Rehabilitation Commission was given responsibility for handling all official foreign relief assistance. To coordinate all of these activities, Gowon appointed one of his most talented and dedicated civil servants, Allison Ayida.[56]

The arrival in Lagos of numerous senior Biafran officials so soon after the war reinforced the belief in federal circles that the government had been well advised to hold a tight reign on international relief activities. Those who returned to Lagos not only appeared well fed, but most reported that no close family members had perished because of the war or a shortage of food. The ability of the Biafran elite to survive relatively unscathed certainly did not erase the specter of millions of malnourished, improverished Ibos, but it probably helped reconciliation between the Nigerian and Biafran elites. For an American living in Lagos at the time, the general lack of recrimination was striking. The federal government declined to hold any victory celebrations or parades, to build war monuments, or to award battle honors or promotions for service in battle.

General Gowon implemented his pledge of a general amnesty on January 15, 1970, and, aside from a handful of junior army officers who allegedly collaborated with the Biafran invasion of the Midwest, there were almost no war-related detentions. High ranking Biafran officers, such as General Philip Effiong, reverted to their prewar rank in the Nigerian army, were placed on immediate indefinite leave, and

[55] Kale Williams actually left Lagos on January 5 with three others and reached the Quaker relief center at Ikot Usen in the Southeastern State on January 10, having visited Asaba, Ibusa, Onitsha, Enugu, and Awgu en route. As Biafra collapsed, Williams and a party of four left Ikot Usen on January 13, traveling to Lagos via Itu, Ikot Ekpene, Aba, Port Harcourt, Umuahia, Bende, Ohafia, Arochukwu, Okigwi, Awgu, Enugu, Awka, and Onitsha. They also met with relief workers from both sides of the conflict who had just been in Owerri, Orlu, Uli, and Ihiala. "Observations on the End of a War," Quaker Headquarters, Lagos, January 21, 1970, pp. 1–3.

[56] Ayida went on an extensive tour of the devastated areas in January 1970, and later said of the thousands of destitute Ibos who had sought refuge in the bush during the final weeks of fighting, "I don't see how they endured for so long. I had never thought the conditions were that bad." Interview: Ayida.

later retired. The only civilian leader known to have been arrested was Ojukwu's chief economic adviser, Dr. Pius Okigbo, and that, according to his associates, was the result of a local and not a federal order. By mid-1971, Dr. Okigbo had been released and was running a consulting firm in Lagos with a large contract from the federal government.

The fate of the three officials who were perhaps most responsible for the development and dissemination of the genocide propaganda is especially interesting. Dr. Ifeagwu Eke, Biafra's commissioner of information, purchased a small fleet of trucks and founded his own transport business shortly after the war. Cyprian Ekwensi, director of information, became chief library officer in the East Central State, in addition to opening a pharmacy in Enugu. Uche Chukwumerije, director of propaganda, launched his own news magazine in Lagos, *Afriscope*, and was soon traveling to OAU meetings as part of the press delegation accompanying Nigeria's head of state.

General Gowon's determination to resist any temptation to extract retribution domestically was consistent with a postwar foreign policy that was devoid of self-righteous indignation or vindictiveness against those states that had been friendly with Biafra. In his January 15, 1970 address Gowon pledged to "maintain correct relations with all foreign governments, notwithstanding the anxieties that they may have caused us."[57] When the federal government staged its tenth independence anniversary celebrations in October 1970, all four African states that had recognized Biafra were invited to send representatives, and all accepted; the resumption of full diplomatic relations quickly followed.

LIMITED EFFECTS OF CIVIL WAR DIPLOMACY

It is too early to evaluate the enduring effects of Nigerian civil war diplomacy, either on the development of that country's foreign policy or on the internationalization of other domestic conflicts. Nigeria still is a relatively young country that had accumulated only six years of diplomatic experience prior to Biafran secession, and postwar domestic concerns have seriously constrained the formulation and implementation of a consistent foreign policy. As for the wider international implications, it remains to be seen whether Biafra's demise will significantly influence policies elsewhere. Because of the importance of unforeseen domestic and foreign variables that affected the duration and intensity of the Nigerian conflict, and given the dearth of in-depth case studies about the international politics of other civil wars, the basis for con-

[57] "The Dawn of National Reconciliation," Kirk-Greene, *Crisis and Conflict*, II, 460.

fident theorizing is rather thin. A review of the immediate impact of Nigeria's wartime diplomacy does suggest, however, several tentative conclusions that deserve further consideration.

One obvious feature of the international involvement in Nigeria's civil war was that it did not escalate into another test of strength between clients of the Soviet Union and the United States. The syndrome of intervention and counterintervention that has frequently intensified the violence of domestic strife in the era of the Cold War was not repeated in Nigeria. The reasons for this were discussed in the first section of the book, and relate to the nature of the issues that divided Nigerians, the absence of ideological cleavages, the sudden birth of the Biafran rebellion prior to the establishment of any formal or covert linkages to foreign governments, and such external factors as the thaw in relations between the two superpowers and the immediate preoccupation with war in the Middle East and in Vietnam. The major powers had very little incentive to meddle and most, including Great Britain, initially adopted a wait-and-see attitude. Unlike other civil-war situations, the Biafran insurgents actually sought to reinforce this tendency toward neutrality as a means of discrediting federal authority internationally, denying Lagos access to traditional sources of military supplies, and further undermining the confidence of the already shaky Gowon regime.

As soon as Nigeria began to demonstrate the military capacity to defeat the secession and to take the further insurance of purchasing Soviet jet aircraft, the Western powers started to embrace the federal cause more openly, and the possibility of non-African military intervention to aid Biafra appears to have been foreclosed. The Nigerian civil war thus became the first post-World War II large-scale armed conflict—between armies representing the interests of more than 50 million people—that was devoid of Cold War overtones. This development, and the containment of several smaller domestic conflicts in Africa in the late 1960s, led one observer to suggest that Africa could become a "strategically sterile environment" by tacit agreement among the major powers.[58] The validity of this rather hopeful notion was unfortunately undermined during the 1975 Angolan crisis, when there was no central authority comparable to the federal military government that could establish a credible nonaligned posture.

The reluctance of non-African governments to become embroiled in Nigeria's civil war was reinforced by the positions adopted in the Organization of African Unity, whose members actively sought to insulate the Nigerian conflict and to arrange a peaceful settlement that would guarantee the territorial integrity of Nigeria. The OAU's behavior,

[58] Nielsen, *The Great Powers and Africa*, pp. 370–373.

in this instance, would tend to confirm what William Zartman refers to as "Rule 1" of African diplomacy: "that intra-system solutions are to be preferred over extra-system solutions to African problems whenever possible."[59]

The reasons why Zartman's norm appears applicable to the Nigerian case are not difficult to discern. Biafra indirectly threatened the security of many fragile OAU states, where disgruntled ethnic groups could have been inspired by the dissolution of Nigeria. Militarily, African states are powerless to block a major intervention from outside the region. This sense of insecurity can easily be aroused, and the risk that foreign aid to Biafra might have helped establish the precedent of a successful secession became another incentive for African leaders to try to contain the internationalization of the Nigerian conflict.

The main means available to African governments were political and diplomatic pressures that were generated primarily through the projection of Organization of African Unity resolutions into the wider international arena. The OAU was able to serve this function because Nigeria chose not to deny the regional body an opportunity to discuss the civil war, even though this could have been vetoed on the grounds that it violated Article III (2) of the charter: "non-interference in the internal affairs of states." The creation of a Consultative Committee on Nigeria, which was also wisely accepted by Lagos, included several of Africa's most pro-western leaders, who appear to have been moved by a desire to arrange a solution that would not only respect Nigeria's territorial integrity but also eliminate the danger that Lagos might become more dependent on the Soviet Union. The continued support of federal policies by committee members who had close ties to Washington no doubt reassured those who may have been apprehensive about the Russian presence in Lagos. Thus, OAU involvement not only enhanced the legitimacy of Nigeria's domestic policies, but also the credibility of her foreign policy.

Whether OAU support for the federal government actually deterred non-African powers from intervening more actively to save Biafra, or merely provided those governments, including the French, with another reason for doing what they were otherwise inclined to do is difficult to determine. Had Biafra failed to penetrate the international system by appealing directly to world public opinion, the question about the importance of OAU support would no doubt be academic. The OAU's political function changed substantially in 1968 when the Western democracies were suddenly confronted with intense domestic pressure to aid Biafra, not because of the prospect of any political, military, or

[59] Zartman, "Africa as a Subordinate State System in International Relations," p. 559.

economic gains, but for moral reasons. It was at this stage in the internationalization process that the Western powers found the psychological force of official African opinion to be a useful antidote to the prointerventionist pressures at home.

The Nigerian conflict appears to have further resolved any doubts about the viability of territorial frontiers in black Africa, at least with regard to the threat of secession. With the possible exception of Eritrea one cannot foresee an insurgency gaining the external support that would be necessary to achieve self-determination. The fusion of two or more states raises other issues; voluntary union would probably be acceptable to African opinion, but wars of aggression certainly run contrary to emerging intra-African norms and, thus far, the region has been notably free of interstate warfare. There are, however, no institutional arrangements for peacekeeping or for the settlement of disputes, including the resolution of any allegations that a change of government has been the result of subversion. In assessing the weakness of the OAU and the lack of means to enforce international norms of conduct, the reader may recall that despite the strength of the pro-Nigerian consensus in the OAU, the organization made no attempt to condemn the four members that recognized Biafra.

Among the international aspects of the Nigerian crisis that are likely to be remembered was Biafra's remarkable success in attracting substantial nongovernmental assistance from Europe and North America. As noted in Chapter 6, one of the few external contacts that Biafra continued to enjoy was with world Christianity. There are no obvious precedents that would have suggested a willingness and ability of the churches to mobilize vast amounts of material aid, as well as pro-Biafran political support in Europe and North America, and it is unlikely that this degree of direct involvement will be repeated elsewhere.

Political and natural disasters have caused severe human deprivation in other parts of Africa since the mid-1960s—in Sudan, Burundi, Ethiopia, and throughout the Sahelian countries, for example—but the reaction of public opinion in Europe and America never approached the concern over Biafra. Several variables, in addition to transnational religious ties, appear to have been important in the Biafran case: the enclave's coastal location that facilitated the delivery of relief and visits by foreign press and film crews; the federal government's decision not to acquire the means to close down Uli airstrip; and the availability of numerous articulate and Western-educated members of the Ibo elite who could appeal directly for external support. Yet if aspiring secessionist leaders elsewhere have been sobered by the Biafran experiment, it is with good reason.

The failure to attract substantial support from Western governments demonstrated the limitations of a strategy that depended on a direct appeal to foreign public opinion that ran contrary to official perceptions of national interest. When pressed, the reactions of the Western democratic regimes, notably those of Britain and the United States, suggest the range of measures available to popularly elected officials who remain committed to defending the international status quo—in this case, the territorial integrity of Nigeria. Through quiet diplomacy in support of the OAU's role as the proper judge of the Nigerian crisis, by promoting peace talks, however devoid of substance, and by supporting the relief efforts while carefully isolating intergovernmental humanitarian cooperation from the regular diplomatic processes and institutions, the Western powers were able to help contain Biafra's penetration of the international system.

Had there been mass slaughter along with the Nigerian military victory, it is conceivable that residual feelings of regret and guilt throughout Europe and America might have encouraged a greater readiness to meet the needs of some future secessionist movement where civilian suffering was a major issue. The federal government's restrained behavior in January 1970 and the reconciliation finally discredited the allegations of genocide. Biafra's leaders continue to claim, however, that by prolonging the war they bought time for the federal army to acquire greater discipline and a sensitivity to world opinion. The argument rests, of course, on the unprovable assumption that had Nigeria conquered Biafra in mid-1968, then many more lives would have been lost than the number who perished during the ensuing months of deprivation.

Postwar revelations have made the humanitarian agencies somewhat defensive about their intervention. Those who were involved with Jointchurchaid and the Red Cross efforts in Biafra believe that the public reaction to apparent exaggerations will make future fund raising more difficult, especially if there is a need to secure government appropriations. Moreover, sentiment within groups such as the World Council of Churches seems to have moved against becoming so deeply involved again with the politics of a civil war. This reluctance, by both actors and financial contributors, already has been demonstrated in other situations, including both natural and man-made disasters, when local political concerns have been raised.[60]

Another key element in limiting Biafra's influence was the flexible and nondoctrinaire conduct of Nigeria's foreign relations. General Gowon may have lacked the charisma and sharp wit of his adversary, but his growing reputation as a compassionate and reasonable leader was an

[60] Interview: Desaix Myers III, USAID, Bangladesh relief program.

important asset for Nigeria. His foreign policy was formulated and carried out by an adroit group of civil servants that strove to maintain good relations with all governments, including that of France. For Nigeria's relatively small diplomatic corps of approximately two hundred officers, nearly all of whom had less than seven years of experience in foreign affairs prior to Biafran secession, the lessons of civil war diplomacy are likely to affect the development of foreign policy for many years.

A framework for Nigeria's postwar foreign policy was actually established in June 1969, seven months prior to Biafra's defeat, when the Ministry of External Affairs summoned its entire corps of ambassadors home for several days of discussion and policy planning. The only previous meeting of this type was the June 1966 meeting of Nigeria's ambassadors in Africa that was referred to in Chapter 1; there would not be another major policy review during the immediate postwar years. Because of the smallness of the Nigerian foreign affairs establishment and the influence of senior diplomats in establishing foreign policy in a military government, the record of the June 1969 discussions provides important insight into how Nigerian diplomats hoped to shape postwar foreign relations.

The tenor of the 1969 ambassadorial meeting was surprisingly similar to that of 1966. The emphasis on modest international aspirations and a pragmatic approach to foreign affairs had not changed during the war. Federal diplomacy had, of necessity, been reactive, but because of an awareness of Nigeria's limited power and influence beyond West Africa, there was a consensus in Lagos that the country's future success in world affairs would depend more on being adaptable than by undertaking any bold, new initiatives. The wartime policy of trying to be flexible while not compromising on matters of substance regarding Biafran autonomy was seen in 1969 as a cause for much self-congratulation. Allowing the OAU to seize the Nigerian issue, going through the motions of peace-talk diplomacy, receiving an international military observer team, and maintaining correct if cool relations with France were viewed as key steps in isolating Biafra internationally. For the future, the ambassadors agreed that twelve principles should guide Nigerian foreign policy, including the pursuit of good relations with all states, especially in Africa; the eschewing of territorial expansion; and the maintenance of strict nonalignment vis-à-vis any military or ideological bloc.[61] The framework was entirely consistent

[61] These principles were: "(1) good neighbourly relations with our immediate neighbours; (2) primacy of Africa in our external affairs; (3) friendship with all states; (4) non-alignment and non-involvement in military and ideological blocs in Africa; (5) adherence to moral and legal principles of international law

with the briefer version formulated at the 1966 meeting, where "pragmatism" had similarly been elevated to a point of principle.

The substance of Nigeria's nonalignment was a major topic of discussion in 1969 because of the civil war experience. Nigeria's expanded ties with the Soviet Union were judged less for their strategic value than for their role in ensuring support from the more radical members of the OAU and in deterring greater interference by Western powers.[62] Anticipating future needs, the ambassadors urged that an effort be made to strengthen the credibility of Nigeria's nonaligned stance. It was noted, for example, that many Nigerian officials uncritically accepted the Anglo-American notion that "only Eastern European countries pose security threats to Nigeria's stability," despite the fact that these Eastern European powers had been strongly supportive of the federal government during the civil war, and had also cooperated with Nigeria "in areas of decolonization in Africa and in trying to alter the existing imperial patterns of trade under UNCTAD (United Nations Conference on Trade and Development) and similar conferences."[63]

In recommending that relations with Eastern Europe and the Soviet Union be expanded, the ambassadors suggested that the government proceed cautiously; they urged, for example, that care be taken not to alienate the Federal Republic of Germany by appearing to support the Russian position on reunification. From Nigeria's perspective, the real value of improved relations with the East was the opportunity to offset Western influence. Indicative of this attitude was a recommendation for specific measures that Nigeria's envoys felt would enhance

---

and friendly relations between states: (a) sovereign equality of all states, large and small; (b) respect for the sovereignty and territorial integrity of all states; (c) non-interference in the internal affairs of other states; (d) peaceful settlement of disputes between states; (e) acceptance of existing boundaries of states inherited from colonialism, subject to mutually agreed adjustments; (f) the right of all states to self determination; (6) inter-African cooperation in diplomatic, economic, cultural and scientific fields and African solidarity based on tolerance; (7) no ambition for territorial expansionism; (8) non-aggression against other states; (9) charity and understanding towards less-developed African states; (10) pragmatism; (11) Africa being declared a nuclear-free zone; and (12) anti-colonialism, anti-racialism." Ministry of External Affairs, Conference of Nigerian Ambassadors, June 1969, Lagos, Nigeria (cited hereafter as MEA/CNA/June 1969), Nigeria's Policy in Africa, Principles, Objectives, and Means, pp. 1–2.

[62] Soon after the war, Nigeria's ambassador to Moscow asserted that Soviet support was "responsible for the Federal victory more than any other single thing, more than all other things put together." *The Times* (London), January 21, 1970. The consensus among Nigeria's ambassadors seven months earlier had been only slightly more restrained: "The Soviet Union has been of immense help and assistance, in terms of hard-ware and diplomatically, during the crisis. Without them the course of the civil war might have been different." MEA/CNA/June 1969, Policy of Nigeria Towards the Eastern European Countries, p. 2.

[63] *Ibid.*

Nigeria's nonaligned status: "Nigeria should consider favorably in principle applications by Eastern European countries to open cultural and consular centers in Nigeria in order to offset the predominance of the activities of Western powers in these fields. The ideal thing, however . . . would be to restrict the activities of Western powers consistent with international practice and reciprocity."[64] When the Soviet Union requested permission to open consular offices around Nigeria in 1970, the federal government declined, and used that rejection as a reason for denying similar applications from Britain and the United States to reopen their missions in Benin and Enugu after the war. Another manifestation of this attitude occurred in relations with the foreign press. A Nigerian diplomat recalls having been approached by Soviet journalist Victor Lewis, who requested an immediate visa to visit Nigeria following Biafra's defeat. The diplomat told him he would have to go through the elaborate clearance process that so exasperated Western correspondents. Lewis reportedly protested what he called Nigerian ingratitude, only to be reminded that Nigeria had paid cash for all of its weapons and therefore had no reason to be grateful.

The desire in Lagos gradually to disengage from Nigeria's traditional friends, notably the United States and Great Britain, reflected not only a desire to enhance the country's nonaligned image, but also a residual bitterness over the attitude that Western powers had exhibited toward the federal government during the civil war. It was the consensus of the 1969 ambassadorial meeting that "the basic attitude of condescension of Western Europe toward Africa has made Western Europe unable to understand that an African country could be fighting for European political concepts of sovereignty, national and territorial integrity."[65]

The Federal Government tried not to antagonize these powers during or immediately after the civil war. Nigeria, after all, has had a continuing need for Western investment and technical assistance, and has sought to expand export markets throughout Europe. Political relations with the West have been based on two fundamental assumptions that Nigerian diplomats believe were confirmed by the civil war experience: first, that most of the Western European countries lack substantial political influence without the active support of the United States; and second, that among Western powers, only France, with its heavy involvement in West African affairs, could pose a direct threat to Nigeria's national security.[66] The intensity of Franco-Nigerian competition in West Africa is discussed below.

[64] *Ibid.*, p. 5.
[65] MEA/CNA/June 1969, Policy of Nigeria Towards Western Europe, Including the Americas (Part I), p. 3.
[66] *Ibid.*, p. 4.

At the level of global politics, notably within the United Nations and its member agencies, Nigeria has continued to move rather unobstrusively through the mainstream of the "group of 77" nonaligned states in their struggle with the industrialized countries for a more equitable distribution of global wealth and technology. Because it has been accepted in Lagos that "with the increased influence of geographical groups in the decision making processes of the United Nations, it was important that Nigeria should maximize her role in the African group . . . as a means of making her views well known to and appreciated by other groups,"[67] Nigerian diplomats have displayed a special interest in those issues before the UN that are likely to affect the cohesiveness of the OAU, or are of vital concern to one or more of the African members.

Despite the prominence given to African diplomatic support in isolating Biafra, there have been no illusions in Lagos about the limited capacity of the Organization of African Unity. Nigerian officials have acknowledged that "in the absence of instruments of power and policy-like sanctions in the use of force, the OAU lacks the means to legitimize its authority and its resolutions."[68] This has not caused Lagos to withhold financial or diplomatic support from the OAU, but rather to augment these efforts at several levels in the African region.

Lagos has tended to mistrust any African subregional bloc that does not include the federal government. Toward the end of the civil war, Nigeria's ambassadors warned that Tanzania and Zambia would somehow use the incipient East and Central African economic community to launch a new diplomatic offensive against Nigeria and, in the long term, that group was seen "to constitute a threat to the predominant role of West Africa in Africa and to Nigeria in particular."[69] The francophone economic group, OCAM, was regarded as a more direct threat to Nigeria's political and economic security, and it was recommended that Lagos seek to undermine OCAM's solidarity by strengthening bilateral ties with Nigeria's francophone neighbors, and by promoting the creation of a new bilingual economic grouping in West Africa that would supplant OCAM and open new markets for Nigeria's industrial products.[70]

Although the concept of the Nigerian-led new West African Economic Community was strongly endorsed at the 1969 ambassadorial meet-

[67] MEA/CNA/June 1969, Foreign Policy of Nigeria Towards the United Nations Organisation, p. 3.

[68] MEA/CNA/June 1969, Nigeria's Policy in Africa, Policy and Attitudes Towards the O.A.U., p. 3.

[69] MEA/CNA/June 1969, Nigeria's Policy Towards African Regional Groups, p. 3.

[70] Ibid., p. 7.

ing, the chances of success were considered slight. These initial doubts were confirmed when thirteen prospective members were quietly canvassed in late 1970 and declined to participate in a major confer- ence.[71] The federal government continued to press the question, how- ever, and in April 1972 General Gowon made a surprise visit to Togo to announce the decision to establish a Nigerian-Togolese Economic Com- munity, which the communiqué issued after the meeting described as "an embryo for a larger West African Economic Community."[72] This was the first time that a former British colony had agreed to establish institutional links with a French-speaking country, and it led eventually to the Treaty of Lagos, which created the fifteen-member Economic Community of West African States (ECOWAS) on May 27, 1975.[73]

A similar history has marked the revitalization of the Chad Basin Commission. In 1969 Nigeria's ambassadors recommended fresh steps to encourage greater cooperation among Nigeria, Cameroon, Chad, and Niger, and by 1972 the Chad Basin Commission reconvened for the first time in eight years to discuss common problems. This was fol- lowed by the establishment of a Chad Basin Fund, to which Nigeria has become the principal contributor.[74]

Federal officials have recognized that Nigeria's relative size and military and economic strength are a source of apprehension to her neighbors. While these smaller states generally welcome bilateral financial assistance, there have already been instances when the activities of the Chad Basin and the more recently reactivated Niger River Commission have been curtailed because the partners feared that if Nigeria assumed a greater share of the financing, she would also exercise undue influence on policy.[75] Lagos also has accepted that these same francophone governments willingly perpetuate the "complex economic, technical, military, and psychic ties"[76] with France, and that blatant pressure from Lagos for demonstrations of greater independence from French domination by these small powers could prove counter- productive should Paris then actively attempt to subvert Nigeria's efforts to forge new political and economic links in the region.

[71] See Aluko, "Nigeria's Role in Inter-African Relations," p. 151.

[72] New York Times, May 7, 1972.

[73] The members of the Economic Community of West African States (ECOWAS) are: Mauritania, Senegal, Gambia, Guinea, Guinea-Bissau, Sierra Leone, Liberia, Ivory Coast, Mali, Upper Volta, Ghana, Togo, Dahomey (Benin), Niger, and Nigeria. West Africa, No. 3025, June 16, 1975, p. 679.

[74] By 1975 Lagos was contributing approximately $1 million to the Chad Basin Commission's Development Fund. West Africa, No. 3078, June 28, 1976, p. 930.

[75] Mayall, "Oil and Nigerian Foreign Policy," p. 327.

[76] MEA/CNA/June 1969, Policy of Nigeria Towards Western Europe, including the Americas (Part I), p. 1.

Although Nigerians are bitter about French support for Biafra during the civil war, this experience was not entirely negative. A major lesson of civil-war diplomacy, as viewed from Lagos, was the limited extent of French control over her former colonies. At the 1969 foreign policy meeting, Nigerian ambassadors noted with satisfaction that several of the economically weak francophone states had apparently flaunted their reliance on Paris and, despite a continued dependence on France for budgetary subvention and other economic assistance, publicly defended the cause of Nigerian unity. With this in mind, the ambassadors recommended that the federal government carefully avoid any break with the French, while actively seeking stronger bilateral ties in francophone Africa through "financial subventions, where feasible; secondment of appropriate personnel; participation in common economic projects; communication and transportation links; sale of power from Kainji dam; and the appointment of Ambassadors."[77] All of the measures were pursued during the years immediately following the civil war.

The good will that the federal government enjoyed in its wartime relations with most of West Africa continued to grow in the postwar years. Had the situation been different, with more states recognizing Biafra, it is difficult to suggest how the federal government would have responded, aside from breaking diplomatic relations—or, in some cases, imposing economic sanctions. In 1969, during the ambassadorial conference, reprisals were discussed, but only in the vaguest terms.[78] How these might have been accomplished was never spelled out, nor is there any evidence that any action was ever taken. To the contrary, a more explicit recommendation "that Nigeria should use every diplomatic means available to win over those inimical to her" was strenuously pursued during the final months of the war. During the 1969 OAU Summit in Addis Ababa, General Gowon held personal meetings with representatives of the four governments recognizing Biafra, including President Julius Nyerere of Tanzania, which helped set the stage for the normalization of relations soon after the cessation of hostilities.

Among Nigeria's immediate neighbors, only Dahomey (Benin) provoked the federal government during the civil war, and the brevity of estranged relations in early 1969 illustrates the resilience of Nigeria's policy toward its weaker neighbors. As noted earlier, Dahomey's agree-

---

[77] *Ibid.*, p. 4.

[78] E.g.: "Nigeria should follow with keener interest some of the centrifugal and divisive forces at work in some of the countries which have recognized the rebel regime [and] . . . Nigeria should not discourage the forces that threaten [their] security." MEA/CNA/June 1969, Nigeria's Policy Towards Africa, Its Application to Individual States, p. 4.

ment to serve as a staging area for Red Cross relief to Biafra caused the federal government to apply economic sanctions which, in turn, finally led to a grounding of the airlift. Given the power disparity between the two countries, Dahomey's boldness was astonishing, and Nigeria's restraint was almost as surprising. Soon after the war, the federal government took quick action to improve relations with this tiny neighbor by issuing Nigeria's first interest-free loan to another government, approximately three million dollars toward the cost of road development from the Nigerian border to Dahomey's capital city. The cautious handling of relations with Dahomey is indicative of Nigeria's conduct in West Africa. Aside from trying to promote greater economic cooperation, the federal government has made little effort to extend its influence, politically or militarily. Since the civil war, the country has been free of external threats to its security and nothing in its international relations has suggested any chauvinistic presumptions.[79]

The permanent secretary of external affairs signaled the postwar drift in Nigeria's foreign policy before a closed-door meeting of senior army officers on July 15, 1971: "We have tremendous prestige in Africa and in Europe, how much prestige of course we honestly don't know. We are one of those outstanding elephants; there are not many that will side with us just to go together. That is why we sometimes press our feelings in order to get other Africans to believe in African unity. We want to press our own views but Nigeria has got to be very careful not to be seen throwing its weight around."[80]

The meeting had been called to consider whether there might be an international role for Nigeria's large military establishment of approximately 250,000; a force that towered over Dahomey's 2,200 man army and Cameroon's 4,300 troops, and that was nearly four times the size of the combined armed forces for the thirteen independent countries that made up West Africa.[81] For a brief period in the early 1970s, military planners in Lagos perceived a legitimate need for a West African regional security pact, if only to protect those governments that feared foreign reprisals for assisting liberation groups in the remaining Portuguese territories. The OAU had recently ruled out the possibility of an African high command because of "the different political backgrounds of member states," but the chairman of the OAU's ad hoc defense commission, Nigerian Colonel Olufemi Olutoye, reported that

[79] For a discussion of Nigeria's post-war relations with West African countries, see Ofoegbu, "The Relations Between Nigeria and Its Neighbours," pp. 33–39.

[80] Senior Military Officers Seminar, Nigerian Institute of International Affairs, Lagos, July 15, 1971, "African High Command—Political and Economic Implications."

[81] See Booth, *The Armed Forces of African States.* Estimate of Nigeria's armed forces confirmed in Lagos by author.

the commission had recommended the establishment of regional defense agreements.[82] When the Nigerian military reviewed this proposal, the practical constraints became obvious: language barriers, poor military intelligence, the absence of standardized military equipment and procedures, logistical constraints—including insufficient air transport—a lack of international procedures for appointing military commanders and financing operations, and even a lack of procedures for determining when an actual act or threat of aggression against an African state had occurred.

Instead of dwelling on the long-range possibilities for taking a more active role in promoting international security or the liberation of colonial areas in Africa, Nigeria's military commanders have had to face more urgent difficulties in managing the armed forces. These have included: integrating the three military divisions that had operated almost autonomously during the war and were plagued by ethnic cleavages, language barriers, and an understaffed officer corps that lacked technical and management skills; providing basic housing and training facilities for thousands of troops that had been hastily inducted and sent off to battle; finding ways to use idle troops for public works projects; and, most importantly, demobilizing the armed forces in ways that would not offend any particular ethnic group or otherwise introduce greater instability to Nigerian society.

Just as the Nigerian military is many times larger than that of other African countries, so too does Nigeria's gross domestic product (GDP) dwarf other black African economies.[83] In 1968, at the height of the war, Nigeria's GDP was approximately $4.8 billion, twenty-five times the size of Dahomey's GDP, and equal to almost three-quarters of the combined GDPs of all West African countries. The strength of the federal economy gained little international attention prior to the country's oil boom, but the wartime economic record was a source of much satisfaction, and perhaps some overconfidence, among federal bureaucrats in Lagos. Despite the loss of the Eastern Region, which accounted for 30 percent of the country's prewar industrial capacity, Nigeria's gross national product actually rose 19 percent during the four years, 1966/67–1970/71, a figure that compares favorably with the 30 percent increase in real terms that occurred over the six years prior to secession. In accomplishing this growth record, the federal government borrowed heavily internally, while the country's external debt was carefully controlled and actually declined between 1968 and the end of the war.

[82] Senior Military Officers Seminar, July 15, 1971.
[83] The following economic analysis is based on Gaston V. Rimlinger, "Nigeria's Economic Outlook for 1970," and "Nigeria Economic Report, August 1974" (mimeographed).

The Central Bank's management of the external debt was an impressive demonstration of the government's determination to finance the war itself and to maintain its independence.

At the height of wartime production, petroleum contributed only twelve percent of Nigeria's export earnings, and barely one percent of the value added to the gross domestic product. A major increase in oil exports was anticipated as the war reached its conclusion, but the post-1973 bonanza from higher prices could not have been predicted. By 1974/75, Nigeria's GDP reached $19.7 billion at current prices, a figure that was larger than the combined gross domestic products of the rest of the black African countries. Whether this preeminent economic position can or will be converted into greater international influence is problematic because, just as the federal army is constrained by internal problems, Nigeria's GDP must be viewed against major dislocations in the domestic economy that, in turn, are affected by political instability.

The aura of national power created by oil wealth pales in reference to the country's per capita income. Nigeria is not only the richest state in black Africa, but it is also the most populous and, by standard measures, remains a less developed country. It is difficult to determine how poor it is because there has been no agreement on a national census. The federal government's census in 1973 produced the much disputed figure of 80 million, while the United Nations projections for that year estimated a total population of around 62 million. With a GDP of $19.7 billion, the country's 1974 per capita income would have been between $246 and $320, depending on the population size.[84] In terms of social equity and productivity, recent increases in the per capita income are deceiving because they have been caused by the petroleum sector, which is an international enclave employing relatively few Nigerians.

Federal civil servants were aware before the war ended that a shortage of neither capital nor foreign exchange would be a constraint on economic development in the 1970s. Oil revenues would be necessary for economic self-reliance, but an insufficient condition for rapid economic development and domestic harmony. Among the problems confronting the federal military government since the end of the war have been severe income disparities, inflation, urban squalor, inadequate food production, lack of rural services, inadequate transport and communication facilities, widespread corruption in government, demands for adjustments in the twelve-state arrangement, the need for a new constitution, and growing pressures for a return to civilian rule. Indeed,

[84] If the per capita income were computed in constant 1962–1963 prices, the real income level would be approximately one half the 1974 figures.

the very existence of unprecedented surpluses in Nigeria's balance of payments has aroused popular expectations for a vast array of new services, such as universal free primary education and health care delivery systems, that far exceed the government's executive and managerial capacity.

The oil boom has also complicated the pursuit of postwar foreign policy objectives, most notably, the promotion of greater international cooperation in West Africa. The quadrupling of oil prices in 1973 caused great hardship for non-oil-producing countries of the Third World. The impact was especially severe for Nigeria's impoverished neighbors, several of whom are among the group of twenty-five poorest countries that the World Bank has called the Fourth World.

Nigeria is a member of the Organization of Petroleum Exporting Countries (OPEC) and has been one of the most outspoken supporters of maximum pricing. Lagos chose not to participate in the 1973 embargo against the Western industrial countries and has become for periods the United States' leading supplier of foreign oil. Federal representatives defend their demands for higher prices in terms of their country's long-term capital requirements, although this has provided no consolation to Nigeria's neighbors. Initial efforts by officials in the federal ministry of external affairs to promote a two-tier pricing system that would give preference to the members of the Economic Community of West African States were not approved by the federal executive council.

Sales to African countries amounted to only 3 percent of Nigeria's petroleum exports in 1974, but federal authorities apparently felt that the two-tier system might be abused and could weaken Nigeria's standing within OPEC.[85] There has been considerable discussion in Lagos about a system of grants and soft loans to alleviate the plight of oil-poor African states but, in the immediate postwar years, the federal government was more concerned about pursuing ambitious domestic objectives than jeopardizing the vague aspirations of its African policy.

Economically, militarily, and demographically, Nigeria would appear to be a dominant regional power and, prior to the civil war, federal diplomats talked easily about Nigeria's "manifest destiny" and her natural sphere of influence in Africa. Ten years later any assessment of Nigeria's latent power or potential for leadership in African and world affairs continues to depend on highly tentative assumptions about the country's internal political stability. When General Gowon was deposed by a military coup d'état on July 29, 1975, he was widely regarded as one of Africa's leading statesmen, and the fact that he was

[85] Mayall, "Oil and Nigerian Foreign Policy," pp. 328–330.

at the time attending a meeting of the Organization of African Unity serves as an ironic reminder of the primacy of domestic concerns. The first executive action taken by the new federal regime was equally symbolic; it was aimed at alleviating traffic congestion in Lagos.

Military victory in January 1970 may have eliminated the threat of secession and established a more viable federal system. Unfortunately, it was not the end of Nigeria's domestic strife, but only a major step in the long struggle to achieve national integration. Many more years will have to pass before the country's leaders will feel secure enough domestically to concentrate on building the international goodwill and respect that will enable them to serve as catalysts for greater economic and political cooperation in Africa—a role that seemed within Nigeria's grasp in the afterglow of civil war diplomacy.

APPENDICES

APPENDIX I

Schedule of Nigerian Interests in Other Countries

COUNTRY	POLITICAL			ECONOMIC			COMMERCIAL				CULTURAL (Educational)							CONSULAR	TOTAL POINTS
	International status	Membership of group of states	Security of defense	Industrial know-how or machinery	Industrial aid	Economic aid	Market for Nigerian produce	Market for minerals	Market for Nigerian manufactures	Agricultural or technical aid	Post-graduate University or technical institutes	University or technical institutes	Scholarships	Nigerian student body	Religious	Racial	Historical or geographical	Resident Nigerians	Maximum possible - 180 minimum - 18
ZONE A **(i) Western & Southern Europe**																			
Eire	5	2	2	4	2	2	4	4	2	4	8	8	6	7	7	6	5	8	88
Britain	9	10	10	10	10	8	10	10	2	10	10	10	10	10	4	10	10	10	163
Norway	4	3	1	3	3	4	4	4	3	6	4	5	6	2	1	7	1	1	60
Sweden	7	7	3	5	5	6	4	4	3	5	5	5	6	2	1	4	1	1	75
Denmark	5	5	3	5	5	5	4	4	3	5	4	4	6	2	1	4	1	1	67
Finland	3	2	1	3	2	2	2	2	2	3	2	2	3	1	1	1	1	1	34
Netherlands	5	8	6	5	5	5	10	7	1	4	6	5	6	3	1	1	1	1	82
Belgium	5	7	4	4	4	4	4	4	1	1	4	4	4	2	1	1	1	1	59
Luxembourg	2	3	1	1	1	1	1	1	1	5	2	1	1	1	1	1	1	1	22
France	9	10	8	8	7	7	7	7	2	6	4	6	5	4	1	1	1	4	101
West Germany	9	9	5	10	9	10	8	7	1	7	4	6	5	5	1	1	4	4	106
Italy	6	7	5	5	5	3	4	4	2	5	4	5	4	2	8	1	2	2	91
Austria	4	3	1	3	3	3	4	4	2	1	4	4	1	1	1	1	3	1	50
Portugal	4	4	2	2	1	1	1	1	1	1	1	1	1	1	1	1	1	1	26

COUNTRY	POLITICAL			ECONOMIC			COMMERCIAL				CULTURAL							CONSULAR	TOTAL POINTS
											Educational								Maximum possible - 180 minimum - 18
	International status	Membership of group of states	Security of defense	Industrial know-how or machinery	Industrial aid	Economic aid	Market for Nigerian produce	Market for minerals	Market for Nigerian manufactures	Agricultural or technical aid	Post-graduate	University or technical institutes	Scholarships	Nigerian student body	Religious	Racial	Historical or geographical	Resident Nigerians	
Switzerland	7	1	1	8	4	8	8	7	4	5	4	6	6	4	1	1	1	3	79
Spain	4	1	1	1	1	1	2	1	4	1	1	1	1	1	1	1	1	3	27
Greece	4	1	1	1	1	1	4	4	4	1	1	1	1	1	1	1	1	1	30
Turkey	5	5	1	1	1	1	2	1	1	1	1	1	1	1	6	1	1	1	32
Cyprus	2	3	1	1	1	1	3	1	2	1	1	1	1	1	1	1	1	1	24
Malta	1	3	1	1	1	1	2	1	2	4	1	1	1	1	1	1	1	1	25
(ii) *Eastern Europe*																			
Eastern Germany	5	5	2	5	5	4	4	4	1	4	4	4	5	4	1	1	1	3	62
Poland	7	8	2	5	5	4	5	5	1	3	4	4	5	3	1	1	1	2	66
Czechoslovakia	7	7	2	5	5	4	7	6	2	3	4	4	5	3	1	1	1	2	69
Hungary	6	6	1	4	4	3	4	3	2	3	3	3	2	2	1	1	1	1	50
Bulgaria	4	4	1	3	2	2	3	3	2	2	3	3	4	2	1	1	1	1	42
Rumania	5	5	1	3	2	2	3	3	2	2	2	2	2	1	1	1	1	1	39
USSR	10	10	6	8	7	8	8	8	2	8	4	6	6	5	1	1	1	4	103
Yugoslavia	7	7	2	4	4	3	6	5	1	3	3	3	3	2	1	1	1	1	62
Albania	2	3	1	1	1	1	1	1	1	1	1	1	1	1	1	1	1	1	21
ZONE B																			
(iii) *North America*																			
U.S.A.	10	10	8	8	8	10	10	10	1	8	10	10	8	8	1	10	7	8	145
Canada	6	8	8	7	7	8	7	7	2	7	8	8	7	5	1	4	1	3	104

COUNTRY	POLITICAL			ECONOMIC			COMMERCIAL				CULTURAL (Educational)							CONSULAR	TOTAL POINTS
	International status	Membership of group of states	Security of defense	Industrial know-how or machinery	Industrial aid	Economic aid	Market for Nigerian produce	Market for minerals	Market for Nigerian manufactures	Agricultural or technical aid	Post-graduate	University or technical institutes	Scholarships	Nigerian student body	Religious	Racial	Historical or geographical	Resident Nigerians	Maximum possible - 180 minimum - 18
(iv) Central America																			
Mexico	7	8	2	3	2	1	3	2	6	1	2	2	1	1	1	1	1	1	45
Guatemala	2	1	1	1	1	1	1	1	1	1	1	1	1	1	1	1	1	1	19
Honduras	2	1	1	1	1	1	1	1	1	1	1	1	1	1	1	1	1	1	19
El Salvador	2	1	1	1	1	1	1	1	1	1	1	1	1	1	1	1	1	1	19
Nicaragua	2	1	1	1	1	1	1	1	1	1	1	1	1	1	1	1	1	1	19
Costa Rica	2	1	1	1	1	1	1	1	1	1	1	1	1	1	1	1	1	1	19
Panama	2	1	1	1	1	1	1	1	1	1	1	1	1	1	1	1	1	1	19
(v) South America																			
Colombia	2	2	1	1	1	1	1	1	1	1	1	1	1	1	1	1	1	1	20
Venezuela	3	3	1	1	1	1	1	1	1	1	1	1	1	1	1	1	1	1	22
Guiana	1	1	1	1	1	1	1	1	1	1	1	1	1	1	1	1	1	1	18
Ecuador	1	1	1	1	1	1	1	1	1	1	1	1	1	1	1	1	1	1	18
Peru	3	3	1	2	2	1	1	2	1	1	1	1	1	1	1	1	1	1	22
Bolivia	3	3	3	4	2	2	1	1	1	1	1	1	1	1	1	1	1	1	24
Brazil	7	8	3	1	1	2	3	1	6	1	2	1	2	1	3	10	8	5	71
Paraguay	2	2	1	1	1	1	1	1	1	1	1	1	1	1	1	1	1	1	20
Uruguay	4	4	1	3	2	1	2	2	1	1	1	2	1	1	1	1	1	1	25
Argentina	7	8	2	1	1	1	3	1	6	1	2	1	1	1	1	1	1	1	45
Chile	4	4	1	1	1	1	1	1	1	1	1	1	1	1	1	1	1	1	24

COUNTRY	POLITICAL			ECONOMIC			COMMERCIAL				CULTURAL (Educational)							CONSULAR	TOTAL POINTS
	International status	Membership of group of states	Security of defense	Industrial know-how or machinery	Industrial aid	Economic aid	Market for Nigerian produce	Market for minerals	Market for Nigerian manufactures	Agricultural or technical aid	Post-graduate	University or technical institutes	Scholarships	Nigerian student body	Religious	Racial	Historical or Geographical	Resident Nigerians	Maximum possible - 180 minimum - 18
(vi) The Caribbean Islands																			
Cuba	6	6	4	1	1	1	2	2	5	1	1	1	1	1	1	8	8	3	53
Jamaica	2	3	1	1	1	1	6	2	5	1	2	2	1	1	1	10	10	2	52
Trinidad & Tobago	2	3	1	1	1	1	5	2	4	1	2	2	1	1	1	8	8	1	45
Barbados	2	3	1	1	1	1	5	2	4	1	2	2	1	1	1	8	8	1	45
Haiti	1	2	1	1	1	1	2	1	4	1	1	1	1	1	1	5	1	3	29
Dominica	1	2	1	1	1	1	2	1	4	1	1	1	1	1	1	5	1	2	28
ZONE C																			
(vii) The Far East																			
China	10	10	6	6	4	3	5	4	5	6	1	2	3	1	1	3	1	1	72
Formosa	5	4	6	3	3	1	2	2	2	1	1	1	1	1	1	1	1	1	35
Mongolia	1	1	1	1	1	1	1	1	1	1	1	1	1	1	1	1	1	1	18
Japan	8	2	4	10	8	7	4	4	1	4	2	2	4	1	1	1	1	1	65
N. Korea	4	3	1	1	1	1	1	1	1	1	1	1	1	1	1	1	1	1	23
S. Korea	4	3	2	1	1	1	1	1	1	1	1	1	1	1	1	1	1	1	24
N. Vietnam	4	3	1	1	1	1	1	1	1	1	1	1	1	1	1	1	1	1	23
S. Vietnam	4	3	1	1	1	1	1	1	1	1	1	1	1	1	1	1	1	1	23
Laos	4	3	1	1	1	1	1	1	1	1	1	1	1	1	1	1	1	1	23
Cambodia	2	2	1	1	1	1	1	1	1	1	1	1	1	1	1	1	1	1	20

COUNTRY	POLITICAL			ECONOMIC			COMMERCIAL				CULTURAL — Educational					Racial	Historical or geographical	CONSULAR	TOTAL POINTS
	International status	Membership of group of states	Security of defense	Industrial know-how or machinery	Industrial aid	Economic aid	Market for Nigerian produce	Market for minerals	Market for Nigerian manufactures	Agricultural or technical aid	Post-graduate	University or technical institutes	Scholarships	Nigerian student body	Religious			Resident Nigerians	Maximum possible 180 minimum 18
Thailand	5	5	1	1	1	1	1	1	2	1	1	1	1	1	1	1	1	1	27
Burma	5	6	1	1	1	1	1	1	3	2	1	1	1	1	1	1	1	1	30
Nepal	3	2	1	1	1	1	1	1	1	1	1	1	1	1	1	1	1	1	21
Bhutan	1	1	1	1	1	1	1	1	1	1	1	1	1	1	1	1	1	1	18
India	7	7	7	2	2	1	1	1	1	1	1	1	3	1	1	1	2	2	42
Pakistan	6	6	4	1	1	1	1	1	1	1	1	1	1	1	6	1	2	1	37
Afghanistan	2	1	1	1	1	1	1	1	1	1	1	1	1	1	1	1	2	1	19
Singapore	3	3	2	1	1	1	1	1	1	1	1	1	1	1	1	1	2	1	24
Malaysia	5	5	3	1	1	1	1	1	2	7	1	1	1	1	4	1	2	1	38
Philippines	5	2	2	1	1	1	2	1	2	3	1	1	1	1	1	1	1	1	28
Indonesia	6	7	2	1	1	1	2	2	2	1	1	1	1	1	4	1	1	1	36
Ceylon	3	4	1	1	1	1	1	1	1	1	1	1	1	1	1	1	2	1	24
(viii) Australasia																			
Australia	6	6	5	4	4	3	5	2	1	5	6	6	6	2	2	4	2	1	69
New Zealand	5	5	3	2	2	1	2	2	1	3	4	5	5	2	1	2	2	1	48
(ix) Middle East																			
Iran	5	4	1	1	1	1	2	1	3	1	1	1	1	1	6	1	1	1	33
Iraq	4	4	1	1	1	1	2	1	1	1	1	1	1	1	5	1	1	1	29
Syria	4	5	1	1	1	1	1	1	1	1	1	1	1	1	4	1	2	1	29

COUNTRY	POLITICAL			ECONOMIC			COMMERCIAL				CULTURAL							CONSULAR	TOTAL POINTS
											Educational								Maximum possible - 180 minimum - 18
	International status	Membership of group of states	Security of defense	Industrial know-how or machinery	Industrial aid	Economic aid	Market for Nigerian produce	Market for minerals	Market for Nigerian manufactures	Agricultural or technical aid	Post-graduate	University or technical institutes	Scholarships	Nigerian student body	Religious	Racial	Historical or geographical	Resident Nigerians	
Lebanon	4	4	1	2	1	2	2	2	1	1	1	1	3	1	2	1	2	1	32
Jordan	4	4	1	1	1	1	1	1	1	1	1	1	1	1	8	1	1	1	31
Saudi Arabia	6	6	3	1	1	1	1	1	1	1	1	1	1	1	10	1	6	4	47
Kuwait	2	2	1	1	1	1	1	1	1	1	1	1	1	1	5	1	1	1	24
Yemen	2	2	1	1	1	1	1	2	1	1	1	3	1	1	4	1	5	1	23
Egypt	7	8	6	6	1	1	2	4	3	1	3	3	5	2	7	1	1	2	60
Israel	5	2	5	1	6	5	3	1	3	6	2	2	4	2	1	1	1	1	58
Sudan	5	5	2	1	1	1	1	1	3	1	1	2	2	1	9	4	7	6	52
ZONE D																			
(x) *North Africa*																			
Libya	4	4	1	1	1	1	1	1	2	1	1	1	2	1	4	4	6	1	37
Tunisia	5	7	1	1	1	1	1	1	1	1	1	1	1	1	4	4	8	1	41
Morocco	5	6	1	1	1	1	1	1	2	1	1	1	1	1	4	4	6	1	39
Algeria	6	5	2	1	1	1	1	1	1	1	1	1	1	1	4	4	6	1	39
(xi) *West Africa*																			
Mauritania	2	1	1	1	1	1	1	1	1	1	1	1	1	1	6	5	8	1	35
Mali	4	2	1	1	1	1	1	1	2	1	1	1	1	1	4	10	8	1	42
Guinea	5	4	1	1	1	1	1	1	2	1	1	1	1	1	3	10	8	1	44
Gambia	1	2	2	1	1	1	1	1	3	1	1	1	1	1	2	10	8	1	39

COUNTRY	POLITICAL			ECONOMIC			COMMERCIAL				CULTURAL							CONSULAR	TOTAL POINTS
	International status	Membership of group of states	Security of defense	Industrial know-how or machinery	Industrial aid	Economic aid	Market for Nigerian produce	Market for minerals	Market for Nigerian manufactures	Agricultural or technical aid	Post-graduate	University or technical institutes	Scholarships	Nigerian student body	Religious	Racial	Historical or geographical	Resident Nigerians	Maximum possible - 180 minimum - 18
Ghana	6	7	7	1	1	1	1	1	3	1	1	1	1	2	2	10	9	7	62
Sierra Leone	2	3	3	1	1	1	1	1	2	1	1	1	1	2	1	10	8	8	48
Liberia	5	2	1	1	1	1	1	1	2	1	1	1	1	1	1	10	8	2	41
Senegal	4	7	4	1	1	1	1	1	2	1	1	1	1	1	2	10	8	4	51
Ivory Coast	5	8	4	1	1	1	1	1	3	1	1	1	1	1	2	10	8	5	55
Togo	2	4	8	1	1	1	1	1	2	1	1	1	1	1	2	10	9	4	51
Upper Volta	2	4	6	1	1	1	1	1	1	1	1	1	1	1	1	10	8	2	45
Dahomey(Benin)	2	5	10	1	1	1	1	1	3	1	1	1	1	1	2	10	10	10	62
Niger	2	4	10	1	1	1	1	1	3	1	1	1	1	1	4	10	10	10	63
Chad	2	4	10	1	1	1	1	1	3	1	1	1	1	1	4	10	10	10	63
Cameroun	4	6	10	1	1	1	1	1	4	1	1	1	1	1	4	10	10	10	68
(xii) Central Africa																			
Ruanda	2	2	1	1	1	1	1	1	1	1	1	1	1	1	1	10	6	1	34
Gabon	1	2	1	1	1	1	1	1	1	1	1	1	1	1	1	10	6	1	33
Congo	3	3	2	1	1	1	1	1	2	1	1	1	1	1	1	10	6	2	39
Congo (Zaire)	5	6	6	1	1	1	1	1	4	1	1	1	1	1	1	10	6	3	51
(Central African Empire)	2	2	2	1	1	1	1	1	1	1	1	1	1	1	1	10	6	2	36
Burundi	2	2	1	1	1	1	1	1	1	1	1	1	1	1	1	10	6	1	34

COUNTRY	POLITICAL			ECONOMIC			COMMERCIAL				CULTURAL Educational							CONSULAR	TOTAL POINTS
	International status	*Membership of group of states*	*Security of defense*	*Industrial know-how or machinery*	*Industrial aid*	*Economic aid*	*Market for Nigerian produce*	*Market for minerals*	*Market for Nigerian manufactures*	*Agricultural or technical aid*	*Post-graduate*	*University or technical institutes*	*Scholarships*	*Nigerian student body*	*Religious*	*Racial*	*Historical or geographical*	*Resident Nigerians*	*Maximum possible - 180 minimum - 18*
(xiii) East Africa																			
Ethiopia	5	10	8	1	1	1	1	1	4	1	1	1	1	1	1	10	6	1	55
Somalia	3	1	1	1	1	1	1	1	4	1	1	1	1	1	2	10	6	1	38
Kenya	6	5	3	1	1	1	1	1	3	1	1	1	1	1	1	10	8	1	47
Uganda	5	3	2	1	1	1	1	1	3	1	1	1	1	2	1	10	8	1	44
Tanzania	5	4	7	1	1	1	1	1	3	1	1	1	1	1	1	10	8	1	49
(xiv) Southern Africa																			
Malawi	3	2	4	1	1	1	1	1	2	1	1	1	1	1	1	10	8	1	41
Zambia	4	3	6	1	1	1	1	1	2	1	1	1	1	1	1	10	8	1	45
Botswana	5	4	8	1	1	1	1	1	1	1	1	1	1	1	1	10	10	1	50
Madagascar	4	5	1	1	1	1	1	1	1	1	1	1	1	1	1	10	6	1	39

Source: MEA, "Working Paper on Administrative Organisation of the Ministry," prepared by E. O. Enahoro, March 14, 1966.

APPENDIX II

Aid to African Countries 1960-1965

Country	Cash grant	Scholarships and training facility	Military and police	Civil service secondment	Others
Angola	£20,191 (to Holden Roberto)	10 Scholarships			Visits to Nigeria by Holden Roberto
Basutoland (Lesotho)	£25,000 Assistance for Development	4 Students for Secretarial Course			
Bechuanaland (Botswana)		2 Administrative Officers			
Cameroun		4 Forestry Officers 3 Agricultural Officers 7 Police Officers 4 Veterinary Officers 5 P & T Officers 4 Cooperative Inspectors 1 Labor Inspector		2 Legal Officers	Advice on Establishment Matters
Chad	£5,000 Contribution to Citrus Plantation				
Congo (Zaire)		40 Police Officers 9 Scholarships	Continuous Military and Police Aid 1961-64		
Dahomey (Benin)	£3,000 Flood Relief				Agreement Nigeria Provide Police Training 200 tons of groundnuts Chief of Police Visit to Nigeria
Guinea	£34 Students F.T.C.				
Kenya	£10,150 for Scholarships & Independence Gift	3 Scholarships for Social Education			Nigeria/Kenya Telecoms. Link
Malawi	£10,000 Independence Gift	1 Community Development 2 University Scholarships 1 Foreign Service, Trainee 1 Information Officer		8 Magistrates and Judges	

Country	Cash grant	Scholarships and training facility	Military and police	Civil service secondment	Others
Niger		1 Museographer 12 Arabic Students 2 Broadcasters			
Sierra Leone		Attachment Legal Draftsman; Training Radio Engineers		3 Medical Officers 1 Broadcasting Officer 1 Prison Director 1 Pathologist	Advice on Salary Structure
Somalia	£10,000 Disaster Relief	30 Ports Authority Students			
South Africa	£931 in small grants to Nationalists £10,000 grant to Nationalist Party				Frequent visits by Nationalist Leaders to Nigeria at Government expense
Southern Rhodesia	£10,000 to Africa Nationalist Congress	20 Secondary Scholarships			Nationalist Leaders visit Nigeria at Government expense
Southwest Africa					Visit of Nationalist refugee at Nigerian expense
Swaziland	£10,000 to Karina Nationalist Leader	5 Scholarships by East for Secondary Education			Visits of Nationalist at Nigeria's Expense for Political Education and Financial Support
Tanzania	£20,000 Independence Gift	1 Treasury Officer 1 Museographer 1 Local Government Officer 1 Scholarship	1 Battalion of Nigerian Army 1964	16 Magistrates 2 Crown Counsels 1 High Court Registrar 1 Marine Officer 1 Marketing Officer	1 Oil Refinery Adviser 2 Tyre Manu. Advisers 3 Foreign Service Advisers 4 Legal Advisers 6 Advisers on Harbor Adm. 150 tons of Groundnuts, Flood Relief

Country	Cash grant	Scholarships and training facility	Military and police	Civil service secondment	Others
Uganda	£15,150 Independence Gift	1 Factory Inspector 1 Education Officer 1 Marketing Officer 1 Law Inspector 1 Scholarship for Secondary Education		1 Chief Justice 1 Lecturer	Advice on Foreign Establishment, Invitation to High Court Official to Visit Nigeria
Zambia	£10,000 Independence Gift £12,440 to U.N.I.P.	3 Foreign Officers trained 1 Animal Husbandry Officer			Diversion of 5 Rail tankers to help supply oil

Source: Working paper prepared for conference of Nigerian ambassadors, Lagos, June 1966.

NOTE ON SOURCES

NOTE ON SOURCES

While interviewing Nigerian and Biafran officials, the following documents were made available to the author without restrictions:

1. Complete set of working papers prepared for the Federal Ministry of External Affairs' Regional Conference of Heads of Mission— Africa, held in Lagos June 9–11, 1966, to review all aspects of the country's foreign policy;
2. Records of the Meeting of the OAU Consultative Committee on Nigeria held in Lagos, Novmber 23, 1967;
3. Records of Discussions between Commonwealth Secretary-General Arnold Smith and the Federal Government represented by Allison Ayida, Philip Asiodu and Ahmed Joda, in London, January 7, 1968, and January 20, 1968;
4. Republic of Biafra, Research Bureau of the Propaganda Directorate, a series of fourteen position papers prepared for the Head of State entitled "Biafra and the World," Spring 1968;
5. Records of Discussions, plus related correspondence, among the Commonwealth Secretariat, represented by the Secretary-General Arnold Smith, the Federal Government, represented by Chief Anthony Enahoro, and Biafra, represented by Sir Louis Mbanefo, in London, May 6–14, 1968;
6. Records of Commonwealth-sponsored Peace Talks held in Kampala, Uganda, May 23–31, 1968;
7. Rcords of Discussions between Lord Shepherd and the Federal Military Government, June 21–23, 1968;
8. Report on the Niamey Session of the OAU consultative Committee, July 15–26, 1968, submitted to the Federal Government by the Federal Delegation, July 28, 1968;
9. Biafran Ministry of Foreign Affairs, Briefing Papers for the Addis Ababa Peace Talks, July 1968;
10. Federal Ministry of External Affairs, cables relating to the progress and substance of talks in Addis Ababa, August 6 through September 9, 1968;
11. Federal Ministry of External Affairs, Brief for the 23rd Session of the United Nations General Assembly, September 7, 1968;
12. Biafran Ministry of Foreign Affairs, Memorandum regarding the Organization of African Unity Meeting in Algiers: An Analysis and Projections based on the West African Political Scene, Abidjan, August 20, 1968;
13. Report of the OAU Consultative Committee on Nigeria, Prepared by His Imperial Majesty for the Fifty Ordinary Session of the Assembly of Heads of State and Government, Algiers, September 1968;

14. Federal Ministry of External Affairs, Record of the OAU Fifth Summit–Algiers, Debate on the Nigerian Crisis, September 15, 1968;
15. Biafran Ministry of Foreign Affairs, "Reviewing our Diplomatic Approach," Summary Conclusions of Heads of Division Staff Meeting, Umuahia, December 1968;
16. Republic of Biafra, Briefing Papers Prepared by the Ministry of Foreign Affairs for use during visits by French and American parliamentarians in the Spring of 1969;
17. Report to the OAU Consultative Committee on Nigeria from the Chairman, HIM Haile Selassie I on his activities in pursuit of a peaceful settlement, 18th April 1969;
18. Records of the OAU Consultative Committee on Nigeria Held in Monrovia, April 17–20, 1969, contained in an Executive Council Information Paper submitted by the Vice-Chairman of the National Liberation Council, J.W.K. Harley to Ghana's National Liberation Council;
19. Federal Ministry of External Affairs, Records of Discussions of the Conference of Nigerian Ambassadors, held in Lagos, June 24–25, 1969, to review all aspects of the country's foreign policy;
20. Summary Minutes of Meeting between His Holiness Pope Paul and Chief Enahoro, Kampala Uganda, August 1, 1969, and Summary Minutes of related meetings between Chief Enahoro and President Milton Obote, President Jomo Kenyatta and Emperor Haile Selassie;
21. Report of the OAU Committee on Nigeria, prepared by HIM Haile Selassie I for the Assembly of Heads of State and Government, 6th Ordinary Session, Addis Ababa, September 1969, AHG/41;
22. Federal Ministry of External Affairs, Organization of African Unity, Sixth Summit, Addis Ababa, September 6–10, 1969, Records of deliberations by the OAU Consultative Committee on Nigeria, September 7–8, 1969, and Summary Record of the Plenary Debate on the Nigeria Question, September 10, 1969;
23. Federal Ministry of External Affairs; Record of Discussion between Commissioner Arikpo and Britain's Secretary of State for Foreign and Commonwealth Affairs, Maurice Foley, Lagos, December 5, 1969.

During the Civil War there was an outpouring of public statements and propaganda by both sides, plus foreign commentaries by journalists, scholars, and public officials. The most important statements by Nigerian and Biafrans have been collected in a two-volume work by A.H.M. Kirk-Greene, *Crisis and Conflict in Nigeria, A Documentary Sourcebook, 1966–1970* (London: Oxford University Press, 1971). Professor Kirk-Greene also has compiled a thorough international bibliography (Volume 2, pp. 482–518) of pamphlets, public documents, propaganda, books, journals, articles, and reports. George B.

Affia of the University of Lagos also has published a bibliography, *The Nigerian Crisis 1966–1970, A Preliminary Bibliography* (Lagos: University of Lagos, 1971), 23 pp. More recently, Christian Chukwunedu Aguolu has produced the *Nigerian Civil War 1967–1970: An Annotated Bibliography* (Boston: Hall, 1973), 181 pp. For a more general list of works by and about Nigerians see: John Harris, *Books about Nigeria* (Ibadan: Ibadan University Press, 1969), 83 pp.

Major foreign policy statements by the Nigerian and Biafran governments were delivered by the respective heads of state, and both Gowon and Ojukwu have published collections of their principal war-time addresses: Yakubu Gowon, *Faith in Unity* (Lagos: Government Printer, 1970), and C. Odumegwu Ojukwu, *Biafra: Selected Speeches and Random Thoughts* (New York: Harper Row, 1969).

The best way to track shifts in the official public positions taken by each side is through a careful reading of the transcripts of *Newstalk* editorials which were broadcast over Radio Nigeria and Radio Biafra. Copies of these transcripts were circulated among officials of the opposing side each morning, and if either government wished to signal the other this proved to be the most readily available medium. Preparation of these editorials was done by parallel committees under the supervision of the respective Ministries of Information. Themes for the editorials were established weekly, but often these were interrupted by changing circumstances. On the Biafran side Ojuwu and his permanent secretary of foreign affairs would participate directly in the formulation of Newstalk themes. The federal officials most influential in supervising the themes of their Newstalks were: Allison Ayida, Philip Asiodu, Ahmed Joda, and Edward Enahoro.

Supplementing official radio broadcasts were the press releases distributed daily by the Federal Ministry of Information in Lagos and the Biafran Ministry of Information through its Geneva outlet, Markpress. Other sets of press releases collected for this study include: International Committee of the Red Cross Press Releases, 1967–1970; Jointchurchaid Releases, 1968–1969; United States Information Service, Lagos; and the British High Commission, Lagos.

No attempt was made to cover the full public debate in third countries, but the reports produced on the Nigerian crisis by the United States House of Representatives International Relations Sub-Committee on Africa and the Senate Foreign Relations Sub-Committee on Africa were searched, and the British Parliamentary Debates regarding the Labour Government's Nigeria policy were an important source. The representatives from several other European governments in Lagos kindly provided copies of relevant debates by their respective parliamentary bodies.

Nigerian press coverage of the civil war and its international aspects was reviewed with the assistance of the library staff of the Nigerian Institute of International Affairs, who maintain a press clipping service dating back to 1965 for the following papers: *Morning Post, Daily*

Times, New Nigerian, Daily Express, Daily Sketch, Nigerian Tribune, Nigerian Observer, West African Pilot.

Research trips to Ghana, Cameroon, Zaire, Liberia, Sierra Leone, and Ivory Coast permitted opportunities to search press archives for coverage of the Nigerian conflict by the major newspapers in those countries. Information from Western European and United States newspapers was gathered with the assistance of the staff at the Royal Institute of International Affairs press library, Chatham House, London. Transcripts of broadcasts by the Africa Service of the British Broadcasting Corporation, the Voice of America, and coverage by the Foreign Broadcast Information Service yielded additional data.

Among the numerous periodicals that reported regularly on the Nigerian crisis, *West Africa* was certainly the most helpful. Other journals that were useful included: *Africa Confidential, Africa Diary, African Research Bulletin, Foreign Report, Nigerian Opinion,* and *Observer Foreign News Service.*

INTERVIEWS

Abraham, Ponnou. *French Embassy, Nigeria*

Achebe, Chinua. *Author and Head of Biafran Political Orientation Committee*

Adefela, Femi. *Director of* News-talks, *Radio Nigeria*

Adegoroye, Victor. *Nigerian High Commissioner to Ghana*

Adeniji, O. *Head of Africa Division, Federal Ministry of External Affairs*

Adigwe, N. J. *Head of Biafran Union in Sierra Leone*

Aferi, N. A. *Ghanaian High Commissioner to Nigeria*

Aggey, John Kwao Amuzu. *Archbishop of Lagos*

Akinsemoyin, O. A. *Senior Information Officer, Federal Ministry of Information*

Akpan, N. U. *Chief Secretary of Biafran Government*

Alim, Hadj Hammadou. *Ambassador of Federal Republic of Cameroon to Nigeria*

Anafulu, Joseph. *Head of Documentation Center, Biafran Directorate of Propaganda*

Ankrah, Joseph. *Ghanaian Head of State*

Anya, O. *Head of Biafran food distribution program for Port Harcourt*

Anyaoku, E. C. *Commonwealth Secretariat*

Arikpo, Okoi. *Commissioner, Federal Ministry of External Affairs*

Arywee, Paul. *Ghanaian Ministry of Foreign Affairs*

Asika, Ukpabi. *Administrator, East Central State*

Asiodu, Philip. *Permanent Secretary, Federal Ministry of Trade and Industry*

Awolowo, Obafemi. *Commissioner, Federal Ministry of Finance, and Vice Chairman, Federal Executive Council; Head of Nigerian delegations to Kinshasa and Algiers OAU summit meetings*

Ayida, Allison. *Permanent Secretary, Federal Ministry of Economic Development*

Azikiwe, Emeka Ayodele. *Nigerian diplomat*

Bamali, Nuhu. *Minister of External Affairs, Balewa government*

Bloom, Bridget. *Correspondent,* Financial Times

Boesch, Christian. *Swiss Embassy, Nigeria*

Brimah, M. B. *Nigerian diplomat*

Carr, George. *United States Embassy, Nigeria*

Chaval, A. *Belgian Ambassador to Nigeria*

Chukwumerije, Uche. *Head of Biafran Directorate of Propaganda*

Chumfong, Sammy. *Director of Program and News, Radio Cameroon*

Ciroma, Adamu. *Managing Director,* New Nigerian

Clark, B. A. *Deputy Permanent Secretary, Federal Ministry of External Affairs*

Cobb, Bruce. *Correspondent, Reuters News Service*

De St. Jorre, John. *Correspondent,* Observer

De Shields, Leonard. *Head of Africa Section, Liberian Department of State*

Dike, Kenneth. *Biafran representative in Ivory Coast*

Dougan, Jose W. Okori. *Ambassador of Republic of Equatorial Guinea to Nigeria*

Dudley, Billy J. *Professor, University of Ibadan*

Ebi, Obi. *Radio Biafra*

Echerue, Michael. *Head of Biafran War Information Bureau*

Effiong, Philip. *Biafran Chief of Staff*

Ekwensi, Cyprian. *Author and Director of Biafran Information Services*

Elias, T. O. *Attorney General and Commissioner, Federal Ministry of Justice*

Emeghara, F. U. *Deputy to Chief Secretary of Biafran Government*

Emordi, Bobo. *Leader of Biafran community in Ghana*

Enahoro, Anthony. *Commissioner, Federal Ministries of Information and Labour; Head of Nigerian delegation to Kampala and Addis Ababa talks*

Eromosele, O. S. *Information Officer, Federal Ministry of Information*

Fakayode, J. A. *Asia Division, Federal Ministry of External Affairs*

Forna, M. S. *Minister of Finance, Sierra Leone*

Garba, J. M. *Nigerian Ambassador to Italy*

Garrison, Lloyd. *Correspondent, New York Times*

Glass, Sir Leslie. *British High Commissioner to Nigeria*

Gowon, Yakubu. *Head of State of Federal Republic of Nigeria*

Haastrup, A. A. *Nigerian Ambassador to Ethiopia and Federal Republic of Germany*

Harriman, Leslie. *Nigerian High Commissioner to Kenya*

Hentsch, Thierry. *International Committee of the Red Cross*

Hoagland, James. *Correspondent, Washington Post*

Hocké, M. *International Committee of the Red Cross*

Hollist, C. O. *Head of International Division, Federal Ministry of External Affairs*

Ibiam, Francis Akanu. *Former Governor of the Eastern Region and Biafran Government Advisor*

Ijewere, G. O. *Head of Africa Division, Federal Ministry of External Affairs*

Ironkwe, Godwin. *Reuters News Correspondent in Biafra*

Issa, Boulama. *Ambassador of Niger to Nigeria*

Iyalla, J.T.F. *Nigerian Ambassador to United States*

Jalaoso, Olujimi. *Nigerian Ambassador to Liberia*

Jemiyo, I. O. *International and Comparative Law Division, Federal Ministry of Justice*

Joda, Ahmed. *Permanent Secretary, Federal Ministry of Information*

Jones, Maurice. *Permanent Secretary, Sierra Leone Ministry of External Affairs*

King, S. J. *Nigerian Cabinet Office*

Kogbara, I. S. *Biafran representative in London*

Kolade, E. O. *Nigerian Consul in Buea, Cameroon*

Legum, Colin. *Correspondent, Observer*

Madiebo, Alex. *Biafran Army Chief of Staff*

Makozi, Alex. *Bishop, Lagos Catholic Secretariat*

Malone, T. P. *Canadian High Commissioner to Nigeria*

Mbanefo, Sir Louis. *Biafran Chief Justice; Head of Biafran delegation to Kampala and Monrovia talks*

Mbu, Matthew. *Commissioner, Biafran Ministry of Foreign Affairs*

McCartty, William. *Defense Attaché, United States Embassy, Nigeria*

Meisler, Stanley. *Correspondent, Los Angeles Times*

Melborne, Roy. *United States Department of State*

Mohammed, S. Z. *Director, Relief and Rehabilitation Office, Lagos*

Mower, Jack H. *United States Embassy, Nigeria*

Mulcahy, Edward W. *United States Embassy, Nigeria*

Munk, Troels. *Danish Ambassador to Nigeria*

Myers, Desaix III. *Bangladesh relief program, United States Agency for International Development.*

Njoku, Eni. *Former Vice-Chancellor, University of Lagos; Head of Biafran delegation to Addis Ababa talks*

North, Haven. *Biafran relief program, United States Agency for International Development*

Nworah, Dike. *Biafran Ministry of Foreign Affairs*

Nworgu, Egbert. *Biafran representative in Portugal and Sao Tomé; Head of Administrative Division, Biafran Ministry of Foreign Affairs*

Nzimero, Ikenna. *Biafran intellectual*

Obi, Luke. *Chief Political Officer, Biafran Ministry of Foreign Affairs; Biafran representative in Germany*

Obiechina, A. *Professor, University of Nsukka*

O'Connell, James. *Professor, Ahmadu Bello University*

Odebode, M. O. *Federal Ministry of Information*

Odumosu, F. O. *Africa Division, Federal Ministry of External Affairs*

Ogbagzy, Ato Araya. *Ethiopian Ambassador to Nigeria*

Ogbu, Edwin. *Permanent Secretary, Federal Ministry of External Affairs; later Permanent Representative to the United Nations*

Ogundere, J. D. *International and Comparative Law Division, Federal Ministry of Justice*

Ogunsulire, E. O. *Nigerian Chargé d'Affaires in Paris; later Ambassador to Zaire*

Ojukwu, C. Odumẹgwu. *Head of State of Republic of Biafra*

Okafor, Raymond. *Biafran office, Ivory Coast*

Okunnu, Olufemi. *Commissioner, Federal Ministry of Works and Housing; Head of the Nigerian delegation to Consultative Committee meeting in Monrovia*

Okwechime, Mike. *Chief of Military Planning, Biafra*

Olson, Clinton L. *United States Embassy, Nigeria*

Olusanya, G. O. *Professor, University of Lagos*

Olutoye, Olufemi. *Under-Secretary (Military), Federal Ministry of External Affairs*

Omolodun, J. O. *Nigerian High Commissioner to Sierra Leone*

Onu, Peter. *Political Officer, Nigerian Embassy, Soviet Union*

Onuoha, J. *Head of the Biafran Public Enlightenment Committee*

Onyegbula, Godwin. *Permanent Secretary, Biafran Ministry of Foreign Affairs*

Onyemelukwe, C. C. *Biafran Officer-in-Charge of operations at Uli airstrip*

Ottah, Nelson. *Principal Information Officer, Federal Ministry of Information*

Preston, Bernard. *Markpress*

Raiski, G. S. *Soviet Embassy, Nigeria*

Ramsaur, Ernest E., Jr. *United States Embassy, Nigeria*

Russell, David. *Galitzine, Chant and Russell*

Scanlon, David. *American Friends Service Committee*

Schioler, John. *Canadian High Commission, Nigeria*

Scott-Emuakpor, L. E. *Deputy Director, Home and Press Section, Federal Ministry of Information*

Shepherd, Lord Malcolm. *British Minister of State for Commonwealth Affairs*

411

Shurtleff, Leonard. *United States Consul, Douala, Cameroon*

Smith, Arnold. *Secretary General, Commonwealth Secretariat*

Stephan, Ralph W. *United States Consul, Kaduna, Nigeria*

Stewart, Michael. *British Foreign Minister*

Sule, Yusuff Maitama. *Minister of Mines and Power, Balewa government*

Tagi, Ibrahim. *Minister of Information and Broadcasting, Sierra Leone*

Tali, Alhaji Yakubu. *Ghanaian High Commissioner to Nigeria*

Trueheart, William. *United States Ambassador to Nigeria*

Udo, Obi. *Director of Programming, Radio Biafra*

Ugoh, Sylvester. *Head of Biafran Central Bank*

Ukwu, Ukwu I. *Head of Biafran Organization of Freedom Fighters*

Volkmar, John. *Member of Quaker peace mission*

Waal, A. de. *Dutch Ambassador to Nigeria*

Wachuku, Jaja. *Minister of External Affairs, Balewa government*

Wagner, Wilhelm. *West German Embassy, Lagos*

Whiteman, Kaye. *Deputy Editor, West Africa*

Williams, Bruce. *Defense Attaché, United States Embassy, Nigeria*

Williams, David. *Editor, West Africa*

Yaccov, Yissakhar Ben. *Israeli Ambassador to Nigeria*

Zinsou, Emile. *President, Republic of Dahomey (Benin)*

LIST OF WORKS CITED

Aboyade, O. and A. A. Ayida. "The War Economy in Perspective." Paper presented to the Nigerian Economic Society's 1971 Annual General Conference, Ibadan, March 1971.

Aitken, William. "On the Airstrip at Uli." *Venture*, XXI (July-August 1969), 13–16.

Akinyemi, A. B. "Nigeria and Fernando Po, 1958–1966, The Politics of Irredentism." *African Affairs*, LXIX (September 1970), 236–249.

Akpan, N. U. *The Struggle for Secession, 1966–1970*. London: Frank Cass, 1971.

Aluko, Olajide. "The Civil War and Nigerian Foreign Policy." *The Political Quarterly*, XLII (April–June 1971), 177–190.

———. "The Foreign Service." *Journal of Administration* (University of Ife), V (October 1970), 33–52.

———. "Nigeria's Role in Inter-African Relations with Special Reference to the Organization of African Unity." *African Affairs*, LXXII (April 1973), 145–162.

Anafulu, Joseph A. "An African Experience: The Role of a Specialized Library in a War Situation." *Special Libraries*, LXII (January 1971), 32–40.

Anglin, Douglas. "Zambia and the Recognition of Biafra." *The African Review* (September 1971), 102–136.

Azikiwe, E. A. "Nigerian Foreign Policy 1960–1965." Master's thesis, School of Advanced International Studies, Johns Hopkins University, 1965.

Azikiwe, Nnamdi. *Origins of the Civil War*. Lagos: Government Printer, 1969.

Baker, Ross K. "The Emergence of Biafra." *Orbis*, XII (Summer 1968), 518–533.

———. "The Role of the Ivory Coast in the Nigeria Biafra War." *African Scholar*, I, No. 4 (1970), 5–8.

Biafra, Republic of. *Ahiara Declaration*. Geneva: Markpress, 1969.

———. *The Case for Biafra*. Enugu: Government Printer, 1967.

Booth, Richard. *The Armed Forces of African States* (Adelphi Papers No. 67). London: Institute for Strategic Studies, May 1970.

Brierly, J. L. *The Law of Nations*. 6th ed. New York: Oxford University Press, 1963.

Butler, B. "Tanzania's Decision to Recognize Biafra: Some Preliminary Considerations." Social Science Staff Seminar Paper, Ahmadu Bello University, Zaria, November 12, 1969.

Carl, Beverly M. "American Assistance to Victims of the Nigeria-Biafra War." *Harvard International Law Journal*, XII (Spring 1971), 191–259.

Cervenka, Zdenek. *The Organization of African Unity and Its Charter*. London: Hurst, 1968.

Coleman, James S. "The Foreign Policy in Nigeria." In *Foreign Policies in a World of Change*, ed. Joseph E. Black and Kenneth W. Thompson. New York: Harper & Row, 1963.

―――. *Nigeria: Background to Nationalism*. Berkeley and Los Angeles: University of California Press, 1958.

Cowan, L. Gray. "Nigerian Foreign Policy." In *The Nigerian Political Scene*, ed. Robert O. Tilman and Taylor Cole. Durham, North Carolina: Duke University Press, 1962.

Cronje, Suzanne. *The World and Nigeria*. London: Sidgwick and Jackson, 1972.

Crowder, Michael. *The Story of Nigeria*. 2nd ed. London: Faber and Faber, 1966.

Davis, Morris. "Negotiating about Biafran Oil." *Issue*, III, No. 2 (Summer 1973), 23–32.

De St. Jorre, John. *The Nigerian Civil War*. London: Hodder and Stoughton, 1972.

Diamond, Stanley. "A Faculty Member's Journey to Biafra." *New School Bulletin*, XXV, No. 6 (January 3, 1968).

―――. "Who killed Biafra?" *New York Review of Books* (February 26, 1970), pp. 17–27.

Dudley, Billy J. "Western Nigeria and the Nigerian Crisis." In *Nigerian Politics and Military Rule: Prelude to Civil War*, ed. S. K. Panter-Brick. London: Athlone Press, 1969, pp. 94–110.

Elias, T. O. "The Nigerian Crisis in International Law." *Journal of International Law* (Lagos), 1971.

First, Ruth. *Power in Africa*. New York: Pantheon, 1970.

Forsyth, Frederick. *The Biafra Story*. Baltimore: Penguin Books, 1969.

Free, Lloyd A. *The Attitudes, Hopes and Fears of Nigerians*. Princeton: Institute for International Social Research, 1964.

Gray, David M. "The Foreign Policy Process in the Emerging African Nation: Nigeria." Ph.D. dissertation, University of Pennsylvania, 1965.

Hanning, Hugh. "Lessons from the Arms Race." *Africa Report* (February 1968), pp. 42–47.

Hatch, Alden. *Pope Paul VI: Apostle on the Move*. London: W. H. Allen, 1967.

Helleiner, G. K. *Peasant Agriculture, Government, and Economic Growth in Nigeria*. Homeward, Illinois: Irwin, 1966.

Hunt, Sir David. *On the Spot: An Ambassador Remembers*. London: Peter Davies, 1975.

Idowu, H. O. "Foreign Policy of Nigeria, 1960–1965." Staff seminar paper, University of Lagos, 1969.

Ijalaye, Daniel A. "Was 'Biafra' at Any Time a State in International Law?" *American Journal of International Law*, LXV (July 1971) 551–559.

International Institute for Strategic Studies, *Strategic Survey 1967*. London: 1968.

Jones, Roy E. *Analyzing Foreign Policy*. London: Routledge, 1970.

Kilby, Peter. *Industrialization in an Open Economy, Nigeria 1945–1966*. London: Cambridge University Press, 1969.

Kirk-Greene, A.M.H. *Crisis and Conflict in Nigeria: A Documentary Sourcebook 1966–1970*. 2 volumes. London: Oxford University Press, 1971.

Klinghoffer, A. J. "Why the Soviets Chose Sides." *Africa Report*, XIII (February 1968), 47–50.

Leapman, Michael. "Biafra: At the Front." *Venture*, XXI (July-August 1969), 11–13.

Legum, Colin. *Pan Africanism: A Short Political Guide*. New York: Praeger, 1965.

Legvold, Robert. *Soviet Policy in West Africa*. Cambridge, Mass.: Harvard University Press, 1970.

Lindsay, Kennedy. "How Biafra Pays for the War." *Venture* (March 1969), 26–28.

Livingstone, W. P. *Mary Slessor of Calabar, Pioneer Missionary*. London: Hodder and Stoughton, 1916.

Lloyd, Hugh G.; Mona L. Mollerup; and Carl A. Bratved. *The Nordchurchaid Airlift to Biafra, 1968–1970, An Operations Report*. Copenhagen: Folkekirkens Nodhjaelp, 1972.

Mayall, James. "Oil and Nigerian Foreign Policy." *African Affairs*, LXXV, No. 300 (July 1976), 317–330.

Mackintosh, John P. *Nigerian Government and Politics*. London: Allen and Unwin, 1966.

Melbourne, Roy M. "The American Response to the Nigerian Conflict." *Issue*, III, No. 2 (Summer 1973), 33–42.

Mezu, S. Okechukwu. *Behind the Rising Sun*. London: Heinemann, 1971.

Miners, N. J. *The Nigerian Army 1956–1966*. London: Methuen, 1971.

Mockler, Anthony. *Mercenaries*. London: Macdonald, 1970.

Modelski, George. "International Relations of Internal War." In *International Aspects of Civil Strife*, ed. James Rosenau. Princeton: Princeton University Press, 1964.

Nafziger, E. Wayne. "The Economic Impact of the Nigerian Civil War." *Journal of Modern African Studies*, X (July 1972), 223–245.

Nelson, Harold D. *et al. Area Handbook for Nigeria.* Washington, D.C.: U.S. Government Printing Office, 1972.

Nielsen, Waldemar. *The Great Powers in Africa.* New York: Praeger, 1969.

Nigeria, Eastern Region of. *The Meeting of the Supreme Military Council, Accra, January 4–5, 1967.* Enugu: Government Printer, 1967.

Nigeria, Federal Government of. *Estimates of the Federation of Nigeria, 1960–61; 1965–66; 1970–71.* Lagos: Government Printer, 1960, 1965, 1970.

————. *Faith in Unity.* Lagos: Government Printer, 1970.

————. *Meeting of the Military Leaders at Peduase Lodge, Aburi, Ghani, January 4–5, 1967.* Lagos: Government Printer, 1967.

————. *Nigeria 1966.* Lagos: Government Printer, 1967.

————. *The Struggle for One Nigeria.* Lagos: Government Printer, 1967.

————. *Training Needs of the Federal Civil Service, A Survey Conducted by the Institute of Administration,* University of Ife. Directed by Professor C. P. Wolle. Lagos: Government Printer, 1968.

————. *Yakubu Gowon, A Short Biography.* Lagos: Government Printer, 1968.

Nigeria, Ministry of Justice. *Nigeria's Treaties in Force.* Volume I, October 1, 1960 to June 30, 1970. Lagos: Government Printer, 1971.

Nwanko, Arthur A. *Nigeria: The Challenge of Biafra.* London: Rex Collings, 1972.

O'Connell, James. "The Anatomy of a Pogrom: An Outline Model." Mimeographed paper, Ahmadu Bello University, Zaria, 1969.

————. "Yakubu Gowon: A Political Profile." Typescript, Ahmadu Bello University, Zaria, 1973.

Ofoegbu, Mazi Ray. "The Relations Between Nigeria and Its Neighbours." *Nigerian Journal of International Studies*, I, No. 1 (July 1975), 28–39.

Ogunbadejo, Oye. "Nigeria and the Great Powers: The Impact of the Civil War on Nigerian Foreign Relations." *African Affairs*, LXXV, No. 2 (January 1976), 14–32.

Ojedokun, O. A. "Nigeria's Relations with the Commonwealth, with Special Reference to Her Relations with the United Kingdom, 1960–1966." Ph.D. dissertation, London School of Economics, 1968.

Ojukwu, C. Odumegwu. *Biafra: Selected Speeches and Random Thoughts.* New York: Harper & Row, 1969.

Onu, Paul E. "Domestic Propaganda in the Biafran Adventure." Unpublished manuscript, Enugu, 1970; to be published by Enugu: Nwankwo and Nwankwo.

Oyewole, Fola. *Reluctant Rebel.* London: Rex Collings, 1975.

———. "Scientists and Mercenaries." *Transition,* XLVIII (1975), 59–65.

Oyinbo, John (pseud.). *Nigeria: Crisis and Beyond.* London: Charles Knight, 1971.

Pearson, Scott R. *Petroleum and the Nigerian Economy.* Palo Alto, California: Stanford University Press, 1970.

Phillips, Claude. *The Development of Nigerian Foreign Policy.* Evanston, Illinois: Northwestern University Press, 1964.

Post, K.W.J. *The Nigerian Federal Election of 1959: Politics and Administration in a Developing Political System.* London: Oxford University Press, 1963.

Rothmyer, Karen. "What Really Happened in Biafra?" *Columbia Journalism Review,* IX, No. 3 (Fall 1970), 43–47.

Schwarz, Walter. *Nigeria.* London: Pall Mall, 1968.

Singleton, Seth. "Conflict Resolution in Africa: The Congo and the Rules of the Game." *Pan African Journal* VII, No. 1 (Spring 1975), 1–18.

Sklar, Richard L. *Nigerian Political Parties.* Princeton: Princeton University Press, 1963.

Tamuno, Takena N. "Separatist Agitations in Nigeria Since 1914." *Journal of Modern African Studies,* VIII, No. 4 (1970), pp. 563–584.

Tanzania, United Republic of. *Tanzania Government's Statement on the Recognition of Biafra.* Dar es Salaam: Government Printer, 1968.

Thayer, George. *The War Business: The International Trade in Armaments.* New York: Simon and Shuster, 1969.

Thompson, W. Scott. *Ghana's Foreign Policy 1957–1966.* Princeton: Princeton University Press, 1969.

Uwechue, Raph. *Reflections on the Nigerian Civil War: A Call for Realism.* London: O.I.T.H. International, 1969.

Wallerstein, Immanual. *Africa, the Politics of Unity.* New York: Random House, 1967.

Webb, Stanley. "Then the War Game." *Shell Magazine,* XLIX (February 1969), 31–33.

Weinstein, Brian. *Gabon, Nation-Building on the Ogooue*. Cambridge, Mass.: MIT Press, 1966.

Wilson, Harold. *The Labour Government 1964–1970*. London: Michael Joseph, Ltd., 1971.

Wiseberg, Laurie S., "Christian Churches and the Nigerian Civil War." *Journal of African Studies* (Los Angeles), II, 3 (Fall 1975), 297–331.

———. "Humanitarian Intervention: Lessons from the Nigerian Civil War." Paper delivered at the 1973 Annual Meeting of the American Political Science Association.

———. "The International Politics of Relief: A Case Study of the Relief Operation Mounted during the Nigerian Civil War (1967–1970)." Ph.D. dissertation, University of California, Los Angeles, 1973.

Zartman, William. "Africa as a Subordinate State Stystem in International Relations." *International Organization*, XXI, No. 3 (1967), 545–564.

———. *International Relations in the New Africa*. Englewood Cliffs, New Jersey: Prentice-Hall, 1966.

———. "Characteristics of Developing Foreign Policies." In *French-Speaking Africa: The Search for Identity*, ed. William H. Lewis. New York: Walker and Co., 1965, pp. 179–193.

Zolberg, Aristide R. *One Party Government in the Ivory Coast*. Princeton: Princeton University Press, 1964.

INDEX

LIBRARY OF CONGRESS CATALOGING IN PUBLICATION DATA

Stremlau, John J.

The international politics of the Nigerian civil war, 1967–1970.

Bibliography: p.
Includes index.
1. Nigeria—History—Civil War, 1967–1970.   2.
Nigeria—Foreign relations.   I. Title.
DT515.9.E3S85   327.669   76–24298
ISBN 0–691–07587–5
ISBN 0–691–10051–9 pbk.